The Unfinished Quest of
RICHARD WRIGHT

Richard Wright. *Photo by Harriet Crowder*

The Unfinished Quest of
RICHARD WRIGHT

by Michel Fabre

*Translated from the French
by Isabel Barzun*

William Morrow & Company, Inc.   New York, 1973

Copyright © 1973 by William Morrow and Company, Inc.

Grateful acknowledgment is made for permission to quote the following:

From "The Leaden-Eyed," from *Collected Poems,* by Vachel Lindsay. Copyright 1914 by The Macmillan Company, renewed 1942 by Elizabeth C. Lindsay. Reprinted by permission of Macmillan Publishing Co., Inc.

From the song "King Joe," copyright 1942 by Bregman, Vocco & Conn, Inc. Used by permission. All Rights Reserved.

From "Between the World and Me," from *White Man, Listen!* by Richard Wright. Copyright © 1957 by Richard Wright. Reprinted by permission of Doubleday & Company, Inc.

From *Eight Men* and *Black Power,* by Richard Wright. Reprinted by permission of Paul R. Reynolds, Inc., 599 Fifth Avenue, New York, N.Y. 10017.

From *Black Boy,* by Richard Wright. Copyright 1937, 1942, 1944, 1945 by Richard Wright. By permission of Harper & Row, Publishers, Inc.

From *The God That Failed,* edited by Richard Crossman. Copyright 1944 by Richard Wright. Reprinted by permission of Harper & Row, Publishers, Inc., New York, and Hamish Hamilton Ltd., London.

Excerpts from *Letters of Richard Wright,* edited by Ellen Wright, Michel Fabre and Edward Margolies. Copyright © 1973 by Ellen Wright. Published by permission of Harper & Row, Publishers, Inc.

From "How 'Bigger' Was Born," from *Native Son,* by Richard Wright (Harper & Row, 1940). By permission of Harper & Row, Publishers, Inc.

From *The Flowers of Friendship,* edited by Carl Van Vechten. Reprinted by permission of Alfred A. Knopf, Inc.

From letters of Paul R. Reynolds, published by permission of Mr. Reynolds.

From previously unpublished material by Richard Wright. Copyright © 1973 by Ellen Wright. Published by permission of Paul R. Reynolds, Inc.

Printed in the United States of America.

Library of Congress Catalog Card Number 73-4227

ISBN 0-688-00163-7
ISBN 0-688-05163-4 (pbk.)

1   2   3   4   76   75   74   73

PREFACE

WHEN in 1961 I began to research the life of Richard Wright, he was esteemed by French critics and public alike as a major writer, not only the greatest Afro-American novelist (Baldwin's *Go Tell It on the Mountain* had gone almost as unnoticed in Paris as the first translation of Ellison's *Invisible Man*), but also as one of the great post-World War II American authors whom Malraux, Sartre and Claude-Edmonde Magny had introduced to the French reader. In underground anthologies, Wright, Caldwell and Steinbeck appeared along with Faulkner, Hemingway and Dos Passos. Partly, perhaps, because Wright had chosen to live in France, his audience here had not diminished at the end of his life. The series of interviews published from October through December, 1960, and his vehement opinions quoted in our newspapers were constant evidence of his presence; at his death not a few Frenchmen felt as if a familiar landmark had disappeared.

Obtaining his works in translation, therefore, was not very difficult, and my discovery of his shrunken reputation among his fellow Americans did not occur until it became necessary to obtain the early original texts. The merest good luck supplied me with the British edition of *Twelve Million Black Voices* in Paris, but I had to wait six years to read *Savage Holiday* in English. When in 1962 I came to teach in the United States and to collect, over a period of two years, documents and firsthand accounts of his life, I noticed that even the name of Richard Wright seemed to have slipped from the memory of his compatriots. A comforting number of Blacks from all social milieus, though belonging primarily to the older generation, had read *Native Son* and *Black Boy*, but my students at Harvard and Wellesley were unwilling to believe that Wright had ever confronted America with more disagreeable and penetrating truths than James Baldwin, their idol of the moment. Many professors of American literature showed polite surprise when I mentioned the subject of my research: perhaps in America one was forced to "publish or perish," but were there not other thesis topics left in France? Among the eminent black university professors, who at that time rarely dealt with Wright (the first seminar devoted to him took place in California in 1964), there were few who seemed to show any deep interest in him. Only a few critics, such as Hoyt Fuller, Irving Howe, Maxwell Geismar and Kenneth Rexroth, were praising him for different reasons. Even obituary notices had been rare and, when they did not coincide with reviews of *Eight Men,* brief. There had been a few allusions to the unpublished episodes of his last novel, "Island of Hallucinations," included in the anthology *Soon One Morning.* There was some mention of *Lawd Today* when it was published in 1963, but because the novel had been written in the thirties it was generally treated as a museum piece.

Nevertheless, Wright had not been buried in total oblivion. I suspected this when I saw a reference to his work in John Oliver Killens's *And Then We Heard Thunder.* I found evidence of it in conversing with William Melvin Kelley and LeRoi Jones, and it was finally proved to me after meeting the people whom Wright had left behind in the United States, friends ranging from Fern Gayden to Frederic Wertham, from Langston Hughes to Willard Maas, from Ralph Ellison to Dorothy Norman, friends and colleagues dating from the thirties and forties, whose memory of him had remained untarnished during the McCarthy era. But most convincing of all was the pride I discovered in those who had known him in Mississippi and in the Chicago ghetto, Blacks who spoke to me about him, sometimes with reserve because I was white, and sometimes with confidence, because I was French.

These were the people who prevented me from doubting the importance of Richard Wright. His poor reputation in academic circles had led me to question my own enthusiasm, especially since I was a foreigner with a mere handful of Americans on my side, but I derived some comfort from the fact that no legend had sprung up about him. Aside from some rumors circulating as to the cause of his death, there was only profound ignorance, especially concerning the reasons for his exile, which tended to cover him with a haze of suspicion. It would be easier to break the silence than to destroy an established myth.

Of course I received conflicting reports about Wright as well as a variety of opinions about his living abroad, which had not been approved wholeheartedly by very many of his friends. It was as if he had somehow betrayed his race and scorned his homeland in settling upon foreign soil. Gradually, however, racial events, totally independent of the literary fashion, began to bring Wright's work back into the limelight. As the civil rights movement tended more and more toward Black Power, its leaders became increasingly aware of the relevance of Wright's message. As the young black writers came to be heard, it was obvious that they had read and understood him. Bigger was rediscovered, not only as a monster to be kept at a distance but as a forerunner of the Watts rebels, the adolescents whose profound human dignity Wright had evoked along with their frustrations and violence. Developments on the international scene also began to bear out Wright's prophecies on the relationship between the West and the Third World, gradually justifying this writer who had been considered dated, an offshoot of a bygone naturalist tradition, totally obsessed by the traumas of his youth.

Meanwhile, my research was leading me, from the yellowed magazines of the Depression to the countryside of Mississippi, from the recollections of his friends to the correspondence files of Paul Reynolds and Edward Aswell, closer and closer to Wright himself. When I returned to France in 1964, I had already collected a great deal of material, but the regulations of the Sorbonne at that time prevented me both from publishing any part of my work before I had defended my thesis and from separating the biography from the critical study.* I therefore worked on both simultaneously until April, 1968, when I submitted the manuscript of the biography alone to the Comité Consultatif des Universités. The student uprising of May, 1968, caused the second of these restrictions to be lifted, but more pressing responsibilities at the University caused me further delay. The next two years were not wasted, however, because Mrs. Ellen Wright had in the meantime put at my disposal her husband's remaining unpublished manuscripts, as well as all his papers, his notes, the successive drafts of his books, carbon copies of some of his own letters, all the correspondence he received from his many friends and admirers, down to the most trivial documents such as train-ticket stubs and hotel receipts,

---

* For instance, my articles "The Poetry of Richard Wright" (*Studies in Black Literature,* Autumn, 1970), and "Black Cat and White Cat" (*Poe Studies,* June, 1971) date from 1963 and 1966 respectively.

which, by some miracle, he had been in the habit of saving. My general conclusions about Wright were not greatly changed after perusing this material, but I found proof for many of my conjectures and was able to make a more detailed and precise chronology of his life. I also discovered his true relationship to some people who had just recently begun to claim a long-standing friendship with him.

This documentation helped to fill a void due to the lack of existing biographies upon which I could depend for such details. The chapters devoted to him in books like Rebecca Chalmers Barton's *Witnesses for Freedom* usually repeated more or less well what Wright himself had set down in *Black Boy*. The only original study then available was in Edwin Embree's *Thirteen Against the Odds,* which was succinct and only brought his life up to 1944.

Although it has been some years since Constance Webb's biography was published, my research for the most part was finished well before hers.* I was therefore alone in defining and filling the gaps in the available material and assessing the new evidence gathered from countless interviews, articles, reviews and letters, all the sometimes tedious, sometimes exhilarating work of reconstructing the history which forms the foundation for any serious study.

One of the aims of my research, which has admittedly been extensive, was to supply a large mass of material on the career of Richard Wright, for the benefit of future scholars. In the realm of biography alone there are details to be verified, approximations to clarify and more source material to be collected, even before the passage of time permits certain more intimate aspects of his life to be explored. It is not my ambition to explain either Wright's life or his work, but to trace his life in detail while placing his

---

* It is perhaps worth specifying that I met Constance Webb in 1962, when she was beginning her biography, and found her knowledge of Wright's life at many points so sketchy that I supplied her with a close and exact chronology. In 1967, Edward Margolies and I made the Wright correspondence we had collected available to her and later, at the request of Mrs. Wright, I spent several weeks going over her manuscript, making a number of particular suggestions for greater factual accuracy. She availed herself of only a few of these for her printed version, where she frequently gives "conversation with Richard Wright" as the source for statements contrary to available evidence. I regret having to be critical in establishing the relation of time and scholarly exchange between her work and mine, for I am indebted to her for the communication of some information, and for making it possible for me to conduct interviews with Ralph Ellison and Chester Himes.

work in perspective, illustrating their relationship to each other.*
This turns out to be particularly necessary for a writer still as
poorly known as Wright—by which I do not mean unknown, but
poorly known in the sense that the reborn interest in him as a
black intellectual has tended to focus only upon the high points
of his life and works. † After having praised him to the skies in
1940 and subsequently dragged him in the mud during the
McCarthy era, people are now beginning to discuss the significance
of his creative and political achievement. My goal, then, will be
to illuminate certain depths of his life and career, which are
generally unsuspected by the average admirer of *Native Son* and
Black Boy, and sometimes even by the friend or competent critic.

In Wright's case, the number of unpublished manuscripts makes
it imperative to take them into consideration, although I am far
from assigning a uniform value to all of Wright's production. In
addition to the unpublished haiku, letters, diaries and novels
("Tarbaby's Dawn," "Black Hope," "Island of Hallucinations"),
certain essays and early poems are still unpublished or difficult
to find. I emphasized many of these because I was anxious to consider everything that Wright was working on at the various stages
of his artistic evolution, to show how an essay perhaps foreshadows
or contradicts a successful piece of work, or how a recurring theme
or metaphor betrays its importance in the subconscious of the writer.
As a general rule, I have tried to assemble in the following pages
a wealth of complementary material so as not to impose a single
meaning upon Wright's career, without, of course, withholding my
own interpretation of the facts. It is possible to support apparently
conflicting theories about certain of his thoughts and actions; it is
possible to see him as torn between diverging tendencies; but this
may actually be a way of acknowledging that he respected the
truth of experience too much to substitute a theory for it, that he
refused to blind himself to reality just because it might contradict
his sense of logic. It is these rich contradictions that I have tried

---

* Having done the research for both the textual and biographical study, I soon
realized that a critical exploration of any value would have doubled the size of
the present volume. I therefore decided to postpone publication of the textual
analyses.
† A notable exception was the seminar organized by the Institute of Afro-American
Studies at the University of Iowa in July, 1970, during which several little-known
works of Wright were the subject of well-deserved discussion.

to retain in the hope that future students of Wright will not unduly privilege any single facet of his personality.

It is as difficult as it is agreeable to give thanks where it is due, but I am nonetheless eager to thank in detail all those who have helped me. First there is Mrs. Ellen Wright, who did me the honor of trusting me to organize and draw upon the several hundred pounds of documents designated as "Wright's personal papers." * She also answered many of my questions and corrected some of my errors without ever attempting to impose her point of view upon me.

Next, I want to single out Madame Margrit de Sablonière, Mrs. Jane Newton, Mrs. Essie Lee Ward Davis and Mr. Jack Conroy for having far surpassed the degree of collaboration which a researcher can hope to expect, sparing neither time nor effort in helping me prepare this book.

It would be so difficult to establish a scale of my indebtedness to the many others who were kind enough to supply me with written or verbal testimony that I have chosen to list them according to the four main periods of Wright's career, a system that will have the added advantage of allowing the reader to place them more easily. I would therefore like to thank the following people (in addition to those who preferred to remain anonymous) for their invaluable contributions. For Wright's childhood in Mississippi: Joe Brown; Rev. O. B. Cobbins; Mrs. Ward Davis; Mrs. Minnie Farish; Mrs. Elenora Gralow of the Natchez Public Library; Mrs. Sarah McNeamer; Mrs. Tillie Perkins Scott; Mrs. Shirley; Mr. and Mrs. Smith; Professor L. V. Randolph, principal of the Smith-Robinson School, for his generous aid in helping me to become acquainted with the black community of Jackson; and the directors of the public libraries of Jackson and Memphis.

For the Chicago period: Nelson Algren, Claude A. Barnett, Arna Bontemps, Alice Browning, Archibald J. Carey, Horace Cayton, Abraham Chapman, Jack and Gladys Conroy, Frank Marshall Davis, St. Clair Drake, James T. Farrell, Hoyt W. Fuller, Fern Gayden, Ed and Joyce Gourfain, the late Langston Hughes, William Jordan, Donald Joyce, Ulysses Keys, Meyer Levin, Lawrence Lip-

---

* Any manuscript referred to in the text as "unpublished" is to be found, unless otherwise specified, in this body of material, abbreviated as WPP in the notes. Other frequently used abbreviations include "AH" ("American Hunger"), *BB* (*Black Boy*), *BP* (*Black Power*), *EM* (*Eight Men*), *GF* (*The God That Failed*), "IH" ("Island of Hallucinations") and *NS* (*Native Son*).

ton, Metz Lochard, Len Mallette, Lawrence Martin, Nathan Morris, Jane Newton, William Patterson, Peter Pollack, Margaret Walker, Theodore Ward, Mrs. Mary Wirth, Jan Wittenber, Harold and Susan Woodson, and the staffs of the Abraham Lincoln Center, the Newberry Library and the Cleveland Hall Branch Municipal Library.

For the New York period: Gwendolyn Brooks, Allison Davis, John Dos Passos, Katherine Dunham, Ralph Ellison, Paul Green, Chester Himes, John Houseman, Irving Howe, Robert Lorenz, Willard Maas, Carson McCullers, Archibald MacLeish, Adele and Marie Mencken, Helen Neville, Anaïs Nin, Dorothy Norman, Philip Rahv, Jay Saunders Redding, Paul Reynolds, Edwin Seaver, John Steinbeck, Oliver Swan, Constance Webb, Henrietta Weigel, Dr. and Mrs. Frederic Wertham.

For the European period: Louis T. Achille, Rudolph Aggrey, Jacqueline Amiot, Georges G. Astre, Sylvia Beach, Simone de Beauvoir, Dr. C. Belfield-Clarke, Olympe Bély-Quénum, Hélène and Michel Bokanowski, Kay Boyle, Aimé Césaire, Mercer Cook, Rosette and Schofield Coryell, Léon Damas, Alioune Diop, Colette and Rémi Dreyfus, Marcel Duhamel, M. Elek, Daniel Guérin, Raymond Las Vergnas, Joshua Leslie, Ruth Liepman, Charles Marks, Jean-Jacques Mayoux, Maurice Nadeau, Dorothy Padmore, William G. Smith, Dr. Victor Schwartzman, Douglas Schneider, Léopold Senghor, Michel Terrier, Jean Wagner, George Whitman, Eric Williams, Sidney Williams and Frank Yerby.

I was also fortunate to be able to exchange information and test hypotheses with several American university professors. Early on, I met Edward Margolies, Keneth Kinnamon and Henry Winslow and had the most rewarding relationship with them. Keneth Kinnamon furnished me with letters from figures like Frank Marshall Davis and Rudolph Aggrey, while Edward Margolies did the same for Paul Green and many others before we collaborated in gathering Wright's correspondence with his editors, agents and friends. Not only was discussing Wright with these men fruitful, but they have proved devoted friends over the years since I began my research. David Bakish, whom I met later, was also kind enough to supply me with further details, and I was able to exchange some revealing information with Horace Cayton shortly before his death.

I would like to thank my thesis adviser, Roger Asselineau, and the members of my defense jury for their pertinent criticisms, and

Professor Robert Bone for his sincere encouragement during a difficult period. I am particularly grateful to Ernest Kaiser of the Schomburg Collection, the librarians of the American Library in Paris, and the libraries of Harvard University and Yale University for their efforts in obtaining rare magazines and newspapers. A Fulbright Scholarship paid for my transatlantic trip to the United States in 1962–64, and one hundred dollars from Wellesley College helped me to get to Jackson, Mississippi, in 1962.

In the preparation of this book in its present form I benefited from the clearsightedness of my editor, Isabel Barzun. Finally, I would like to thank my father for his help in the original preparation of my thesis, and Geneviève, my wife, whose advice partly determined my choosing this subject, for having patiently endured the presence of Richard Wright in our home for all these years.

CONTENTS

LIST OF ILLUSTRATIONS

INTRODUCTION

W<small>HAT</small> justification is there for a biography of Richard Wright? even considering his life in its historical or cultural context, his literary achievement alone is reason enough for such a study. One novel (*Native Son*), his autobiography (*Black Boy*) and a dozen stories in *Uncle Tom's Children* and *Eight Men* distinguished him as one of the most significant American prose writers, and certainly the most important, if not the most brilliant, Afro-American novelist. In addition, his work raises broader issues because he was black, because of certain aspects of his life that are not specifically literary. This fact alone would be enough reason to devote a book to the development of a person for whom literary achievement was not the only goal in life, or the sole governing principle. A man's writing is certainly never a series of unrelated acts any more than it is the résumé of his life. Rather, it represents stages in the evolution of an intellect sometimes formed by an ideology and sometimes directing it, reorienting it according to the personal demands of the moment, of which the author may be only subconsciously aware. In short, Richard Wright the man transcends Richard Wright the novelist, even though he would certainly never have been the object of such a study if he had not been a novelist.

"I am a very average Negro, and that may be why I'm exceptional." How can this remark, delivered to interviewers on the publication of *Black Boy*, be believed when another of Wright's favorite statements—"The Negro is the metaphor of America"—immediately brands him as exceptional? According to Wright, the experience of the black American crystallizes a more universal problem of Western culture created by the transition from a family-oriented, and still somewhat feudal, rural existence, to the anonymous mass civilization of the industrial centers. The history of the black people of the United States reflects the material progress and cultural evolution of the country at the same time that it anticipates (by years, decades or even centuries) a similar evolution in other nations of the world.

In fact, Wright's own life can be viewed as a metaphor of this transition, since he accomplished the social progress of three generations in one lifetime, he himself linking the emerging Third World to the Old South still slumbering in the racist dogmas that governed his Mississippi childhood. His life could be compared to a bridge, of which the three arches reached first to the Chicago ghetto of the Depression, then to the artistic and intellectual circles of New York during World War II and finally to Europe during the fifties. This geographical progression coincides curiously enough with his spiritual itinerary, which lends at least a superficial unity to his career: America and *Native Son* representing the Communist phase; Paris and *The Outsider*, the existentialist phase; Africa and *White Man, Listen!*, the anticolonialist phase. This rather facile division is extremely deceptive, however, first, because Wright's thought turns out to be much more of a continuum, revealing many inner complexities, and second, because it tends to restrict his contribution as a writer to that of being merely a witness of his times.

Could Wright have been, rather, a precursor, as is often claimed? Since the recent demands for Black Power, many have attributed to him the honor of inventing this nationalist slogan, but his explanation of the term to his Dutch translator proves, to the contrary, that he meant it merely as a way of designating the future Ghana as a black nation. Was he really an innovator? Certainly the literary forms that he used for his writing were not original. His works fit into traditional, even fixed molds, and were the result of a wide variety of influences. His early poetry stemmed from Whitman, T. S. Eliot, the surrealists and the blues; his first novel (*Lawd Today*, published posthumously) drew on Dos Passos and James T. Farrell, and his first short stories (collected in *Uncle Tom's Children*), on Joyce, Hemingway and Stein. *Native Son* borrows from both Dreiser and Dostoevsky and *Twelve Million Black Voices* was modeled upon *As Long as the Grass Shall Grow,* a photographic study of Indians by Oliver LaFarge and Edwin Rosskam. The absence of novelistic techniques and the frequent melodrama in *Black Boy* only make it a more classical form of autobiography. James Baldwin was led into supposing that "Man, God Ain't Like That" and "Man of All Works" represented a new departure in the art of short-story writing only because he did not know that they were written as radio plays, and the haiku, of course, owe their splendor precisely to Wright's scrupulous respect for the Japanese models. He never sought originality for its own sake but rather borrowed what he needed from wherever he found it, in order to gain better control of his reader, to create a new synthesis which bears his original stamp, to deal more blows to his adversaries, to convey his message more forcefully and thus "to build a bridge between men."

The same observations could be made about his ideologies, both personal and political. Marxism, existentialism and pan-Africanism were all concepts that others had discussed before him, and more brilliantly than he. He had also been introduced to these ideas by other people such as Abraham Aaron, Dorothy Norman and George Padmore. In his life as in his work, the progress of an influence, the repercussions from a discussion or the reading of a book can be traced step by step. In spite of Wright's very European love of intellectual discussion, in spite of his extraordinary thirst for abstract ideas, which, in his case, was accompanied by the advantages and disadvantages of being self-educated—he perceived things with originality and freshness but had a tendency to emphasize the obvious because he had only just discovered it—in spite of his political fervor, which sidetracked him from literature at various times, and in spite of the almost religious intuition that led him to the heart of Kierkegaard and Heidegger, it would still be hard to prove that Wright was an original thinker.

A precursor he was, however, and not only in the obvious sense of having been the first black novelist to achieve fame and fortune in the United States; this was material success, and hence transitory. In addition, the questionable honor of being the "first Black" in America to have accomplished a certain thing only serves to indicate the status of an oppressed minority within its historical context. In history, therefore, Wright may be more widely known as one of the first to have thrown the truth of his resentment in the face of white America. *Native Son* was an act of defiance, an ideological bomb with which Wright frankly proclaimed his fear, sense of deprivation and hatred. But the wide success of *Native Son* was largely due to a propitious historical situation, since other Blacks had through their actions and writings done the same thing before him with some, though lesser, results. Richard Wright's career is linked to a very specific moment in Afro-American history, and if he refused to be considered an exception to the rule it was because all the Blacks of his generation who had survived the hardships put in their way had, in his opinion, accomplished something exceptional, something that even the stories of Brer Rabbit already proclaimed. William Faulkner acknowledged this fact in saying of his Negroes, "They endured." *Invisible Man* later presents the same truth metaphorically. Wright's originality, then, is that he completely understood and often reiterated (although his listeners did not often find it possible, or pleasant, to pay attention to him during his lifetime) that the situation of the Black in the twentieth century, and in particular during the crucial period from the Depression to the advent of Black Power, was exceptional. These years saw the awakening of the Third World and with it the enormous mutation of our civilization. "The liberation of the colored peoples of the world is the most important event of our century," is a refrain that runs throughout Wright's work. The same message, delivered half a century before by W. E. B. DuBois, did not have the same existentialist dimension. For Wright, its symbolic meaning came from his own experience as much as from humanist philosophy: if the black man is awakened, and if everyone accepts the "black man" in himself, will not mankind as a whole eventually accept itself?

This became the goal of Wright's quest, which continually broadened, starting with increasing personal liberation from racism and materialism, and progressing toward a general liberation from the diverse forms of totalitarianism and oppression. In this sense, if it is fair to call *Native Son* prophetic because it foretold the uprisings in cities and the violence of the extreme black militants that would come thirty years later, *The Outsider*, in my opinion, deserves the distinction even more. It depicts the explosion of the social unit, the civil anarchy that results from the growing concentration of power, the weakening of faith, the secularization of man, the advent of the Nietzchean man who has become his own "little god"—all characteristics of the crisis in our civilization, a crisis so serious that it is debatable whether the West is undergoing the throes of an evolution or the agony of a decline. That Wright was the author of these books was not fortuitous. He had suffered the traumatic experience of oppression and his intuition was subtle enough, his historical culture rich enough to enable him to feel all of this perhaps more vividly than any one else. The wound of racial oppression and the negative aspects of his education actually endowed him with a special insight, the double vision of belonging to two cultures (American and Afro-American), which he was then able to convey in forceful and understandable language, even if rapid historical and social change sometimes prevented him from creating the most adequate symbols for it. Wright gave his opinion of these two cultures that he knew from inside and out, and tried to define, if not resolve, their problems. From his revolutionary poems to his appeal in *White Man, Listen!* he sought, with noble impartiality, to unite them. His family heritage, though in many instances a distinct disadvantage, certainly helped him to overcome the provincialism that handicapped other Afro-American intellectuals. His grandmother's Adventism and the severity of his family toward his rebellion against the Southern way of life forced him very early to question the rules of his environment. He could, for instance, sympathize nostalgically with the nationalism of a Garvey without being hampered by an incapacity to view the situation in nonracial terms. Likewise, after he had adopted a Marxist perspective, he was still able to reject the discipline of a party that forbade him to fight for his own people at the same time. I do not intend to deal here with the question of whether he was right or wrong—whether his Marxist ideas prevented him from making any positive contribution to black culture, as Harold Cruse maintains; whether they harmed him as an artist, as Robert Bone believes; or even whether, on the other side, his nationalist sympathies prevented him from becoming anything more than a "marginal revolutionary," as the Communists insist. I only want to stress that with his broad point of view he constantly, and sometimes desperately, tried as a militant writer to make a synthesis between class and race, between White and Black, between Marxism and nationalism, between the individual and society. Whether or not he succeeded, Wright deserves credit for raising one of the main ideological problems of our century and never ceasing to search for the values that would lead him to its solution. Toward the end of his life, when he favored total support of African nationalism against neocolonialism, he defined himself as a "non-Communist revolutionary," but he never stopped thinking of himself as an American, and a Western man. This implied the lawful right to speak out on issues that concerned the West, as well as those that concerned Afro-Americans in particular, on issues that concerned the world as well as those that concerned America. In his effort at universality, Wright wanted nothing human to remain foreign to him; his favorite line from Walt Whitman, "Not till the sun excludes you do I exclude you," shows the place in his heart which was reserved for the disinherited and the oppressed.

This type of humanism owes nothing to the concept of the

"honnête homme" of the Renaissance or the Enlightenment, nor does it stem from the academic neohumanism popular in the United States at the turn of the century. Wright's humanism, in fact, constitutes one of the most cogent reasons to consider him a prophetic writer. Instead of hailing him as a pioneer of Black Power, it would perhaps be better to regard him as a precursor of what Black Power could lead to, and as an accurate, observant and involved critic of his times. He did not envision a mythical America, totally integrated, where enemies would be united in an apotheosis of brotherhood. Rather, he saw a possible America where, should the Whites give up using Nazi solutions to racial problems, federalism would be understood as a more or less peaceful coexistence of various ethnic groups and cultures which, since their individual values were not denied them, could choose to mix freely or to remain separate. Wright claimed this right to coexistence for each one of us when he claimed the black American's right to express himself without a label, without being limited to a role as representative of a race, nation, class or religion. For the sake of all Americans, he wanted, as an American, to be allowed to criticize America. He dared, as a Black, to criticize the nascent state of Ghana; he made it his duty, as a Westerner, to denounce the West. After having asserted, in both his fiction and his political writing, the individual's right to survive against any system, Wright attempted to act as a critical conscience of our world. If he was never wholly successful, the partial replies to his questions and his incompleted projects still represent a greater gain for mankind that a more perfect success as a traditional writer would have brought. For this reason, Wright must not be judged on his writing alone; his career as a militant intellectual must also be put on the scale. He can then be evaluated as one of Ralph Waldo Emerson's living pillars of an era, a "representative man."

ONE

Some people pride themselves on their ancient and noble lineage; Richard Wright used to recall with a mixture of pride and bitterness that his family began with his four grandparents, born in slavery. Far from wanting to reconstruct his genealogy, he readily accepted the mystery shrouding his distant family origins with as much detachment as he did the fact that his birth was never officially recorded. He preferred to have come out of nothing. In the biographical information which he included with his first manuscript submissions, he mentioned only his various jobs and the poverty of his family after the desertion of his father, while in *Black Boy* he says nothing at all about the Wright branch of his family.[1]

The Wrights, who came from a Delta plantation on the Mississippi River, had black, white and Indian, probably Choctaw, blood. Richard's paternal grandfather was one of the few freed slaves in the region who, on the day after the end of the Civil War, was given by the military government the plot of land which he had worked as a slave. More remarkable still, he managed to hold onto it. With his many children, born to him of his wife, whose maiden name was Walker, Nathaniel Wright was able to make a living at the beginning of the century on this small farm in the northwest of Adam County, situated in the village of Stanton, about twelve miles east of Natchez. If some of his neighbors are to be believed, "Old Man Nathan" was something of a patriarch. Strong, surly, with very black skin and opinions to match, he was respected in the community because he had succeeded in combating certain cunning white neighbors who had tried to cheat him out of his piece of land.

Nathaniel's sons soon scattered. Like their father, they were illiterate and, disillusioned with working in his fields from an early age, they preferred to hire themselves out as day laborers on the big plantations. One of the oldest, Salomon, did stay home to help on the farm, but Nathan, who had been born a little before 1880, left home at the beginning of the century to be a sharecropper in a nearby village. There, at a party given by the Cranfield Methodist Church, he met Ella Wilson, the young schoolteacher who became his wife.

Although Richard Wright spent his first three years around his paternal grandparents, he does not seem to have retained a very clear impression of them. Perhaps when he later vowed to forget his father, he rejected all memory of that branch of his family. Whatever the reason, he was much more vividly and profoundly affected by his mother's relatives, with whom he spent the later, more significant years of his childhood.

The Wilsons were much more numerous than the Wrights. They were not farmers, and by their way of life, their education and even, for a time, their income they belonged to the black lower-middle class. Ella Wilson's father, Richard, had led a colorful youth. He was born in slavery on March 21, 1847, on a plantation near Woodville, Mississippi, in Wilkinson County, belonging to a certain John Charles Alexander. At the age of eighteen, he escaped from his master and crossed the Southern lines with a band of slaves in order to join the Union Army. At Cairo, Illinois, he was authorized to enlist for three years in the Federal Navy and so served in the Mississippi Flotilla from April 22 to July 27, 1865, as a landsman on the U.S.S. *General Lyons*, then at Memphis Hospital before returning to civilian life with an honorable discharge. He then settled in Wilkinson County and during the period of Radical Reconstruction seems to have belonged to a black militia set up by the Freedmen's Bureau to insure free elections. He was soon obliged to curtail his militant activities. He lost the sight of one eye, and being somewhat frail, he began to suffer from chronic rheumatism. He moved to Natchez in 1894 and supported his family by jobbing around, since the "black codes" of Mississippi had prevented him from getting the type of work that would have suited him, an intelligent though illiterate man. It is, then, easy to imagine how much his resentment of the Whites must have increased when the Washington government, due to an error in copying his name, repeatedly refused him the pension to which he was entitled as a veteran.

A half century later, when his grandson came to live with him, Richard Wilson, who might have become a hero in the young boy's eyes, seemed little more than an irascible and crippled old man. Despite his gun, his volley of swearwords and the frightful grinding of his teeth, he inspired more pity than fear in his young namesake.

On February 26, 1871, the pastor of the Woodville church, William Haynes, had married Richard Wilson to Margaret Bolden of the same village. Margaret had taken her name from her former master. Born in 1853 or 54, she was, as a result of being more Irish and Scottish than African, ". . . nearly as white as a Negro can get without being white, which means that she was white," according to Wright, in *Black Boy*. Possibly because of her light skin, she had not had to work in the fields but was brought up instead to be a house slave. After Emancipation she learned the trade of midwife-nurse, even though she could not read, so that when the Wilsons settled in Natchez around 1895 she became an assistant to a white doctor. She was competent and scrupulously honest, and her devotion to her work was equaled only by her propensity to preach morality to others, which earned her an indisputable prestige among her friends and acquaintances. At this time a slender young woman whose brown eyes sparkled with intelligence behind steel-rimmed glasses and whose pale face was framed by smooth black hair, she was a lady in more ways than one. Although Richard came to loathe her tyrannical authority, he was still able to recognize that she was the most influential and impressive member of the family.

Whether Richard Wilson was attracted by the proud bearing of this slight woman, by her inexhaustible energy or by her respect for God, it is certain that their union was peaceful from the moment he abandoned to his authoritative wife the responsibility of earning their living, keeping the house and educating their children. Since his bad health obliged him to remain inactive, Richard increasingly found refuge in remembering his glorious past, while Margaret gave more and more of herself to keeping the family alive in their large wooden house on 10 Woodlawn Street, in a respectable Natchez neighborhood.

The nine Wilson children were strongly marked by their mother's influence and at one point or another during his youth Richard came into contact with all of them, except the youngest, Lonnie, who went off to be a sailor. Richard received part of his education from them and, almost as much as his mother and his grandmother, they were the adults who either encouraged or opposed him in his initial efforts to assert himself in the world.

Born in February, 1872, the eldest Wilson child, Thomas Booker, decided to remain a Baptist rather than follow his mother, who had converted and become a stern Seventh Day Adventist. At the time of Richard's birth, Thomas was a teacher in Hazlehurst, Mississippi. He and his wife, Julia Dukes, already had two daughters, Velma and Gladys; from 1920 on, they lived in the same house as Richard. Velma, only three months younger than her cousin, meant much more to him than a mere playmate, in that she was the only relative for whom he felt any affection who also returned it.[2] Uncle Thomas, on the other hand, was an example of what to avoid most in life. Since he was out of work at that time, he had a temporary job re-stuffing chairs, and represented to Richard both failure and sub-servience to the Whites. In *Black Boy* Wright is as devoid of feeling when he paints the picture of this uncle as Thomas was lacking in understanding for his nephew.[3]

Richard scarcely knew his other uncles. Clark Wilson, the third child, born in June, 1880, had become a carpenter and, thanks to the independent income of his wife, was able to set up business as a contractor. He was therefore comfortably off by the time Richard visited them in Greenwood, Mississippi, toward the north of the state, for a disastrous few weeks in 1920.

Uncle Edward, the seventh child, had taught at Carters, Missis-sippi, before becoming a Methodist pastor in Ohio. He later moved to California, so Richard had little opportunity to see him except for a few family reunions. He only met his uncle Charles many years later, when he left his wife, Felicie Kipper, and his carpentry business in Mobile, Alabama, to be at Ella's bedside during a serious illness.

Cleopatra, the eldest Wilson daughter, was born in January, 1876. Originally a teacher in Natchez, she had moved to the Middle West during World War I, so that Wright did not get to know her until 1927, when he went to Chicago to seek his fortune. By that time "Aunt Sissie" was an old, crochety woman suffering from a weak heart. She died in 1942.

Richard's mother, Ella, was born in June, 1883. She was elegant and pretty in her youth. Of medium height and fairly light-skinned, she had great courage and intelligence, and an attractive personality supplemented by a love of order, perseverance, discretion and a reserved, reflective nature. By far her best friend was her sister Margaret, three years younger and completely different. Maggie was robust and full of energy. Combined with her iron will, these quali-ties enabled her to adapt to any situation throughout her turbulent life. Cook, dressmaker and factory worker by turn, she eventually left her parents in 1910 to settle in Elaine, Arkansas, where her husband, Silas Hoskins, ran a saloon. It was with them that Ella and her two sons stayed from 1916 until Maggie's departure for Detroit immediately following the death of Uncle Hoskins. Later, in the thirties, Wright again lived with her while she devotedly looked after both Ella and their ailing mother. In spite of her down-to-earth spirit, which prevented her from sympathizing with Richard's literary aspirations, she was his favorite aunt, and their affectionate relationship ended only with her death.

On the other hand, Richard had a memorable if not altogether peaceful relationship with Addie, the youngest of his aunts. Perhaps because she was somewhat unfortunate-looking as an adolescent, Addie was not distracted from her schooling by suitors, and was the only one of the family to complete her secondary education. An ardent believer, like her mother, she attended the Adventist high school of Huntsville, Alabama, and later taught at the Adventist school in Jackson, where Richard, only nine years younger than she, came up against her excessive severity, showing in return a redoubtable spirit of rebellion.[4]

The size of the Wilson family was not remarkable, since large households were the rule in the South at the time; nor was the mother's power in the home unusual since economic discrimination often left the black male unemployed; rather, the Wilsons were distinct from their neighbors primarily because of their religion, living as they did in the midst of a largely Baptist and Methodist community. For one thing, the Adventist rules forbidding work on Saturday and prohibiting pork made the religion an almost unheard-of luxury; Blacks, more than others, needed to work on Saturday to compensate for their low wages, while pork was the staple meat of the Southern country diet. Mrs. Wilson was almost fanatic in her evangelist zeal, from which even her closest friends were not spared, but they respected her too much for her excellent manners and her unquestionable moral authority to make fun of her somewhat laughable religious eccentricities. In Natchez, the Wilsons inhabited the neighborhood reserved at that time for the best mulatto society of the city, where, for instance, the white aristocrats used to establish their mistresses and the colored bourgeoisie aspired to live. When the Wilsons were economically ruined and had to move to Lynch Street, in Jackson, none of Grandmother Wilson's acquaintances used the customary form of address that would have made her "Aunt

Maggie," but out of deference they all addressed her as "Mrs. Wilson." In spite of their obvious poverty, the family remained eminently respectable and the brothers and sisters demonstrated striking solidarity on many occasions. They had received excellent moral instruction and, what was even more valuable, the kind of education that would enable them either to teach in country schools, become preachers, or at the very least choose professions requiring more specialized training than that of day laborer, which would be the only choice for the Wrights.

When Richard, for emotional reasons, chose to reject his father's heritage, the decision was made easier by the rich tradition of his mother's family. If Richard did not become the delinquent that poverty and racial discrimination could easily have made of him, it was largely due to the influence of his maternal grandmother, although he did not fail to revolt against her in due course. He also learned from his mother, uncles and aunts to value learning. As the author of *Black Boy*, he wanted to see himself as a child of the proletariat, but in reality he attached greater importance to the honorable position of his grandparents in their town than he did to his peasant background. Although he later lived in abject poverty, he never adopted the values of his companions in the street.

2

Even if the general standard of personal responsibility and loyalty practiced by the Wrights could have been said to correspond to the high moral and religious tenor of the Wilson family, there was nevertheless a social gulf between the lower-middle class families of Natchez and the farmers of the surrounding areas, even those farmers who owned their own land. For this reason, Ella Wilson's family considered her marriage to an illiterate laborer a step down. Despite this disapproval Ella, who was teaching in Cranfield at the time, accepted Nathan Wright shortly after their first meeting. They were married in Natchez in 1907 and settled right away as sharecroppers on a farm near the Wrights, twenty-two miles east of Natchez in the village of Roxie with its two hundred inhabitants.

Wright explains in *Twelve Million Black Voices* that share-cropping was for black farmers at the time almost a feudal system. Living in small, ramshackle houses, the farmers put in long days of hard work and were chronically in debt. Perhaps the life was not so gloomy for the young couple since their families were near, able to give moral as well as material support, but, except during the winter, Ella had to give up her teaching to take care of the farm. Nathan, who had long been used to such frustration, suffered much less than Ella in the narrow confines of their existence.

On September 4, 1908, in the midst of these difficulties, Ella gave birth to her first son, who received the Christian name of his two grandfathers, Richard and Nathaniel. Since there was no Office of Vital Records at the time, the event was simply recorded in the family Bible.

A little over two years later, Ella gave birth to a second son, Leon Alan. Since Ella found that she could not take care of two children and the farm, in the autumn of 1911 she went to live with her family in Natchez, while Nathan abandoned farming, which had hardly been profitable, to become an itinerant worker. He thus lived apart from his family for a while before finding a job in the city at a sawmill.

Richard remembered little of his first three years of life on the farm but he recorded a few impressions in an unpublished draft of *Black Boy*:

Vision is what I remember most from my first years, vision in terms of people, objects, landscapes, movement, color, black faces, trees, bonfires, plowed fields, barnyardfowl, movements of birds and leaves. . . .

I seem to remember—always as in a dream—a doorway looking out towards fields and sky. . . . The sight of fields seen framed through a doorway that caught a portion of sky was what has stuck and lingered in my memory.

This is undoubtedly the doorway of the house he was born in, with its wooden floor, two rooms, and the three steps onto the porch. And finally, he preserved one image, of two women, probably his mother and grandmother, chatting and arguing in the courtyard covered with red clay dust; the heady smell of laundry boiling over a wood fire in two black pots; the child not being allowed to get near the flame; a pang of hunger; and words that he spoke without understanding what they meant.

The opulence of the Mississippi countryside was there, with its glorious sights, but he went to live in Natchez with the Wilsons too soon to get a real idea of plantation life, and his subsequent move to Memphis completed his metamorphosis into a city boy.

Natchez had only twelve thousand inhabitants although it was at the time equal in size to Jackson, the capital of the state. The city took pride in its ancient Indian origins, in the vivid memory of its heroic resistance to the Yankee troops, and in the few colonial houses whose names, Devereux, Melrose, Monmouth, for the most part recalled to the black inhabitants only the rigors of slavery on the large plantations. In addition to being an administrative center, Natchez was also a port on the Mississippi second only to New Orleans, and boasted the most flourishing cotton trade on the Delta. The river, wide and rolling with its yellow, muddy waters at the foot of the bluffs, offered an impressive spectacle, with barges and boats going up and down stream and sailors busy on the docks, working under the casual gaze of the idlers. Each Saturday, the motley crowd of noisy farmers from the surrounding countryside would come to sell their produce, do their errands and amuse themselves in the bars. The heart of the black section of town was Saint Catherine Street, which served as a sort of meeting place and cultural center for the colored population of the Upper Delta.

The Blacks accounted for about half the population of the city and, although segregated by law, were often blood relations of their white neighbors. The black community remained on guard, united by a mixture of prudence and resentment, although this did not prevent its members from forgetting their problems in the revelry of market days. In this closed but lively atmosphere, Wright received those first memorable impressions of life which, as a mature writer thirty years later, he evoked only to destroy his illusions about the childhood universe falsely idealized in his memory by the distance of time. In "How Jim Crow Feels," Wright emphasized the rampant disease, filth, vulgarity and apathy of this rural existence because he wanted to show how an overlay of seeming "exoticism" often masked the actually atrocious life of Blacks in the Old South. On the other hand, the few lyrical pages in *Black Boy* glorify these simple earthly pleasures, portraying the world and wonderment of the four-year-old child, with his fresh sensations. It was a land of animals, black and white horses, flocks of wild geese, snakes shining in the damp grass, sparrows poking about in the dust. It was also an elemental world of sun and nighttime, dew and wind, and a world of work in the fields, haymaking, hog killing, and the smell of burning hickory. Crowning all these sights and sensations was the "vague sense of the infinite" that Wright claims to have felt in contemplating the Mississippi from the height of the green bluffs of Natchez. This year spent in the large house on Woodlawn Street allowed the child to enjoy the surrounding nature as a poet, rather than as a farmer's son. He had left the miserable sharecropper's dwelling but not the sights of the countryside. Living in a small city but enjoying the wonders of nature certainly permitted his sensibility and imagination to develop early.

For such an exclusive personality as Richard's, who had apparently been a difficult baby, the birth of Leon might have been seen as a threat. He now had to share his mother's affection not only with his father but with his new brother. Statements in *Black Boy* regarding his opposition to his father at a later date would point to a particularly great longing for the exclusive love of his mother; Nathan's long absences due to his work as a day laborer seem to have been welcomed by the young boy. But in a large household where several women were in charge of looking after the children, he necessarily came in for a larger share of affection and care than he might otherwise have known; and the conversation between the two brothers during the episode of the fire leads us to suppose that Richard had already attained enough strength of character to dominate his younger brother to the point where he no longer needed to be jealous of him. In any case, it seems that only one trauma, albeit a large one, marred that happy year.

One of Wright's earliest memories was of a momentous scolding he received for having set some curtains on fire and burning up a section of the house, which necessitated hastily evacuating his sick grandmother.[5] He may simply have wanted to amuse himself or to imitate the grown-ups, like all children attracted by fire. Or perhaps he consciously disobeyed to prove his superiority over his brother or express his resentment at finding himself neglected in favor of his sick grandmother. Whatever the reason, he was more afraid than hurt by the accident, but his mother's despair upon thinking she had lost him tripled her severity. She beat him fiercely, and he was confined to his bed for days with fever. Whether he really did have the nightmares, described in *Black Boy*, about white, udderlike sacks looming over his bed about to drench him with a horrible liquid, an image that he used to illustrate the transformation of the maternal breast into a threat, he certainly did regard the punishment as a betrayal. It not only seriously inhibited his independent spirit but also caused him to doubt his relationship to his mother. How could the source and object of all love turn into a fury, capable of punishing him so painfully and rejecting him so totally? This episode brutally shattered the emotional security he had derived from the exclusive affection of his mother; the same treatment from his father would certainly not have been as upsetting. The sudden deprivation of his mother was the first in a series of recurring experiences which, although the child was less than four years old at the time, caused a chronic frustration. Every author with a character unbalanced in some respect owes it to some dramatic event which occurred at such an early age that he could neither understand it nor come out of it unscathed. If it is true, as Wilhelm Steckel maintains, that neurosis is an attempt at self-expression, of which the man of genius is the embodiment, then it may well be that Wright's original estrangement and deep insecurity are rooted in this incomprehensible punishment for a transgression he did not accept as such, an experience which long predated his first encounter with racism.

3

It was on the Wrights' trip to Memphis in 1911, that Richard apparently made his unforgettable voyage on the *Kate Adams*, one of the last of the paddle-wheel river boats. Since the family could no longer live at the expense of the Wilsons, and there were very few job opportunities in Natchez, Nathan decided to take his wife and children with him while he tried his chances in a true industrial center.

The population of Memphis by that time was close to a hundred thousand, with the black workers settling between Beale Street and the outlying areas to the southeast of the city. The Wrights rented two rooms in a brick house at California Flats, somewhat south of the famous Blues Street. In this dreary and dirty atmosphere, where bricks and stone replaced the wood and greenery of Natchez, the children had only a small courtyard in front of the house as a play area. Nathan had found a job as a night porter at the Lyle Drugstore, and the restriction on making noise during the day when he slept rapidly widened the gap already apparent between father and son.

Richard was not a wild child in any sense, but he was very willful. His parents showered him with attention. In an early version of *Black Boy*, he admits that they bought him many mechanical toys, among them a monkey and a dog, which he immediately took apart to see how they worked. His father once gave him a drum, which delighted him, but since he never stopped playing on it, it was put on top of a closet where he could not reach it. Characteristically, Richard refused ever to touch it again. What with the constraints due to lack of space and to the presence of his father at home, the boy came to regard his father solely as an incarnation of authority, which his own weakness prevented him from escaping, and in no way saw him as an example to follow or a figure to be proud of and love. Moreover, Nathan's large appetite sometimes made him almost repulsive to Richard, as reported in *Black Boy*, although this could also be a hidden way of suggesting the son's sexual rivalry.

Instead, then, of basing a final judgment of Nathan on the uncompromising picture given in the beginning of the final version of the book, consider these impressions jotted down in an earlier version:

I cannot even remember having established any kind of relationship with my father at all, when I think back to this period. I am dimly aware that I felt a vague dread of him. Though he was real and tangible enough, he always seemed, in my mind, to exist far away. He was the law-giver in the family, I felt. I do not recall his ever having said anything kind. His violence was loud. He was a big man and I still have memories of his drinking beer and eating long and hard at the kitchen table. My mother called my father "Mr. Wright," a strange relic of manners she had inherited from the whites of the South where all men were "Misters."

Wright states in *Black Boy* that his father was "always a stranger to me, always somewhat alien and remote" (p. 9).

Richard's resentment of his father and scorn for him is beautifully illustrated by the story of the kitten. Wright claims that he actually strangled the little creature, whose meowing had elicited the angry comment, "Kill that damned thing!"—taking the words literally so that his father could not punish him without compromising his authority. This may be an overly rational explanation, but Richard's moral victory here foreshadows his future relationship to power in general, and to the power of white society in particular. He rejected his father's authority as tyrannical and unreasonable, and later asserted himself more and more in relation to the rest of his family. Ella remained his only source of values, because she respected his individuality and could appeal to his moral sense. His revolt against his father accompanied a transfer of admiration to his mother, both as an object of affection and a source of authority. Soon, because of her devotion to him, Richard even ceased to fear her.

Memphis was an initiation for Richard in several areas. There was the world of the streets to contend with, where for the first time the boy had to hold his own against his contemporaries. His first fight, in which he was robbed of money given him to do an errand, left him the choice of learning to defend himself or having his mother turn him out of the house. He asserted his rights with his fists, but his need for tenderness was increased as a result. Although he learned to use violence as a survival tactic, he found that it was only a façade to hide his underlying timidity, a weakness of which his frequent silence in front of strangers was a recurring symptom.

It was not long, however, before Richard and his brother preferred to live in the streets rather than in the quiet, empty house. Their mother left every day to work for the Whites, and Nathan returned less and less frequently, choosing the happy atmosphere of Beale Street, with its blues singers, bars and the company of girls, over married life and family problems. He came home rarely and ceased altogether to maintain the household financially. When Ella was away, the children were left to their own devices, perhaps in the casual charge of a neighbor, but free to discover the world within the neighborhood. In this way, Richard would play in all innocence with a used condom, or attach a dead snake to a string in order to frighten the women, or even amuse himself in the company of drunks. He would watch these disreputable grown-ups for hours on end from the doorway of a nearby bar, following them, fascinated, as they staggered off. It is safe to assume that Richard remained a mere observer, as the published version of *Black Boy* does not corroborate the story told in an earlier draft that the child, tempted by one of the drinkers, developed an irresistible craving, linked with eroticism, for alcohol, which turned him into a buffoon to amuse the adults. He was never really a delinquent, despite his effort to make us believe so by exaggerating his depraved behavior to underline the harmful effects of racial and economic oppression.

If living in Memphis offered Richard the world of the streets, circumstances also facilitated his sexual enlightenment. Observing the adults relieving themselves in the open latrines, the young boys naturally grew curious about their sexual habits, although a perverted interest in scatology cannot be deduced from this (*BB*, p. 17). The young girls, too, who would take the child home for something to eat, did not hesitate to kiss and caress their adorable playmate, who had already acquired a feeling of shame and fear about sex. This fear perhaps dates from an episode, not included in *Black Boy,* which had taken place earlier, probably in Natchez. A cousin of Ella's named Laura, who was separated from her husband, was keeping Richard with her for the day and asked him to look at and touch her vagina.[6] He was terrified by this experience, and the fear was reinforced when his mother forbade him ever to see the young woman or her child again. As a result Richard very early felt the taboo surrounding sex and became fearful of women. This terror could have sprung from an exceptionally strong Oedipal conflict in which every woman, and in particular his cousin Laura, was the incarnation of his mother, but it is more likely that in constantly living in crowded quarters, Richard was an unwilling and guilty witness to sexual relations between his parents, a scene which recurs in his novels almost obsessively.

Because of this traumatic and false initiation by Laura, later experiences that might otherwise have appeared normal only reinforced the guilt and fear accompanying any relationship with a woman, and sexuality in any form revolted him for many years to come. Much later notes reveal that Wright had a terror of homosexuality, associating it with the term hermaphrodite; he has a vague memory of wandering through the streets of Memphis, drunk or maybe drugged, imagining that he had become a hermaphrodite, a kind of devil without a tail, in order to revenge himself on the strict religion of his family.

With Nathan's desertion of the family came Richard's first experience of hunger. After two years in Memphis, Nathan was no longer content with staying away from home for merely a few days or weeks; he went to live permanently with his mistress. Ella had already sacrificed her career as a teacher to become a cook for the Whites, just as she had to sacrifice her pride a year later to take her husband before the courts; this was a humiliating episode for Richard, who watched his father smilingly claim that he was doing all he could for his family, his irresponsibility his only reply to the tears of his wife. Richard already associated his father with the horrors of hunger, a moral as well as physical resentment nourished by Ella, who lamented to her boys that they were no longer like other children because they did not have a father. Richard used his mother's bitterness to justify his own disgust, and after the scene in court he totally rejected his father: "I tried to forget my father. I did not hate him; I simply did not want to think of him" (*BB*, p. 24). When poverty forced Ella to send the children to beg Nathan for money, Richard refused the proferred coin, in spite of his hunger; instead he felt like grabbing a poker to strike this person who thus insulted the poverty that he had caused. He never forgot this confrontation, in which the presence of the mistress added sexual guilt to the moral ugliness of the situation:

Many times in the years after that image of my father and the strange woman, their faces lit by the dancing flames would surge up in my imagination so vivid and strong that I felt I could reach out and touch it; I would start at it, feeling that it possessed some vital meaning which always eluded me (*BB*, p. 30).

In fact, Nathan's behavior was not unusual. Job discrimination favored infidelity by forcing the black man to look for work far from home. Under these circumstances he would often be unable to assure the support of his family and would see his authority usurped by his wife, who could more easily get a position as a servant. In any case, Nathan's voluntary desertion had two consequences, one of obliging Ella to support the family herself, and the other of forcing Richard to assume some of the responsibilities of the missing father too early. By the age of six Richard was looking after his younger brother and trying to act as the "man of the house."

The ensuing strained relationship between mother and son was due to circumstances and not to Ella. Richard naturally blamed Nathan's desertion and the subsequent deprivation on the remaining adult. In addition, sensing somewhat confusedly that his mother expected him to be a substitute for his father, he must certainly have been torn between the guilt of having his desire to get rid of his father realized and the fear of not meeting his mother's expectations. His fear of failure caused him to be almost completely paralyzed by shyness, not only with women but in every situation in which he had to speak or act in front of other people.

Then, to his disappointment, Richard discovered that his new position in his mother's affections also meant that, as the sole arbiter of what he was and was not allowed to do, she had to be more severe toward him. Frustrated, the child reproached his mother with having changed roles and tended to rebel. Nothing up to this time had led him to submit to the rules of his milieu, and he questioned the wisdom of these new restraints. Nevertheless, since Ella was the one person whom he respected and admired, his hostility and rebellion were for the time being directed, at least outwardly, against authority figures other than his mother.

This was also a time of initiation into the wonders of reading. If Wright depicts himself as a delinquent, he also credits himself with a curious and lively mind. He learned to count in a single morning, with the coal man as teacher, and he pestered his mother with questions about the world around him while eagerly thumbing through the school books abandoned on the sidewalk by more fortunate children. His first reader was the Sunday paper, deciphered with Ella's help. According to a draft of *Black Boy* in which Wright says that he read about the sinking of the *Titanic,* this must have been the spring of 1912. In spite of this instruction at home, he did not actually go to school until he was seven or eight years old.

He first attended Howe Institute, a small private school in the neighborhood. He was overcome with shyness whenever the teacher asked him to write on the blackboard, to read out loud or even to say his name. In addition to accentuating his emotional problems, school emphasized the shame of being poor and without a father, different from other children, and thus increased the feelings of inferiority that he expressed with explosions of violence or attacks of muteness. Throughout his life Wright was a brilliant storyteller and lecturer, but he continued to be fearful when speaking before an audience to which he could not relate.

Richard acquired his share of learning in class and his share of swearwords and obscenities during recess. Proud of his new knowledge, he scribbled the words with soap on the windows of all the houses on his street, only to be forced, beside himself with rage and shame, to wash them off under the malicious gaze of the neighbors. Already morality was curtailing his rights, and soon religion would, too. In fact, after Nathan left, Ella began to seek refuge in religion, perhaps influenced by her mother, who had come to visit. She sent Richard to Sunday School where, if the savory episode of the pastor who ate all the chicken is to be believed, he came to loathe religious constraint as much as the gluttony of the Reverend.

In 1915, just after Grandmother Wilson had left, after putting a little order into the household, Ella fell suddenly ill. The family became destitute overnight. It was midwinter and, living on the charity of the neighbors, Richard had to take care of his mother and Leon until his grandmother's return. Then the two boys were sent to the Settlement House, a Methodist orphanage where Ella promised to work, as soon as she was better, to pay for their board. It was here that the directress, Miss Simon, terrified him with her advances almost as much as Laura had before her. Constant hunger, the iron discipline and the tricks and intrigues of the other children, combined with the sudden separation from his mother, made this period a long nightmare to Richard. He eventually ran away, only to be caught by a white policeman and whipped by Miss Simon. He had to stay at the orphanage until Ella had enough money to pay for the trip to Elaine, Arkansas, where Aunt Maggie had invited them to live with her.

This difficult time seemed to be coming to an end, but Richard had been permanently affected by it.

Dread and distrust had already become a daily part of my being and my memory grew sharp, my sense more impressionable; I began to be aware of myself as a distinct personality striving against others. I held myself in, afraid to act or speak until I was sure of my surroundings, feeling most of the time that I was suspended over a void (*BB*, p. 26).

His father was dead in his eyes, and he could not depend upon his brother. His mother was the sole object of his admiration, his only source of tenderness and security, and suddenly he didn't know if these, too, might not be taken from him.

4

Before leaving for Elaine, Ella decided to spend several months with her parents. For the children this summer of 1916 was a glorious escape from their long ordeal.

At the beginning of the year the Wilsons had left Natchez for Jackson to spend the rest of their lives near their son Clark, who had bought them a one-story frame house at 1107 Lynch Street, just over a mile southwest of the Capitol. Richard spent the best moments of his childhood in this seven-room house with the back garden, where his grandparents lived in dignity despite their advanced age and their poverty. For the first time he knew the joy of having space:

Its white plastered walls, its front and back porches, its round columns and banisters, made me feel that surely there was no finer house in all the round world (*BB*, p. 33).

After the gray industrial buildings of Memphis, the city of Jackson was a rural paradise. Although the population had doubled in ten years, Jackson had only twenty thousand inhabitants and remained a commercial and administrative center, with no industry to speak of beyond a few sawmills and brickyards. Except around the new Capitol, built in 1903, and in the white sections, the streets were not paved, ditches served as gutters and the shabby wooden houses were built on stilts above the rain-soaked earth. Yet the many trees and gardens, along with the nearby fields and plains, lent the city a restful and picturesque air. The true countryside began only a few miles from Lynch Street. To the east, across the railroad tracks toward the sinuous Pearl River, and to the west, down the Illinois Central line toward Moorehouse, were forests and swamps, stretching all the way to Forest Hill.

The two brothers went on long walks and fishing parties with their grandfather, as well as on expeditions to pilfer blackberries, nuts and peaches. Due to his superior experience of having traveled about the state and lived in Memphis, Richard soon became the leader of a band of children. This summer and autumn in Jackson resulted in one of the few lyrical passages in *Black Boy*, evoking the intoxicating perfume of the magnolia, the tall grass gleaming in the wind, the hot nights dotted with flickering fireflies, and a detail, important above all others, "the drugged, sleeping feeling that came from sipping glasses of milk, drinking them slowly so that they would last a long time, and drinking enough for the first time in my life" (*BB*, p. 40).

A most significant episode of these happy months was the discovery of the wonderful world of fiction. Grandmother Wilson had staying with her as a lodger a young teacher, Eloise Crawford, who one day told Richard the story of Blue Beard to satisfy his incessant demands. This was a day of revelation: "The tale made the world around me be, throb, live. As she spoke, reality changed, the look of things altered, and the world became peopled with magical presences. . . . My imagination blazed. The sensations the story aroused in me were never to leave me" (*BB*, p. 34).

The untimely arrival of his grandmother cut short these delights, since she considered all the great works of fiction to be inventions of the devil. Accused of corrupting youth, Eloise was soon packing her bags, but Richard secretly swore that he would know the end of the story some day and possess the key to this enchanted world.

Richard also became better acquainted with his grandparents at this time, and formed an opinion of them which was confirmed several years later. He speaks of his grandfather with a certain affection, although he was at first terrified by the sudden outbursts of anger of this usually taciturn veteran who kept a loaded gun next to his bed. In fact, since Richard Wilson never beat his grandson, the boy regarded him as practically another playmate and was thankful for the initiation into the pleasures of fishing. His feelings toward his grandmother were more qualified. She was still lively and authoritative despite her diminutive size and advanced age, and believed more than ever in the effectiveness of corporal punishment as preparation for spiritual salvation. She therefore

Nathan Wright.
*Photo by
Richard Wright*

Ella Wilson Wright

Margaret Bolden Wilson

CERTIFICATE OF DISCHARGE.

42-906.
R

ISSUED UNDER THE PROVISIONS OF THE ACT OF CONGRESS APPROVED APRIL 14, 1890.

This is to Certify that *Richard Wilson*

who served under the name of *Richard Vincent*

was discharged from the naval service of the United States,

July 17 — 1865

By order of the Secretary of the Navy: March 10. 1896.

NAVY DEPARTMENT,

BUREAU OF NAVIGATION,

Washington, D. C., March 13, 189 6

Chief of Bureau.

DESCRIPTIVE LIST.

ENLISTED AT			WHERE BORN, AND PERSONAL DESCRIPTION.						
WHEN	TERM.	RATING.	CITY, TOWN, OR COUNTY.	AGE AT ENLISTMENT.	OCCUPATION.	EYES.	HAIR.	COMPLEXION.	HEIGHT. Feet. Inches.
1865			Mississippi	18	None			negro	5 7½
April 3									

Marks and scars: *None*

Richard Wilson's discharge

immediately set about reforming her grandson, who had for too long been left to himself in the streets of Memphis. From the very beginning Richard had good reason to resist her authority.

At this time Richard also seems to have become aware of the customs and laws of the white world. He had certainly seen Whites before and had vaguely held them responsible for the tortures of hunger, but due to his youth and the size of the black quarter in Memphis, he had been spared frequent contacts with them. The rough draft of *Black Boy* indicates that after his escape from the orphanage, he spent hours talking with the white policemen who found him and entertained him by showing him their revolvers and badges. This episode, therefore, was not in the least frightening for the child. In Jackson, however, Lynch Street was quite close to the Capitol and shopping had to be done in white quarters, which also had to be crossed to get to the other black enclaves in the city. This automatically meant more contacts with Whites, and Richard had "the bitter amusement of going into town with Granny and watching the baffled stares of white folks who saw an old white woman leading two undeniably Negro boys in and out of stores in Capitol Street" (*BB*, p. 40).

As he indicates here, he was greatly misled about race and color by the fact that Grandmother Wilson was as white as any white person. For a long time Richard did not understand the difference between the races, since a member of his own family seemed to belong to another race. At a time when the majority of Blacks were aware of segregation and discrimination almost from the cradle, Richard's confusion was all the more terrifying, since he was already eight when he discovered them and he naturally looked for a rational explanation. He thus developed a psychological defense against potential racial violence.

True, I had heard that colored people were killed and beaten, but so far it all had seemed remote. There was, of course, a vague uneasiness about it all, but I would be able to handle that when I came to it. It would be simple. If anybody tried to kill me, then I would kill them first (*BB*, p. 43).

This is the typical, though naïve, reaction of a child discovering oppression and segregation. The very next traumatic episode of his life educated him in its dangers, when Ella took her two sons to Elaine, Arkansas, to live with Maggie.

Aunt Maggie had just married Silas Hoskins, a divorcé who had made a little money with his brother building a number of the new houses in Elaine, a large, recently industrialized town in the northeast of the state. "Buster" Hoskins owned a saloon that served the hundreds of black workers from the surrounding sawmills. Business flourished and the couple lived in a one-story house, surrounded by a large garden, close to the center of town. There, once again, Richard enjoyed the luxury of eating as much as he wanted. He even broke the habit of stuffing his pockets with bread for fear of not having enough the next day. Here he finally felt at home, living with his favorite aunt, far from the reprimands of his grandmother, free to run wild in the glorious autumn countryside. His uncle often took him in his buggy to Cherry Street, the main

street of Helena, a small center on the banks of the Mississippi
protected by enormous dikes. In spite of the fact that Ella forbade
it, Uncle Hoskins undoubtedly also took him to the saloon. Although his uncle terrified him one day when he had had too much
to drink and drove the horse right into the river, Richard became
so fond of him that the tragedy that was about to hit the family
affected him deeply.[7]

One day Silas, who used to spend the night in his bar armed
with a revolver, and come home at dawn, failed to appear. After
the family had spent a day of agonizing suspense, one of the
neighbors informed Maggie that Silas had been killed by some
Whites who had threatened to murder the entire family. Without
taking the time to weep for Maggie's husband, or even to collect
his body, they all fled to West Helena, taking only their personal
belongings with them. Much later Richard found out that his
uncle had ignored the threats and was killed in cold blood by
some Whites who were after his property. The shock of this sudden
death, with the direct threat to the rest of them it implied, crystallized once and for all his vague dread of the white world into hatred:

We, figuratively, had fallen on our faces to avoid looking into that
white-hot face of terror that we knew loomed somewhere above us.
This was as close as white terror had ever come to me and my mind
reeled. Why had we not fought back, I asked my mother, and the
fear that was in her made her slap me into silence (*BB*, p. 48).

Among the familiar specters of hunger and emotional insecurity,
fear of Whites had found its place.

5

Defenseless and penniless, the two horror-struck sisters decided
to return to their mother, and once again, at the beginning of 1917,
Richard headed toward Jackson. It was a quick journey, but one
incident did engrave itself on his mind, one of the scenes cut from
the final version of *Black Boy*. After the stop at Clarksdale, in the
compartment for Blacks, a beautiful mulatto woman placed her

feet on the seat opposite and, by exposing the inside of her thighs, sought to excite the male travelers. Whether Richard was thinking of Laura or not, it did bring home the omnipresence of sex, he admitted in a rough draft of *Black Boy*: "I had never felt so keenly, so achingly the dark terror of the beauty of woman." He could not tear his eyes away, in spite of his mother's disapproval, and it became a memory of capital yet mysterious importance. This scene is characteristic of Wright; the presence of his religious-minded mother and her disapproval of the situation did not succeed in stifling his desire, but this desire, in being suppressed, turned into a feeling of shame. The image of such "bad" women (in whom Laura, his father's mistress and the mulatto girl are combined) is perceived as simultaneously prohibited by his mother, the moral figure in his life, and desirable as a substitute for her.

This time Richard probably stayed no more than three months in Jackson, which was just long enough to learn about the war, since he saw the troops marching by, and to see a chain gang for himself when a group of prisoners came to repair the sidewalk on Lynch Street. According to Richard, Ella soon became so tired of living with her mother that she and Maggie set off again to look for work in West Helena.

This small town of four thousand people, an industrial suburb of Helena, was only about ten years old. It consisted of private houses, workshops, canneries and packaging factories, with food stores sprinkled here and there. The black population was large. Joined to Helena by Route 20, which wound between the gentle hills of Crowley's Ridge, the town was surrounded by small farms, which mitigated the stark aspect of the industrial center.

The family lived there for almost two years, although they frequently moved from house to house and changed neighborhoods. Originally they rented a corner house near the railway station, where the two brothers, with ten cents each for lunch, continued their education in the streets while Ella and Maggie cooked or cleaned for Whites. Leon and Richard joined the children who used to insult the local Jewish grocer, or fish for refuse in the sewers where they launched homemade boats, or scout the alleys of this poor but picturesque section of town with its beggars, prostitutes, thieves and fortune-tellers. Richard also fell in love with the trains. His favorite pastime was watching the mechanics clean

Richard and Leon

or repair the boilers. Sometimes the children would slip between the cars and climb up into the cabin of the locomotive, "imagining that we were grown-ups and had got a job as an engineer running a train and that it was night and there was a storm and we had a long string of passenger cars behind us, trying to get them safely home" (*BB*, p. 53).

In circles where Casey Jones was as famous as John Henry, the engineer was a hero of black folklore, as well as a childhood idol. This love of trains and the escape that they symbolized, the desire to be a leader of men, a superman on an iron monster, crops up throughout Wright's work, as in, for example, the escapes by train in "Big Boy Leaves Home" and "Almos' A Man," and the dream sequence at the beginning of *The Long Dream*.

In this atmosphere of play and popular culture occurred the amusing episode in which Richard, encouraged by a little girl to watch what was going on in an apartment next door, unwittingly pursued his career of voyeurism. Perched upon a scaffolding, he was learning about whorehouses until he fell and attracted the attention of the owner who, unfortunately, happened to be the family's landlady. After an argument of epic proportions between Ella and this woman (yet another confrontation between the mother and a woman of ill repute) the family was thrown out and had to move to a wooden house on the same street.

This house was the scene of another incident that indirectly increased Richard's hostility toward white people. Aunt Maggie had a mysterious suitor, a certain "Professor" Matthews, who wore an impeccably starched white shirt and used to heap presents on the children to gain their confidence. One night Richard overheard a conversation which revealed that this man had just robbed a white woman, then killed her and set fire to her house in order to cover his crime.[8] Richard knew enough to keep silent when a sheriff came to the house, after Maggie and Matthews had fled northward. In spite of his fear, racial solidarity, born of repression, triumphed over his moral scruples and education. Nevertheless, he felt guilty that he had participated in a crime by not denouncing it. As a result he hated the white people who so terrorized him that he was forced to act against his better nature.

Richard's exposure to local community life clarified the implications of his color. The common fear of lynching and the hatred of Southern institutions that favored racism and segregation cemented racial unity. The situation, in fact, was already very explosive. Having proved themselves on the battlefield in Europe and known some equality in France, black veterans were no longer willing to suffer the harassment designed to keep them down at home. The return of the troops brought with it outbreaks of violence. In the autumn of 1919, under the pretext of suppressing a riot, the white mob and militia of Elaine killed several dozen Blacks who had been disturbed at the renewal of white terrorism and had formed farmers' syndicates and a self-defense group.

By that time Richard was already back in Jackson, but the stories from previous years of outrages in other cities had already increased tension in the black section of West Helena. Just as the young boys tried to outdo each other with obscenities in order to proclaim their growing virility, they modeled their attitudes upon those of their elders to prove their courage. Thus Richard adopted pride in being black, and hatred of the Whites:

I had to pay for my admittance to their company by subscribing to certain racial sentiments. The touchstone of fraternity was my feeling toward white people, how much hostility I held toward them, what degrees of value and honor I assigned to race. None of this was premeditated but sprang spontaneously out of the talk of black boys who met at the crossroads (*BB*, p. 68).

Conversations, reveries, boasting and long discussions among Blacks on the porches at nightfall, as well as battles against the children of bordering white neighborhoods, all turned ordinary childhood rebellion into racial resentment. This period supplied Wright with a wealth of experiences and stories which he eventually used as original material in his novels; for example, the ruse of a certain black woman who hid a gun under a blanket in order to kill four of her husband's murderers, when ostensibly she had come to beg humbly for his body, is used in "Bright and Morning Star." Richard's already developed sensitivities could not help but become more extreme:

These fantasies were no longer a reflection of my reaction to the white people, they were a part of my living, of my emotional life. . . . It was as though I was continuously reacting to the threat of some natural force whose hostile behavior could not be predicted (*BB*, p. 65).

Wright also was heir to a wealth of legends, surviving ancestral beliefs, proverbs, folk sayings, tales and superstitions ranging from voodoo to Christianity, all of which form a rich repertory in *Black Boy*. In addition to this heritage and the conversations with his friends whose tone he recaptured so well, Wright fed his imagination on endless fantasies:

Because I had no power to make things happen outside of me in the objective world, I made things happen within. Because my environment was bare and bleak, I endowed it with unlimited potentialities, redeemed it for the sake of my own hungry and cloudy yearning (*BB*, p. 64).

This need for personal as well as racial compensation led him to believe more fully in the truths of these creations of his imaginings than in reality itself, an indisputable source of his literary gift.

As Richard began to accept the values of the black community and adopt its popular attitudes, he was detaching himself from his mother. He respected her moral authority in principle, but he no longer did more than appear to obey her. He swore, for instance, after being wounded in the head during a fight with some white children, that he would never fight again, but of course he was lying. As he wrote later, "If I kept my word I would lose my standing in the gang, and the gang's life was my life" (*BB*, p. 73). Subsequent experiences made him a loner, but at this age he was heavily influenced by his environment, despite the claim of certain critics that he had always been in revolt, cut off from the masses and incapable of participation in communal life.[9] He did not want to be set apart, different from the group; he was, in fact, happy for once to belong to a band of boys, to a clan and to a neighborhood. When his mother found a job working for a white doctor at five dollars a day, Richard was able to attend the community school, where he never called attention to himself or showed a desire to be distinguished from the others. In fact, now that he was finally able to wear suitable clothes, he began to lose some of the shyness that had gripped him in public; at Sunday School he made fun of the hymns and the pastor, like the other children, although he was, like them, fascinated by the Bible stories. In many ways, then, Richard seemed to have become an integral part of the black community.

Fate was against him, however. Ella's health took a sudden turn for the worse and she had to quit her job. By this time Maggie was in Detroit and, despite the generosity of the neighbors, Richard had to leave school to earn a few cents here and there, carrying lunch to the railroad workers and selling food to passengers on the trains in the station. He soon discovered that he was too young and too frail for these jobs. Since the Wrights could not pay their rent, they moved to one of the houses built on stilts next to the river, only to return nearer to the center of town when Richard got a job as delivery boy for a laundry. A third move saw them in a ramshackle house next to the railroad tracks, where the two boys would sneak between the trains in order to collect the lumps of coal fallen from the tenders. Meanwhile Ella's health continued to deteriorate; she fainted frequently and had difficulty talking. "Al-

ready there had crept into her speech a halting, lisping quality that
. . . was the shadow of her future" (*BB*, p. 73). One morning
Richard found her chained to her bed by paralysis, and the wild
terror of losing his mother now joined his sufferings from poverty.
Once again the neighbors took care of the family, since Ella was
unable to speak or feed herself, until the arrival of Grandmother
Wilson, who had been notified instantly.

Meanwhile Richard had become physically exhausted and un-
done by the cruelty of his fate. He was unable to eat the food
offered to him, because he did not want to be indebted to the
charity of others, and he collapsed completely when his grandmother arrived:

I went through the days with a stunned consciousness; unable to
believe what had happened. . . . The utter loneliness was now
terrifying. I had been suddenly thrown upon my own. Within an
hour the half-friendly world that I had known had turned cold
and hostile (*BB*, p. 78).

The courage and affection of his mother had helped him to
survive Nathan's desertion, as the support of his friends had defended him against racism, but now his mother's terrible illness left
him defenseless and, though he was only ten, suddenly much older.
He henceforth lived with the constant, and gnawing recognition of
human frailty, the deep insecurity of knowing that fate could so
easily break the thread of life—he had, at age ten, what could
almost be called an existentialist perception of life.

Grandmother Wilson collected from the family the money necessary to take Ella and the children to Jackson. Maggie came all the
way from Detroit to take care of her sister while Cleopatra, Charles,
Clark, Thomas, Edward and Addie arrived from the four corners
of the state. They each contributed so that specialists could be put
on the case, but Ella remained paralyzed.

In the meantime, Grandmother Wilson was too poor to keep the
two children with her for very long, so Leon happily accompanied
Maggie back to Michigan. Richard was disappointed that he could
not go with them and reluctantly chose to go live with his Uncle
Clark in Greenwood, Mississippi; that way he could at least be
close to his mother.

Greenwood was on the Yazoo River, a few dozen miles north of
Jackson, and took pride in being the world center for long-fiber

cotton. One third of the total population of seven thousand was black and formed a "black belt" around the commercial center and the bourgeois quarter of Guitney. Uncle Clark ran a small carpentry business and owned an attractive four-room house on Walthall Street where Aunt Jody, who was a quiet and neat little mulatto woman, kept herself busy. The household was calm and Richard, who for a long time had not sat down to such a well-provided table, was able to go back to school, but he did not soon get over the shock of Ella's illness. Despite his terrible nightmares and his bouts of sleepwalking, he might have improved had he been given a consistent dose of affection but, if the account in *Black Boy* is to be believed, Aunt Jody's cold and reserved personality made him ill at ease. He was oversensitive to criticism of his poor manners and surprised to be assigned specific chores; he was considered a good-for-nothing whom everyone expected to improve:

Both Uncle Clark and Aunt Jody talked to me as though I were a grown up and I wondered if I could do what was expected of me. I had always felt a certain warmth with my mother, even when we had lived in squalor; but I felt none here. Perhaps I was too apprehensive to feel any (*BB*, p. 78).

This fear of failure was only secondary when it came to Uncle Clark, since Richard was convinced that it was his mother whom he had let down as a dutiful older son replacing his father. He had not only been too young and too weak to earn any money, but he had been unable to prevent bad fortune and illness. He felt responsible for what had happened to his mother, and he was suffering for it. At the same time he was jealous of his younger brother, having gone north with Maggie, even if—or, in fact, especially since—his attachment to Ella had denied him the same choice. Thus his involuntary separation from Ella was his punishment for failing her. Perhaps when he realized that he could not help this person to whom he owed everything, he unconsciously turned against her in order not to feel guilty, a classic example of powerless love turning into resentment.

The immediate result was that Richard became an emotional wreck, and he continued to sleepwalk for more than a year. He did not seem to be frightened, however, of going to a new school. In fact, once he had gained the esteem of his classmates by proving his physical courage, he found school to be a salutary diversion from the long hours spent in Aunt Jody's house. He was more afraid of being alone with his thoughts. When he found out that a little boy had died in his bed, he imagined that the ghost was coming back to haunt him, this being perhaps another manifestation of his diffused feeling of guilt toward his mother. He did not improve until he had rejoined Ella; her presence was his pardon. Once again, as at the orphanage, their separation proved disastrous for Richard, demonstrating his exclusive attachment to her as well as his inability to accept anyone else's authority.

Under these conditions, Uncle Clark's advice was useless; on the verge of a nervous breakdown, Richard was finally allowed to go back to Jackson.[10] His turbulent childhood was over and he went to live out the crucial years of his adolescence on Lynch Street.

TWO

R ICHARD had left his mother thin, unable to walk and "star-
ing quiet as stone," so the joy of coming home was doubled when
he found her in much better health. Nevertheless, she was still bed-
ridden and the doctor advised a second operation. Accordingly,
Richard went with his Uncle Edward, who had come to fetch her,
and put her into the hospital at Clarksdale. Segregation in Jackson
meant that the best-equipped clinics were closed to Blacks and even
in Clarksdale, with the specialist as an accomplice, Ella had to be
admitted as an emergency patient, bandaged from head to toe to
hide her color. Following this humiliation came an anxious wait in
a hotel, the return to Jackson with Ella on a stretcher in the baggage
car, and another period with doctors filing in and out of the house.
The general chaos due to the prostration and groans of the sick
woman was followed by disappointment, since another blood clot in
the brain had caused a relapse.

Once, in the night, my mother called me to her bed and told me that
she could not endure the pain, that she wanted to die. I held her
hand and begged her to be quiet. That night I ceased to react to
my mother; my feelings were frozen (*BB*, p. 87).

Thus, Richard managed finally to accept Ella's paralysis as no
longer a dreaded and unique scandal but a sad state of affairs destined to continue through improvements and relapses until her death
or complete recovery. In writing *Black Boy*, twenty years later, he
interpreted the molding of reactions and feelings that had taken
place at this time:

My mother's suffering grew into a symbol, gathering to itself all
the poverty, the ignorance, the helplessness; the painful, baffling,
hunger-ridden days and hours; the restless moving, the futile seeking, the uncertainty, the fear, the dread; the meaningless pain and
the endless suffering (*BB*, p. 87).

Ella's state of health determined his outlook. The constant prey of morbid thoughts, he became taciturn and purposely avoided showing his joy too openly. His lack of security and his desire to escape increased. He developed an inflexible idea of life, which combined a thirst for reality with the conviction that only a heated struggle would give existence a meaning wrenched from suffering. Skeptical in spite of his curiosity, and eager to get to the bottom of problems, he was attracted by people whose exciting lives seemed likely to clarify his own. His fascination with these personality traits soon became a passion nurturing in him "that enthralling sense of wonder and awe in the face of the drama of human feeling which is hidden by the external drama of life" (*BB*, p. 88). Even if Wright exaggerates his precocity when writing his autobiography, it is important to remember that the future stages of his development all proceeded from his intensely tragic sense of human existence, which was existentialist long before he knew the word. Stemming from poverty and the insecurity resulting from his father's desertion, fostered by racial pressure, this feeling took on a metaphysical dimension with the discovery of the suffering undergone by the person dearest to him. This existential anguish in the face of the human drama remained with him determining his behavior and inspiring his work.

Meanwhile, Ella's illness was causing difficulties for the Wilsons. It was 1920 and Grandmother Wilson, who had never been rich, now had two more mouths to feed, while her age made it more difficult for her to exercise her profession; her husband, of course, was incapable of any exertion on account of his rheumatism. The family had ruined themselves in having Ella cared for and there was no hope of more money coming from anyone.

So once again any superfluous purchase that might have cheered this drab existence was out of the question. Richard wore shabby, patched clothing and suffered the tenacious agonies of constant hunger, which stunted his growth and made him irritable. He had wild dreams of vanilla wafers and would fill his stomach with water to stop the pangs. With only a little beef or fish on Sunday, the family's daily meals consisted of cornmeal mush, hash made of flour and lard, fried peanuts and the traditional greens. Pork was of course forbidden. Furthermore, Richard's right to partake even of this meager fare was contested, since he had refused to stay with Uncle Clark and was not earning a living. As a child he did not have a say in the household, while he was only able to claim support if he subscribed to his grandmother's religion, at least in appearance. Since religion was the principal motive as well as the ultimate goal of Margaret Wilson's life, and her belief was the more ardent in that she was late to convert, she lived her faith and imposed it on her family with unbelievable force. In an unpublished piece, "Memories of My Grandmother," Wright explains his position:

My mother being an invalid, I lived in my grandmother's house and ate her bread and automatically this dependence obligated me to worship her God. My grandmother practised the Seventh Day Adventist religion, a ritual of worship that reaches down and regulates every moment of living. (I sometimes wonder—even though I have abandoned that faith—if some of my present-day actions are not derived, in whole or in part, from the profound and extreme effects of the emotional conditioning which I underwent at that period.)

Richard himself had not been baptized, and his brief attendance at Sunday School, along with the rare and unsatisfactory contacts with pastors, had not led him toward any faith, while the way religion was imposed at home made him hate anything connected with it. At the same time that Grandmother Wilson considered her grandson a stray sheep for her to present to God, she treated him as an evil presence that might contaminate her household. This contradictory desire to draw him into the bosom of the Adventist Church and to keep him at a distance because of the danger he represented, prevented her from trying to understand the child himself. As a result, Richard became increasingly resistant to any kind of restraint, unwilling to perform any outward sign of devotion. He deliberately protected himself with insensitivity and indifference against any metaphysical preaching. This became an open war that lasted for years. Richard was fighting for his survival. First, his deprived childhood had taught him to value the material satisfaction of his appetites, as he goes on to say in "Memories of My Grandmother":

I longed for happiness here and now, in the form of feeling with the feelings of my body. Yet I think I understood with my mind the feelings of religious happiness that surrounded me as I grew up. But I was too sensual for Protestantism; maybe some other form of religion would have snared me.

In rejecting Adventism, Richard proclaimed his individual right to renounce the principle of renunciation itself. Second, and more important, the theological basis of this religion placed such a burden of guilt on the boy that he could not have survived. In *Black Boy* he claims:

Granny intimated boldly, basing her logic on God's justice, that one sinful person in a household could bring down the wrath of God upon the entire establishment, damning both the innocent and the guilty, and on more than one occasion she interpreted my mother's long illness as the result of my faithlessness (*BB,* p. 60).

For him to accept the responsibility of his mother's shameful paralysis, a situation that was already hard to bear since she was the dearest person in the world to him, would have been emotional suicide.

As it was, he suffered an intellectual death, since Grandmother Wilson regularly burned the books that he brought home and smashed the crystal radio that he had made with outstanding ingenuity simply because she would not admit that the music coming out of it had a natural origin. Nature also ordained that everyone had to rise and go to bed with the sun. Every meal was an opportunity to recite verses from the Bible, and every reprimand a pretext to call upon the Almighty. Even if Richard could get out of reading prayers, using homework as an excuse, and merely pretended to kneel, he could not escape the Saturday worship. While all his friends were playing or working, he grouchily followed his grandmother and Aunt Addie to church, a simple wooden building without a steeple at the corner of Rose and Pascagoula streets, only three hundred feet from home. Since Mrs. Wilson was one of the most respected members, she could not let Richard neglect his religious duty without impugning the sincerity of her own belief as well as her ability to persuade, and, as Wright saw it, her power and self-esteem. This was how Richard came to spend the nights preceding the major religious holidays, when the faithful stayed up to pray and sing hymns, curled up on one of the pews where, having devoured his sandwich, he would fall asleep, soothed by the sensual harmony of the music.

Although Richard was revolted by this faith which seemed meaningless to him, completely opposed to the immediate joys of life, he was not impervious to the force of religion. The dogmas of the church did not succeed in breaking his spirit, but their form did leave their mark:

I responded to the dramatic vision of life held by the church, feeling
that to live day by day with death as one's sole thought was to be
so compassionately sensitive toward all life as to view all men as
slowly dying, and the trembling sense of fate that welled up, sweet
and melancholy, from the hymns, blended with the sense of fate
that I had already caught from life (*BB*, p. 97).

The extraordinary stories in the Bible were also bound to capture
his imagination, in the same fashion as fairy tales and horror stories.
Although the austere Adventists did not go in for dramatic sermons,
the elders in the parish often preached with direct inspiration from
the Bible:

The elders of her church expounded a gospel clogged with images
of vast lakes of eternal fires, of seas vanishing, of valleys of dry
bones, of the sun burning to ashes, of the moon turning to blood,
of stars falling to the earth, of a wooden staff being transformed
into a serpent, of voices speaking out of clouds, of men walking
upon water, of God riding whirlwinds, of water changing into wine,
of the dead rising and living, of the blind seeing, of the lame walking; a salvation that teemed with fantastic beasts having multiple
heads and horns and eyes and feet. . . . A cosmic tale that began
before time and ended with the clouds of the sky rolling away at the
Second Coming of Christ; chronicles that concluded with the
Armageddon; dramas thronged with the billions of human beings
who had ever lived or died as God judged the quick and the
dead . . . (*BB*, p. 89).

This compulsory church attendance, in fact, provided early instruction in the understanding of fiction. Wright learned to decipher
the system of representation set forth in these sermons and parables.
Later he borrowed some of his most beautiful images from these
preachers, while many a symbol in his work is taken directly from
the biblical mythology with which he became so familiar.[1]

In addition to this system of poetic representation, Richard also
acquired an increasing respect for the power of ideas, which made
one strong enough, for example, to ignore personal appetites for the
sake of another, broader reality. In "Memories of My Grandmother,"
he goes on to say,

The first and foremost thing that puzzled me about my grandmother's religion was her callous disregard for the personal feelings of others and her inability to understand—and her refusal to

even try—anything of social relationships. Yet this callousness towards others, this stern disregard of things relating to the life of society as a whole was related with an abstract, all embracing love for humanity.

This is a somewhat surprising criticism coming from Wright since with the passage of time, he himself, came to be reproached for using his energies in the interests of humanity, to the neglect of his love for individuals. In any case, Wright did not fail to stress the effect of the Adventist vision, the detached, "outside the world" vantage point that may have caused his later interest in existentialism, while the theme of the "tragic elites" that recurs in his books is partially explained in "Memories of My Grandmother":

Their teachings and their religion, by encouraging me to live beyond the world, to have nothing to do with the world, to be *in* the world but not *of* the world, . . . implanted the germs of such notions in me. . . . These events which create fear and enchantment in a young mind are the ones whose impressions last longest; perhaps the neural paths of response made in the young form the streets, tracks and roadways over which the vehicles of later experience run. Perhaps a man goes through life seeking, blindly and unconsciously, for the repetition of those dim webs of conditioning which he learned at an age when he could make no choice.

At thirteen, Richard of course did not appreciate the knowledge that he was unconsciously acquiring. Religious services were merely a painful waste of time.

The church later became the setting for his awakening sexuality. In spite of a diet that, he ironically claims in *Black Boy,* "would have stunted an average-sized dog," Richard had arrived at puberty. More and more interested in the opposite sex, he regarded church as an ideal place to contemplate feminine charms. He amuses himself in *Black Boy* (with not a trace of the remorse that would have tortured a conscience-ridden James Joyce) recalling the happy combination of religious atmosphere and desire. He fell idealistically in love, as is usual at that age, with the wife of an elder, who sang in the choir:

I felt no qualms about my first lust for the flesh being born on holy ground; the contrast between budding carnal desires and the aching loneliness of the hymns never awoke any sense of guilt in me. It was possible that the sweetly sonorous hymns stimulated me sexually, and it might have been that my fleshly fantasies, in turn, having as their foundation my already inflated sensibility, made me love the masochistic prayers. It was highly likely that the serpent of sin that nosed about the chambers of my heart was lashed to hunger by hymns as well as dreams, each reciprocally feeding the other (*BB,* p. 98).

Although Wright is being ironic, his adolescent experiences could easily have led him to interpret worship as a disguised expression of sexuality and later to propound this psychoanalytical view of religion in *Pagan Spain.*

Richard was under constant pressure to convert. The entire family ranged itself against him, alternately threatening and supplicating him, enlisting his friends against him as well as hurling all the rhetorical thunderbolts of the preacher at his head. Prayers, revival meetings and parish services were in vain. It was not so much that he refused to believe in the existence of God, but that religion as it was practiced seemed like tyranny, or an empty ritual. He limited his faith to what he could understand and associate with his immediate environment; thus, even the daily spectacle of his mother's suffering, which frightened him so much, could not force him to bow down before an invisible power.

If he could have found somewhere else to live he probably would have done so, since he depended upon his grandmother and his aunt for subsistence and could not refuse indefinitely to convert without antagonizing them.

One incident in particular precipitated the final crisis in his relationship with his grandmother. During a sermon about Jacob fighting the angel, Richard tried to explain to her that he, too, would have to see an angel in order for him to believe. She misunderstood and thinking that he had already seen an angel, proclaimed the miracle to her friends. Richard hastily disabused her of this idea, thus disappointing her dearest hopes and making her ridiculous in public. Although he promised to pray for his own conversion, Grandmother Wilson never forgave him; she considered her grandson a lost cause in the eyes of God. For his part, Richard performed his duties and even tried to write hymns to compensate for his lack of fervor, but when nothing came of this she relegated him to the ranks of the damned. In one sense this implacable coldness from his grandmother was a release, since he could finally escape the world of Adventism and spend more of his time at school and with his friends.

2

Richard had never yet attended school for a full year. After only a few months at the school in Greenwood, in 1920, he was unable to return to class in Jackson for lack of proper clothes. He waited for vacation to be with his friends, devouring everything he could lay his hands on, textbooks belonging to his young neighbors, old almanacs and local weekly papers.

In September, 1920, when he would have preferred to join his friends in the Jim Hill public school, he was sent to the Adventist school by his grandmother, who wanted to supplement the religious instruction he received at home. The school was actually one room in the Rose Street Church and the only teacher was Aunt Addie, who had just finished secondary school in Huntsville, Alabama. As devout as her mother, she was soon made secretary of the parish and put in charge of over thirty children ranging from five to fifteen years old. With their polite and retiring manners, her pupils seemed pretty dull to Richard, who had for so long been knocked about in one city or another, participating in adult life, sometimes in its least recommended aspects.

Richard's relative maturity and unruliness made him the only threat to Addie's authority, so she immediately resolved to punish him as a lesson to everyone. When his neighbor, who had cracked nuts in class, refused to confess, Richard took his beating for an offense he had not committed without complaint. On the other hand, when Addie started in on him again at home, Richard, outraged at so much injustice, grabbed a kitchen knife to make her respect him. During this epic scene, related in *Black Boy*, even Grandfather Wilson could not disarm him.

That day the undersized boy did more than win a battle. He learned how to overcome the authority of the family, discovering that violence would also earn him respect in the adult world. He totally ceased to respect Addie, who now treated him with scorn and coldness. She never called on him again in school and he ceased to study with any regularity.

To his immense relief, he was allowed to go to public school the next year, although all his worries were not over. He had long been responsible for mending his clothing, which was now threadbare, and had to wait for weeks before he could buy his books. He also had to prove his physical courage when forced to fight someone who had thrown his new straw hat to the ground. Nevertheless, he had a burning desire to go to school in order to balance his own experiences with his knowledge from books. He also yearned to become more a part of the black community from which his family's religion isolated him.

On this score, his school years in Jackson were satisfying. Jim Hill School was just to the east of where he lived. When he was admitted to fifth grade in September, 1921, he was about four years behind an average white boy who had gone to school regularly, and about two years behind his own friends; but the teacher, Miss Lucy McCranie, soon recognized his true intellectual capacity and after a few weeks put him into sixth grade. Richard was uncontrollably happy, and he already dreamed of being a doctor. In sixth grade Miss Alice Burnett taught arithmetic, reading, English composition, history and geography,[2] while Mrs. Johnson gave classes in singing and music for the entire school. With his lively intelligence, Richard had a great natural desire to learn and a respect for teaching instilled at home, yet he did not refuse to play hookey on occasion. This was more out of boredom than laziness, since he used to study by firelight when there was no more kerosene in the lamp. He rapidly exhausted the material in his books and would take an illustrated magazine into class, which he perused while half following the lesson in progress.

As he had in West Helena, Richard also mingled happily with the other pupils who, for the most part, continued to attend school with him. Ten years later in Chicago he was still friendly with some of them, such as Dick Jordan, the undisciplined son of the Clifton Street grocer; Joe Brown, who lived in Washington Addition; Perry Booker, D. C. Blackburn, Lewis Anderson, Sarah McNeamer and Essie Lee Ward. He states proudly, "I was now with boys and girls who were studying, fighting, talking; it revitalized my being, whipped my senses to a high, keen pitch of receptivity. I knew that my life was revolving about a world that I had to encounter and fight when I grew up" (*BB*, p. 110).

The joy of doing well in class and being part of a gang also meant that Richard began to resent the things that differentiated him from the others—his poverty and, above all, the eccentricity of a religion that forbade him to work on Saturdays to earn the necessary dollar that would have made him equal to his friends. Accordingly, he would often shy away at the last minute from a chance to begin an intimate friendship, from a sudden reflex of embarrassment and mistrust. He refused invitations to parties because he was ashamed of his clothing. He bravely pretended not to be hungry while the others gobbled down enormous sandwiches.[3] Luckily this pride and reserve, which some people misinterpreted as conceit, did not fool his best friends, who tried to make him share both their meals and adventures. On many an evening he would forego his plate of vegetables so as not to be kept in the house by his grandmother and join the group wandering about the streets and the fields, to watch the workers at the brickyards and the cotton mills, or organize a baseball game, or figure out how to sneak into the Alamo to see a Western at the only movie house in the neighborhood.

In order to satisfy both his thirst for knowledge and his hunger for food, Richard looked for a job as a newsboy after class. Although Grandmother Wilson burned all the magazines that came into the house, she gave him permission to do this and his friend Dick Jordan provided the opportunity. Besides the few extra pennies he would earn, Richard could read the illustrated literary supplements of the Chicago *Ledger* and the *Saturday Blade* he delivered every week. He was thrilled by the crimes of an imaginative scientist who diabolically tortured his victims in "The Copper Room," and he devoured *Riders of the Purple Sage*, Zane Grey's recent success, which the *Ledger* was putting out in installments.[4] Since he was interested only in the fantastic tales and horror stories, Richard did not realize that the paper was totally run by supporters of the Ku Klux Klan until Essie Ward's father pointed it out to him.

According to *Black Boy*, Wright had already tried to write himself the year before. He had written a story mixing his memory of a series of books on Indian history with overtones of sensuality. Apparently inspired by the death of a girl who had lived next door, he wrote a few pages about a young Indian girl who, when her lover broke his promise to return to her, walked into a river and drowned herself.[5] Proud of his work, he rushed over to read it to a girl friend, whose surprise and complete failure to understand what he had tried to do was oddly flattering. He realized that literature offered him more than an escape; he could actually compensate for his feeling of inferiority. Thus Richard probably made the most of his talents as a storyteller in order to impress his friends. At any rate it is certain that his imagination and verve astounded them.[6]

Since there were no summer jobs that did not require working on Saturday, Richard spent his vacation doing nothing, bored and frustrated. Since he was at home most of the time, old quarrels came alive, but now when Aunt Addie would start to scold him, he would simply grab a knife while Grandmother Wilson stood by helplessly. Ella, meanwhile, had slowly gained enough strength to be able to walk with crutches. As she helped with the daily chores, she tried her best to reconcile the adversaries and to calm her son's violence, even though she often shared his irritation.

At the end of the summer, Richard reaped the rewards of his education. A Lynch Street neighbor, Mr. W. Mance, needed a secretary-accountant to accompany him on a trip to the south of the state in order to sell insurance. They traveled by train, car, and carriage from one Delta village to another.

Richard knew very little about life on the backward plantations of Mississippi, so these were his lasting impressions of the rural South before he started writing in the thirties. His descriptions of the black sharecroppers prior to 1940, when he briefly returned to his birthplace, were based on what he had observed in the Delta in 1922. In *Black Boy*, he was struck by the monotony and stupidity of this "bare bleak pool of black life." While he slept on corn-shuck mattresses and filled up on salt pork, black-eyed peas and milk, he was observing the conditions in which his parents had lived at the beginning of the century.

On Sunday, Brother Mance would go to church and preach a mixture of religion and insurance sales talk. He vividly conjured up the ever-present specter of death to sell a guarantee of a handsome burial to the impressionable farmers. Richard became familiar with this sort of sermon, which he later used to effect in, for example, Pastor Ragland's funeral speech for the victims of the dance-hall fire in *The Long Dream*.

Richard also learned the value of education from this trip. The poverty of these illiterate farmers from whom he was descended was far worse than his. The sharecroppers gazed admiringly as he filled out the insurance forms and encouraged their timid children to say hello to him, and the wives were awed by his erudition.

Richard was convinced once and for all that a good education was the only path to salvation.

During that summer Grandfather Wilson fell ill. Richard Wilson had for a long time been immobilized by rheumatism. His meals were brought to him in a first-floor room overlooking the street, where he lived with his memories. Sometimes he came down to warm himself in the sun, musing for hours while he sharpened his knife and hummed old military marches. Young Richard had long since ceased to be afraid of his former playmate, and the old man no longer even answered questions about his campaigns in the Civil War.

Grandmother Wilson was still fond of relating her husband's exploits, so Richard learned from her how his grandfather had joined the Union Army to take revenge on the South. Now that he was older, Richard's fertile imagination could conjure up a hero to replace the fast-declining veteran he knew. Since Grandfather Wilson had been discharged from the Army under the name of Vincent, he was never able to prove to the authorities that he had served and thus never received the pension due him for having been wounded. His old age was clouded by the conviction that he was the victim of a Confederate plot, and he died on November 8, 1922, without having been able to convince the authorities of their mistake.[7] Richard was called to say a final good-bye to the old man, who died the same night. Later he was to remember him as a symbol of both the constant black resistance to the white world and the unjust defeat of the black people.

By this time, the young boy felt increasingly isolated from his family and persecuted by his grandmother's restrictions. One day, tortured by the shame of having to go to school in rags and determined to earn money enough to be able to buy a sandwich at lunchtime, he packed his belongings and threatened to leave right away if he was not allowed to work on Saturdays. Whether or not Margaret Wilson's feelings triumphed over her principles, Richard reports that she yielded. "Now I was truly dead to Granny and Aunt Addie, but my mother smiled when I told her that I had defied them. She rose and hobbled to me on her paralytic legs and kissed me" (*BB*, p. 126). Even in his solitude Richard always derived strength from his mother's moral authority, which supported his own revolt. He lived in the hope that one day she would be well enough to take him somewhere else and make a real home for him.

Upon his return from the Delta, Richard went into seventh grade, the last year at Jim Hill School, which was taught by the director himself. Samuel Brinkley was an excellent teacher. He had one paralyzed arm but stood up as straight as a ramrod and maintained as much discipline with his cutting remarks as with corporal punishment. He seems to have been interested in Richard, who was a gifted and conscientious student, and this final year of school was profitable and without noteworthy events.

This was the first year that Richard was allowed to work, and he used the hours after school as well as on the weekend to help pay for his keep. His first job paid $2 a week and consisted of running errands and doing chores; but the hard work and the scorn of his mistress, combined with the meal of moldy molasses that he could no more eat at breakfast than he could when it was served up again at dinner, were enough to make him quit after a few days. Since he had never before worked for white people, he naïvely thought that this was simply a piece of bad luck, little imagining the harassment he would later learn to expect. His second job was on an outlying farm where he milked cows, took care of the poultry, cleaned house and served breakfast. Richard was under great strain in this job, which naturally showed up in class, but he was somewhat compensated for this by being able to make himself a breakfast of hastily scrambled eggs and gulping down enormous glasses of milk. He was able at last to pay for books, lunch, some new clothes and occasionally something that he had coveted for a long time and was able to buy on credit, such as his watch. Most exciting of all, he was finally equal to his friends. During recess he could exchange jokes with them about white employers and boast about how much he could get away with.

Because of his superior intelligence and imagination, Richard was made the head of a Dick Wright clan, to which the most lively and independent sons of the neighborhood bourgeoisie belonged. The group, which included Dick Jordan, Perry Booker and Joe Brown, met in the cellar of Frank Sims, the son of a respectable black citizen of Pearl Street. They had their password and their ritual games (playing "snake" and other tricks on women passersby), not altogether innocent pastimes, which Wright describes in "Tarbaby's Dawn" and *The Long Dream*.

On summer afternoons, they often went southwest of the city to swim at Rock Bottom Creek, which belonged to Mr. Barrett. The elderly white man sometimes threatened them with his gun, but without much success, although they themselves drove the white boys away with stones on the theory that, since the municipal swimming pool was for Whites only, Rock Bottom Creek should be for Blacks. These swimming parties provided the setting for Fishbelly's battle with clay balls and it is likely that Robert Ellis' accidental drowning in the swift current of the creek under the horrified eyes of his friends was later elaborated into the tragedy of "Big Boy Leaves Home." [8]

Now that he worked for white people, Richard was himself prey to a tension which never abated with time:

I was tense each moment, trying to anticipate their wishes and avoid a curse, and I did not suspect that the tension I had begun to feel that morning would lift itself into the passion of my life. Perhaps I had waited too long to start working for white people; perhaps I should have begun earlier, when I was younger—as most of the other black boys had done—and perhaps by now the tension would have become an habitual condition, contained and controlled by reflex. But it was not to be my lot. I was always to be conscious of it, brood over it, carry it in my heart, live with it, sleep with it, fight with it (*BB*, p. 131).

While Richard was endeavoring to satisfy the whims of his employers, he had to accept another compromise: he finally agreed to join his mother's church. Ella was almost well. She was able to walk without canes and she may even have gone back to her teaching.[9] Thrilled at the thought that they would soon have a home of their own, Richard smothered her with attentions, which included accompanying her to the Methodist church. Ella had remained faithful to this church whose congregation differed greatly from the handful of rigorous Adventists who attended the Rose Street Church. Various sections of the black bourgeoisie found a dignity in the Methodist church that bathed them in an agreeable feeling of self-contentment. The rituals were not austere, and the sermons often reached a pitch of frenzy. Richard was thus exposed to a flamboyant group which he describes in *Black Boy*, somewhat condescendingly, as a crowd dedicated to

snobbery, clannishness, gossip, petty class rivalry, and conspicuous display of cheap clothing. . . . I liked it and did not like it; I longed to be among them, yet when with them I looked at them as if I were a million miles away. I had been kept out of their world too long ever to be able to become a real part of it (*BB*, p. 152).

During the numerous services for the "revival," Ella entreated Richard to be baptized. Innocently drawn in by the earnest deacon, who then trapped him with the weapons of sentimentality and shame, he lacked the courage to break a silence which was the equivalent of an affirmation, and he found himself among the group to be baptized in the Episcopal Methodist Church of Lynch Street.[10] Although he was old enough to see through the farce of which he was an object, he loved his mother too much to disappoint her in public.

It was a simple, urgent matter of public pride, a matter of how much
I had in common with other people. If I refused it meant that I did
not love my mother, and no man in that tight little black community
had ever been crazy enough to let himself be placed in such a position (*BB*, p. 135).

After several months of boredom at Sunday School, Richard naturally returned to the streets and the countryside. Perhaps he had hoped, in converting, to remove some of the barriers which still seemed to separate him from other people, but in fact this formal submission to the laws of the black milieu did not help him to become a part of it, since the barriers were within himself. First fear and shyness had caused him to turn inward because he came from a family that was "different" from others. Now he scorned the religion which the Blacks used to forget their human condition. The church was nothing more than an outlet, like women and alcohol. Richard's only salvation was learning, which seemed to separate him from his own people but would later enable him to combat the Whites on their own grounds. If his critical sense rejected mediocrity and provincialism, he paid for his intransigence with painful isolation. He was rejected more often than he rejected others. This became even more noticeable in the spring of 1923 when Uncle Thomas, who had lived on the outskirts of Jackson for a year, came with his wife and two daughters to live in a few rooms in the large Lynch Street house. This posed an additional financial strain, because Thomas could no longer find work teaching and only managed to survive by repairing furniture and restuffing chairs. Meanwhile, the family's resources had been completely drained when Ella had yet another relapse, which left her once again paralyzed. So when Richard's fondest hope of going to live elsewhere with his mother was dashed, he had to contend with this uncle who, accustomed to being obeyed, determined right away to take a strong stand against his rebellious nephew. Once again Richard resorted to violence, arming himself with razor blades this time in order to avoid an undeserved punishment. It is only fair to say that Richard could not imagine how humiliated Uncle Thomas had been by trying to survive in the South, and apparently he was not aware that the fifty-year-old man was already suffering the first symptoms of Parkinson's disease. To Richard he seemed only a mixture of servility and failure. Whether or not Wright is correct in saying in *Black Boy* that Thomas was compensating for his own failure by crushing those weaker than he, he did seem totally incapable of respecting the qualities and personality of the young adolescent, and he made no effort to show Wright any affection.[11]

Summer. Bright hot days. Hunger still a vital part of my consciousness. Passing relatives in the hallways of the crowded home and not speaking. Eating in silence at a table where prayers are said. My mother recovering slowly, but now definitely crippled for life. Will I be able to enter school in September (*BB,* p. 141)?

This was the situation at home in June, 1923. Richard had just finished Jim Hill School, and if he wanted to go on to eighth grade at Smith-Robinson he had to find a full-time job immediately. He first worked as water boy in the Bullard brickyard, a few blocks west of Lynch Street. For $1 a day he carried a zinc pail of water under the hot sun and endured the insults of his boss, whose dog, according to *Black Boy,* bit him severely one day. At first Richard had been afraid of Kate, the mule he had to work with, but one day he screwed up his courage to actually climb onto her back and from then on he ran races with Perry Booker, at the risk of being fired by the foreman.[12] When the yard closed, Richard spent some time as a caddie at the municipal golf links, some miles from town, but he soon had to give this up because he tired too easily and could not follow the balls with his eyes.

In September, Richard got a job with a white family named Wall in order to pay for books and supplies. Although *Black Boy* was designed to describe the effects of racism on a black child, which meant omitting incidents tending to exonerate white persons in any way, there is no doubt that the Walls were liberal and generous employers. For almost two years Richard worked before and after class, earning three dollars a week bringing in firewood and doing the heavy cleaning. Mr. Wall, the foreman of a sawmill, lived with his young wife and mother-in-law (a former teacher called Dr. Johnson) who were, therefore, the first friendly white women of Richard's acquaintance. Since they respected his qualities as an individual, he sometimes submitted his problems and plans to them and soon considered their house a second home where he met with more understanding than from his own family.

One traumatic incident took place at the Walls' which, as Doctor Wertham, who made a study of psychological determinants in *Native Son*, remarked, reappeared in the central scenes of the novel. One day when he was bringing in some wood, Richard entered Mrs. Walls' bedroom without knocking. He found her getting dressed and was, for once, severely reprimanded. Undoubtedly this caused him to become aware of the sexual significance of his intrusion, which in his fantasies he connected with an earlier memory of being scolded by his mother for looking at a nude little Mexican girl in a city park. He had, in fact, inadvertently broken the barrier protecting white women from black men and, on another level, the mother from the son. The sin of being a potential, if not intentional, ravisher only reinforced the guilt deriving from his first disturbing sexual experiences. Wright agreed with Wertham that the episode is reproduced in *Native Son*, when Bigger kills and burns Mary. All the elements are there; the disapproving presence of the girl's mother, the virginal bedroom, the possibility of rape and finally the fire. (Wright was bringing wood to light a fire; Bigger took care of the furnace of the central heating system.) [13]

Perhaps the embarrassing and intimate nature of his memories of them caused Wright not to describe these people in detail, as well as the fact that they did not conform to the image of how white Southerners were supposed to treat Blacks. Nevertheless, he must have acquired a certain knowledge of the white world and its manners from these friendly people. This entailed its own set of difficulties, however. Although his self-confidence was increased, since he was encouraged to treat white people as equals and to expect mutual consideration, he was at the same time sheltered from the evils of the racism around him, and this left him totally defenseless against the general hostility of white Southern society toward the Black. At the same time Richard learned to appreciate the positive and desirable aspects of life in a white family like the Walls'. Furthermore, this warm relationship with white women accustomed him to look to them for guidance and help. Later, in Chicago, when Wright's attitude toward the white woman had crystallized, he sought in her not only the sexual satisfaction and revenge that she afforded him, but also a companion who, more than anything else, would be a teacher and a sort of mother. He preferred the white woman, with her ease and brilliance, cultivated by her background, to the black woman, whose intellectual capacity he was prone to underestimate.

For the time being this job enabled Richard to continue his studies at Smith-Robinson. The black children usually spent two years there, after elementary school, and graduated at age fifteen or sixteen. Every morning, with his friends Dick Jordan, Joe Brown, Essie Lee Ward, Wade Griffin and Varnie Reed, he crossed the center of town and the fringes of the railroad station to reach the school at the corner of High and East Monument streets. There Mrs. Mary L. Morrison taught eighth grade and Reverend Otto B. Cobbins, the ninth. According to Wright, they were both competent and dedicated teachers despite their limitations.[14] The principal, W. H. Lanier, ruled the establishment with almost military discipline and inspired Wright's assiduity and obedience, which contrasted markedly with his behavior at Jim Hill. He was soon at the head of the class, distinguishing himself particularly in history, English and anatomy, but bowing to Minnie Farish and Dick Jordan in mathematics and civics.[15] Since he learned easily, he quickly became bored with the textbooks he had read many times, so his private reading of the old illustrated magazines filled in the empty hours at school.

Meanwhile, Richard's literary attempts produced his first published story, "The Voodoo of Hell's Half Acre." Wright describes it in *Black Boy* as

a plot about a villain who wanted a widow's home. . . . It was crudely atmospheric, emotional, intuitively psychological and stemmed from pure feeling. I finished it in three days and then wondered what to do with it (*BB*, p. 144).

According to the typesetter who made up the issue of the *Southern Register* where the story appeared, in the spring of 1924, the tale, entitled "Hell's Half Acre," began like this:

Gone are the days when I attended Jim Hill School. . . . Professor S. Brinkley was my principal: Mrs. Alice Burnett, my 6th grade teacher, often took my friend Bigger Thomas and I to the office of Professor Brinkley, for playing marbles, behind Jordan's store next door to the school and not knowing our lesson. Often times we would pick daisies and take her a bouquet, to keep her from taking us to the office, as our next move would be punishment by Professor Brinkley, as he would put one hand in his pocket, rear back in his chair as tho' he was going to have a talk with you, and his next word was: "Give me my hickory! Let your suspenders down and give me your back." I cared very little for books as my method of study was poor. I lived only one block West of the school on Lynch Street. We had no lights and so I would often get my lessons as best I could by fire light if we had no kerosene.

I remember one day in March in flying a kite, our kite alighted in a tree in Mr. Diamond Cox's backyard. I was afraid to go in after it, so I got Bigger to go in for me and Mrs. Cox said she would have Bigger arrested and tell my mother as soon as she came home from school. My mother was teaching the rural and it was always after dark when she came home. . . .[16]

This does not agree at all with Wright's own recollection of the story; it even seems that the word "Voodoo," so heavily charged with atmosphere, did not actually appear in the title. In any case, the story consisted mainly of personal experiences, without much imaginative embroidery. More important than this discrepancy, however, is that the typesetter's reconstruction indicates that Wright used James "Bigger" Thomas as his hero. This boy was the neighbor whose name Wright used fifteen years later for the protagonist of *Native Son*. He was also called "Biggy," a shortened form of "big-gity," a pejorative term used by southern Whites to describe any black person who was not sufficiently humble. Ella and Grandmother Wilson deplored Bigger's influence over Richard, since he would bully children weaker than himself and even defy adults. Richard both feared and envied his strength, but he soon learned to tame Bigger's brutality with cunning and would flatter him into aiding and abetting some of his more reprehensible plots, such as the excursions into Mr. Cox's orchard. Although Bigger did not go on to the Smith-Robinson School, Wright never forgot him, and he made him the literary symbol of black revolt suddenly exploding after a long period of oppression.[17]

Richard could not hope to find an audience within his family, so he went to see Malcolm D. Rogers, for whom he had sold and delivered papers. In addition to owning a store, Rogers was the editor and printer of the *Southern Register*, an eight-page weekly that had been started in the autumn of 1923. This was one of the first attempts to establish a black press in Jackson, since the local daily papers naturally ignored news of the black population. Rogers was educated, dynamic and militant, and he appreciated these same qualities in Richard. To encourage him, therefore, he agreed to publish the story in three installments.

Richard soon enjoyed a small fame among the readers of the paper who knew him. Not unexpectedly, the word "Hell" in the title brought the wrath of Grandmother Wilson down upon him. She was afraid that the director of the school would turn against Richard because of the story; Uncle Thomas merely scorned Richard for this literary attempt. Richard's friends, at first surprised, admired him mightily, although in *Black Boy* Richard mentions noticing a certain distrust as well.

The mood out of which a story was written was the most alien thing conceivable to them. They looked at me with new eyes, and a distance, a suspiciousness came between us. If I had thought anything in writing the story, I had thought that perhaps it would make me more acceptable to them, and now it was cutting me off from them more completely than ever (*BB*, p. 146).

It is conceivable that Wright exaggerates this new barrier. The class could boast members of equal education and intelligence, and several came from fairly cultivated middle-class families. He certainly did not stand out as a solitary genius amid a mass of mediocrity. Furthermore, since Richard knew nothing of literary techniques, his story was a completely instinctive creation. It would therefore be premature to mention a gap between the writer and his public. Those who knew him at the time remember him admiringly as an extremely talented storyteller.[18]

What Richard's friends were unable to fathom was his seemingly excessive ambition. He dreamed that as soon as his mother got well, he would take her away from Jackson. He knew that a black person could not expect to find a decently paid job in the South. The North, therefore, glamorized in Aunt Maggie's letters and the reports of men returned from cities in the Middle West, seemed like a Promised Land. For these enterprising young people, the large cities meant adventure, which was, of course, glorified in popular novels. Richard was an avid reader of Horatio Alger. He believed implicitly in the Wallingford series of ways to "Get-Rich-Quick," in the myth of the self-made man, in the great American dream whereby everyone had an equal chance.[19] If the South flagrantly denied this ideal, perhaps the North would allow a creative and ardent personality to flourish, even if it lived in the skin of a black man.

With summer came the problem of finding a full-time job again. Richard was not strong enough to work at Mr. Wall's sawmill, and he lamented the fact that everyone seemed to be able to get work but him. A shocking event that summer depressed him deeply for weeks. Ray Robinson, "Chunky," as he was called by his friends, was married with two children. He worked as a bellboy at the Edward House, the large hotel in Jackson. Attractive and charming, he had for several months had a white mistress whom he refused to give up in spite of threats from certain Whites who knew about the affair. Eventually "Chunky" was arrested and reportedly "shot while attempting to escape" as he was being transferred from Jackson to the prison in Raymond. In fact, he was tortured to death in the woods southwest of the city. Richard did not know the man very well, but since he was the older brother of his classmate Carl, he was terribly frightened by his murder. He, too, was at an age where women attracted him, already perhaps those who were protected by the terrible taboo. He could, therefore, feel just as guilty as the actual victim, and just as threatened. In several of his stories, Wright later used this episode whose bloody details made the rounds of the black community. For the time being, however, it provided yet another reason to despair:

Indeed, the white brutality that I had not seen was a more effective control of my behavior than that which I knew. The actual experience would have let me see the realistic outlines of what was really happening, but as long as it remained something terrible and yet remote, something whose horror and blood might descend upon me at any moment, I was compelled to give my entire imagination over to it, an act which blocked the springs of thought and feeling in me, creating a sense of distance between me and the world in which I lived.[20]

Contrary to the chronology of *Black Boy,* it seems likely that it was during the summer of 1924 that Richard worked for the American Optical Company. Mr. E. C. Ebert gave him fifteen dollars a week to clean the workshop and make deliveries on a secondhand bicycle. Whether or not the optician was actually from Illinois and, therefore, against racial prejudice, as Wright describes him in the book, Richard did indeed antagonize the two white employees by trying to learn the trade. He does not seem to have quit in the face of their threats, however, as he states in *Black Boy,* but apparently left only to return to school in September.[21]

Whatever the case, the white terror exposed to Richard the frailty of his plans and the emptiness of his hopes. The racial system excluded him from achieving the American ideal, while his family's religion and background somewhat prevented him from sharing the uncomplicated existence of the Blacks among whom he lived, whose only aspirations were for material happiness. Moreover, Richard was not even a part of his own family. Addie and Grandmother Wilson barely spoke to him. Uncle Thomas forbade his daughters Velma and Gladys to play with him.[22] Leon, who came home from Detroit at the beginning of the winter, to Richard's great joy, was easily persuaded to criticize the intransigence of his elder brother. His mother was the only person who did not totally shun him, since she understood his fundamental shyness and delicacy. It is no wonder that Richard came to think that taking her with him to the North was the only solution. In the meantime, though, he had one more year at Smith-Robinson.

4

Going back to his part-time job at the Walls', Richard entered ninth grade, and among the thirty-six students in his class were his best friends Dick, Joe, Essie, Minnie and Hattie. Arthur Leaner, a lively and clever boy, joined the group, and his turbulent adventures were later a constant source of interest and literary inspiration.

The Reverend O. B. Cobbins said that he never had to threaten Richard with the belt he used whenever someone earned more bad points than good ones. Besides getting a total of ninety-eight out of one hundred on his school work, Richard still found time to read his cherished magazines, and even novels, in class. His only insubordinate act was refusing to join in a general prayer that was supposed to avert a long dry spell. Richard fought in the name of science and demonstrated so intelligently that the cycle of water in nature could not be changed by Providence, that he was not punished. More than any of the others, Richard was often chosen to speak in front of the eighth and ninth grades together, perhaps presenting a report on something he had read, or telling a spellbinding story that he had discovered in some magazine. His hopes soared with this reassurance of his talents. Reverend Cobbins was, in fact, struck as much by the boy's reserve as by his intelligence and therefore tried to offer him these opportunities of asserting himself. Richard's consciousness of being different was somewhat reinforced by his classmates. They were surprised that he did not have any known girl friend and that he refused their invitations to birthday parties. At the time, however, Richard was secretly enamored of two schoolmates. Charlotte Metcalf, who turned everyone's head with her delicate manners and her clear, translucent complexion, was Richard's passion for a long time, until one day the wind blew up her hair and he discovered a raw scar on her scalp, which inexplicably repelled him. For Birdie Graves, a charming mulatto who wore a pleated skirt and white frilly blouse, he experienced a distant and idealized love.

If he refused invitations to parties, it was because he did not own any long pants and was afraid of looking ridiculous. His schoolmates apparently did not see through his tough-guy exterior to the deep insecurity and shyness beneath. Nor were they always able to understand him, since his dreams of escape and of a literary career were so foreign to them. His appearance, both the shabby clothes and the thinness, caused him to keep apart, and he did not always realize that his classmates, in spite of their teasing and mocking, felt a real respect for him. In these circumstances any teacher's recognition of his intellectual ability was precious encouragement, even if it separated him still further from his friends.

The motto for the graduating class of 1925 was "We finish

to begin." The solemn awarding of diplomas took place in May, and Richard had the honor of being valedictorian. Dick Jordan was salutatorian and wrote his welcoming speech on black achievement in Ethiopia. Minnie Farish, Essie Ward and Hattie Crawford were the three other speakers.

The principal got permission to hold the ceremony in the municipal party room on Congress Street, usually reserved for white schoolchildren, because the open-air ceremonies the year before had been interrupted by a violent storm. As a theme for his speech Richard had chosen "The Attributes of Life" so that he could show how the educational system of the South tended to deprive the black population of an intellectual life and human qualities. Thus, when W. H. Lanier summoned him to his office in order to give him a prepared speech to read, Richard refused to accept it.

It is important to understand Mr. Lanier's difficult position. His dignified appearance—silver-gray hair, Indian profile and fine features—along with his qualities as an astute diplomat had enabled him to gain the confidence of the white community. Thanks to his excellent administration of Smith-Robinson, he had received the mayor's permission (something which, given the racial situation, no one else could have managed) to start a secondary school past ninth grade for black students. It was to open on Ash Street the following September. This was an enormous feat, which Mr. Lanier had had to maneuver and sometimes compromise to achieve. Richard was unaware of, or did not want to admit, the reasons for this apparent submission to the established order of things. Neither the risk of having his diploma denied him, nor the promise of a teaching position, the example of his friend Dick Jordan, or the wrath of his Uncle Thomas would shake him. Finally the principal capitulated and allowed Richard to read his own speech; in return Richard agreed to cut certain passages that might have antagonized the authorities.[23]

Meanwhile, Richard had borrowed enough money from Mrs. Wall to make a down payment on a real suit. His graduation picture shows the intense gaze on his thin face with the slightly protruding ears over the white shirt, striped tie and new pearl-gray suit with the first long pants he had ever worn. He gave his speech, which he had spent weeks memorizing, and marched out of the room during the applause, without even staying for the performance of "Climb Though the Rocks be Rugged." It was May 29, 1925.

Richard at the time of his graduation

Class graduation picture

5

Richard had only himself to rely upon for completing his education, while he was responsible for supporting himself and his mother if he planned to leave for the North. His conflicts with Adventism led him to declare, in "Memories of My Grandmother," "Indeed it was my grandmother's interpretation of religion—or perhaps I should say that it was my religious grandmother's interpretation of life—that actually made me decide to run off from home at the age of fifteen." In 1925, his dreams of independence went far beyond this liberation from religion.

Richard decided that before leaving Jackson he had to have enough money to pay for his trip and to keep himself going while he looked for work. Aside from teaching, which was now open to him because of his diploma but which would mean abandoning all hope of escape, only badly paid jobs requiring neither education nor prior training were available.

In June, he started work as a delivery boy and sales clerk in a clothing store run by Mr. W. J. Farley; this was the beginning of a painful period of adaptation. He soon realized that his part-time jobs had not given him any idea of the difficult working conditions that Blacks endured. Richard was not only a witness to but also a victim of the brutality that was the daily fate of colored people. He tried to learn to behave humbly and to wear a contented smile to hide his true feelings. Later, when Wright was putting together a series of autobiographical episodes called "The Ethics of Living Jim Crow" in order to demonstrate how racism modified the psychological reactions of the black man, he chose almost all his incidents from this final formative year in Jackson.

His friend Dick Jordan taught him how Blacks ought to behave before Whites but, as Wright declared:

It was simply utterly impossible for me to calculate, to scheme, to act, to plot all the time. I would remember to dissemble for short periods, then I would forget and act straight and human again, not with the desire to harm anybody, but merely forgetting the artificial status of race and class. It was the same with whites and blacks; it was my way with everybody (*BB*, p. 163).

In spite of the omnipresent and unpredictable violence, and the constant feverish discussions about Whites among neighbors and classmates, Richard had been too long protected from the white world to immediately adopt the tricks of self-protection that were second nature to many Blacks. The painful, or at least disconcerting, experiences of his first months of work gave him the practical education that he had not received at school. After two years, he had finally learned to keep his thoughts to himself, to feign innocence and contentment; he even developed the habit of covering the books he borrowed from the library with newspaper and concealing his ambition to be a writer.

This education never ceased. Richard witnessed the brutality of his boss toward a black customer who staggered out covered with blood after being beaten in the back of the shop for "not having paid her debts." He himself was a victim when some young Whites gave him a lift, only to throw him off the moving car because he had forgotten to say "Sir." Once, when his deliveries took him into the white section of town late at night, armed policemen stopped and searched him. Each lesson was a shock to a boy who could not become an "Uncle Tom," and as a result he lost a number of jobs either because he was so paralyzed by his inner tensions that he was clumsy, or simply because he was not sufficiently deferential.

He was fired from Farley's in September, and then from a drugstore. Convinced that he would never be able to keep a job, he decided to continue his studies. At the new Lanier High School, he rejoined some of the more fortunate of his old friends. There Mr. Cobbins taught him math, Mr. William Peterson, English and Miss Theresa Thorp, history. In spite of his enthusiasm, Richard did not profit a great deal from their teaching; in any case, he had to leave school after a few weeks of irregular attendance because he needed to earn money again.

Once again thanks to his steady friend Dick Jordan, who was then working in a jewelry store on Capitol Street, Richard controlled the tensions which had become almost an illness and got a job as a hallboy at the Edward House. While washing the marble halls of this large hotel, he learned not only about the white world,

but about the world of black servants who so easily accepted the
role society assigned them. Their worries were limited to their
work, and their hopes consisted of earning enough to drink, chase
girls and go dancing. Richard could not become a part of this
group, but life with his fellow workers was easy since in their
simplicity they demanded nothing of him. Following their example,
he learned to dissimulate. Soon he was promoted to bellboy and
began working on room service, where he came into contact with
the clients. Prohibition had closed the bars, but Richard used to
carry contraband whiskey to the prostitutes of the hotel under the
nose of the police. Since these girls did not consider the black
servants human beings, they wandered about naked and completely
uninhibited in their presence. There is no way of telling what effect
this had upon the adolescent tortured by sex, but certainly some
revealing passages in *The Outsider* and *The Long Dream* are based
on Wright's observations as a bellboy.

Every week Richard gave his family a large portion of his salary
and the profits from contraband liquor, causing him to despair of
ever amassing the hundred dollars he needed to leave. Gradually
the idea of stealing it took hold in his mind. He was not held back
by his conscience, since in a way the Whites themselves had placed
him beyond the law because of his color. He was, on the other
hand, terrified by the risk involved. His desire to leave finally
triumphed, and thanks to his friend Arthur Leaner, who had recently used the talents of the Dick Wright Club in a minstrel show,
he got a job as ticket collector for the Alamo Theatre. This was
the small movie house on Amite Street run by a Jew for the Blacks
of the neighborhood. A friend of the girl who sold tickets had a
plan whereby Richard would hold out a certain number of tickets,
which she would resell during peak periods. They had to wait a
few days for Mr. Lehman's vigilance to subside, but even so, the
three of them collected enough money in two months for Richard
to save a sizable sum.

In order to speed his departure, Richard stole a gun from the
house next door, raided the storehouse of Jackson College and
sold the stolen canned fruit to restaurants in town. Richard sometimes played tennis and baseball with the students at this state
college for Blacks, and the president's sons, Zack and Giles Hubert,
were his classmates at school. It was undoubtedly they who con-

trived this plan of contributing to the fugitive's nest egg. The next day, after a secret good-bye to his mother, Richard boarded the Illinois Central for Memphis, his only luggage a cheap suitcase containing a few articles of clothing and a pair of new shoes.

THREE

T HE quiet and deserted streets that greeted Wright early one
Sunday morning in the autumn of 1925 did not belong to the same
Memphis he had left ten years before. The rapidly expanding city,
with its 160,000 inhabitants, was unchallenged as the industrial
capital of the Deep South. Blacks constituted more than a third of
the city's population, and Beale Street had been its principal attraction ever since the blues of W. C. Handy had made it famous in
1909. Stretching from De Soto Fish Dock more than a mile to East
Street—the city itself now extended east beyond Chicasaw Bluff—
it was a cultural center where a vibrant popular Negro tradition
flourished and where, on a Saturday afternoon, all elements of
black life were available for enjoyment. Along the docks teeming
with stevedores, where the old *Kate Adams* rotted at anchor, stood
the saloons and whorehouses. Underworld activities were carried
on between Hernando Street and Fourth Street, including Gayosa,
"the street of shame," lined with its prostitutes, professional blind-
men and banjo players. There was the Daisy Theatre for gangster
films, Sim's Beer Garden, where stabbings occurred, the New
Orleans Ballroom, the "Hole in the Wall," Elmer Atkinson's bil-
liard room and Joe Raffanti's Midway Cafe, pervaded since prohibition by an aroma of grain alcohol and bathtub gin. Further
along were the preachers of Handy's Park, the old-clothing and
fruit vendors, photograph shops, hairdressers, drug peddlers, charlatans and healers by the dozen, and soul restaurants like Piggly-
Wiggly and The Greek, where day laborers flocked from the
surrounding countryside to haggle over their chops and chitterlings.

On that cold autumn morning, Richard was simply looking for
a place to live, painfully aware of the dangers of the city for a
provincial boy, thinking perhaps of his mother's cautionary advice
and the temptations to which his father had succumbed. As he
gazed circumspectly at a sign advertising a room for rent on 570
Beale Street, Mrs. W——, an honest baker's wife, opened her

60

door and motherly heart to him, for two and a half dollars a week.

Wright deliberately stresses the warm atmosphere at this household. Here he no longer felt the constant pressure to justify his presence; merely by sitting down at the table he had become a member of the family.

> I learned the full degree to which my life at home had cut me off, not only from white people but from Negroes as well. To Bess and her mother, money was important but they did not strive for it too hard. They had no tensions, unappeasable longings, no desire to do something to redeem themselves. The main value in their lives was simple, clean, good living, and when they thought they had found those same qualities in one of their race, they instinctively embraced him, liked him and asked no questions (*BB,* p. 187).

Unfortunately, Richard had lived alone with his thoughts for too long not to be somewhat afraid of this intimacy, and although he had finally found the family he had never had, he discovered that he could not be satisfied without his own "unappeasable longings." Despite his gratitude to these kind people, he lived totally isolated in the world of his own personal plans. His relationship with R——— (the girl whom he calls Bess in *Black Boy*), therefore, is just another manifestation of this fear. Richard apparently had not had many girl friends and he was taken aback by the abandon of this young girl who spontaneously threw herself into his arms simply because she liked him. The girls from the black lower-middle class whom he had known at school seemed reserved and calculating compared with his uninhibited new companion. It is not necessary to take literally the account of their relationship given in *Black Boy,* for an earlier version of the autobiography shows that with this pretty girl in his arms he was less sophisticated and scrupulously restrained than he admits.[1] Nevertheless, it reveals his attitude toward a certain type of black woman. Why else would he resist his desire to take what R——— so freely offered (even Mrs. W——— was in favor of a "trial period") if he were not afraid of being trapped? They were, in fact, already speaking to him of marriage, which would have ruined all his plans, yet his strict moral education forbade him to enjoy the girl only to abandon her. Later, Wright's heroes show this same propensity to mock, even to strike, the women who unwittingly hold up an ironic mirror of their situation; Bigger feels this in making love

to Bessie, Cross in relation to Dot, Fishbelly to Gladys and Wright
himself toward his illiterate mistress in "Early Days in Chicago."
This indicates the male desire for superiority as well as the despair
at still being imprisoned in a solitude which even sexual relations
cannot destroy.

Richard discovered that he was more surprised by his own inhibitions than by the frank sensuality of the young girl. R——'s
natural, almost primitive, behavior caused him to reevaluate the
austere upbringing, which had engendered in him both a religious
and a sexual taboo. He also was able to measure the disparity
between their educations and must have felt a certain satisfaction
at the contrast between her simple concept of life and his own
infinitely complex plans for the future. He was, on the other hand,
incapable of enjoying the moment for what it was worth in itself,
and, instead of acting on impulse, he meditated on his own complexity. He was as alone as he had been at school or working at the
Edward House. In this episode with R—— it is clear that Wright
hated her as much as himself for their failure to communicate. This
reaction is characteristic: he might not expect a woman to understand all his problems, but he could not love her for any length of
time if she were not in some way his intellectual equal.

2

On his first day in Memphis, Wright managed to raise a few
dollars on the stolen gun and find a job as a dishwasher at $12.00
a week including two free meals at the Lyle Drugstore, on the
corner of Main and Beale streets, where his father had once worked.
Somewhat later, he thought of looking for work with another optical company. Mr. J. R. Horseley, of the Merry Optical Company
at 144 Madison Street offered him a job at ten dollars a week as
an assistant and delivery boy. Richard made out a strict budget
in order to save for his family's arrival, which meant that he often
went without proper food. He breakfasted on bread and milk and

bought a can of vegetables for dinner, after having a hamburger and peanut butter for lunch. In this way he was able to live off the tips he earned during lunch hour running errands for his white co-workers.

Wright noted in *Black Boy* that because the Whites in Memphis did not resort so frequently as those in Jackson to physical violence or insults to express their scorn of the Blacks, he was able to adapt more easily to that city's less rigorous code of Jim Crow behavior:

It was fairly easy to contemplate the race issue in the shop without reaching those heights of fear that devastated me. A measure of objectivity entered into my observations of white men and women. Either I could stand more mental strains than formerly or I had discovered deep within me ways of handling it (*BB,* p. 196).

Thus Richard coped with his tensions, but he still had problems in any situation that did not allow him to act openly, as is illustrated by the story told in *Black Boy* of his distrust of a Yankee who offered him a dollar. Because he could not openly admit to his hunger and poverty, he resented the act of generosity that had brought his feelings to the surface. "The safety of my life in the South depended on how well I concealed from all whites what I felt" (*BB,* p. 204).

Even if the boxing match that the foreman and other workers forced him to fight against another black employee never took place as he describes it in *Black Boy,* it is nevertheless an accurate testimony to the interracial tensions in the company. Its significance for Wright was that he was unable to refuse, and that, in spite of himself, he came to hate his adversary.[2] Usually the atmosphere at work was calmer. Wright would observe the white employees, learning their habits and weaknesses by running their errands, takin their suits to the cleaners or delivering their love letters to the secretaries across the street, but he was at ease only in the company of other Blacks. Isidore, the night watchman; old Dupree and his son, Alan; Dixon, the janitor at the American Bank on the ground floor; and Shorty, the elevator man, were more open, alert and aware of their situation than the black personnel at Edward House. They often got together during lunchtime in a small room overlooking the street, where Richard could finally say what he felt while the others chatted about the details of the day or vented

their anger and scorn for the Whites. These talks were similar to
the bull sessions Wright used to enjoy at school, but there was now
less boasting and more fierce and emotional condemnation of the
state of race relations. For the time being at least the Blacks could
accept the ignominy of being without civil rights, but they were
adamant about the indispensability of economic rights. Many
topics normally unmentionable were broached at these midday
meetings:

American white women; the Ku Klux Klan; France and how Negro
soldiers fared while there; Frenchwomen; Jack Johnson; the entire
Northern part of the United States; the Civil War; Abraham Lincoln; U. S. Grant; General Sherman; Catholicism; the Pope; Jews;
the Republican Party; slavery; social equality; Communism; Socialism; the 13th, 14th and 15th Amendments to the Constitution;
or any topic calling for positive knowledge and manly self-assertion
on the part of the Negro (*BB,* p. 202).

Nevertheless, these discussions probably never ranged much beyond the daily preoccupations and vexations of the men, which
might have revealed to the seventeen-year-old his own already well-
developed group consciousness. In any case, his determination to
head for the North was only strengthened. In Jackson he had been
a prisoner of a closed system, but Memphis put him within reach
of the fuller existence that he eventually found in Chicago.

Shorty, the "clown," was a fund of common sense and managed
to teach Wright some self-control as well as the relative value of
self-esteem. Since Shorty was "hard-headed, sensible, a reader of
magazines and books," he and Richard probably discussed what
they had read.[3] Perhaps the elevator operator was even able to
advise the future novelist on what books to read, because by this
time Richard had given up popular magazines and detective stories
in favor of the major literary magazines of the period, which he
could buy secondhand and sell again. In this way, he discovered *Harper's Magazine,* the *Atlantic Monthly* and *The American
Mercury,* whose enlightened and liberal, if not exactly avant-garde,
editors were publishing some of the best writers of the period. Did
Shorty actually suggest the theme of a story to Wright? In some
preliminary notes for *Black Boy,* Wright is uncertain whether or
not he wrote a story called "The Memphis Monster," although at

one point he was haunted by the idea that he was a criminal, guilty of murder and hunted by the police. Elsewhere he says that this was only a dream that he had told Shorty, but further along he states that Shorty had dictated the story to him in their lunchtime retreat. Whatever the truth, there is a link between crime and fiction on the one hand, and Shorty's suggestions and Wright's compositions on the other. The latter may have been accidental, but the former was a constant element in Wright's fiction, since he had come to regard literature as a forbidden activity, and hence, the writer as a criminal.

3

      Every morning before work, Wright would stop at the American Bank to see his friend the elevator operator and read the *Memphis Commercial Appeal*. It was probably in May, 1927, that he read an editorial in that paper lambasting H. L. Mencken, who was then editor-in-chief of *The American Mercury*.[4] Although Richard had never heard of Mencken, he was immediately intrigued by him for the simple reason that the South seemed so hostile to him. Since the Cossit Public Library, where Wright sometimes borrowed books for Whites, was closed to Blacks, he resorted to the subterfuge described in Chapter Thirteen of *Black Boy* which became an oft-quoted anthology piece. An Irish Catholic who worked at the optical company lent Richard his library card so that he could pretend to borrow books in his name.[5] He must have handed this carefully forged note with a pounding heart to the librarian, who read, "Dear Madam: Will you please let this nigger boy have some books by H. L. Mencken?" This was how Wright obtained *A Book of Prefaces* and one volume of *Prejudices*.

      That night transformed Wright's life. It was a revelation for the young boy to finally discover the power of words, not as just an escape or a compensation, but as a tool for rebuilding the world.

I was jarred and shocked by the style, the clear, clean, sweeping sentences. Why did he write like that? And how did one write like that? I pictured the man as a raging demon, slashing with his pen, consumed with hate, denouncing everything American, extolling everything European or German, laughing at the weaknesses of people, mocking God, authority . . . Could words be weapons? Well, yes, for here they were. Then, maybe, perhaps, I could use them as a weapon? No. It frightened me. I read on and what amazed me was not what he said, but how on earth anybody had the courage to say it (*BB,* p. 218).

If this conversion to militant literature and the choice of writing as a career—something he had only dimly envisioned prior to that night—seems sudden, it is because Wright has condensed a long evolution into one symbolic episode of his autobiography. As a child Richard had discovered that literature meant escape and compensation; as a boy he had learned that his education and special talent for storytelling would win him the admiration of his friends, and this in turn encouraged him to let his imagination expand into the world of fiction. Even though this alone took years, he, who had once dreamed of becoming a doctor, had never yet thought of making a career of writing. Thus, during the crucial Memphis period, which unfortunately is poorly documented, Wright did not suddenly discover his literary talents so much as he discovered good literature, represented by the great novelists of the nineteenth and twentieth centuries, in opposition to the detective stories, dime novels and popular fiction that had been his usual fare. With Mencken as his guide, the first serious writing he was exposed to consisted of realistic novels and embattled journalism, the very forms to satisfy those critical and militant appetites that escape literature had lulled to sleep. This transformation of literary tastes, of course, also corresponds to his new freedom, both psychological and physical. He was older and more mature and hence had more control over his destiny, while he was now living in a less constricting environment. Nevertheless, his sophistication at that time was not so great that he could judge the realistic novel as anything more than an astounded newcomer. If the text of "The Memphis Monster" were available, it would certainly resemble "Hell's Half Acre" more than "Superstition," a traditional suspense story that he wrote much later in Chicago. It was a full six years, in fact, before Wright even discovered his career, and only after many hesitations and trials along the way.

Prejudices taught Richard how a writer can fight; *A Book of*

Prefaces introduced him to the contemporary novel. Although he probably looked up the strange words in the dictionary that he had brought from Jackson, he must have been overwhelmed by the unfamiliar proper names on every page. In defending Conrad, Dreiser and James G. Huneker, for instance, Mencken passes rapidly from one author or country or period to another. The almost forty authors listed in *Black Boy* as having awakened Wright's literary taste do not correspond exactly to those in Mencken. Rather, he selected from *A Book of Prefaces* about twenty, to which he added fifteen others who, it is safe to assume, must have figured in his early reading. It was natural that Wright should avoid the unfortunates whom Mencken attacks (of Kipling, Chesterton, Ibsen, Maeterlinck, Tagore, Selma Lagerlöf, Bernstein, Bergson, Wells, Charles Morgan and Arnold Bennett, Wright only includes the last four), and it would have been difficult to get hold of Romain Rolland, Lord Dunsany, Renan, Sudermann, or Hauptmann in Memphis at that time. But why was he not struck by other names that crop up repeatedly in *A Book of Prefaces:* Shakespeare, Swift, Molière, Washington Irving, Hawthorne, Bret Harte, William Dean Howells, Oliver Wendell Holmes and Henry James? Undoubtedly these people did not appear essential to Richard in 1927, but since we know that Wright did not discover T. S. Eliot, Baudelaire, Gide, Stendhal, Thomas Mann, Nietzsche, Flaubert, Poe, Edgar Lee Masters or Gogol until he reached Chicago, the five novelists who remain (Alexandre Dumas, Frank Harris, O. Henry, Sherwood Anderson and Sinclair Lewis) must also have become part of the literary background he acquired in Memphis. Dumas was a natural favorite because of his color and his talent as a raconteur. The sensationalism of Frank Harris and the famous O. Henry blueprint for a short story attracted Wright, while Anderson and Lewis satisfied his thirst for realism.

My first novel was Sinclair Lewis's *Main Street*. It made me see my boss, Mr. Gerald, and identify him as an American type. . . . I felt now that I knew him, that I could feel the very limits of his narrow life. And this had happened because I had read a novel about a mythical man called George F. Babbitt (*BB,* 218–19).

Wright reacted so strongly to *Babbitt* that he made a note to encourage his fellow workers to read such books.

Possibly Wright managed to find works by the other novelists whom Mencken recommended: Balzac, Anatole France, Zola, Maupassant, Thomas Hardy and George Moore, the author of *Sister Teresa*. Turgenev, Gorky, Conrad, Shaw, Crane and Huneker he read later, but by 1927, he had finished *Poor Folk* by Dostoevsky, *McTeague* by Frank Norris, and had discovered Dreiser, the most influential of all, whom Mencken had praised highly for his two books "about women."

I read Dreiser's *Jennie Gerhardt* and *Sister Carrie* and they revived in me a vivid sense of my mother's suffering; I was overwhelmed. I grew silent, wondering about the life around me. It would have been impossible for me to have told anyone what I derived from these novels, for it was nothing less than a sense of life itself. All my life had shaped me for the realism, the naturalism of the modern novel, and I could not read enough of them.[6]

The American realistic novel provided Wright with the means to analyze the society he lived in, to bridge the gap between himself and the white world created by ignorance alone. It also enabled him to start separating white people, who had hitherto appeared collectively as a unified threat, into social and psychological categories. Finally, he came to view his own claim to humanity in less personal terms. Admittedly, though, literature was still at times an invitation to dream and lose himself.

The plots and stories in the novels did not interest me so much as the point of view revealed. I gave myself over to each novel without reserve, without trying to criticize it; it was enough for me to see and feel something different. And for me, everything was something different. Reading was like a drug, a dope. The novels created moods in which I lived for days (*BB,* p. 219).

More important, reading the novels of Dreiser and Lewis, along with the stories of Anderson, encouraged him to use his newly acquired way of thinking to alter his life. But in trying to do so he felt depressed by the unbearable realization of everything that was out of reach both for him and his people because of their color.

In buoying me up, reading also cast me down, made me see what was possible, what I had missed. My tension returned, new, terrible, bitter, surging, almost too great to be contained. I no longer felt that the world about me was hostile, killing; I *knew* it. A million times I asked myself what I could do to save myself, and there were

no answers. I seemed forever condemned, ringed by walls (*BB,*
p. 220).

More than ever, he felt imprisoned in a cultural ghetto. Could he
possibly become a writer like Dreiser? Local black papers like the
Memphis Times and the *Western World Reporter* never mentioned
anyone with such ambitions. Even his landlady was frightened by
how much he read. None of his friends owned any of the books that
interested him and Shorty had never heard of most of them, so
Richard felt as criminal as if he had stolen fire from the gods. If
he were venturing onto forbidden territory, would he be punished
for trespassing?

I could not conquer my sense of guilt, my feeling that the white
men around me knew that I was changing, that I had begun to regard them differently. . . . A vague hunger would come over me
for books, books that opened up new avenues of feeling and seeing
and again I would forge another note to the white librarian. Again
I would read and wonder as only the naive and unlettered can read
and wonder, feeling that I carried a secret, criminal burden about
with me each day (*BB,* pp. 220–21).

Nevertheless he continued to revel in the sin of educating and cul-
tivating himself with these novels, which he covered with old newspapers in order to conceal them like contraband.

He tried hard to imitate his idols—Mencken, who could wield
words like bludgeons, and Dreiser, who dissected society with a
scalpel, but platitudes and clichés seemed the best he could do.[7]
He therefore decided to study the language itself. He always had
his dictionary with him, but reading several grammars and books
on style was less satisfying to him than concentrating on the novels
themselves. He would first try to grasp the author's viewpoint to
help him get to know people so well that he could describe them.
In the process he learned that he would have to control his feelings
before he could write about them; but his repeated failures only
increased his frustration.

The year 1927 was a momentous one in Wright's life because
these discoveries were foreshadowing his own career. Was he equally
aware of the startling domestic and international events recorded in
the *Commercial Appeal*? Charles Lindbergh was visiting one city
after another on his triumphal tour across the United States; one

protest followed another in a vain attempt to save Sacco and Van-
zetti, who were finally executed on August 23; and Marcus Garvey
was exiled on November 23. Since the Memphis papers ignored most
news of the black population and openly condemned radicalism,
it is quite possible that Wright remembered 1927 mostly as the year
the *Kate Adams* burned and a terrible flood (mentioned in his early
stories) devastated the Delta region during the spring.

In any event, he was profiting from the abundant black culture
offered on Beale Street, although he says little about it. Secular
music had been forbidden in his grandmother's house, but he made
up for lost time by listening to Gertrude Saunders and others sing
blues at the Palace Theater on Saturday nights. In "Memories of
My Grandmother," he mentions recognizing "this quality of freely
juxtaposing totally unrelated symbols and images and then tying
them into some over-all concept, mood, feeling," as being characteristically black American, although it would be wrong to credit
him with having had a sense of cultural nationalism at that time.
As he became increasingly fond of blues, he also became interested
in black folklore, city folklore in particular, perhaps because he
lived so near Beale Street or because he spent so much time with
Shorty and his other black friends. Curiously enough, this immersion
in black culture was all taking place during the very period when
he was most inspired by the white novelists whose world was so far
removed from his. The sirens on Beale Street must have revealed
certain sources of his culture, regardless of whether his reading and
discussions with friends had yet opened his eyes to the complexities
of the political and social scene.

In any event Wright's own worries were still largely financial,
since he had to support himself and save for the arrival of his family.
He had moved out of Mrs. W——'s home after one year and was
now staying with a Pullman porter, Ted W. Martin, on Griffith
Place. By the fall of 1927, however, he had doubled his original
sum at a rate of ten dollars a week, so that despite his mother's
uncertain health, she and Leon were now able to join him. Leon
soon found a job and they rented a small apartment on Washington
Street, which they furnished on credit. With a more regular diet
replacing the eternal pork and beans, Richard calmed his impatience
by making definite plans for departure. Aunt Maggie, meanwhile,
had been abandoned by Uncle Matthews and also joined them in

Memphis, at the beginning of the autumn of 1927. She was once again out of work, but she brought back from Detroit a mine of information about life and job possibilities in the North; she herself hoped to start a hairdressing salon somewhere in the Middle West. Her arrival, in fact, spurred them on to action. There was no reason to wait until they could all afford to leave at once. Accordingly, it was decided that Richard and Maggie would go to Chicago, while Ella and Leon would await their turn back in Jackson.

When Wright agreed to end *Black Boy* with his departure from Memphis, he added the vibrant and prophetic final paragraphs, which provide the best possible summary of both the meaning and the effect of his childhood in the South. Of course his perspicacious and lucid conclusions belong to the established writer of 1944 and not to the wounded adolescent of November, 1927, who probably had no such clear idea of why the South could never allow him to develop, or that he was "taking a part of the South to transplant in alien soil," or that he was, first and foremost, fleeing for survival.

In the main, my hope was merely a kind of self-defence, a conviction that if I did not leave I would perish, either because of possible violence of others against me, or because of my possible violence against them. The substance of my hopes was formless and devoid of any real sense of direction; for in my southern living I had seen no looming landmark by which I could, in a positive sense, guide my daily actions. . . . My flight was more a shunning of external and internal dangers than an attempt to embrace what I felt I wanted (*BB,* p. 227).

Having already diverged from the path of his family, and refusing to adopt his father's solution, which had inspired him with unforgettable disgust, he now realized that he was physically and morally incapable of continuing the two-faced existence indispensable for survival in the South. His was just another example of the attraction of the Northern states for thousands of former slaves; he had been influenced by the great American myth of equal opportunity popularized by Horatio Alger, criticized by Mencken and made into a tragic destiny by Dreiser. Whereas most Blacks migrated north in order to find better paid jobs in a less volatile racial climate, Wright went above all in search of spiritual enlightenment, hoping to live the life of the mind, to give free rein to his feelings and beliefs and, in short, to reach the level of the spiritual masters whom he had just chosen for himself. Several long years, however, still separated him from his irrevocable decision to become a writer.

FOUR

My first glimpse of the flat black stretches of Chicago depressed and dismayed me, mocked all my fantasies. Chicago seemed an unreal city whose mythical houses were built of slabs of black coal wreathed in palls of grey smoke, houses whose foundations were sinking slowly into the dank prairie. Flashes of steam showed intermittently on the wide horizon, gleaming translucently in the winter sun. The din of the city entered my consciousness, entered to remain for years to come. . . .

I looked northward at towering buildings of steel and stone. There were no curves here, no trees: only angles, lines, squares, bricks and copper wires. Occasionally the ground beneath my feet shook from some faraway pounding and I felt that this world, despite its massiveness, was somehow dangerously fragile. Streetcars screeched past over steel tracks. Cars honked their horns. Clipped speech sounded about me.[1]

At the time of Richard Wright's arrival, Chicago's population had almost reached three million and was swelling so fast, with immigrants from all directions, that Memphis was a small town in comparison. It was no wonder that he felt like a complete provincial in these new surroundings.

He had also been aware throughout the journey of a gradual feeling of liberation. The all-too-familiar signs "For Whites—For Colored" started to disappear. On the streetcar that he took to his Aunt Cleopatra's, the Whites whom he sat next to paid no attention to him, and little by little the tension that had seized him dissipated. An atmosphere of indifference, in which everyone acted as if the other people did not exist, was slowly replacing one of intense racial consciousness and fear. Soon this somewhat disconcerting lack of personal relationships and human kindness began to weigh upon Wright, but for the moment everything was new and appealing. He had no fond memories of his childhood home to regret; he had left no one he cared for behind, since his family was going to join him soon. His only uneasiness was caused by the unfamiliarity of this urban world. Reading Dreiser had prepared him for the ways in which unscrupulous city-dwellers set ambushes for inexperienced provincials; it was like adventuring into a jungle: "I knew that this machine-like city was governed by strange laws and I wondered if I would ever learn them" ("AH," p. 2). He would have to adapt to the pulsing atmosphere of Chicago, but he could still hope for a better life in the big city; he had been hardened by a childhood of deprivation and humiliation and expected nothing from anyone except a job.

Although there were subtle forms of segregation in Chicago, it was not a rigid institution like the Southern Jim Crow. The newly arrived Black was overwhelmed by his freedom: freedom to vote, freedom to apply for any job, to sit down where he wanted in buses and parks, to be waited on in shops and cafés, to go to museums and libraries. Most important of all, he no longer had to conceal his real feelings. Yet the promise of enlightenment and endless opportunity that the large city offered inspired an equivalent fear. Richard found his aunt just as aged and worn by city life as Ella had been by illness. When her husband had left her, she had moved to a rooming house. Here Richard also took a room and was struck by the dreary and dispiriting atmosphere of the neighborhood. In the kitchenettes where the Blacks gathered,

everything seemed makeshift, temporary. I caught an abiding sense of insecurity in the personalities of the people around me. . . . Wherever my eyes turned, I saw stricken, frightened black faces trying vainly to cope with a civilization that they did not understand. I felt lonely. I had fled one insecurity and embraced another ("AH," pp. 2–3).

Chicago was still the teeming, ever-expanding city that Carl Sandburg had immortalized, but for a black person Chicago was above all the South Side, the immense "Bronzeville." Except for four or five separate enclaves around the stockyards and steel mills near Blue Island and Evergreen Park, the black ghetto formed a solid rectangle, one and a half miles wide and seven miles long. Twenty-sixth Street on the northern border separated it from the new residential section that had replaced the slums south of the Loop, the commercial center of the city. The tracks of the Central and Western Illinois Railroad formed another boundary along Wentworth Avenue to the east of the stockyards, separating the Blacks from the Mexicans, Poles and Irish. White neighborhoods east of the University of Chicago blocked expansion toward the lake, so that the inroads of one hundred thousand Blacks during the twenties had pushed the ghetto to the west of Cottage Grove Avenue between 31st and 47th streets. The main expansion was southward, however, from 47th Street to 65th Street beyond Washington Park, along the railroad tracks beside South Chicago Avenue.

This, a city within a city, was Wright's environment. Two hundred thousand Blacks lived, slept, ate and amused themselves there, although shopkeepers and gambling-house owners were the only ones who worked there. Wright had some restrictions in looking for a job; he could not have become a factory worker, for instance, since he was too thin and weak. He was eligible to train for a job with the post office, police, fire or highway departments, or the city government, but in the meantime he looked for a job in a shop.

He started as a delivery boy in a delicatessen. The Jewish couple who ran the store treated him very kindly, but he had difficulty understanding Mrs. Hoffman's thick European accent since he was used only to the speech of the Deep South.

A girl friend from Jackson then found him a job washing dishes for a Mrs. Crooks, who had just opened a cafeteria on the ground floor of the Hotel Patricia on Fullerton Street in the north part of town. The fifteen dollars a week and free meals were welcome, and Wright kept the job off and on until February, 1929. He first helped set the place up and later carried breakfast trays to the clients in the hotel. He was the only black employee. The cook was an elderly, red-faced and angular Finnish woman, whom Richard finally got fired because she spit into the soup. The white waitresses were open and friendly with him, which never would have been true in the South, where any relationship with a white woman was fraught with the traditional danger, and he only gradually got used to the inevitable intimacy created by working together in the kitchen. Since he was a good listener, he learned a great deal about the lives of these girls:

During the lunch-hour which I spent on a bench in a nearby park, the waitresses would come and sit beside me, talking at random, laughing, joking, smoking cigarettes. I learned about their tawdry dreams, their simple hopes, their home lives, their fear of feeling anything deeply, their sex problems, their husbands. They were an eager, restless, talkative, ignorant bunch, but casually kind and impersonal for all that. They knew nothing of hate and fear, and strove instinctively to avoid all passion (*EM*, p. 220).

In spite of his relaxed relationships with Connie, Bess, Maybel and Jane, Wright was a long time abandoning the caution that he had acquired so painfully in Jackson. With his smiling reserve, he remained on guard, observing, comparing, criticizing and concluding. He had dreamed of having the same life as the Whites, sharing the same dreams and riches, only to find that their dreams and riches were illusory.

Their constant outward-looking, their mania for radios, cars and a thousand other trinkets, made them dream and fix their eyes upon the trash of life. . . .

Perhaps it would be possible for the Negro to become reconciled to his plight if he could be made to believe that his sufferings were for some remote, high, sacrificial end; but sharing the culture that condemns him and seeing that a lust for trash is what blinds the nation to his claims, is what sets storms to rolling in his soul.[2]

He supplemented his analysis by studying the liberal critics like Mencken, whom he continued to read avidly. He had bought a secondhand copy of *The Book of Prefaces* and always had some book borrowed from the public library with him. When Mrs. Crooks could not hide her surprise at seeing a black dishwasher reading *The American Mercury,* Wright went back to his habit of wrapping up books in newspaper and reading in private or on streetcars.

Even after the arrival of his family, Richard never really mingled with the people of the neighborhood. Although he did not openly criticize their unabashed and single-minded search for cheap amusement, they were able to sense that he had little in common with them and scorned their way of life. Since he knew how to get along by himself, he hardly felt the need of friends. Perhaps his education and background should have brought him closer to the respectable middle class, but he could not afford to join in their social life, and participation in church or club activities merely to attain a certain social standing repelled him. His financial status ranked him with the class below, and he suffered the deprivation, promiscuity and filth of the "kitchenettes" that went with it, but he shunned the compensation of their amusements. He hated drinking, gangs and the popular game of policy, although from time to time he would make an effort to be neighborly and attend a local house-rent party, where each guest contributed to help the hostess pay her rent.

At these affairs I drank home-brewed beer, ate spaghetti and chitter-lings, laughed and talked with black, southern-born girls who worked as domestic servants in white middle-class homes. But with none of them did my relations rest upon my deepest feelings. I dis-cussed what I read with no one, and to no one did I confide ("AH," p. 18).

With his charming half-smile, Wright concealed his true feelings. The only pleasures he freely indulged in were solitary communica-tion with other minds, through books, and his own attempts at literary expression. As he admitted, "Conversation was my way of avoiding expression; my words were reserved for those times when I sat down alone to write" ("AH," p. 19).

In the spring of 1928, he took an examination for work with the central post office and was hired for a summer job. Since he had to work only eight hours a day, he could devote the rest of his time—four or five hours—to reading and writing. His salary, sixty-five cents an hour, came to just twice what he had been making as a waiter and was about the best he could have expected at the time. The whole family benefited from this change. Wright moved to a room in Aunt Maggie's apartment, where his family joined him at the beginning of the summer. The three of them slept in the single windowless room, and they shared the kitchen with Maggie.

In order to continue working for the post office, that autumn Wright had to have a medical examination which he failed, as he had feared he would. More rest, and a diet of milk and steak had not compensated for twenty years of undernourishment; he did not weigh the minimum one hundred and twenty-five pounds required. When he lost the chance of this stable employment, Richard became subject to his Aunt Maggie's recriminations. Though a powerful, courageous and good woman, Maggie could not understand her nephew's obstinate passion for books. She besieged him with advice and warnings, and blamed him for her electricity bills. The confined space soon made the atmosphere unbearable, particularly since Leon used his feeble health as an excuse not to look for a job, at least not hard enough to suit his brother. Richard therefore decided to return to his dishwashing job in Fullerton Street and to rent with his

Aunt Cleopatra a tiny two-room apartment where "in the kitchen a wall-bed fitted snugly into a corner near the stove. The place was alive with vermin and the smell of cooking hung in the air day and night" ("AH," p. 22).

He also determined that he would not be done out of a good job just because circumstances had prevented him from having had enough to eat as a child. He prepared himself for the next examination by stuffing himself unmercifully in an attempt to gain weight, and in March, 1929, he was finally hired as a substitute clerk and mail sorter, pending a permanent appointment. His relative affluence now meant that the family could get a larger apartment, four rooms at 4831 Vincennes Avenue, and that he could go back to his reading and writing.[3]

Wright used the details of his duties at the central post office in his novel *Lawd Today*. The enormous brick building on the corner of Clark Street and Jackson Boulevard bore the unfortunate distinction of having the worst working conditions of all United States post offices. The discipline was worthy of a penitentiary. The chapter entitled "Squirrel's Cage" follows each step of the protagonist's endless eight-hour shift and accurately describes Wright's daily routine and drudgery in 1928. Having become a mere number after passing the armed identification control guards, he would first sort the mail by category, then the letters by destination, then cancel the stamps before finally putting the mail into bags, all under the constant supervision of a foreman. Dust rose from the bags, the lighting was harsh. The constant noise of the stamping machines and the fumes from the ink only made matters worse. Every minute spent in the bathroom was recorded, and the penalty for being caught dawdling or smoking a cigarette there was two hundred demerits.

Wright had learned the names of the stations and trains and the schedules of the eighty counties and thirteen hundred cities and towns which were his responsibility so rapidly that he was soon promoted to sorting by destination, where he acquired the automatic and accurate gestures that permitted him to chat with a fellow worker while throwing the mail into the proper pigeonholes. Like Jake in *Lawd Today*, Wright even had a box at home to practice for his examination. After a mere half hour at the cafeteria, the process of stamping began. The ordinary letters had only to be slipped by machine into a chute, but the "fat" mail had to be stamped by hand so quickly that the worker was totally exhausted by the end of his shift.

Work ended either at 12:30 in the afternoon, 8:30 in the evening or 4:30 in the morning, and Wright would immediately go home to sleep a little before starting to write. The routine and the stagnant air of the post office soon disgusted him, although he made some of his true friends there. The workers were united not only by their common sufferings, but by common aspirations as well. Many white students, for instance, worked there to support themselves, and the post office was jokingly referred to as "The University." Among the Blacks, too, were some who hoped to change their jobs and pursue a career. In his new position Wright found two friends, a young Irishman named Tim McAuliffe, and a Jewish student named Abraham Aaron, who shared his interest in literature and current events; they introduced Wright to a number of modern authors. Among the Blacks were Len Mallette, who was trying to get a college education, and Dan Burley, who was determined to become a newspaper reporter. They often got together over a glass of beer, sometimes reviewing the racial and political situation, but most often discussing literature. Wright was the only one whose interest in books took priority over everything else. His active mind astounded his friends, as did his determination to write.

By this time he was seriously contemplating a literary career.[4] He in fact wrote a number of short stories, one dealing with a black woman gradually going insane under the pressures of her life, and another about a janitor with a severe cold. A third story centered upon a Negro woman who frequented fortune-tellers, and ended in a death fraught with revenge and superstition. Taking his cue from Henry James (and especially from his technique in *The Awkward Age*), Wright believed that his dialogues should carry as heavy a "burden of reference" as possible. From the lush descriptions of Conrad he tried to derive guidelines for the evocation of the landscapes of the Deep South. In an unpublished version of *Black Boy*, he recalls that the general atmosphere of this early writing was gloomy, replete with "death, poverty, nervous collapse and hysteria."

At about the same time, Wright briefly attended the meetings of a kind of black literary society. It was made up of

a dozen or more boys and girls, all of whom possessed academic learning, economic freedom and vague ambitions to write. I found them more formal in manners than their white counterparts; they wore stylish clothes and were finicky about their personal appearance. I had naively supposed that I would have much in common with them but I found them preoccupied with twisted sex problems ("AH," p. 25).

Wright felt very different from these young Blacks because of his background, his seriousness about his career and his horror of affectation. Unlike them, he had no fear of committing himself to something he believed in, nor did he need to fake passion or play the bohemian to make up for an inner emptiness. He also discovered that social success as defined by the black bourgeoisie could never satisfy him. If he wanted to become a writer, he would have to escape from the ghetto, meet more cultivated people and rival the masters of thought and writing whom he admired, that is to say, the Whites. His real friends then were the few fellow workers whose interests he shared and a certain number of old schoolmates who had also fled to Chicago because of the tense situation in the South. Among these were Essie Ward, Arthur Leaner and Joe Brown.

While Wright abhorred the entertainments of the lower classes, the pretensions of the bourgeoisie and the illusions or consolation of the church, he apparently did admire a certain set of people at the time:

The one group I met during those exploring days whose lives enthralled me was the Garveyites, an organization of black men and women who were forlornly seeking to return to Africa. Theirs was a passionate rejection of America, for they sensed with that directness of which only the simple are capable that they had no chance to live a full human life in America. Their lives were not cluttered with ideas in which they could only half believe; they could not create illusions which made them think they were living when they were not; their daily lives were too nakedly harsh to permit camouflage. I understood their emotions, for I partly shared them ("AH," pp. 25–26).

The Universal Negro Improvement Association had been founded after the war and had reached its height in 1922 with its grand parades and the fine-sounding titles of its semimilitary organization. In addition, it could boast several million shareholders in its nascent transatlantic company. Marcus Garvey had enjoyed an unprecedented popularity despite the opposition of the other leaders because he endowed the disinherited masses with a new dignity, promising a new African empire and exalting its ancient glories. Even though he was deported to Jamaica in 1927, numerous followers continued for years to believe in his utopian vision. The movement was fast declining, but Wright did meet some of these people in dingy apartments where the walls were covered with maps of Africa and color portraits of the U.N.I.A. dignitaries. Without agreeing with their ideology, Wright admired their dynamism and pride, which indicated to him the Afro-American revolutionary potential.

His refusal to join the Garvey movement was caused by a general skepticism. He and Aaron, for example, would ridicule sacrosanct American institutions and the stupidity of political leaders, but they had no idea what or who would replace them. They may have scorned the established political system by refusing to vote, but they also distrusted the grandiloquence of the various revolutionary proposals. On the threshold of the Depression, Wright admits, "I sensed that something terrible was beginning to happen in the world, but I tried to shut it out of my mind by reading and writing" ("AH," p. 26). The economic crisis soon forced him to face the situation squarely.

One evening in October, 1929, when Wright was returning from the public library, he could read the news of the Wall Street crash in the newspaper headlines. He might not have been concerned to learn that millions of investors had been ruined, but the stock market crash soon caused the post office to reduce working hours. Additional appointments were suspended just when Wright, with a brilliant score of 94 per cent on the competitive examination, would have been permanently hired. Soon the substitute clerks were called upon only one or two days a week. The reduction of Richard's salary from thirty dollars to five plunged the household into financial straits again. In a few months the exuberance of the South Side was entirely extinguished. Evicted tenants' furniture on the sidewalk, bread lines, workers hunting for odd jobs, the unemployed sleeping in the parks, famished children scrounging in garbage cans —all this was the new face of ruined America. While the tenants organized to defend themselves, the unemployed began their protests to demand help from the city government. The skirmish of August 20, 1930, which claimed the lives of two workers, was only one of many such confrontations with the police.

By the spring of that year, Wright was totally out of work. After weeks of fruitless searching, he was called back to the post office for a part-time job during the summer. Meanwhile the family was struck by illness. Aunt Cleo had a heart attack, Leon developed stomach ulcers and Ella suffered another relapse. Autumn brought the final blows. Richard's job ended, the banks were closing for an unlimited time, factories and offices were cutting their personnel and welfare organizations had not yet even been thought of, much less planned.

2

Circumstances favored less than ever Wright's ambition to become a writer, nor were his literary talents likely to keep him fed. Nevertheless, using his friend Dan Burley's connections, he tried to get himself known among the black press so that he might become an editor or a reporter. The most he accomplished, however, was placing a story in *Abbott's Monthly Magazine,* which had recently been founded by the famous editor of the *Chicago Defender.* This was the only magazine catering to the large black public, and it printed almost 100,000 copies an issue, amounting to around one hundred heavily illustrated pages. A great variety of articles appeared beneath the cover on which a sepia belle displayed herself: there were serious political analyses, following the bent of the *Defender*; reports on Africa; sensational confessions; and stories with provocative titles.[5] The tone of "Superstition," which came out in April, 1931, signed by Richard Nathanael Wright, and written exclusively for money, was probably influenced by the audience of the magazine, while it boasted the rudimentary techniques of a beginner modeling himself on Conrad, Poe and "dime novels." Nevertheless, certain interesting characteristics of Wright's style are already apparent.

"Each year the family held a reunion, each year death claimed its toll—was it superstition—or was it fate?" This sensational subtitle, reminiscent of the Gothic mood of "Hell's Half Acre," accurately summarizes the story. At the end of a good meal, a group of black businessmen each decide to tell a story. The last speaker, Fentley Burrows, chooses to describe his two successive and disturbing visits to a small Southern town. On his first trip, he is obliged to spend the night with a black family, having been told that all the hotels are full. Meanwhile, all the children of the family have come home unexpectedly to celebrate Christmas. Lilian, who had earlier mentioned the superstition surrounding the family next door, whereby a complete family reunion always spelled the death of one of its members, dies that day of pneumonia. The next year, out of curiosity, Burrows again goes to stay with the family and is present at the sudden death of the mother, whose sons have again arrived unannounced.

Wright cleverly exploits the intrigue generated by the two possible explanations for these tragic deaths, the natural and the supernatural. He scrupulously builds up a case for the natural causes. Lilian has frequent coughing fits; the bloodstain on her handkerchief and her feverishly bright eyes lead the reader to assume she is in the advanced stages of tuberculosis. Mrs. Lancaster's heart attack, considering that she was described as a small and frail old woman, is also understandable. At the same time, Wright draws on disturbing points about the scene to create a propitious atmosphere for the intervention of fate. But his impressionistic and superficial portrayal of the characters turns them into puppets. The pallor and mystery that envelop Lilian recall the heroines of Edgar Allan Poe, but in fact Wright announces the tragedy without much subtlety. Lilian herself is the one to recount the double deaths that struck the neighbors on successive family reunions, and on the second occasion her portrait falls from the wall and breaks on the mantelpiece shortly before her brothers' arrival. The tale's major faults, though, are the meaningless repetitions and abundant clichés. The style is bogged down by metaphors poorly evoking the nameless evil.

A silence,—deep and awful—a silence fraught with the meaning of something dreadful seemed to freeze the entire room. I shall never, as long as I breathe, forget that silence. In that silence there was revealed, hideously and repellently, the stark nakedness of the fearful hearts of a primitive folk,—fearful hearts bowing abjectly to the terror of an unknown created by their own imaginations. The outside world had fallen away, leaving only that room and its superstitious implications present. It was as if a long, skeleton-like hand

had reached upwards through an unknown past and claimed the
hearts of these primitive folks. It was awful. I felt as if I was floating out upon a cold and naked space! The very contents of their
inmost hearts were laid bare in that very moment: the unreasoning
fear of death.[6]

One of the faults that later plagued Wright as a novelist—the
compulsion to explain while describing—appears here, but some
of his future strong points are also in evidence. He creates the impression of reality with a few telling and poetic details. In addition
to Wright's mastery of Gothic techniques, "Superstition" reveals
that he is beginning to think about the origin of his own anguish.
In his guise as the narrator, whose detachment and skepticism he
emphasizes, Wright is outraged at the damage superstition causes
in primitive minds. He thinks that he is cured of "the childish sickness of metaphysical fear," which fosters traumas and religions, yet
his belief in the rational is apparently shaken by some troubling
coincidences.

The style of the story neither corroborates nor disproves Wright's
own judgment, given in "American Hunger," of the development
of his writing at this time. Even if certain sentences seem to correspond to what he declares to have written then, it would be useless
to assume the influence of Dostoevsky or Proust. Conrad and Poe
are more likely. Burrows is a double of *Lord Jim's* Marlow; while
seeming to express their own feelings, they are both instruments
for the transmission of the authors' views. A different setting might
have made even the subject Conradian. In any case, "Superstition"
is a Gothic story owing its most obvious techniques to Poe's *Tales*.[7]

With the vague dates that Wright supplies for this period of his
literary development, it is difficult to distinguish the various possible influences from his wide reading since arriving in Chicago.
Of course, any author mentioned in *A Book of Prefaces* had an
automatic introduction; Mencken spoke well of "The Blue Hotel,"
so Wright read the stories of Stephen Crane as well as *The Red
Badge of Courage*. He sampled Dostoevsky with *Poor Folk* and
went on to devour *The Possessed* and *Notes from Underground*.
He was rapidly finishing Dostoevsky when he started on Tolstoy.
He also read a number of Conrad's novels: *The Arrow of Gold,
Chance, Nostromo, Typhoon, The Shadow-Line, Victory* and
Youth, which he bought second hand. He read *The Genius* and
The Titan by Dreiser, *Three Soldiers* by Dos Passos, *Emperor Jones*

by Eugene O'Neill. Sometimes it was chance and the price of the book that guided his choice, but usually it was the wise advice of William Harper, a good friend who later owned a bookstore in the ghetto.[8] Thus Wright provided himself with a number of classics as well as several avant-garde works written at the beginning of the century. Among English writers such as Shakespeare, Swift, Dickens, Carlyle, Galsworthy and Hardy, George Moore became one of his favorites because of *Confessions of a Young Man* and *Esther Waters*. He also bought at that time H. G. Wells's *Outline of History* and *Undying Fire*. However, he preferred D. H. Lawrence, especially after absorbing the mother-son relationship in *Sons and Lovers*. He read, among other translations from the French, Balzac's *Seraphita*, to which he alludes in unpublished essays; he had already discovered *The Three Musketeers* by Alexandre Dumas, his racial brother who had become famous in a saner society, but he now added *Iceland Fisherman* by Pierre Loti, *Mademoiselle de Maupin* by Theophile Gautier, and Anatole France's *The Revolt of the Angels* and *The Gods Are Athirst*, a story about the French Revolution. Although he bought *The Divine Comedy* and *Decameron*, there is no telling if he read them all the way through. He did read the plays of Lessing and Ibsen, and Arthur Schnitzler's *Theresa*. Among American authors, his slender library featured only old and incomplete editions of Whitman and Poe, in addition, of course, to his favorite great masters.

Conrad and Dreiser undoubtedly dominated Wright's writing at this time. In fact it was Conrad who tempted Wright to sacrifice realism to romanticism in "Superstition," although the bourgeois audience he was catering to may have been responsible for the flagrant lack of social realism. The fact that the Depression was at its height did not prevent the three Negroes in the story from being successful businessmen, while the entire episode could just as easily have taken place in an exclusively white setting. Furthermore, the narrator says that he had to stay with a family because two conventions had filled the hotels of Koogan. Would it not have been more accurate to mention that the white hotels would not take him and that this small Southern town had no black hotels? In fact, this papier mâché setting was written to please those who wanted to live vicariously in the world of Horatio Alger. Two years later Wright came to regret that he had not followed his own principles but had stooped to the level of his audience. He was ashamed of this "blood and thunder story," which he in part disowned by never again signing anything he wrote with his middle name.[9]

In spite of this Conradian and Gothic story, Wright had by 1930 already attempted to model some writing on Dreiser as well. He hoped to write something with the South Side as a setting and the Blacks who lived there as characters. To this end, he practiced recording their speech and describing their customs, referring to the available sociology books in order to characterize different types of black people. Len Mallette remembered how carefully Richard observed what went on at the post office in order to write the novel whose broad outlines were already those of *Lawd Today*. His dedication was total. One day after work, Mallette took Richard to a striptease show at the Rialto, nearby. When it was over, Richard had nothing to say about the girls; he didn't thank Len, but said, rather, "Well, I've lost two hours now and I could have worked at my novel." [10]

This novel was only a simple attempt at fiction, but it represented a significant and continued effort for Wright. For the first time he was trying to transform, via dialogue and description, both his rudimentary sociological knowledge and his own experience. Since he had chosen to portray ordinary life, his adolescent penchant for the imaginary and the supernatural gave way to verisimilitude. At the same time, he achieved a certain detachment. *Lawd Today* is written in the third person, which tends to keep Jake Jackson at a distance, but it does not suffer from the author's omniscience, although there are didactic passages enumerating the rules of the policy game or describing the mail sorting table. The characters are free to enjoy their own feelings, with Wright's often ironic commentary achieved merely by the juxtaposition and contrast of their points of view. There is no way of telling what portion of the novel he actually wrote at this time since he totally reworked it five years later to complete the final version; it would therefore be wrong to overemphasize Wright's conversion to realism at this stage. Nevertheless it is certain that he was already making an effort to get at the truth of things, however painful. When, for instance, a black journalist during that same period described the gaming houses and prostitutes of 47th Street in terms arousing the wrath of the ghetto inhabitants, who accused him of siding with critics, Wright surprised his friends by defending the author in the name of objectivity. He felt neither slighted by the article nor akin to the people it stigmatized; he merely hoped to achieve a similar detachment in his first novel.[11]

3

"Superstition" should have earned Wright thirty or forty dollars, but the economic crisis killed the magazine; it stopped publication in 1931, and he was never paid. When his summer job at the post office came to an end, he got special permission from the Board of Education to enter the Hyde Park Public School in the tenth grade but was not able to attend for more than a few weeks. After many days of fruitless job hunting, the help of a distant cousin got him a position as an insurance agent for a funeral home.

Wright received a 10 per cent commission on receipts, plus fifteen dollars per dollar on new policies, although he would be penalized at the same rate on unrenewed policies. In spite of the economic crisis, the funeral-insurance business continued at an only somewhat slower rate because so many Blacks preferred to do without in this life in order to be assured a proper funeral. Nevertheless, most people failed to pay their premiums as soon as they were strapped for money, even at the risk of having to begin again with another company. Thus, agents would roam around the South Side looking for a family with a new money supply who were ready to start another policy. The competition was fierce and Wright fared poorly.

In return he did acquire a detailed knowledge of lower-class life, which he describes in "Early Days in Chicago": "Each day now I saw how the Negro in Chicago lived, for I visited hundreds of dingy flats filled with rickety furniture and ill-clad children. Most of the policy holders were illiterate" (*EM*, p. 228). He drew upon this material later, in, for instance, *Twelve Million Black Voices*, where he denounced the system of "kitchenettes," and in *The Long Dream* where, for a while, his hero has the same kind of job Wright had. For the time being, though, he was scarcely able to find time to study or read, much less write, since he was so exhausted by the time evening came.

This hateful life did have one compensation. Until this time Wright had only seen girls sporadically, but this year he probably had his first steady, if not serious, affair:

There were many comely black housewives who, trying desperately to keep up their insurance payments, were willing to make bargains to escape paying a ten-cent premium. I had a long, tortured affair with one girl by paying her ten-cent premium every week. She was an illiterate black child with a baby whose father she did not know. During the entire period of my relationship with her she had but one demand to make of me: she wanted me to take her to a circus (*EM,* p. 228).

Wright was not satisfied with a purely physical relationship with M—— W——, and he was subject to ambivalent feelings. He was jealous of his mistress's other lovers while pitying her simplicity, which was so close to stupidity; he was irritated when she made fun of his professorial efforts to teach her to read; and, worst of all, he declares, he was "angry that I was sitting beside a human being with whom I could not talk, angry with myself for coming to her, hating my wild and restless loneliness" (*EM,* p. 229). Even though he could not be satisfied with a girl who was unable to share his intellectual aspirations, he was at the mercy of his desire.

Besides resenting the sordidness of his job, Wright found that the funeral company was dishonest. In order to reduce the services guaranteed to its clientele, the company would send an inspector to pretend to verify the contract and then substitute a less advantageous one while the client was not paying attention. Wright knew that he would lose his job if he revealed the fraud, but he suffered under the degradation of this compromise.

The economy was still getting worse and the black population was sorely affected. During the summer of 1931, more than eight hundred destitute ghetto families were evicted from their homes; neighbors would unite and resist by putting the furniture back in place. Then on August 31, two black workers, Abe Grey and John O'Neill, were killed during a confrontation with the police in which a crowd protested the eviction of a widow and her children. The ten thousand people who marched through South Side on the day of their funeral successfully frightened the police away. By this time the League of Struggle for Negro Rights, a radical Communist group, was condemning the law-abiding tactics of the NAACP and had organized an effective movement to protest the evictions.

During the twenties, a number of Blacks may have refused to join the Communists for fear of losing their jobs, but by now they had nothing to lose, so the Party's antiracist slogans were well received. Furthermore, the campaign to defend the Scottsboro Boys, which had begun in 1931, had become very active by the following year when the International Labor Defense chose the black lawyer William Patterson to defend the accused. This aroused some outright sympathy for the Communists, whom the Blacks had until then regarded with a mixture of curiosity and distrust. In Chicago, black and white organizers working together had succeeded in mobilizing the masses. In February, 1931, black Communists such as Joseph Gardner, Bob Ware, Ed Williams and Jack Tilford had led a demonstration of the unemployed. Charles Banks became the expert in charge of resisting evictions. Speakers rose up on street corners to hail the imminent proletarian revolution and the need to unite.[12] The size of the movement in 1932 should not be exaggerated; of the two hundred thousand Communists there were only five hundred Blacks, but the group was so active that most of the ghettos could not help but come into contact with them.

During his free afternoons or evenings, after he had finished his route, Wright would listen to the orators in Washington Park.

As I went from house to house collecting money, I saw black men mounted upon soap boxes at street corners, bellowing about bread, rights and revolution. I liked their courage but I doubted their wisdom. The speakers claimed that Negroes were angry, that they were about to rise and join their white fellow workers to make a revolution. I was in and out of many Negro homes each day and I knew that the Negroes were lost, ignorant, sick in mind and body. I saw that a vast distance separated the agitators from the masses, a distance so vast that the agitators did not know how to appeal to the people they sought to lead ("AH," pp. 33–34).

The crowd often considered these black Communists charlatans like the rest. The haranguers naïvely copied the affectations of their Russian comrades, wearing the same kind of open-necked shirts and the visors of their caps folded back, while they assumed the stance of a Lenin and summoned God to strike them dead to prove His existence. But among them were some speakers who could present a coherent Marxist analysis of the situation. Thus, it was more difficult to resist the arguments of Brown Squire, Sol Harper or David Pointdexter as they denounced the corruption of the black millionaire Oscar de Priest or the Republican mayor "Big Bill" Thompson.

Wright admired the militant Communists. When the unemployment relief centers were opened, many meetings took place at the one on Oakwood Boulevard, located at the Abraham Lincoln Center that Wright used to visit regularly. A demonstration in Washington Park was a great success in June, although Bob Reed and David Pointdexter were arrested. Herbert Newton, on the other hand, managed to address the crowd from the top of a tree, while the police tried to dislodge him by throwing bricks. These confrontations between Communists and police slowly forced the most skeptical to admit the courage of this fistful of extremists, so that whenever its immediate concerns were involved, the crowd supported their actions. Wright himself shared their idealism as well as a large part of the Marxist perspective. He liked the characteristic Communist preference for action, but he still distrusted anything that did not correspond to his own experience, and he certainly did not believe in the coming revolution.

Because of his job as an insurance agent, Wright was hired, in the summer of 1931, as an assistant to Ben "Doc" Huggins, the owner of a beauty parlor and a precinct captain in the ghetto. Huggins was collecting Republican votes for Mayor Thompson so that he himself would get the position of city personnel inspector. A demagogue with a powerful personality, Thompson depended upon his relationship with the city's minorities to keep his seat; the Blacks were particularly helpful since they were on principle faithful to Abraham Lincoln's political party. In return for their support, he gave them small jobs, favored them as candidates for various city services and chose not to see the countless infringements of the law in the ghetto, such as gambling and drinking. Thus, ten dollars and the promise of a job as a librarian's assistant lured Wright to participate in the political campaign, distributing drinks, buying the votes of the "policy" players, saloon owners and pimps. Having no particular Republican leanings, Wright was disgusted by the seamy side of the electoral system and even more outraged when Huggins only procured him a job sweeping the public parks. The next year, he had no scruples in assisting the captain of Democratic Precinct 4, since it was merely a question of earning a few extra dollars and not of doing his civic duty.[13]

A series of failures made the year 1932 particularly difficult. While he had been recruiting votes, Wright and his friend Joe Brown had tried to start an insurance program for the *Herald American*. When that folded they worked for a black company, the Supreme Liberty Life Insurance, that was trying to launch a program of commercial and industrial insurance, but once again the enterprise collapsed after only a few weeks. The two then got together with their versatile friend Arthur Leaner, whose fertile mind had conceived the notion of exploiting the gullible public by selling miracle cures through the mail. The "Three Star-Gazers" never executed their fraud; no sooner had they bought "lucky dust" from the local medicine man than Wright's true nature triumphed. He abandoned the dangerous undertaking, less perhaps from a sense of honesty than from the simple fear of being caught, and the episode remained an amusing memory for later use.[14]

The Wrights' poverty continued. By November, 1932, when Franklin D. Roosevelt was elected President, Chicago had as many unemployed as it had workers. After two years of struggling to

Richard Wright (sixth from the right) as assistant precinct captain with the Courtney group. *Photo by T. Oyama*

find and keep a job, Wright was at the end of his tether. To avoid eviction, the family moved to a filthy, decaying slum.

The place was dismal; plaster was falling from the walls; the wooden stairs sagged. When my mother saw it, she wept. I felt bleak. I had not done what I had come to the city to do.

One morning I rose and my mother told me that there was no food for breakfast. I knew that the city had opened relief stations, but each time I thought of going into one of them I burned with shame. I sat for hours, fighting hunger, avoiding my mother's eyes. Then I rose, put on my hat and coat, and went out. As I walked towards the Cook County Bureau of Public Welfare to plead for bread, I knew that I had come to the end of something ("AH," p. 39).

In an early version of *Black Boy*, Wright confesses that he resisted the temptation to resort to illegal activities at that time by becoming a policy-ticket collector. Humiliating as it was, his desperate visit to the Public Welfare Bureau represented a moral victory. But it was also the end of a dream, the end of the American myth, which had promised at least a living if not a Horatio Alger success story. By the time the unemployed were planning their first hunger march on Washington, Wright had come to the conclusion that the whole American system had finally proved its incompetence and injustice. The Depression cast this intelligent and enterprising young man among the jobless, vagabonds and bums whom he had hitherto looked down upon because they were not earning a living. Now he realized that their common destitution could not be conquered by personal qualities and personal effort alone. He now belonged to the huge class of the exploited and disinherited as much as he did to the black community:

The day I begged bread from the city officials was the day that showed me I was not alone in my loneliness; society had cast millions of others with me. But how could I be with them? . . . I was slowly beginning to comprehend the meaning; a sense of direction was beginning to emerge from the conditions of my life. . . . My cynicism slid from me. I grew open and questioning. I wanted to know (*EM,* p. 235).

Public Welfare eventually supplied food; a social worker assured family support and secured Richard a job as a street cleaner until the influx of Christmas mail meant that he could return temporarily to the post office. There he found that if the desperate economic

situation broke down the barriers between individuals, it also lowered them between the races. He could now consort more freely with
the white students who had flocked to the post office with their
useless diplomas. For the first time they invited him home and he
observed how common misfortune obliterated certain prejudices;
a class perspective had replaced the racial one.

Early in 1933, when his temporary job was over, Wright was sent
to dig ditches for the Cook County Forest Preserves. He kept his
spirits up, despite his sore hands and aching back, by reading books
on aesthetics and going to see the girls he had known while selling
insurance. Finally, he got a job at the Michael Reese Hospital,
unaware that he owed this favor to Mrs. Mary Wirth (the wife of
the famous sociologist at the University of Chicago), who was doing
social work in his area. Impressed by the appearance and manners
of this young black boy whom she would have liked to see continue
his studies, she had approached a friend, the director of pathology
in the serology center, who hired Wright and another Black to work
in his laboratory. To save their pride, their unemployment benefits
were paid directly to the hospital, which put them on the payroll.

The hospital occupied a complex of gray brick buildings from
Ellis Avenue to 29th Street in the northwest of the ghetto, and
Dr. Thalheimer had one of the most modern laboratories. In this
medical sanctuary the Blacks had no status. "Four of us Negroes
worked there and we occupied an underworld position, remembering
that we must restrict ourselves—when not engaged upon some task
—to the basement corridors, so that we would not mingle with white
nurses, doctors, or visitors" (*EM*, p. 237).

Wright's job was to clean the stairs and the operating rooms and
take care of the guinea pigs. Since he had once dreamed of becoming
a doctor, he suffered from this segregation and disdain, which prevented him from learning about the scientific world that surrounded
him. He was even more hurt by the ironic replies of the Jewish doctors whom he sometimes dared to question about the Wassermann
or Aschheim-Zondek tests, because he knew that they, too, were up
against racial prejudice. It was torture to find himself clocked by
an intern, an efficiency nut, who wanted to see him clean a room
in seventeen minutes. He was personally insulted by careless people
who would walk on the steps he had not yet rinsed. Overhearing
a lesson which he could have followed himself addressed to a group
of interns, he could not suppress a feeling of revolt at being kept

aside. He did his work conscientiously, but perhaps his pride and questions to the doctors gave his superiors a less favorable impression of him than of the other colored employees.[15]

In spite of these humiliations and the routine that forced him to get up at dawn, the work had its good moments. Once, out of curiosity, he inhaled some fumes of Nembutal, and his friends nearly succeeded in convincing him that he had poisoned himself. On another occasion two Blacks who had worked there for fifteen years and had become inseparable enemies came to blows in an epic battle over their favorite daily paper. On February 9, 1933 (the coldest day in fifty years, according to the meteorological archives), Brand and Cooke, armed with knife and ice pick respectively, knocked a row of guinea pig cages to the floor. The four men, fearing for their jobs, feverishly tried to efface all traces of the disaster. Their meager knowledge of the experiments under way must have entailed numerous errors in getting the animals back into the proper cages and perhaps resulted in unexpected scientific findings. The need to retain his job, along with his resentment of the doctors, kept Wright silent about this catastrophe. Once again he had sacrificed his scruples to self-interest, as he had done in working for the insurance company and for "Doc" Huggins. Years later, the episode was the subject of the story aptly entitled "What You Don't Know Won't Hurt You." [16]

FIVE

1

T HE year 1933 was an eventful one for Chicago. In February, a bullet intended for President Roosevelt fatally wounded the Democratic mayor; he was replaced by the Irishman Kelley, who eventually won the South Side vote from the Republicans by giving the Blacks more positions in the city. On March 4, Roosevelt opened the banks and created the Federal Emergency Relief Administration to fight the economic crisis. In May, anarchist bombs shook the offices of five large companies while, as if to deny the hard times, the second Chicago World's Fair opened to commemorate a "Century of Progress." For Wright, too, the year was a landmark, since he began his literary career as a revolutionary poet.

The year before, several Communist intellectuals, led by Henry Allan Potamkin, had expanded a leftist literary and artistic club originating in New York to national scale in the hopes of inspiring and uniting radical young people. Named after the militant American author of *Ten Days That Shook the World,* who had died in Russia in 1921, the John Reed clubs were an immediate success and there were now over thirty of them in the large cities. Their members were affiliated with The International Union of Revolutionary Writers in Moscow, to which such people as Alan Calmer, Bob Reed, John Howard Lawson and John Wexley were representatives.

The Chicago club had organized a meeting of all the Middle Western groups at the beginning of August, 1932, where it was decided to establish three types of clubs: one for those interested in literature and the plastic arts; another focusing on music and dance; and a third functioning as a political information center open to all Communist sympathizers. The newly opened club belonged to the first category and, in June, 1933, started to publish a small literary magazine. As opposed to *New Masses,* the Party magazine, which as a rule accepted only established authors, *Left Front,* like the similar club organs of Indianapolis, Detroit and Cedar Rapids,

95

catered to beginners, who thereby found, in those times of economic crisis, an invaluable means of reaching some kind of audience. Thus, many young intellectuals and writers joined the club to participate in its literary, rather than political, activities.

Wright was recruited by his friend Abraham Aaron, who was acting according to a plan adopted during the summer of 1933 to deliberately enlist black members. Aaron had already recruited some white former post-office employees and had just had one of his stories accepted by *Anvil,* Jack Conroy's proletarian magazine; he therefore enjoyed a certain reputation. Aaron was working at the reception desk of the Troy Lane apartment hotel and invited Wright to discussion groups at his apartment. Later he recommended that Wright attend a regular meeting of the group, which might help him on his way to becoming a writer. Accordingly, Wright went one autumn evening to a single room at 1475 South Michigan Avenue.

Paper and cigarette butts lay on the floor. A few benches ran along the walls above which were vivid colors depicting colossal figures of workers carrying streaming banners. The mouths of the workers gaped in wild cries; their legs were sprawled over cities.[1]

In a paragraph that appeared in "I Tried to Be a Communist," mainly criticizing their unrealistic aspirations, Wright mentions a number of club members who, in fact, provided some of the first enduring literary friendships he had ever known. About twenty of them were particularly active. Bill Jordan, former editor of *The Left,* a brilliant but short-lived magazine, had left Davenport, Iowa, to take over *Left Front.* The other writers included, of course, Abe Aaron, who published short stories under the pseudonym Tom Butler; William Pillin, a fairly good poet; Maurice Merlin; and Irving Yaffa. Nelson Algren, who was writing *Somebody in Boots* and whose story "The Hunters" had just been accepted by *The American Mercury,* joined this group soon afterward. The artists were more numerous and more politically active. One of them, Gilbert Rocke, was secretary of the club and a staunch Communist, efficiently supported by Jan Wittenber, known for his accurate pencil and his black beard that lent him a Christ-like air. Herbert Klein was then a promising stage and movie director, and probably the most genuinely talented person there was Morris Topchevsky. Wright predicted that "Toppy" "was to become one of the nation's leading painters." *Left Front* was also proud of printing Mitchell Siporin's satirical lithographs, while Abraham Weiner, Nicholas Cheskin, John Groth and Ray Breinin also contributed along with sympathizers whose talents were less specific. Many of these were women like Edith Margo, who was treasurer of the magazine; Nucia Castle, who succeeded her; Eva Teitel; Olga Ziegler; Eleanor Zwimmer; a social worker; the wife of a university professor; and an Irish girl who worked in advertising.

Wright felt immediately at home, since everyone treated him courteously but without condescension. He left the magazine's editorial-board meeting with a few recent issues of *New Masses* and *International Literature,* in which the poetry of Langston Hughes appeared along with articles by Gorky and André Gide.

The passage in "I Tried to Be a Communist" describing his enthusiasm on reading these magazines condenses an entire series of events into one crucial episode, just as do the lines in *Black Boy* on his discovery of Mencken seven years earlier in Memphis. Although he was somewhat torn between his new sympathies and his mother's religious beliefs, he came to see in Marxism an organized search for truth about the life of oppressed peoples, and this convinced him that the Communists were sincere. Wright had long yearned to participate in American intellectual life, to become part of the Western culture in which he lived, but the strangeness and hostility of the white world had discouraged him. Now he concretely realized that the oppressed classes of all colors were united by a common suffering, and that as a writer, he could play a particular role within the group:

The revolutionary words leaped from the printed page and struck me with tremendous force. It was not the economics of Communism, nor the great power of trade unions, nor the excitement of underground politics that claimed me; my attention was caught by the singularity of the experience of workers in other lands, by the possibility of uniting scattered but kindred peoples into a whole. It seemed to me that here at last, in the realm of revolutionary expression, Negro experience could find a home, a functioning value and role (*GF,* p. 118).

It was perhaps the first time that Wright had felt needed. Although he still wondered about the sincerity of the other Communists, his own was not in question. He totally lived for the idea that he had a place in this newborn world.

Here, then, was something I could reveal, say. The Communists, I felt, had oversimplified the experience of those whom they sought to lead. In their efforts to recruit masses, they had missed the meaning of the lives of the masses, had conceived of people in too abstract a manner. I would try to put some of that meaning back. I would tell Communists how common people felt, and I would tell common people of the self-sacrifice of Communists who strove for unity among them (*GF*, p. 120).

This mission, which governed Wright's work for years, certainly had scope as well as its share of naïveté. He already thought of himself as a mediator and had so much confidence in the revolutionary ideal that he addressed his first poems not to the confirmed radicals, but to the people, so that they might share his recent discovery. The club not only provided a justification of his desire to write "à la Mencken"—that is, with commitment to a cause—not only a group of people with common human and intellectual interests, but also the opportunity of reaching a well-defined public.

Feeling for the first time that I could speak for listening ears, I wrote a wild, crude poem in free verse, coining images of black hands playing, working, holding bayonets, stiffening finally in death. I felt that in a clumsy way it linked white life with black, merged two streams of common experience (*GF*, p. 118).

Like his momentous discovery of literature through H. L. Mencken, described as taking place in one moment of revelation, it does not matter whether or not the composition of "I Have Seen Black Hands" was actually inspired by a single night of reading Marxist literature, as Wright claimed. What does matter is that at the club Wright was accepted at face value as a writer who was openly expressing his feelings as a black man.[2] This in turn supplied the ideological unity to his work that marked the beginning of his career as a revolutionary poet.

At one of the next meetings, Wright submitted several poems— "I Have Seen Black Hands," "Rest for the Weary" and "A Red Love Note"—to the criticism of his friends. Abe Aaron was enthusiastic and Bill Jordan was in favor of publishing them; although they lacked polish, the strength and purity of their inspiration was exactly what *Left Front* was looking for. They therefore decided to submit the first and best of the group to *New Masses* and to print the second two themselves.

The revolutionary spirit of these poems is not surprising. Each covered one aspect of the social struggle: the inefficiency of the liberal ideology, in "Child of the Dead and Forgotten Gods"; the failure of capitalism, in "A Red Love Note," "Rest for the Weary" and "Everywhere Burning Waters Rise"; and the unity of the workers, in "Strength." Among these Communist propaganda pieces only "I Have Seen Black Hands" brings up the racial question. The tone of these passionate exhortations, aimed in turn at the pacifist, the decadent bourgeois, the ruined financier and the eager revolutionary, fits into the tradition of radical poetry appearing in *The Rebel Poet* and *New Masses*. The metaphors are not always apt, and Wright offers some well-worn clichés as discoveries, but the language is most often original. The surprising abundance of biblical allusions in this political context indicates Wright's early love for the language of sermons, and the images come naturally: the capitalists are Pharisees, guardians of the temple of Mammon, erected by greed and, like the temple in Jerusalem, to be devoured by flames because the merchants have transformed it into "bargain counters of justice."

In "A Red Love Note," Wright satirically puts the institutions that he condemns on trial, mingling the language used in a court proceeding against an insolvent debtor with the saccharine phrases of a love letter. When Wright ceases to sermonize, as in "Child of the Dead and Forgotten Gods" and "Rest for the Weary," the message is more poetic. The individual's revolt in "Strength," for example, is "a gentle breeze, ineffectually tearing/at granite crags," which is then transformed into "a raging hurricane vast and powerful/wrenching and dredging by the roots the rotting husks of the trees of greed." [3]

"Everywhere Burning Waters Rise" shows more obvious artistry. The concrete beginning, a description of economic inertia, is supported by a rigid rhythmic structure. In describing the poverty of the oppressed the poet mingles the concrete with the abstract. Further along, the accumulation of present participles and the repetition of near synonyms transform the fog of discontent into a stream of blood and fire. The prophetic hymn celebrates the torrent of the revolution in a passionate finale contrasting with the restraint at the beginning.[4]

"I Have Seen Black Hands" is the real success of this group of poems, almost a fresco in free verse representing the stages of Afro-American experience, somewhat like Shakespeare's soliloquy, the

"Seven Ages of Man." The poem traces the process of growth from the innocence of the cradle, through the games of childhood and studies at school, to the wiliness of adolescence. Then comes the harsh life of the adult—the hands of the soldier who fights in foreign lands, of the worker who increases the nation's wealth only to find himself unemployed, of the rebel, the defeated, the imprisoned, the lynched black man convey the message:

> I am black and I have seen black hands
> Raised in fists of revolt, side by side
>   with the white fists of white workers
> And some day—and it is this only which sustains me—
> Some day there shall be millions and millions of them
> On some red day in a burst of fists on a new horizon.[5]

Since this poem was inspired by Wright's own experience, it is more moving than his diatribes against the capitalist system. Without irony or forced juxtapositions, he achieves a sometimes picturesque, sometimes pitiless enumeration, propelled by the rapid succession of conjunctions and the repetition of "black hands." He limits himself to the suffering of his own people, without making any explicit accusations—this, with the open Marxist interpretation, assures the power of the poem.

2

Wright had finally made his true literary debut by offering his works to this supposedly enlightened audience, and it was not long before he became one of the mainstays of the Chicago club. His increasing attraction to the club matched the members' own enthusiasm for him. The variety of club activities, among them a campaign to get the government to subsidize artists, exhibitions and debates, impressed him as much as the fervent idealism of his new friends. For their part, the most experienced and influential members—Topchevsky, Rocke and Wittenber—welcomed the polite interest of this somewhat timid but amazingly self-controlled young Black. The painters accepted him because he was unassuming, while the writers admired his talent.

Within this ostensibly harmonious group there was some rivalry. Since the painters were predominantly Communist, they faithfully obeyed the Party directives. They were politically very active and therefore used most of the money that actually belonged to the entire club. The writers, who had to move heaven and earth just to publish their magazine, were naturally loath to see their economies pay for projects that meant less to them. When a change of officers took place, about two months after he had joined the club, Wright found that he had been elected secretary without having aspired to the position. The writers had wanted to get rid of Gilbert Rocke and cleverly assumed that the charge of "racial chauvinism" would be enough to prevent the artists from voting against a black member. Wright had personal reasons for accepting this responsibility, since he wanted to have some control over the shaky magazine that printed his poetry. Reassured by his moderate nature, the painters soon came around to him even though he was not yet politically committed.

By the spring of 1934, the new executive secretary had already accomplished so much with his enthusiasm and zeal that even his original detractors were surprised. He had inaugurated the season by leading a discussion and giving a lecture on "Negro Culture in a Marxist Perspective" at the club on September 8, 1932.[6] Wright also organized the weekly Tuesday meetings and started the Saturday lecture program to which the club would invite progressive professors such as the sociologist Ernest Burgess, who spoke on "Art in Soviet Russia"; Lawrence Martin, of Northwestern University, speaking on "The Collapse of Liberalism"; the historian Lewis Gottschalk on the French Revolution; John Strachey, of the University of Chicago; the anthropologist Melville Herskovits; and Robert Morss Lovett. As well as being highly informative, these lectures provided the only avenue by which Wright could have met these prominent older intellectuals. At the beginning of March, 1934, he himself went to speak at the Indianapolis John Reed Club. His subject, "Black revolutionary poetry," was one that he frequently discussed during the thirties and forties.

During regular meetings, the artists may have preferred to spend their time criticizing the Works Progress Administration, but the writers, when they were not discussing literature, concentrated on the future of *Left Front*, which was, by 1933, the official publication of the John Reed clubs of the Middle West.

After the January, 1934, issue containing "A Red Love Note" and "Rest for the Weary" came out, Wright became a member of the editorial board, just under Bill Jordan, with Pillin, Siporin, Merlin, Aaron and Edith Margo. They were beset with difficulties. A few new subscriptions, as well as lectures and a "Jungle Ball" for the benefit of the magazine, meant they could pay the printer. But the Party had jeopardized the publication with its money requirements and the May issue, in which "Everywhere Burning Waters Rise" appeared, was to be the last. This issue also included a scene from "John Henry," by Herbert Klein; "Jurgen's Folly," by Herbert's brother Marvin, who wrote under the name Mark Marvin; the final section of a long report by Edith Margo on the Communists in the South Side; and an article by the poet-farmer H. H. Lewis. *Left Front* probably did not rival the literary quality of its predecessor, *The Left*, but it was certainly above average and to have been both an editor and a contributor was to Wright's credit.

Wright was soon more famous than his original sponsor. It was Aaron, in fact, who had encouraged Wright to send his poems to Jack Conroy, the editor of *Anvil*, which published both "Strength" and "Child of the Dead and Forgotten Gods" in March.[7] *New Masses* then accepted a slightly revised version of "I Have Seen Black Hands." Even though this poem may not have been judged entirely on its own merits, since it was also in the magazine's interests to publish the work of one of the few black members of the John Reed Club, there is no doubt that having his name appear in the great leftist journal of the period considerably increased Wright's prestige. In only a few months, his handful of poems had earned him a secure position in the club, a group of friends— some of whom he kept for years—and even recognition by the national Communist press.[8] Surely Wright had discovered the spiritual family that would recognize and appreciate his talents.

After his original elation had passed, however, he did not fail to notice some of the club's weaknesses, particularly from his vantage point as a mere sympathizer.

The demands of the local Party authorities for money, speakers and poster painters were so great that the publication of *Left Front* was in danger. Many young writers had joined the club because of their hope of publishing in *Left Front,* and when the Communist party sent word through the fraction that the magazine should be dissolved, the writers rejected the decision, an act which was interpreted as hostility toward Party authority.

I pleaded with the Party members for a more liberal program for the club. Feeling waxed violent and bitter. I was informed that if I wanted to continue as secretary of the club, I should have to join the Communist Party. I stated that I favored a policy that allowed for the development of writers and artists. My policy was accepted. I signed the membership card *(GF,* p. 122).

Although he did admire the Party's fight for racial equality, and his poems glorified the need to unite, it seems that Wright's motives for joining (at the end of 1933 at the earliest, and not in 1932 as he sometimes intimated) were more literary than political. Since he had never had the chance to escape his total intellectual isolation by going to college or associating with his white contemporaries, the club was the only bridge between his cultural ghetto and the American intellectual world. *Left Front* assured him, and many other club members, a certain audience at a time when the economic situation was forcing many publishers and magazines to go out of business.[9] So, even disregarding any of his political reasons for joining the Party, Wright's literary survival depended on continuing to publish the magazine, whatever it cost him.

Wright knew enough not to get caught between the painters and the writers or between the Communists and the sympathizers. The club was the scene of fights and some amusing, some extremely irritating incidents, but it was in his South Side C.P. unit that Wright found himself under real attack. His black comrades labeled him an "intellectual" because of his educated speech, shined shoes and clean shirt. His reply to their distrust and patronizing tone was to cut himself off and assert more than ever that his literary career took priority over his administrative duties. The others called him an "incorrigible bourgeois" because he spoke like a book even though in his working hours he cleaned the city streets. As he later confessed in "I Tried to Be a Communist," he was tempted to listen to these people only to collect material for his future novels.

For Wright, as for the majority of his radical colleagues, the conflict between a writing career and political activity posed a problem. At the August, 1934, Middle West Writers' Congress,

which was held in Chicago, the participants were much less interested in professional problems than in ascertaining the latest
Party stand on this point. For a long time the writers had been
complaining because organizational work left them no time to write.

The question debated was: What does the Communist Party expect
from the club? The answer of the Communist leader ran from organizing to writing novels. I argued that either a man organized or
he wrote novels. The Party leader said that both must be done. The
attitude of the Party leaders prevailed and *Left Front,* for which I
had worked so long, was voted out of existence (*GF,* p. 135).

A second national congress of the John Reed clubs was then set
for September 28–29 in Chicago. Forty delegates, representing
about a thousand members, attended and Wright got a chance to
meet some of the best-known young radical writers. From Minneapolis there was Meridel Le Sueur, whose short story "I Was Marching" had just won the *New Masses* prize; from Missouri came Jack
Conroy, who was just publishing his first novel, *The Disinherited;*
Joseph Balch, a tireless traveler who wrote lively stories; and Joe
North, also from *New Masses.*

Wright, who represented Chicago along with Merlin, Rocke and
Bill Jordan, was in charge of reporting on the functions of the
various clubs. A. B. Magil, the force behind the Detroit club and
an older Communist from the early days of *New Masses,* appealed
at the end of the meeting for the organization of clubs on a national
scale. Finally Alexander Trachtenberg, a member of the Central
Committee and director of International Publishers, delivered the
Party directive in ambiguous terms. Wright was delighted to hear
a leader apparently supporting his own proposition. He could hardly
believe his ears, therefore, when Trachtenberg announced that the
clubs were not going to be reorganized, but would be dissolved
altogether.

The reasons for this were due to changes in Russian foreign
policy. When Hitler refused to enter a pact for mutual nonaggres-
sion, Stalin needed to ally himself more closely with the Western
democracies in order to protect the young Soviet Republic. Little
by little the slogans of the Popular Front against fascism replaced
those calling for an open war against capitalism. Since club members were not sufficiently well known to serve Party propaganda
purposes, a national organization restricted to noted writers and
artists would replace them. Meanwhile Richard, unaware of the

Party's interest in the color of his skin, thought he was going to be among those left out in the cold. He protested vigorously.

I asked what was to become of the young writers whom the Communist Party had implored to join the clubs and who were ineligible for the new group, and there was no answer. . . . It was not courage that made me oppose the Party. I simply did not know any better. It was inconceivable to me, though bred in the lap of Southern hate, that a man could not have his say. . . .

Before the congress adjourned, it was decided that another congress of American writers would be held in New York the following Summer, 1935. I was lukewarm to the proposal and tried to make up my mind to stand alone, write alone. I was already afraid that the stories I had written would not fit into the new, official mood. Must I discard my plot ideas and seek new ones? My writing was my way of seeing, my way of living, my way of feeling, and who could change his sight, his sense of direction, his senses (*GF,* pp. 136–37)?

If Wright is not attributing events to 1934 that actually occurred a year later (as is probably the case), there is no telling which completed stories he is alluding to here. Just prior to going to the Public Welfare Bureau in 1932, he had finished writing the life story of Myrtle Bolden, plantation-born, who had taught school in the Deep South before migrating north with her four children, and who ended in destitution and neglect. This he later considered awfully crude and lacking both plot and inspiration. His plans for novels consisted only of the first version of "Commonplace"—the future *Lawd Today*—and "a psychological study of bronze-sepia, firm-fleshed Jack Johnson, the Negro prize-fighter." [11] Neither of these would have conformed to the new Communist perspectives since he did not use the black American to symbolize the forces of revolution. The reference must have been to some other stories, since that year Wright hoped to complete his plan to show the Communists what life was like for Blacks and tell Blacks what communism represented. When working at the Michael Reese Hospital he had envisioned a series of biographical sketches on the labor movement, "Heroes, Red and Black," which would indicate the kind of experiences that might lead a black person to join the Party. There was ample precedent for this literary genre in proletarian literature, but Wright also had a personal reason for choosing this mode of expression.

At the time of the John Reed Club

He got the idea from his own experience and from his friendship with David Pointdexter. "Dex" was dark-skinned, tall, thin and energetic. He had worked as a stevedore the length of the Mississippi before settling in the North. A facile speaker, he fascinated Wright with anecdotes from levee camps, countless stories of tricks he had played upon white people and tales of the daring exploits of local anarchists. By the end of 1934, Wright was spending many evenings at the Pointdexters', sometimes taking notes on the sheets of yellow scratch paper that he always carried with him. The friendship between the two men was built on something of a misunderstanding. As a writer, Wright saw that "Dex" was a special character who could supply unique material, while Pointdexter hoped that Wright would share his anarchistic vision of communism. In joining the Party, Wright had not bothered to study the theoretical basis of Marxism, although he was familiar with the economic side of the analysis. It was several years before he read *Das Kapital* and, except for the pamphlets distributed by the Party, he was familiar at that time only with Stalin's *Colonial and National Question*, because it concerned him directly as a member of a minority group.[12] Pointdexter probably taught Wright more about Trotskyism and the Party's opposition to it. In fact, the formation of the Popular Front did not prevent Pointdexter from defying the Communist leaders by continuing the revolutionary agitation sanctioned in previous years. While he supported his friend's freedom of expression, Wright was far from sharing his political opinions, since human problems interested him more than subtleties of doctrine.

At that time Pointdexter was under indictment on the charge of inciting to riot, and his lawyer, Oliver Law, the South Side representative for the International Labor Defense, became suspicious of Wright when he saw him taking notes on his client's past. Perhaps he imagined that he was a spy. In any case, Wright had to refrain from asking questions in order not to aggravate the situation. Finally the Party advised him not to see "Dex" at all, since he opposed the Popular Front and was therefore guilty of ideological separatism. Oliver Law, a self-educated and narrow-minded local official whose military career had left him with a peremptory manner, demanded that Wright frequent only orthodox Communists and that he stop writing novels in order to devote himself to work as a propagandist. Law considered Wright a spineless and sentimental intellectual.[13] In Wright's eyes, the dilemma was insoluble: either he would have to conform to the Party directives and thus sacrifice his integrity as a writer, or he would once again be cut off and isolated. For the time being, he tried to stall, in order to remain part of the cultural organizations of the Left without becoming a mere political tool.

3

In the summer of 1934, the hospital was forced to lay off personnel and Wright was once again out of work. The family, which had increased with the arrival of Grandmother Wilson, moved to 4804 St. Lawrence Avenue, a slum next to the tracks of the Illinois Central. After sweeping streets and digging ditches again for the Cook County Forest Preserves while his Communist friends were calling him a bourgeois, he was hired to supervise a Youth Club organized to control delinquency in the ghetto. This was another source of fascinating material, which the future author of *Native Son* acknowledged much later in "How Bigger Was Born." In his autobiography, he recorded his immediate impressions.

Each day black boys between the ages of eight and twenty-five came to swim, draw and read. They were a wild and homeless lot, culturally lost, spiritually disinherited, candidates for the clinics, morgues, prisons, reformatories, and the electric chair of the state's death house. For hours I listened to their talk of planes, women, guns, politics, and crime. Their figures of speech were as forceful and colorful as any ever used by English-speaking people. I kept pencil and paper in my pocket to jot down their word-rhythms and reactions. These boys did not fear people to the extent that every man looked like a spy. The Communists who doubted my motives did not know these boys, their twisted dreams, their all too clear destinies; and I doubted if I should ever be able to convey to them the tragedy I saw here ("AH," p. 134).

Here Wright was not only able to acquire the social and psychological background that was later crucial to the creation of Bigger Thomas, but also to share without condemning the passions of the delinquents and, for once, to give free rein to his own antisocial feelings. Although his education and code of behavior would have predisposed him to favor honesty and morality, he realized that the Youth Club did not attack the root of the problem but only served to lessen its effects. Thus he sided more with the young rebels against society.

Compared to his new friends, his work and political activities, home now represented a backward milieu, as well as a hindrance to his ambition. Richard was technically the head of the family and he never shirked his responsibilities, contributing his entire salary to their support. Ella was still partially paralyzed after a recent attack of encephalitis. While Richard still respected her because of her indisputable moral authority, her devoutness irritated him more and more, along with her resigned attitude toward social injustice and hatred of communism. Since in Richard's opinion Leon was still malingering, Wright spent increasingly less time at home in order to avoid the friction between them.

Some of his old pals from Jackson were his best friends at this time. Joe Brown shared his political enthusiasms; Dick Jordan supplied information about his job with the railroad and his contacts with Whites for a short story Wright was planning; [14] Essie Ward was continuing her studies while working in a garment factory, and Wright often had dinner with her family. He used to advise her on what to read, help her write her sociology papers and on occasion dictated essays, which invariably received A's. They sometimes attended the Metropolitan Community Church to hear the spirituals, which Richard greatly enjoyed, although each time he seemed surprised by the singers' enthusiasm and wondered about their reasons for being so happy.[15]

Among the members of the John Reed Club, Wright was most relaxed with Bill Jordan, who enjoyed discussing literature (Wright himself talked about little else at the time) and looked at Wright's poems and stories:

He showed me numerous manuscripts, but all I remember about them is an impression of a tremendous flow of words, like Thomas Wolfe, quite undisciplined, impelled by an obvious urge to communicate a deep sense of wrong. He seemed to think my advice was useful. At any rate, he listened; and came back. I remember going over one manuscript with him and cutting it in half. What the story (or poem) was, I do not remember.[16]

Wright listened to the criticisms of this literary elder brother who on occasion helped him to improve the structure of a poem or gave him a shirt when his was in shreds. Abraham Aaron, Wright's perspicacious friend and sponsor, left for Pennsylvania in 1934. Abraham Chapman, Howard Nutt, Lawrence Lipton and Nelson Algren were among his favorite companions because of their common and sincere interest in the underworld and the "underdog."

Wright saw less of the painters. Gil Rocke had a kind of studio in "Rat's Alley," under the arcades of a World's Fair pavilion looking out onto Cottage Grove Avenue. Rocke had done a portrait of Pointdexter as an orator and Jan Wittenber, who had used Wright as a model for a painting exalting the unity of the proletariat, had several times invited him to his parties.[17] One evening, for instance, along with Bernard Goss and some black female fine arts students, they had gone to hear Harry Belafonte, who was then just beginning his career. In Wittenber's eyes Wright did not participate enough in political demonstrations and the two had a reserved friendship at best. Wright was more intimate with Morris Topchevsky, who taught him to appreciate modern painting and had introduced him to the Conroys, who had come to visit the World's Fair Exhibition, in May, 1934. Toppy lived and worked in a studio in the Abraham Lincoln Center, where Wright regularly attended the cultural events, in particular the Friday lectures. There he could hear Franz Alexander speak on psychiatry; Anna Louise Strong, John Haynes Holmes and Esther Perez de King lecture on politics; and Zona Gale and Lou Allen Jones talk about modern literature. He also used the library and so had many opportunities to visit Toppy. This was the beginning of his lifetime interest in nonrepresentational painting.

That year Wright made friends with two young couples, the Gourfains and the Newtons, who both helped him in their separate ways. He had met Joyce Gourfain at the club, and become very close to her. He continued to see this witty woman and her husband, Ed, until he left for New York. He often had dinner with them, conversing more openly in this friendly atmosphere than he would among the Communists.

He often discussed literature with Joyce and, somewhat later, read to her successive versions of "Big Boy Leaves Home" and "Down by the Riverside." She in turn interested him in Henry James, who was then the butt of criticism from the progressives, who condemned him as a decadent. She urged him to read *Daisy Miller, Portrait of a Lady* and *Roderick Hudson*. James fascinated Wright to such an extent that he borrowed from him the idea of a symbolic or representative hero. After reading James's *Prefaces*, for instance, he developed the fight between Big Boy and the dog in "Big Boy Leaves Home" and transformed Mann's attempt in "Down by the Riverside" into a confrontation of Man against Nature or Fate.[18]

Wright's other favorite haunt was the house of Jane Newton. Her husband, Herbert, had been a good friend of Pointdexter but had been one of the Communist leaders who suggested that Wright stick to more orthodox politics after "Dex" had been condemned. In the spring of 1935, the Newtons moved to a house on Prairie Avenue that Jane had wanted because she was expecting her second child. She entertained a good deal, inviting anyone who enjoyed chatting over a cup of coffee: students, musicians, welfare workers, artists. Jane came from a white middle-class family that had given her a good education, and she had a certain literary talent of her own. Thus Wright acquired an adviser and competent critic as well as a friend, while her guests provided a willing and receptive audience.

At that time Dick was a slim, fresh-faced young man. He smiled often when he spoke, his voice softly shaded with tones of the speech of the Mississippi Basin. When he used slang, it had audible quotation marks around it. He had two common expressions when he listened to criticism: in one, he leaned forward, his mouth a little open, his eyes on the face of the speaker; in the other he drew his shoulders up, lowered his eyes and set his jaw, making him the perfect picture of a person rejecting a proposal and withdrawing in the comfort of his own opinion. His spoken vocabulary was not large, but his words came easily and freely in conversation. His speech, however, was marked by the conventional stammer of the river valley Negro, which took the form, besides the repetition of syllables of words, of the interjection of the sound "er-r-r-ah" at the beginning of sentences and before important words. This did not appear when he read, of course. His written vocabulary was slightly larger than that of his common speech and one could observe its growth and the transition of words from his written language to his spoken one.[19]

Largely on the advice of his new friends, Wright started to read the avant-garde writers of the period: Proust, Joyce, Faulkner, Gertrude Stein, E. E. Cummings, T. S. Eliot. His reading had by now progressed from dime thrillers, through the American naturalist novels, and the international classics of the nineteenth century, to the revolutionary writings in *New Masses*. The authors of these latter works could not help him resolve his problems of form, so he turned back to the great English and Russian novelists at the same time as he studied the avant-garde experiments. Abe Aaron had given him Cummings' translation of *Red Front* by Louis Aragon, which led him to buy *The Enormous Room* and *Eimi*. He read *Portrait of the Artist as a Young Man* and *Ulysses*, which he discussed at length with several members of the club. Even though "decadent bourgeois" was the Marxist label for T. S. Eliot, who now influenced him as much as Whitman, Wright knew enough to imitate, half-consciously perhaps, Eliot's tone and rhythm.

He also mentions his accidental discovery of *Three Lives*, by Gertrude Stein, on the library shelf. The repetitive and sinuous prose of this eccentric woman who lived in France recalled the harmony and rhythm of Negro speech in the Deep South so vividly to him that suddenly he started to bombard his previously ignored Grandmother Wilson with questions for the sole purpose of transcribing her replies, conducting what he described as "experiments in words." [20] He then practiced copying the periodic structure and word combinations of Miss Stein's story "Melanctha," using the sound and repetition of the words to create a state of mind that would prolong the meaning of the words themselves. He describes working on this technique, which he tried to incorporate into his forceful style, as a demanding exercise:

My purpose was to capture a physical state or movement that carried a strong subjective impression, an accomplishment which seemed supremely worth struggling for. If I could fasten the mind of the reader upon words so firmly that he would forget words and be conscious only of his response, I felt that I would be in sight of knowing how to write narrative ("AH," pp. 20–21).

At this time Wright expanded his meager library with *Many Marriages*, by Sherwood Anderson; *Lady Chatterley's Lover*, which he used to recommend to his friends along with the other great novels of D. H. Lawrence; *Permanence and Change*, by Kenneth Burke; and a volume of *Men of Good Will*, by Jules Romains. He also bought at great expense the four-volume translation of Proust's masterpiece.

I spent my nights reading Proust's *A Remembrance of Things Past,* admiring the lucid, subtle but strong prose, stupefied by its dazzling magic, awed by the vast, delicate, intricate and psychological structure of the Frenchman's epic of death and decadence. But it crushed me with hopelessness for I wanted to write of the people in my environment with an equal thoroughness, and the burning example before my eyes made me feel that I never could ("AH," p. 22).

This disciplined apprenticeship in literary technique and his new revolutionary zeal were enough to make Wright's first awkward attempts at writing past history. He was soon considered better than any other member of the club. By nature capable of writing with passion, he now learned to use each word accurately, for a specific purpose; there was no longer anything random about his choice. Meanwhile, since the few Marxist books he had read told him nothing about Blacks in America, the subject he had selected, he started to read in sociology, psychology, and history. He bemoaned his lack of the general theoretical knowledge that would have sustained his creative attempts:

Something was missing in my imaginative efforts: my flights of imagination were too subjective, too lacking in reference to social action. I hungered for a grasp of the framework of contemporary living, for a knowledge of the forms of life about me, for eyes to see the bony structure of personality, for theories to light up the shadows of conduct.[21]

Apart from Marxist interpretations, the books he actually owned in these various areas were ridiculously few: *Napoleon*, by Emil Ludwig; *Principles of Economics*, by F. W. Taussig; *Murder Made in Germany*, by Heinz Liepmann; and *Modern and Contemporary European History*, by J. S. Shapiro. At first he was at the mercy of his chance discoveries in the public libraries, but later his student friends at the University of Chicago guided his reading. By 1936, Wright was able to give a Marxist analysis of the social situation, while he was far more than a beginner on the sociology of minorities and the racial problem. He considered psychology and psychoanalysis his most serious weak points.

4

At that time Wright abandoned his plan to do biographical sketches of black Communists and started to write short stories, based either on his own memories or on the tales of Pointdexter and Dick Jordan. In 1935, he read a version of "Big Boy Leaves Home" at Jane Newton's. He had originally intended it to be a novel but did not know how to continue, so he condensed it into a story without changing the plot.[22] On another evening he read a four-page open letter to President Roosevelt entitled "Repeating a Modest Proposal," in which he suggested that the racial and economic problems of the country would immediately be solved if all the black people were eaten. Although in his subtitle he apologized for imitating "old Jonathan" and was not making any attempt to be original, he used every weapon at his disposal and was extremely inventive as a result. He railed simultaneously at conformism, big business and xenophobia, and attacked the horrors of lynching and segregation as well as the apathy of the "good Negroes," such as Robert R. Moton, Congressman Mitchell, the NAACP and the Urban League, while quoting the Bible in support of cannibalism. Although this was written for a satire issue of *New Masses*, it was never published, apparently to avoid alienating the church associations and the black moderates whom the Party hoped would attend the National Negro Congress. In December, *Esquire* rejected the manuscript, and *Race* eventually buried it somewhere in their files.[23]

Since the autumn, 1934, Party decision concerning the John Reed clubs granted them another full year, Wright continued to organize events for the Chicago club, which had moved first to an attic on North Avenue and then to a spacious room on South State Street. He was really the one who kept the group going at the time, doing all kinds of things from sweeping the floor to answering a telegram sent by Gorky and protesting attacks against the club's artists by a *Daily News* columnist. Partly due to him, a number of fine writers like Lawrence Lipton and Algren began to attend more regularly. It was Wright who welcomed Earl Browder, national chairman of the Communist Party of the United States, when he came to Chicago for the Second Congress against War and Fascism; he also greeted a number of speakers who appeared in the lecture series, among them Mike Gold, who spoke on "The Crisis of Modern Literature," and John L. Spivak, who discussed "Pogroms in the United States." In this fashion Wright became better acquainted with a few established left-wing authors and could therefore assess what he too might attain within the leftist camp. Wright recalls with amusement the visit of Maxwell Bodenheim, then a Party member, in an early version of his autobiography: Bodenheim talked about the situation of the writer in San Francisco, where he then lived, and read some of his poems, all scribbled on brown paper bags cut into pieces. Between poems Bodenheim would retire to the men's room, where he would take a drink from his flask; he came back so drunk from his last trip that he just remained standing there, unable to utter another word.

Meanwhile Wright's own reputation as a poet was growing, and more of his poetry was getting into print. On November 23, 1934, he had given another lecture at the Indianapolis Club, tracing the career of Langston Hughes from *The Weary Blues* up to *The Ways of White Folks*. The tickets sold that evening were for the benefit of a new magazine, *Midland Left*, whose first issue appeared in February, 1935, and contained two of Wright's poems, chosen by the editor, Rebecca Pitts. "Rise and Live" was a meditation on oppression, somewhat reminiscent of a blues song. Had Eliot's *Murder in the Cathedral* been published by June, 1934, the chorus of Canterbury women might well have been Wright's model, but his originality is unquestionable:

Is this living?
Is this living here idle living?
Is this living here holding our empty hands
Feeling with our senses the slow sweep of time
Rising, eating, talking and sleeping,
And every so often crawling to plead for a handout of crumbs?

Is this living?
Is this living here lost living?
Is this living here wondering why we have no future,
Enduring with our nerves the dread drone of our days,
Dreaming of a past irretrievably gone,
And feeling the dull breath of death in the wan flow of time?

"Obsession" was the first of Wright's many pieces using the theme of lynching:

This haunting American symbol
Of fire cooking human flesh
The dreadful frame that will not die

. . . .
The dragon of my dreams.

The refrain "How long" again borrows a blues rhythm. The poem is effective on a purely emotional plane totally free of radicalism.

Although Rebecca Pitts had asked Wright for other manuscripts, she decided not to publish his group of prose vignettes in the first issue because the propaganda was somewhat blatant. One of these, "Grain Elevator," was scheduled to appear in a future issue, but by that time the magazine had folded. On November 12, 1935, *Monthly Review* wrote to Wright rejecting an article on militant literature called "Where Do We Go from Here?" [24]

Two poems were published, however, in the April, 1935, issue of *International Literature*, the monthly publication of the International Union of Revolutionary Writers. "A Red Slogan" was probably accepted for its value as propaganda. In it Wright treats a dozen slogans, comparing each in turn to the torch that lights up the march of history, the hatchet that cuts the Gordian knot, a flower, a red star, and the crest of the victorious wave. The use of black dialect makes the second poem more interesting. The title line, "Ah Feels It in Mah Bones," repeated as a blues refrain, refers to the musings of a poverty-stricken man on the social upheaval that he can feel in his bones as surely as an approaching change of weather.

The January 22, 1935, *New Masses* contained Wright's "Red Leaves of Red Books," a short piece about finding a second Bible in Marxist writing. This is less a defense of communism than an effort to show an entire people's craving for learning, a thirst of which he, of course, had firsthand experience.

Wright was at that time gradually becoming known and accepted in Chicago's progressive literary and intellectual circles, but this was perhaps due less to the genuine value of his work than to the color of his skin. Everyone seemed so surprised to meet "such an intelligent Negro" that they went into ecstasies about even his mediocre work. The Party wanted above all to add another black name to the roster. The January 22 issue of *New Masses*, for example, also printed Granville Hicks's appeal to "all writers who have achieved some standing in their respective fields; who have clearly indicated their sympathy for the revolutionary cause and who do not need to be convinced of the decay of capitalism, of the inevitability of the revolution" to attend a national congress. Richard Wright's signature appeared along with those of Dreiser, Waldo Frank, James Farrell and Nathanael West. He was even invited to be an official delegate with William Pillin, Paul Romaine, Nelson Algren and Howard Nutt. "It might have been to 'save' me," he remarked ironically, eight years later. Yet his presence was probably required more to complete the quota of colored participants than to insure his loyalty to the Party.[25]

SIX

Despite the somewhat disillusioned tone of "I Tried to Be a Communist," the first American Writers' Congress had a particular interest for Wright. Not only would he get a chance to see New York, but he could actually meet his favorite novelists, such as Dreiser and Dos Passos, as well as some of the critics and men of letters who could make or break a literary career. Since he had only just signed up for the Illinois Federal Writers' Project in the spring of 1935, he eagerly called upon Mrs. Wirth for help in obtaining a leave of absence to attend the Congress.

At the opening session, held in Carnegie Hall on April 26, 1935, Earl Browder, speaking on "Communism and Literature," said the very words to ease Wright's mind:

The first demand of the party upon its writer members is that they shall be good writers, constantly better writers so they can really serve the party. We do not want to take good writers and make bad strike leaders of them.[1]

Saturday was devoted to section meetings held at the New School for Social Research. The morning debates on the proletarian novelist, led by John Howard Lawson, were stimulated by statements from Joseph Freeman, Jack Conroy and Edwin Seaver, the literary critic for the *Daily Worker,* whom Wright was meeting for the first time.

The only notable speech of the afternoon was Meridel Le Sueur's report on the current literary situation in the Middle West, although later, after the debate, Wright was enthralled to hear James T. Farrell speak on the revolutionary story. Farrell was the most famous of the younger writers, having already published the first two volumes of *Studs Lonigan.* His point of view had always been individualistic, and here, as a prelude to his subsequent systematic attacks against literary Stalinism, he gave a true defense of art against propaganda and political tyranny. Wright had never met Farrell before,

118

but he knew that his reputation at the Chicago John Reed Club was rather poor.[2] Since Wright was becoming interested in the short story at this time, Farrell's rigorous observations could not help but influence him, especially because he had his own reservations about the political demands of the Party. This was the beginning of a literary friendship that benefited Wright enormously.

At the final meeting on Sunday morning, after Granville Hicks's paper on "The Dialectic Evolution of Marxist Criticism" and the statements of Alfred Hayes and Robert Gessner, it was Wright's turn to speak. The day before, Eugene Clay, another black delegate, had ranked Wright with Langston Hughes, praising his rapid development and mastery of poetic techniques. In response, Wright evoked the loneliness of the young writers for whom the John Reed clubs had been the only salvation. His own case was a perfect example.

You may not understand it. . . . I don't think you can, unless you feel it. You can understand the causes and oppose them, but the human results are tragic in peculiar ways. Some of the more obvious results are lack of contact with other writers, a lack of personal culture, a tendency toward escape mechanisms of ingenious, insidious kinds. Other results of his isolation are the monotony of subject matter and becoming the victim of a sort of traditional Negro character.[3]

Here Wright was already stating his opposition to any "literary ghetto" and formulating principles that he clarified in "Blueprint for Negro Writing" two years later. Although he was one of the very few who dared voice regret at the closing of the clubs, many people sympathized with him.

The meeting ended triumphantly with the founding of the League of American Writers, and Wright, along with Chicagoans Algren, Conroy, Farrell and Robert Morss Lovett, figured among the fifty members of the national council, essentially an honorary position. It thus seemed that the Communists had not been angered by his plain speaking; he was being given a chance. The intransigence of the Chicago officials and their severe treatment of writers now appeared to have been a local error. In New York writers were applauded and respected. To enjoy their friendship, share their enthusiasms, become a part of this elite was well worth the price of adapting to Communist discipline. Wright even joined the League's contingent of the May Day parade and knew the exhilaration of

participating in a mass demonstration.[4] The distrust of his cell
comrades had often kept him from joining the ones on the South
Side. Wright had defined his role primarily as that of a writer, a
function which had been amply recognized by the Congress. He
wanted to be a writer first, but since he was black his only option,
for the moment at least, was to be a Communist writer. He therefore consented to remain a Communist in order to remain a writer.

New York itself had been an education of another sort. After a
grueling trip hitchhiking, Wright was surprised and taken with the
city as he discovered it.

Long used to the flat western prairie, I was startled by my first view
of New York. We came in along the Hudson River and I stared
at the sweep of clean-kept homes and grounds. But where was the
smoke pall? The soot? Grain elevators? Factories? Stackpipes? The
flashes of steam on the horizon? The people on the sidewalks seemed
better dressed than the people in Chicago. Their eyes were bold and
impersonal. They walked with a quicker stride and seemed intent
upon reaching some destination in a great hurry ("AH," pp. 86–
87).

Broadway was a veritable feast. Wright saw the recent hits by Clifford
Odets—*Waiting for Lefty, Till the Day I Die* and *Awake and Sing.*
He admired Jack Kirkland's theater adaptation of *Tobacco Road*
as well as another radical play, *Black Pit*, by Albert Maltz, whom
he had just met a few days earlier. The undeniable success of these
plays, which were all inspired by left-wing ideology, must have reassured Wright that militant literature had commercial potential,
yet another encouragement for him to stick to writing as the only
possible future for him. He expressed only enthusiasm and satisfaction with his trip in his May 10 letter of thanks to Mrs. Wirth on
his return.

His assessment of the literary successes of the moment and the
few contacts he had made combined to instill in Wright a new
attitude toward the Party. The closing of the John Reed clubs would
diminish the power of the different regional groups in favor of the
strong personalities. A member of the nationwide League had every
chance to make himself heard, but only if he had sufficient talent.
In Chicago, however, there was no way of being heard as a progressive writer independent of the Party. For the time being, then, he
would continue to write, in spite of his difficulties with the Communists in Chicago; he would become one of the stars whom the

Party, profiting from his renown, would be anxious to help. He would then be on his way to becoming independent. New York, the one place where such a prize could be won and enjoyed, therefore represented for the adult writer, as Chicago had for the adolescent, the next stage of his journey.

2

The South Side Youth Club had closed at the beginning of the spring, and with it disappeared Wright's job. The family had moved again, to 2636 Grove Avenue, but luckily by this time Wright's old friend Mrs. Wirth had returned to welfare work and had immediately entered him in the Illinois Federal Writers' Project, a newly created branch of the Works Progress Administration. Since Wright had been paid for the poems published in *New Masses,* he qualified as an "unemployed writer," and he was put to work doing research on the history of Illinois.

On May 25, 1935, Wright gave a brilliant report on the American Writers' Congress to the John Reed Club before returning with renewed vigor to writing, in what little time he had left from his new job. "Big Boy Leaves Home" had now been completed, but probably on the advice of Bill Jordan, or because of James Farrell's speech at the Congress, Wright decided to revise it and in particular to lessen the violence of the opening scenes. He had got the idea for "Down by the Riverside" while glancing at Burrows' *Basis of Social Consciousness* in the Chicago Public Library:

A passage in the book told of a woman standing on the edge of a lake in Switzerland. The woman saw a man on the lake in a canoe. The canoe capsized and this woman plunged in to save the man. The author pointed out that this showed that social consciousness, the desire to save and serve others, is more powerful than one's own sense of self-preservation.

That was the spark that set going a whole train of thought—the Mississippi River, the excitement and the fear that accompany flood waters. I decided to use a flood to show the relationship between the two races in the South in a time of general tragedy. The story practically wrote itself.[5]

Again Wright had recourse to Pointdexter's reminiscences as well as his own recollection of the 1927 floods. In his autobiography he says that he envisioned at that stage a whole series of stories linked by a common theme and treatment.

The short story "Big Boy Leaves Home" had posed a question: what quality of will must a Negro possess to live and die in a country that denied his humanity? There took shape in my mind—as though an answer was trying to grope its way out of the depth of me—the tale of a flood, "Down by the Riverside." I waded into it, feeling my way, trying to find the answer to my question. But it dissatisfied me when I had finished it; so, casting it aside, I tried to say the same thing in yet another way in "Long Black Song" ("AH," p. 81).

Wright comments about this third story from the same period:

When I was employed on the Federal Writers Project in Chicago, practically all of us young writers were influenced by Ernest Hemingway. We liked the simple, direct way in which he wrote, but a great many of us wanted to write about social problems. The question came up: how could we write about social problems and use a simple style? Hemingway's style is so concentrated on naturalistic detail that there is no room for social comment. One boy said that one way was to dig deeper into the character and try to get something that will live. I decided to try it. I took a very simple Negro woman living in the northern hills of Mississippi and tried to construct a story about her. I tried to conceive of a simple peasant woman, whose outlook upon life was influenced by natural things, and to contrast her with a white salesman selling phonographs and records.

I tried to make out of that story a social comment implied in the very nature of the story itself. You might call it an indictment of the conditions of the South, letting the consciousness of the woman speak for the Negro people.[6]

Wright's first novel, roughly outlined some years earlier, had also described, although from a somewhat different perspective, the buried humanity of the black man who lives in a country which deliberately suppresses it. It focused on the black, middle-class post-office employees who inhabited comfortable homes on 63rd Street or Stony Island, the borders of the South Side at the time, and dreamed of becoming doctors or lawyers but never even managed to complete their education before starting to practice "the three 'A's': Automobile, alimony and abortion." [7]

"Cesspool" (the title for the future *Lawd Today*) had already been rejected by Knopf on April 5 and by Scribner's on April 25, while on James T. Farrell's advice Vanguard Press recommended a great many cuts including the radio announcements, an ironic commentary on the action; the dispute at Doc Higgins' tonsorial palace; one episode at the post office; and the final quarrel with the prostitutes.

Wright was having better luck with his poetry. "A Salute to the USA" had been submitted to *New Masses* in October, 1934, and, with a new title and slight revision by Orrick Johns, it appeared in July, 1935, as "Spread Your Sunrise." Here Wright hailed the advent of socialism, drawing heavily upon the folklore of the Frontier, the obvious source for his revolutionary giant. The July–August, 1935, issue of *Partisan Review* published "Between the World and Me" which, according to Kenneth Fearing, had been unanimously approved by the editorial board. It is a full evocation of a lynching, as opposed to the sketch in "Obsession." The narrator gradually identifies with the victim as, one by one, he notes the traces of the gruesome scene, somewhat the way Big Boy reacts at watching Bobo's torture from his hiding place at the end of "Big Boy Leaves Home." Without succumbing to the easy expedient of the pathetic, Wright deepens his own emotion and the reader's with a series of admirable images:

> And my skin clung to the bubbling hot tar, falling
>   from me in limp patches.
> And the down and the quills of white feathers sank into
>   my raw flesh, and I moaned in my agony.
> Then my blood was cooled mercifully, cooled by a
>   baptism of gasoline.
> And in a blaze of red I leaped to the sky as pain
>   rose like water, boiling my limbs.
> Panting, begging I clutched childlike, clutched
>   to the hot sides of death.
> Now I am dry bones and my face a stony skull staring
>   in yellow surprise at the sun. . . .

After rejecting an article on "The Way of Angelo Herndon," *New Masses* accepted "Hearst Headlines Blues" in January, something Wright had composed in a different vein the preceding autumn. Wright had wanted to use "materialized" language in his poetry, so the various headlines of the reactionary newspaper magnate form an ironic commentary on the government's illusory solutions to the economic crisis. A few months later, the December 15, 1937, issue of *New Masses* contained "Old Habit and New Love," a return to a simpler style without political undercurrents, where the worker's need for a job, the beauty of his accomplishments and the desire for a harmonious world are extolled. The rich language and dense images slowly unfold in a visionary finale:

O Creators: Poets, Makers of Melody! Some first-shift dawn shall
find us on equal ground, holding in our hands the world's tools,
drafting the hope-prints of our vision on canvases of green earth!

Here Wright approaches Whitman and Sandburg, although elsewhere he leans more toward T. S. Eliot and the imagists. He oscillates, in fact, between the use of black speech and folk material and a more sophisticated style, irreconcilable influences that are the result of his diverse background. This eclecticism was characteristic of a number of the young radical poets, Edwin Rolfe and Horace Gregory among them, who thought it fair enough to use the forms of bourgeois society to serve socialist ends.

Wright was meanwhile becoming more interested in the essay than in poetry as a medium for his revolutionary writing. In August, he won second prize in a contest organized by the magazines *New Talent* and *Silhouettes* for an article entitled "Avant-Garde Writing," which unfortunately was never published. It was, in fact, a few pages on his definition of avant-garde. Since art reflected the social conditions of a given period, it must necessarily change constantly to correspond to the spirit of the times. To be avant-garde, one had to introduce a "new consciousness" into the old forms, if only to make them stand out. Thus, a magazine like *New Talent* should have a double function.

It not only represents the new consciousness in creative terms, but
seeks to extend and deepen it among all classes of the population.
. . . This new consciousness, if the groups in question are in the
"stream of things," is a higher one than espoused by preceding
groups.

Those whom this avant-garde literature would have to reach were not the traditional intelligentsia, but rather the masses and the young intellectuals, those whom the recent economic upheavals had affected the most.

The October 8, 1935, issue of *New Masses* contained "Joe Louis Uncovers Dynamite," Wright's first piece of journalism. Wright had once written over a hundred pages of a novel whose hero, Tar Baby, was modeled on Jack Johnson, and Louis, a younger black boxer, had interested Wright for some time. The article described the psychological reactions of the Blacks when Joe Louis beat Max Baer in Chicago on September 24, 1935. Every member of the ghetto identified with this champion of the race, trembling with excitement as the quintessence of black triumphed over white.

Except for the final paragraph, which the editor, Miller North, probably added to insure its Communist orthodoxy, this is a vibrant expression of purely personal feeling, tinged with, if anything, a spirit of nationalism. The simple and sometimes poetic style recalls certain phrases in "Everywhere Burning Waters Rise," although elsewhere the dialogue, spiced with slang, is reminiscent of *Lawd Today*.

3

Since Richard was now receiving a regular salary from the Federal Writers' Project, the Wrights (now reduced to four after Grandmother Wilson's death) were able to leave their miserable apartment on Grove Avenue and move to "La Veta," a somewhat dilapidated stone mansion on 3743 Indiana Avenue. According to his autobiography, Wright finally had a room of his own on the ground floor, although he was rarely able to use it for his writing since he did not qualify for the reduced work week enjoyed by the "creative writers" who had already published a book; he had to spend most of his time continuing to do research on the history of Illinois and the Negro in Chicago.[8]

The demands of the Party were more burdensome than those of the F.W.P., even though Wright avoided cell meetings and the Club no longer met. By this time he had stopped seeing his old friend Pointdexter, partly because of his increasing coldness, but also to forestall further criticisms from the local authorities. His interviews with Oliver Law and Herbert Newton had finally made Wright realize that their positions were irreconcilable. Less understanding leaders like the narrow-minded Harry Haywood (who had been sent to supervise Chicago organization in February, 1935) had obliged him to justify himself at a higher level, that is, before John P. Davis himself. Under pressure to participate in more political activities, Wright was put in charge of organizing a protest against the rising cost of living. When he proposed instead to reassemble the young writers of the South Side to replace the defunct Club, he came up against the brick wall of "a Party decision." For a time, then, he tabulated the daily price of pork chops and held meetings on the housing crisis.

Perhaps reassured by his obedience, the Party asked him to help prepare for the National Negro Congress scheduled for Chicago in February, 1936. It was the Popular Front era, and the Communists wanted to unite all the Blacks belonging to religious organizations, political groups, unions and movements protesting segregation and discrimination. If they were careful not to antagonize the NAACP and the black clergy, they would be able to dominate this coalition.[9] John P. Davis, who was in charge of organizing the Congress, personally delegated Wright to preside over a special session on black history and culture and to write a foreword for the program of the debates. They also wooed him with the possibility of attending the American Youth Congress in Europe, to which the Party would pay his way. He refused for the time being, both because he was the sole support of his family and because he did not want to abandon his writing.[10]

The Congress opened on February 16 under the chairmanship of A. Philip Randolph, the leader of the famous Union of Sleeping Car Porters, and Wright was one of the national delegates. He participated in discussions on "The Role of the Negro Writer and Artist on the Social Stage," along with Langston Hughes, Arna Bontemps, Morris Topchevsky and Mark Marvin.

Perhaps more significant than the Congress itself was Wright's report on it for *New Masses*. Ostensibly an informative article, it also managed to convey the enthusiasm he was supposed to have experienced. Using literary gimmicks in the service of journalism (such as stage directions to indicate time and place [11]), he cleverly caught the essence of every speech, described the hopeful delegates coming from all backgrounds and states and urged the Blacks to have confidence in the "Farmer Labor Party." By juggling statistics, he implied that the Congress and its audience were a true representation of the black masses.

This was, in fact, a rare example for Wright of precise political journalism. When he wrote regularly for the *Daily Worker* two years later, he seldom used this direct style, and only after a lapse of twenty years did it reappear in his account of the People's Party Convention, in *Black Power,* and in his report on the Bandung Conference, published as *The Color Curtain.*

4

In November, 1935, the regional director of the F.W.P., Clark Slover, had put a young geography professor named Nathan Morris in charge of preparing a guide to Illinois, an idea which other states subsequently adopted. Wright was one of forty field workers of a total of three hundred fifty writers assigned to this project, which meant that now he had more free time for writing, since he only went to the office twice a week to report on his findings and pick up a new assignment. At the Wells Street office Wright found old friends like Nelson Algren and made some new ones, such as the novelist William Attaway. He spent most of his time in either the public library or the Newberry Library, a gold mine of local archives opposite the picturesque Bughouse Square, where speakers and bums would vie for attention at lunch time. Although he usually went home to do his writing, he would sometimes write up his reports at the main office of the F.W.P. on the fourth floor of the Abraham Lincoln Center, which was the nucleus of much of Chicago's cultural activity at the time.

In addition to regular meetings, the Sunday night debates and lectures presented a variety of distinguished people. Sociologist Louis Wirth spoke on the use of political slogans, Elizabeth Drew lectured on film and Henry Johnson on the C.I.O., while foreign experts often gave talks there on their way through the city. Wright not only attended these lectures avidly, but also organized weekly meetings of young Negro writers and artists. Thus began the South Side Writers' Group in April, 1936. The twenty members of this literary club would read and discuss their work as well as analyze their common problems. Fenton Johnson, one of the first black free-verse poets, came several times, although as a rule he avoided participating in the new wave in literature. The "elder" of the group, Frank Marshall Davis, whom Wright had met at the National Negro Congress, was an editor for the Associated Negro Press and author of *Black Man's Verse* and *I Am the American Negro*. Wright also associated with Margaret Walker, a student at Northwestern University and later a member of the Society of University Poets. She was writing the first poems of *For My People* and fervently admired Wright, with whom she had a close relationship until 1939. Wright also made friends with Marian Minus, whom he worked with the following year in New York. Theodore Ward had worked for the Federal Speech Project before becoming Wright's colleague at the Federal Theatre Project and was writing *Big White Fog*. The group also included the poets Robert Davis, Edward Bland, Russell Marshall, Fern Gayden and Dorothy Sutton; the essayist Theodore Bland (who wrote under the name Allyn Keith); Julius Weil and Barefield Gordon, as well as other less talented beginners.

These writers took their literary and social role seriously, as had the members of the Negro Renaissance whose heirs they wanted to be. Wright was the principal leader of the group and, along with Claude Lightfoot (a Communist of the International Negro Youth Organization), represented the most radical viewpoint, but many others also considered themselves militant writers. It was, in fact, difficult not to be caught up in the wave of social realism and proletarian literature at the time. Wright submitted his critical essays for his friends' opinions, as well as, and apparently for the first time, "Down by the Riverside" and "Long Black Song." One version of "Bright and Morning Star" was also read aloud toward the end of the year.[12] Nevertheless Wright was still considered primarily a poet; he had spoken and read his poetry at the Roosevelt Road Cultural Center, under the aegis of the Writers' Group, and on April 10, 1936, he gave a talk on Negro literature at the Evanston Library.

During this time he also attended other literary get-togethers, not only at the Gourfains', but more recently at the home of Silvia and Irving Eisenstein, who lived near the Newberry Library. Among the members of this mostly Jewish group were Sam Ross; the author Ben Gershman; Samuel Lipschultz; Ray Jones; William McBride; Peter Pollack, who worked for the Artistic Center of Chicago; the black sculptor Marion Perkins and his wife, Eva; and a platinum blonde named Virginia, who typed Richard's stories. The star of these evenings was without a doubt Lawrence Lipton, an inveterate bohemian, a dynamic storyteller and already the author of two books. He was a kind but severe critic of Wright's prose and also showed his own work to Wright, who came to admire him greatly and formed a long-lasting friendship with him.[13]

These various literary circles provided Wright with the friendly and challenging atmosphere of the old John Reed Club. In an article for the June 8, 1937, *Daily Worker,* Wright recalled that his plan, if not the group's, had been to lead the black writers toward radicalism:

Following the National Negro Congress in Chicago, a year ago, a group of writers . . . formed the first group whose aim was to render the life of their race in social and realistic terms. For the first time in Negro history, problems such as nationalism in literary perspective, the relation of the Negro writers to politics and social movements were formulated and discussed.

Accordingly, Wright used to ask leftist writers like Robert Morss Lovett, a member of the League of American Writers Council and a writer for the *New Republic,* to speak. He also introduced Arna Bontemps to the club. A graduate student at the University of Chicago and author of *Drums at Dusk*, he was then publishing a novel that Wright reviewed for the June, 1936, issue of *Partisan Review and Anvil. Black Thunder* was about the slave rebellion led by Gabriel who, in spite of his failure, never renounced his role of liberator, even at the end. Although Wright's review, entitled "A Tale of Folk Courage," showed his ignorance of a large portion of Afro-American literature, or at least his refusal to consider anything that was not social realism, his analysis of the symbolic and mythical importance of the main character indicated the direction of his own search. In any case, the article showed his interest in closely studying the folk material to which he soon afterward called black writers to return.

Wright had met the editors of *Partisan Review* during his trip to New York, and Jack Conroy, the editor of *Anvil*, had been his friend for a long time. When the two magazines merged in February, Wright was listed as an associate editor along with Nelson Algren, Jack Balch, Alfred Hayes and Erskine Caldwell. This was only an honorary title, however, and the New York board, headed by Philip Rahv and William Phillips, actually made all the decisions.[14]

In the June, 1936, issue of the magazine appeared Wright's reply to an article by Sidney Harris. Rahv had asked him to respond to Harris who had described the Chicago literary scene in the preceding issue, and in attacking *Poetry* magazine's "aesthetic tea parties," had added the name of Meyer Levin to the leftists' proverbial list of pet peeves. Admittedly Levin did work for *Esquire*, but he was also a member of the League of American Writers and, as Wright pointed out, the city had prevented his play *Model Tenements* from being produced at the Federal Theatre on the grounds that it was too radical. In fact, "In Defense of Meyer Levin" was a vindication of Wright's own group as well as of Levin himself.

There are young writers and artists in Chicago who stand clear of the mire. . . . There are left-wing theatre groups doing fairly good work in spite of the Kelly-Hearst-*Tribune-Poetry-Esquire-Daily News*-University atmosphere. Some of these countertendencies are as yet raw, green, and in a certain way ineffective. But if there is any hope for a vital and well-knit cultural life in Chicago, it is coming from their direction. . . . The job is a big one, it is nothing less than the task of building our own organs of expression, mobilizing our own audiences, maintaining our own critical standards, and nursing and developing our own talent. And the beginning of such a movement has already started.

At this time Wright was also taking an active part in the Middle West Writers' Congress, which took place in Chicago on June 14–15, 1936. As part of the Communist electoral campaign, the Federation of Arts and Professions was again attempting to regroup writers and artists, and the Chicago Congress resulted in the formation of a new magazine, *Midwest*. It was to act as a liaison publication directed from Minneapolis by Meridel Le Sueur, known for her proletarian stories; Dale Kramer, who had just relinquished administrative duties on a small magazine; and Mitchell Siporin, a former Chicago John Reeder. *Midwest* had a very short life and Wright never contributed to it.

In any case, more important magazines were now claiming his attention. In January, 1936, *International Literature* had published his six-page poem, "Transcontinental," the longest and perhaps the most ambitious he ever wrote. Three years before, Minna and Abe Aaron had given him E. E. Cummings' translation of "Red Front." Thus, with the dedication "To Louis Aragon in praise of 'Red Front,' " Wright proceeded to use the same breaks, variety and contrast of tone used by Aragon: the affected speech of high society, the breathless advance of the red locomotive, and the prosaic style reminiscent of a radio announcement. In Aragon's piece, the relentless train of the proletariat led to the downfall of capitalism and the liberation of the masses. Wright's revolutionary automobile takes him across an America where Soviets flourish. He enlarges upon certain of Aragon's themes but adds an original tone to his glorification of socialism. Aragon was inspired by the tradition of the French Revolution, Wright, by the revenge of the repressed minorities: the Black, the Indian and the tramp can finally raise their heads as the revolution, like Robin Hood, sweeps in to bring justice to all. Most important, however, Wright infuses the poem with some personal bitterness, openly expressing his hatred of the rich Whites and using certain autobiographical details.[15] He finally seems to have defined his resentment and his need for vengeance so clearly that he feels almost forced to put it into words. In addition, Wright borrows certain techniques from experimental poetry, such as collage, superimpression, insertion of prose, typographical variation, and onomatopoeia. The lyrical movement of this ambitious and varied poem, sometimes tender, sometimes epic in the style of Whitman, provides a symphonic unity that prevents it from crumbling under the profusion of its multiple and contradictory elements.

Due to the influence of his friend Theodore C. Robinson, a drama critic for the Federation News Agency, Wright was transferred in the spring of 1936 from the Federal Writers' Project to the Federal Theatre Project, to act as literary adviser and press agent for the Negro Federal Theatre of Chicago.

The immediate goal of The Federal Theatre, which Hallie Flanagan had organized the year before, was to reemploy the people of the profession, and one of its first effects was a renewed interest in theater throughout the United States. The Chicago Theatre Project was originally run by E. C. Mabie and later by M. Stevens. Theodore Viehman directed the troupe that had planned to put on Meyer Levin's censured play, and worked in the Great Northern Theatre. Peter Kessler directed the Experimental Theatre; Harry Minturn, the American Repertory Theatre at the Blackstone; and Mary Merril, the Negro Federal Theatre. Because they had had a certain success in parks, schools and hospitals with vaudeville and minstrel shows, they were allowed to use the large auditorium of Igoe Hall, the Palace of the Guards, where Robert Dunmore and Ruth Corpening's stage adaptation of *Romeo and Juliet* opened on April 1, 1936. *Romey and Julie* mixed episodes from Shakespeare's play and scenes of the rival colored gangs in the style of *West Side Story*. Then Lou Peyton's *Did Adam Sin?* ran until the middle of May, and July and August were spent on Miss Merril's production of *Everyman*, an unsuitable choice, as Wright points out:

The skinny white woman who directed it, an elderly missionary type, would take a play whose characters were white, whose theme dealt with the Middle Ages, and recast it in terms of Southern Negro life with overtones of African backgrounds. Contemporary plays dealing realistically with Negro life were spurned as being controversial (*GF,* p. 150).

Since Wright had no intention of limiting himself to his job as press agent, he worked on the productions themselves and may even have written his two unpublished one-act plays at this point, since they were definitely written prior to 1937 and in the same year. The first of these was based on the opening chapters of *Lawd Today*, describing Jake and Lil's turbulent married life. The other sketch later became part of an early scene in *Native Son*, only here Mrs. Burke is not troubled by her son but by her daughter, Vera, who has been made pregnant by Willie Boy.

On May 15, Wright was chosen as a judge for a theater contest organized by the Education Committee of the Y.M.C.A. Several black plays had been submitted: Theodore Ward's "Sick and Tiah'd," Langston Hughes's "Soul Gone Home" and Paul Green's "Hymn to the Rising Sun." Green was an already established playwright very familiar with black life, and this play about a July 4th celebration in a Southern penitentiary was a denunciation of the chain-gang system.

During the summer Wright, probably again with the help of T. C. Robinson, managed to have Miss Merril replaced by Charles de Sheim, a young and dynamic Jewish producer. De Sheim was responsible for the troupe's rehearsing three one-act plays, among them Paul Green's, which Wright and Theodore Ward were helping to produce for the Princess Theatre in the Loop before a combination of events made the eventual performance impossible. According to Ward, a personal rivalry developed between de Sheim and the actor-playwright Robert Dunmore, who had hoped to succeed Miss Merril. In "I Tried to Be a Communist," Wright maintains that the actors balked at playing roles that did not correspond to the "good Negroes" of vaudeville and, more important, that there was a Communist plot against him personally. Despite these difficulties, rehearsals continued until the night of the dress rehearsal, in November, when the city censors finally prevented the play from being presented to the public.[16]

Nevertheless, Wright reported that Communist pressure and threats caused him to ask for a transfer to the Experimental Theatre. Apparently during the winter and perhaps even after taking a job in the stockyards, he was transferred back to the Writers' Project.[17] By this time the Illinois guide was well-advanced, but since none of its sections were signed and the preliminary reports were destroyed in 1960, it is impossible to determine whether Wright was responsible for the picture of the South Side underworld or this poetic description of the Carnegie Steel Corporation:

At night, like a huge firework sparkles, almost instantly consumed fountains of sparks leap from the Bessemer converters into the sky, projecting a weird quavering glow on the clouds visible for miles along the lake shore.[18]

Meanwhile, Wright's own compositions were receiving some attention. "Big Boy Leaves Home" had been accepted in January, 1936, for *The New Caravan*, an anthology edited by Alfred Kreymborg, Lewis Mumford and Paul Rosenfeld, which was published the following November. Although Wright received less than fifty dollars, which quickly vanished in dental bills, he was for the first time being noticed by the non-Communist white press.

The story had already been much admired by the limited public to whom Wright had read it. The *Daily Worker* reported that the only exception had been the Literary Society at the University of Chicago where, as he was reading the manuscript, he saw the audience gradually leave the room, apparently shocked by his language. Professor Lawrence Martin, who was giving a course in literary composition at Northwestern University, had been so enthusiastic that T. C. Robinson had asked him to join Napier Wilt and Robert Morss Lovett in helping Wright apply for a Houghton Mifflin grant. Martin in turn had secured him a recommendation from Melville Herskovits.[19]

Most encouraging, however, were the favorable reviews in some of the major newspapers. Not only did Wright's friends Edwin Seaver of the *Daily Worker* and William Phillips in *New Masses* praise his dramatic talent, but Robert Van Gelder in *The New York Times*, Gorham Munson in the *Saturday Review of Literature* and Robert Coates in the *New Republic* agreed, claiming that "Big Boy Leaves Home" was the best piece in the anthology.

This came at a time when the young writer was having his first novel rejected by one publisher after another. But to have had a story published meant that he could be reclassified as a "creative writer" by the F.W.P. Accordingly, he became the coordinator of a group of writers at a salary of $115 a month, and in November he was put on the editorial board of *Prairie Pages*, which encouraged the members of the Illinois Project to send in their work. The magazine was never published, and Wright's only prospective contribution was the outline of a play, "Song of the Prairies." He had envisioned a heroine, "through whose actions and reactions the material can be felt and emotionally evaluated. . . . This one woman's concern, the motive of the drama, will be for the preservation, enrichment, sustaining, and enlargement of all those conditions which support life." [20] He would place this character outside of time to give continuity, destroying the chronological sequence by "telescoping" events. This technique foreshadowed the "mood" that Wright suggested would unify the various themes of an ambitious series of novels he had outlined during the fifties.

The success of "Big Boy" probably encouraged Wright to give up poetry in favor of short stories. He had by this time finished "Down by the Riverside" and, according to John Trounstine, his literary agent in New York, it would be published in the third issue of *New Writing*. "Long Black Song" was also completed by July, 1936, if not before, when Wright submitted the broad outlines of "Fire and Cloud" to his friend Abraham Chapman, who found it excellent, title and all. Since "Fire and Cloud" was expressly designed to show the development of political awareness among Negroes, Chapman suggested that Wright read a recent article by Deborin on the problem of genius and social consciousness in order to apply its principles

to his story. In a sense, "Fire and Cloud" was in Wright's eyes a
fictional treatment of the theme of "The Way of Angelo Herndon,"
the article that *New Masses* had rejected at the beginning of the
year.

The fourth story in the book came about as a desire on my part to
depict in dramatic fashion the relationship between the leaders of
both races. Of course among the Negro people the preacher is the
acknowledged leader . . . I represented the preacher in a very
crucial moment, a moment in a relief crisis when he had to tell his
starving flock that the relief people would give him no food. What
happens to him, and how his character underwent a change, will be
found in the fourth story.[21]

In November, 1936, *Story* rejected the first version of "Almos' a
Man." Like the story of the same title published in 1941, it was
taken from the final chapters of "Tarbaby's Sunrise," the first section
of a novel probably written the year before or even as early as
1934, describing the childhood and early career of a black boxer.[22]
Existing notes indicate that even the novel never went beyond the
hero's adolescence.

Wright was also busy revising "Cesspool," which had suffered so
many rejections, and retitled it "Lawd Today." Norton, Vanguard
Press and Simon & Schuster were still considering it. The 1936 version, which represented a second or third draft, is fairly close to
the final version published in 1963. The novel was heavily autobiographical: the naturalist scenes at the Central Post Office, Jake's
wanderings during the morning, the scene at Doc Higgins' tonsorial
palace, the black nationalist parade, were modeled on Wright's own
life and habits, his interest in Garveyism, his work for the Republican precinct captain. Even the episode with the charlatan recalls
the abortive attempt of the "Three Wise Men from the East" to sell
charms by mail. Reading *Studs Lonigan* and talking with Farrell
had inspired Wright to borrow a number of his techniques by 1935,
such as the use of dreams, fragmented conversations between friends
and a minute description and chart of a bridge game, paralleling
that of the football game in Farrell's *Judgment Day*. Moreover, the
stylistic evolution of Wright's poems indicates the order in which
he adopted certain techniques that seem to be superimposed on the
rough outline of his novel. The division of the novel into sections
of time and the visit to Rose's saloon are reminiscent of *Ulysses*.

The choice of Lincoln's birthday for the action of the novel, to emphasize ironically the hero's lack of liberty, seems to be the result (although it could predate the play) of Wright's having read "Hymn to the Rising Sun" in 1936. The radio announcements also appear in "Transcontinental," and the newspaper headlines commented on by Jake appear in "Hearst Headlines Blues," both techniques derived from Dos Passos. By this time Wright had abandoned the American and Russian realists not only for Henry James but for T. S. Eliot and critics like Joseph Wood Krutch, Van Wyck Brooks and Waldo Frank. Thus, quotations taken from *The Modern Temper, America's Coming of Age, Our America* and *The Waste Land* reflect this mixture of influences, from which Wright gleaned a certain conception of writing. Throughout these years, he had been trying, in verse or in prose, in one style or another, to communicate the same message—to show the transition from life in Mississippi to life in Chicago with its initiation into city routine, intellectual awareness and political responsibilities. On this level, the evolution of his characters follows closely upon his own.

Spring brought new disappointments. John Trounstine eventually returned "Down by the Riverside," asking him to cut it by at least a third. Then the publishers started returning *Lawd Today*. Norton rejected it in April. "This artificially blown up and drawn out story" was returned by Vanguard Press along with "Tarbaby's Dawn," which they had wanted to read before coming to a decision. In May, Maxim Lieber, Jack Conroy's agent, wrote that he considered neither of them worthy of publication; they were both just a series of episodes without any real plot; Wright wrote excellent stories but did not have any talent for the novel. Finally Simon & Schuster and Random House turned them down.

5

Possibly the repeated rejection of his novels contributed to Wright's decision to go to New York and defend his interests as his agent had failed to do. More immediate, however, was his desire to definitely break away from political and cultural surroundings that he found increasingly restrictive. His growing reputation in left-wing literary circles now allowed him more freedom from the local Communist organizations that in 1934 had been his sole way of escaping the cultural ghetto. On the other hand, his relationship with the local Party apparatus had become difficult. Even when the formation of the Popular Front against War and Fascism had somewhat relegated the black cause to second place, Wright did not oppose the new Communist policies. Instead, his quarrel was still over the same old issue: he wanted to write and not to organize. He says in his autobiography that he told John P. Davis:

I simply do not wish to be bound any longer by the Party's decisions. I should like to retain my membership in those organizations in which the Party has influence, and I shall comply with the Party's program in those organizations (*GF,* p. 148).

The national leaders were not hostile to this attitude in practice, but the local authorities considered it contrary to the principles of discipline and obedience, and this set them against Wright. Certain confrontations described in "I Tried to Be a Communist" are placed in a biased context and out of chronological order, making them difficult to date. This, of course, is because the article was written in 1943 to answer accusations of former friends who had been plaguing him ever since he had left their midst, so that even if he was faithful to the psychological truth of what happened, he often combined several episodes into one for effect. Nevertheless, it can safely be assumed that the thirties was a period of definite evolution for Wright in relation to communism. Successive disillusionments had transformed his original enthusiastic and total dedication into wariness. His individualism was against him; he was at the mercy of leaders like Oliver Law and Harry Haywood, ostracized from unit 205 by certain black comrades and even denigrated by the Communists on the W.P.A. in spite of his union activities. Certain insults and public humiliations that he claims to have suffered in Chicago during the thirties seem actually to have taken place in New York during the forties. Yet Wright's friendship with the "Trotskyite traitor" Pointdexter and later with people like Ted Robinson, James Farrell and Jack Scher, who repudiated Stalinism, caused him to be spied upon at the meetings and parties he attended. There is no available evidence to corroborate. Wright's account of the violence against him at the Federal Negro Theatre, but Margaret Walker remembers that he was actually prevented from walking in the May Day, 1937, parade.[23]

In a letter dated October 6, 1959, to his editor, Wright states plainly:

The American Communist Party tried strenuously to convince me that writing was not my forte and that I would serve better as an organizer. I refused to accept this and withdrew from the Communist Party. . . . Feeling that the Communist Party in New York was more liberal and intelligent, I left Chicago for New York in 1936, and upon arrival, I was reinstated into the Communist Party and given charge of the Harlem Bureau of the *Daily Worker*.

In fact, he did not leave Chicago until 1937, but since James Farrell wrote him on February 9, 1937, saying, "I'm glad to hear you left the Party," the importance of this first break, which is also mentioned in Wright's correspondence with Margaret Walker, does not seem in the least exaggerated. Nevertheless, Wright was not prepared to abandon completely the ideal that had so inspired and even sustained him for several years. He still believed that Marxist theory was valid and he, as opposed to Farrell, still felt that Stalinist discipline was necessary, despite the Trotskyist trials of the thirties. Personally, however, he was ready to do without the restraint and, having shed the enthusiasm and naïveté of the neophyte he had been, he quietly left the Party in order to be able to write more freely.

Meanwhile, Wright had devised an elaborate plan for doing a historical report on the Blacks and the racial situation in Chicago. He had submitted the idea to Sterling Brown, then a Washington official of the F.W.P., who replied that he would like Wright to direct a similar project that he himself had been considering. Wright had been waiting for two years for a chance to try his luck in the intellectual and artistic circles of New York, and he welcomed the implication in Brown's letter that he would have to leave Chicago. In addition, the F.W.P. was being threatened with a severe cut in funds; the director for the State of Illinois, Jay Du Von, a former staff member of *The Left*, was himself at the mercy of the new campaign to economize and could no longer help his friends. Accordingly, Wright had been looking for a more secure job. He failed to be hired as a journalist for the Associated Negro Press in Chicago, but the post office now had openings. When Wright took the examination again, he ranked first. He thus had to choose between a stable though routine job at an annual salary of around $2,000, and the risk of trying to make a living by writing. The main deterrent was his feeling of guilt at leaving his family. Fortunately, Leon had finally found a job at the Works Progress Administration and could assume some responsibility for them, and Wright's friend Fern Gayden, who had been working for a while at the welfare office in the neighborhood, could look in on them from time to time. Except for a vague promise of work from *New Masses* and perhaps some occasional reporting for the *Daily Worker*, Wright had no job prospects in New York until he could qualify for transfer to the local F.W.P. But he was ready to take any risk in the hope of finding something better, and accordingly he chose the path of adventure. "I thought I ought to give myself a chance," he wrote later, "and that's what I did." [24]

SEVEN

"**I** tore up the notice of appointment, thumbed a ride to New York—and have had hell and satisfaction ever since." [1] Up until this moment, Wright had used only his free time for the pursuit of his literary career, and had always given priority to finding a steady job in order to support his family. Now he was free to organize his own life, and the risk involved only kindled his desire to succeed as a novelist. During the next ten years, the most productive of his life, the publication of his first four books earned him an international reputation. The most he was hoping for at the time, however, was to find a publisher and, with luck, a job that would allow him to write.

Dressed in a suit borrowed from Ed Gourfain, and carrying in one suitcase all his worldly possessions—some clothing, a few books and his typewriter—Wright left Chicago by car with Piro and Isabella Caro toward the end of May, 1937. Once in New York, he spent two days with their friends the Weigels, some young artists who lived on Bleecker Street.[2] He then moved in with his friend Abraham Chapman until, in mid-June, he rented a furnished hotel room at 809 St. Nicholas Avenue in Harlem. The owner, Mr. Douglas, was a great help at the beginning, extending him credit and scouting out odd jobs for him, such as cleaning the streets and delivering phone books.

Wright had arrived in New York only a few days before the second American Writers' Congress, to which he was a delegate. In contrast to the theme of the 1935 Congress, the appeal published on May 4 in *New Masses*, signed by many well-known authors, primarily liberals and Communist sympathizers, stressed the professional rather than the political goals of the meeting. At that time the Communists contented themselves with defending cultural and pacifist institutions, and even freedom of speech, since, in view of the Popular Fronts, they were anxious to enlarge the membership of the League of American Writers.

Archibald MacLeish opened the meeting on the evening of June 4 in Carnegie Hall. Several scenes were shown from "The Spanish Earth," a film made by Joris Ivens on the front lines of the Civil War, with a script by MacLeish, Lillian Hellman and Ernest Hemingway. Hemingway then spoke about the responsibilities of the writer toward war and fascism. At the end of the session, Wright probably took the opportunity of expressing his admiration for Hemingway in person.

The section meetings took place on Saturday, with talks by Kenneth Burke and Malcolm Cowley. The next day the delegates divided up into special committees according to literary genre, with Wright attending the discussions on fiction, led by Leane Zugsmith. During an exchange on the bearing of political aims upon a writer's technique, the eternal problem for the militant author, the question arose as to how a writer from a bourgeois background could paint realistically the life of a worker. In disagreeing with Ben Field, Wright was certainly thinking of his problems in cell 208 when he proclaimed the danger for a writer of devoting too much time to organizational work as a way of fulfilling his political responsibilities. "There is no backwardness on the part of the trade-unionists in accepting the writer as a writer. They realize his function if the writer realizes it." [3] This idea, which was also expressed by Nancy Bedford Jones, John Hyde Preston, Benjamin Appel and George Albee in their successive statements, revealed how determined Wright was not to sacrifice his artistic integrity to restrictive political imperatives. Max White, a young delegate from San Diego, was so struck by Wright's remarks that he wrote to Gertrude Stein describing Wright as "the clearest and hardest of the minds present." [4]

Presiding over the second part of the session, Wright introduced Henry G. Alsberg, the director of the Federal Writers' Project, who briefly described its activities. That same evening the 350 delegates elected a new board of directors. Because of his vigorous protest against the Trotskyist trials Waldo Frank, the president, was replaced by Donald Ogden Stewart, a completely dedicated Party member. Wright's name, too, did not reappear on the national council. Perhaps because Earl Browder was currently selling communism as twentieth-century Americanism, better known, albeit less radical, writers were preferred. In any case, Wright was active throughout the Congress, although it differed from the previous one in being less a literary opportunity than a chance to meet up with old acquaintances. Along with the Chicago delegation, he spent a memorable evening at the Farrells', and the last evening he escorted Algren, Conroy and Lawrence Fallon from the St. Louis W.P.A. to a Harlem nightclub before doing the rounds of Greenwich Village.[5] He also met some other writers for the first time, among them Willard Maas and Marie Mencken, who became two of his best friends.

Two days later, the *Daily Worker* contained an article by Wright announcing the launching of a quarterly called *New Challenge*, intended to "present the literature and conditions of life of American Negroes in relationship to the struggle against war and Fascism." Describing the South Side Writers' Group, Wright said that a similar group would be formed, with Dorothy West and Marian Minus in charge of its magazine. This would not necessarily be closed to white writers and would also explore the relationship between folk tradition and literature.[6]

The magazine was actually a reincarnation of *Challenge*, which Dorothy West had started in March, 1934, "to permit new Negroes to make themselves heard," according to James Weldon Johnson's foreword to the first issue. Along with the work of writers like Langston Hughes, Arna Bontemps, Claude McKay and Countee Cullen, *Challenge* had published the first poems of Frank Yerby, Waring Cuney and Owen Dodson.

The project was part of a rather belated Party effort to unite the literary elements of the Left, but considering the brief career of *Left Front* and the almost immediate failure of *Midwest*, there was no telling whether *New Challenge* would finally realize Wright's dream of bringing together a group of progressive black authors. Although the *Daily Worker* apparently sanctioned the enterprise, and it had the support of Benjamin Davis, it would not be directly controlled by the Party and would not be financed by it.

The outline for the new magazine was finally completed in July, 1937. Although Dorothy West's March editorial for *Challenge* had already indicated her progressive tendencies and interest in the South Side Writers' Group, Wright played a vital role in the radical orientation of the new magazine. In fact, Wright's correspondence with Margaret Walker reveals that he eventually did most of the work for the publication and made almost all the editorial decisions.

During the sometimes stormy meetings, Wright even disagreed

with Claude McKay on political grounds, but he had the support of the most zealous of the New York group: Louis Burnham, Henry Lee Moon, Louis Sutherland and George Waugh. Loren Miller and Langston Hughes were willing to make the magazine known to younger writers on the West Coast, while Sterling Brown, Arthur Randall and Alain Locke would use their influence on its behalf in Washington and elsewhere.

Wright's arrival in New York, corresponding as it did with the planning for *New Challenge*, also marked the time when he defined his attitudes on the relationship between ethnic literature and the black writer's political commitment. These ideas first showed up in his critical writing. For the October 5 issue of *New Masses* he reviewed two Afro-American novels: *These Low Grounds*, by Waters E. Turpin and *Their Eyes Were Watching God*, by Zora Neale Hurston. He was hard on Turpin, whose attempt to present the social rise of the Negro seemed to lack finesse, but he was even fiercer in attacking Miss Hurston because, though she wrote with facility, her vision was corrupt and perpetuated the "minstrel show tradition and the clichés about black life so dear to the white reading public." The artist's technique and his message were inseparable for Wright. Sincerity without artistic unity could never make a work of art, nor could elegant writing without the commitment of the artist.

Wright had already propounded this point of view in his essay on avant-garde literature, as well as in a somewhat curious unpublished article entitled "Personalism," in which he stated:

There is among the petty bourgeois writers no class solidarity, no economic interests to preserve, no ideology or psychology to maintain. They have only themselves and . . . the consciousness that their values and hopes are receding. Therefore the only expression possible in the initial stages is one of personal protest, or *personalism*. . . . Personalism as a means of literary expression will emphasize tendency rather than form or content. . . . Personalism will be anti-aesthetic insofar as it will seek to push art beyond mere contemplation. . . . It will seek to make those who come into contact with it take sides for or against certain *moral* issues, and these issues will be elementary ones.

"Blueprint for Negro Writing," which appeared in the Autumn, 1937, *New Challenge*, nevertheless remains the most complete, coherent and profound statement of Wright's theories on Afro-

American writing. The lead editorial specifies the magazine's clearly radical orientation, announcing its intention to combat the reactionaries and fascists through the creation of a contemporary social, realist literature, and to decrease the black writer's isolation while also encompassing Whites.

Having had his point of view adopted in the editorial, Wright then develops it in his essay. He opens by criticizing the traditional trends of black writing, which he categorizes as either attempts to achieve a flashy and artificial style, or as appeals from the cultured black bourgeoisie for justice as a class within white America. He advises the young writer to stop aping the white majority and to turn to his ethnic community for material. Since his culture springs from folklore, from the wisdom of his race's popular and oral tradition as much as from the black church, he should hold up new objectives for the black masses rather than undermine his own and his people's humanity by accepting the stereotypes imposed by white society. Thus, he should assert his own nationalism without shame, but only in order to transcend it by means of the Marxist vision, infusing it with the meaning of this wider perspective. The ideology should only be a point of departure, however, and should culminate in a work of art that would portray the "complex simplicity" of the Afro-American existence and, using all available techniques, reveal the interaction of social, economic and political forces. Once the writer understands his nation's history as if he had lived through each stage himself, he will find that themes for his creations will automatically spring to mind.

Wright was advocating a stricter literary discipline than that of the Harlem school, which was apt to sacrifice realism to the clichéd, the picturesque or so-called primitive qualities of the race, and he urged greater autonomy for the writer and a more precise definition of the profession than did the proletarian school. In today's terms, the nationalism he favored would be thought more "revolutionary" than "cultural."

He was also bent upon balancing a class perspective with a racial one, stressing both the complexity and the individuality of Afro-American culture. Of course the writer could use any literary techniques and forms that suited his needs, remaining receptive, for instance, to the innovations of Joyce, Kafka and Eliot, but Wright maintained that he should be drawing equally upon folklore. Finally, he asserted that a writer should never try to accomplish any function other than writing; the message of the work should not overwhelm the medium he has chosen. Knowing that the individual's progress would benefit the community, Wright urged the Afro-American writer to work toward destroying the cultural ghetto and triumphing over the rivalries, jealousies and factions within his own race.[7]

Although Wright had expressed various of these ideas in the past, this was the first time he had formulated a complete program, emphasizing the ethnic and popular tradition, insisting that art be independent from politics and that the black writer not aim primarily at a white audience. For a large part of his career Wright followed his own program, and this inspired many black writers of this generation, like LeRoi Jones, who are writing today for an Afro-American audience from a nationalist point of view.

New Challenge was supposed to have come out in September but did not appear until November. The contents were homogeneous, and included stories by Norman McLeod and Benjamin Appel, poems by Frank Marshall Davis, articles by Sterling Brown, Alain Locke, Loren Miller, Collins George, Robert Hayden, Eugene Holmes and Russell Marshall—all friends or acquaintances of Wright's.

The two new talents to appear in print were Margaret Walker and Ralph Ellison. After Wright's departure, Margaret Walker had become the most active member of the South Side Group, and since he had been the one to introduce her to literature, she returned the favor many times over by getting subscriptions for the magazine, sending him constant news, doing research for him and occasionally comforting him during their frequent correspondence, which lasted until 1939.

Ralph Ellison had just graduated from Tuskegee Institute and, despite his interest in contemporary literature, was then most drawn to sculpture and music. In Wright's work he had been able to discover for the first time in a black poet's writing the sensitivity and technique of modern poetry. After reading "I Have Seen Black Hands" and "Between the World and Me," he asked Langston Hughes to put him in touch with Wright. They met almost as soon as Wright reached New York and began a literary friendship that lasted for years. Surprised by Ellison's intellectual curiosity and talents, Wright was only too happy to act as mentor to this slightly younger man so predisposed to admire him. Ellison had studied literary technique for some time and had even written some poetry, but he had never dreamed of becoming a writer. The two met often that year to exchange views on literature. Wright recommended his own favorite authors—Conrad, Joyce, James, Eliot and Malraux —but he was perhaps less of an initiator than a stimulus, since Ellison had already read a great deal. He was inhibited about writing because of his high standards, but Wright forced his hand by asking him to review *These Low Grounds* for the magazine. He even got him to write a short story, "Hymie's Bull," which showed Wright's influence, but there was no second issue of the magazine in which it could have appeared. After completing the story, Ellison actually began a novel, "Slick Gonna Learn," but he soon abandoned it, feeling that he had not yet completed his apprenticeship. He thereafter devoted himself to writing critical articles, although he never ceased to delve into the problems of form. His solution eventually produced *Invisible Man*, ten years later.[8]

Meanwhile the Left had hailed the first issue of *New Challenge* with enthusiasm. Malcolm Cowley in the *New Republic* and Mike Gold in his *Daily Worker* column both congratulated Wright on his achievement, but the Party refused to support the venture. Without advertising and an assured audience, not to mention regular subscribers, the magazine was doomed. In addition, a rift apparently had occurred between Dorothy West and Marian Minus, with the result that Wright abandoned the enterprise altogether, though he had already collected a good number of manuscripts for the February, 1938, issue, among them more poems by Margaret Walker, the story by Ellison and "Ann Witke," by Henrietta Weigel.

2

Absorbing as the launching of *New Challenge* was, it in fact represented one of Wright's secondary activities. He had left Chicago with no definite promise that he would be transferred to the F.W.P. in New York, and he was fully aware of the financial risk if he were refused. As it turned out, in spite of his friends' efforts on his behalf he had to wait over six months, because he had not been a resident for the required length of time.[9] He had, of course, considered other possibilities of employment and was provided with several letters of recommendation, one from his friend Herbert Caro, who was then president of the technicians' and researchers' union of the New York City Projects Council. Since Wright's rupture with the Chicago Communists had been kept a secret, the New York group still considered him one of themselves and Benjamin Davis, one of the most influential of the Party intellectuals, suggested that he might work as an editor for the Communist press. Thus, it was probably right after the L.A.W. Congress that Wright was admitted to a local cell and started writing for the *Daily Worker*. He was appointed "Director" of the Harlem Bureau, a pretentious title since he was often the only editor and reporter, and badly paid at that. Nevertheless, he had his own tiny office on the newspaper's single floor, where he could write in privacy and keep his manuscripts, proud to show them to colleagues and visitors.

His co-workers saw little of him, mistaking his prudent reserve for disdain and regarding him as someone brought in from the outside, despite Benjamin Davis' sponsorship.[10] They were suspicious, too, of this writer whose attitude unmistakably emphasized the distinction he made between journalism and literature.[11]

Wright meanwhile chafed at being restricted to interviewing and political reporting. He had hoped to write a few lead articles rather than merely assure coverage of the minor headlines, but he rarely got the chance. During the six-month period from June 6 to December 26 he composed more than two hundred articles. Sometimes he collaborated with other editors (among them Alan Max, an official appointee from the Washington office), but most often he was on his own, gleaning bits of information in the ghetto and soliciting interviews himself, only to submit his articles to other editors who would censure, change or print them, with or without a by-line. The subject matter was naturally dictated more by the demands of the moment and the political situation than by the personal taste of the author. More than half the articles dealt with meetings and demonstrations of concern to Harlem residents, while the rest were divided almost equally between politics and protests against the living conditions of the ghetto. A few treated cultural, literary and artistic events of note, a subject more to Wright's liking, as might be expected.[12]

Predictably, the political pieces did nothing more than set forth the official Party position, particularly in regard to the racial question. Wright's personal contribution was kept to a minimum, even, for example, in his October 24 article, "New Negro Pamphlet Stresses Need for U.S. People's Front," a review of *Road to Liberation for the Negro People*, which had been written by sixteen leaders. Such articles usually consisted of simple propaganda, or, at most, elementary instruction, not requiring extensive political background or frequent contact with political leaders. Wright certainly did not complete his Marxist education at this period. On the other hand, he was forced to familiarize himself with the major problems of the day, and in particular with the intricacies of the famous Scottsboro case. The trial of the nine Negroes from Scottsboro, Alabama, accused of raping two white girls, was at that time a cause célèbre from which the Communists reaped valuable propaganda. The Harlem Bureau mentioned it at least once a week, either to announce a judicial victory, or to invite its readers to attend a demonstration or contribute funds. If Wright later alludes to the "Scottsboro Boys" in his books, it is because he became so involved with the case at this time.[13]

The competition on page three of the paper in 1937 was between this trial, ghetto problems and news of Negro volunteers fighting in the Spanish Civil War. Two of Wright's articles on these latter subjects are of particular interest. One is a report of the black secretary's conclusions about the English section of the I.W.B., assessing the contribution of several black Americans in the Loyalist forces. These included Harry Haywood, Wright's former adversary, who had enlisted in the Abraham Lincoln Brigade, and Oscar Hunter, a friend from the Chicago stockyards, who was fighting at Murcia.[14]

"Harlem Spanish Women Come out of the Kitchen," which appeared in the September 20, 1937, *Daily Worker*, is an original, almost poetic evocation of a "Pasionaria" cell meeting.

Each Wednesday at 1 P.M. some 70 women in Spanish Harlem lay aside their aprons, turn off the gas in their cook stoves, tell their children to be good (or better, take them with them), and go to a small, dingy meeting, at 84 West 111th Street. They are not going to a women's sewing circle, or to a temperance meeting or to a Bible class; these dark-haired, bright-eyed women are about much more serious business. They are members of the Communist party and the ideal in their hearts is la Pasionaria, the heroine of the Loyalist Spanish masses. Some of the women are elderly; some are young; almost all of them have children; eleven of them have husbands in the Loyalist trenches. . . . They assemble in the room and wait for their comrades. The room is quiet. Soon is heard a faint humming; it grows louder, then finally breaks into song. NO PASARAN! More come in, bringing their children whose grubby hands are filled with tin foil.

Some of the lyrical passages in *Pagan Spain*, written twenty years later, must assuredly be a distant echo of Wright's admiration of the Spanish women, expressed here in language that the humblest reader could understand.

Among his propaganda articles aimed at the Harlem audience were "Born a Slave She Recruits Five Members for Communist Party," tracing the career of Mother Ross who, just like the heroine of "Bright and Morning Star," was still militant at the age of seventy-two (August 30, 1937), and "Mrs. Holmes and Daughter Drink from Fountain of Communism," in which he extols the merits of the Workers' Alliance (September 7, 1937).

Wright particularly excelled in portraying the daily life of the Negro with stories such as "Negro Who Escaped Lynching in South Ordered to Return by Harlem Relief Official" (December 26, 1937), and "Protests Against Slugging Grow, Butcher Who Attacked Negro Boy Is Fired" (July 15, 1937). The chronic poverty of the ghetto dwellers also provided ample material. "Santa Claus Has a Hard Time Finding Way in Harlem Slums" (December 27, 1937) was inspired by a sign he had seen on 120th Street: "Merry Christmas— Room for Rent—For Whites Only." Here Wright introduces the reader to Mrs. Grover, whose small son Raymond suffers from bronchitis and whose daughter will never be able to study music and dance, in spite of her talent; the purchase of even a few toys for presents has aggravated their desperate situation. In another vignette, " 'He Died by Them': Hero's Widow Tells of Rescue of Negro Children" (December 6, 1937), he praised the daring of a white truck driver who rescued two ghetto children from a burning house before he himself perished in the flaming furnace. The human touch enlivening these reports and the techniques arousing the reader's sympathy reveal the storyteller behind the journalist.

In the final category of articles on cultural life in Harlem belongs "Huddie Ledbetter, Famous Negro Folk Artist Sings Songs of Scottsboro and His People" (August 12, 1937). Ledbetter gave a recital in August that prompted Wright to do a feature story on his career and talents. He placed the famous singer's repertoire of over five hundred songs in the Negro popular tradition and went on to describe his youth in the South, the pride that had earned him the nickname Leadbelly, his long years in prison and the principal themes resulting from his experience of cane cutting, backbreaking days picking cotton, nighttime escapes from lynch mobs, friendships with humble people and the solidarity with his fellow convicts. Wright's respect for this man who used words as weapons was equaled by his indignation that the white impresarios should be exploiting such great Negro artists. John A. Lomax, a folklore expert at the Library of Congress, had used Leadbelly to collect songs from the black prisoners, and despite the huge success of his recording "Irene," the singer had earned only $200. After his marriage, Leadbelly had returned to the South and joined the Workers' Alliance, which explains the militancy of his later compositions such as "Bourgeois Blues," attacking segregation in Washington, and "The Scottsboro Boys Got Here," sung at a benefit for the accused on a nocturnal cruise of the *Mayflower*. The article reflects Wright's continuing interest in songs and black folklore, and "Irene" was for years his favorite song. His conversations with Leadbelly at this time supplemented his knowledge of blues, a form that he later used himself.

"Negro Tradition in the Theatre" (November 15, 1937) summarized the past difficulties of black theater and traced its recent progress. The creation of the Federal Theatre, bringing Harlem a subsidized cultural program, allowed black playwrights and actors to ignore financial imperatives for the time being and gradually caused the decline of "minstrel shows" and vaudeville in favor of realistic, serious theater. Initially *Walk Together Chillun* by Frank Wilson, dealing with labor struggles and the problems of Negro unity, somewhat disconcerted audiences still accustomed to the traditional genres, but *Macbeth*, with an entirely black cast, was a national success. Then J. A. Smith added a new note with *Turpentine*, a drama about lumberjacks in the South, and this was soon followed by Conrad Seiler's *Sweetland*, in which sharecroppers appeared on stage. Wright arrived in Harlem just in time to see *The Case of Philip Lawrence*, the story of a black teacher in search of a job. Thrilled by this revolution in black theater, which matched his own ambitions for the Negro Theatre of Chicago, Wright was angry that half the actors at the Lafayette Theater were fired for financial reasons. Later he himself helped in an attempt to start a new black theater group.

Writing these articles was an opportunity, if not a professional duty, for Wright to keep abreast of everything that happened in the black community, whether it was Joe Louis' victory over James Braddock for the boxing championship, the second National Negro Congress in Philadelphia on October 15, or the innumerable tenant strikes, consumer boycotts and protest demonstrations. Except for a few stories in which his treatment outshone the interest of the subject matter, he was not a particularly brilliant journalist, and he was certainly never a *Daily Worker* star like Edwin Seaver, the literary critic; his friend James Dugan, who wrote lead articles; or Mike Gold with his column "Change the World" and background articles on Mexico and the war in Spain. In addition, Wright had no political influence and merely followed the Party line.

Even though the Harlem Bureau had rarely been as well managed, these months as a journalist were more important for Wright than for the paper. Besides an extensive knowledge of Harlem life, he acquired the skills of reporting and learned the propaganda techniques of the Party, lessons which served him well later in life.

3

Since Wright had no intention of devoting himself solely to journalism, he had continued to publish his own work. On his arrival in New York, he was able to read his poem "We of the Streets" in the April 13 issue of *New Masses*. This work, in Whitmanesque couplets, glorified the life of the poor and the strength of the urban proletariat. On August 24, the magazine printed "Silt," a two-page story, simple but poignant, narrating the dilemma of a black sharecropper who, though ruined by a sudden flood, is obliged to honor his contract although he will have nothing left for himself. In 1961, this appeared as "The Man Who Saw the Flood" in a volume of Wright's stories entitled *Eight Men.*

American Stuff, a voluminous collection of works written by the
Federal Writers in their spare time and prepared by the publication
guild, came out soon afterward. Appearing alongside contributions
by Robert Hayden, Kenneth Rexroth and other new talents was
Wright's "The Ethics of Living Jim Crow—An Autobiographical
Sketch," which he had written in the fall of 1935 for the stillborn
magazine of the League of American Writers. Jack Conroy had been
so impressed with it that he had written Wright on October 10,
1936, suggesting that his agent, Maxim Lieber, could place "this
autobiography of which you have sent me several chapters." The
twenty-page piece is divided into nine episodes covering the most
painful racial conflicts of Wright's youth. Later incorporated into
Black Boy, they include the battle against the white children in
Elaine, the brutal workers who chased him out of the optical company in Jackson, the boys who threw him off the moving car, the
policeman who searched him as if he were a criminal and the more
subtle racism of his co-workers in Memphis. The New York critics
greeted this vigorous condemnation of racism as enthusiastically as
they had welcomed "Big Boy Leaves Home." [15]

In the meantime, Wright was having no luck with his novels.
From June to December, *Lawd Today* collected rejections from
Random House, Reynal and Hitchcock, Simon & Schuster and even
Stackpole Sons, and he totally gave up the idea of submitting "Tarbaby's Dawn" after Viking, Modern Age and Norton had rejected it.
After several revisions, this novel totaled 323 pages and was divided
into two parts consisting of from five to seven scenes or episodes,
each including at least one dream, usually a nightmare. The tone
thus achieved was meant to indicate the physical, intellectual and
emotional development of the protagonist, but in fact the absence
of discernible plot, if not the fragmented action, reduced the whole
to a group of scattered events, not the steady unraveling of a destiny.
This view of black life in the South as seen through the eyes of an
adolescent was probably too close to Wright's own experience in
spite of his revealing statement on page one that the book was not
autobiographical and the situations were purely imaginary.

The hero of this unpublished novel is fifteen-year-old Daniel Mor-
rison, the son of a black day laborer working on the property of
Jim Hawkins. Despite his mother's pleas and his father's beatings,
Daniel plays hookey more often than not and is only in fourth grade

at public school; the pressure from his group of friends proves greater than that of his family's principles. Dan is, however, proud of his physical strength and ability to do heavy work, and so he dreams of becoming a boxing champion. He is therefore immensely relieved when his father decides he should go to work for Jim Hawkins: he had already helped feed the animals, milk the cow and collect eggs; now he would also work with Jenny the mule.

Dan is still a child, however, joining his friends in games of baseball, clay-ball fights, flying kites and frightening women with dead snakes attached to strings. Although his work with animals has initiated him into the secrets of sex, he knows nothing of love and girls and soon begins to suffer the agonies of puberty. A strict religious education received from Pastor Hopkins, aided by his army of deacons, has taught Dan that the Bible prohibits the satisfaction of natural instincts. Biblical myths and characters haunt Dan's simple spirit, giving him dreams and nightmares. He yields to his mother's wish that he be baptized. Somewhat later, the death of his aunt Lulu, who had been his symbol of freedom because she lived in the city, reinforces his terror of the life to come, while his father's refusal to let him go to see the girls of a traveling circus reinforces the taboo on sex. Meanwhile Bill, a sexually experienced and Mephistophelian friend, urges Dan to affirm his virility, which he does with a childhood friend named Mary, the daughter of a neighboring farmer. Mary soon discovers that she is pregnant; given the impossibility of an abortion, her angry parents insist they marry to preserve the family honor. The rigid principles of the rural community, his poverty and now these new responsibilities all contrive to imprison the inexperienced adolescent in his milieu. In addition, Dan is just becoming aware of the white threat; he hears at the barbershop that a laborer in the next county has been lynched. Finally a wise farmer explains to both Dan and the reader the racial situation in the South, quoting from Booker T. Washington.

Now that he is head of a family and a sharecropper, Dan realizes that he will never become a boxer like Jack Johnson but continues to daydream of a power to compensate for this disappointment and buys an old revolver to enhance his security and personal dignity. It is at this point that "Almos' a Man," published in 1941, begins. Apparently by accident, but in fact through an unconscious desire to hurt the white man by attacking his possessions, Dan kills the mule one day during his target practice. With fifty dollars' worth of debts, and a child to be born, Dan answers the call of the passing train and heads North.

The obviously autobiographical elements—the games, the restricted atmosphere of a small community, the religious life, the departure on a train—present a feebly disguised version of Wright's own odyssey, but "Tarbaby's Dawn" is more than just the story of Dan's youth. Wright focuses on Dan's situation in order to paint a realistic and sometimes touching tableau of rural existence. The slow rhythm of the seasons, labor in the fields and chores on the farm, the infrequent amusements and the ever-present atmosphere of racial prejudice all have the white menace as a background, constantly reinforcing black solidarity. The novel also attempts, though often awkwardly because of the heavy-handed symbolism contrasting real life with dream life, to reveal the progressive inroads of society as it gradually warps the development of a personality. This clash between individual aspirations and social imperatives becomes a central theme in Wright's later work and is actually the basis for the *magnum opus* he outlined to Ed Aswell in a letter of August, 1955.

The concrete personal experiences that later proved to be the strength of *Black Boy,* and the well-executed structure elaborated with good dialogue were not enough to counterbalance the overwhelming faults of "Tarbaby's Dawn" nor to lessen the trail of rejection letters in its wake. Since the *Bildungsroman* had not then come into fashion, this kind of novel about a Negro was doomed to failure.

Wright had meanwhile tightened the plot of *Lawd Today* and pruned some of the dialogue, at the suggestion of James Farrell and Maxim Lieber. He had also added a few pages reintroducing Lil in the final scene, thus rounding out the vicious circle of his black post office worker's life and making this version very close to the one eventually published in 1963. Wright had two main objectives in composing this unique picture of Southern immigrants recently settled in a Northern ghetto. First, he wanted to show the Blacks themselves how the shallow, materialistic American ideals actually harmed their community, and second, by unveiling the prejudices of the black bourgeoisie, to reveal the necessity for political education to make the masses aware of their plight.

Publishers, unfortunately, thought that a "Negro" novel should be exotic, not informative, while the Communists, repudiating this picture of black life, since it naturally destroyed all their clichés, actually discouraged Wright from trying to get it published.[16] Margaret Walker, one of the few among Wright's friends to appreciate the novel, clearly understood his intentions, as she explained in her letter of November 24, 1937.

Most colored folks have even less [than their white friends] and they strain to fill their houses full of matched suites of furniture and I am beginning to see more and more every day the tragedy of *Lawd Today:* It's right in my face. I can see the wisdom and need for such a book. Everything is just as you have written it. The debts, the liquor, the frustrated women, superficial and unconscious. Drinking and playing bridge, and living above their means, straining and bragging. It's part of their living and they're really miserable; yet if you go in their homes you think they ought to be happy, they live in such luxury.

EIGHT

BECAUSE Wright's transfer to the F.W.P. of New York was still pending, these autumn months of 1937 were financially difficult; he had to move several times and make even more demands upon his friends for help, not only to hasten his acceptance by the W.P.A. but to apply for a literary grant. In October he actually completed an application for a Guggenheim Fellowship but thought his chances were so slim that he never sent it in.

Nevertheless, the year ended on a happy note. In September, Wright had entered his short stories only a few days before the deadline for a contest sponsored by *Story* magazine for all F.W.P. members. On December 14, Whit Burnett told him confidentially that "Fire and Cloud" had just won the first prize of $500, having been chosen from among six hundred entries by a jury consisting of Sinclair Lewis and the critics Harry Scherman and Lewis Gannett.[1] This significant sum of money, as Wright told numerous interviewers after the awarding of the prize on February 15, would first go toward buying the coat and shoes he had needed for so long, and an enormous steak dinner.[2] He then planned to spend all his time working on a "novel of Negro life in Chicago" and perhaps, if the money lasted, eventually go to Mexico on vacation.[3]

Numerous Negroes wrote to him expressing their pride in his brilliant literary debut, and several black girls even proposed marriage.[4] He could not hide his own satisfaction at this success as he wrote triumphantly to his old friend Essie Ward on February 26:

Maybe by now you have heard the news that I won the National Fiction Contest sponsored by the Story Magazine. My book will be published next month, March 23rd, by Harpers. I hope you get a copy and see what your old pal has done.

The most important result of the prize had, in fact, been that Wright no longer had any difficulty in finding a major publishing house to accept his work. Since John Trounstine had fulfilled his responsibility as literary agent with empty promises, Wright had decided to go elsewhere. He first approached the Ann Watkins Agency, and then, with Aletha Elting, a friend of the Weigels' who worked for Paul Reynolds, as intermediary, he went so far as to ask Reynolds, the well-known agent of Paul Laurence Dunbar, to represent him. According to the rules of the contest, "Fire and Cloud" would come out in the March issue of *Story*; meanwhile the Story Press offered the whole collection to Harper's, where Eugene Saxton and Edward Aswell accepted it for publication under Wright's chosen title *Uncle Tom's Children*. At that time, Reynolds obtained a good contract for Wright's next novel and he submitted an outline for it to Harper's at the end of the month.

The four stories of *Uncle Tom's Children* had been written in Chicago and were inspired by varying influences. They had, however, been planned as a collection, and as such they showed not only how far Wright had come since "Superstition" but also offered a striking new perspective on the Southern Negro experience, which explains the surprised but enthusiastic reactions that followed its publication.

All of Wright's stories, as well as the novel "Tarbaby," evoke the terror that racism instilled in the Blacks of Mississippi, by focusing on the consciousness of the principal character. "Big Boy Leaves Home" opens with an idyllic scene which is soon shattered by a brutal drama. Four young black boys have been roaming about the countryside, singing and playing on a fine summer day. They decide to risk taking a swim on the land of the irascible Mr. Harvey and are discovered, naked, by a white woman. Her cries summon Harvey's son, her fiancé, who kills two of the innocent boys before Big Boy manages to overpower and shoot him. Big Boy is forced to flee while the desperate Negro community tries futilely to avert the lynchers on their way to avenge the murder. Concealed in a damp hole for which he had battled first a snake and then a bloodhound (symbolically killing the monsters to nestle in the bosom of Mother Earth), Big Boy witnesses the torture of his friend Bobo before a truck driver helps him on his way North at dawn.

An adolescent's initiation into violence is a common theme in American literature, but in this case it corresponds almost exactly to one of the author's own traumatic experiences, and Big Boy is a pathetic character. These black children, guilty in their innocence, have lost their paradise; when the wrath of the white gods descends upon them, the primitive harmony of their life is replaced by the obsession to escape. The woman and the serpent merely reinforce this symbolism.

The steady crescendo of violence is a model for the stories that follow, while the emphasis on realistic details and the use of the countryside as a stage set save the plot from being bogged down in it. Wright uses this correspondence between nature and the hero's state of mind, an application of Eliot's theory of the "objective correlative," to link Big Boy's feelings to his thoughts, as well as to construct a simple symbolism that nevertheless remains within the limits of realism. In addition, he switches from the third person to the first person for the painful episodes that Big Boy suffers alone, resuming the objective point of view at the end. A similar, though somewhat modified, technique is used in the other three stories.

"Down by the Riverside" opens in the middle of a flood. Mann, a black farmer, has shown remarkable courage and initiative in getting his wife to the hospital to have her baby, but even though he has conquered nature, the evil of the white man still awaits him. Since there were no boats for sale, Mann's brother had stolen one belonging to a postman. This act sets into motion a chain of events beginning with Mann's murder of the postman when he tries to recover his stolen property. No sooner has Mann seen his wife die in childbirth because of the delay in reaching the hospital than he is called up by the troops to serve on a rescue squad. As chance has it, he finds himself saving the family of the man he had killed. The postman's son recognizes him, but at the end of this night of tragedy, Mann no longer has the courage to kill him, nor the will to flee the village. His guilt exposed, and threatened with lynching, he is shot on the banks of the river.

Although the plot often hinges on coincidence (the second encounter with the postman's family seems somewhat unlikely), the whirlwind pace of the story propels along the reader who is constantly either sharing Mann's sufferings or judging him, due to the alternation of first- and third-person perspective.

Wright analyzes with great accuracy the instinctively egotistical actions, dictated by prejudice, of the white population toward Negroes who, even in a time of danger, are not treated as humans. Given their similar environment, however, Mann represents progress in relation to Big Boy. The young boy fled, while the mature man victoriously confronted nature. Nevertheless, Mann is still unable to overcome his helplessness and submission to the Whites; he considers his cause lost ahead of time, a feeling that has become almost second nature to him. Only by the third story does the black hero resist, fight and die with dignity, beaten in an unequal struggle.

The farmer Silas in "Long Black Song" is treated somewhat differently, however, in that he is not the only protagonist. The story first focuses on his wife, Sarah. While waiting for her husband to return from a fair, Sarah yields to the advances of a white man, a young and eloquent phonograph salesman. Furious at this betrayal, whose traces are obvious, Silas beats his wife, who then flees for refuge to a nearby hill, her baby in her arms. The real crisis occurs when the white men return. Silas shoots the adulterer but the man's friend escapes and gives the alarm, bringing back a crowd of lynchers who set fire to the farm. Deaf to the entreaties of his wife, Silas refuses to escape to safety, fighting to the very end and dying in the flames rather than give himself up.

Silas's story is partially filtered through Sarah's point of view. This farmer's wife is passive and primitive, a dreamer whose instinctive and sensual rhythm corresponds to that of the revolving seasons, the alternation of night and day, reverie and action. The pendulum of the clock versus the rising and setting sun is a simple symbolism Wright uses to accentuate the cultural gap between Sarah's life in the fields and the salesman's existence in the city. Speaking as a native of the South, Wright offers here a notion of happiness similar to that of the Agrarians.

Even more than Mann, Silas retained his human dignity in death, but both stories contain an "original sin" that initiates the ensuing crisis; in this case Silas was guilty of neglecting his wife in order to get rich and equal the Whites, thus partially justifying her infidelity. By contrast, the hero of "Fire and Cloud" is totally innocent and, as a result, totally triumphant.

Over the years, the Reverend Daniel Taylor has become the recognized leader of the black community in his town. With the country in mid-Depression, the white city government and the local welfare services refuse to provide aid to his parishioners. It becomes his job to pressure them to do so. But his own freedom of action is restricted by contradictory forces. The white mayor and his men insist that he use his influence to prevent a protest demonstration being planned; the Communists want him to support it, while the allegiance of his parish is divided between him and Deacon Smith, a "black Judas" ready to betray him.

Taylor's physical ordeal, a symbolic baptism in fire and blood when the Whites beat him in the woods to intimidate him, translates him to a higher plane of strength and wisdom. He opposes his faith in the solidarity of the masses to the concept of personal revenge advocated by his son Jimmy, a typical young, individualistic militant. Taylor thereby achieves a union of the oppressed, both black and white, whose number assures the success of the demonstration. "Victory belongs to the strong" is the lesson, learned from Lenin, that Wright proclaims here via Taylor.

This fourth story adds a wider scope to the entire collection and is an appropriate conclusion. Uncle Tom's children, the new generation of Blacks, will no longer turn the other cheek and submit to white harassment as their parents had. Taylor was an "accommodating leader" until he acquired a broader understanding of his responsibility toward his people. Economic necessity and racial conflict changed his conception of duty from a purely religious to a political one; God came to be identified with the oppressed masses. The literary techniques may be theatrical, the uniting of poor Whites and Blacks improbable despite the precedent of Angelo Herndon, and the scene with mayor, Communists and deacons all assembled in Taylor's house unintentionally comic, but the consistent biblical symbolism in the hero's character enables the moral of his maturation to satisfy the laws of aesthetics. Moreover, the dialogue is realistic and lively, without didactic speeches, and the time sequences, unencumbered by flashbacks, preserve the drama of Wright's narrative in all its glory.

The progression from Big Boy, through Mann and Silas to Taylor adds another dimension to the individual stories. Each protagonist is more committed to the social struggle than the last, more responsible and hence more victorious because he acts less from purely personal motives. He is therefore less isolated in his actions. The fact that this statement comes out only implicitly from the book's perspective is in itself an artistic achievement, since explicit theorizing or propaganda could have been embarrassing, as it later proved in *The Outsider*.

2

The subject matter of *Uncle Tom's Children* alone assured it a chorus of praise from the radical critics. Granville Hicks, who reviewed the collection for *New Masses,* was particularly proud to see a new star on the revolutionary horizon, but Alan Calmer, in the *Daily Worker* of April 4, was intelligent enough not to stress the political significance of the collection, instead devoting a great deal of space to the merits of Wright's prose. James T. Farrell, in *Partisan Review,* called it a "genuine literary achievement," praising the skillful use of the vernacular and the courageous realism of the stories. The more conservative press reacted somewhat differently. While the liberal Malcolm Cowley said, in the April 16 issue of *New Republic,* that it was ". . . both heartening as the evidence of a vigorous new talent and terrifying as the expression of racial hatred," a good number of critics, in particular those of *The New York Times* and *The New York Times Book Review,* deplored the fact that Whites were presented in such a uniformly bad light.[5] No one, however, remained unmoved by the dramatic quality of the stories. Most enthusiastic on this score was Frederic T. March in his article "Hope, Despair and Terror" for the May 8 issue of the *New York Herald Tribune* magazine section, *Books.* He intimated that Wright could win a Pulitzer Prize and, although unaware that in addition to Gertrude Stein and Hemingway Wright had certainly been influenced by his early reading of Chekhov, even compared him to the famous Russian.

The black press was not so unanimous, although in general they were pleased with the success of one of their race. Sterling Brown unhesitatingly ranked Wright's stories with those of Erskine Caldwell, William Faulkner and Jean Toomer in *Cane.*[6] Alain Locke had to excuse himself later for his grievous error of having referred to the book as *Uncle Tom's Cabin,* but his review was almost dithyrambic.[7] The only unfavorable comment came from Zora Neale

Hurston in the April 2 *Saturday Review of Literature*. She was
as much shocked by the violence that Wright attributed to interracial relations in the South as by his Communist message. This
hardly came as a surprise, however, since Wright's criticisms of her
novel had shown how divergent their viewpoints were.

Uncle Tom's Children was even mentioned somewhat later by
Eleanor Roosevelt in her column for the *New York Post*. She said
that she had found it "beautifully written and so vivid that I had
a most unhappy time reading it." [8]

The Book Union, a radical book club, bought the collection as
their April selection, and Wright was able to write Reynolds on
February 26, 1938, that he had received two proposals for theater
adaptations, one from George W. Lattimore's agency and the other
from James G. Johnson, who wanted to write an opera using
Wright's themes.

Meanwhile the Party was getting valuable publicity from this
success, so that those who had been somewhat hostile toward or
distrustful of Wright at the *Daily Worker* now attempted to make
amends. Christmas, 1937, finally marked Wright's transfer to the
F.W.P. in New York, and he had immediately quit his job, proving
how impatient he was to give up journalism for creative writing.
Nevertheless, since the critics on the Left had praised him so generously, he was not about to deny his debt to Marxism and the
Communist Party, which had "shaped [his] thought and creative
growth," as well as to the radical literary groups in which his career
had been launched.[9]

Wright had now become one of the literary stars of the Party
and attended various political functions and activities as a result.
On March 5 he was guest of honor at the annual ball given for
New Masses which, the same week, published his review of a novel
by William Rollins on the Spanish Civil War.[10] On April 5, as a
representative of the antiracists, he wrote an open letter to the
New York Post called "Readers' Right: Writer Asks Break for
Negroes," in which he denounced the segregation that was usual in
American sports at the time. It was not a political act when, with
Whit Burnett presiding, he spoke to the Writers' Club of Columbia
University about the commitment of a radical author and traced
the genesis of the four stories in *Uncle Tom's Children*.[11] At the
end of April, however, he signed an important declaration pub-

lished by the Party in the *Daily Worker*. A group of anti-Stalinists including Robert Coates, Malcolm Cowley, Marc Blitzstein, Stuart Davis and Paul Strand had been requesting signatures on a petition to protest the Moscow Trials. In response to this, the paper prepared a statement in which various authors, among them Wright, agreed that there had been sufficient evidence to establish the guilt of the accused Trotskyists. Wright, in other words, had swallowed the Party verdict.[12]

On May 10, *New Masses* published "Bright and Morning Star," which Wright had completed in Chicago and which he wanted to perform as great a propaganda function as possible, even though he was well aware of the literary problems this posed. He had just been putting the finishing touches on it when he received the *Story* prize. On the advice of Whit Burnett, who had written him on January 27, 1938, he cut all references to the Scottsboro trial and the International Labor Defense. He also shortened some of the heroine's meditations and her long tirade in response to the obscenities of the sheriff, attempting, as in "Long Black Song," to blend the ideology of the characters with the instinctive movements of their thoughts and the realistic details of their lives.

The story clarifies the theme of Christianity evolving into political commitment first treated in "Fire and Cloud," with the influence of the heroine's sons, who are both Communists, pushing her further in this direction than the Reverend Taylor.

Since Sug is in prison for his political activities, his younger brother, Johnny Boy, has taken over organizational activities. A secret cell meeting is about to take place when Johnny's white girl friend, Reva, arrives to warn him that the sheriff and his men are on their way to arrest the members of the Party. The race-oriented viewpoint of the mother is clearly contrasted with the Marxist vision of the son when Sue suspects Booker, a newly recruited White, of having denounced them, while Johnny refuses to distinguish between Whites and Blacks, seeing only rich and poor.

Johnny is arrested as he tries to warn his comrades, but the sheriff cannot get their names from him and prepares to take him to the woods to be tortured. Meanwhile, Sue unfortunately lets herself be persuaded by the smooth talk of Booker and gives away the vital names. She soon realizes her mistake and, by taking a short cut, beats the traitor to the clearing, where she sees the sheriff's men torturing her son. With a gun hidden in a sheet, she shoots Booker before he has a chance to relay his knowledge, and she herself is killed.

There are three immediate conclusions to be drawn: first, that the mother was right to adopt her son's Communist vision to replace her own religious convictions; second, and more important, that Johnny's trust is the cause of his downfall; and third, that the traitor is a white man. Wright may have wanted to make the point that forming an underground labor organization in the South was such a difficult task that, if caution prevailed, the Party would never attract any new members—that a generous political deed therefore had an attendant risk. Nevertheless, Wright destroys the nice balance achieved in "Fire and Cloud." Although he cleverly substitutes revolutionary images that are not, in form at least, intrinsically different from the religious symbols and thought processes, an ambiguity remains. The inconsistent character of Reva does not convince the reader that the oppressed of both races have united. Furthermore, Sue's heroic character dominates the plot at the expense of the Communists. Thus, when she gives her life to save her son's comrades, her primary motive seems to be because they belong to her race. This fundamental hesitation between the ethnic and the Marxist perspectives certainly reflects Wright's own ambivalence at the time of composition, in spite of his firm propagandist intentions. The plot also lacks the unified symbolism that characterized "Fire and Cloud," but the melodrama is sustained by an almost epic narrative style, which elevates the biblical characters of mother and son to the level of the heroes in the Red Army of the 1917 revolution so vividly depicted in Eisenstein's films and Gorky's novel *The Mother*.

The story was ready in time to appear in *Uncle Tom's Children,* to which it could have been a fifth act, but it was decided to publish it separately. *Harper's Magazine* actually rejected it, but since it fit Party specifications even better than had the four previous stories, *New Masses* published it as part of a special literary supplement on May 10, hailing it as the latest triumph of a great writer.

Under the Party's aegis, Wright received countless honors, which often meant suffering numerous ordeals, during the months following the publication of *Uncle Tom's Children*. With a respite for a summer vacation, every few days of the spring and fall he would be attending a meeting, reception, ball, theater or lecture, or himself be giving a speech for some benefit.[13] Despite his simple tastes and his horror of social functions, he was leading almost a "public" life, never refusing for that period, along with his political activities, to play the role which the Party expected of him as one of its best-known writers. Half-flattered, half-irritated, he conscientiously paid for his success with his time and energy, although it is hard to say whether the author or the Party reaped more publicity from this campaign.

3

Wright had meanwhile become acquainted with a good number of authors at the New York Federal Writers' Project, most of whom had also attended the American Writers' Congress. The New York section alone employed around thirty supervisors to coordinate the over 450 authors, journalists, poets and playwrights who for the most part worked as researchers, secretaries, proofreaders, photographers and even clerks. Like the F.W.P. in other states, the New York section was preparing a volume for the American Guides series. Under the direction of Harry L. Shaw, and later Harold Strauss, the "recognized" writers were free to work at home, dividing their time between their own work and research for the Project. Since Wright's native honesty prevented him from accepting his hundred dollar a month salary as an unemployment benefit, he plunged into the laborious research necessary for the guide. He was part of a team working under Joseph Gaer on a book called *New York Panorama,* which Random House was supposed to publish later in the year.[14] It emphasized the achievements during the Depression of which the New Deal could justly be proud. Wright did all the research for a chapter entitled "Portrait of Harlem" and wrote it virtually unaided, retracing the origins of the ghetto, its economic conditions and distinctive social structure before summarizing its artistic life.[15] He was able to speak from intimate knowledge in this documented study, which added weight to his denunciation of the discrimination that persisted in spite of recent

With fellow writers of the New York F.W.P.

progress. The quarter of the space he devoted to cultural life was not free from echoes of his *Daily Worker* articles and hints of his personal experiences at the time, and even his literary tastes peep through. "Joyce's *Ulysses* influenced some of the Negro writers, and even the gospel of Gertrude Stein claimed a number of Negro adherents." [16] Is he not referring primarily, maybe even exclusively, to himself in this sentence?

When his essay for *New York Panorama* was completed, Wright worked on another guide to New York City, this project directed by Lou Gody, Chester Harvey and James Reed. Although he helped do the research for the section on Harlem, it is impossible to ascertain whether he covered all aspects of it and what sections of the chapter entitled "The Harlems" he may have written.[17]

The ghetto also provided the subject of an article that *New Masses* published on July 4, 1938, under the title "High Tide in Harlem: Joe Louis as a Symbol of Freedom." Wright had gone to the

Louis-Schmeling fight on June 22 as a special reporter for the *Daily Worker*, where his enthusiastic coverage appeared two days later as "How He Did It—And Oh!—Where Were Hitler's Pagan Gods?" His *New Masses* article was somewhat of a repeat of "Joe Louis Uncovers Dynamite," which James W. Ford had praised so highly when it was written in 1935. The second essay, though like the first largely devoted to the delirious enthusiasm of the audience when the victory of their hero was announced, reveals different political implications. The match is presented here more as the struggle of democracy against fascism than of one race against the other.

After a pompous opening (a reference to Greek Tragedy gives Mike Jacobs the right to wear the purple robe of Sophocles and Euripides), Wright evokes in almost Rabelaisian language the wind of liberating madness sweeping through Harlem and the feverish joy of the Blacks. Unfortunately, he spoils the literary effect of the people's spontaneous delirium with his belabored interpretation of its political significance.

Wright's opinions at this time, in fact, rapidly earned him a reputation as a militant at the F.W.P., whose offices were the scene of many conflicts between the employees and the federal administration. This was a time of incessant claims and protests, largely because Congress was questioning the value of the F.W.P. and people were being laid off for lack of funds. The writers were thus fighting to get a better salary while living in constant fear of losing their jobs altogether. Meanwhile, because the Writer's Union there included a number of Communists who favored Wright, Hiram K. Smith, Ralph Ellison and Alfred Russel for office, Wright was elected and played an active role until the beginning of the summer, once even organizing the strikers to occupy the F.W.P. offices.[18]

In spite of these activities, the F.W.P. was more important to Wright as an ideal brotherhood of intellectuals than an arena for political and union combats. Although there was bound to be dissension and jealousy, the solidarity was unquestioned and Wright seldom refused to help a colleague, since colleagues so easily became friends.[19] Many of Wright's old friends also worked for the Project at one time or another. Willard Maas, Marie Mencken, Helen Neville, Ralph Ellison, Claude McKay and Roi Ottley were there, and although no one came into the office regularly, they would get together at someone's house to attend the theater, a party or political meeting. They were Wright's new spiritual family, the stimulating and varied company he enjoyed when tired from writing *Native Son* in the Newtons' quiet household where he was living at the time.

NINE

1

BEFORE he left Chicago in 1937, Wright had not only considered the idea of writing the story of an adolescent growing up in the ghetto but had even sketched the broad outlines of a novel, drawing upon his experiences at the South Side Youth Club. It was not until he moved to Brooklyn, however, that he actually completed *Native Son*.[1]

After his appointment to the F.W.P. in the winter of 1937, Wright had rented a furnished room at 139 West 143rd Street from a very obliging woman named Mrs. Sawyer, who let him use her kitchen as well, to save him money on meals. Unfortunately, Wright let himself become romantically involved with the young daughter of the house and only barely escaped marrying her, a significant experience in light of Wright's eventual choice of a wife.

For the moment, however, he was concerned only with leaving the Sawyer family, and the day after the final rupture with them moved in with his friends Jane and Herbert Newton, who had themselves just moved to 175 Carlton Avenue in Brooklyn and let him have the use of one room in their new apartment.

The composition of his novel absorbed the major part of Wright's time and energy that year, and he kept to a rigorous schedule. Once the sun had taken the chill off the morning air (around five thirty during the summer) he would get up and, armed with a thick pad of yellow paper, head for Fort Greene Park. Surrounded by lush greenery, he would install himself top of a slight hill where a monument stood honoring local heroes of the Revolution who had been killed in the port below. Around ten o'clock, after Herbert had gone to work and the children were out playing in the small courtyard, Wright would come in for breakfast. Jane would be busy in the kitchen, which was large enough to serve as the center of family life, and while Wright had breakfast, the two would discuss what he had just written in his nervous and almost illegible hand. Sometimes he would go right up to his room to polish and type up the morning's rough draft. If Jane had time, he would show her this new version and perhaps give her an idea of what he planned to write the next day.

On the afternoons he did not go into the city and to the F.W.P., he might take a nap in his room, in which case he ate at five o'clock with the children. He enjoyed talking to them and often told them stories simply to observe their reactions. He would then either return to his room or go out for the evening, which sometimes meant that he was there when Herbert came home from work, around eleven or twelve o'clock. Otherwise, the two men rarely ran into each other except on weekends.

Wright was able to talk very freely with Jane; in fact he was more open with her than he had ever been with his own family. Never before had there been someone with whom he could discuss his reading or examine each stage in the creation of a novel. At that time Jane was more widely read than Wright in many areas, and had a broad cultural experience, which enabled her to make certain corrections in the text as well as suggest useful reading. Wright actually owned only a few dozen books, but he was an avid reader of all genres: magazines, Westerns, literary and progressive political journals, novels (by Caldwell, Dos Passos, Hemingway and Gorky), essays by Stalin and theoretical works on Marxism. It was Jane who encouraged him to reread with close attention to technique and detail *The Possessed* and *The Brothers Karamazov*.

Jane did not always agree with Richard about certain points or episodes in the novel, for instance his insistence upon naming Bigger's victim Mary Dalton because it had been the "nom de guerre" of a New York Communist sent to Chicago as a Party official in 1934. Without knowing her very well, Wright had heartily disliked this girl, and it gave him pleasure to think that people like Harry Haywood and John Davis would get the subtle allusion if he used her name in this context.[2] A practical detail occasioned another disagreement. In his first draft, Wright had Bigger use his knife to cut off Mary's head so that her body would fit into the furnace. Jane finally had to make Richard try to decapitate a chicken with a kitchen knife in order to persuade him to put an axe in the cellar for Bigger to use at the crucial moment.

In general, the author would hotly defend his own conception of his characters, their actions and their motives. He would always start by arguing the exigencies of the plot or the need to foreshadow some future event, before eventually admitting the justice of some of his friend's suggestions.

The novel was well along when, one June afternoon, Wright declared that he was now forced to get rid of Bigger's friend, Bessie. Jane begged Wright to spare the girl, since she considered the murder both unnecessary for the development of the plot and insufficiently motivated. Although Wright recognized the logic of Jane's remarks, a deep-seated conviction prevented him from yielding on this point. He was inspired by two literary traditions: that of American realism, as exemplified by Dreiser's *American Tragedy,* and the Russian existentialism of Dostoevsky's *Crime and Punishment.* His writer's imagination saw no obstacle to combining in one character two types of people—the murderer who kills as an act of creation and the one who kills in response to a social determinism. If Bigger resembled Clyde Griffiths at the beginning of the novel, he was by now gradually turning into another Raskolnikov. Bigger's murder of Bessie marked a new stage in Wright's literary evolution; everything that he had learned from his naturalist models up to this point had prevented him from allowing his characters to give in to these demonic temptations, but now Bigger claimed his right to "create," in the existentialist meaning of the word, by rejecting the accidental nature of his first murder with this further proof of his power to destroy.

Jane and Richard went on to discuss Bigger's eventual capture and the events that led up to it. Since Jane knew the South Side as well as Richard, she was able to suggest the exact location of the capture, though she was still arguing for Bessie's life at the time. Richard had just cried out, "But I have to get rid of her. She must die!" when Mr. Thomas Diggs, the owner of the house, a very quiet young man who had been living on rent from his tenants since the death of his mother, happened to knock at the door and come in. The poor man had undoubtedly heard this sinister declaration, since he withdrew immediately, very embarrassed, while Richard roared with laughter at the idea that someone thought he was planning a murder.

Wright considered himself fortunate not only because he had Jane to discuss the novel with but because current events seemed to be conspiring to supply him with additional material.

I was about half way through the novel when a big case broke in
Chicago that almost duplicated the story I was writing. I modeled
the newspaper releases in the book on the actual news stories of
this case.[3]

Wright told this to Edwin Seaver, and he also pointed out that
Max's defense had been modeled on Clarence Darrow's famous defense of Leopold and Loeb. In "How Bigger Was Born," Wright
stressed how closely real life approximated fiction and sometimes
even surpassed it. In fact, however, he only borrowed a few minor
details from the case of Robert Nixon. On May 27, 1938, this
eighteen-year-old black boy had taken a brick and murdered a
woman, the mother of two, apparently because she surprised him
in the act of robbing her apartment. He was immediately identified
by his fingerprints and caught with bloodstains on his clothes while
still in the vicinity of the crime, at which time he denounced an
accomplice, a boy his own age named Earl Hicks. The Chicago
police subsequently got him to confess, probably under torture, to
another crime, two attacks also on white women as well as five
attempted murders of which it was not at all certain he was guilty.

Wright took an interest in Nixon's case more out of a desire to
study the behavior of Whites once they turned against a black man
than out of curiosity about the psychology and motivation of the
murderer himself. He asked his friend Margaret Walker to cut out
the reports of the investigation and trial published in the *Tribune*
and other Chicago daily papers. The *Tribune* had immediately
transformed the murder into a sexual crime and made a great deal
out of a charge of rape, although the prosecution never explicitly
brought this charge against Nixon. If the articles that Bigger read
about himself in prison seem unduly exaggerated, it is well to remember that Wright was quoting word for word from the *Tribune*
reports of the Nixon case, which made him out to be an apelike
and repulsive creature.[4]

In addition to the black lawyers already on the case, the International Labor Defense appointed a white lawyer, Joseph Roth,
to defend the accused. Wright's model for Buckley was Attorney
General Thomas Courtney (even their names are similar), whom
he had actually helped get elected when he was assistant to Republican precinct captain Doc Huggins. Courtney later proposed
a law intended to decrease the number of assaults committed by

the mentally unbalanced, which was passed unanimously because of the Nixon case alone.

Wright had originally gone to Chicago to talk to Ulysses Keys, one of the defense lawyers, but once there, he evidently picked up additional material from the trial itself: the charged atmosphere of the courtroom, the hostility of the public toward the accused during the reconstruction of the crime, the briefness of the debates, and the fact that the jury found Nixon guilty and condemned him to death after only one hour's deliberation. Wright must have thought the striking similarity of his fiction to real life was a good sign. Had not Dreiser used the murder of Grace Brown by Chester Gillette to write *An American Tragedy*? The Nixon case certainly resembled that of Bigger Thomas to a comparable degree. Nevertheless, the desire to approximate reality did not lead Wright to modify the basic structure of *Native Son* in the slightest, perhaps because the novel was so close to his own emotional experience.

The first third of the manuscript was finished by the beginning of the summer, and a few months later Jane and Richard were having heated arguments on the subject of the third book, which dealt with Bigger's trial. Wright admitted that he had planned this section in order to express certain ideas which the nature of his main character made impossible to set forth earlier. Bigger, a black adolescent without education, could not possibly have the insight or perspective to equal the Marxist vision of the lawyer Max, experienced as he was in the juggling and formulation of ideas, but since Wright had certain opinions of his own that he wanted at all costs to incorporate into his novel, this last section was to serve as a repository for his ideological views, as articulated by Bigger's lawyer. The model for Max was not Robert Nixon's lawyer but an International Labor Defense official whom Wright had seen something of in Chicago during 1934; the name was probably taken from one of Wright's colleagues at the *Daily Worker*, Alan Max.

Wright also had difficulty deciding on the character of Mary's boy friend, Jan Erlone, and was not at all satisfied with the portrait of him that had emerged by the end of the second book. Erlone is the homonym of "alone"—the lone rider, in a certain sense— and Jan was in fact the only person who eventually managed to elicit a friendly reaction from Bigger. (His first name seems to have been taken from Jan Wittenber, Wright's old friend from the John

Reed Club.) Perhaps Wright had acquired a better opinion of white Communists from staying with the Newtons, mixing with their friends and working at the W.P.A. According to Jane, he wanted in any case to present a more favorable picture of this boy. He could feel the critical eyes of certain members of the Party—people whom he considered his friends and whose judgment he respected and even depended on—fixed upon him. He admitted, though, that he did not expect them to praise him for the novel, even if he finally succeeded in presenting Jan Erlone in a more favorable light.

Jane Newton criticized Wright not only for some technical errors in the depiction of court procedure and Communist activities in this section but, more generally, for the inauthenticity of these activities, considering the personality of the present leaders and character of American communism at that time. Wright saw the strength of Jane's argument but made no changes in his presentation; when confronted with suggestions that would have altered the course of events, he preferred to preserve his own text even though he was not totally satisfied with it, something which demonstrates how much the novel was the product of one author's mind and sensibility. It was as if Wright intended to speak his mind, free himself from the burden of his message, even at the expense of the story.

Toward the beginning of the fall, the Newtons' house was sold and they moved into an apartment at 522 Gates Avenue, above a store and right next to the streetcar tracks. In spite of the noise, the cramped living conditions and the absence of a park nearby, Wright followed his friends, since the cost of a room of his own was prohibitive and the atmosphere of their home helped him to write. He worked very hard at fixing up the third book. He was now somewhat less pressed for time and got to know his friends even better as he adapted to their new life. Since the weather was forcing the children to play indoors, his discussions with Jane were shorter and less literary, and Wright became familiar with the everyday problems of running a household. At the same time, he was coming to identify more and more with Bigger and thus tried to steer clear of too great an intimacy, just as he had formerly withdrawn within his own family. In the long run, however, the differences separating him from Jane turned out to be more regional and social than specifically racial.

It was after a long critical discussion with his friend Ralph Elli-son that Wright completed the final third of the novel, which was already entitled *Native Son*. Nelson Algren had been thinking of using this title himself for *Somebody in Boots* and had mentioned it at the time to Wright, although the expression originally came from a song satirizing a presidential candidate from California:

> The miners came in forty-nine,
> the whores in fifty-one,
> They jungled up together
> and begot the Native Son.[5]

Since he took "native son" to mean a person who was neither an immigrant nor a foreigner, Wright was emphasizing that Bigger was 100 per cent American and that as such, he had been deeply wounded to find himself excluded from a higher social class. At the same time, Wright was blaming the country itself, and not some foreign ideology, for inspiring so much hatred and violence in one of its citizens. The title was not to the taste of Wright's editor, but the novelist could not find another that was more to his liking.[6]

While Wright was continuing the revision of the first complete draft of the novel, his material situation took a turn for the better. *Uncle Tom's Children* had sold moderately well, and "Fire and Cloud" was going to be made into a play by Langston Hughes. The two of them planned to collaborate on the adaptation, and Paul Reynolds even sent them a proposed contract on August 5, but the project eventually fell through. On the other hand, Edward As-well, Wright's editor at Harper's, managed to get him a $400 advance on *Native Son* in November. In spite of his strict summer schedule, Wright had found the time to send off his application for a Gug-genheim Felowship, and he was now assured of a number of strong recommendations from figures such as Professor Lawrence Martin, critics Lewis Gannett, Granville Hicks and Harry Scherman, his friend Claude Barnett from the Associated Negro Press, and a female admirer of his—no less than Mrs. Eleanor Roosevelt.[7]

A few weeks before Christmas, the Newtons moved once again, this time to an apartment at 87 Lefferts Place, a small, once-fashionable street near Bedford-Stuyvesant. The buildings re-sembled private houses, the streets were lined with trees and the neighborhood was quiet, the only business in the vicinity being Frank Campbell's funeral home across the street. In these ideal surroundings, Wright resumed his work with renewed intensity.

He now aimed to improve his almost completed first draft by shaping it according to a coherent theoretical point of view. To this end, he buried himself in books and periodicals devoted to literary criticism, among them an essay by Henry Seidel Canby on the art of the short story. He also read the stories of Hemingway and critiques of them. Jane urged him to read *Man's Hope* by Malraux and Tolstoy's *War and Peace,* although he was already familiar with both authors, and the two of them discussed at length the technique and structure of *Man's Fate.*

Wright had very definite ideas about the form of a modern novel. A meticulous description of setting and an orderly, methodical presentation of each character in turn were all very well for a Victorian novel, but nowadays, he felt, the action should take off from the very first line and move ahead rapidly, without interruption. For this reason Wright was not at all satisfied with his opening scene—the dialogue between Bigger and his friends, who are looking for a way to find some money for the movies—but so far he had not been able to think of anything better.

Wright's friend Theodore Ward was also around at this stage of composition, and although he may have exaggerated the help he provided, there is no doubt that he acted as a stimulus. Ted had come to New York to work for the Federal Theatre and, as a result of visiting Richard the day after his arrival from Chicago, had rented an attic room in the Newton house. Ward was a great traveler and more of a man of the world than Wright at that time, and perhaps he had a more practical view of the writer's profession. He suggested some stylistic changes and dug out a recording of "Life Is Like a Mountain Railroad" so that Wright would use the correct words for the song that Mrs. Thomas sings to herself. Wright enjoyed listening to Ward's records because they fired his imagination, and soon after this period, early in 1939, he was proudly able to read to his friends the splendid opening scene in which Bigger kills the rat in the kitchen of his family's small apartment. He recalls this moment in "How Bigger Was Born":

At first I rejected the idea of Bigger battling with a rat in his room; I was afraid that the rat would "hog" the scene. But the rat would not leave me, he presented himself in many attractive guises. So, cautioning myself to allow the rat scene to disclose *only* Bigger, his family, their little room, and their relationships, I let the rat walk in and he did his stuff (p. 50).

Paul Reynolds had meanwhile had time to read the first version of the novel very carefully. He pointed out several weak points, among them the character of Jan and his pardon of Bigger, some unbelievable aspects in Mary's character, the very small number of servants in the Dalton household and, in particular, their extreme naïveté in trusting a new chauffeur to bring their daughter home alone in the middle of the night. Wright valued the intelligent and penetrating comments of his agent and tried to adapt his own vision to the demands of verisimilitude. He did not, however, modify his text to any great extent, although he promised to produce a better balance between the two conflicting forces in a new novel that he was already contemplating.[8]

With the completion of the short scene in which Bigger takes leave of his family and the world in his prison cell, the second draft was finished, leaving only minor revisions to be done. Every day a typist would come and gradually copy the manuscript to be delivered to Harper's. The floor was strewn with papers and the air reeked of glue, since Wright used to type out even the smallest correction and paste it onto the second draft so that his typist would find it easy to read. He used this system with practically all his subsequent books. In this revision, the author condensed the novel a good deal at the same time that he emphasized certain points, developing in particular the theme of guilt.[9]

On June 10, 1939, Wright wrote to Reynolds that the final manuscript would be ready to send to Aswell. That evening, Richard, Ted, Jane and a few neighbors read the entire novel out loud, celebrating the occasion far into the small hours of the night to the sound of a prelude by Shostakovich, which shook the walls as the phonograph blared it forth.

Native Son was handed in the following day and Wright received the galleys the very next month, since the Book-of-the-Month Club had decided to make it their September selection. They then put it off until December. With the help of Frances Bauman, Wright feverishly went over the proofs during October, only to have the publication again postponed until February and finally March. Members of the Club were given a choice between *Native Son* and, to satisfy the more conservative readership, *The Trees* by Conrad Richter.

In this way Wright became the first black novelist to benefit from the Book-of-the-Month Club's large circulation. In addition, Harper's announced the publication of their future best-seller with a sizable publicity campaign, while Dorothy Canfield Fisher wrote an introduction to the novel pointing out the significance of Wright's social message and his greatness as he grappled with a truly Dostoevskian theme.

2

The publication of *Native Son* on March 1, 1940, made Richard Wright one of the great names among American novelists of the forties. Expecting the worst, Wright discovered that his dire predictions had been totally unfounded.

Since a book which presented racial and social problems in such direct and scathing language would never be judged on literary merit alone, the critics were bound to use different criteria depending upon their political leanings, their conception of literature and their race. The first extremely favorable reactions set the tone, however. The *New York Post* announced on the very day of publication that *Native Son* deserved all the literary prizes, and on March 25, as part of a clever publicity campaign, both *The New York Times* and the *Herald Tribune* saluted "*The Grapes of Wrath* 1940" and "a black *American Tragedy*." The time was right for a great success; the public was finally ready to face the enormous problem which the economic crisis had revealed in all its urgency, while, in the literary domain, the realism of Steinbeck, with his sympathies for the "underdog," had paved the way for Wright's big-hearted naturalism. The enthusiasm of Henry Seidel Canby, who introduced the book to the Book-of-the-Month Club readers, was echoed in numerous magazines and daily newspapers. Lewis Gannett, Charles Poore, Clifton Fadiman and Malcolm Cowley, along with the critics of *Newsweek* and *Time*, all sang its praises, comparing Wright with Dreiser, Dostoevsky, Steinbeck and Dickens.[10] They particularly stressed the importance of his message and the irresistible force of

Signed photograph at the time
of *Native Son*

the prose, which compelled the reader to finish the novel in one
sitting. Wright was acclaimed as one of the most perceptive social
critics of his time and hailed for his exceptional command of dramatic narrative.

The first reactions of the black press were just as enthusiastic,
although sometimes less unequivocal. The *Chicago Defender* and
the *New York Amsterdam News*, as well as a few daily papers with
wide black circulations, published their reviews only toward the
middle of March.[11] Black readers were often torn between their
legitimate pride in the literary fame of one of their own people
and regret that he should have destroyed their protective shield of
respectability. The choice of such an antisocial black protagonist,
so near the bottom of the social ladder, was bound to confirm the
racists' prejudice that the black man was a beast lusting after white
women. The more enlightened understood, however, that the novel
might bring at least the liberal whites to realize the gravity of the
problem. Certain people's reactions were anxiously awaited. Alain
Locke finally applauded Wright's sincerity and James Ivy, speaking
for the NAACP, found nothing with which to reproach the novelist.[12]

Meanwhile, the encouraging reception from the critics rapidly stimulated sales to an unexpected high. In many bookstores stock was depleted in a matter of hours. The novel sold 200,000 copies in under three weeks, breaking a twenty-year record at Harper's.[13] Wright suddenly found himself famous; he was called the "sepia Steinbeck," two pages of *Current Biography* were devoted to him [14] and the citizens of Memphis cabled congratulation to their "adopted son," although their warmth was by now superfluous. When the New York World's Fair opened two months later, Wright's name figured on the "Wall of Fame" reserved for Americans of foreign, Indian or Negro origin, next to those of Phyllis Wheatley, Paul Laurence Dunbar, James Weldon Johnson, W. E. B. DuBois, Marian Anderson and Ethel Waters. Everyone asked Wright for interviews, talks, autographs. His fan mail was voluminous, ranging from strangers offering their friendly congratulations, to readers asking him agonizing questions on how they could help "solve the black problem," although he also received some letters of protest and insult.[15]

This whirlwind of activity left Wright hardly any time to write. His review of Erskine Caldwell's *Trouble in July* for the *New Republic* had been completed some time before, as had the text of his lecture for the Schomburg Collection in Harlem. He had agreed to give a talk there, although he had refused to give other lectures that would have been more prestigious and well-paid, because the curator, L. D. Reddick, and the librarians, Miss R. Rose and Miss Jean Blackwell, were his friends and because he wanted to reach a select and influential black audience. The *New York Amsterdam News* of April 16 reported that after being introduced by Henry Seidel Canby, Wright spoke on the creation and writing of *Native Son*, which later became the article "How Bigger Was Born." On March 12, he gave the same lecture at the Institute of Arts and Sciences at Columbia University, before attending an enormous cocktail party given by Harper's in his honor at the home of Eugene Saxton.

Meanwhile the novel was being eagerly and passionately read, criticized or defended in all regions and social circles of the country. Libraries placed it next to the Afro-American classics and it even helped a lawyer prevent the eviction of his unemployed client.[16]

The actual drama of *Native Son*, which sometimes attains an unbearable intensity, is deliberately kept simple in order to symbolize as forcefully as possible the plight of black immigrants in the ghetto.

Born in Mississippi, Bigger Thomas lives with his widowed mother and sister in one of the South Side's miserable "kitchenettes." Bigger's discovery of a rat in the kitchen one morning, and his violence in killing it, quickly establish the poverty of this family and the tensions racking the adolescent torn between the religious resignation of his mother and the revolt of the gang to which he belongs. A conversation between Bigger and his friend Gus then reveals the common hatred of Whites that motivates them, while their hysterical fight, ostensibly to prevent the gang from robbing the store of a Jew but really to hide Bigger's lack of courage, shows how much the ever-present terror keeps their hatred under control.

Bigger finally is offered a job, via welfare, which his duty to his family as well as a certain pride lead him to accept, although he is reluctant to join the very society that is oppressing him. During an interview with the wealthy family whose chauffeur he is to be, he sees the luxury of the white world, which he had previously only known from the movies. Mrs. Dalton, who is blind, is a typical liberal while her daughter Mary, in her adolescent revolt against the bourgeois life of her parents, has a Communist boy friend and fancies herself a progressive. Her well-meaning but ignorant intentions as she affects to treat Bigger as an equal only confuse him and increase his resentment. It is an unbearable ordeal for Bigger when Mary and her boyfriend, Jan, invite him to eat at their table in a restaurant in the ghetto where everyone knows him. When Mary gets back home and is too drunk even to walk, Bigger takes it upon himself to carry her upstairs to her room. He is panicked by the unexpected and ghostly appearance of her blind mother, and in order to prevent Mary from crying out he inadvertently suffocates her.

Realizing the full meaning of his action, which he accepts as murder, Bigger struggles with the problem, then reacts to the urgency of his situation and burns the body in the furnace, using all his ingenuity to turn suspicion away from himself. His crime, however, has become his first creative act, and in his euphoria he dreams of further revenge. Thus he asks for ransom, not so much to get rich as to prove his power, and his second murder—to silence his black mistress, Bessie, whom he beats to death with a brick for fear she will give him away—confirms his criminal destiny. With the dis-

covery of Mary's remains, a manhunt of gigantic proportions has
been initiated. The fugitive is tracked, trapped and finally captured
by a hysterical crowd among some ramshackle houses of the ghetto.
The third and final section of the novel, consisting of Bigger's sor-
rowful meditations, goes from the capture to the execution and
contrasts with the excitement and drama of the preceding scenes.
He reaches a new understanding of his fate as explained through
his lawyer, Max. Rejected and oppressed all his life, can Bigger still
be saved? Can he be reached and helped to rejoin society, thus
preventing his execution from being a simple annihilation? The boy
had always scorned religion because of his mother; here, embodied
by Pastor Hammond, it fails. Jan's friendship and pardon, on the
other hand, encourage Bigger to accept the help of Max, a lawyer
from the International Labor Defense, although his family's visit to
the Daltons fills him with shame. It is during this final ordeal, in
which Bigger is led from the reconstruction of his crime to the death
sentence, that he gradually discovers the meaning of his life and
plants the seeds of a positive relationship with Jan and Max.

In the structure of the novel and portrayal of the characters
Wright made few innovations, depending primarily upon the proven
techniques of the realistic novel. He had also returned to Chicago
for the setting in order to insure the accuracy of the topography,
thus showing a concern for naturalism that the critics did not fail
to appreciate. But just as important, though not as obviously so,
was the role of symbolism, which was inspired by Wright's reading
and carefully examined during numerous discussions at the Newtons'. Wright weaves a network of themes through the use of tem-
perature, color and certain objects. The hostile color white, for
example, is associated with blue and yellow in opposition to the
warmth of red and black. The snow and icy blasts of wind contrast
with the comforting warmth of milk and the devouring red heat
of the coal, while the plane, the pigeon, the priest's cross (and also
the Cross of the Ku Klux Klan) and the rat all assume a metaphoric
meaning that prolongs their role in the action of the novel. This,
in fact, is the basis of one of the most striking if not original devices of Wright's narrative: the use of a symbolic detail or episode
to announce a crisis or future event. The killing of the rat in
the first scene foreshadows other murders, while the rat itself sym-
bolizes the family's poverty as well as Bigger's fierce hatred and
the enormous forces that confront him. Eventually, too, Bigger

himself will be caught like a rat. Along with these metaphoric underscorings the repetition of key words contributes to the unity of the rapid and tight prose, while one scene leads into the next less from causal relationships than from the continuity (or discontinuity) of the physical and emotional reactions of the protagonist. This results in their being united in the same stream, so that the story profits from additional speed and momentum.

Perhaps the most controversial literary device was the deliberate and exclusive use of Bigger's point of view. This automatically caused the black characters to come alive, while reducing the Whites to stereotypes, since Bigger always remains an outsider to their world. Although it implies a bias, this limitation is in fact an end in itself, almost a symbol, since no other technique could have emphasized so effectively the gap between the two races. The white audience, unused to making the necessary effort to see the world through the eyes of a black man, misunderstood the author's intention, and on artistic grounds some reviewers felt they could reproach him for his superficial portrayal of the white characters. Since the novel did lose in depth and texture what it gained in unified perspective, Wright planned to use more than one point of view in his next novel.

The use of Bigger's point of view also inspired criticism on ideological grounds. Assuming that Wright, a reputed Communist, would adopt the official Party viewpoint, critics were confused by a certain ambiguity, or vagueness, in Wright's intentions, caused, it appeared, by the use of this perspective.

In fact, Wright's first ambition was to shock his public, largely the white liberals, into realizing the truth of the racial situation. He mentioned specifically, following the publication of *Uncle Tom's Children* and later in "How Bigger Was Born," that he hoped the daughters of bankers who had wept upon reading his stories would no longer have that release in his novel. He therefore felt compelled to include all the ingredients that would make *Native Son* an ideological bomb in case it would be his last chance to speak out. Thus he vehemently denounced American racism, more subtly criticized the blindness of the Communists, made pessimistic predictions about the evolution of the human personality as it underwent rapid urbanization and scorned the pious lies and solidarity of the black bourgeoisie. Wright wanted to destroy all the accepted ideas: the majority's refusal to see the extent of racism and the hatred it engenders, the illusions of the liberals, the naïvely clear conscience of the radicals and the myths of black "high society." He was, in other words, perfectly aware of the condemnation he invited. The novel, he thought, would serve as both a measure of and a judgment upon the different currents of American opinion.

Nevertheless, Wright does use Max as the spokesman for his Marxist analysis of the social situation in the United States, and he is inclined to equate racial and social prejudice as both being fostered by economic exploitation. Yet the Communist characters are not presented as faultless heroes. This is due to Wright's fundamental honesty, and not to clouded political thinking as some left-wing critics concluded during the enormous speculation on this question. Wright's liberal admirers have tended to minimize the extent and sincerity of his commitment to the Party, while many Communists reproached him for not adopting a true Communist perspective because he did not portray the masses as revolutionary. If, however, Bigger's limited perspective is adopted without reservations the ambiguity dissolves, since Wright viewed communism as only a means for black liberation. The novel in fact becomes extremely coherent, but both liberals and Communists were white and alike failed to see that Wright gave priority to his point of view as a black man. In any case, what critics pointed out as weaknesses in certain characters cannot be blamed upon the author's limitations as a writer but were rather his means of achieving a certain effect.

At the time, of course, it was not surprising that the Communist Party was not totally satisfied with its prize writer, although the reaction was delayed for a time. Mike Gold waited almost a month before stating noncommittally in his *Sunday Worker* column, "Dick Wright Gives America a Significant Picture in 'Native Son' " (March 31, 1940). Then Samuel Sillen, for *New Masses*, decided to avoid direct criticism, while inviting controversy, by publishing a series of contradictory reactions from real and imaginary readers. This ran from April 23 to May 21, 1940, and included Chester Himes's very favorable comments. Black Communists like Benjamin Davis, Jr. (who was more powerful and intransigent than Sillen), and James W. Ford fully realized what they called the "nationalist racial spirit" of the novel and took Wright to task. Earl Browder, on the other hand, actually had no fault to find with the novel when his judgment was called upon to put an end to certain attacks.

The fact that Wright more often adopted the black point of view than that of the union of exploited workers could have been sufficient reason for official blame from the Party, but at the time they could not do without one of their most prestigious black writers.[17] On April 29, 1940, after a long silence, Mike Gold finally came to the defense of the novel in his column for the *Daily Worker*. This constituted the official Party verdict, but Wright had not missed the significance of the delay, as is apparent in this letter to Mike Gold.

To be quite frank, until you spoke up in its defense, I'd all but given up hope that our movement could look deeper into the book, that we could doff our set of stock-reactions and think creatively about it. . . .

Now, in relation to the Communist Party, there are other notions regarding writing which I had to write off before I could feel free to write. There is a proneness on the part of many Party officials to believe that the novel ought to be used in the units with the directness of an organization letter. They encourage the creation of types of writing that can be used for agitprop purposes, and they have a tendency to sneer at more imaginative attempts. . . .

There is still another notion prevailing among ninety per cent of all party members that all party comrades should be represented in fiction as white knights charging heroically into the enemy. Well, life just ain't that way; people just don't act that way. . . . An assumption which says that a Communist writer must follow well-established lines of perception and feeling, must deal with that which is readily recognizable and typical, must depict reality only in terms of how it looks from a common and collective plane of reality, . . . might seem sound. But I think those who put forward this reasoning forget the international framework in which we live and struggle today. We are in a race with the Nazis, who today possess the offensive. . . . Are we Communist writers to be confined merely to the political and economic spheres of reality and leave the dark and hidden places of the human personality to the Hitlers and Goebbels? I refuse to believe such. . . . Not to plunge into the complex jungle of human relationships and analyze them is to leave the field to the fascists and I won't and can't do that. If I should follow Ben Davis's advice and write of Negroes through the lens of how the Party views them in terms of political theory, I'd abandon the Bigger Thomases. I'd be tacitly admitting that they are lost to us, that fascism will triumph because it alone can enlist the allegiance of those millions whom capitalism has crushed and maimed.

In this long letter, probably written in May of that year, he supplies a passionate but coherent vindication of his plan.

I do not agree with Ben Davis when he implies that the majority of the Negroes are with the labor movement. Such an implication can become a tragedy as grave as that which the German working class made in estimating Hitler's chances for success. My aim in depicting Jan was to show that even for that great Party which has thrown down a challenge to America on the Negro Question such as has no other party, there is much, much to do, and, above all, to understand. . . .

Despite all the heroic struggles the Party has put forward to win the Negro, it is still possible for a wave of nationalism to sweep the Negro people today.[18]

Wright complained that Bigger's humanity, so obvious to him, meant so little to them, and that Ben Davis thought Max should have pleaded "not guilty." He even blamed the narrow Communist vision for fostering illusions.

The *Daily Worker* certainly could not publish such a letter, but it does reveal the realism of Wright's political vision and the scope of his literary goals. These words also contain the germs of dissent, hidden but growing, which eventually caused his rupture with the Party.

After the first wave of enthusiasm had passed, other discordant voices began to be heard among the chorus of praise that had greeted the publication of *Native Son*. In *The American Mercury* of May, 1940, Burton Rascoe stated,

Sanely considered, it is impossible for me to conceive of a novel's being worse, in the most important respects, than *Native Son*. . . . There are faults in this novel which even a tyro in fiction should not be guilty of.[19]

According to him, the message should have emerged from the action and dialogue so as not to appear as the commentary of the author. Ignorant and oppressed by society, Bigger would never have been able to perceive so clearly the forces overwhelming him, and since his reactions differed from those that the author would have had under similar circumstances, Wright had violated a fundamental principle of the Aristotelian aesthetic. After this partially valid criticism, Rascoe lost all control, declaring that Wright was very wrong to vilify the Whites who had recognized his talent so enthusiastically and were making his fortune. He went on to deny that an American Negro would encounter any more obstacles than the majority of Whites and to declare that the moral of the novel was not only shocking but unsubstantiated. Wright's scathing reply condemned American pseudo-liberalism, while Rascoe, to have the last word, accused the author of Stalinism.

At the same time, and conceivably as part of a simultaneous attack, the *Atlantic Monthly* published a review dismissing *Native Son* as the expression of an unjustified hatred, since, it claimed, the Blacks were not deprived of their political rights in the South. The article concluded that since the racial problem was insoluble anyway, everyone for the time being should adjust to the status quo during the continuing search for longterm justice, using the patience of the Jewish nation as an example. Wright's reply, "I Bite the Hand That Feeds Me," [20] combined an almost prophetic vehemence with another excellent statement of his position on the racial question and his intentions in creating the character of Bigger. This was a partial recapitulation of his lecture at the Schomburg Collection, which the *Saturday Review of Literature* published with a few minor cuts on June 7 as "How Bigger Was Born." The following month Harper's published the complete version of thirty-nine pages, indicating March 7 as the original date of composition. Wright was not merely giving the behind-the-scenes story of the several stages in the composition of the novel, nor a reminiscence of his youth. Rather, he wanted his public to realize the dangerous potential of the black *Lumpenproletariat,* wavering between fascism and communism. As a sophisticated analysis of the psychology of oppression and the possibilities of adapting literary techniques to social and political protest, this essay is one of the most valuable that Wright ever produced in the period between "Blueprint for Negro Writing" and *White Man, Listen!*

TEN

ALTHOUGH the writing and reception of *Native Son* occupied a good deal of Wright's time and energy during 1939–40, additional literary and political activities were vying for the attention he spared from his personal life, which was also in a state of flux.

At the beginning of 1939, he had received an O. Henry Memorial Award of $200 for his story "Fire and Cloud." The jury, made up of the critics Irita Van Doren, Frederic March and Edward Weeks, gave the first prize to Albert Maltz's "The Happiest Man on Earth" but gave Wright's story second prize in preference to "The Promise" by John Steinbeck, which won third prize.[1]

In April, 1939, Eleanor Roosevelt was one of the first to congratulate him for getting a Guggenheim Fellowship; other winners were John Steinbeck, Robert Penn Warren and Harold A. Sinclair, but Wright was the only black recipient. The $2500 was to cover a year's work starting from May 18, 1939, and since he had almost finished *Native Son,* the reason he had given for applying the previous year, he had to begin work on another novel. This book, he stated at the time, would be set in Harlem and Brooklyn and would have three principal themes: the situation of women in the big cities, the working conditions of the domestic help, and the role of religion in the feminine mentality.[2]

In fact the project was already fairly well advanced, since Wright had sent Reynolds his outline summary of five pages before the end of March, soon after his preliminary letter of March 7, in which he had explained,

I'm already gathering material for a new novel, another long one. Most of my characters are already definitely in mind and the bare outline of the plot is taking shape. . . . I'm working out a scheme whereby white and black characters can be shown on an equal plane and with equal emphasis and detail. In "Native Son" I gave the picture of the world from the point of view of Bigger alone and

188

the unreality of the white characters was part of the movement of the story, that is, they formed the motive for Bigger's acting towards them in such a strange way. Had Bigger seen them as *people,* the deeds, the crimes he committed would have been impossible. What I've done is to give the black world at the expense of the white. I felt, when I first started writing, a sort of personal need to do this, a need which I don't feel now.[3]

The plot was also more ambitious and complex than that of *Native Son*, covering many years and including eleven characters. Six of these would play a major role, and five of the eleven were white.

Maud Hampton, a twenty-seven-year-old mulatto woman, becomes ill and is prohibited by her doctor from continuing the job as a welfare worker that she has held since she graduated from college. She then decides to pass as a white woman in order to get a job as companion to a banker, Cleveland Spencer, who is paralyzed. In this capacity she hires Ollie Knight, a black girl, as a servant via a shady employment agency that allows her to keep part of the woman's salary. One day Maud's race is discovered by accident and disclosed to the servants as well as to Spencer's lawyer, Henry Beach. The chauffeur, Freddy, who is in love with Maud and hopes to gain her favor, persuades everyone including his mother, Clara, the cook, to keep the matter quiet. Meanwhile, the banker has made Maud guardian of his daughter and heiress to his fortune, a fact which Beach uses to pressure Maud: she should poison Spencer, he urges, and, profiting from his wealth, begin to enjoy her life. Maud follows this advice and starts to mingle in New York society. She cannot, of course, maintain her position without the complicity of Beach and all the Negro servants, while she loves Freddy without being able to bring herself to abandon everything and flee with him. Tortured by remorse, unable to extricate herself from Beach's blackmail and in pain from the progressive deterioration of her health, she finally commits suicide, leaving her possessions to Ollie, the poor servant whom she had originally exploited. Her magnificent house becomes the office for an interracial union of domestic servants.

This outline shows a variation on the "tragic mulatto" theme so popular with the early-twentieth-century Afro-American novelists. Although Maud finds herself caught between the two races, her principal concern is her role as a woman, and the racial aspect of her dilemma merely supplies the pivot for the plot. Wright did not set out to describe the place of women in modern society as a piece of "feminist" propaganda, but he cannot help concluding that they are victims more often than not. The moral of the ending, with its socialist implications, does not submerge Wright's main interest in portraying Maud's inner conflicts, which are aggravated but not produced by her social and racial position.

Considering Wright's difficulties in portraying Jan, Reynolds advised him to stick to the types of Whites that he knew well. He also emphasized how difficult it would be to portray Beach and introduce a woman like Maud into New York society realistically. Wright was grateful for these warnings and gave his agent carte blanche to negotiate the contract for the novel, which he then entitled "Little Sister."

By December, 1939, he had written more than five hundred pages of the rough draft and a letter to Reynolds on February 6, 1940, indicates that he gave him a first version of nine hundred pages on that date. His plan had changed somewhat. What he had originally intended as the study of a particular black woman he now hoped to turn into a study of the feminine personality in general, as it developed from feudalism to fascism. He hoped to do this not by changing the plot a great deal, but by lending certain characters a more symbolic dimension.

I spoke of inserting a section dealing with Maud's early life and childhood. Well, that section can depict a picture of feudal life that exists right here in our own America, that is, the present plantation system in the South. I can trace the developing growth of Maud from the plantation to the time when she meets Beach, who gradually turns fascist in the novel.[4]

Wright was counting upon the enlightened comments of his agent to help him accomplish this.

The relationship between the two men had always been good and they were now on excellent terms. Carl Van Vechten's photograph of Wright occupied a prominent position in Reynolds' office, and to the great joy of his friend the curator L. D. Reddick, Wright had persuaded Reynolds to give to the Schomburg Library a large collection of Paul Laurence Dunbar's letters to Paul Reynolds, Sr. Wright, in any case, never hesitated to ask his agent's advice on literary questions, and Reynolds' wise and tactful suggestions were valuable to a young writer still ignorant of the demands of editors and of many facts about the white world that he was trying to describe. Reynolds in fact thought the novel somewhat ungainly, and he suggested certain changes in his letter of January 18, which Wright made immediately, although he eventually abandoned "Little Sister," as well as a later version, "Black Hope."

At about the same time, Reynolds told Wright that a company in Hollywood needed someone to write the screenplay for a film on Booker T. Washington. Admitting that he had never read *Up from Slavery,* Wright did not commit himself on the worth of the project, but he was particularly afraid that he would not be able to speak his mind on what he considered the unjustifiable gradualism of this former leader.[5]

2

Although Wright's grant meant that he was able to quit working for the F.W.P. on May 18, 1939, he had fought long and hard under the auspices of the union for the Federal Arts Bill, which was supposed to prolong the life of the Project. In February, 1939, he had even helped Albert Maltz, Millen Brand and George Seldes organize the "Pink Slip Cabaret" to set up an emergency fund for writers who were laid off. He was also still on the list of lecturers for *New Masses* at that time, but he does not seem to have spoken for them. However on April 20, he participated in a round table radio discussion on "Can We Depend upon Youth to Follow the American Way?" He offered one long contribution, speaking as both a young Black and a young writer, in which he deplored the effects of massive industrialization on the new generation and eloquently condemned economic and racial discrimination.[6]

Now that he had the Guggenheim, Wright was even more in demand for literary and cultural events. On May 6, he presided over a meeting of the Harlem Cultural Congress held at the Black Community Art Center, taking part in a debate on Afro-American arts and letters with Alain Locke, Countee Cullen, Langston Hughes and Warren Cochrane. On May 12, he spoke on "Negro Contributions to American Culture" at an evening organized by the Committee on Civic Affairs at the YMCA in Brooklyn, which was followed by a reading of black poetry and a program of spirituals sung by Leonard Franklin, the star of *Four Saints in Three Acts* by Gertrude Stein.

Among the signatures on the appeal to attend the third American Writers' Congress published in *Direction*, its new official organ, Wright's figured prominently, along with those of seventeen other Party authors. The Congress itself was more than ever before a great Party meeting rather than a cultural event. Thomas Mann, who had fled Nazi Germany, was the honorary president of the opening session on June 2, 1939, and Donald Ogden Stewart, Louis Bromfield and Louis Aragon, representing France, were speakers. In his report on the activities of the League for the June 20 issue of *New Masses*, Samuel Sillen remarked on its significant expansion, but less than three months before the German-Soviet pact, the Communists were already being criticized by the intellectuals on the Left. Disputes flared up more frequently and a certain number of writers had actually left the party and were openly attacking Stalinism. In the spring a half-dozen of them, among them John Dewey, Sidney Hook and Eugene Lyons, had founded a Committee for Cultural Freedom and had published an anti-Soviet statement signed by one hundred and fifty writers including Louis Adamic, Max Eastman, Sherwood Anderson, Sinclair Lewis, Claude McKay and John Dos Passos, to name a few. Thus, the Congress was partly intended to rally those writers who were still faithful to the Communists.

By this time Wright was no longer on the editorial board of *New Masses* or a member of the lecture committee, but if he did not participate in many official activities, he at least did not balk at letting the Party use his name, as on a statement drawn up by the Defense Committee of the U.S.S.R. and which appeared in the *Daily Worker* of August 10 and *The Nation* of August 23. This "Letter to All Active Supporters of Democracy and Peace—answering those who are attempting to destroy the unity of the progressive forces by spreading the false idea that the Soviet Union and the totalitarian states are fundamentally alike" was prompted by an attack from the new Committee for Cultural Freedom. Ironically, the same issue of *The Nation* announced the signing of the Soviet-German pact, and a few days later several more Communist intellectuals, including Vincent Sheean, Ralph Bates and Granville Hicks, resigned from the Party. Although Wright, too, was far from agreeing with all the Party's decisions, he saw that the Left in America was divided and he did not think it would be possible to combat fascism efficiently without belonging to a large and well-run Party organization.

It was during this summer, then, that Wright wrote an unpublished article entitled "There Are Still Men Left," a defense of the most superficially upsetting aspects of Stalinism.

What does fasten my attention upon Communist action is whether it overcomes settled and ready-made reality, whether it effectively pushes outward and extends the area of human feeling, not like a book or a work of art, but *really,* whether it illuminates new possibilities for human life (sometimes I find myself most deeply attracted to it when most people are repelled—that is, for instance, when the USSR signed the pact with Nazi Germany) and creates incalculable surprises.

Wright already had the conception of communism that he later developed in *The Outsider,* although by then his conclusions were negative. Communism was an ideology, a way of life, which went beyond the boundaries of existence to approach a true cultural revolution. In a sense, it was not subject to moral judgments:

The rightness or wrongness of a given set of tactical actions by the Communist Party does not strike me as being of any great ultimate importance. . . . It takes a more integral order of feeling to accept what is happening in Europe from the angle of the USSR than the Hicks, Sheeans and Bateses possess. They are rebels against capitalism; the ones who . . . are contemptuously referred to as the "faithful" are rebels against the limits of life, the limits of experience as they know it. They are (and not in a mystical or religious sense) striving against the world.

Thus, for the time being, although his opinions were not always orthodox on the subject of recent events, Wright remained faithful to the Party. He welcomed Paul Robeson back from Europe at a reception given in his honor on October 13, and he opened classes at the Writers' School of the League, speaking on "Problems for the Writer of Today." During the winter he differed with Dreiser, who was a staunch defender of Russia's intervention in Finland,[7] nevertheless, he let the *Daily Worker* publish his statement against black participation in the war and aid to occupied Finland.[8]

As far as his literary career was concerned, the year ended well. "Bright and Morning Star" was chosen for two anthologies—*Best Short Stories of 1939,* which was dedicated to Richard Wright and Jesse Stuart, and *Fifty Best American Short Stories (1914–1939),* both edited by Edward O'Brien. Theodore Ward had meanwhile written a stage adaptation of it, and together they had approached Ethel Waters, one of the wealthiest black actresses of the time, for financial help in putting on the play. She unfortunately was afraid to risk supporting a project that might offend the white audience. Later, when Miss Waters, who had given each actor appearing with her in *Mamba's Daughter* a copy of *Native Son,* asked Wright to come and autograph them in the theater, he excused himself by saying that he was going to be out of town, perhaps not unhappy at the chance to make the famous actress feel how ill-advised she had been to refuse to help produce a militant play.[9] Meanwhile, the Harlem Suitcase Theatre, which had been founded with Wright's help, decided to put on "Fire and Cloud." Rehearsals began at the Little Theatre on August 11, 1939, but the undertaking fell through from lack of funds. On the other hand, *Uncle Tom's Children,* which was already being studied in courses at Columbia University, was chosen by the editors of *The Nation* as one of the ten best books of the year, and the national press of the U.S.S.R. printed 75,000 copies of the translation during the winter, with an enthusiastic preface by Isidor Schneider.

Since Wright was busy writing *Native Son* during that year, he published very little. But "Red Clay Blues," a short poem that he wrote in collaboration with Langston Hughes, did appear in the August 1 issue of *New Masses.* Using a blues rhythm, it describes the nostalgia of a black immigrant whose sensitive feet cannot get used to the pavements of the ghetto after the clay of the Georgia fields. The South was also a setting for a story that Wright sold to *Harper's Bazaar* in November, 1939. It was actually his friend Willard Maas, head of the literary section when *New Masses* had published "Bright and Morning Star," who persuaded George Davis, the editor of *Harper's Bazaar,* to ask Wright for a manuscript. Wright brought out the end of "Tarbaby's Dawn" and, for lack of time, asked Marie Mencken, Maas's wife, to extract a story from it.[10]

3

Margaret Walker was among the Chicago friends whom Wright saw again during the L.A.W. Congress. The two had corresponded regularly since he had come to New York, and she had done a great deal for him during this time, not only getting subscriptions to *New Challenge* but writing comforting and perceptive letters to him during the period when his novels were being rejected, and sending him clippings about the Nixon case for the documentation of *Native Son*. As far as he was concerned she was a devoted friend with deep feelings for him, but in her frankness, she apparently committed indiscretions which almost lost Wright some of his friends in Chicago, with the result that her visit, which could have been a happy reunion, in fact marked the date when Wright withdrew from her. She would certainly not have suffered such shock and disappointment if Wright had admitted to her sooner that he was in love with and on the point of marrying someone else.[11]

Wright's emotional and sexual experiences up to this point not only determined his eventual choice of a companion but even affected his literary career. They are often reflected in his fiction, especially in *The Outsider,* where in contrast to the somewhat negative characters of Damon's black wife and black mistress, Eva emerges as the portrait closest to Wright's idealized, if not ideal, woman.

In Chicago, apart from his affair with the illiterate young black woman during the several months that he sold insurance, he had had other affairs, numerous though brief, usually with the white progressives or Communist sympathizers of the John Reed Club. He also knew a number of well-educated, pretty, intelligent black girls, such as Fern Gayden, Alberta Sims, Deborah Smith and Margaret Walker, who corresponded to the type of woman he could have married.[12] Since his arrival in New York, he had had many relationships with girls and married women of both races, and in February, 1938, he was even on the point of marrying a girl from a black bourgeois family in Brooklyn; her father, however, would not consider a "penniless writer" for a son-in-law.

When Wright rented a room from the Sawyers in Harlem, he found that his landlady was extremely obliging and that her house was a real home for him. The daughter, Marion, a frail and gracious adolescent with a pale olive complexion, was the object of attentions from another older lodger. Since she was timid and reserved, Wright got into the habit of acting as her chaperone, coming down into the kitchen if he thought the other man might be importuning her. In return Marion took him into her confidence, telling him about an unfortunate sexual experience she had suffered in her childhood. In this way they soon became intimate, although Richard scarcely realized that he was emotionally involved. He introduced her to Jane Newton as "a girlfriend," but soon afterward, to Jane's complete astonishment, he told her that they had decided to get married.

For Wright, who was by now a famous author, to choose a practically illiterate girl from a very modest Harlem background was in itself surprising, but it was possibly his resentment at having been rejected by a middle-class family that caused him to look for a wife among the people. Now that he was thirty and had never known the joy of family life, he would naturally want to start a home of his own, but even supposing that he had a strong physical attraction to Marion, the girl's self-effacing personality was not at all likely to impress him. He was not the type of man to give in to pure compassion, nor did they have to get married. Nevertheless, Mrs. Sawyer soon sent out cards to their friends announcing the wedding for Sunday, May 22, 1938.

On May 12, however, Richard burst into the Newton household announcing that according to the prenuptial physical examination, Marion had an advanced case of syphilis. Wright seemed simultaneously outraged that he had been deceived and relieved that he had escaped from such a grave danger. He broke completely with Marion, although her illness was congenital and not communicable. His physical and moral revulsion, no doubt, was due to his puritanical upbringing, in which shameful diseases were associated with "bad women," but it also indicated that he had little true attachment to Marion, much less love. Perhaps he felt that fate had saved him from falling into a trap. In any case, as Mrs. Sawyer wrote to Jane Newton a few days later, the wedding was "postponed indefinitely." [13] This episode left only a faint literary trace in Wright's work. Perhaps a belated feeling of remorse inspired him, shortly before his death, to create a hero (in "A Father's Law") who feels guilty for having morally murdered his fiancée after abandoning her when he discovered that she had syphilis; his subsequent criminal career is the result of his need to be punished for this original crime.

Wright's immediate reaction was flight, not remorse, since a few days later he moved in with the Newtons in Brooklyn.

It is understandable that Wright would take care not to get involved soon again, and he went back to having short and casual affairs. After the end of his friendship with Margaret Walker, he seems to have become interested in Jean Blackwell, a librarian at the Schomburg Collection. She had visited Russia and been a member of the John Reed Club, but did not belong to the Party. Wright found her attractive and intelligent, but it was symptomatic that he associated her with the black bourgeoisie, which he still resented. He felt ill at ease in that milieu, which seemed false and pretentious. Nevertheless, during the same period, he had a passionate affair with the beautiful wife of a funeral home director. Tired of her pedestrian husband, she fell deeply in love with her imaginative admirer, and although he eventually tired of this beauty without brains, her gaiety afforded him all the tranquility and relaxation he could have hoped for during the composition of *Native Son*.

There is no doubt that Wright's hesitations were caused by his attraction to the many different attributes which he hoped to find in one woman, and, with time, he turned more and more toward white women. This was his revenge for the years of sexual and emotional frustration during adolescence; he certainly felt additional pleasure in flouting the taboos that, for a black man in Mississippi, were the equivalent of a castration. To possess a white woman was a way of eradicating painful memories, even though a black man suffered many humiliations in her company at New York restaurants and other public places. Such interracial affairs represented, therefore, adventure in both meanings of the word.

In addition to being a means of revenge and easy prey, women fascinated Wright as an author; he wanted to know how adulterous wives were able to live with their dull husbands. He himself was demanding and tyrannical, often pitiless, with anyone who loved him unreservedly, and he never scrupled to accept what was offered him. He asked for a great deal but gave a great deal of himself in return to those who knew how to appreciate it. Apparently he was still unsure of his own feelings, and while he posed as a mature man, he actually charmed everyone with his distinction, reserve and the somewhat timid adolescent air that he carefully sought to conceal. His apparent coolness was in fact his way of preserving privacy, and it masked a great need for tenderness, although he disliked any open motherliness in a woman. A woman had to retain some aura of mystery (an intricate and calculated style of dress fascinated him, for example), but she also had to be his intellectual peer, although he rarely talked about politics and literature outside of male company. He could not completely relax in an atmosphere of feminine frivolity, and this once caused him to exclaim somewhat regretfully: "I cannot rest, I can only write."

Certainly Wright's behavior differed according to the woman he was with, but it does partially explain how his past determined and restricted his choice of wife, although he may not have realized it then.

In fact, the time was coming to an end when adventures that merely satisfied his desire and flattered his vanity would be enough for Wright. He wanted to find a companion for life. By this time it was clear that his wife could never be a black girl, whether a bourgeoise or an intellectual. She would have to have a well-defined personality and, in addition to being cultured and intelligent, she would have to be interested in politics, while also being affectionate and desirable.

At the beginning of 1939, Wright met two women who seemed to fulfill most of these requirements. He first saw Ellen Poplar at the Newtons' after a political meeting. Ellen lived in Brooklyn and was in charge of the local Party organization, a position of great responsibility, under the direction of James W. Ford himself. With her lively air, hazel eyes and bright face framed by auburn curls, she was extremely attractive, while her well-adjusted personality, the seriousness of her commitment and her reserve impressed Wright, who was somewhat accustomed to young girls, and Whites in particular, making advances toward him. When Ellen came back to report to Jane about other cell meetings, Wright found that she put her political responsibilities ahead of romance. Weeks passed before he finally got a chance to chat romantically with her at a party, but by spring, 1939, he was so in love that he attended the political meetings of Ellen's sections and went to hear her speak in public just for the pleasure of being in her company.

At about the same time, Wright became fascinated by Dhimah Rose Meadman, a young divorcée. He was impressed by her noble bearing, strong personality and artistic talents. Dhimah shared a large apartment on Hamilton Terrace with her mother and her two-year-old son, Peter Woolman, whose father was English. Her mother, Utis, had formerly been an actress and now worked in the administration of the Ladies Garment Workers Union. Although Dhimah was a Jewess of Russian origin, she actually looked rather Egyptian, tall, with dark brown hair and a distinguished presence.[14] Like her mother, she was attracted to the glitter of theatrical life and had become a ballet dancer. She had studied choreography in the U.S.S.R. and now ran a small modern dance class more or less under the aegis of the Party.

Richard probably felt that as an artist, she would have no reason to envy him, and as an experienced woman, she would have no need for his protection. He admired her independence and would expect her to feel the same toward his. Physically he was very attracted to Dhimah, but he still hesitated to marry her. When Wright moved into the room next to his friend Theodore Ward at 809 St. Nicholas Avenue in May, 1939, he confided his indecision and asked Ward to meet Dhimah and give his impression of her. He also asked his friend Ralph Ellison to advise him in a similar way.[15]

Apparently Wright was more drawn toward Dhimah at this crucial time because he felt that Ellen would refuse to marry him. He had never openly asked her, but they had had a long conversation about the qualities and the strength necessary to maintain an interracial marriage. In addition to mutual love and tastes, the couple needed unusually strong nerves and powers of self-denial. A white woman who married a black man would, in most cases, cut herself off from her family and many of her friends. She would also expose herself to the jealousy of black women and the scorn of both racial communities. It was a choice more difficult for the woman than the man and Ellen wanted time to think about it.

The youngest of three children, Ellen had been born in Manhattan, in 1912 (making her four years younger than Richard), only a short time before her parents, Polish Jews, were naturalized.[16] She lived at home and her parents did not approve at all of her political activities, which had already created a great deal of tension. She had fallen in love with Richard the first time she had met him, and in spite of her family's opposition, had proved her affection by often spending the night with him in his room in Harlem. The basis of their relationship had always been clear; since they were united by their common interest in communism and literature, Wright seemed to be sure that he had found the kind of woman he wanted as a life companion. Meanwhile, Ellen had also made up her mind but was asking for a little time to extricate herself from her family's influence before proclaiming her choice to the world. Some of this uncertainty may have been communicated to Wright, who mistakenly interpreted it as deep indecision, although he may have been in a hurry for Ellen's answer merely to resolve his own uncertainty over Dhimah. In any case, Ellen postponed giving an answer until after her summer vacation, which she was going to spend as a counselor at Unity Camp, a Party organization in upstate New York.

On her return, Ellen left her family and rented a room in Manhattan. She made a date to see Richard and tell him her decision, just in time to be told, to her complete dismay, that he was going to marry Dhimah. The wedding took place at the beginning of August, 1939, in the sacristy of the Episcopal Church on Convent Avenue, with Ralph Ellison as best man.[17] At first Richard and Dhimah lived in the enormous apartment on Hamilton Avenue, but they later moved to Crompond, New York.

In spite of the deluge of compliments, honors and fan letters that followed the publication of *Native Son,* Wright apparently remained true to himself. From among the sometimes contradictory sketches of his character drawn by interviewers there emerges a slightly different portrait from that of the aspiring but timid young writer of Chicago. Reporters tended either to remark his affability, his talents as a conversationalist and as a raconteur, or else his serious expression, cold look and resolute set of his jaw. Describing himself as "self-educated like Lincoln," he told his interviewers that from the time he had begun to devote himself seriously to writing, in 1935, he had set himself the task of exploring the virgin territory of black life in America. The public also learned about his lifelong passion for reading and his recent interest in photography and films—he sometimes went to as many as three movies a day. He also described his work habits, how slowly he wrote, the simplicity of his life and the tranquility that was necessary for a regular and conscientious life as an author.[18]

Wright mentioned his planned trip to Mexico at this time. The full life of the newly married couple, and perhaps the postponed publication date of *Native Son*, had prevented them from taking a honeymoon, but during these first few months of World War II, Wright was longing to get out of the tense atmosphere of New York. Coming upon an article by his friend Professor Lawrence Martin, who praised the charm and relatively low cost of life in Mexico, Wright became convinced that they should go there to live. He apparently left all household decisions to Dhimah who, excited by the idea, had already decided to take her son, her mother and her pianist along with them by the time that Wright asked Martin to rent them a villa in the colony of American tourists at Cuernavaca. Wright intended to relax down there while finishing up the first version of "Little Sister." [19]

In February, 1940, Wright had to lecture in Philadelphia as well as spend a few days in Chicago, where he had decided to buy a small house for his family, still living on Indiana Avenue. Even with the help of his friends Ed Gourfain and Ulysses Keys it was difficult to avoid being swindled by the real-estate brokers, who resold at exorbitant prices old houses, abandoned by Whites, that were now in the confines of the ghetto. He finally bought a suitable house at a reasonable price on Vincennes Avenue.[20] March was spent going to all the parties, interviews and lectures resulting from the publication of *Native Son*. Richard and Dhimah, who were hoping to keep this to a minimum, had moved up their departure date from April 5 to March 22 when *Life* magazine asked Wright to provide the text for an article on the South Side. Since this publicity for the book was too good to miss, he boarded his first plane on March 18, heading for Chicago with the *Life* photographers. Two days of nonstop work finished the article and the captions. During his tours around the ghetto, Wright was accompanied by the sociologist Horace Cayton. Although Wright had met Cayton in Professor Wirth's office, during the days when Mrs. Wirth was helping him, it was this second encounter that marked the beginning of their long friendship.[21]

The Wrights were finally free to leave and embarked on the *Monterey* for Veracruz, planning, after a brief stop in Havana, to enjoy the existence described by Lawrence Martin in "Life Among the Escapists." They settled into a comfortable villa at 62 Madero Street in the Miraval Colony, but quickly found the house too small to contain both Dhimah's dance practice, to piano accompaniment, and Wright's own work. Accordingly they moved to number 33, a huge villa in the middle of a big park, with ten rooms and a swimming pool.[22] They immediately received visits from American neighbors such as the famous Mabel Dodge Luhan, and somewhat against his will Wright found that he was involved in the social life of the colony.

He was nevertheless delighted by the climate and the total absence of segregation. He certainly shared the normal reactions of a foreigner in a strange and sometimes disconcerting country, remarking to Paul Reynolds on May 21, 1940, "Accident, theft, murder seem to be the order of the day in this unbelievable land. Life here is cheap. This morning I saw four dead on the highway—auto accident."

He nevertheless evinced a real desire to get to know the country. He emphasized the dignity of the Indians as they sold their pottery and baskets, while the scrawny children gazed for hours at the open-air restaurants and rummaged in the trash cans. Happening to meet his old friend Herbert Klein, who was filming "The Forgotten Village" with John Steinbeck, he joined up with the crew and traveled all over the countryside as they collected material on Indian culture.[23]

Mexican politics also impressed him. The agrarian reforms, the recently built university and the unions boasting a million members gave him renewed faith in social democracy, particularly when, during the July presidential elections, Manual Avila Camacho, the union candidate, defeated Juan Andreu Almazán, the favorite of the American business interests and the Catholic bourgeoisie. Wright also discovered a new kind of peace:

I write from a country—Mexico—where people of all races and colors live in harmony and without racial prejudices or theories of racial superiority. Whites and Indians live and work and die always resisting the attempts of Anglo-Saxon tourists and industrialists to introduce social hate and racial discrimination.[24]

In spite of his social engagements, Spanish and guitar lessons and visits to the capital, Wright also worked, and on June 1, he finished

With his first wife, Dhimah Rose Meadman

In Mexico, 1940

turning his Schomburg Collection lecture into the article "How Bigger Was Born," for the *Saturday Review of Literature*.[25]

Meanwhile Wright never stopped spreading his ideas on democracy and racial problems. His mission as a writer was "to create a new life by intensifying the sensibilities and to work towards world understanding by improving living conditions." [26] He advocated that intellectuals of the entire American continent unite, and he still supported the activities of the Party. In the April 2, 1940, issue of *New Masses* he had signed the "Open Letter to President Roosevelt" protesting the seizure of documents from the offices of the Abraham Lincoln Brigade and the Dies Committee attacks against the unions. According to the April 25 issue, he, along with Dreiser, also served on an emergency committee to save *New Masses*. In May, he defended Earl Browder, who had been imprisoned because of a passport problem, and, along with three hundred members of the League of American Writers, he signed a petition printed in *New Masses* on June 25, 1940, against the United States joining the war.

Despite the many pleasant aspects of life in Mexico, Wright decided to return to the United States after less than three months. The need to meet with Paul Green for the stage adaptation of *Native Son* and to do more research on American Negroes in Chicago were the apparent reasons for his return, but most of all, he found it impossible to work on "Little Sister" in existing circumstances. He was irritated by the parties where snobbery passed for intelligence, by the false local color of the Miraval Colony and by the close proximity of his wife's mother, son and accompanist. Moreover, in this honeymoon paradise, the difference in tastes and character between Richard and Dhimah only became more apparent. Wright now longed for simplicity and tranquility. He had hoped to have more time with his wife, only to find that she reveled in this worldly and artistic circle of which she was the center. He suddenly discovered that Dhimah was preoccupied with herself, whereas he would have liked her to be more completely devoted to him. He now saw her as just as indolent and insensitive to him as she was to their servants and the natives. One incident shows how hostile Wright had become toward his new wife. Dhimah had been bitten by a scorpion and was crying in the bathroom, but he did not go to her rescue. As he later confided to his friends, "She was mean to me. At last she found a beast that stood up to her." [27]

Dhimah returned directly to New York, but Richard decided he would rather pass through the South to see his family. On June 14, as he recalls humorously in "How Jim Crow Feels," he crossed the border with Marx's *Capital* in his suitcase, to the stupefaction of the custom official, who could not imagine that a black man might be a writer by profession. He again experienced the humiliation of traveling "Jim Crow," going by train from San Antonio to New Orleans. His first stop was Natchez, where he found everything pretty much as he remembered it from twenty-five years earlier. The moss-covered oaks, the yellow river, the pigs wallowing in the dust around the cabins, the greasy, indigestible food, the clouds of mosquitoes in the humid air and the backward farmers living without hope, all filled him with sadness.[28] He stayed with his cousins on Beaumont Street and visited his Uncle Thomas' family as well as his father, who was still working as a day laborer on a farm near Stanton. He no longer saw him as the tyrant of his youth but as a victim of white tyranny like all the others.

I discovered that blood and race alone were not sufficient to knit people together in a community of feeling. The psychological gap between us that had been wrought by time made us regard one another with tension and forced smiles, and I knew that it was not the myth of blood but continued associations, shared ideals and kindred intentions that make people one.[29]

Father and son, naturally, did not have much left to talk about; it was primarily a chance for Wright to measure how far he had come, how much of a gap now separated him from the world of his childhood. The house in which he had been born had been destroyed in a fire, and since there were no civil records before 1912 he could not get a birth certificate. After a dreary Sunday in Natchez, he went to Alabama in another "Jim Crow" train, where he had to go without food because a group of white soldiers monopolized the waiter. From Birmingham he headed for Chapel Hill in order to see Paul Green about the stage adaptation of *Native Son*.

Wright (center) with father and relatives, summer, 1940

He returned to New York for several days, then left for Chicago at the beginning of July, 1940, to do research on Blacks who had migrated to the city for a Viking Press book in collaboration with Edwin Rosskam, a former photographer for the Farm Security Administration. He had no sooner plunged into the files of his friend Horace Cayton, to see what documents were available, than he was besieged with invitations from all quarters.

He was a guest of honor along with Langston Hughes at a reception given by their mutual friends Jack Conroy and Nelson Algren for the launching of *New Anvil*. The editorial of the first issue proclaimed its intention "to reveal to the public the Richard Wrights and the Jesse Stuarts of tomorrow." [30] On July 7, he gave a lecture at the Church of the Good Shepherd for the Pan Hellenic Council, of which his friend Ulysses Keys was president. He visited the American Negro Exhibition with Horace Cayton, Arna Bontemps, Claude Barnett and Langston Hughes, and the interview he gave at the Coliseum on that occasion indicates how militant he was on the subject of racial equality.[31] Two days later he was on his way back to Chapel Hill to begin work with Paul Green on the play.

Meanwhile, Dhimah had moved to Hamilton Terrace, near her mother, after her return from Mexico. She was sharing the apartment with Rose and Ralph Ellison in the hope that Richard's friendship with them would give them more chances to see each other and become reconciled. Richard, however, moved back with the Newtons, who now lived at 343 Grand Avenue in Brooklyn. As time passed, he was even less inclined to get back together with Dhimah. He was further aggravated during his one visit by the impression that she was living in excessive luxury at his expense. All hope of reconciliation was gone and the divorce proceedings were soon begun.[32]

ELEVEN

Before Wright had even finished *Native Son*, Theodore Ward had stated his interest in doing the stage adaptation, but Wright had more ambitious plans. The first serious offer to have the play done on Broadway had come from Edward Lasker and Eddie Camtor, and various other offers had been refused by the time Paul Green suggested that he adapt the novel with the collaboration of the author himself. Wright became seriously interested in this plan, since he considered Green's *Hymn to the Rising Sun* one of the most realistic black plays ever written by a white man.[1] Since Lasker had waived his option when Clifford Odets had refused to write the script, Irene Lee, who represented Orson Welles and John Houseman, went directly to Mexico in order to urge Wright to give them the rights. Thus on June 15, 1940, Wright signed a contract with United Productions—that is, Welles, Houseman and John Mankievicz—specifying that the play would be put on at the beginning of the winter, at which time Wright and Green expected to have finished the script.

Using this as a pretext to shorten his stay in Cuernavaca, Wright made a preliminary visit to Green on his way to New York and returned on July 10 to start the actual writing. Working in Bynum Hall (which had formerly been used as slave quarters), two miles outside of Chapel Hill, they first made an outline that retained the dramatic passages of the novel, then added a few scenes and changed the emphasis of certain sections. Thus the political aspect was easily reduced by making Jan a minor character, an ironic portrait of a militant Communist, who appeared only after Mary's death, while Mary herself symbolized the rich upper-middle class. The main problem was what significance to attach to Bigger's fate. Welles apparently wanted him to be the passive victim of the society that had conditioned him, although the motive of his actions would still be hatred, born of fear, but inspiring revenge worthy of a more positive character. Green envisioned the new Bigger as less exclusively the product of his milieu; he felt that he should seem more conscious of his actions and hence more responsible for them. His free will would therefore be more apparent and he would be able to discover his own identity sooner than in the novel and thus gain the sympathy of the audience more quickly. The denouement would then provide a real catharsis, with Bigger accepting his fate as representing the fate of all Blacks. The attacks on an ineffective religion—as seen in Mrs. Thomas' references to the religious picture on the wall and Bigger's blasphemies—were characteristic of Green, but he would have liked to turn the hero into an expiatory victim, a sort of black Jesus. Wright originally helped him formulate this new image but eventually preferred a version that remained closer to the novel.[2] One scene in an abandoned building to which Bigger had just brought Clara (Bessie in the novel) showed him trying to externalize his view of the world and, through the exaltation he felt at murdering her, arriving at a profound understanding of his own actions. This scene was also discarded.

Wright found Paul Green an understanding companion during these stimulating but exhausting weeks, and they were able to talk with ease on subjects other than the play.[3] Sometimes the two men worked feverishly with Green lighting one cigarette after another in the excitement of the moment and Wright buried in his armchair shored up against the wall, concentrating on the words that poured out of his mouth. At other times they conversed more calmly during the languid summer afternoons.

As the play gradually took shape, Wright also got to know the liberal South at Chapel Hill which, although segregation was rampant, contrasted so greatly with the fields of Mississippi that economic and social progress had bypassed. On July 28, he spoke to the Negro Youth Club of Durham, North Carolina. He added to the story of how Bigger was born his beliefs on the functions of literature and criticized the less militant black leaders, expressing himself more freely than he ever could have in Mississippi.[4] He also reviewed *The Heart Is a Lonely Hunter* for *New Republic*. He was excited by the novel, placing Carson McCullers alongside Gertrude Stein, Sherwood Anderson and Ernest Hemingway on his private list of great masters. He considered her more skillful than Faulkner at expressing the despair of the human condition and, most important, hailed this young writer as the first Southern novelist capable of portraying a black character as easily and with as much accuracy as a white.

Toward the end of September, when Paul Green joined Wright in New York to continue work, they cut certain scenes and condensed some dialogue to conform to Orson Welles's demands, reducing the play to two hours. The episode that was to transform Bigger into a black Jesus by having him take upon himself the sins of his race was cut, Jan's role was shortened even more and it was at this time that Bessie's name was changed to Clara for the convenience of the actors.[5]

Since Wright had to go to Washington at the end of January, just before the play was finished, to work on *Twelve Million Black Voices* with Edwin Rosskam, Paul Green hurried to visit him there to put the finishing touches on the third act. The two authors then discussed with John Houseman how the play should be acted, and rehearsals finally began on February.[6]

By that time the text corresponded almost exactly to the version that Harper was going to publish that same year, 1941. The difficulty of adaptation had been less in presenting the audience with the black man's tragedy than in transforming the 350 pages of powerful prose into a dramatic sequence. With its monolithic structure, density and repetition, the novel had the same power as *An American Tragedy*. It had therefore been necessary to reduce what amounted to a sociological study into a handful of telling events. The trial and defense, for instance, are both covered in one scene where Max actually pleads Bigger's case in front of the audience. The final episodes, in which the pathos creates a kind of mercy for the condemned, are also condensed into one scene. A sudden and abrupt decline in the dramatic tension at this point allows a catharsis to begin.

Naturally an objective viewpoint replaces the subjective one. Bigger's behavior is limited to actions that take him from his abortive attempt to rob the grocery store to Mary's murder, and from there to the electric chair. His fate alone creates the drama, and the secondary plots with their various themes—Buckley's election, the hysteria of the white crowd, the anti-Communist prejudice of the press—are either drastically cut or omitted altogether. The final version had only ten scenes, all intended to illustrate the psychological evolution of the hero as economically as possible.

The first scene presents simultaneously the poverty of the Thomas family, the Christian resignation of the mother and the rebellion of the son. The episode at the movies was omitted, so that the conversation between Bigger, Gus and G. H. comes next, with the airplane in the sky left as the one symbol of their desire for power and escape. Then, as the new chauffeur at the Dalton house, Bigger meets Mary. A big cut here, leaving out the car ride and the evening with Ernie, means that Bigger is next seen bringing the inebriated girl back to her room, leading to the murder itself. Only in scene five, when Bigger is replying to Brittens' interrogation, does the audience meet Jan for the first time and learn what preceded the murder. Scene six includes the visits to Clara and the subterfuge of the ransom note, before the body is discovered in the furnace. After the manhunt among the abandoned houses, during which Clara is killed by a policeman when Bigger uses her body as a shield, the fugitive is captured, wounded by a bullet. Max's speech is the only opportunity left to retrace Bigger's past (in the novel this was also accomplished through the newspaper articles), to explain that he is in fact a victim of the system, which is only partially implied by the plot. The last scene condenses almost sixty pages of the novel into fourteen, eliminating the pastor and the reconstruction of the crime altogether; Bigger is thus left alone to face his destiny after his family's visit, becoming a wholly pathetic character in his solitude until he realizes that his crime has given his life some meaning.

The trial and prison scenes seem insufficient to balance the first eight scenes, especially since the defense is too short to be quite convincing. The line of argument does not attack the root of the problem and is thus too vague to gain in power what was lost in length. Furthermore, Bigger has very little time to emerge in the one prison scene, although the modification of the character compensates for this, since throughout the play he is less limited and less negative than in the novel and does not need such a long evolution to find his identity. As Wright mentioned in the program notes, Bigger's story alone was now enough to convey the moral.[7]

The necessary funds to produce the play were raised by Ben Bernard, Jerry Lavin and William Herz, but they were counting on the sale of tickets to assure a continued run. Although the price of the seats was kept down to $3.30, the St. James Theatre could bring in $18,000 a performance.

Wright had confided to Langston Hughes on January 29, 1941: "Everybody around here seems to be excited about how Bigger is going to be received, but I'm keeping my fingers crossed, as usual, waiting to see what will happen." He had conquered his apprehension and consented to all the changes that Orson Welles had wanted, overwhelmed by this "human locomotive." Although Welles had sometimes browbeaten him, Wright praised his courage and originality in the program, and his correspondence indicates the same admiration.

The theater was rented on February 14 and three days later the rehearsals began, with Orson Welles and John Houseman directing. A cup of tea in one hand, his red scarf around his neck, interrupting himself repeatedly to look for his tobacco pouch, Welles was already a somewhat legendary figure. Wright had not intended the adaptation to be a hit in the theatrical sense, because he considered his denunciation of racial injustice more subtle and sustained than mordant or shocking. He wanted to show the inherent evil of the American way of life without descending to melodrama, but Orson Welles went ahead and exploited the dramatic aspects of the play, even at the expense of the text.

The last-minute problems were numerous, according to *The New York Times* of March 30. Lionel Stander had to put up extra money in return for 8 per cent of the profits just to get them through opening night, although technical problems obliged them to postpone it because the crew was not yet able to change the scenery fast enough to satisfy Welles. The original opening date was therefore postponed to March 17, then to the 19th and finally the 25th. Three days before the opening they had a preview for the New York critics and the members of the NAACP, covered by Marvel Cooke in the March 22 issue of the *New York Amsterdam News*. Everyone praised Canada Lee's performance as Bigger and in general admired Welles's production. Most people, in fact, were familiar with the novel, so they were more concerned with the way in which the play represented the book than with the message or plot. Wright had won the battle with the reading public and now it was up to Welles to do the same with his Broadway audiences. He had advised how the scenes should be cut, had chosen and directed his actors and, finally, imbued the production with spirit and brilliance, making it both rich and full of contrasts, in a style that clashed with the refined tradition of Broadway. The technical director, Jean Rosenthal, made use of the entire range of light and sound effects and James Morcom, who had accompanied Wright and Welles to the South Side before designing the set, created the somber scenery whose symbolism complemented the realism.

The moment the curtain went up the audience was irresistibly absorbed by the drama, and to maintain the spell the play continued for two hours without an intermission. This was also why Welles had insisted that the scenery changes take less than one minute, although the stage crew had to be almost completely retrained and the opening postponed. To accomplish this, Jean Rosenthal had the sets suspended above the stage instead of using the traditional scenery on wheels.[8] In addition, all the lights were turned off for several seconds before the curtain rose to insure the receptivity of the audience; programs were handed out after the performance so that no one would be tempted to leaf through them during the action.

The surprise of the opening scene was due more to the spectacle itself than to the ring of Bigger's alarm clock. Welles had wanted the entire stage to be framed in yellow brick to suggest the inhumanity and ugliness of the big city as well as to represent the metaphor of the wall, which ran through the novel. This huge frame was then left in darkness for the scenes at the Daltons', to emphasize the constant presence of the social destiny. Not only was there a different set for each scene, but the size of the stage itself was changed to give symbolic variety. The one room in which the Thomases were crammed, with its broken furniture and drying laundry, was seen through an opening of fifteen feet (so narrow, in fact, that Joseph Wood Krutch, in his review for the April 5 issue of *The Nation,* complained that he got a crick in his neck) to symbolize the narrow limits of their life. The street was hardly any wider, but its extreme height drew the eye upward to the sky and the airplane: symbols of hope for these young black boys. The maximum opening of the stage was thirty by forty feet, which allowed by contrast for the profusion of sofas, knickknacks, bird cages and green plants in the sumptuous Dalton living room, with a window at the back opening onto a park. To minimize the realism of the murder, Mary's bedroom was on a three-foot platform and the bed on a pedestal, making the room into a sanctuary. The long filmy curtains hanging over the windows in the back were lit from the other side by the pale dawn, emphasizing the unreality as well as the purity of this murder committed in a state of trance, almost like a ritual sacrifice. The next scene, in Clara's tiny room, immediately suggested by contrast the sordid facts of everyday life, with all its realistic details.

Welles saved the full extent of the theater's resources for the trial. Up to this point the brick wall had kept the audience at a distance; now Welles joined the spectators to the stage by placing Max on an extension over the orchestra, forcing them to participate in the judgment. They were not allowed to reestablish the distance and hence attain relief from the tension, nor to experience a catharsis, until the heavy structure of iron and stone descended to enclose Bigger in his cell forever.

Welles had stressed the symbolism at the expense of the picturesque and the import of Max's defense at the expense of the characteristic overtones of Negro life. The details that had given the novel its warmth were absent, particularly in the first and final scenes, in which the pathetic nature of life in the ghetto creates most of the emotional impact. The dramatic elements, therefore, somewhat overshadowed the typical. As Muriel Draper pointed out, it was most effective to show evil as inherent in a socioeconomic situation for which each person in the audience was responsible, although to present Bigger in psychological terms, outside of his social context, would have assured an easier theatrical success.[9] Welles counted upon the actors to establish the balance and nuances, since he had decided to use the atmosphere for symbolism alone. Sound effects accompanied the dialogue, just as the bricks surrounded the action; bells ringing, clocks striking, cars rumbling, blues, hymns, telephones, and shouts all reminded the audience of the social context. Welles had even suggested that the orchestra of modern life continue while the sets were changed, in order to link two scenes with sound as a "fade-out" would in cinema. Sometimes this noise was annoying, as in the menacing roar of the furnace and the manhunt scene in which the shots, cries, whistles and sirens almost destroyed the dramatic illusion. The lighting was used for the same purposes but was subject to the same excesses. The dawn gave the impression of unreality, the last beam from a spotlight cut the bars of the cell, but even if the intermittent flash of neon signs during the manhunt accomplished the same thing as the wild drumbeats in *Emperor Jones*, there was the danger of stupefying the audience even before the end of the episode with the violent noises and lighting designed to convey the racial hysteria.[10]

Canada Lee deserves the credit for maintaining the balance and, therefore, enhancing the drama, the human warmth, the pathos and refined psychology of the play. Welles and Houseman had preferred the former boxer to better-known actors. Lee had already played Blacksnake in *Stevedore,* Jean-Christophe in *Haiti* and Banquo in the black *Macbeth* that Welles had produced for the Federal Theatre. No one noticed his broken nose and cauliflower ears when they saw how his stances, gestures, intonations and even silences expressed to perfection Bigger's frustration and hatred, which, boiling under cover of his fear, would suddenly explode in his family's face. Canada Lee's vivid imagination enabled him to use all the tensions and releases of the plot to elicit an intense sympathy for Bigger although he never resorted to self-pity. He had met the model of this character a thousand times and his performance, which made his name, earned him a long ovation on opening night as well as the enthusiastic praise of Charlie Chaplin.

The rest of the cast provided excellent support for the lead. Evelyn Ellis played the pious and self-sacrificing Hannah Thomas with as much conviction as she had played Bess in *Porgy and Bess,* which had been put on by the Theatre Guild. Whittaker Chambers and Helen Martin—Buddy and Vera—were pathetic innocence itself. Doris Dudley had been cast in the difficult part of Mary, but she quit the play on March 8, perhaps because she feared the unfavorable publicity it might bring her.[11] She was replaced by Ann Burr, who was able to convey the necessary simplicity and frivolity. Formerly a model, she had had some walk-on parts for Fox-Movietone and had been a vaudeville actress at the World's Fair, but she had only appeared on Broadway during the three performances of Irwin Shaw's *Quiet City.* The rest of the cast were mostly established actors who had worked with Welles in *Citizen Kane*: Everett Sloane (Britten), Erskine Sanford (Mr. Dalton), Paul Stewart (the newspaper reporter) and Ray Collins, who replaced John Berry as Max and forcefully conveyed Wright's message in the vibrant tones of Bigger's defense. Philip Bourneuf played Buckley without being excessively unctuous, and Nell Harrison played the delicate Mrs. Dalton, dignified in her blindness.

With the notable exception of the "Hearst press," the New York critics were all the more enthusiastic about *Native Son* because the theater season had so far been unexceptional. The play opened in the middle of the war between Orson Welles and William Randolph Hearst that had been raging since the filming of *Citizen Kane*.[12] Despite Welles's statement that any resemblance between his hero and the newspaper magnate was accidental, Hearst did not let up on his campaign of silence until May, 1941. Thus, the *Daily Mirror*

Wright with Canada Lee, 1941. *Photo, New York Post*

made no mention of *Native Son* at first and later, having rejected
what they considered a too favorable review by Robert Coleman,
reprinted a devastating article by John Anderson of the *Journal
American*. This caused Burns Mantle, the famous critic of the
New York News, and Arthur Pollock, of the *Brooklyn Eagle*, to
defend the play publicly against the flagrant injustice of the Hearst
papers. On June 6, the *Daily Mirror* was even forced to print an
advertisement for *Native Son*, in order not to jeopardize their business relations with the other daily papers.[13] All the support that
Wright and Welles had attracted, as well as the quality of the play
itself, managed to triumph over these unfortunate circumstances,
which could have been fatal to the play despite its merit.

Meanwhile Metro-Goldwyn-Mayer made an offer for the movie
rights that Wright refused with understandable indignation, since
they wanted to change the title and substitute white characters for
the black ones. At the same time, black intellectuals argued over
the wisdom of making a play out of a novel that portrayed a Black
in such a crude and uncomplimentary light. The most cowardly of
these envisaged disastrous economic repercussions, claiming that
black servants would lose their jobs because their white employers

would begin to distrust them. Others thought it extremely audacious to show a white actress in the arms of a black man and feared the typical racist reaction to the intolerable flouting of a Broadway taboo. Some went so far as to ask the Harlem Labor Union to picket the St. James Theatre until performances were stopped as a protest against the offensiveness of Bigger's character. Rev. O. Clay Maxwell, from Mount Olivet Baptist Church, excoriated the play, while Forrest McKeen, director of the Long Island Institute of Sociology, and Walter White, a personal friend of Wright's, defended it in the name of the NAACP.

The important papers praised the play on artistic grounds, the Left hailed it on ideological grounds and because it represented an innovation for Broadway, and even the Communist press was mostly favorable in spite of Jan's insignificant role. On May 24, 1941, Ruth McKenney, Albert Maltz, Marc Blitzstein and Alvah Bessie met on Theatre Night at the Manhattan Center for a discussion of *Native Son*. Reassured by this support, Wright felt free to tell the public his intentions and problems as a playwright in numerous interviews and on a radio program entitled "Native Son: From Novel to Play." [14]

The play stayed until June 15 at the St. James, but even the 115 performances to sizable audiences did not manage to cover expenses. Apart from the initial crowds, attracted by curiosity and admiration, the play was never able to draw those theatergoers who preferred light entertainment to a confrontation with reality.

Yet Wright had never identified so completely with the black masses; it almost seemed that he was speaking from the stage on their behalf, and apparently his message was often heard. At the beginning of July, Harlem greeted the play enthusiastically at the Apollo Theatre before it moved to the Maplewood Theatre in New Jersey. On August 2, the play broke all records at the Windsor Theatre in the Bronx, where the thirteen hundred seats were sold out and a hundred people bought standing room. The next night they moved to the Flatbush Theatre in Brooklyn, where they played to a full house until the beginning of September, interrupted only by a few performances in the Bronx and in Atlantic City.

A few weeks later, the troupe set off on a tour of several states, and on October 7, at the Nixon Theatre in Pittsburgh, Pennsylvania, the play finally broke even. Despite the fears of Burns Mantle, the play was not affected by censure either in Boston or in Chicago where, in fact, it ran with great success at the Studebaker Theatre from October until January, 1942. Max's defense became as famous as Charlie Chaplin's speech in *The Great Dictator*. Most of the original cast stayed with the troupe and, in going from city to city, they realized more fully the power of their message. Canada Lee was justified in stating: "We're making history in the theater. The Negro has never been given the scope that I'm given in this play. . . . Now they'll think of the Negro as an actor and not as some butler-valet type, some ignorant person." [15] His personal success was astounding. His background, determination and present career united him with Wright, and their friendship, which dated from that period, lasted for the rest of the actor's life.

According to John Randolph, who played Jan, the Baltimore performances of *Native Son* were the most memorable. After performing from Boston to Milwaukee, and from Detroit to St. Louis, the troupe finally crossed the Mason-Dixon line to present the South with an antiracist point of view. Although the police had forbidden them to post in the lobby pictures of black and white actors side by side, and a group of Quakers were refused first-balcony tickets for their black members, the director of the Ford, the main theater in Baltimore, did not dare prevent three black soldiers from sitting next to their white friends. The police guarded the orchestra and the lobby, and the colored audience was jammed into the second gallery, but there were no incidents. When Max's defense elicited shouts of enthusiasm, the actor could have been speaking for Wright when he remarked, "You can't imagine what it means to say what you've always wanted to say and to say it precisely to the people it was meant for." [16]

2

The Mexican trip in the spring of 1940 and the time spent writing the play had not prevented Wright from attending cultural events and propaganda meetings, some organized directly by the Party and others by progressive intellectuals who might assemble for reasons not specifically political. Wright's recent but active interest in photography, for example, had led him to enter the national contest "Youth in Focus," organized by the American Youth Congress and *Friday Magazine*, both under Communist control. Since May, Wright had also been working with Langston Hughes, Paul Robeson, Theodore Ward and a few others to start a theater group that would put "authentic Negro life on stage" without the old stereotypes and prejudices. Directed by Powell Lindsay, the troupe was planning to put on Ward's *Big White Fog* at the Lincoln Theatre. Thus on September 6, 1940, Wright spoke at a dinner given at the Golden Gate for the benefit of the Negro Playwrights Company; five thousand people came to hear Paul Robeson sing, to admire Hazel Scott from Café Society and to learn about "how Bigger was born." [17]

This effort to promote an ethnic theater was part of Wright's intention to use his own reputation to help both black cultural endeavors and other writers. In his review of *The Big Sea* for the *New Republic*, Wright in fact came out more strongly in favor of Langston Hughes's autobiography than he really was. He presented his friend as the precursor of the realistic Negro novel, as Dreiser had been for the Whites, and called him the cultural ambassador for his race to the court of world opinion.[18] He was more genuinely enthusiastic about *Special Laughter*, a collection of quite talented poems by Howard Nutt, an old white friend from the Chicago John Reed Club. Wright sent the poet a letter, which was going to serve as the introduction, and in which he emphasized the prophetic and social role of the poet, whom he describes as:

Slyly draping in the guise of humour an awful secret which our generation shares in common, a secret which makes us chronically aware of a class that does not know that

> Anticipation
> Of disaster
> Has its own sort
> Of special laughter.[19]

The disaster here was no longer the economic depression, but the Second World War.

Wright, who had been vice president of the League of American Writers since July, was also elected to the board of the American Peace Mobilization. This was a Party organization which had set up "a perpetual peace vigil" opposite the White House, although by December, 1940, after several months, they had not succeeded in organizing a march on Washington to protest the United States' entry into the war. The *Daily Worker* of September 30 published under the headline "Native Son Author Backs Ford, Browder" an antiwar statement made by Wright as a leader of this organization:

We must think clearly, act quickly and unitedly to ward it off. Trouble lies ahead for all of us, but especially for the Negro. . . . As fast as the days run, Congress grinds out reactionary laws to repress and enslave those who question or protest. Today, even more than in the First World War, is the time for fearless, forthright leadership to protect and voice the fundamental interests of the Negro people. . . . That Ford should be a candidate for Vice President of the United States is an achievement for the Negro people, an achievement recognized and supported only by the Communist Party.

Although Wright supported the Communist candidates and policies publicly, he never neglected what he considered the interests of black Americans. In the present situation, the Blacks had nothing to gain by fighting in an army where discrimination and segregation were rampant, only to find on their return, as in 1919, the racists more than ever determined to put them "back in their place." Wright was planning to speak on this very subject at the National Negro Congress, which met at the end of October, but he eventually did not attend at all.[20] In any event, the Communists proved their strength during this Congress by taking over the organization in spite of A. Philip Randolph's efforts to prevent them. Two more years were to elapse before the war situation had developed to a point that forced Wright himself to revise his position.

At that time, however, even Wright's personal life seemed to be run by the Party. Ralph Ellison, who had been sent by *New Masses* as a reporter to the Congress, ran into Ellen Poplar there and gave her news of Richard. She was far from having forgotten him, while he had never stopped thinking about her since his marriage and divorce, blaming himself for his impatience and injustice toward her. He secretly hoped that they could be reconciled, and the opportunity arose when Ellen came to visit the Newtons. They literally fell into each other's arms; explanations would have been superfluous. Their union started that very night when Ellen, too, moved in with the Newtons.[21] In February, they moved to 467 Waverly Avenue with the Newtons, and it was only after they were married in March, 1941, that they got an apartment of their own. Wright changed none of his plans. The previous year he had been thinking of going to live in Russia for a while and had made inquiries about the possibility of Dhimah's getting a job, since he thought he could live there on his royalties. In November, Theodor Rokotov, an official of the Revolutionary Writers' International, had assured him that his wife could find a temporary job fairly easily, so during the winter Wright continued making plans for departure, although now, of course, he would be taking Ellen. The military situation in Europe and his problem getting a passport led him to offer his services to the Associated Negro Press as a war correspondent to the Soviet Union, China or India.[22] He wanted to leave toward the middle of March, with Ellen as secretary. Although they never actually made this trip, Richard and Ellen, since they participated equally in every activity from the very beginning of their life together, were doubly united by their mutual affection and their political convictions.

The witnesses at their marriage, which took place on March 12 in Coytesville, New Jersey, were Abraham Aaron, Richard's old friend who had introduced him to the John Reed Club, and Benjamin Davis, Jr., the Party official who had both sponsored and kept Wright in line since his arrival in New York. By this time, however, Davis had certainly somewhat revised his critical and intransigent attitude of the preceding year, and to all appearances Wright was on good terms with the Communist leaders. The relationship was not always easy, though, and Wright often had to be nagged to perform his duties. At the thirtieth anniversary celebration for *New Masses*, held on February 16 at the Manhattan Center, Wright sent his heartfelt good wishes, but in fact the Communist leaders had sent him a letter and two telegrams reminding him to do so.[23] On March 2, he was supposed to meet with Earl Browder, Benjamin Gold, Ben Davis, Louis Budenz and some others at the Party office to congratulate Mike Gold on his twenty-fifth anniversary as a militant, but there is no evidence to show that he actually went. That same month he agreed to give the rights of his story "Bright and Morning Star" to the Earl Browder Defense Fund, and the story was reissued, separately, by Inter-

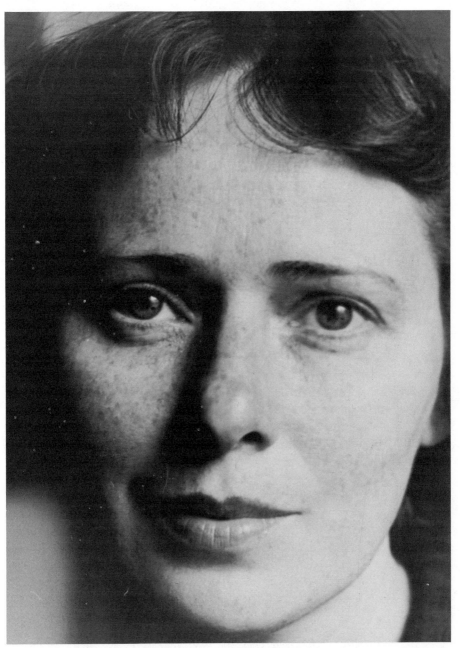

Ellen Poplar Wright, 1941. *Photo by Richard Wright*

national Publishers. In his letter, dated March, 1941, which was used as a preface, Wright stated:

It is not my story, it belongs to the workers. I would never have written it unless I had felt that I had a workers' audience to read it. Ever since it was published in the pages of *New Masses,* some two years ago, I've wanted to see it published alone and cheaply enough for the workers to buy and read.

Actually, his correspondence with Paul Reynolds indicates that he had held out for more than a year, waiting for several magazines and anthologies to buy the story, in order not to lose money before complying with the increasingly urgent requests from the editors of *New Masses.* At the end of March, 1941, he somewhat more willingly participated in a book sale for European Intellectual refugees, organized by the Exiled Writers Committee. At this point his lack of enthusiasm and desire to keep a certain distance did not imply any split from the Party line.

As a leader of the American Peace Mobilization, he participated with Vito Marcantonio and Theodore Dreiser in the pacifist demonstration at Randall Stadium on May 5. When the Communist writers sent their congratulations to Earl Browder, who was celebrating his fiftieth birthday in prison, the *Daily Worker* of May 20 quoted Wright as saying:

Earl Browder's recent imprisonment has grown a thousandfold in political meaning with the rapid spread of the imperialistic war. . . . The Negroes' position towards the war belies all the frantic efforts of the Roosevelt administration to justify the war on idealistic grounds.

Once again he was arguing against the black masses' supporting the war by associating their stand with the anti-imperialist pacifist movement.

There were many reasons for Wright's pacifism, starting with the Party line. After the signing of the German-Soviet pact, the Communists condemned the capitalist war, thinking that peace would safeguard "the world's lone socialist state." [24] In addition, the war had engendered such tension that individual liberties in the United States were being threatened and radical groups subjected to increasing repression; Wright was therefore not just defending democracy in its bastion overseas, but attempting to preserve it on American soil as well. Finally, Wright identified with numerous Blacks who remembered how little they had benefited from their participation in World War I and who now saw the politicians using the conflict at hand as an excuse to ignore legislation on racial problems. Wright stressed this third point more and more, and although he only touched upon how hateful it was for the Blacks to fight the Nazis in a segregated army, "The Negro People and the War" was the subject of the lecture he gave at Columbia University on April 23 and of his speech at the fourth American Writers' Congress a month later.

Wright had contributed only sporadically as a member of the national council of the L.A.W., but he did attend the preparatory meeting at which they formulated an appeal published in the May 27, 1941, issue of *New Masses* and the April–May, 1941, issue of *Direction*.[25] This time the forty writers who signed it, including Wright, stressed the pacifist mission of the writer. They urged everyone to oppose military propaganda and censure, to help the victims of fascism and to transform the F.W.P., already in its decline, into a "People's Art Project" in order to enrich American democratic literature and broaden its audience. The program was ambitious. However, despite its 750 members, the League had lost since the last Congress some of its most famous members such as Thomas Mann, Louis Bromfield, Van Wyck Brooks and Malcolm Cowley. The opening session, on June 6, was run by other union organizations and was nothing more than a political meeting. Following Dashiell Hammett, Wright spoke at length on the refusal of black Americans to fight in the war. The complete text of "Not My People's War" was printed in the June 17, 1941, *New Masses* and contained a synthesis of his thoughts on the subject. He deplored the necessity to speak about war during a writers' congress but recognized the omnipresence of the conflict, which created "a new and terrifying subject," and stated the position of his race:

Indeed, the Negro's experience with past wars, his attitude towards the present one, his attitude of chronic distrust, constitute the most incisive and graphic refutation of every idealistic statement made by the war leaders as to the alleged democratic goal and aim of this war.

It seemed that the prohibitions, humiliations and lynchings of 1919 were going to be repeated in the segregation of the Negro units and discrimination in the armament factories, in view of President Roosevelt's recent statements. Furthermore, the war was clearly imperialistic and was of no concern to the Blacks:

Our primary problem is a domestic problem, a problem concerned with the processes of democracy at home. We need jobs. We need shelter. We urgently need an enormous increase in health, school, recreational, and other facilities. We need to see the Thirteenth and Fourteenth Amendments to the Constitution enforced. We need to see the Bill of Rights translated into living reality.[26]

Wright refused to wait until the war was over to continue the fight for racial equality. Fortunately, his point of view as a black militant was the same as that of a militant Communist, but he went further. Since the Black would not benefit from his heroism, Wright was even more indignant about the vexations that he would suffer while at war than he was about the simple fact that he would be obliged to fight in the first place. Actually, he formulated the slogan of the "double victory."

If this is a war for democracy and freedom, then we fight in it, for democracy, for freedom. We shall fight as determinedly against those who deny freedom at home as we shall fight against those who deny it to others abroad.

Here Wright almost commits himself to saying that the Blacks would fight for democracy, which might seem contradictory if he had not also emphasized that the war was antidemocratic. The duty of a black writer, therefore, was not to prepare for war but to prepare the millions of readers to respond to an appeal for peace when it came. This is the clearest public statement of Wright's inner conviction that his own fight against American racism was a crucial manifestation of his position as an anti-Fascist pacifist. Wright felt that the step from an unjust capitalist war to a war for liberty and democracy would be hard to take. The essential thing now was what progress the black Americans could make because of this international conflict.

At the various section meetings on June 7, celebrities were rare, and the debate among the critics, traditionally the most important part of the program, was not lively. Mike Gold reviewed the record of the literature of the thirties, and Herbert Aptheker evaluated the Negro's contribution to national culture. Wright himself did not attend. He was noticed at lunchtime next to Donald Ogden Stewart at the head of a group of writers who had joined the journalists' union and were picketing the *New York Day*.[27] At the drama session the next day, Eleanor Flexner discussed *Native Son* in a speech significantly entitled "Broadway Battleground." During the general assembly that same afternoon, Dashiell Hammett was elected president, replacing Donald Ogden Stewart, who became a vice-president along with Wright, Dreiser, Caldwell, Meridel Le Sueur and Albert Maltz. Dreiser received the Randolph Bourne Prize for "exceptional service given in aid of culture and peace," while *Native Son* was declared the best novel published since 1939.[28] They adjourned to the sound of music, since Joshua White, Leadbelly, Burl Ives and the Golden Gate Quartet were the guests of honor at the dinner dedicated to poetry and music. The Congress, however marked the semifailure of the League. Not only had most of its famous members resigned, but the majority of the American writers did not follow its resolutions; it had become the instrument of the Communists, whose shifting policy eventually discredited not only the Party but also the organizations associated with it.

On June 22, 1941, the day after the American Peace Mobilization organized a National Peace Week, Hitler invaded Soviet Russia. The A.P.M., shamelessly renamed overnight the American People's Mobilization, immediately organized an aid program for Great Britain. Wright's pacifist speech "Not My People's War" had come out in *New Masses* on June 17, and three weeks later the July 8 issue contained the reaction of other writers under the heading "Why This is Our War."

Two years earlier Wright had accepted the invasion of Finland, with difficulty, but this time, the turnabout that the Party forced him to make was one of the most mortifying events of his career. In January, 1941, he had been awarded the Spingarn Medal, the highest distinction reserved for a black American, for "his powerful depiction, in his works *Uncle Tom's Children* and *Native Son*, of the effects of discrimination and segregation and the denial of his rights as a citizen on the American Negro." [29] Hailing him as one of the most forceful American novelists, the Spingarn committee was also, in fact, acknowledging his achievements as a courageous militant who never hesitated to do his duty, even if he did not spare the black bourgeoisie and the moderate stance of the NAACP. The solemn presentation of the medal took place in August during the thirty-second annual meeting of the NAACP in Houston. Wright's acceptance speech had been given to the press a few days in advance. Its tenor was so close to "Not My People's War" that the Party leaders forced him to change it at the last minute into an appeal for Blacks to volunteer to defend democracy. He had so many reservations about the conditions of black participation in the war that he submitted very unwillingly; this episode marked the beginning of both his ultimate split with the Communists and the hatred of authoritarianism that inspired so much of *The Outsider*.[30]

In spite of this humiliation due to Party requirements, the actual moment when Wright was presented with the heavy medal, engraved with his name and hung on a red and black ribbon, was a solemn one. His response to the presentation speech and the subsequent ovation was dignified and moving.

It is with a deep sense of responsibility that I accept the Spingarn medal. I accept it in the name of the stalwart, enduring millions of Negroes whose fate and destiny I have sought to depict in terms of scene and narrative in imaginative fiction. It cannot be otherwise for they are my people, and my writing—which is my life and which carries my convictions—attempts to mirror their struggle for freedom during these troubled days.

To be more explicit, I accept this award in the name of my father, a sharecropper on a Mississippi plantation and in the name of my mother who sacrificed her health on numerous underpaid jobs, and in the name of millions of others like them, whose hope for peace and security reflects the aspirations of the common people everywhere during this period of war and cataclysmic social change.[81]

Wright assumed the role of spokesman for the most under privileged member of his race at the same time that he emphasized the value of his own success as an example. As he himself often remarked, it had only taken him one generation to achieve the social position normally attained in three. His sense of responsibility led him to accept the role of "leader of his race," a position which gave him added strength and even a certain independence from the Communists. He could do without them: the Blacks needed no one else—neither the unions nor the white proletariat—to formulate their protest.

The Party attitude toward the war had, of course, completely changed since July, and the bombing of Pearl Harbor on December

7, 1941, finally gave Roosevelt a specific reason to declare war on Japan. During September and October, Wright had refrained from making any statement on the war and even refused to write a few words to boost the sale of savings and defense bonds, but on December 16 his signature appeared on an L.A.W. petition in *New Masses*, a "Communication to All American Writers" demanding immediate action against Germany, Italy and their satellites. Now he finally spoke unequivocally.

I pledge my loyalty and allegiance, without mental reservations or evasions, to America in her fight against the unprovoked totalitarian attack launched by Japan and her allies. I shall through my writing seek to rally the Negro people to stand shoulder to shoulder with the administration in a solid national front to wage war until victory is won.[32]

He was not happy about the American entry into the war, but he accepted his share of the responsibility in the hope that the world would be a better place after it was over. He immediately offered his services to the government, not as a way of proving his patriotism but in the interest of efficiency. In an introduction written in December, 1941, for a condensed version of *Twelve Million Black Voices*, he tried to prove that it was in the best interests of black Americans to fight.

In the present world struggle, the American Negro is allied with the anti-Axis powers. To put it bluntly, while there are many things wrong with America's democracy as far as the Negro is concerned, his wrongs *will not* and *cannot* be righted by Hitler, Mussolini or Hirohito.

We are fighting to defeat those enemies. But we must also fight to preserve the kind of America where the struggle for the extension of democracy can be taken up with renewed vigor when our enemies are crushed.

Still there lurks a danger to our war effort: we may accept too readily a unity built upon the suppression of those who petition for a redress of authentic grievances. We forget that it is not the oppressed who produce the best warriors for freedom. . . . The best way for America to ensure against any Negro listening to the pipe-dreams of treacherous Japanese agents is to see that the Black Belts are eliminated. To end the evils depicted in these pages is a measure of national defense.[33]

While he sincerely supported the national war effort, Wright did not retreat in inch when it came to civil rights. He clearly indicated his belief that America's strength depended upon the unity of her citizens, which, in turn, was only valid if everyone enjoyed equal opportunities. It was up to black Americans to win the "double victory" against Nazism abroad and racism at home. The war, in other words, in no way justified a halt in social progress, a point that soon led him to disagree with the Communists.

The military authorities, who distrusted Wright because of his Communist sympathies, were certainly not aware at the time that he sought a special commission that he was gradually pulling away from the Party, if not dramatically at least irrevocably. Many people had left the American Communist Party in response to one or another of the abrupt changes in policy dictated by Moscow, but Wright was drawing away during a period of calm, when it was no longer dangerous for an American to be a Communist since the United States was allied to Soviet Russia against the Axis.

On February 13, 1942, the *Daily Worker* published Wright's "Letter to Sender Garlin," warmly congratulating the paper for providing its readers with a heated and instructive debate on jazz. The letter ended with an appeal:

Every issue of the *Daily Worker* should carry some common discussion about vital problems. In this way, multiple points of view, expressed from varied environmental class angles, will afford the basis for a true, sound, Marxist discussion. . . . Let us encourage the expression of the opinion of the man in the street; we can learn from him and he from us.

This was obviously a clear and urgent plea for a wider point of view on all issues but it was not heeded, and, a few months later, Wright refused Benjamin Davis' repeated requests to give a lecture for the Party. The previous spring, the Communists had decided to oppose A. Philip Randolph (the president of the Union of Sleeping Car Porters, who had played a key role in the National Negro Congress) when he organized a march on Washington. Wright was indignant that he could not participate in this demonstration against discrimination in armament factories and segregation in the army. Although mobilization had made Blacks eligible for numerous jobs in industry, they received lower salaries and fewer benefits. In the armed services themselves, the Navy would accept them only as stewards, the infantry had separate units and camps for them and the Air Corps did not allow them to fly. In addition, the Red Cross had originally refused black blood donors, and later, constrained to accept them because of the large number of wounded, kept their blood in separate bottles. (Ironically, it was a black doctor, Charles Drew, who conducted the experiments with plasma that led to the process of blood transfusions.) The march on Washington, then, was amply justified, but the Party, in its recent stance unconditionally supporting Roosevelt's war, did not want to antagonize the government on these points, no matter how vital such a confrontation might be in the fight against racism. Accordingly, James W. Ford reprimanded Wright for defending the interests of his own people, and Ben Davis suggested that he go back to his novels and leave politics to the Party.[34]

When his friend Horace Cayton disclosed that the Communists would withhold their support from any attempt to combat government discrimination in the courts, Wright withdrew from the Party without a scandal. He now limited himself to supporting the NAACP and other organizations that were working in this direction, and his undeclared break was kept a secret for several months. In March, 1942, Wright was one of the sponsors of a "Communist" dinner in honor of Paul Robeson; on July 14, a review of *Negro Caravan* by Samuel Sillen mentioned Wright favorably, as did the article "The Negro in American Theatre" in *New Masses* the following week. On the other hand, on October 20, the magazine collected under the title "The Negro and Victory" statements by Hughes, Ellison, Ford, L. D. Reddick and Saunders Redding, and there was nothing by Wright, which was the only clue that he had refused to contribute. At the end of the year, a critic who reviewed *No Day of Triumph*, for which Wright had written the introduction, showed that he, too, was not aware of any break, since he came out against Wright and those imitators of his Communist ideology . . . who forsake the possibility of speaking sincerely and convincingly in their naive attempts to set a class of Negroes against the others." [35]

Since Wright had made no public declaration embarrassing to the Party, his decision was not irreversible. As a result, they made little effort to discredit him except for a few insinuations, and merely spied closely on him, hoping for a reconciliation. Wright, for his part, was not about to turn against his old friends, as so many ardent Stalinists had done, and clear his name with a startling conversion to anti-Communism. No doubt he wanted to avoid the possibility of a campaign against him from the Communist press, but most of all he recoiled from being the aggressor.

It is important not to overestimate Wright's emotional reaction to this break, which was, perhaps, not as significant as its effect upon his literary career, although in 1945 even this was deliberately exaggerated by certain critics belonging to both sides. The Left wanted to attribute Wright's success to his political commitment and the Right sought to prove that the same influences had been detrimental. Although Wright's statements on this subject are also contradictory, his letter to Edward Aswell of August 21, 1955, seems to explain his motives and feelings most accurately.

As you know [he wrote] I broke with the Communist Party in 1942; I left under my own steam. I had intuitively realized much of what is now in the daily press about the Communist Party, including its infiltration by the F.B.I., agents, etc. In short, when I was a member of the Communist Party, I took that party seriously, and when I discovered that I was holding a tainted instrument in my hands, I dropped that instrument.

The physical act of my severing my connections with the Communist Party was not at all difficult, despite the fact that I caught brick bats from both Right and Left. Being a Mississippi-born Negro, I survived all that with an ease that most people would not imagine. Indeed, I've been so conditioned that I actually thrive (at times) under conditions of hostility. So, unlike many others who have broken with the Communist Party, I felt no need of excessive amounts of alcohol, mysticism, Catholicism, Christian Science, or anything else. In fact, I felt a kind of grim exhilaration in facing a world in which nothing could be taken for granted, a world in which one had to create and forge one's own meaning for one's own self.

There were other things, however, that did bother me. And those things stemmed from the ramifications of the racial question in the United States. As anyone with common sense could easily guess, I was a Communist because I was Negro. Indeed the Communist Party had been the only road out of the Black Belt for me. Hence

Communism had not been for me simply a fad, a hobby; it had a deep functional meaning for my life. Therefore when I left the Communist Party, I no longer had a protective barrier, no defenses between me and a hostile racial environment that absorbed all of my time, emotions, and attention. To me the racial situation was a far harder matter than the Communist one and it was one that I could not solve alone.

It is clear from this that Wright did not abandon his Marxist point of view. He was merely forced to admit that the socialism practiced by the American Communist Party did not give enough attention to the fight against racism and the development of the individual. He discovered that the Communist Party was no more idealistic or honest than any other political party. If the Blacks could not count on its support, then he, personally, must now expect the Party to attempt to destroy him, since the concept of mercy was foreign to it. As he states somewhat pathetically and exaggeratedly in "I Tried to Be a Communist," he now had to forgo a certain type of literary inspiration such as that which had sustained *Uncle Tom's Children*, but there were alternatives just as satisfying in the literary sense, were he to adopt a more exclusively black nationalist perspective. Nevertheless, he could not accept this switch from a class to a racial point of view as anything but a limitation, a regression to "provincialism." He could not believe in the revolt of the Bigger Thomases, since they were as likely to espouse fascism as socialism; he despised the black bourgeoisie, who were totally wrapped up in themselves; and the rural South had never meant much more to him than a "swamp of civilization," cowering under the scepter of religion. Only the radical intelligentsia might help the masses, but now, without the support of the Party, the Blacks could count only on the progressives and liberals, and only in a very limited way. As a "leader," Wright was alone with his people, who were themselves divided, and alone as an individual as well, since his integrity was bound to invite attacks from all sides. Although he would miss the warmth of solidarity, his "grim exhilaration in facing a world in which nothing could be taken for granted" was a challenge as well as a new beginning. If Wright had escaped the ghetto thanks to Communism, he could now go back there in spirit, both to promote racial equality and to draw inspiration and strength from his sense of duty toward his race.[36]

3

Wright had just decided to go ahead with the stage adaptation of *Native Son* when he also agreed to write the text for an illustrated book on black Americans that Edwin Rosskam, a former photographer for the Farm Security Administration, was preparing for the Viking Press. The book was to be somewhat similar to Oliver La Farge's study of the Indians, *As Long as the Grass Shall Grow*, and Wright's trip to Chicago in the summer of 1940 was partly in order to ascertain what sources and documents would be available. He also accompanied Rosskam to Washington at the end of January, 1941, to consult the archives of the Department of Agriculture, and he returned to Chicago to study the ghetto in depth because he considered his experience of Harlem too limited. His friend Horace Cayton was now director of the recently opened Parkway Community House on 5120 South Parkway, where the Good Shepherd residential and cultural center was located. Wright collected a great deal of material for the book, interviewing the young people who used the library or the clubs and consulting the notes of his friend Cayton, who generously shared the information he had gathered for *Black Metropolis*, a monumental study of the South Side, which came out four years later. Cayton also provided him with some broad general concepts, such as the sociological differences between urban capitalists and large landowners, on which Wright based his chapters "Lords of the Land" and "Bosses of the Buildings." [37] Besides his family, to whom he introduced Ellen for the first time, Wright found many old friends. On April 12, the Caytons gave a buffet attended by Arna Bontemps, the attorney Charles Schwartz, Edward Rodriguez, Dr. Edwin Embree, president of the Julius Rosenwald Fund, and the Wirths. Wright had not seen Mary Wirth since he knew her as a social worker in 1933, and this party provided a chance for Wright to become better acquainted with Professor Louis Wirth, who obliged him by providing a program of readings in sociology that Wright conscientiously followed.[38]

Throughout their stay at the White Way Hotel, Richard and Ellen were sought out by old friends such as Nelson Algren, the Conroys, Metz Lochard, Peter Pollack and Langston Hughes.[39]

Meanwhile this "folk history of Negro Americans" required a great deal of serious preparation, and as time went on Wright became increasingly fascinated and absorbed by the study of his own origins. As with *Home Town* and *As Long as the Grass Shall Grow*, which Rosskam had also worked on, the commentary was supposed to fill a mere twenty pages. Horace Cayton's files as well as Professor Wirth's advice provided Wright with an indispensable theoretical foundation and a quasi-professional approach to doing research, both of which caused him to far exceed the requirements for the commentary. To explain the origins of the ghetto he felt that he had to describe the poverty of the rural South, which, of course, had its roots in slavery. To provide historical perspective for the documentary he added a final chapter inspired by his socialist vision, in which he looked forward from the present desolation of life in the urban centers to a future full of struggles and hope. These four chapters, arranged in chronological order, soon amounted to 150 pages.

Although this was Wright's first nonfiction book, the stages of composition, which are easy to reconstruct from the several versions of the manuscript, nevertheless reveal the author's characteristic methods. He began with a conceptual framework, incomplete and without a logical sequence. Then he would either explain these concepts so that their contrasts and similarities would emerge, or he would work on formulating them in language whose poetic qualities would suggest further associations and oppositions not contained in the concepts themselves. Later, while reorganizing the paragraphs within the chapters, he continually worked on his style, polishing the prose to make it flow so that the rhythm and sonority of the language would clothe and enhance the ideas, elevating them from the purely intellectual level to that of the imaginative and figurative.

Mrs. Birdoff, whose sister was a friend of Ellen's, worked as Wright's secretary at this time. Generally he worked alone in the morning, writing a first draft in pencil (he had about twenty, all well sharpened). In the afternoon he would dictate, either to her or into an Ediphone. He would then make from four to six revisions on long sheets of yellow paper, triple-spaced with huge margins.

I noted curiously that the first draft had his description of how the early slaves were tied up and transported "like spoons laid out in the holds of the ships." In the final revision it became "stacked like cord-wood in the foul holds of clipper ships." [40]

The final title for the book was chosen in June and the manuscript handed in to Viking Press by mid-July, 1941, when Wright immediately asked for it back because he was not entirely satisfied with some of his wording and images. Meanwhile a remark in a letter to his friend and editor Edward Aswell, on July 21, indicated that he already intended to use *Twelve Million Black Voices* as the basis for a much larger project. "As I explained to you earlier," he wrote, "this text forms the outline for a long series of novels which I hope to write some day." They would form the saga of the black nation in the United States. The evolution of this one ethnic group would illustrate a striking but representative aspect of a general twentieth-century phenomenon: the technological and social change, caused by industrialization, resulting in urbanization becoming a way of life. The Afro-Americans typified a colonized people coming upon industrial civilization, and their fate would exemplify a crucial stage in the development of all mankind moving from the feudal state to the age of technology.[41] This was the meaning of Wright's later statements on the symbolic character of the black man in America.

There is no way of telling when Wright conceived this plan and whether he was already planning new novels or intending to include those he had already written. *Twelve Million Black Voices* itself, with a printing of 5,000 copies priced at $3.00 each, came out in October. In addition to writing the more than fifty pages of text, Wright was responsible for a photograph showing a "For Rent" sign in the window of a Chicago slum. All the other photographs were taken by Rosskam. The reviews were uniformly enthusiastic. The commentators on the radio program "Men and Books," from "Nothwestern University of the Air," represented the general opinion, with John T. Frederic, the professor of modern literature, only mentioning a few minor faults, such as one historical chapter that was somewhat too schematic and heavy. He did not find the Marxist orientation in the least harmful and ranked the book alongside *Let Us Now Praise Famous Men*, the study made by James Agee and Walker Evans of Alabama tenant farmers.[42] Arna Bontemps, repre-

senting the Blacks on this program, hailed Wright as a master of
poetic prose, belonging to the fine tradition of the Negro spiritual.

In December, Wright wrote the foreword to a selection from the
book that appeared in the April, 1942, issue of *Coronet* magazine.
This included approximately fifteen pages of the text as well as thirty
couplets composed by Wright to accompany photographs by Rosskam and Fritz Henle. Written in the colorful folk style of Paul
Laurence Dunbar's *Lyrics of Lowly Life*, they begin with a
nostalgic evocation of the peaceful and deeply-rooted life on the
plantations, which the ghetto immigrants regret. A description of
the slums then leads into a plaintive lullaby in which the mother
blames the system:

> You toil and sweat day after day
> To pay de white man rent
>
> You'll find no matter where you go—
> No matter how you figger
>
> De rule is: everythin' for whites
> And nothin' for a nigger

But there are simple pleasures, too, like the Saturday dance and
church on Sunday, and the ending contains a note of hope, when
the mother begs the Almighty to give her son

> half a chance
>
> To play a bigger part than she
> In America's advance

Wright had never refused to help a friend or stranger in need,
especially a fellow writer if he felt that his recommendations or advice might be useful. During the year 1941 alone he wrote a lyrical
paragraph as an advance quote for the jacket of Henrietta Buckmaster's *Let My People Go*; he advised Harry Birdoff, who was
looking for a publisher for his history of *Uncle Tom's Cabin*; and
he was instrumental in getting Harper's to publish the novels of his
friends Nelson Algren and Laurence Lipton.[43]

He did much more, however, to help two prisoners. Professor
Morris V. Schappes, sentenced to eighteen months in jail for pro-
Communist activities, had sent his wife a series of moving letters,
to which Wright composed a preface at the insistence of the Party,

which published them as *Letters from the Tombs* in order to rally support.[44] Wright was a more willing benefactor in the case of Clinton Brewer. Since the publication of *Native Son* he had, in fact, received many pleas for help from black prisoners who identified with the hero of the novel, but during the autumn of 1940 an extraordinary letter from an elderly woman requesting the release of Clinton Brewer did cause him to pay closer attention. Brewer had already served eighteen years of his life sentence for the murder of Mrs. Wilhelmina Washington, mother of two, who had refused to marry him. Wright visited Brewer in prison, which he had entered in 1923 at age eighteen, and whether or not he saw in him a reincarnation of Bigger, as one newspaper article implied, he eventually wrote the governor of New Jersey, Thomas A. Edison, Jr., on March 30, 1941, asking that Brewer be released on parole.[45] This letter described Brewer as a sensitive and intelligent man, who had apparently succeeded in maintaining contact with the outside world by means of books and periodicals. He had, moreover, been studying music composition and thought that he could now earn his living in this field. Wright had sent one of Brewer's pieces, "Stampede in G Minor," to his friend John Hammond, Jr., of Columbia Studios, and Count Basie had made a fairly successful recording of it. Wright therefore felt convinced, as he told the governor, that Brewer had established through his art an organic social relationship to the world, making a second offense highly unlikely.

Unfortunately, Wright was completely mistaken. Brewer was released on July 8, had apparently readjusted and was planning to do musical arrangements for Count Basie on a regular basis when, three months later, he stabbed another young woman in circumstances similar to those of his first crime.[46] This time he was supposed to be executed without delay.

Meanwhile, however, Ella Winter had sent Wright a book that had come out in September, 1941, called *Dark Legend*, by the psychiatrist Frederic Wertham. Wright was fascinated by this Freudian analysis of matricide, which Wertham linked with the story of Hamlet. Wright immediately got in touch with the doctor, as he wrote on October 24, 1941, in order to determine which factors, motives or psychological abnormality had made this second murder possible. Although Brewer had known his second victim for only two months, Wright was convinced that this crime was deeply rooted in his past. On November 9, Wertham retained a lawyer for Brewer and agreed to give expert evidence himself. Since Brewer's behavior did reveal a pathological obsession, the intervention of the psychiatrist saved his life. Wertham and Wright's common cause formed the basis of a close friendship between them.[47] Wright also used Brewer's story in *Savage Holiday* and perhaps started from it to outline another, much more extensive, work, which would explore the areas of conflict between society and the inner world of the individual.

John Hammond, who had given Brewer a chance in the world of music and records, one day suggested to Wright that he himself write some blues. In three hours, as Wright boasted to Paul Reynolds on September 25, 1941, he had written thirteen stanzas glorifying Joe Louis, who had just won a match against Nova. The form of "King Joe" was classical. The first two verses of each three-line stanza were practically identical, while the third formed a conclusion. To hail the "big black bear cat" Wright used the objects and talking animals from black folklore: corn bread, black-eyed peas, Brer Rabbit, the Bull Frog, Bumble Bee and the Boll Weevil, characters worthy of any "tall tale" of the frontier. The automobile maker, a new John Henry, himself became an invincible machine:

> Old Joe wrestled Ford engines, Lord, it was a shame;
> Say Old Joe wrestled Ford engines, Lord, it was a shame;
> And he turned engine himself and went to the fighting game.

Racial hostility and pride is laconically expressed:

> Wonder what Joe Louis thinks when he's fighting a white man
> Bet he thinks what I'm thinking, cause he wears a deadpan.

Just as in "Joe Louis Uncovers Dynamite" and "High Tide in Harlem," the song resounds with the overwhelming triumph and superiority of the black people on the day after their champion's victory. Wright clearly thought of the blues as songs of struggle and revenge.

John Hammond directed the recording, which took place on October 1 at Liederkranz Hall. Count Basie and his orchestra set the couplets to music, and Paul Robeson, who was singing the blues for the first time in his life, had Jimmy Rushing stand by his side to beat time. Wright, Max Yeargan and the other guests were there to hear the typical blues chords, the trumpet introduction by Buck Clayton—which seemed as if it would break the loudspeakers—and Robeson's powerful bass voice. The record sold fairly well, with an advance order of 40,000 copies.[48]

The preceding autumn Wright had also written an introduction to *Southern Exposure*, a three-record album of songs on segregation and the economic exploitation of the Blacks by the famous folk singer Josh White, whom Wright and Hughes had recently asked to sing their "Red Clay Blues." The title song, "Southern Exposure," was followed by "Defense Factory Blues," "Uncle Sam Says," "Hard Times Blues," "Bad Housing Blues" and "Jim Crow Train," whose subjects are obvious. Wright's interest in blues, of course, reflects his political commitment and his fight for racial equality, as well as a renewed fascination with the folk origins of his own culture.

The blues could be called the spirituals of the city [he wrote]. They are the songs of simple people whose life has been caught up in and brutalized by the inflexible logic of modern industrial existence. . . . Since the best-known blues have love as a main theme, people have a false idea, because an incomplete one, of their true range and role in the life of Black people. There also exist blues which indict the social system and they have been judged not commercial enough because of this satirical bent. . . . Common, everyday life, the background of our national life, is to be seen through the blues: trains, ships, trade unions, planes, the Army, the Navy, the White House, plantations, elections, poll tax, the boll weevil, landlords, epidemics, bosses, Jim Crow, lynchings. . . . All such blues are as natural for the Black people as eating and sleeping, and they come as a rule out of their daily experience. Their very titles indicate the mood and state of mind in which they were written.[49]

While he was finishing up *Twelve Million Black Voices*, Wright was also working on two novels. In the spring of 1941, the papers had announced that he was writing a short novel on Negro life in Harlem and Brooklyn. This had been inspired by a story which had appeared two years earlier in Edward Zeltner's column for the *Daily Mirror*. In one fashionable quarter of Brooklyn there was apparently a beautiful house, which was, in fact, the one attraction sure to be pointed out to every visitor. But there was a mystery about it: no one ever saw the owners, only a great many black servants. Kitchen help came and went, while every morning the chauffeur would bring out a magnificent limousine from the garage and go off alone. One day, of course, it was discovered that the Blacks actually owned the house and that they only pretended to be servants to avoid the outraged protests of their white neighbors.

This was a second departure from the old theme of black servants that he had used the year before in "Little Sister," and it became the principal subject of the new novel. By March 6, 1941, Wright had already written half of a first version that he was planning to continue for several hundred pages in order to cut and revise it down to the desirable density.[50] He verified the details with as much care as he had the topography of Chicago for *Native Son*. He interviewed judges, welfare employees and city officials. He visited the Union of Domestic Employees on Third Avenue, jotted down hundreds of episodes from the lives of maids encountered there and spent the mornings in an employment agency taking notes as the Blacks were asked for their previous experience and references.[51]

At the beginning of 1942, Wright sent a first version of the novel to Paul Reynolds, who wrote back on February 12 suggesting a number of titles: "Native Daughter," "Slave to the Whites," "The Life That Failed," "Another World." In March, Wright finally decided upon "Black Hope," perhaps inspired by Nelson Algren's "White Hope," the abandoned title of his novel *Never Come Morning*. Wright was somewhat discouraged by Reynolds' numerous objections in matters of detail, and although Reynolds did everything in his power to reassure him about the novel and his literary career in general, he spent a good part of the year cutting scenes, rewriting dialogue and changing the characters.[52] During the summer he completed a second version, but it pleased him so much less than the first that he admitted agonizedly that "Black Hope" was still far from finished.

Wright was very discreet about the other novel, which he was writing at the same time. Despite his increasing intimacy with Reynolds (they were now on a first-name basis), on June 6, 1941, he wrote merely that he was waiting to finish *Twelve Million Black Voices* before seriously settling down to it. Then he decided to wait until he had moved. On July 24, he wrote again to say that he had started it but had also begun to think about writing a group of short stories, although the idea had not yet "shaped up." With all these irons in the fire, it must have been a real bout of inspiration that enabled him to write the complete, 150-page manuscript of "The Man Who Lived Underground" before the end of the year.

This was the story of Fred Daniels, a black servant who is coming back from his employer, Mrs. Wooten's, counting his weekly salary, when a policeman stops him and searches him. At the station he is handcuffed and taken to General Headquarters. There, while he tries to convince the officers that there are respectable and in-fluential people who will vouch for him, he finds that he is accused of murdering a certain Mrs. Peabody. He is beaten, blinded by a light aimed at his eyes and punched in the stomach as he swallows a glass of water, but although he replies to the ques-tions, while bleeding profusely, he will not confess to the crime. He is then hung by his feet from a hook and faints as the police batter his body with kicks and blows. When he comes to, early in the morning, he is presented with a paper that he cannot read but must sign if he wants to see his wife, who is expecting a baby. He faints again and, finally, exhausted and foggy, he signs.

During this first section, the dramatic unfolding of the action alternates with the flow of Fred's thoughts. He has nightmares and hallucinations about Rachel, his job, and Mrs. Wooten; his inner world, which suffering has reduced to pure sensation, seems more real than the murder of which he is accused and the actual presence of his torturers. In the second section, Fred's inner world disappears and he is capable of action. Taken to Mrs. Peabody's for the re-construction of the crime, he realizes the seriousness of the situation and vainly tries to escape. The police allow him a final visit with Rachel; she has to be rushed to the hospital to have the baby and he is taken with her to the maternity ward. Everything now seems unreal to him again. He naps on a hospital bench under guard, but when left alone for an instant he jumps out the window, runs wildly through the rain and hides in a doorway. He finally slips into a man-hole, thus beginning the third section of the novel, which was even-tually published as a story in 1944. The action now takes place in a subterranean universe in which Fred sees, not reality in reverse, but the reverse of reality; he is still within the world, but because he is a spectator freed from himself and invisible, he is now omnipo-tent. This novel that began like any police story, concerned with the life and feelings of a completely average black character, suddenly becomes a surprising existentialist metaphor of human and divine existence, when removed from its original setting. The hero is an outsider whose color is no longer important, moving Wright to re-mark to Reynolds on December 13, 1941, "It is the first time I've really tried to step beyond the straight black-white stuff. . . ."

This sudden step from the racial novel to the metaphysical para-ble, which Wright seems to have accomplished so easily, required a distinct broadening of his themes and techniques. Certainly he acknowledged his debt to Dostoevsky, whose *Notes from Underground* perhaps inspired him, but Dostoevsky's secret universe was completely spiritual and unreal compared with the maze of sewers that Fred Daniels traverses like Jean Valjean in *Les Miserables,* and the conflicts of the Dostoevskian underground man were rooted in bitter opposition to humanity.[53] Fred, on the other hand, who maintains his position in relation to society, is like Bigger, whom the Whites did not at first suspect since they were incapable of imagining that he had motives similar to their own. Fred's situation mirrors the dilemma of all black Americans, who are both part of America and excluded from it. He does escape from his racial definition by escaping the system, but he is still on the sidelines, not because he is black in a white context, but because he is now a human being in an unreal, inhuman context. "The Man Who Lived Underground" contains the germ of the philosophy that inspired Wright in *The Outsider* of 1953. This "outsider" portrayed in 1941 evinces characteristic features of Camus' *Etranger* (although this book had not yet been written) and he is in a way close to the "exile" of the French existentialists. Indeed, Fred is responsible for a suicide and brutalities that result from some undiscovered thefts he committed while "underground," as well as guilty of abandoning humanity by transcending his condition. At first he is able to enjoy his freedom and irresponsibility, but soon the urge to rejoin society and share his divine knowledge of its laws triumphs over his pleasure in breaking those laws. Fred therefore turns himself in to the police, not because he feels the slightest guilt for the deaths that he has indirectly caused, but because it is his only chance to have other people participate in his inverted world. The police, of course, shoot this dangerous man who "would wreck things."

Wright sent the novel to Harper's immediately so that it might be published the following spring, but they rejected it. Perhaps Aswell was not confident that its newness and richness would be sufficient to win a public expecting something more similar to *Native Son.* It may also have been too short or lacking unity, considering the abrupt change from the realistic style of the police brutality in the first chapters to the more metaphoric, though equally detailed, evocation of the underground world. During 1942, *Cosmopolitan, McCall's Magazine* and the *Atlantic Monthly* all followed Harper's lead, and not until 1944 did "The Man Who Lived Underground" find a publisher.[54] Edwin Seaver, who had vainly tried to help

Wright place it, used the last part for his anthology *Cross Section*. Without the first two sections it was now a short story, and the remaining tale of Fred Daniels' underground existence lost the motivation supplied by the police brutalities, which had forced the hero to descend into the sewers, although it acquired mystery and its universal meaning was emphasized.

The deleted passages, however, not only show Wright coming out against police brutality toward Blacks but explain the denouement, when Daniels is killed in the sewer after returning to give himself up in order to share his extraordinary world.

The sensation of unreality that overwhelms the black man in the white world was later the theme of "The Man Who Killed a Shadow," while both *The Outsider* and *The Long Dream* describe police brutality toward Negroes. Here, however, Wright apparently sacrificed the realistic beginning of "The Man Who Lived Underground" in order that the story might take on a symbolic and metaphysical dimension, yet nothing indicates whether this extremely fortunate change was Wright's own idea.

In December, 1941, Wright gave two extracts from the first version of "The Man Who Lived Underground" to his friend Kerker Quinn, who was starting the magazine *Accent*.[55] He also wrote an enthusiastic introduction for Nelson Algren's *Never Come Morning*, which was published by Harper's in 1942. This short essay, in fact, presented an entire program for a realistic literature of the people:

Many competent novelists would not have considered its subject material as legitimate material, would have condemned this subject matter, no doubt, as being sordid and loathsome. Others would have treated it lightly and humorously, thereby implying that it possessed significance. Still others would have assumed an aloof "social worker attitude" toward it, prescribing "pink pills for social ills," piling up a mountain of naturalistic detail. A militant minority, shooting straight to the mark, would have drawn blueprints and cited chapters and page in a call for direct action. I think, however, Nelson Algren's strategy in *Never Come Morning* excels all of these by far, inasmuch as he depicts the intensity of feeling, the tawdry but potent dreams, the crude but forceful poetry, and the frustrated longing for human dignity residing in the lives of the Poles of Chicago's North West Side, and this revelation informs us all that there lies an ocean of life at our doorsteps—an unharnessed, unchannelled and unknown ocean.

Algren's hero, Bruno Bicek, obviously appealed to Wright be-cause, like Bigger Thomas, he represented a true American liberated from the uniformity of modern society.

If I were asked what is the one, over-all symbol or image gained from my living that most nearly represents what I feel to be the essence of American life, I'd say that it was that of a man struggling mightily to free his personality from the daily and hourly encroach-ments of American life. Of course, *Native Son* is but one angle of what I feel to be the struggle of the individual in America for self-possession.[56]

This statement is indicative of Wright's transition from what could be called a somewhat restricted racial perspective to a general con-demnation of American values. Perhaps hastened by his recent in-tensive meditations on Afro-American history, apropos of *Twelve Million Black Voices*, it might even have caused the sudden veering toward an existential and metaphysical philosophy in "The Man Who Lived Underground." It certainly helps to explain his increas-ing difficulties with his novel about black servants, which he eventu-ally abandoned altogether.

There was no doubt that Wright had by this time become a personage in New York intellectual circles and a big name in the American literary world—and could thus safely consider himself "successful." In 1938, his salary from the F.W.P., combined with his prize money, earned him at the most $2,000. In 1939, he declared $2,585 to the Internal Revenue Service, but in 1940 he earned close to $30,000, of which more than half came from royalties on *Native Son*.[57] Even after deducting the cost of his divorce and the sum paid to Dhimah, which he preferred to settle all at once, plus the expense of setting up a new household, he still found himself about $10,000 ahead. He was accustomed, however, to a simple life and foresaw that this year of comparative wealth would probably be an excep-tion, so he did not change his frugal habits. A few weeks after their marriage, Richard and Ellen moved into a two-room apartment at 473 West 40th Street. Ellen now had time to learn Southern cook-ing, to please her husband, while Richard established the work routine that he maintained throughout the rest of his life. He would spend a long morning at his typewriter or desk, taking a short break at noon for lunch in the kitchen. The afternoon was then devoted either to puttering around the house and writing letters or, more often, to going out either to see friends, attend a meeting or see a film, do research at the library or simply take a walk. In any case, he generally did not work during the evenings.

On July 10, 1941, the Wrights went back to live in Brooklyn, in a three-room apartment at 11 Revere Place. Richard's relations with his parents-in-law had always been very strained, if not nonexistent, but in August Ellen was able to tell her mother that she was expecting a baby, which improved the situation somewhat. Mrs. Poplar abandoned some of her prejudices for a reconciliation that developed into a relationship of extreme courtesy, if not warmth, on both sides.

Wright spent the summer writing and arranging his new apartment. He left the city once, to receive the Spingarn Medal in Houston, while Ellen went to visit her brother, who had been drafted. In September, they both went to Skywood Manor, a magnificent estate in the wilds of Jefferson County, New Hampshire, where Wright gave a talk at the White Mountains Conference, a summer school for L.A.W. writers. Then they started their real vacation from September 4–15 on the seashore of Halibut Point in Pigeon Cove, Massachusetts.[58]

On April 15, 1942, Richard was able to watch the birth of his daughter, Julia, through the glass windows of the delivery room. He doted on the baby from the moment she was born, and his friends smiled to see him literally standing guard against germs in his solicitous tenderness. Mrs. Poplar, meanwhile, was won over by the new arrival and immediately tried to run the household, until the courteous firmness of the young couple broke her of the habit of giving unnecessary advice.

At the beginning of the summer the Wrights moved once again, this time into a rather curious artistic colony. In October, 1940, George Davis, who was then editor of *Harper's Bazaar*, had invited Wright to dinner in the house that he had just started to share with Carson McCullers, whose novel Wright had recently reviewed. Here, Wright had met W. H. Auden and a good number of other artists, some of whom came to live at "Seven Middagh" at one time or another. This enormous Victorian house with gray shingles and a gingerbread porch, right next to the Brooklyn Bridge, became during the forties a sort of general headquarters for a group of artists and writers even larger than the Brook Farm colony. The Wrights moved into the ground floor, with George Davis just above them and the painter Oliver Smith on the top floor. The azaleas and Pavel Tchelitchev's frescoes were somewhat overwhelming to Richard and Ellen, who were by far the least eccentric of the "February house" inhabitants.[59]

They certainly did not see regularly all the former residents and visitors who came and went, among them Salvador Dali, Leonard Bernstein, Aaron Copland, Louis MacNeice, Virgil Thompson, Christopher Isherwood, Benjamin Britten, Paul Bowles and Golo Mann. They were, however, very friendly with George Davis and Carson McCullers and saw a certain amount of Lotte Lenya, Anaïs Nin, the tenor Peter Pears and Gypsy Rose Lee, who was an enlightened connoisseur of surrealist painting as well as a talented actress. At first Wright enjoyed the somewhat bohemian life because it was a constant source of stimulating intellectual exchanges. The quarter also had its curiosities. The spinster of the house next door collected lost dogs and kept them with her monkey; Mrs. Parker, the drugstore owner on the corner, and Miss Kate, the antique dealer, always had some worthwhile piece of gossip to relate, and in the evening the Sand Street bars and the whorehouses on the port lent color to the otherwise respectable neighborhood of brownstone houses. In addition Willard Maas and Marie Mencken lived nearby and Wright made some new friends in the area like the Richard Roveres,[60] but after a year the atmosphere became too noisy for them. Carson McCullers drank a great deal and owned a troop of performing dogs that got her into all kinds of trouble with the other tenants, while George Davis used to befriend sailors and dock workers who frequently beat and robbed him. These were certainly not ideal surroundings for Julia and, since Wright needed an additional room for a study, they once again thought of moving.

Since Wright was the sole support of his family he was not draftable, but he did want to participate in the national effort and was particularly anxious to get a special commission in the psychological or propaganda services of the Army. He reasoned that since he might not be exempt from the draft forever, he would encounter less discrimination in such work than as a simple soldier. In April, 1942, he sent Paul Reynolds an article entitled "Mobilization of Negro Opinion" and directed to the attention of Colonel Welles, head of army press relations for the New York area. He outlined an extensive propaganda campaign (using specific facts conveyed by radio, the press, church, schools, posters, songs and black intellectuals and artists) aimed at convincing the black population that the Fascist regimes were fundamentally racist.[61] Reynolds' work on Wright's behalf had still accomplished nothing by July, and Wright was so worried that his political opinions might cause his request to be refused that he offered to give a complete explanation of his position to the local draft board.[62] He finally approached Truman Gibson, who was then an aide in the office of the assistant to the Secretary of War, asking for work in the Radio Section of the armed forces. He went to Washington and filled out the necessary forms, only to find out in the autumn that no decision had been made on his case.[63]

Wright never did get the special commission, although he was not drafted as a soldier either. He thought for a while, as he confided to Ed Aswell in a letter on August 7, 1942, that his racist neighbors might have given the Army investigators unfavorable information about him. Certainly his Communist sympathies and criticisms of the government's racial policy were not in his favor, but it seems most likely that Colonel Welles was not in a sufficiently powerful position to be of help. The boxer Joe Louis, who had been recommended to him at the same time, turned out to be in trouble with the Internal Revenue Service, which caused some unfavorable feeling toward black applicants, and finally, at the crucial moment, Welles was transferred to another post.[64]

TWELVE

After a twenty-eight-week tour that ended in Pittsburgh on March 31, 1942—in fact its third visit to that city—*Native Son* returned to the New York area in mid-April and attracted a certain amount of attention as a revival. It played in Flatbush until the middle of May, was performed in various New Jersey theaters, then moved back to Flatbush and the Bronx, returning to Broadway on October 23. In the meantime Wright had made several changes in the text. Soon after Pearl Harbor he had added some allusions to the war and the Blacks' readiness to volunteer, but at the same time he did not fail to attack the segregation practiced within the Army.[1] Most of the original actors resumed their parts at this time with the exception of Alexander Clark, who replaced Philip Bourneuf as Buckley, and John Berry, who played Max, and was replaced as the reporter by John Ireland. The critics all mentioned that Canada Lee had perfected his performance, which, considering that public interest in the subject had somewhat abated, was the principal reason for what success it enjoyed.[2]

Broadway was at that time being subjected to a "clean-up" censorship campaign organized by various citizens' and religious groups with the support of the mayor as well as Paul Moss, director of the Censure Commission. *Native Son*, described as "obscene and strongly not recommended," was soon the butt of attacks by the Catholic Movement for the Theater. Lee Schubert (the man who had lost the Ambassador's license when *Wine, Women and Song* had been condemned for obscenity) was nervous enough to substitute *My Sister Eileen* for *Native Son* at the Majestic, with the excuse that the play was still in the red after its sixtieth performance.[3] As a result, the New York Theatre League launched a protest campaign on December 7, which united diverse groups of progressive opinion such as the Drama Artists Guild, Actors' Equity, the Negro Youth Congress and the National Congress for Constitutional Liberties. Rev. Adam Clayton Powell presided over a meeting in support at the Golden Gate Church; A. Philip Randolph, Lester Ranger, president of the Urban League, and Horace Cayton offered their services; Elmer Rice and Howard Lindsay provided financial support. The Communist press and the Party, through Ben Davis, also came out against the proscription. Meanwhile Wright's name figured prominently on the "Schomburg Honor Roll" of 1942.[4] Walter White, in the name of the NAACP, even called upon the mayor to justify himself, but La Guardia claimed that he did not know why Lee Schubert had made such a decision. The play continued its run despite the letter posted in churches around the city condemning it as "the glorification of license and crime." In spite of this publicity and Canada Lee's excellent performance, the financial success was only moderate, primarily because, as the critics often mentioned, Julius Loewenthal had taken over from Orson Welles. In his defense it must be said that Loewenthal had been forced to economize by omitting the rapid changes of scene, because the price of the tickets had been lowered from $2.75 to $1.50 in order to attract a popular audience. The rhythm of the play was thus broken, especially because of the intermission added after the fifth scene, while the lighting was sometimes insufficient and the original sound track quite scratchy after five hundred performances. It was no surprise, therefore, when the play closed on January 2, 1943.

2

In August, 1942, Wright happened to tell a friend the amusing story of the overturned guinea pig cages at the Michael Reese Hospital in Chicago. On this friend's advice he turned the anecdote into a short satirical piece, which was published by *Harper's Magazine* in December, 1942, as "What You Don't Know Won't Hurt You."[5] The tone was ironic and sometimes bitter, telling of the segregation of the few black hospital employees and how the animals had been randomly replaced in their cages, possibly causing an important theory to be abandoned or some questionable discovery to be announced. Nevertheless, this was the first use of humor in Wright's fiction, and it was unexpectedly powerful. The story turned out to be very successful among black readers when Wright gave it to *Negro Digest* for publication in January, 1943, in aid of this new magazine.

For two years running, Wright had refused invitations to speak at Fisk University in Nashville, either from lack of time or because he judged that professors at black universities must belong to the black middle class that he often attacked in his articles. In 1943, Horace Cayton finally persuaded him to accept the invitation of Charles S. Johnson, the head of the sociology department, to speak to the students. He had not even chosen the subject of his lecture by the time he got on the train with Horace Cayton for the South, so he decided to speak on his own problems and beliefs as a writer and a black American. He later described this talk that he gave on April 9, 1943, at the Commemorative Chapel:

I gave a clumsy, conversational kind of speech to the folks, white and black, reciting what I felt and thought about the world; what I remembered about my life, about being a Negro. There was but little applause. Indeed, the audience was terribly still, and it was not until I was half way through my speech that it crashed upon me that I was saying things that Negroes were not supposed to say publicly, things that whites had forbidden. What made me realize this was a hysterical, half-repressed, tense kind of laughter that went up now and then from the white and black faces.

After the speech I stood sweating, wanting to get away. A Negro educator came rushing down the aisle, his face tight with emotion: "Goddam," he panted in a whisper, "you're the first man to tell the truth in this town!"

A white man, a Southerner, came and stood a few feet from me and murmured ironically, uneasily: "You've brought the racial problem to Nashville."

There were more of these reactions from both white and black, so many more of them that I resolved that night I would stop writing my novel and string my autobiographical notes, thoughts and memories together into a running narrative.[6]

Horace Cayton was astounded by Wright's oratorical powers. Everyone was left gaping after Wright had revealed the false pretensions of both races and predicted the evolution of their relationship up to the time when Blacks would no longer be prevented from voting in the South.[7] The next day, after an exhausting evening with the students, who assailed him with questions about his own life, Wright visited the University's Bethlehem Center and attended a performance of *Green Pastures* put on by the Fisk Stagecrafters at the Little Theatre. On Sunday Cayton was not feeling well, but Wright went to lunch as a guest of the sociology and English students at Jubilee Hall, before a final gathering of friends at the Johnsons'.

This visit, though brief, had far-reaching effects. Wright was exposed to a new generation of university students and abandoned certain of his prejudices against them. He had a chance to see the specific problems of an institution like Fisk, which was situated on the frontier of the Deep South in a city where the liberals were so timid as to be mostly ineffective in their efforts. The trip itself also renewed the experience of segregation. Wright and Cayton had to eat in a separate section of the dining car, and Wright spent the night fully dressed on the bottom bunk of the Pullman. In answer to Cayton's surprise at this, he replied, "You never can tell what might happen in the South. I'd just as soon have a stone wall between myself and these Whites." He had been so conditioned and scarred by his childhood that he had no trouble reassuming the defenses and emotions he had learned as a "black boy." Most significant of all was the public's reaction to his speech, which was the spark that kindled his vague ideas of writing an autobiography into a burning desire to begin at once. Although this desire was not at all new, Wright returned to New York with the incentive to devote himself to the project and had finished a first draft in about eight months.[8] Over a period of ten years of literary activity, Wright's memories had become partially pruned and organized. A biographical sketch intended for *New Caravan* (where he gave 1909 as his birthdate, causing many a mistake in reference books) was the first instance in which he exaggerated the poverty of his origins and emphasized the lack of contact with civilization that had characterized his itinerant childhood. "The Ethics of Living Jim Crow," written in 1937, described his first experiences with racism, which he repeated almost word for word in *Black Boy.* Finally, the numerous interviews since 1940 had brought out the principal stages of his career, his love of Mencken, his varied reading and his many jobs. In 1940, at age thirty-two, he asked Paul Reynolds for time to consider his friend's suggestion of writing his autobiography, but in 1943, his reception by the mixed audience at Nashville gave a new meaning to this material that he had previously considered too personal.

Wright had been trying for a long time to make white Americans understand the black world they refused to confront partly because they were responsible for it. He was convinced that knowing reality was itself the beginning of progress, and hence that it was an indispensable step toward solving the racial problem. Wright was fully aware of his own fear and aggression, which came out in his stories and first novel, since he tended to identify with his characters and make them up out of himself. The reception of *Native Son*, however, had shown Wright that Bigger had been considered a special case, by both Whites and cautious Blacks who still clung to their stereotyped image of the Negro. They were frightened by Bigger and so rejected him by denying his humanity. At Fisk, Wright had noticed the panic in his audience as he systematically destroyed the veils that protected their easy consciences and revealed both hostile and fearful feelings that no one had dared express aloud. This, then, was his point of departure. He would not allow the pseudoliberal Whites and the black bourgeoisie to continue any longer in their bad faith. Although they might be able to ignore Bigger as a monster of fiction, they would have a difficult time rejecting the experiences of his creator. Wright himself was just as confident in the symbolic truth of his hero, but he had finally admitted that his public would be more easily convinced by autobiography. He was, therefore, far from setting himself up as a model, nor was it a whimsical expression of false modesty when he suggested: "One of the things that made me write is that I realize that I'm a very average Negro . . . maybe that's what makes me extraordinary." [9] He is merely asserting the value of every human being and using his own life as the most convenient source of truth with which to reclaim the dignity of every black man.[10]

Although Wright changed the "he" of *Native Son* to "I" in *Black Boy*, he emphasized that he was describing a universal black childhood, since the privilege of being able to express himself implied the responsibility of speaking for others who could not. "I wanted to give, lend my tongue to the voiceless Negro boys. I feel that way about the deprived Negro children of the South. . . . 'Not until the sun ceases to shine on you will I disown you.' That was one of my motives." [11] This solidarity was as much intellectual as emotional, since Wright, like Whitman, who considered the poet a prophet, felt that the "representative" writer should remove the shrouds of ignorance and thus remove the evil. His book should have a therapeutic function. But only a sincere confession could bring about the solution of the racial problem; a very high degree of self-knowledge was needed, and this might be painful for Blacks and Whites alike, since such knowledge presupposed both a moral and political judgment.

I wrote the book to tell a series of incidents strung through my childhood, but the main desire was to render a judgment on my environment. . . . That judgment was this: the environment the South creates is too small to nourish human beings, especially Negro human beings. Some may escape the general plights and grow up, but it is a matter of luck and I think it should be a matter of plan. It should be a matter of saving the citizens of our country for our country. [12]

The double function of revealing and judging determined Wright's method. He searched in his past for the implications of his memories, not shying away from the baldest detail or the most compromising insight. He was quite ready to take sides, even though he sacrificed nuances by this open, even simplistic, support of a thesis.

Wright delved into his past for months, sometimes working for ten hours at a stretch in his office. He would record his earliest memories on the Ediphone before typing them. Some later episodes he scribbled down and others he typed directly, depending upon the time and place in which the incident came to mind. He did not, as formerly was his custom, have a secretary type his rough draft, but took the time himself to make a clean copy. He made so many corrections, in fact, that every revision meant a new version of an episode. He continued this process until he had retraced his first twenty-five years of life. [13]

Writing this biography was therapy for the author, as well as a test. He considered it an inner adventure, akin to psychoanalysis, by which he could come to reevaluate his personality and his career at the very moment when his break with communism was causing him to question himself and seek in himself a new direction. He discovered himself as a black man, scarred by his hatred, alienated as much from his family as from those American "lovers of trash" whose only preoccupations were material. He evaluated his mistakes and weaknesses and his somewhat unjust rejection of his father. He acquired a clearer conception of his capacity as a writer. He no longer considered it a career happened upon by chance. Originally a sublimation of his bitterness as a passion-ridden adolescent, a channel for his aggressiveness, it finally gave way to an idealism. By the end of this period of self-probing, Wright was enormously relieved at having made the effort and changed as a result of it.

If you try it, you will find that at times sweat will break out upon you. You will find that even if you succeed in discounting the attitudes of others to you and your life, you must wrestle with yourself most of all, fight with yourself; for there will surge up in you a strong desire to alter facts, to dress up your feelings. You will find that there are many things that you don't want to admit about yourself and others. As your record shapes itself up, an awed wonder haunts you. And yet there is no more exciting an adventure than trying to be honest in this way. The clean strong feeling that sweeps you when you've done it, makes you know that.[14]

On December 17, 1943, he sent Reynolds the manuscript, which covered his life up to his departure from Chicago in 1937; he also enclosed a letter expressing both modesty and the conviction that he could do little to change or improve "American Hunger."

Here is another manuscript, the value of which I do not know. Read it and if it is worth showing to Harper's, then let them see it; if, however, you think that such a book ought not to be published by me at this time, then hold it. I don't think that there is much that I will ever be able to do on this script. Perhaps a section or two here and there will have to be pulled out. But, on the whole, the thing will have to stand as it is, for better or worse.

He had meanwhile gone back to work on his novel about black servants from a new perspective and had finished 125 pages of a new version by the end of the year. He had completely given up the original idea but used the same material to elaborate the same theme in what he considered, as he confided to Reynolds in his letter of December 17, a more dynamic and coherent fashion.

It may seem that I'm not working, but I am. The truth is that I've had trouble getting my writing to jell right. And of course, that is something that a writer has to fight out with himself and settle and solve.

Reynolds was enthusiastic on reading the autobiography and at the beginning of January, 1944, Aswell, who was just as keen, accepted it with the intention of publishing it before the end of the year; he did suggest, though, that it might be better to limit the book to Wright's experiences in the South because it would then be more closely knit. In addition, the second section, which took place in the North, should logically end, he felt, in another volume, with the New York years. Aswell also wanted to add an explanatory subtitle, "The Biography of a Courageous Negro," but Wright wrote back on January 22 saying that he wanted the reader to be the judge of his courage and suggesting as an alternative "Biography of an American Negro." The story of the Chicago years, too short to be published as a book, was offered to *Harper's Magazine*, which rejected it in February. "American Hunger," however, was due to come out in the autumn, and in May Wright received the galleys for the entire autobiography.

Even the jacket had already been designed—with red and black lettering on a white background—when Wright wrote Reynolds on August 10 suggesting that the title be changed to *Black Boy*:

Now, this is not very original, but I think it covers the book. It is honest. Straight. And many people say it to themselves when they see a Negro and wonder how he lives. Black Boy seems to me to be not only a title, but also a kind of heading of the whole general theme.

At the same time he submitted eight possible subtitles, in order to avoid labeling the book an autobiography if it only went up to his eighteenth year.[15] He now preferred to emphasize the particularity of life in the South, and the chronic anxiety of his childhood. At this time *Black Boy* became a Book-of-the-Month Club selection, which postponed publication until the following year. In his August 24 letter to Reynolds approving the new jacket design, Wright also expressed his satisfaction with this decision and suggested that the introduction to the book be extracted from the review that Dorothy Canfield Fisher had just written for the Book-of-the-Month Club *Bulletin*.

The *Atlantic Monthly* accepted the second section of the book, which had just been rejected by *Cosmopolitan*. They used only the passages relating to Wright's Communist experiences, although this was not an attempt on their part to emphasize Wright's condemnation of authoritarianism. In fact, the editors of the magazine had first thought of publishing the whole piece in one issue, which would have involved more extensive cutting, but since they finally decided to publish it in two installments, they included everything from the original text dealing with communism. They added only a few transitional sentences with the result that "I Tried to Be a Communist" does not distort the message of the complete autobiography as it was originally written in 1943.[16]

Wright dealt with his experiences in the Chicago C.P. unit and at the John Reed Club in terms that could just as well have applied to his difficulties with the New York leaders from 1941 to 1942. The article questioned the sincerity of the Communists and revealed the "terrorist" methods used at the very heart of the Party toward the somewhat undisciplined members, emphasizing the total scorn for individual liberty which such disciplinary action betrayed. Wright did not attack the Party itself but criticized individual leaders, among whom it is easy to recognize Oliver Law, Harry Haywood and John P. Davis. He made some withering comments, and although he limited himself strictly to his own experience, he caused considerable damage to the Party image.

"I Tried to Be a Communist" came out in the August and September issues of the *Atlantic*, and the response was almost immediate. Up to this point, the Communist hostility had been subtle. It was understandable that Wright might want to take revenge on certain Communists for their spying, denigration, humiliation and insults, but, though insidious, this campaign against him had not been much publicized. In his article "Richard Wright in Retreat," which appeared in the August 23, 1944, issue of *New Masses*, Samuel Sillen was only moderately critical of Wright, claiming that he had crossed over to the reactionary camp.[17] James W. Ford, on the other hand, was much more brutal in "The Case of Richard Wright," written for the *Daily Worker* of September 5.

He declared the irremediable exclusion of the "renegade" whom he now held up for public scorn, and for almost the next ten years everything that Wright wrote or said was systematically denigrated by the Party press, whenever they did not feel it would be even more effective to condemn him by total silence. Not only was Wright without allies in his fight against racist attacks, he had now to protect himself against his former friends. From now on, he rejected both communism and fascism as two equally insidious and brutal methods of seizing power.

The conservatives certainly did not fail to congratulate themselves on Wright's defection. The September, 1944, parish bulletin of the Church of St. John in New York was not the only one to rejoice at Wright's "conversion":

A new Mr. Wright makes his appearance. How different he is from the author of "Native Son." He is still pulling no punches, but this time his adversary is not the whole world but only a group of the world's inhabitants, those who call themselves "Communists."

It is evident that this young writer has had a sad disappointment; that he has been disillusioned and, too, that he is thoroughly disgusted with his experiences as a Communist. As Mr. Wright concluded (and, we think, quite correctly): "Communism is certainly not a panacea for the American Negro." Instead, Mr. Wright says: "Communism is selfish, intolerant, bigoted and insincere,"

the author proclaimed without batting an eye at his misquotation. Wright shuddered to see the Church use his writing for its own ends, but it was inevitable. The nuances of his presentation, his enthusiasm for certain accomplishments of the Party, his nostalgia in saying good-bye to his former beliefs—everything, in fact, which softened his criticism of the Party—was ignored in favor of polemic; public opinion held that deserting one camp was synonymous with moving to the other.

Most of Wright's Communist friends and, in particular, certain of the *New Masses* critics, refused to desert him, but they did have to refrain from openly defending him. Others, like Langston Hughes, Dorothy Norman, Willard Maas and John Hammond, who believed in the common action of radical and intellectual forces outside the Communist Party, provided Wright's new political and intellectual milieu, while he also came closer to the intellectual and artistic circles of New York, and even to the black bourgeoisie.[18]

3

At the beginning of August, 1943, Ellen, Richard and Julia had left "Seven Middagh" for the more respectable atmosphere of Lefferts Place, still in Brooklyn Heights. Number 89 was a big brick building divided into apartments, where they stayed for two years. They themselves designed and decorated the six-room apartment, C-23, hiring Ad Bates, a well-known Harlem cabinet maker, to do the necessary work.[19] Wright finally had a room for his library, which now numbered over six hundred volumes. He had acquired a great many treatises on psychology, anthropology, psychoanalysis and sociology, and soon the Encyclopaedia Britannica and the Encyclopedia of Social Sciences joined his collection of modern novels and books on Afro-Americans. He continued to read voraciously, almost five books a week, but these he usually borrowed from the public library.

It was at this time that the riots started in Harlem. In June, violent interracial outbreaks in Detroit had already caused thirty-four deaths and hundreds of injuries. On August 1, a black soldier was protesting the arrest of a woman in the hall of the Hotel Braddock when he was wounded by a policeman. Violence immediately broke out in Harlem, where white stores were looted and police action caused five deaths and sixty wounded, a tragedy that moved Wright to give one of his rare interviews for that year. He described what he had observed from 100th to 120th streets along Eighth Avenue, the border of the ghetto. He emphasized the fear and tension of the Blacks to whom he spoke, explaining that, rather than a racial riot, in which organized groups of Blacks and Whites entered into the action, this had been a spontaneous outburst of anger, primarily caused by a difficult economic situation.[20] He suggested that the position of Afro-Americans in the armed forces be improved and that a program of economic aid to the ghetto be instituted. In September, he helped to organize The Citizens' Emergency Conference for Interracial Unity, which assembled representatives from both races at Hunter College.

This troubled summer must have further inspired Wright to take action on his commitment to articulate necessary social criticism as a representative of the black community. He had certainly been cherishing for some time the idea of starting a magazine devoted to improving the understanding between Blacks and Whites.

As early as 1940, with the help of the "Progress Publishing Company" and in association with Louis Adamic, Emmett Gowen, William Carlos Williams and Leonard Goldsmith, he had tried to launch an inexpensive magazine that would counteract the reactionary influence of the popular magazines, but they had not been able to raise the necessary funds.[21]

In the meantime, Wright had been impressed by the orientation and format of the daily newspaper *PM*, which had been started by his friend Roger Pippett in 1941. Wright therefore worked out a proposal for a monthly publication along the same lines, which would run to about two hundred pages and have a printing of five thousand copies for a start. He sent out his detailed plan for "American Pages" (or "These States") toward the end of the summer.

Wright's aim was to "clarify the personality and cultural problems of minority groups" for the white middle class, by "using the Negro question as an abstract and concrete frame of experience to reflect a constructive criticism upon the culture of the nation as a whole." [22] His method resulted largely from his study of psychoanalysis. If he could "psychoanalyze" the white reader and his culture, make him question his beliefs by confronting him with the truths about American industrial society, he would demolish his racial prejudices as well as the American myths of democracy and happiness. He would then be ready to discard his familiar, and racist, thought patterns. It would almost be the beginning of a cultural revolution on the ethnic level.

Wright started from the assumption that an industrial society is unable to satisfy man's most creative and constructive tendencies, the frustration of which will, therefore, show up in various pathological actions such as problem drinking, cruelty, violence and racial hatred. Nevertheless, the magazine would aim less at emphasizing these failures and blaming them on the system than at painting in concrete terms the compensations and life-styles that social unbalance had caused—"the restlessness, the crazy fads, the inescapable loneliness, the adoration of cheap movies, cheap pathos, cheap morals, cheap art, cheap journalism, cheap aspirations, and the whole dismally lowered tone of American personality expression." This plan, in fact, embodied Wright's disillusionment with the United States. As a child, he had imagined that the Whites lived a more beautiful and profound life than the Blacks, but now that he had ascended the social ladder himself, he saw only a vulgar existence, devoid of personal dignity. This was a disillusionment that never ceased to grow.

As differentiated from *PM*, the future magazine would use biographical sketches, simplified academic studies, extracts from novels and, something that became one of Wright's lifetime interests, criminal case studies. Wright made up a list of more than one hundred possible issues and themes.[23] Among the most interesting were articles on folklore, pieces of typical Negro humor, a regular report on the evolution of race relations, portraits of Whites who passed themselves off as Blacks and vice versa, and biographical sketches of prostitutes, black champions and celebrities, as well as white fascists. A review section would briefly list recent books but might devote several pages to the work of a particular author. In this way all aspects of racial experience would be covered and the myths of American society scrutinized.

A paragraph deleted from the final version of the plan indicates that Wright's personal motive was to express his own special insight into the problem. He perceived not only the cultural problems implied by the situation of minorities in the United States but also the problems of the nation as a whole, as revealed in its attitude toward minorities. Through his selection of the material and collaborators he wanted to express his own understanding of the nature of such problems. He believed, in fact, that he belonged both to the minority culture and to the dominant culture, and his aim was to bring them together, help them to understand the implications of the situation. Here Wright is already formulating his theory on the privileged position of the black American, an outsider living on the fringe of two cultures and therefore able to understand both points of view better than anyone else. This was a theory he supported in later writings on Africa and the Third World, but even in 1943 he had already foreseen the ultimate failure of the "melting pot" and the traditional conception of American democracy. At the same time he proclaimed the right to live in a pluri-ethnic and pluri-cultural society in which the minorities would play a significant role.

> If America can be brought to understand the nature and meaning of minorities, whether as individuals or groups, she will have taken the first step toward a unified culture, and it will be the first instance of a true circulation of basic ideas from one place of American consciousness to another.

Thus Wright's conception of the black man's role in the United States actually foreshadowed that later held by advocates of Black Power in the sixties. Wright himself never opposed integration and in fact did everything in his power to promote it. By integration, however, he did not mean a more or less disguised form of amalgamation, but rather an equality among the several ethnic cultures in American society that would permit them not only to survive but also to enrich the national culture precisely because they had retained their individuality and not been reduced to a common denominator.

Wright's plan did not lack scope or foresight, but the magazine never got started. Several of Wright's influential radical and liberal friends, like Edwin Seaver, E. R. Embree, Bernard Wolfe, St. Clair Drake, George Davis, Horace Cayton and Ralph Ellison, supported the idea, but those who tried to interest some enlightened millionaire in the progress were without success. Of these, Horace Cayton came the closest.

In March, 1943, Cayton had suggested to Marshall Field III, the owner of the *Chicago Sun*, that the paper reserve a column in which well-known writers could express themselves on racial issues, and had specifically mentioned Wright at the time. Embree's book *Thirteen Against the Odds*, biographical sketches of notable black Americans, had come out in January, 1944, and Wright had participated with Etta Motten, the wife of his friend Claude Barnett, in a critical broadcast on this collection, which contained the best account of his early career written in his lifetime. He saw Embree again that spring in Chicago, where Horace Cayton had Wright invited to attend a convention on black Americans organized by the Rosenwald Foundation.[24] There the plan for the magazine was officially presented to Marshall Field. Mrs. Clara Florsheim, the widow of a rich shoe manufacturer, had already agreed to partially finance it (the total sum required was $16,000), provided that Marshall Field was also interested, but despite Embree's earnest pleas, Field thought the enterprise too much of a risk.[25] "American Pages," therefore, represented nothing more than another excellent attempt on Wright's part to perform his function of a committed black intellectual. It proves, however, that he had clearly realized the implications of his position as a critic of American culture and the world importance of the black American, while his failure convinced him that, despite the assurances of white liberals to the contrary, a black intellectual had little chance of being heeded; America was not disposed to fight efficiently against its racist prejudices.

As part of Wright's mission to show the white world another piece of reality about black life, Wright had applied to the National Film Board of Canada for a job at the beginning of 1942. He wanted to make a film on the underground railroad, an idea suggested to him perhaps by reading Henrietta Buckmaster's book, in order to give a more accurate and complete picture of black resistance to slavery. Through his friends Norman McLaren and Guy Glover, he wrote to Film Board officials John Grierson and Ernest Borneman on February 4 and 18 respectively, explaining this idea which "its very nature rendered impossible to accomplish in the United States," but Grierson could not, or would not, agree to the request, although Wright had specified that the question of money was secondary.

When he returned to New York from Chicago on April 6, 1944, Wright told Reynolds about yet another project, this one to show the contribution of popular black culture to American culture in the form of a screenplay probably inspired by his trip to Fisk University the year before. "Melody Limited" was modeled on the adventures of the Jubilee Singers and told the story of a group of recently emancipated slaves who, during Reconstruction, tour America and Europe to earn money to save and expand their school, which had been started by a Southern liberal plantation owner, Colonel Weatherby.[26] Wright himself explains the goals and possibilities of his screenplay in the opening pages of the unpublished sixty-page outline. He wanted

to tap the almost untouched archives of religious and secular songs of the Negro; . . . The advantage of going to the sources for this material is to recapture the old dignity, grandeur of Negro folk music, much of which has been watered and deleted. The old contagion and enjoyment which these songs evoked in the 70's could be revived and there is no better medium than the movies for doing so. . . .

The aim of the story is to depict the romantic and adventurous manner in which the Negro educational institutions were built and the role that religion and Negro folk songs played in their building. Inasmuch as Northern and Southern whites both contributed in the building of the educational institutions, I feel that they could be presented on the screen with Negroes in a manner not yet done in the American film, showing them as men and women who tried against odds to build a bridge of understanding between the races.

It is noticeable that Wright's political opinions did not lead him to minimize the role of religion in this scenario, written out of the same desire to stress the folk tradition as were *Twelve Million Black Voices* and his blues songs. Wright felt that the old melodies had been adulterated by the white singers of the day to suit popular taste, and that no one was better qualified than Arna Bontemps to help him restore some of their original force and authenticity. In addition, he wanted to point out that interracial collaboration had taken place during the Reconstruction period.

The love interest of the plot predominates, but the simple dramatic outline also includes many lyrical passages making use of freedom songs, hymns, children's rhymes, the syncopated rhythms of African dances and, of course, the spirituals sung at all the concerts, which punctuate the scenes and heighten the dramatic climaxes. These spirituals are, in the order in which they were sung, "All God's Chillun Got Shoes," "This Train, This Train," "They Crucified My Lord," "Get on Board, Chillun," "Let My People Go" and "Sometimes I Feel Like a Motherless Child."

The spirituals are, in fact, responsible for the eventual success of the band. On their first stop, Chicago, their audiences in regular theaters quickly diminish as they sing their classical program, but when they gather near a fountain and spontaneously express their despair in spirituals, people flock to hear them and offer money. They donate this sum to the mayor in aid of the homeless of the city, which is being ravaged by the great fire. In return, he sends them on to Cleveland, where, again, their classical concert fails but a spiritual, sung in bitterness, attracts an enormous audience. They are now on the road to success, which leads them to Washington,

Baltimore, Buffalo and New York. They have already assured the future of Colonel Weatherby's school, but in response to an invitation, they visit England, where they are awarded the trophy in the Crystal Palace Festival, a singing contest, by no less than the Queen of England.

Wright gave the manuscript to Columbia Films, through M. Spingold, at the same time that he offered it to the National Film Board of Canada, but, having been read by Miss Emily Brown of the Columbia Film Board on April 18, it was finally rejected, and later, in July, Lena Horne refused the lead role. The outline was never used, despite the efforts of Arna Bontemps, who worked hard to place it.

Considering how interested Wright had become in lessening the gap between the races and presenting the so-called Negro problem to the American public, he was obviously surprised and delighted when Mr. Leston Huntley, a radio producer, asked him to write and organize a series of programs on the life of a black family. By June, 1944, only two months later, he sent in a general plan for the series, entitled "Sunny Side of the Street," along with descriptions of all the characters, texts for three programs and outlines for a dozen others, all of which came to about one hundred pages. His imagination was so stimulated by the prospect of working in this new domain that he wrote steadily for three solid weeks. He was not able in that amount of time to determine the exact progression of the episodes, but the characters he created were suitable for serial treatment and each one could be the central character for an entire program. The general theme was the daily life of a black family, its relationship with the outside world as much as its intimate home life. Danny, the young son, would embody the theme of childhood in Harlem; Ruby, age fifteen, would show the world of adolescence; the world of jazz among the "swingers" would be revealed through Larry; and Uncle Caesar would provide colorful humor. Miranda, the mother, would be a continuing character, since she would appear in each episode, and the major subject of one of them. Foreseeing that the speech of the black actors would automatically add flavor and piquancy to the written text, Wright did not bother to write the dialogue in Negro dialect, but merely made sure to use characteristic phrases and expressions of the ghetto. He wrote Leston Huntley on June 5, 1944, that he was very satisfied with his accomplishment:

I feel [it] conveys a good feeling for Negro life itself, over and above plot, emotion, humor and suspense. I have put a great deal of time and energy into this, and the further I proceeded the more enthusiastic I became.

Leston Huntley spent the entire summer trying to place the program, but he ran up against a great many obstacles. The greatest opposition seemed to come from a number of influential Blacks (a certain Professor Dent in particular), who were radically against this project, since, according to them, it would show their race in an unflattering light. In a letter of December 6 to Huntley, Wright was sympathetic but indignant.

It never occurred to me that you were encountering the same brand of trouble from so-called Negro leaders that I've had to deal with ever since I've been writing. . . . It is not the Negro race that cannot see this in the way you wish. It is a very small and prejudiced minority whose objection you are assuming is that of the entire race. . . . Mr. Dent sees Negro life and America from the topmost rungs of the academic world. Men like Mr. Dent are usually so throttled and frustrated with dealing with the Negro problem that they easily lose their sense of proportion, their sense of reality, and they finally drift into a neurotic state of mind in which they think and feel that every utterance must plead their cause. . . . Where the Dents always go wrong is that they mistake how this job should be done. They seem to feel that the only way in which the Negro's humanity can be asserted is by showing the Negro wearing a claw hammer coat, white shirt, black tie, and, incidentally, reading classical literature! Only a few people in any race do that.

Wright even suggested conducting a contest to determine, ahead of time, which type of family most Blacks imagined they belonged to, but Leston Huntley did not dare confront the powerful prejudices of American radio at the time. Perhaps, too, he was being denied the necessary money, and so this magnificent project (which only today has been achieved on television) was dropped. Once again Wright was thwarted because of the limits imposed by the backwardness of the American public.[27]

At the request of Edwin Seaver, Wright let his name be included from February, 1944, to August, 1945, among the associate editors of *Direction,* the monthly publication formerly run by the L.A.W., but, unlike Kenneth Burke, John Gassner, William

Gropper and other editors, he published nothing in the magazine. He preferred to give his interviews and reviews to *PM*, the excellent newspaper of Ralph Ingersoll and Elmer Rice, since they shared his opinions, and he had complete confidence in his friend, Roger Pippett, the book review editor.

In May, 1944, he participated actively in Harlem Week, one of the great achievements of the city-wide "Harlem Week Committee," an interracial organization to help the ghetto and improve relations in the different New York communities. Dorothy Norman, known for her editorials in the *New York Post* and her work in this area, presided. Wright had met her four years previously at Theodore Dreiser's and the two of them, both anti-Stalinists, had seen each other frequently since then. In 1944, they began to see more of each other, and Dorothy, the editor of *Twice a Year,* a magazine inspired both by the liberalism of Randolph Bourne and the aesthetics of Alfred Stieglitz, introduced Wright to those progressive writers and painters in New York who also refused to submit to political authoritarianism in their fight for civil liberties and individual rights.

On June 2, 1944, Wright attended a good-bye party given by Dreiser at the Commodore Hotel. Dreiser had been living in Hollywood since the beginning of the war and had come to New York to receive the Medal of Merit of the American Academy of Arts and Letters. Among his friends who had just attended the ceremony and were assembled for a large dinner were George Seldes, Kenneth Miller, Doris Dudley, Robert Elias, Edwin Seaver, Eric Weiss, George Duthuit, Lotte Jacobi and Isidor Schneider. At that time Wright had still not published any formal declaration of his break with the Party and he had not been put into quarantine by the Communists. Margaret Tjader recounted the conversation between the two authors in "Dreiser's Last Visit to New York," which appeared in the 1946 issue of *Twice a Year*, following Dreiser's death.

With Richard Wright, Dreiser talked long about Chicago; they agreed that it had been a stimulating place to them both, because of the realistic vision of life that flourished there, the youth, the rawness of the city. The Chicago of their day was changing so fast that there was no time for traditional attitudes to form and harden.

"When I talked to Dreiser," said Wright later, "I was never conscious that I was in the presence of a writer. The small, vicious habits of writers never clung to him. He did not discuss his latest book, or the book he was about to write. Listening to his simple, direct descriptions, you felt that he was above all a man, sensitive, creative, intensely interested in everything—bigger than a writer. He could melt his mood into that of those surrounding him. . . . If you asked him a question, he would say a little something in reply; and later, a little more, and perhaps later, still more—as if any idea was enough to start some deep, emotional, psychological movement in him."

It was during this evening that Dreiser was informed of the death of his sister Mamie, which was such a shock that he had to lie down for a few moments before asking his guests to leave. He went to Chicago three days later, and Wright never saw him again.

In August, the Wrights went to Canada for their vacation, first spending a few days in Montreal with their friend Frieda Lewis, then going to Ottawa, where they stayed until September 9, after a trip to the Gatineau country of Quebec. As Wright confided to a friend, they were, in fact, looking for a place to live, making excursions from Ottawa to inspect the houses and land for sale, but they never found their ideal home. Despite the heat, which was even greater than that of the New York furnace he had left, Wright found the countryside lush and beautiful, and he regretted leaving this peaceful area where the animals came to eat on the threshold of his house and where it was so agreeable to do nothing. He saw Norman McLaren and Ernest Borneman and met for the first time William O'Connell, a young writer with a lively and sensitive style, whom he recommended to Ed Aswell. He was even asked to be a member of a jury on films, an honor that delighted him.[28] He was still in Ottawa when he heard the sad news of Paul Reynolds, Sr.'s death at the age of eighty-four. This man had been the literary agent of Shaw, Conrad, Galsworthy, Stephen Crane and Paul Laurence Dunbar, but it was his son who usually took care of Wright.

When he came back, Wright had to face the first attacks following the publication of "I Tried to Be a Communist" in the *Atlantic Monthly*. He did not reply directly to these attacks, but shortly after, he corresponded with Antonio Frasconi, a painter from Montevideo, and in letters to him passionately claimed his independence of thought and action from the Communist Party as well as from American institutions. Although Wright had always supported other writers (that very month he had recommended *Count Me Among the Living* by Ethol Kossa to Aswell), he had never had the opportunity to counsel an artist in the same way until Antonio Frasconi wrote him in November, 1944, because he was hesitating, in spite of his own antiracist opinions, to publish a volume of about fifty wood cuts on the American Negro. His friends considered that the book would weaken the union against fascism in Uruguay and that the allusions to the riots in Detroit and to the racial inequality in the United States would bring American democracy into question. Since Wright had just solved a similar dilemma by leaving the Party that would endorse the segregation of blood by the American Red Cross, he strongly denounced all attempts to camouflage the racial problem, especially if this "united front" was so fragile that the simple truth could break it. He concluded that the artist must always give priority to his own perspective, regardless of circumstances or political imperatives.[29] This was henceforth Wright's own program, outlined in a letter to Frasconi, who used it as an introduction to his book, _Los Infrahumanos, Problema Del Negro en America_, published in January, 1945.

At that time Wright had two major plans, which he described to Ed Aswell in a letter of November 27, 1944. The first was a photographic documentary about the children of Harlem. After having tried in vain to find a black photographer who would have free access to the resources of the ghetto as well as a firsthand knowledge of the subject, he got in touch with Helen Levitt, who was known for her exhibitions of 1943 at the Museum of Modern Art and had already published numerous photographs of black children. The principal theme of the collection was to be the delinquent—his life at home, at school and in the street, as well as in the juvenile courts and houses of correction—but the project was never realized.

The second project was to assemble under the title "The Meaning of Negro Experience in America" over a dozen studies by black writers and sociologists on black culture and the racial problem. Wright explained to Aswell that he had refused, the year before, to contribute to Rayford Logan's book _What the Negro Wants_ because of a disagreement between the white liberals and the Blacks assigned to write it. Wright's collection would not be merely a new arrangement of monographs and personal impressions. Each author would have his own domain assigned him from the list of specific subjects so as to eliminate repetition, while the black writers, who would on the average be more radical and scientific than Logan's collaborators, would provide unity through their common point of view. In the spring of 1944, Wright had even thought of organizing what he called a "thinking coterie" and of assuring the collaboration of certain friends and acquaintances; J. Saunders Redding, Horace Cayton, St. Clair Drake, Melvin B. Tolson, Manet Fowler, Lawrence D. Reddick, C. L. R. James, E. Franklin Frazier, all accredited writers, would first agree upon their common viewpoint and then each write an essay. Wright himself planned to write a long conclusion, "The Meaning of Negro Experience in America," which was also the subject of an upcoming lecture tour.[30]

This plan was not at all definite by the end of 1944, since certain projected contributors had not yet even been asked, but Wright wanted to know what possibilities Aswell thought such a book might have. The project failed, on its own, it seemed, because the principal organizers could not agree on certain points. On January 1, 1945, Wright had a meeting at his house with Cayton, who was visiting him for the holidays, James, Drake and Reddick. According to Wright's private diary, it was Drake who balked at any general definition of the Blacks, ascribed their racial situation in America to exclusively economic causes and more or less equated racism with mere aversion. Wright was almost ready to give up the project altogether, although Redding discussed and accepted the outline on February 26. Somewhat later Wright, Cayton and James tried once again to revive the project by themselves, but Wright's departure for Paris put a definite end to what could have been one of the principal works of the period on the black American.

Despite the group's difficulties in achieving a common perspective, Wright enjoyed the support of several good black friends at that time. Cayton stayed with him every time he came to New York. Michael Carter, the editor of the *Brooklyn Eagle*, worked with him toward integration and they exchanged impressions, books and information. Ralph Ellison often came over to discuss literature and, since he was then working for the Merchant Marine Union, to tell of the latest racial incidents on the high seas. He was also trying to get exempted from the draft and Wright helped him by referring him to Dr. Wertham. Ellison's brother had been reported missing, and he naturally felt disinclined to serve in a segregated army. Nevertheless, he was drafted, but was fortunate in serving in the Merchant Marine.[31]

Elizabeth and St. Clair Drake lived in the same building as the Wrights and so visited frequently; sometimes they watched Julia when the Wrights went out to dinner or to a play such as *The Tempest*, where they went on January 31, 1945, with Mark Marvin, Herbert Klein and a few other friends, an evening which Wright mentions in his journal.

By God, how this Shakespeare haunts one! How much of our speech comes from him. . . . One is awed. And feels afresh the power of the spoken word and the power of the living image on the stage, and again I longed to try to do plays, dramas. How bleak I felt in my own life after seeing *The Tempest!* Yet, how possible it felt that I could do such as that! I recalled when I last saw *Hamlet* and told my friends that some day I'd make thunder like that on the stage, and by God, not a year had passed before *Native Son* was on that very same stage.

Wright, in spite of his run-ins with Drake, enjoyed his friendship and helped him, notably in placing *Black Metropolis* with Harcourt, Brace and writing the introduction for the book. Although Cayton had apparently done most of the work on the book, Drake's name came first and Wright made sure not to look as if he were favoring his friend Cayton.

Wright's relations with other black writers were less friendly, with many people reproaching him for preferring to stay at home and avoiding black social events. On February 1, he wrote in his journal:

Ralph called. . . . Velaco's wife told him I had been the subject of a long discussion at Roi Ottley's house, and that, of the people who took part, most of them agreed that I was a bad one, that I never went anywhere, but just stayed home and wrote. No doubt they are hearing about my *Black Boy* and this is their way of expressing their hate and jealousy of me. To hell with them.

In the journal he kept during the first two months of 1945, he constantly deplored these petty maneuvers and jealousies among the Blacks, which weakened their enterprises and wasted his precious time. For instance, two entries in January mention a certain Neil Scott, who asked him to write the biography of Joe Louis under Scott's name. He was seriously tempted by the $1,000 and his interest in the boxer, only to find out that Scott had neither the permission of the military authorities which Louis needed, nor the boxer's complete support, much less a publisher. Wright was also filled with a sense of waste and futility at the news that two black

writers had committed suicide, and disgusted by the endless discussions of the racial problem, the utopianism of the proposed solutions, the cowardice of the war correspondents who would not
expose the extent of the segregation and the many interracial incidents in the Army. His journal shows that he tended to refuse
invitations to most social functions in order not to be disappointed
once again, as he was when he met Madame Pandit at Dorothy
Norman's. He describes his conversation in the January 4 entry:

When I arrived, the drawing room was full of people. Mrs. Pandit,
grey and black haired, brown olive skinned, was answering questions with a quiet sense of personal indignation, but with no sense
of the sprawling suffering that lay behind her in her vast and teeming country. The crowd was New York's intellectual world.

I take it that you are not for non-violence, I was asked. No, definitely, I am not, I replied. Each and every Indian ought to learn how
to make gunpowder in his kitchen just like a girl learning to cook.
. . . If you are ever free, it will be because you butcher enough
English-men to get them off you. . . . No exploiting power ever
out of the goodness of its heart let a captive people go free.

Most people were there, of course, out of curiosity and snobbism.
Wright felt that he was embarrassing the Indian visitors when he
asked why their country resisted Western influences. Since he
favored industrialization, which would allow colonized countries to
free themselves economically, he opposed the doctrine of non-
violence. As an energetic and individualistic American, he deplored
India's lack of resourcefulness.

At the Dissenters' Club, where United States foreign policy was
analyzed, he complained, in fact, that he had never met an American
with a clear picture of the situation and not an overly pessimistic
or optimistic view. When a Frenchman pointed out that American
life was contrary to its own egalitarian and democratic ideals, as
Gunnar Myrdal had stated in *An American Dilemma*, which Wright
so admired, he concluded that foreigners were the best critics and
that perhaps the United States would only accept an opinion which
came from Europe or elsewhere. On the racial question, Wright
vacillated between an enthusiastic desire to act and a pessimistic
disillusionment. This was most marked in his dealings with the
Chicago Council on Interracial Relations. To prevent riots, a committee consisting of leaders of both races had met in March, 1944,

and, with the help of Embree and Robert Weaver, persuaded the Council to vigorously oppose "restrictive covenants." A report on Negroes in Chicago was then prepared by the Mayor's Committee.[32] As a guest at a Council luncheon on January 12, Wright was appalled by the futility of the meeting. The true solutions were ignored; the Blacks themselves were so anxious to become white that they did not exploit what advantages they had.[33] Nevertheless, Wright agreed to serve on the committee, since he could be useful; he also wanted to try to get Marshall Field and the Rosenwald Foundation to subsidize his friend, the psychiatrist Benjamin Karpman, so that he could make a synthesis of his study of black patients, or to give financial aid to the Wiltwyck School for juvenile delinquents.

For months Wright had been visiting schools, houses of correction and juvenile courts with a West Indian welfare official attached to Wiltwyck. Mr. Gibbons was so well informed and free of inhibitions that Wright learned more from his clear insight into the problems than he could from any specialized treatise on the subject. Having once again reworked his story of black servants, since the fall Wright had been collecting interviews and attending sessions of the juvenile court in Brooklyn incognito.[34] He wrote Aswell on November 27, 1944, that he had "hit upon a man, a terrible creature, by the name of Butts Basin, to do my evil deeds" and serve as protagonist, but he later abandoned this idea, too. At one point, in answer to a request for a juvenile edition of *Black Boy*, he had thought of retelling his experiences in a series of letters, as a way of overcoming the difficulty of writing for a predetermined audience, but he eventually spent the winter of 1944 on a novel about delinquent children. By January 9, he had written more than one hundred pages of "The Jackal," which he intended to revise, heightening the realism and improving the flow of the style. The story centered upon a gang of Negro boys who kidnap a woman and then are afraid to let her go lest she turn them in. In this way Wright planned to study the pathological behavior resulting from fear and anger. He wrote a twenty-five-page scene without stopping. He would use the captive as a symbol to unite his characters, and the leader, Treetop, as the incarnation of the preschizoid type that Mr. Gibbons had described to him.[35] Encouraged by Aswell's decision to publish, Wright read widely to increase his knowledge of sociology and psychology. Among other books Gibbons lent him *The Psycho-Analytic Study of the Family* by Fluegel, and he talked to the children in Harlem. He even thought of spending his vacation at Wiltwyck. His friend Dr. Ben Karpman, of St. Elizabeth's Hospital in Washington, sent him an abundant sheaf of clinical cases, and he visited Dr. Wertham regularly. His activity was motivated less by the desire to write a naturalistic novel than by a desire to help juvenile delinquents and combat nervous disorders in the ghetto. When Wertham asked him to help found a free psychiatric clinic in Harlem, Wright immediately got in touch with Marshall Field's lawyer. He also solicited aid for Wiltwyck from the wealthy Mrs. Adele Levy, Harry Scherman and the Book-of-the-Month Club. He had Mrs. Roosevelt preside at a benefit tea and he promised to write a new brochure for the Foundation.

When he began "The Jackal," Wright was also thinking of writing the last part of his autobiography, as well as a collection of stories entitled "Seven Men," although at the same time he claimed that he was more and more interested in writing a play.[36] He was currently collaborating with George Crosby on a screenplay called "The Last Flight," the story of an American Nazi working for the German radio who tries to return home as he sees Hitler's power disintegrate. Wright was delighted by his visit to Crosby in Far Rockaway, Long Island, and by Crosby's finishing touches on the piece, but it was rejected a month later by Eve Ettinger of Columbia Studios, for whom it had been written.

In his journal, Wright continually worried about the evolution of his art and career as a writer in relation to his struggle with the racial problem. He was never satisfied with what he had accomplished but always started a new project the minute he had determined the fate of the preceding one. It may be amusing to see him regret that he could not "write in serenity, like Shakespeare," just as his plan to produce an enormous work of a million words perhaps seems overambitious, but his grandiose dreams did give a new direction to his work. In 1941, Wright had already thought of using *Twelve Million Black Voices* as the conceptual and historical framework for a series of novels, and on January 20–21, 1945, he describes having confided a similar idea to George Davis.

I explained to him that I wanted to write before I die a series of novels, something like Proust's *Remembrance of Things Past*. I do not want to do it in Proust's style, but in some manner native to America and the Negro. After all, Proust was a Jew living in

Paris, rich and in touch with all the latest developments in art and science; he found that associational thinking and memory, which he borrowed from psychoanalysis, could form the scaffolding of his massive work; and so he took it for his own and used it. I must find something likewise to hang my theme of Negro life upon. It has not been to many people that I have spoken of that great dream of mine. But I want to take the Negro, starting with his oneness with his African tribe, and trace his capture, his being brought over in the Middle Passage, his introduction to the plantation slave system, his gradual dehumanization to the level of random impulse and hunger and fear and sex. I want then to trace his embracing of the religion of protestantism, his gradual trek to the cities of the nation, both North and South; and his gradual urbanization UNDER JIM CROW CONDITIONS, and finally his ability to create a new world for himself in the new land in which he finds himself. I do not want to do this in terms of a family for my aim is not to depict moral customs and traditions and social changes, so much as the subjective voyage spanning centuries. It is a spiritual journey that I wish to depict, not a material one. When the war is over and if I'm lucky, I want to leave the hatreds of race and the pressures of the United States behind and go and live in a foreign land where the currency is cheap and give myself up to this great work. I call it great, but it is simply at bottom my own story. I've not had of course a sense of oneness from the past of Africa; but I feel the need for one now in the future and I'm looking toward it. The book will really be an expression of my own spiritual hunger. I had once thought that Communism was an instrument for that, but now I don't know. They beat you down too much with dictatorial methods of work and feeling and thought. I've still been thinking of my theme for the Negro, the theme in which I'll express and try to assuage my hunger for some sort of unity in my life. I've been urging myself that my next novel ought to be my last unplanned work. I mean a novel that does not fit into the scheme I've devised for myself. The more I think of the word VOYAGE, the more I like it. The title should have that word in it. If I can write my version of this theme, I'll be able to overcome my sense of a poem that's haunted me whenever I pass through or live in a Black Belt, a stanza from a poem by [Vachel] Lindsay:

> Not that they starve, but starve so dreamlessly,
>   Not that they sow, but that they seldom reap,
> Not that they serve, but have no gods to serve,
>   Not that they die, but that they die like sheep.

Oh, God, how lonely I am with this burden of consciousness! If only there were supporting minds about me, kindred feelings! Why do I feel so deeply that this theme I want to write is so important? Yet I hear no voice about me even hinting of like matters. My main energies are sucked into this preoccupation . . . Yet I've lived this long without help and I will and can live on. What has happened to me that makes me feel the necessity of stating so vast and broad a statement of life? Some deprivation? Well, whatever it was it has now been filled with an outward guise that sweeps up the meaning and passion of five hundred years of the world's history . . . Maybe I ought to see about stating this theme from [this] point of view. Perhaps English history provides a better point of view? I don't know. But this I do know. In no other country under the sun was the Negro so stripped as in this. Yes, this is the country, for this is where the Negro was changed, completely, totally; where he was cast unwittingly into the mold of Western civilization . . . Somewhere, yes, in the life of the American Negro lies a clue, a cue for me. I must seek it more fervently than ever.

This is Wright in his entirety—his insatiable longing to find unity and identity by rejoining his ancestral heritage inspiring him to live elsewhere so as to contemplate America from a distance, and the painful realization of the solitary nature of his task combining with an almost mystical need to capture the meaning of life in his work. He always thought of the future and would try to use his personal experience and that of the black man in general to unite these aspirations with his own life, to unite the past and the future. To bridge a gap was the leitmotif of his work, the unspoken legacy of Bigger and the last word of Cross Damon. On February 12, his meditations took a metaphysical turn.

When the feeling of the fact of being a Negro is accepted fully into the consciousness of a Negro there's something universal about it and something that lifts it above being a Negro in America. Oh, will I ever have the strength and courage to tell what I feel and think; and do I know it well enough to tell it?

Such thoughts had little to do with the current war situation. The headlines were full of the German offensive into the Ardennes, the victories of the American troops, the swift Russian advance on Berlin—while Ollie Harrington, Roi Ottley and Ralph Ellison, recently returned from Europe, added concrete details. Rationing would soon be over (which occasioned in Wright the child-ish joy of buying a dozen pairs of white wool socks in order to dye them all colors of the rainbow), even if the approaching end to those hostilities brought with it uncertainty as to the effects of postwar life on the Blacks. In contrast, his personal life was serene. Julia would soon be three years old. He still worried about the slightest sign of a cold, but he was now fascinated by watching her grow and form-ing a bond of companionship with her.[37] Ellen had become the essential element of his stability, and he left more and more of the practical responsibility for their life to her. She was as fine a hostess as she was an intellectual companion, and she was still for him the "most beautiful." [38] Mrs. Poplar rarely came to visit, since Richard was strongly against any intrusion into their household, but she telephoned frequently and their relationship was courteous.

The Wrights wanted to live in Greenwich Village, both because the atmosphere would be more stimulating for a writer and because hostility toward mixed couples was minimal there. However, the re-strictions among landlords and real-estate agents made it difficult for a black person to move there, much less buy a house. Jacob Salz-man, the Wrights' lawyer, discovered a large house for sale at 13 Charles Street, right near Washington Square. Without mentioning the race of his client, he prepared a contract and the first deposit was made on January 26, 1945. The house cost $18,000 and Salz-man got an $8,000 mortgage from a local bank, still without di-vulging Wright's color. Meanwhile, Wright had received a $7,500 advance for his next novel and he borrowed the rest, using, thanks to Paul Reynolds, his contracts with Harper as collateral.[39] A few days after the deposit had been made, the Communist press revealed the sale in progress in the hopes of arousing the hostility of the neighbors, but the contract was signed on February 13. After sev-eral days of anxious waiting, the new owners finally started to make plans for the two floors in which they planned to live. They had set themselves up as the "Richelieu Estate Company" so that any hostile tenants could not turn directly against them. On March 8, Salzman had deposited a portion of their rent and threatened to evict Franklin Folsom, a tenant who wanted to start a rent strike.[40] When the neigh-bors failed to get rid of the Wrights with belated pressures, they actually offered $20,000 for the house on March 22, but Ellen and Richard continued their arrangements with their decorator, and told the Office of Price Administration in April that they intended to move into the two bottom floors. One of the leases did not expire until October, but none of the tenants actively resisted any further.

Although Salzman had succeeded in outwitting residential segregation in Greenwich Village, the Wrights were not as lucky in Vermont, where they wanted to buy an old farm to spend their vacations. They had given a Mrs. Watkins a deposit on a small property, but before the closing, Wright was told that the legal situation of the seller turned out to be so complicated that Wright decided not to go through with it. He was, therefore, greatly surprised to see some time later that the farm was still for sale, which meant that the whole affair had been a farce, intended merely to keep a Black from buying the land.[41]

In these trying circumstances due to racism, Wright's old friendships were a great comfort. He enjoyed evenings with the Werthams, the Maases, the Kossas and other artists, intellectuals and members of the liberal or medical professions with whom he did not have to waste his time in empty socializing.[42] It was perhaps with Dorothy Norman that he had the most stimulating discussions. Since her courageous liberalism was not for her merely a way to an easy conscience, he could confide in her without restraint. He was not excessively suspicious, but there were too many pseudoliberals who used the "Negro problem" as a remedy for their own neuroses, and too many Communists who were supposed to report on the opinions of the "renegade" in those circles where political and personal intrigues automatically engendered an atmosphere of suspicion. Wright, in fact, was the victim of some insidious attacks. Leo Cherne, who himself had been criticized by Mike Gold for having published *The Rest of Your Life,* told Wright that the Party had done everything in its power to prevent the Book-of-the-Month Club from taking *Black Boy.* Wright was also "chilled," as he wrote in his journal on January 16, to hear that the widow of his good friend Hank Johnson claimed that her husband had been assassinated on Party orders. Wright later used Hank and his death in *The Outsider,* along with other experiences and impressions formed at this time. As a result, Wright fully appreciated the rare visits of Max Yergan and Richard Moore, and was satisfied to find an irrefutable criticism of the Soviet Union in W. L. White's report on the Russians. He noticed, too, that Ella Winter was disillusioned after her return from Russia and hoped that someone would eventually proclaim the truth about the American Communists.

Government spying turned out to be just as upsetting as the Party's maneuvers. The FBI had forced one of Wright's friends to show them a play he was writing based on the development of atomic energy, and Wright himself received a visit from the military police. Wright, it seemed, had volunteered, along with Paul Robeson and Carlton Moss, another black Communist, to set up a radio staff for the Office of War Information, and had already taped some programs for the soldiers in the Pacific when Moss had declared that the Party forbade him to collaborate with Wright. The government investigators, who by this time knew more than Wright about Moss's activities, had come to ask him to inform on his old colleague.[43]

THIRTEEN

N INETEEN FORTY-FIVE was the year of *Black Boy*. It was the March selection of the Book-of-the-Month Club, with *Apartment in Athens* by Glenway Wescott, and Harper's had planned a lavish $20,000 publicity campaign. Edward Aswell's suggested subtitle, "A Record of Childhood and Youth," and Wright's ideas for the introduction had been adopted. The first reviews from the major New York papers came out before publication and the liberal critics were immediately enthusiastic. It was a propitious moment for a discussion of racial problems. Everyone was thinking about the "double victory" campaign led by the Blacks, the new efforts toward equal employment in industry and the need for postwar reforms. In *Strange Fruit* Lillian Smith had just written about an interracial marriage—in fact, one of the slogans of Harper's publicity campaign was "*Black Boy* starts where *Strange Fruit* and *Freedom Road* end"; *Kingsblood Royal* by Sinclair Lewis had shown his concern about the topic; and now *Black Boy* provided a frank and well-written exposé of the psychological effects of racial oppression in the South. The power and sincerity of *Black Boy* had few predecessors, and the quality of the writing made it a new *Portrait of the Artist as a Young Man*. The influence of Joyce may not have been obvious, as with *Lawd Today*, but the parallel immediately noted between his concerns and those of Wright was justified by many common features in their work: the protagonists' realization of belonging to a minority; the horror of a religion haunted by sex, and the difficulty of escaping from it; the conflict between obedience and liberty. *Black Boy*, too, hinted more strongly at the literary calling to which the hero was destined than to the fact that he was, as Wright liked to say of himself, "an ordinary Negro." Since he had made his own experience a universal one, he attracted a widespread audience, readers throughout the world finding in him a part of themselves.

The style of the book partially determined its reception. Even

278

W. E. B. Du Bois in the *New York Herald Tribune* of March 1, indignant as any good Communist sympathizer at the pessimistic viewpoint and shocked as any Victorian at the dirty language, claimed that he was charmed by the occasional poetic flights. The serious intent of *Black Boy* contrasted with the insistent humor of *The Big Sea* by Langston Hughes. Wright would not spare the reader the slightest revealing detail, no matter how sordid, which once again moved the Catholics to accuse him of obscenity.[1] But the genuinely shocking effect of the autobiography comes from its message and viewpoint, which was what the critics considered.

The liberals read *Black Boy* as the author intended them to, Sinclair Lewis first among them with an article for *Esquire,* and Wright particularly appreciated Lionel Trilling's review in *The Nation.*[2] He was nevertheless disappointed to see that few critics understood exactly why he had emphasized the deprivation and narrowness of black life. He had meant to destroy the myth of the innately "happy Negro," a stereotype used excessively to argue the minimal effects of racist oppression; but the critics were in fact surprisingly attached to this notion of irrepressible Negro vitality and reproached Wright for not subscribing to it himself. Certainly one passage in *Black Boy,* above all others, aroused this controversy:

I used to mull over the strange absence of real kindness in Negroes, how unstable was our tenderness, how lacking in genuine passion we were, how void of great hope, how timid our joy, how bare our traditions, how hollow our memories, how lacking we were in those intangible sentiments that bind man to man and how shallow was even our despair. After I had learned other ways of life, I used to brood upon the unconscious irony of those who felt that Negroes led so passional an existence! I saw that what had been taken for our emotional strength was our negative confusions, our flights, our fears, our frenzy under pressure (p. 33).

After "I Tried to Be a Communist," the Communists were, of course, unanimous in their attacks. While granting the justice of Wright's vigorous condemnation of "Jim Crow," many deplored his "intense confusionism," "the narrow subjectivity" and the "counter-revolutionary perspective of a renegade." Since Wright had refused to overlook the passivity of certain Blacks, he had become a sort of enemy of the people. In the April 3, 1945, *New Masses*, his friend Isidor Schneider was more perceptive when he recognized the autobiography "as a powerful observation of neurotic behavior brought

on by racial oppression." Benjamin Davis, Jr., under the headline
"Richard Wright in Retreat," reproached him in the April 8 issue of
the *Sunday Worker* for saying "wholly unacceptable things about the
Negro's capacity for genuine emotion . . ." and for omitting "the
biggest new thing that is happening in the world today—the main
progressive currents from which even the South is not immune. . . ."
He particularly held Wright "responsible for his own voluntary act
of withdrawal from the forces which are among the leaders of the
fight for a better world."

Black Boy was forcing the American reader to consider the
South from the black point of view, to understand that the social
structures, the legal measures, the interracial etiquette of the country
were all expressly designed to relegate the black man to a position
from which it would be impossible to escape. A prisoner of the black
taboos and white restrictions, Wright reacted very early by revolt-
ing: against his family, against preconceived ideas, against his milieu.
It was a revolt in words and actions, and literature soon became the
avenue of escape. His mother had enabled him to grow in sensitivity
and imagination (a debt already acknowledged in the dedication of
Native Son), and Wright finally succeeded in his revolt by substitut-
ing for unquestioning acceptance and docile obedience the search
for his own values. In so doing Wright placed himself outside the
socio-ethical norms of the South, becoming and accepting himself
as a criminal without the least regret, because he did not consider
the laws that so defined him legitimate.

Then, by lending his voice to all the Blacks who had not had the
freedom and the talent to express themselves, Wright was discarding
the entire culture of the South, which smothered spiritual development for his people. He thus exposed himself to the wrath of all
partisans of the racist system. In addition, he included a part of
the black community in his criticism—those who had learned the
manners of Uncle Tom all too well through years of oppression—
and he attacked the parents and neighbors who had wanted to make
a "good Negro" out of him. As a result he not only alienated himself from those of his own people who found it easier to maintain
the status quo, but also from those who were insulted by his way of
minimizing the actual richness of Afro-American culture on the
grounds that it could have been much greater. He in fact regarded
the submissive members of his race with a certain revulsion (the
word *obscene*, which he always used in a moral sense, describes his

feeling about them exactly) and with an undisguised scorn, which perhaps led him to minimize and underestimate his cultural heritage, and fail to see that in other cities and states, even in the South itself, there were Blacks who used this very tradition as the basis for their own development. Just as he had generalized outward from the case of Bigger, Wright had perhaps used his somewhat special experience as a universal example of cultural poverty, when it may have been caused largely by his particular family relationships and atypical religion.

Wright was somewhat disconcerted to find the black critics, except, of course, for friends like Horace Cayton and Michael Carter, almost agreeing with the Communists. The first article in the *Chicago Defender* was favorable, but later, on March 3, Ben Burns called the book "a sorry slander of the Negroes generally," maintaining that "the essential bleakness of black life of which he speaks is more an accurate chronicle of his own life. . . . In *Black Boy* he is again erring as he did in *Native Son* in his emphasis on the hopelessness of the Negro's lot, in his total failure to see that the clock of history is moving ahead, not backward."

Wright was expecting such attacks, but mostly from the black bourgeoisie, from the leaders or academics who were so anxious to preserve their hard-won status that it upset them to see a black man admit to the inferiority of his situation.[3] Poet Owen Dodson, a friend of his, had told him of the reactions of Alain Locke, who had read the manuscript well before publication, and in his journal on January 6, Wright remarked with assurance:

Dr. Locke said that he did not know why Wright wanted to drag up all that old stuff; that I had tossed away good writing; that I had assumed a direct, elementary style instead of fancy writing; and that the book made him shiver. Well, he needs to shiver a little, life is cold. . . . I suspect that Negroes will pick my bones for this book, that they will hover over me like vultures and hack away at me; for I'm convinced that they cannot as yet fathom the motives that made me write this book; they are not emotionally independent enough to want to face the naked experience of their lives.

It was this "naked experience" that Wright had thought to expose in all its horror, in order to denounce the forces responsible for it. Perhaps, however, he did not anticipate such an outcry from the

Blacks as well when he destroyed the myth of the "contented Negro." [4]

Fulfilling the social obligations resulting from the publication of *Black Boy* was an ordeal for Wright, but the publicity was extensive. Mary Margaret McBride and John Mason Brown immediately made the book the subject of their radio programs. On March 5, Wright was called upon by Sterling North and Lewis Gannett to "Meet the Critics," and *Life* magazine rushed its photographers down to Mississippi for a nine-page story.[5] The public, meanwhile, was more enthusiastic than Wright had dared to hope. Hundreds of fan letters, congratulations and pleas for advice came from all sectors of the black and white population; but there were, of course, attacks as well. The pseudoliberals, congratulating themselves that American democracy had allowed an oppressed Negro from Mississippi to succeed, were indignant that he described oppression as the rule. Obscene letters informed Wright that the book was also being read in the South. One store in Nashville refused to carry the book, the *Natchez Democrat* would not print any ads for it, and the commander of the air force base at Deming, New Mexico, would not allow it in the library. Wright was even given the dubious honor of being mentioned in the Congressional Record, thanks to Mississippi congressmen Bilbo and Rankin:

It is a damnable lie from beginning to end. It is practically all fiction. There is just enough truth to enable him to build his fabulous lies about his experiences in the South. . . . It is the dirtiest, filthiest, lousiest, most obscene piece of writing that I have ever seen in print. . . . But it comes from a Negro and you cannot expect any better from a person of this type.[6]

A letter from Edward Aswell to the Parker House Bookshop in Boston, written in April, 1945, indicates that Harper's was promising legal aid in the event that *Black Boy* was censored. The advance sale was close to 30,000 copies and on March 18, *Black Boy* was eleventh on the best-seller list, moving to fifth place on April 1, fourth place on April 8, and second place on April 15. It reached first place on April 29 and remained there until June 6, was in second place until August 6, in third until the beginning of October, and was down to eight again by November. Among all the nonfiction sales of the year it ranked fourth. On May 10, with a first printing of 50,000 copies, World Publishing Company took over from Harper's when it had sold over half a million copies; this measure was conceived by Aswell and Reynolds so that the shortage of paper would not restrict sales. The Book-of-the-Month Club had sold 325,000 copies by August 1.[7]

During the period of literary debates about *Black Boy,* Wright took advantage of his additional opportunities to speak out on the seriousness of the racial situation.[8] He had been scheduled to speak at Columbia University on February 13, and had done a great deal of research without evolving a suitable plan for his lecture, which was supposed to be on black American literature. Although the date was moved up a week, he finally got an idea that caused him to change his subject, which became "The Black American Discovers Himself," an account of his trip from Texas to Chapel Hill during the summer of 1940.[9] A few days later, he spoke again, this time at the New York Institute of Arts and Sciences on the black contribution to American literature. Although still convinced that educating the public was a step in the right direction, he, unlike Gunnar Myrdal, was also sure that in the near future violence would be the necessary prelude to a lasting solution.[10]

At the beginning of March, during a program inaugurating a Red Cross campaign in New York, Wright spoke about race relations in the South, not mentioning his own reservations about the Red Cross itself. He also agreed to have a brief appeal to the reader printed on the jacket of a new edition of *Black Boy,* to stimulate the sale of war bonds.[11] He had hardly recovered from the flu, which kept him at home for three weeks, when he spoke at a famous authors' luncheon given by the Association of Philadelphia Booksellers on April 9. On April 16, he presented a vigorous opposition to the optimism of senators Voorhis and Ives, of the New York State Assembly, and the gradualism of Elmer Carter, of the Urban League, in a debate entitled "Are we on the way to solving the racial problem?" during the radio program "Town Meeting of the Air."

I take issue with Mr. Elmer Carter's dangerous theory of a gradual solution of the race problem. . . . It is true that under the stress of war the nation was compelled to admit Negroes to a few areas of life heretofore reserved exclusively for whites. But let us not be deluded into thinking that these gains will be lasting. . . . The race problem is not being solved. Indeed, it is becoming more acute. Witness the recent outbreaks in Beaumont, Texas; Detroit and Los Angeles.

What do we mean by a solution of the race problem?

It means a nation where there will exist no residential segregation, no Jim Crow army, no Jim Crow navy, no Jim Crow Red Cross Blood Bank, no Negro institutions, no laws prohibiting intermarriage, no customs assigning Negroes to inferior positions. We would simply be Americans and the nation would be the better for it.[12]

On April 23, Wright participated along with Aubrey Williams and Josephine Wilkins, from the national bureau of the sharecroppers' union, in a debate at the Roosevelt Hotel, on "What the peace will bring to the South," during the National Sharecroppers' Week. On April 30, he spoke in Pittsburgh for the NAACP and then went to Washington to try and interest Maxwell Hahn, of the Marshall Field Foundation, in publishing Dr. Benjamin Karpman's collected material on the psychopathology of the Negro American.

Despite this enormous activity, he often felt discouraged by the overwhelming nature of his task. Visits from European friends like Ivan and Claire Goll merely reinforced his conviction that Americans planned to enjoy the return of peace as satisfied consumers with easy consciences; they lacked his urgent concern for humanistic issues, which, he claimed, proved his greater affinity with the Europeans. Under these conditions, he wondered whether criticism could only be effective if it came from outside.

At least the translation rights of his books were selling well abroad. He received $1,000 from the Scandinavian countries alone, and soon England, Brazil, Palestine, and Argentina would be able to read *Black Boy*. *Native Son* was to be published in Paris, and Manuel Barbera's adaptation of the play had run for over one hundred performances at the National Theatre of Buenos Aires, with Ibanez Menta as Bigger, the big role of the Argentina theater season. In the United States, there were already plans to put *Black Boy* on the stage. In July, Klein and Marvin took an option, but Philip Yordan, who had been asked to write the adaptation, could not come to an agreement with them. Wright refused John Wexley's offer, even though he had proven his ability with *They Shall Not Die*, for fear that he might give the play a pro-Communist slant.

Abe Kendal started work on the adaptation, but since Marvin and Klein had not been able to raise the necessary money, the option came to end before he was through.[13] In view of the huge sale of the book, Wright was not that interested in an adaptation for the time being. Two chapters from the end of "American Hunger," originally accepted by *Harper's Magazine* in January, came out in *Cross Section*, in 1945, under the title "Early Days in Chicago," while Wright gave George Davis some other unused passages from the manuscript, which *Mademoiselle* published in September, 1945.[14] *Liberty Magazine* and *Coronet* both came out with condensed versions of the autobiography; magazines, anthologies and textbooks all vied to publish something by Wright, so that by the end of the spring, any debts for the Charles Street house were easily repaid.

Wright had agreed to do several reviews for *PM*, and at Harry Scherman's request he worked for a while as a reader and adviser for the Book-of-the-Month Club. During his illness in March he yawned over *Heritage of the River* by Muriel Elwood, savored a history of Scottish fishermen by Neil Gunn—in spite of its title, *The Silver Darlings*—and was outraged by the sloppy style of *Dragon Harvest,* the latest work by Upton Sinclair.[15] He reviewed *The Brick Foxhole*, an antimilitarist novel by Richard Brooks, and he read almost all of John O'Hara's works in order to discuss *Pipe Night* during another broadcast of "Meet the Critics" on April 16.[16] The review which most affected his own future was his piece on Gertrude Stein's *Wars I Have Seen*. He was so sensitive to her prose that he actually wrote an entire essay for *PM* on February 19, which had to be condensed to one-third its length. Carl Van Vechten brought Wright's review to Gertrude Stein's attention, and she in turn devoured his books with as much enthusiasm as he had hailed her achievement, in a sentence worthy of Stein herself:

Wouldn't it be strange if in 1988 our colleges made the reading of *Wars I Have Seen* mandatory, so that our grandchildren would learn how men felt about war in our time? Wouldn't it be simply strange if Miss Stein's grammarless prose was destined for such a strange destiny? Would it not be strange if anything strange like that did happen? [17]

Black Boy so impressed her that she wrote him in May, and he answered in a long and lucid letter on the American attitude toward the racial problem and postwar materialism, mentioning his own desire to visit France. *The New York Times Magazine* then came out with Gertrude Stein's impressions on Wright:

I said the trouble is, as long as the Negro was just a native race, the white man's burden point of view, it's all right, but now when one Negro can write as Richard Wright does, writing as a Negro about Negroes, writes not as a Negro but as a man, well the minute that happens, the relation between the white and the Negro is no longer a difference of races but a minority question and ends not in ownership but in persecution. That is the trouble, when people have equality there can be differences but no persecution; when they begin to have equality then it is no longer separation, there is persecution." [18]

This was the beginning of a friendship enhanced by mutual affinities. Wright sent to Paris via Carl Van Vechten copies of *Twelve Million Black Voices* and "How Bigger Was Born." He wrote on June 23, 1945, that he was also sending "two little documents on Harlem and Negro life" (*Handbook of Harlem Jive* by his friend Dan Burley, and a few issues of Father Divine's newspaper), which he thought might interest the author of "Melanctha" in the linguistic creativity of the ghetto, since she had been the first to fascinate Wright with the beauty of the Negro language.[19]

2

The Wrights wanted to rent the house of their friend Dr. Safford, in Wading River, Long Island, for the summer, but it was only available for the month of May. Then, thinking that they might go back to the house they had rented the previous summer in the Gatineau, they left for Quebec on June 25. On June 27, they were the dinner guests of Jean-Charles Falardeau, professor of sociology at Laval University, and the next day they settled in Sainte-Petronille on the Ile d'Orleans, a small village whose quaint atmosphere had preserved the warmth of the former French province. Accustomed to the rationing imposed in New York City, Wright rejoiced that he could buy filet of beef for 25¢ a pound, and as a poet, it made him happy to contemplate the sunsets over the St. Lawrence River and the port of Quebec from his bedroom window. French Canada, in fact, was a foretaste of Europe. He who had always advocated modernism, the triumph of the rational over tradition and superstition, now discovered the dignity that man gains from a sense of the past. He became nostalgic, wanting to belong to a heritage that would consolidate the "perpetual present" Americans live in, as he later explained to Gertrude Stein on October 29, 1945:

Living with such a landscape one gets used to it. Then huge battle-ships and aircraft carriers steam into the harbor. . . . The sensuous landscape is chopped and bitten by sharp angles and lines, and then one knows that the landscape of French Quebec is terribly old-fashioned, and one too remembers then the landscape of New York City and at once one knows what modern art is. Quebec is slow and ripe and organic and serene; there is no hurrying and no straining to attain the impossible or unique or the different. But when one returns to New York City, one is struck by the hurried, the green, the vague and the frantic. Everything is romantic, abstract. In Quebec man has found a way of living with the earth: in New York we live against the earth.

Wright was using this time to write the long introduction to *Black Metropolis*, which he had promised his friends Drake and Cayton. He spoke freely and forcefully, using this sociological study on the Chicago ghetto as a point of departure for a panoramic view of the whole racial problem.[20] While Ellen contentedly indulged her taste for antiques in the local shops, Richard also put the final revisions on a lecture he was scheduled to give at the Bread Loaf Writers' Conference on August 17. After an unpleasant journey on a dirty and crowded train, the discovery of the natural beauty of Vermont revived Richard's regret that he had not been able to buy a farm there. "If the past were still alive in the U.S.," he was moved to write Gertrude Stein on August 23, "everyone everywhere would be happier for it." He saw a piece of old America in the area of Bread Loaf Mountain, but although he met Louis Unter-meyer and Catherine Drinker Bowen at the Conference, he did not find enough interest in the racial problem among this somewhat blasé group of writers who met each summer under the aegis of Robert Frost.[21]

After another visit to the Falardeaus in Quebec, Wright returned to New York and its headaches—contracts to sign; an article on the play *Deep Are the Roots*, which *Life* was clamoring for; the failure of the plans for the stage adaptation of *Black Boy*—but also to the certainty that his autobiography would support him for some time.[22] This material success did not prevent him from attacking the myth of the "self-made man" in his September 16, 1945, review for *PM* of the complete works of Horatio Alger (the creator of his childhood heroes), in which he denied the Puritan morality that claimed wealth was the recompense of virtue.

Wright then set out on a huge lecture tour, organized by Harold Peat, to enlighten his fellow citizens on the "so-called Negro problem." On October 8 he was in Baltimore, on the 9th in Lewisburg, Pennsylvania, on the 11th in Ashland, Wisconsin, and on the 12th at Eau Claire, speaking on "The American Negro Discovering Himself" to the members of the Teachers' Association of Northwest Wisconsin. On October 15 he was in Boston, and in Hartford on October 26 he addressed a convention of Connecticut teachers on Afro-American literature. He mentioned Phyllis Wheatley, Alexandre Dumas and Pushkin, quoted from *Twelve Million Black Voices* and presented Afro-American literature as a continuous protest against racism, in words that he often repeated in later years.[23] Back in Brooklyn on October 27, he expressed his satisfaction to Gertrude Stein, advising her to return to the United States herself to speak about the racial problem. On October 29, he took up his tour again and spoke at the West Side High School in Newark. On the first of November he went to Washington, to the Howard University Forum, and after Eleanor Roosevelt spoke on the international scene and the plan for peacetime, he described the "unfinished task of democracy." His lecture to the students on black literature violently attacked the stereotypes in which the black man was represented either as a faithful servant, a stupid beast or a child of nature.

It is the Florian Slappeys that I protest against most. Mr. Cohen is a widely read writer in the popular magazines and he sticks to the oldest and most dishonest trick of the writing trade when he types Negroes—and does the most damage. The Uncle Remus stories of Joel Chandler Harris fall somewhat into the folklore class, but even there I stamp my foot down where possible.[24]

Wright contrasted the falseness of those authors who wrote only to please with the lucidity of *Strange Fruit* and the realism of *Kneel to the Rising Sun*. On November 7, he spoke on "The Negro Contribution to American Civilization" in Camden, New Jersey. On the 12th he was in Kankakee, Illinois, and on the 14th in Des Moines, Iowa, where he spoke in the afternoon at the women's club on "The Role of the Negro in the Arts and Sciences." That same evening, after a dinner at Hoyt Sherman's home, he spoke to the members of the Negro Community Center on the cultural backwardness of the United States and the problems created by industrialization, then responded to the attacks of Congressmen Bilbo and Rankin, quoting several black poets to back up his argument. The next day he spoke at Cornell College in Mount Vernon, Iowa, on the situation of the black Americans, and gave the same speech three days later to the men's club of Temple Emmanuel, in Duluth, Minnesota. On the 19th he gave a lecture at John Marshall College under the auspices of the Association of the Jewish Educational Center of Saint Paul, Minnesota, and on the 20th he was at Anshe Emmet Settlement House of Chicago, where he ran into his old friend Joe Brown.

Wright was doing a marvelous job in spite of this hectic schedule, but his manager, Harold Peat, had overestimated his strength. After the fourteenth of the fifty engagements planned over a four-month period, Wright was physically and mentally exhausted by his efforts to literally captivate his audience, because he could not give his best without that indispensable current of mutual sympathy. On December 3, Reynolds had to send Harold Peat a medical certificate on Wright's behalf to bring this triumphant but debilitating tour to an end, at least for the time being.[25]

The tour had suggested another plan to Wright; his lecture would provide both an outline for and an introduction to an anthology of Afro-American literature as racial protest. Edward Aswell read the text and wrote on December 5, 1945, urging Wright to get started as soon as possible.

While Wright was using his energies and reputation as a foremost American writer for the benefit of his race in general, he did not fail to encourage individual young writers of either color. "Two Novels of the Crushing of Man, One White, One Black" was a review of his that appeared in the November 25, 1945, issue of *PM*. He disposed rather quickly of Arthur Miller's *Focus*, the adventures of a man who, because he had been taken for a Jew and persecuted, came to side with the Jews. Although Wright found the book "reasonable and intellectual," he was more excited by Chester Himes's first novel, which, he believed, had qualities similar to his own. He was impressed by this "sea of prose so blindingly intense that it all but hurts your eyes" and by his using "words like a soldier shooting at you from a foxhole." [26] However, he preferred the narrative episodes, which were less brutal but more authentically dreamlike, to the overelaborate style of the dreams that began each chapter. Altogether, he felt that Himes was not just a new black talent but a new genre of writer. Wright went further, when Himes needed a $500 loan, and obtained $1,000 from Reynolds on the rights of *Black Boy*. This may have been the magnanimous gesture of an established author, but it was effective and Himes remembered it as the beginning of a lasting friendship.

Wright did a similar favor in the autumn for another aspiring young black writer whom his friend Henrietta Weigel had recommended. This young man was looking for a grant, which was how Wright came to invite James Baldwin to his house and to agree to read the sixty pages he had written of his first novel. Through Aswell, who was one of the directors of the Eugene Saxton Foundation, Wright got Baldwin the grant that launched him upon his brilliant career.[27] In November, 1944, Aswell had sent Wright the manuscript of *A Street in Bronzeville* by Gwendolyn Brooks, for which he wrote a very enthusiastic advance quote. He put Reynolds in touch with the young Esther Carlson, whose story he had admired at the Greenwich Village Writer's Club, as well as with Marianne Oswald, who had written *A Small Voice*; and thanks to Wright, Harper's published Ethol Kossa's first novel, *Count Me Among the Living,* with his complimentary quote.[28]

This generosity was motivated largely by a general desire to help promising young talents, but his enthusiasm over Jo Sinclair's *Wasteland* reveals his special pleasure in discovering a writer after his own heart, someone who used realism to grapple with the current problems of the country. Aswell had asked him to read the galleys and Wright (whose recommendation helped to win it the Harper Prize for 1946) could not say enough in its praise. The novel, in fact, fulfilled the very wish he had expressed in his journal, when pondering the prejudices of his mother-in-law, to have a white novelist explore the psychology of the immigrant.

I'm sure that when Ellen's mother was a peasant in Russian Poland, she did not hate so many people of other races; but since coming to the land of the free and the brave she has had a lot of trouble keeping her sons and daughter from marrying Negroes, Japanese and what not, folks whom she has learned to hate since coming to our great and noble land. . . . She swapped her ancient age-old culture for the American cult of material success and its parallel of color hate and moral imperialism, and it has not worked out. Oh boy, what a theme for a novel! She has come to worship what she is now hating in this land. . . . Why don't white writers write these things up? I'm too far from them to know them intimately enough to write about them. There's great tragedy in this land and most of its artists are blind.[29]

Wasteland, he rejoiced in his review for *PM*, forced the reader to accept the reality of minority cultures that he would otherwise be inclined to reject or misinterpret; this in fact was the goal that Wright himself had set for "American Pages." Considering its successful psychoanalytical approach, Wright compared the novel with *The Making of Americans* by Gertrude Stein and also mentioned Proust and *Finnegans Wake*. Certainly Wright had no desire to please the author (since he had never met Ruth Seid, who wrote under the name of Jo Sinclair, although Himes had recommended her), but he had suddenly come upon the justification of one of his own deep conceptions of literature. In such cases, his unshakable belief in the power of words often led him to attribute the failure of a given, perhaps unremarkable, novel to its audience and not its author.

In homage to Countee Cullen, Wright made it a point of honor to attend the poet's funeral at Woodlawn Cemetery on January 12, 1946. Three thousand people flocked to the service at the Salem Methodist Episcopal Church. In spite of their political differences, the two writers always felt a great deal of respect for each other, and Wright was affected by this death, which followed only a few months after that of his old friend Burton Barnett.

As usual, Wright was one of the guests of honor at the annual
Harper dinner during Book Week in Philadelphia, on March 12,
1946. He also agreed to give two lectures during the spring and
worked a little on the anthology, but he spent most of his time on
a project with his friend Dr. Frederic Wertham. The two had become so close that Wright agreed to lend himself to an experiment
in association of ideas, since Wertham was interested in the relationship between writing and psychoanalysis. As a result of his experiments with Wright, the doctor had written, in 1944, "An
Unconscious Determinant in *Native Son*," an article giving a sexual
interpretation of the famous scene where Bigger burns Mary's body.
The episode apparently went back to the day when Wright, age sixteen, saw the daughter of his employer nude; while the murder was
more accidental than deliberate, it symbolized a rape.[30] Later,
Wright described to Wertham the dreams and daydreams that obsessed him. In writing "American Hunger," for instance, he had
never been able to tell whether he had imagined or had actually
experienced certain events. Sometimes he had asked his family and
friends to confirm certain memories, and at others he had depended
upon Wertham's opinion.[31]

In any case, these two men were already bound together by their
common interest in literature and the fight for racial equality. As
the director of the mental health clinic of the General Hospital in
Queens, Wertham had taken care of black juvenile delinquents for
years; now he wanted to open a free psychiatric clinic in Harlem,
in which qualified personnel would provide the care that no hospital, public or private, offered in the ghetto, where the living conditions, the paucity of black psychiatrists and the segregation in
hospitals made this an urgent need. For a while Wertham, Wright
and the journalist Earl Brown tried to interest philanthropic foundations and public organizations, but the state was not ready to
provide social security of this type, and no foundation was willing
to alienate the medical community opposed to the idealism of a
practitioner who wanted to take care of the poor for free. Nevertheless, a few volunteers founded the Lafargue clinic (named for
the French negrophile) without the money and in the face of the
opposition. The Episcopalian minister Shelton Hale Bishop offered
them the basement of the St. Philip's Church parish house, where,
starting April 8, 1946, delinquents and the sick could come and

confide their problems to a devoted staff for 25¢, if they had it. Dorothy Norman made an appeal for money in her *New York Post* column, and with what they received they were able to buy a little furniture and start some files. The clinic was never empty.

In aid of the clinic Wright wrote "Psychiatry Comes to Harlem," an article combining an objective report on the beginnings of the clinic with a passionate attack on the complacency of America, the lack of social conscience of the medical profession and the bad faith of those who were allegedly fighting racism.[32] A second article, "Juvenile Delinquency in Harlem," which did not come out until the end of the year, also resulted from Wright's concern with psychiatry as well as from his research for "The Jackal," which included interviewing gangs with Mr. Gibbons and Dr. Wertham. The article revealed both the extent of Wright's knowledge of psychopathology and the seeds of certain psychoanalytical themes that later appeared in his novel *Savage Holiday*.

Meanwhile, Wright's eloquent introduction to *Black Metropolis*, which was published at the end of 1945, refueled the Communist campaign against him. The sociological approach of Wright, Cayton and Drake, close to that of Gunnar Myrdal, was opposed to the strictly Marxist perspective of Herbert Aptheker, who accused them of overemphasizing the moral aspect of the racial problem and neglecting its economic basis. Wright was somewhat vindicated in the February 11, 1946, *New Masses* when Albert Maltz courageously reopened the debate on the relationship of politics to literature that had been the rage in the heyday of proletarian literature.

It has been an accepted assumption in much of left-wing literary thought that a writer who repudiates a progressive political position (leaves the intellectual orbit of *New Masses,* let us say) must go downhill as a creative writer. But this is not true to sober facts— however true it may be in individual cases. Actually it is impossible to predict the literary future of Richard Wright at this moment. He takes political positions which seem to many to be fraught with danger for his own people. He may continue to do so. But *Black Boy*, whatever its shortcomings, is not the work of an *artist* who has gone downhill. It is to the credit of *New Masses* that it recognized this in dealing with the book. Equally it is impossible to predict now the future achievements of J. T. Farrell, of Kenneth Fearing, of Lillian Smith.

Maltz was immediately called to task by Howard Fast, Alvah Bessie and John Howard Lawson, who expressed the official Party line and forced him to recant and to admit that he had made "an error in [his] dialectical attitude" and that Wright was actually a "perverted talent" and an "agent of reaction." [33] Aptheker chimed in again in the May 14th issue with "A Liberal Dilemma," ridiculing the introduction of *Black Metropolis* before stating categorically:

All history and all life is composed of the dreams and the struggles of the very people who, Wright says, "starve so dreamlessly and die like sheep." Hear the songs, read the poetry, listen to the folk-tales of the Negro and say he is without dreams! . . . What non-sense is this! What slander! The oppressed are the heroic. The dis-possessed are the uncorrupt.

Aptheker's bad faith was flagrant but Wright did not reply, since he was already in France, far away from these polemics, when the article came out and the magazine eventually allowed Horace Cayton to explain and defend his intentions.[34]

3

Since Richard and Ellen had not wanted to evict their top-floor tenant for fear of Communist campaigns against them or merely social reprisals, they had waited until his lease expired before moving into their Charles Street house. They had left Brooklyn in October, 1945, however, to move into 82 Washington Place, just west of Washington Square. Their apartment was somewhat too small, but the atmosphere of Greenwich Village and the certainty that they would soon be living in their own house, of which they had already arranged and decorated the ground floor, made it easy to wait, so that 1945 finished in security, glory and comfort.

Black Boy had triumphed, yet Wright was not totally satisfied even after becoming *the* great black American writer, since the color of his skin still imposed limits upon him. His climb up the social

Richard and Ellen, a few years after their marriage. *Photo by Carl van Vechten*

At his typewriter, with Julia

Relaxing

At work, in New York. *Photo by Hart Preston*

ladder had only caused him to confront the racial problem on a larger scale. He realized that he would never enjoy all his rights as an American citizen, and that not all the readers of his country were ready to consider him a full-fledged author. Doubtless the continual humiliations which Wright suffered contributed to this feeling: the fact that he had to go all the way to Harlem to have his hair cut, that he could not buy a farm in Vermont, the hostility of his Charles Street neighbors, to name a few.[35] In view of barriers at home, he started to look outward, toward the rest of the world, to find a place where he might be able to assert his human dignity. He was particularly attracted by Europe, which, now that the war was over, was open and more welcoming to visitors from across the Atlantic. Wright had first felt the need for a past in Quebec, and his few contacts with Europeans revealed to him a way of thinking that appealed to him more than Americanism. The pessimism that accompanied his militancy soon became a growing conviction that American civilization on the whole had lost the primary humanistic values. Thus his sense of the tragedy in life, which he had had since childhood, was now joined by a feeling of alienation, constantly reinforced by racism and further nourished somewhat later by his contacts with existentialism. Without a doubt, Wright had already begun in spirit the trip of which he dreamed, to live in a country where the low cost of living, the absence of racial tensions, the atmosphere of liberty and a harmonious civilization would enable him to write his great work.

"I Choose Exile" was written in 1950 to give the reasons for his departure for Paris, but it was not an ex post facto justification of his decision, since he had clearly revealed his motives to Gertrude Stein in the spring of 1946. As early as May 27, 1945, he had written her:

Maybe next year we will come to France and I hope that Paris will be like so many have said it used to be. Will it? For a reason I don't know, I've always felt that France would mean something to me, and that I'd live there. So I'm honor bound to see France. . . . Really, next year, I want to bring my wife and child to France, to Paris. I'm going to try my best to do that.

In hoping that Paris would be the same as it used to be, Wright was referring to what people like the war correspondent Ollie Harrington had told him: in Paris, it seemed, a black writer was treated as a writer and not as a "nigger."

Although this prospect appealed to Wright as a black man, he was equally interested in France as a writer, since he felt spiritually akin to the expatriate novelists of the "lost generation," especially Hemingway and Gertrude Stein, who was a literary godmother to them both. If he, too, went into exile, he would become part of a literary tradition; he would have a past as well as a future. His color had not entirely prevented the "American Dream" from coming true for him, but at most it would be a material dream. He, however, scorned people who did not use their wealth to good ends, and he had by now discovered with horror the mediocrity of "mass democracy." Yet he was not simply motivated by a desire to escape the racial nightmare or Henry Miller's "air-conditioned nightmare." [36] On the contrary, he was actively looking for a concrete position from which to work in full awareness of the international significance of American cultural and ethnic problems.

When he announced his intention of living in Paris for a time, artists and intellectuals of both races tried to dissuade him. Some even asked Dorothy Norman to intervene on their behalf, although she was actually doing everything she could to forward the plan. According to them, Wright would lose his American identity in Europe, and furthermore, his duty was to remain in his homeland to be on the spot in the fight against racism.[37] Nevertheless, Wright's mind was made up, and he entered his request for a passport in January, 1946. Since permission to leave the country was not granted without good reasons and proof of a source of income abroad, Wright obtained a statement from Gallimard, which was publishing *Black Boy,* specifying that he would be giving lectures in Paris. In addition, Dorothy Norman created for him the special position of "Paris correspondent" for *Twice a Year*; his name was on the editorial board in any case for having helped the magazine, and he would only have to get in touch with a few French writers and bookstores in Paris, a job which, though unpaid, would help him obtain his passport.

The family made arrangements for a several-month visit, since postwar difficulties of transportation and lodging, as well as rationing, were still uppermost in people's minds. Dr. Sidney Pelage, a native of Martinique sent to the United States by the French government, offered his Paris studio to them for the duration of his stay in America, and Wright also asked Gertrude Stein to reserve two rooms in a small hotel for a few weeks. Language presented yet another problem. In Canada, Wright had been proud of his ability to make himself understood by shopkeepers, but in spite of preparatory lessons he had taken in New York, his progress was slow. He wrote Gertrude Stein that lecturing in French was certainly out of the question and that he still had trouble understanding the spoken word. In fact, he was full of fears on that score. He was counting on Gertrude Stein as a sort of guardian angel, and she patiently reassured him and answered his many questions. This exchange of letters further cemented their friendship, and Wright was as enthusiastic as ever upon reading more of her books. Shortly before his departure, he asked Bennett Cerf for the proofs of *Brewsie and Willie* in order to review it for *PM*.[38]

In March, 1946, at Dorothy Norman's home, Wright had the opportunity to meet Jean-Paul Sartre, who was visiting the United States for seven weeks with a group of French journalists. Wright certainly found him interesting but regretted that the Frenchman would not say what he really thought of America.[39] Wright was hoping that he would soon meet Camus, who was also in New York at the time. Existentialism was beginning to catch on in American intellectual circles and Wright found that it fit in with his intimate vision of the world, as well as corresponding to the philosophy of the Russian novelists whom he so admired.

In 1940, he had discussed Miguel de Unamuno's *Tragic Sense of Life* with Ralph Ellison, who had since called his attention to the development of an existentialist theater in France. Then, at the end of 1944, Wright had asked Dorothy Norman to instruct him on existentialism and the writings of Kierkegaard, Nietzsche and Heidegger, whom she had read. She had invited Paul Tillich and Hannah Arendt over so that they could discuss the topic with him. He had also recently bought the English translation of Kierkegaard's *Concept of Dread,* published by the Princeton University Press, and always kept the book with him.

With all his preparations and increasing desire to leave, Wright became more and more anxious about the continued silence of the State Department concerning his passport. In mid-April, via the journalist Michel Gordey, a relative of Marc Chagall, whose exhibition at the Pierre Matisse Gallery Wright had visited, he appealed to the French cultural attaché, Claude Levi-Strauss, to see if he could hasten the delivery of his passport. Gertrude Stein was also busy on her side, and Wright eventually received an official invitation from the French government to come to Paris for a month with his family. The document specified "all expenses paid," a formality intended to reassure the Washington authorities that Wright would have enough money.[40]

Meanwhile, the overseas radio division had asked Wright to prepare a program to be broadcast in France. The hour and the date had already been set when he learned suddenly by phone that it had been canceled. It seemed that the radio people had investigated him and, not knowing of his break with the Party, were fearful of what he might say. Perhaps the State Department's delay with his passport was also due to the fear that official propaganda might suffer if Wright were allowed the opportunity to give frank answers to Paris reporters. Thus, when he called the passport bureau, he was told that his official invitation by the French had not been received, and a copy, sent immediately, was lost in the same mysterious manner. Finally Wright himself went to Washington and (apparently thanks to the support of Evelyn Walsh McLean) finally obtained his passport a mere three days before the *Brazil* was scheduled to sail. He therefore had no time to relax and missed hearing Ray Rosenthal's radio adaptation of *Black Boy,* which was broadcast on the evening of April 30. He was so anxious to leave that, although he had been a witness to a fight between some Italians the previous month, he had not appeared in court lest judicial complications prevent his departure, and for fear the police would come find him he stayed with his friend George Davis for the remaining two days; at the last minute he leapt into a taxi to embark on the morning of May 1. James Baldwin, who visited Wright a few days before his departure, described his Greenwich Village apartment as

dismantled, everything teetering on the verge of oblivion. . . .
Richard did not seem, though he was jaunty, to be overjoyed.
There was a striking sobriety in his face that day. He talked a
great deal about a friend of his who was in trouble with the
U.S. immigration authorities, and was about to be, or already had
been, deported. Richard was not being deported, of course, he was
traveling to a foreign country as an honored guest.[41]

Baldwin did not know about Wright's recent difficulties. He was not yet aware that the freedom of a black writer was limited by his own fear of the consequences of revealing his view of American life. America had done little to fan the flame of Wright's patriotism and was correspondingly unwilling to trust in it.

FOURTEEN

Having finally allowed Wright to leave, was the American
government then going to try to make him into a cultural ambassador? He was, in fact, officially accompanying several paintings
that the National Gallery of Art was lending to France for a special
exhibition. The crossing was uneventful, however, and on May 8,
1946, Wright experienced the vague feeling of guilt, on beholding
the half-sunken ships and the chaotic ruin of Le Havre, that the
reality of the war inspired in American visitors. Soon, too, he
learned about the black market when, on disembarking, he was
approached on three occasions by people wanting to buy American
dollars.

Paris produced an entirely different reaction in him. Gertrude
Stein had alerted her friend Douglas Schneider, cultural attaché at
the American Embassy, so that an official limousine was waiting
at the Gare Saint-Lazare to detach the Wrights from the eager crowd
of reporters and critics, among them Maurice Nadeau and Claude-
Edmonde Magny. Wright was already entranced with the beauty
of the city by the time he reached the Trianon-Palace, their hotel
in the heart of the Latin Quarter. In the December, 1960, *France-
Etats-Unis,* Douglas Schneider recalled that first morning in a
"Souvenir de Richard Wright."

It was very early, around seven o'clock, on a clear sunny morning.
The travelers seemed wide awake, so, instead of taking these new
friends of mine directly to their hotel on the rue de Vaugirard,
we went the long way around, down the Champs Elysees, past the
Tuileries on the rue de Rivoli and back along the quais. Richard
Wright was sitting next to me, and as we entered the Place de la
Concorde, facing the Louvre, and later all along the Left Bank,
I heard him exclaim under his breath, "How beautiful! How absolutely beautiful! . . . I had no idea that one city could contain
in so little space so many treasures, so many flowers, so many
grey stones, all beautiful . . . so very beautiful."

During the first few days, Gertrude Stein introduced Wright to the Luxembourg Gardens and the other delights of the neighborhood. She received him at 5 rue Christine and managed as best she could to moderate his boundless enthusiasm. He meanwhile paid a visit to Sylvia Beach, another patroness of exiled writers, the "bookseller" of Shakespeare & Company who had helped Joyce and Hemingway make a start. He tried to get her to share his latest literary enthusiasms: Nelson Algren, Lawrence Lipton and Jo Sinclair.[1]

After an official reception at the Hotel de Ville, where Wright was named an honorary citizen of Paris, invitations poured in, which led him to declare in "I Choose Exile":

My first week in exile disclosed a smooth flow of Parisian public politeness that imbued me with a sense of social confidence. The sharp contrast between French and American attitudes demonstrated that it was barbarousness that incited so militant a racism in white Americans.

On May 30, the publisher Gaston Gallimard gave a huge reception in Wright's honor, where he again saw Sylvia Beach and Gertrude Stein, who had just returned from a lecture tour of the American bases in Germany. He also met the literary lions of Parisian society: Roger Martin du Gard (who had actually decided to brave the photographers in order to meet him); Maurice Merleau-Ponty; Jean Paulhan; Jean Schlumberger; Roger Caillois; Michel Leiris; Raymond Queneau; Jean-Jacques Mayoux, who was then director of the Coopération Intellectuelle; and Marcel Duhamel, who was to translate *Black Boy* and was thinking of adapting *Native Son* for the stage.[2] A few days later, Albin Michel, who was going to publish the translations of *Native Son* and one volume of *Uncle Tom's Children*, gave a dinner in Wright's honor.[3] Next, he was invited to lunch by the Ministry of Foreign Affairs Office of Cultural Services. A *New York Herald Tribune* interview on June 2 indicates that Wright was taking French lessons in order to chat more easily with the writers he met at the Café de Flore, and working only slightly on his novel.[4] He never hesitated to tell the truth about the racial situation in the United States and to reply frankly to the reporters, even at the cost of perhaps seeming anti-American. On May 25, *Samedi-Soir* published his first impressions of France, under the significant headline "In Paris, the black G.I.'s have come to know and love liberty." He commented on the G.I.'s whom he had met, the devastation of the war and the difference between Europe and America. Wright had been spending most of his time enjoying the capital and the absence of racial tension, and in talking with some Frenchmen, and trying to fathom the psychology of these people who had just rejected the new constitution. Nevertheless, his conclusions in a journal entry of May 25 undoubtedly summarize his hopes more than his findings.

In saying "no" the French are actually saying "yes" to life, a life which they are dreaming about but have not yet envisioned in its proper form. France has an opinion on the way in which men ought to live in the world, and she realizes more clearly than any other nation in the West, the dramatic importance of what can be won or lost, depending upon which political or social decisions are made.

Clearly, France was then the symbol of a humane and harmonious civilization to Wright, who later supported this opinion by repeating André Gide's reply when asked why this should be so: The more secure man feels and the more ancient and cohesive his society, the less he is motivated by fear of what is different to make strict laws, to exclude originality and to practice xenophobia and racism. In fact, André Gide, whose *Travels in the Congo* Wright greatly admired, was among his new friends at the time, along with Sartre and Simone de Beauvoir, although his preferences in French literature were still Flaubert, Maupassant, Proust and "that wonderful Malraux." [5] He did not enjoy his official reception by the Société des Gens de Lettres, which had been postponed from June 6 to June 22 because Ellen was sick. Speaking before the group of embassy and ministry representatives and a large female contingent headed by Mme. Catulle-Mendès, after Gérard Bauer had attempted to define his work, Wright made some remarks on Dos Passos, Faulkner, Hemingway and Caldwell before being presented with a "diplome d'amitié Parisienne" from a representative of the Préfet de la Seine. Paris feted Wright unstintingly, if not always discerningly, and in return he attended these functions politely if not willingly.

His literary friendships could not help but lead him to commit himself to certain activities. Thus, he donated a manuscript to be sold at the Galerie Pierre on rue des Beaux Arts for the benefit of Antonin Artaud; Claude Max, editor of *Les Nouvelles Epitres,* a collection of letters by writers on current events, solicited four pages on "the Negro problem in the United States"; and Wright's series of articles on racism in the South came out in *Paris Matin*.[6] Once again he used the material from his summer trip of 1940 for these articles. On July 2, 1946, the entire thirty-minute program of the Club d'Essai, entitled "A Man and a Book," was devoted to Wright, and the following day the P.E.N. Club welcomed him at a reception given by Raymond Schwab and Jean Schlumberger. He was considered a representative Afro-American and everyone was eager to pay homage to his talent.

This social whirlwind died down with the arrival of summer vacation, and Wright had the leisure to settle his contracts with Mrs. Bradley, his literary agent in France, who had just returned from America. Meanwhile, since his search for an apartment had been unsuccessful, he finally moved to an apartment which a French professor, who was now off to Australia, had rented furnished. There among the stuffed crocodiles at 38 Boulevard St. Michel he installed his typewriters and dictaphone, but he wrote only one story during the entire summer. He had already finished "The Man Who Killed a Shadow," which Paul Reynolds was having trouble placing in the United States, when it was taken by *Les Lettres Françaises*.[7] The plot was based on a true story that Charles H. Houston, a prominent lawyer for the NAACP in Washington, had told Wright in 1945. Julius Fisher, a black man, had killed a white woman because she had made advances toward him and then started to yell for help; he had simply wanted to get her to be quiet. This time Wright explored the unreality of the white world to a black person, after having depicted the black man's invisibility in "The Man Who Lived Underground." Saul Sanders, who has been batted about from one city to another as a child, is sometimes reminiscent of the protagonist of *Black Boy,* but Saul is fated to be a murderer. Instinctively and involuntarily, purely to overcome his terror, he murders the white librarian because of her cries. Tension is created by the linking of racism and sexuality—not Saul's sexuality, for he is a well-conditioned, almost mechanical person, but the frustrated desires of the spinster. The style is a mixture of cold monotone and shrill urgency, presenting a horrible crime in a banal and unreal light while still allowing the reader to share Saul's singularly detached and absent state of mind, that of yet another "outsider" whom Wright created before meeting Camus' Mersault. The story did not come out in

English, however, until 1950, in the first issue of *Zero,* a small magazine that Wright helped Themistocles Heotis to launch.

On July 21, 1946, *PM* published, under the heading "Letter from
Paris," Wright's review of *Brewsie and Willie,* which he had finally
finished. "American G.I.'s Fears Worry Gertrude Stein" also included a description of the seventy-year-old author just as Wright
had found her in her apartment, still active in spite of her age,
surrounded by her objets d'art, her Cézannes and Picassos, her enormous dog—Basket II—and the no less faithful Alice B. Toklas.
Wright's next visit was one of the last Gertrude Stein received before
she went into the American Hospital on July 19. At that time she
gave him some advice which he eventually followed eight years later
and acknowledged in the opening pages of *Pagan Spain.*

"Dick, you ought to go to Spain."
"Why?" I had asked her.
"You'll see the past there. You'll see what the Western world is
made of. Spain is primitive, but lovely. And the people! There are
no people such as the Spanish anywhere. I've spent days in Spain
that I'll never forget. See those bullfights. See that wonderful
landscape . . ." (p. 4).

She died on July 27, following an operation for cancer.

Returning to Paris at the beginning of October, after a few weeks'
vacation with his family in the South of France, Wright already
began thinking about when he would leave. Granted, he was not
needed in New York, where his affairs were in good hands—Jacob
Salzman, who was in charge of the house on Charles Street, had
freed the second floor, while Reynolds kept in touch and continued
to represent his professional interests.[8] He was, moreover, completely won over by France, as he had written to Aswell on May 15:

Paris is all I ever hoped to think it was, with a clear sky, buildings
so beautiful with age that one wonders how they happen to be,
and with people so assured and friendly and confident that it took
many centuries of living to give them such poise. There is such an
absence of race hate that it seems a little unreal.

Of course, as a true American, he sometimes became irritated by
the slow rhythm of life and a certain lack of efficiency, as when the
post office and shops closed for a two-hour lunch. In fact, he blamed
this atmosphere and his hectic social life for the delays in the writing
of his new novel. But above all, as he wrote Reynolds, he was drawn

back to America by the possibility of finally settling into his new house, which would provide the comfortable and peaceful setting he needed for his work.

In November, the Wrights left for Switzerland to visit the environs of Zurich, where he gave a few interviews and got in touch with a publisher for the German edition of *Black Boy*. Once back in Paris a new round of receptions preceded his departure. At a meeting organized by *Carrefour*, he met René Maran, from Martinique, whose African novel *Batouala* had received the Prix Goncourt, and Hélène Bokanowski, an admirer of his work who later became a faithful friend. He saw again Gide and Prévert, as well as Aimé Césaire, whom Léopold Senghor had arranged for Wright to meet in June. Although Wright was somewhat distrustful of the existentialist set of Saint-Germain-des-Prés, he admired Sartre a great deal, and was particularly intrigued by his latest play, *The Respectful Prostitute*, which was based on the Scottsboro case.

His efforts to learn French had been more laudable than successful, but his visit had nevertheless revealed to him the essential differences between Europe and America. As contrasted with the complacency of America, which had been spared by the war, the vitality of ruined Europe filled him with admiration.

I would not go so far as to say that the American citizen is one of the most miserable beings in the world. . . . In America, the material life of the worker has become easy but it leaves the individual facing a void, feeling an uneasiness which he cannot manage to overcome; he does not know where to turn to recover his balance and his good spirits. As a general rule, Americans are particularly resourceful in times of crisis; they know what to do in order to win and survive, but all of them are now suffering the great depression which comes after the victory.[9]

He had been touched by the unexpected warmth of his reception, flattered by the respect that he had commanded as a man of letters and impressed by "the humanism which was so deeply embedded in the customs and habits of everyday life" in France. He would have liked to see culture keep pace with progress in America, now exclusively preoccupied with success, yet his trip to France did not at the time represent to him the first step toward expatriation. While criticizing America, Wright felt profoundly American, and so in exclaiming "My life is over there," he was indicating that this trip to

France was merely an enjoyable experience which he planned to repeat, the prelude to other travels meant to broaden his horizons.[10]

Wright was already stating at that time his interest in Africa. He had been struck by the fact that the French colonials no longer thought as Africans but reacted as Frenchmen, and he was curious to see for himself how this psychological and cultural mutation came about.

It is not surprising, then, that at the end of 1946, during his trip to London to see Innes Rose, his literary agent for Great Britain, Wright made a point of visiting the Jamaican George Padmore. C. L. R. James had suggested that he get in touch with Padmore, who had been fighting for over a decade for the liberation of the black people. The two men, already united by their non-Communist Left political allegiances, quickly became friends. The night before he set sail, Wright was invited to dinner by the Colored Writers' Association. In a Soho restaurant he met many progressive intellectual figures of the Third World, among them the young South African novelist Peter Abrahams; the West Indian poet Peter Blackman; Mohammed Mahgoub, from Sudan; the Eurasian Cedric Dover, president of the Association and author of *Half Caste*; Birman Maung Ohn; R. T. Makennen, secretary of the Pan-African Federation; and Dr. Malcolm Joseph Mitchell, representative of the League of the Colored Peoples.[11]

This one evening had two significant and long-range effects upon Wright's future. His friendship with Padmore influenced his political thinking and further increased his interest in Africa, and for the first time he met black militants from all the English-speaking countries. Only the year before he had occasionally lost courage during his solitary combat against racism in the United States, but now he had found a reason to hope, as he declared upon returning to New York, that the general attitude toward the racial problem was entering a new phase. The voice of the black American was now being echoed throughout the other non-white continents of the world in countries such as Burma, China and South Africa, whose citizens accounted for three-quarters of the world's population.[12]

On January 11, the Wrights sailed from Southampton on the *Queen Elizabeth* and were back in Manhattan after more than eight months' absence. They immediately moved into their house on Charles Street and spent the first few weeks getting it organized. Enormous bookshelves covered the walls of the library, and while

Ellen was busy decorating and arranging furniture, Richard settled down in the agreeable atmosphere of being home at last. France would always be the setting of his marvelous vacation, but he felt deeply attached to "this particular hell" where he had been born. All he had to do now was to work as quickly as possible, taking up his friendships and habits where he had left off.

The Lafargue Clinic, which had just opened before he left, was now going full steam ahead. In February, 1947, General Bradley, director of Veterans Administration, gave the clinic new prestige by assigning it the care of all veterans, regardless of race. As a member of the board of directors, Wright continued to follow its progress, and that of all psychiatry in Harlem.[13] He also served as Harlem guide to Simone de Beauvoir, who was spending part of the spring in New York, between trips down South and to the Middle West. She had originally made contact with the Wrights again at the end of January, when she attended a lecture Richard gave on his experiences in Europe. On February 3, he escorted her to the Savoy, the famous Harlem dance hall.[14] On April 9, they attended a service of the Abyssinian Baptist Church, where they had a long talk with Rev. Adam Clayton Powell, Jr. On April 13, they went with Nelson Algren to listen to spirituals in a small church in the ghetto, where Wright was invited to speak. The series of parties, political discussions among Leftist intellectuals and nightclub rounds continued right up until her departure.

On May 8, she accompanied Wright to an Authors' League luncheon at the Town Hall Club, where they saw Juan Goyanarte, Marc Connelly and Fritz von Unruh. Wright had run for the executive committee of the League that winter in the hopes of rescuing the organization from extremist factions whose representatives had already obtained a ruling to force the League to publish the membership list and wanted to take over its direction entirely. Wright had been elected on the official slate with, among others, John Hersey and Irwin Shaw. Several board meetings had taken place after his return from France, but there were no significant results and Wright soon lost interest in working exclusively on the essentially peripheral problems of the writing profession.[15]

Wright was still not working a great deal on his novel, and his anthology of Afro-American literature remained in the planning stages, but he did write two reviews for his friend Roger Pippett of *PM*. He was forced to treat E. M. Forster's *Aspects of the Novel* on its own merits rather than as a perspective on the author, since he had never read anything else by Forster. As a result his praise was somewhat vague, in contrast with his enthusiasm for Fritz von Unruh's *The End Is Not Yet.*

His comprehension of the involved and recondite nature of the problem of fascism lifts him, at one stroke, out of the class of fictioneers and onto that plane of writers who, through the prophetic power of their vision, legislate new values for mankind.[16]

He compared the novel with *Crime and Punishment* and declared it "the most important novel yet to come out of devastated Europe."

On May 23, 1947, he appeared once again on the WNBC radio program "The Author Faces the Critics," this time to discuss John Gunther's *Inside U.S.A.* with Fiorello La Guardia and Harold Stassen.

This was the extent of Wright's literary activity during the five months since his return from France. He was, in fact, having difficulty readapting to America despite his enjoyment of his new home, old habits and friends. The lack of prestige of the literary profession in America was even more apparent to him after the honors he had received in France. He had been delighted to return to the abundance of food and the comfort and efficiency of the United States, but he saw his pessimistic predictions about the cold war coming true as state pressure on the individual conscience and the materialism of a consumer society became increasingly oppressive. In an interview on existentialism for the July 11, 1947, issue of *Combat*, Maria le Hardouin asked him a question that elicited the following response:

An American is forced to live in exile from himself, in order not to see that he is in despair. This allows him to ignore the discrepancy between his actions and his principles which are handed down from one generation to the next. . . . In fact, thousands of interests and necessities oblige him to turn up his nose at these noble theories which is why everyone takes care not to ask himself the great fundamental questions again and lives as a prisoner of his complexes.

Nevertheless, his worst and most immediate vexations were racial. In 1947, New York had not yet eliminated segregation, much less brutal discrimination. He still had to have his hair cut in Harlem,

On the steps of his Greenwich Village house, 1947.
Photo by Hella Heyman, Studio Gallery

With Manhattan in the background

With Knobby. *Photo by Studio Gallery*

With Ellen on Long Island, 1947.
Photo by Studio Gallery

go only to certain restaurants he knew would serve him and be called "boy" by the neighborhood shopkeepers. His Italian neighbors were unabashed in their hostility, making disagreeable remarks and muttering threats against the "nigger." In the spring of 1947, gangs of young white hoodlums began to invade Greenwich Village, throwing Blacks out of the restaurants and molesting interracial couples. Richard began to be afraid for his family. He was just as enraged to be insulted on the streets when walking with Ellen or another white woman as he was when served salted coffee (a popular trick played on Blacks at that time), but he contained himself.[17] Nevertheless, fear for the safety of his family brought the violent reactions of his Mississippi childhood to the fore again. He was especially worried about Julia who, at age six, could be forever traumatized by the racism that she had already experienced. (A department store had refused to let her use their bathroom because of her color.) The war had not saved America from its racist habits. Republicans and Southerners were, in fact, regaining some of the influence that they had lost during the New Deal, and Wright feared that the beginnings of the cold war would stimulate any fascist tendencies in the system. Even if the tide turned toward liberalism again, it might be too late for Julia. In June, Wright reserved space on the *United States* so that the family could once again leave for Paris.

Wright had no idea how long this second visit would last, but he took enough with him for a long stay. The royalties on *Black Boy* assured him a regular income, which Reynolds would pay quarterly via American Express, and he would also send Ella her monthly check.[18] A lawyer, Harry Nassberg, was put in charge of Wright's business affairs and Odette Lieutier, an acquaintance, was to receive the Wrights as tenants in her Paris apartment on the rue de Lille. As a result, they immediately put the Charles Street house on the market and, with an easy mind, took a few weeks' vacation in Dr. Safford's cottage at Wading River, Long Island. Since Wright had not been able to have his lawyer send him a car the previous summer, due to customs formalities, he now bought an Oldsmobile and proceeded to take driving lessons. In this way, Wright had an unexpectedly good time during this final reprieve before his coming exile and he was already beginning to remember only the agreeable aspects of America. They spent their last few days in New York with George Davis, whom Richard enjoyed as much for his somewhat melancholy sensibility as for his conversation. On July 30,

1947, Ralph Ellison, the Maases, the Kossas, Bernard Wolfe and the Jameses were among the many friends who came aboard to drink a farewell glass of champagne. The Oldsmobile and seventeen trunks of books, clothes and supplies were in the hold.

The somewhat contradictory impressions to be found in Wright's diary, ranging from relaxation and wonderment to irritation bordering on indignation at the practical problems he encountered in readapting to Europe, testify to the unsettled state of mind that apparently delayed work on his novel for several more months.

On August 5, after a somewhat disagreeable crossing, the Wrights were met at Southampton by Peter Abrahams, whose autobiography Wright was in the process of reading.[19] In spite of having to concentrate on driving on the left, Wright reveled in the trip to Folkstone and the view from his hotel window, which he described in poetic and almost painterly terms in his journal entry for August 6, 1947:

I must admit that I've never seen anything so beautiful as the English countryside in August; it was like a series of water-colors with all descriptions of color. Up hill, down hill, around curves which could not be called curves because the whole trip was a curve, and around roads bordered by green hedges. . . .

Outside of [my] window is the English Channel, misty blue and wide and calm. . . . The sun has gone down; the sky is a soft, pearly grey. People are walking along the water front slowly; there is no noise, and in the Channel is a single tiny boat with two people in it, and it is surrounded by mist blue and faint; and behind it a curtain, blue and grey and white, hangs with delicate precision. The glaring light of Southampton which hurt my eyes is gone here in this beauty.

After a long wait at customs and a rough crossing, the Wrights arrived the following evening at 9 rue de Lille. They immediately made arrangements to fetch their Siamese cat, Knobby, which had been sent directly via Cherbourg so as to avoid the English quarantine, and began to unpack their numerous trunks. Alice, their maid from the preceding year, returned to work for them. Michel Bokanowski lent them money for moving expenses, and Bill Gremley stocked them with provisions from the PX, but there were numerous annoyances: the lack of hot water, the delays before

they could get food coupons, the breakdowns of the Oldsmobile—
which stumped the French mechanics—the almost semiweekly
electricity failures, the closing of many stores for the summer vacation. These daily problems irritated Wright all the more because
he was constantly thinking about his novel, as his journal musings
for August 11 reveal:

While standing around today waiting for trunks and other things,
I felt more than ever that the kind of book that I'm writing is
needed and comes right out of what people are feeling. Freedom
and how can one be free. We seem to live on the sheer edge of an
old world going to pot and the new one whose outlines are yet to
be seen. Which of course means that the old set of feelings which
fitted one situation is going and the situation is gone and since there
is not yet a clear set of new relations the new set of feelings is not
clear and defined. So, any idea as to the future, then, is of great
value, of general value and need, and any rejection of the past of
great value is therefore precious.

Wright finally rented a hotel room across the street so as to have
some peace in which to write, but inspiration deserted him. Gradually, however, he developed a certain fatalism so that delays and
lack of efficiency were not so bothersome to him. He also became
less mistrustful, something that had been partly due to not understanding the language.[20]

Another unforeseen inconvenience, which wasted a good deal
of time, was the constant stream of friends who kept dropping in
on him at home. He was happy to see them, but he did not consider an evening well spent unless he got some new idea or had an
enlightening conversation. Bill and Mary Gremley, whose Army
contacts were valuable for shopping; Catherine Dudley, on her way
to Italy; Nancy Norman, heiress to a New York fortune; Edith
Schroeder, Ellen Weinstein, and Claude-Edmonde Magny and some
of Odette Lieutier's French friends were the most frequent visitors.
At the end of August, George and Dorothy Padmore spent several
days in Paris, and Richard and George engaged in interminable
conversations while one of George's Indochinese friends introduced
them to the exotic restaurants of Paris. Then Carson and Reeves
McCullers arrived. Carson, who was in a pitiful state, half-paralyzed
and blind in one eye after a recent stroke brought on by her excessive drinking, required constant attention; by September she
had to spend several weeks in the American Hospital while Reeves,

footloose, frequented the cafés. On August 29, Peter and Dorothy Abrahams also came to Paris, and Wright showed them the city. They sat chatting at the tables of the Flore or the Deux Magots, went out to dinner, listened to jazz at the Tabou bar, had onion soup at Les Halles, went to the greyhound races and canoed in the Bois de Boulogne, but Wright quickly tired of this tourist life.[21] He would have liked to get up at dawn to write a few pages before it became hot, but the late evenings exhausted him. He wanted more than ever to avoid all social obligations, but how could he devote less time to friendship without looking like an ogre?

Meanwhile, the apartment on the rue de Lille turned out to be much too small for two families, and Odette's lack of common sense, along with the discovery that she took drugs, was only an added incentive to leave. At the end of August, the Wrights moved into 166 Avenue de Neuilly, where they had unearthed a six-room apartment after much searching.[22] Sylvia Beach returned the refrigerator that had been lent to her, Ellen bought furniture at antique stores and the flea market and Richard built bookshelves in the library, for which he bought a secondhand radio-phonograph. The only things left to do were to stock up on coal, in anticipation of the rigorous winter, and for Richard to start writing again. On September 9, he wrote to Paul Reynolds:

I did, to my surprise, get a chance to do some work on the ship, but I've had a chance to do but very little since being in Paris. All of our time was taken up with getting the new apartment and moving into it, getting identity cards, rations, etc. But that is now over and I'm beginning to poke into the novel again.

On board he had actually done no more than reread the first draft and rewrite a dozen pages. He had been in a hurry to make it a "great" book, that is, "a book one can read feeling the movement and rhythm of a man alive and confronting the world with all his strength," but he admitted in his journal entry of July 31 that he had lacked the inspiration.

While waiting until he had envisioned more clearly how he would deal with the concept of freedom, Wright decided to familiarize himself with existentialism. What he had learned in Dorothy Norman's living room was insufficient, but the more he learned, the more the philosophy seemed to correspond to his own vision of life and human responsibility. Thus, each day brought him closer to the existentialist ideal of the committed intellectual, the man who was always willing and able to testify to and fight against injustice. For Wright this began a period of diversified but intense activity. While he neglected his novel to engage in political action or to search for philosophical certainties, he also discovered other domains of true aesthetic expression, films in particular. This has often been labeled Wright's "existentialist period," leading up to the composition of *The Outsider* in 1953, but it was actually a richer and more complex experience than that implies. He certainly published very little during this half-decade, but he lived an intense spiritual life, each day further removing himself from purely American preoccupations by acquiring a more European, more global, view of his own situation in particular, of the black situation in general and of the situation of contemporary man. These years, which could be called a second maturation, or a reorientation, were, in fact, the somewhat confused beginnings of Wright's new view, in the fifties, that the salvation of humanity could come only from the Third World. Although he continued to be interested in writing novels, they were still the result of his prior interests in psychoanalysis and ideology. Even *The Outsider* was a means of obliterating the past, not of announcing the future.

Wright's major projects during these years indicate the principal directions of his thought: the participation in a third and neutralist force in order to fight against racism more efficiently; the condemnation of totalitarianism in the name of existentialism; the filming of *Native Son*; and his support of the *Présence Africaine* group. Since all these activities are chronologically and often philosophically interwoven, it is therefore important to remember that Wright pursued them all simultaneously, moving ahead to another when one did not turn out, ready to go back to the first if a further development opened up new possibilities. Even though Wright's activities seemed as orderly at the beginning of the forties as they appear feverish and dispersed by the end of the decade, Wright himself had not fundamentally changed. It was just that his hesitations as the unknown author of *Native Son* had been more hidden, and it was unity of purpose alone which was later lacking in the author of *The Outsider*. This apparent disorder actually was the precursor of an important shift in direction, in which Wright eventually turned his energies toward African liberation after confirming the futility of European attempts to confront the cold war.

2

During the summer of 1946 in Paris, Wright had met Léopold Senghor, the best known of the French-speaking black African writers, and through Senghor he met the West Indian poet Aimé Césaire. In postwar Paris, some of these pioneers of negritude were worried about the survival of traditional African culture in a rapidly industrializing society. It was, however, the Senegalese teacher Alioune Diop who, with the group of intellectuals who had collected around him, crystallized the movement and launched the magazine *Présence Africaine*. Diop's editorial for the first issue stated that the magazine was "open to the collaboration of men of good will (white, yellow and black) who are willing to help us define the African's creativity and to hasten his integration into the modern world." [23] André Gide; Emmanuel Mounier; Jean-Paul Sartre; Albert Camus; Michel Leiris; Father Maydieu, the Dominican director of *La Vie Intellectuelle*; Pierre Naville; Paul Rivet—all Africanists or "Africanizers"—represented metropolitan France on the list of sponsors with Paul Hazoumé and Wright. Wright, in fact, was present at the historic first board meeting at the Brasserie Lipp in October, 1946, and contributed Boris Vian's translation of "Bright and Morning Star" to the impressive contents of the first issue. In addition, he was responsible for the decision to publish one of his favorite poems by Gwendolyn Brooks, "The Ballad of Pearl May Lee," and his friend Sidney Pélage's article on the so-called primitive mentality. He also worked with Thomas Diop on preparing an English version of Alioune Diop's editorial and *Un Enfant du Pays* was reviewed in Madeleine Gautier's column, "Reading Notes."

During the next few years *Présence Africaine* devoted itself to clarifying and explaining the conflicts of the young African intellectuals unable to return completely to tradionalism, unwilling to assimilate themselves completely to Europe and not yet sure

of how to confront Western technological civilization with the African culture which, as Alioune Diop concluded in his original editorial, could and should contribute humanism to the world.

> We men of overseas, from ancient China, from pensive India to
> silent Africa, possess immense moral resources which constitute
> the substance to be fecundated by Europe. We are indispensable
> to each other.

The Africans, Diop stated, considered the spiritual vitality and
creative power of the black Americans indispensable to the black
world, even if these Blacks had almost totally forgotten their ancestral customs and had not escaped the influence of their confined
and dehumanizing social setting. Of course, this opinion struck a
responsive chord in Wright, and his admiration for France impressed Diop, who planned to devote a special issue of the magazine
to Afro-Americans.

Wright thus became the spokesman for his black compatriots and
accordingly published Frank Marshall Davis, a few of Samuel
Allen's more remarkable poems (thereby encouraging him at the
start of his career) and articles by Horace Cayton and C. L. R.
James. He remained an active member of the board until 1950,
attending gatherings for important black personalities and artists
who passed through, among them Louis Armstrong and Duke
Ellington, who was welcomed on July 21, 1948, at Gallimard's
the day after a group of stars had squeezed in to see him at the
Club Saint-Germain. He also introduced E. Franklin Frazier and
black folk singers to the French public, but most important was
the material aid he was able to provide. With Camus and a few
others, he worked hard to establish an effective liaison with
UNESCO, and in the autumn of 1948 he actually approached the
Baronne de Rothschild for a loan so that the magazine could survive while awaiting the subsidies promised by some African states.[24]
He soon made good friends in the Société Africaine de Culture and
in January, 1948, Jacques Howlett was one of the first to defend
him against the attacks in *Poésie 47* made by Jean Kanapa on
behalf of the French Communist Party.

Wright was, in fact, interested in everything concerning Africa.
Sidney Pélage had returned from there with shocking stories of
the poverty and the feelings of the people. Wright conversed with

Peter Abrahams, a fierce opponent of apartheid whose autobiography he brought to the attention of Harper's, and corresponded regularly with George Padmore. On November 18, 1948, along with Abrahams, Diop, René Char and Audiberti, at the Palmes Bookstore he opened the exhibition "Evidence de l'Art Nègre," consisting of works of art, for the most part lent by Madeleine Rousseau, and books on Africa. As he stated on the invitation to the opening:

The vitality, the unconventional bravery, the freedom of invention of these sculptures all testify to the power and originality of Negro expression, and in particular, of the African artistic expression which is offered to you in this exhibition. What the Negro has accomplished in art is only a measure of what he is capable of, and what he might be able to accomplish in other realms of life, if only he is given a chance. In the meantime, he offers the world tangible images of a life which is nowhere near over, even though, often, it must still be led in slavery or oppression.

During that same month, his introduction to a special issue of *Musée Vivant,* which Cheik Anta Diop and Madeleine Rousseau devoted to "Negro Culture," expressed the same convictions.

In the summer of 1950, he worked with Aimé Césaire organizing "Revelation of Negro Art," an exhibition of works from the Musée de l'Homme and performances of ritual songs and dances at the Cité Universitaire. Although he had resolved in 1953 to refuse any further demands in order to work on *The Outsider,* he nevertheless agreed to inaugurate the exhibition of the sculptor Ben Ewonwu at the Palmes Bookstore on October 3—still another indication that the need to disseminate African culture was a priority for Wright.

Through this kind of collaboration, and from his conversations with African intellectuals, Alioune Diop in particular, Wright explored his kinship with those he called "marginal men," torn between two worlds. He, too, belonged to two cultures, was the offspring of a new race born of a cross between two mentalities, which scarcely realized its own originality but owed it to itself to express it. Wright found that this concept not only encompassed his own mission as a black American, but also afforded him the opportunity to join a worldwide culture in which his participation would be more significant than any he could achieve in the United

States. If this group to which he belonged had enough perspective on white civilization (as both participant in and spectator of it) to denounce its abuses and foresee its errors, then perhaps it could infuse the West with the vital resources, the humanism, of another culture. Wright was discovering that the fate of the black American was not only linked with the fate of America and Africa but with that of the West and the entire world as well. The problem of defining the American nationality and Western culture was inseparable from that of redefining African culture and world coexistence. Wright had wanted, in a way, to save America, but in order to do so he had to save the world, so that from this point onward, he worked more with his new African, European and West Indian colleagues—with all those, in fact, whose culture contained the antidote to the dehumanizing poison of industrialization. Since he now saw his struggle to free America from racism as part of a much larger fight, his activities with *Présence Africaine* and the intellectuals from the French-speaking Third World represented a stage of his spiritual evolution just as important as his contacts with existentialist philosophy and the writers of *Les Temps Modernes.* For the time being, these two allegiances overlapped rather than conflicted; had not Jean-Paul Sartre just written "Black Orpheus," the preface to Léopold Senghor's anthology of black poetry?

3

Wright had originally been passionately interested in the French existentialists. Before his first trip to Paris he had become familiar with Camus, Simone de Beauvoir and Sartre by reputation at least. He had been able to read Camus' important lecture "The Crisis of Man," which *Twice a Year* published in the winter of 1946; *Caligula,* which he bought in English the next year; and, later, in 1948, *The Plague;* but *The Stranger,* which he read in the autumn of 1947, made the strongest impression on him, as he testified in his journal on September 6, 1947:

Took Camus' *Stranger* into the Bois de Boulogne and read. I finished the book and found it interesting. It is a neat job, but devoid of passion. He makes his point with dispatch and his prose is solid and good. In America a book like this would not attract much attention for it would be said that he lacks feeling. He does however draw his character very well. What is of course really interesting in this book is the use of fiction to express a philosophical point of view. . . . There is still something about this Camus that bothers me. Maybe because he is the artist and Sartre and De Beauvoir are not primarily.

Unaware of the personal conflicts and contradictions in Camus' life, Wright retained this opinion and worked with him on occasion until the day when, as a last resort, Camus sided with the French colonials in the Algerian war. By that time Wright had moved so far away from this attitude, somewhat reminiscent of Faulkner's "racism," that he never saw Camus again.

Simone de Beauvoir was more accessible than Sartre and became a closer friend of the Wrights, originally because she had been their guest on her visit to the United States, and later in the early fifties because Ellen became her literary agent. Of her books that he had read, Wright was only interested by *The Second Sex*. Since he did not know Merleau-Ponty except for having run into him at various parties, French existentialism, for Wright, was represented by Sartre. In this case Wright's regard for the man seemed to outweigh his admiration for his work. Between 1949 and 1951, Wright did read Sartre's novels and plays, as well as some minor essays like "The Psychology of the Imagination," but it was not until 1957 that he read *Being and Nothingness*. In 1946 *Partisan Review* had published passages from *Anti-Semite and Jew* and the next year Wright read *Existentialism as Humanism*. For him, Sartre was the author of this last work, just as Sartre considered Wright the author of *Black Boy* (not *Native Son*)—that is to say the type of committed author, torn between two audiences, whose work owes its greatness to its ability to transcend this tension.[25]

It was on political issues that the two eventually worked best together. Sartre's position, somewhere toward the Left, combined a desire to renew in the Communists the political morality they had lost since Stalinism, with the hope of working with the non-Communist Left against reactionary forces.

Wright was surprised and delighted that Sartre associated his own experience of oppression, the Nazi occupation of France, with that of all oppressed and colonized peoples. On August 27, 1947, he wrote enthusiastically in his journal:

Sartre is the only Frenchman I've met who has voluntarily made this identification of the French experience with that of the rest of mankind. How rare a man is this Sartre! His ideas must be good for they lead him into the areas of life where man sees what is true.

This, in fact, was the time when Wright, Sartre and Simone de Beauvoir often met to discuss political and philosophical matters, sometimes far into the night. On September 7, the topic had been freedom, as Wright confides again to his diary: "Sartre is quite of my opinion regarding the possibility of action today, that it is up to the individual to do what he can to uphold the concept of what it means to be human. The great danger, I told him, in the world today is that the very feeling and conception of what is a human being might well be lost. He agreed," as well might the author of *Existentialism as Humanism*.

On existentialism itself, Wright's opinions became better defined but varied depending upon whether he adopted the metaphysical and religious definition of Heidegger and Kierkegaard, or the concept of commitment advocated by the French school. Since his rupture with the Communist Party, Wright had been humanist in both ethics and politics, but while he had evolved from politics toward morality, Sartre had proceeded from morality to politics. In any case, the two agreed when it came to committed action, which both of them felt imposed upon them by the beginning of the cold war, with its disturbing international political tensions. Although Wright claimed a certain detachment, his tendency to dramatize finally overcame him. After a conversation with Winthrop Rockefeller in the fall of 1947, his fear of war between the United States and Russia led him to book passage on the *Queen Elizabeth* just in case he needed to leave France in a hurry.[26]

The political and economic situation in France was also precarious. The floods during the fall of 1947 had made many staples even scarcer and aggravated the rise in prices. The situation was no better in the rest of Europe. *Native Son* was supposed to be performed in Prague; when Ellen went there in December and

In front of the Gaité Bookstore, 1948

In Paris

In Rome. *Photo by Fedelli*

With the Padmores, Paris, 1947

wanted to do some shopping with the royalty money that had been held there since the Communist take-over, she could find nothing to buy except a few glasses, a doll and some Christmas decorations.

Wright came back with similar impressions from his trips to countries where his books were being translated. He went to Milan with Ellen to celebrate the Pellizi publication of *Native Son,* attended a huge reception in Turin given by Einaudi, which was having *Black Boy* translated, and so consorted with the principal Italian critics—Aleramo, Bontempelli, Jovine, G. Baldini, Bellonci and Massino—as well as with several authors. During his stay in Rome, from February 10–15, 1948, Wright gave his lecture on Afro-American literature to which Mondadori bought the rights as well as to a collection of stories, *Cinque Uomini.* He toured the city, visiting the Trinita dei Monti and the villa Medicis, and gave a few interviews at the Trinity Bar. He was struck by the splendor, animation and the light in Rome, particularly after the gray streets of Paris, but the chronic poverty, the shabby little cigarette vendors and the innumerable beggars made as strong an impression on him as the presence of hope and gaiety and resourcefulness amid so much apparent corruption and confusion. Carlo Levi, whom he had been happy to find "as jolly and laughing as ever," gave a luncheon in his honor at which several Italian intellectuals made Wright realize how determined they were to rebuild Europe but how little they could accomplish without the help of the Marshall Plan. A letter addressed to Dorothy Norman on February 28, 1948, in which he describes the sometimes contradictory diversity of this shifting society, reflects some of his own uncertainties: "Ideologically, the people are without a keen sense of direction. They are in favor of some of the ideas of both the Left and Right, but their daily worries absorb all of their emotions and intellectual energies." [27]

Wright then went to London, via Belgium, the only prosperous country in Europe at the time because the United States, which also made use of Belgian ports, was buying uranium from the Belgian Congo. The wealth was more frightening than comforting, however. He noted in the same letter to Dorothy that "the most innocent looking produce has MADE IN USA stamped on it. The Belgians are fat, dull, and their minds are as narrow and devious as their winding streets." While criticizing Belgian materialism, Italian corruption and French apathy, he found England positively depressing. Certainly the famed British spirit of solidarity had allowed belief in a former way of life to survive, but the slogans of the Labor Party were not enough to feed this impoverished and starving nation. In fact, Wright had only gone to London because the Bolton Theatre, a small playhouse in Kensington, was putting on *Native Son*.[28]

From Wright's letters to Dorothy Norman of February 28 and March 9, 1948, it is clear that he was fairly well informed on the true economic and political difficulties of this continent that had been devastated by war. As usual, he was inclined to dramatize and, because he was American, to underestimate small nations by judging them too hastily, but he was sincerely worried about the ideological complexities of the cold war. In place of the superficial condescension of a citizen of the greatest world power came the anxiety of a humanist who could not find clear reasons to hope for the survival of individual values in the old world. In France, De Gaulle was patiently waiting backstage while M. Schuman was trying to prevent the Right and the Left from tearing each other to pieces. After the coup in Czechoslovakia, the Communists could no longer dissociate themselves from Stalinism, and the Right was pro-American only because it was anti-Russian. In the mounting antagonism Wright saw the thousands of individual tragedies as a prelude to a general upheaval of society. Beyond the obvious split caused by the cold war, he envisions a worse state of affairs in which America and Russia would unite in their totalitarianism, their exaltation of power, and annihilate the individual altogether, as he prophesies in his letter of March 9:

The Right and Left, in different ways, have decided that man is a kind of animal whose needs can be met by making more and more articles for him to consume. If man is to be contained in that definition and if it is not to be challenged, then that is what will prevail; and a world will be built in which everybody will get enough to eat and full stomachs will be equated with contentment and freedom, and those who will say that they are not happy under such a regime will be guilty of treason. How sad that is. We are all accomplices in this crime. . . . Is it too late to say something to halt it, modify it?

As he observed unrestricted industrialism becoming the criterion for all values, Wright denounced a deeper problem than that of the confrontation of the two major powers, which was, essentially, "the total extinction of the concept of a human being which has prevailed for 2,000 years," and, with its passing, the advent of the consumer society. This is the first clear formulation of one of Wright's major themes during the fifties: the individual versus society, the mind versus materialism. He was trying to resolve this dilemma in the novel he was working on, which became *The Outsider*. He had come to France to find a humanist tradition; he thought he had found it in 1946, only to have it retreat in 1948 before the advance of Americanization. This not only changed his concept of the racial question, which he had already begun to see in a broader perspective, but it forced him, even as he sought to elicit a final spark of comprehension in Western minds, to look elsewhere for reasons to believe in mankind. The Third World represented not only an area still to be freed from colonial oppression, but also the last hope for the survival of world civilization, just as the liberation of the American Negro would be the salvation of America. At this time, therefore, Wright decided to go to Africa as a journalist in order to look for answers to these problems.[29]

The letters in which Wright expressed these fears and forebodings were not destined for publication but, with his permission, Dorothy Norman printed them in the 1948 tenth-anniversary issue of *Twice a Year*, which included essays by Camus and Simone de Beauvoir as well as—thanks to Wright—articles by Carlo Levi, Stephen Spender, Ignazio Silone, André Malraux, and Claude-Edmonde Magny, in a magnificent effort to bring America and Europe face to face. The symposium, entitled "Art and Action," began with a translation of Sartre's *The Respectful Prostitute*, preceded by the author's reply to his American critics and an introduction by Wright, who defined the so-called Negro problem as "a white problem, a phase of the American problem in general."[30] He asserted that this subject would have to be treated as comedy or as a farce by a foreign observer and claimed the artist's right to pronounce a moral judgment. Considering the number of intellectuals who contributed their views, the issue was remarkably homogeneous; everyone was concerned with defending the individual (while demonstrating to Europe the benefits of American technology) and ultimately resolving the problems of democracy.

It was toward this end that Wright agreed to work with Sartre to transform the Rassemblement Démocratique Révolutionnaire, which already had more than a thousand members among the non-Communist Left, into a powerful movement. Although Wright would not allow himself to risk being deported by becoming involved in the affairs of a country that was protecting him, he could help the group of *Les Temps Modernes* and the RDR by taking a public stand against certain aspects of American policy to which his nationality alone would lend weight. He agreed with Sartre that the individual could, even by himself, act effectively and that a militant intellectual should always be ready to become involved when events called for it, as a person, not as a member of a party or a nation.

Thus, his participation in the large RDR Writers' Congress held on December 13, 1948, was widely remarked upon. Under the chairmanship of David Rousset, Sartre, Camus and André Breton, a large number of writers including Theodore Plievier, Carlo Levi, Guido Piovene, Abdallah Ibrahim and M. Ratsimanango gathered in the Salle Pleyel to discuss the theme of the internationalism of the mind. Wright spoke at length, criticizing both America and Russia on the grounds that neither one was worthy of guiding humanity if all it offered was purely material happiness. Although his speech might now ring hollow to someone who could not catch the allusions to current events—the coup in Czechoslovakia and the incipient threat of McCarthyism—the rhetoric itself was moving. On December 16, 1948, *Franc-Tireur* published this speech in which Wright condemned American antiintellectualism as much as the Soviet intellectual dictatorship, and exalted the writer who fights against totalitarian propaganda for individual liberty, "the freedom to save oneself from something, and look ahead to something." He was faithful to his Marxist perspective, but his wording was existentialist when he emphasized the need for action and individual values. The newspaper went on to remark, "Is it wrong to say that this torrential stream of violence in Wright's magnificent cry leads him into a certain injustice, as much toward the United States as toward Russia? Probably not, but at least he protests and his malediction is heart-rending in its beauty." [31]

Was Wright's new political commitment no more than a diversion or would it permit him to understand himself better? His letter to the *New York Herald Tribune*, which appeared on April 4, 1949, in reply to a series of articles by the Communist leader Anna Louise

Strong, marks a stage in his evolution. It was almost as if Wright were settling an old account. In "Comrade Strong, Don't You Remember?" the agonized Communist whom Miss Strong had refused to support ten years earlier seemed now overjoyed to see her expelled from Russia.[32] The diatribe transcends the personal level, however, attacking the methods of totalitarianism, the press campaigns, the calumnies, and the ceaseless fights setting one leader against another in the struggle for power, and actually outlines the subject of *The Outsider*—a denunciation of the tyranny by which one man arbitrarily decides to play the role of God and control the destiny of others. If Wright, as he admitted, was enraged at reading Miss Strong's articles on her recent arrest and expulsion on charges of being a spy, it is because they "so rekindled [his] sense of the moral and ethical problems involved in membership in the Communist Party." He did not, in fact, reproach her for being a spy, but rather for the ruthless inhumanity in currying Party favor by falsely accusing other Communists. Wright denounced the double-dealing of these leaders who had formerly refused to adopt the proper policy toward the Blacks, but more striking than his indignation at such exploitation of "the contradictions existing in the sentimental bourgeois mind" is the almost naïve idealism of his final appeal.

You are in a position to help cleanse the soiled political instruments which the oppressed want to use in their struggle for a better life. . . . You can still confess openly, honestly, completely, and with a deep sense of responsibility toward the oppressed of this earth and their future. You are toward the end of your span. One of the miracles of life is that we can alter the meaning of events by changing our attitude toward them. Can you do that, Anna? Are you that free? The right to act is yours in the most absolute sense.

Wright wanted morality to triumph by introducing the truth into the practice of politics and by refusing to let the end justify the means, which had been his reason for leaving the Party. He emphasized how he himself had kept silent during the Communist attacks on him and, after 1944, had decided not to write anything more on this subject because he realized that anticommunism could entail as much psychological slavery as communism itself. Having earlier refused to join in the Party's persecution of "deviationists," he could not now denounce former comrades to the Un-American Activities Committee, yet this did not spare him from now being attacked by the French Communist press. This time, however, he fought back, but on a different level from his adversaries. He wanted the public to understand the duplicity and maneuvering that party leaders had to employ in order to stay in power, or in other words, the intrinsic corruption of politics. Finally, as an existentialist he claimed the primacy of individual choice as the source of humanist values.

As part of his RDR activities, Wright was to participate in the International Day Against War and Fascism, scheduled for April 30, 1949, the same day as the Communist-sponsored International Anti-war Day. The group of peace partisans that assembled consisted of progressives ranging all the way from Ingrid Bergman and atomic scientist Francis Perrin to delegates from the Bolshevist-Leninist Party of Ceylon, and received beneficial support from several workers' movements. The huge gathering that evening at the Vel' d'Hiv', following the afternoon debates at the Sorbonne, was marked by the obvious absence of Sartre, Merleau-Ponty and Wright, who, fearing that David Rousset might change the event into an anti-Soviet demonstration, had sent the following message:

We condemn for the same reasons both the more or less disguised annexions in Eastern and Central Europe by the USSR and the Atlantic Pact. It is by no means certain that this pact will slow up the coming of war. It may, on the contrary, hasten it. What is certain, on the other hand, is that, a little sooner or a little later, it will contribute to make it inevitable.[33]

This was read following the speeches of the American delegates who favored the Atlantic Pact—Sidney Hook, James T. Farrell and Karl Compton—and after the Dutch delegate De Kadt had shamelessly extolled the atomic bomb as an instrument of peace. Rousset, who was soliciting funds from the CIO and generally playing into the hands of the United States, had tried in vain to get Wright to share his views, but the day before the meeting Wright had told Farrell that he would not speak against his own feelings.[34]

Wright's statement provoked a deep resentment among his compatriots, especially those from the American community in Paris. He also alienated certain members of the American non-Communist

Left whom, according to an interview with Michel Salomon, he had particularly wanted to criticize for collaborating with a capitalist and racist regime, professions of faith and principles notwithstanding. Sartre and Wright were, in fact, more progressive in their position than Sidney Hook, who never stopped insisting upon his Marxist orthodoxy. In any event, the nearly ten thousand people assembled for the evening were generally opposed to American policy. Karl Compton was booed for trying to defend the principle of the American bomb, and M. Fontaine, of the French Anarchist Committee, took issue with him in a long speech. On the other hand, Gary Davis, leader of a peace movement Wright had recently given his support, was universally applauded. Perhaps his success on that agitated evening was due to the vagueness of his plans, although his idea of declaring himself a "citizen of the world" certainly corresponded to Wright's view of international affairs.

While Wright came out against the non-Communist American Left at the RDR Congress, he also disagreed with Paul Robeson's declarations at the Anti-War Day Congress, where he maintained that black Americans would never fight against Russia.[35] Wright reminded everyone that the Blacks would not forget that the Communists had relegated their claims to second place during World War II and that they could only count on themselves in the fight for equality. Even the NAACP had done more for the Blacks than had the American Communist Party.

Thus, Wright more or less agreed with the anti-American positions of RDR until the summer of 1949, when Sartre himself resigned on the grounds that it had become too exclusively anti-Soviet.

This did not mean, however, that Wright and Sartre had agreed to play along with Russia. In 1949, *Les Temps Modernes* was, in fact, the first magazine to publish the French translation of "I Tried to Be a Communist." Wright had gone to London from May 21–26 of that year, primarily to deal with the inclusion of this piece in an anthology entitled *The God That Failed*. The editor of this collection was Richard Crossman, a Labor MP from Coventry since 1945 and member of an Anglo-American commission on the Palestine question, an issue on which he opposed the policies of Ernest Bevin. Arthur Koestler had suggested the idea of the book to Crossman, who planned to reprint articles by Ignazio Silone, Louis Fischer, André Gide, Stephen Spender, Koestler and Wright. When he was approached in November, 1948, Wright had made only one condition, which he explained in a letter to Paul Reynolds on December 20. He felt that the anthology would have to include opinions from workers, union leaders and, in general, people other than writers, if it was to be meaningful, but he eventually relented, partly, perhaps, because of his recent skirmishes with the French Communists, and partly in order to counteract some of the recent Party apologies along the lines of "Why I Became a Communist." In any case his motivation in this instance was the same as that which had led him to reply to Anna Louise Strong. He did not formulate a new attack, nor did he change the text, which by now, of course, was quite old, but like Gide and Silone he was merely trying to reintroduce morality into politics.

While these political activities were distracting Wright from the composition of his novel, he also seemed ready to participate in certain literary and social events required of a leading Paris intellectual. The Albin Michel publication of *Native Son* in the autumn of 1947 had immediately followed that of *Uncle Tom's Children*, and in the middle of January, 1948, Gallimard published *Black Boy*, which was awarded the French Critics' Award. All this entailed public appearances of one kind or another. He signed books at the Daphne Adeane Bookstore on the rue de Seine, attended parties at either the offices of Gallimard or *Les Temps Modernes,* and accorded innumerable interviews to both French and foreign newspapers. He spoke freely about the racial problem, the industrial civilization of the United States and his reasons for becoming an exile.

He also gave lectures. In February, 1948, he spoke about the relationship between America and Europe at the American Church in Paris, whose minister was one of his best friends. On March 6, he gave his lecture on Afro-American literature at the Club Maintenant. On March 17, Wright and Gaston Monnerville, deputy of French Guyana and president of the Senate, were guests of honor at an Anglo-American Press Association luncheon held at the Club des Blindés.

Although Wright continued for years to represent the ultimate authority on racial matters in the United States, he was, with time, becoming more integrated into Parisian life, at the risk of losing the immunity that had protected him on his first trip: the press of the Right no longer spared him their cutting remarks, while the Communists had totally let themselves go. In return, it was not unusual to see friends defend his position and works either in *Présence Africaine, Les Temps Modernes, Combat* or *Franc-Tireur*. He found, in spite of himself, that he was being adopted by certain groups, but that also implied a sense of belonging, of having roots, that was not likely to be disagreeable to him.

When the Wrights moved to 14 rue Monsieur le Prince in the middle of May, 1948.[36] Wright finally achieved the setting he had hoped for when looking for a place to live in Greenwich Village. They were in the middle of the Latin Quarter, close to the American school that Julia attended at 207 Boulevard Raspail, and Wright could see his publishers and most of his friends without leaving the neighborhood. In short, he now lived in the heart of an intellectual capital, within reach of everything that mattered to him.

When Fernanda Pivano, his Italian translator, came to interview Wright in his new apartment, she found him comfortably ensconced amid his typewriters, binoculars, records, long sheets of yellow scratch paper, Siamese cat and innumerable books. But he was also the man about town who appeared at the salons of Marie-Louise Bousquet and Lise Deharme, for whom Peggy Guggenheim, in a necklace of Calder mobiles, prepared a dish of pineapples and rice when she gave a party in his honor, the celebrity whom Anna-Marie Cazalis chose to collaborate with on a short film on Saint-Germain-des-Prés. First and foremost, however, he was a Parisian intellectual who interested himself in the problems of his time. He would praise the poetry of Gwendolyn Brooks; mention Kafka, Heidegger and Jaspers, whom he had just read; or comment upon his favorite novels: *Moby Dick, Ulysses, The Sound and the Fury*. What is more, he now could do so with the contemplative calm that comes with being established. He was writing very little at the time, but he was maturing, rethinking his political and philosophical beliefs. Paris was not so much the saving grace of culture that he had somewhat naïvely hoped to find, as a center for intellectual exchanges and new ideas from Africa, Europe and America.[37]

Although Ellen went back to New York in June, 1948, to decide what furniture and possessions she should bring back to France, Richard had no desire to see the United States again so soon. He also wrote Reynolds on June 7, 1948, that he considered Maxwell Geismar's plan to publish his "selected works" premature. While his horizons were broadening along humanist and existentialist lines, the American critics might trap him into a black "provincialism," especially since no part of his new book would be ready in time to be included. Thus he already thought of himself as much more than the author of *Native Son* and *Black Boy*, even if the main body of his work was still to come. He clearly demonstrated the widening of his perspective when he spoke around the time of the publication of *Black Boy* to the French press. At the time he was living and writing in Paris, he was "already looking towards Africa, India, and the East, and beginning to discover that the aspirations, the need for change, and the gropings of the black man were not [his] alone, but those of all mankind." [38]

Nevertheless, his new "philosophical" novel, which he had started before his first visit to Paris, had not progressed. He had been reading extensively, especially among the German existentialists, and studying the basic works of Heidegger and Kierkegaard, taking notes and pondering the more obscure and difficult passages. He even went so far as to have his copy of Husserl's *Phenomenology* rebound in black leather so that he could take it with him wherever he went, like a priest with his prayer book, evidence not of affectation but of a concentration that he had never equaled before. Each time that he felt obliged to mention his novel to Reynolds, it would be with a series of excuses to justify the fact that he had not finished it. The year 1947, of course, had been largely spent getting settled in Europe. But he remarks on his thirty-ninth birthday that he has "not accomplished much." [39] The inactivity for which he reproached himself was not a passing lack of inspiration, but rather represented the distance separating a huge project from its achievement. He needed to look back into himself so that his mind could blossom again; he had been battered by racism, disillusioned by Stalinism and now, in Europe, no longer found the nourishment that he had counted upon to provide some miracle. The result was an unsettled state of mind, which he evokes in his journal entry for September 17, 1947:

In the morning I shall stay in bed late, I hope, and think and dream some so that my own DEEP RESTLESS AND HURT SELF CAN COME ONCE MORE TO THE FORE, SO THAT ONCE AGAIN I CAN STOP FEELING LIKE A HUNTED

BEING AND FEEL LIKE A BEING HUNTED. There is a
subtle but profound difference, you know.

He was also physically tired after a six-week bout of flu and, on
the advice of his friend Dreyfus, decided in November, 1947,
to take a vacation on the Côte d'Azur. The gambling in Monte
Carlo did not interest him and the tourists irritated him, but his
spirits improved with the warm climate and the distance from Paris,
so that he was able to take up the novel again on his return. He
managed, this time, to get himself one-third of the way through
before he abandoned it again.

By the autumn of 1948, Wright was again exhausted. During the
winter he had traveled, and the following spring he suffered from
sinus trouble and more attacks of the flu before finally having his
tonsils out. Nevertheless his poor health, the necessity to attend
political meetings and cultural events, the writing of various articles, and family obligations, do not explain his feelings of guilt,
which seemed to spring from a sort of repugnance to finish his
novel. He spent Christmas, 1948, with his family, but instead of
writing, he prepared for the birth of his second daughter, Rachel,
who was born on January 17, 1949, at the American Hospital.
From February 25 to March 6, he was in Rome, and then went
to Switzerland for the publication of *Black Boy*.

In April James T. Farrell, who had come for the RDR Congress,
stayed near the Wrights for several days and was soon followed
by Nelson Algren. On May 3, Wright delivered a message at the
Peoples' Congress Anticolonialist Day. On May 5, he gave a lecture at the Union Universitaire Américaine on the Negro's contribution to literature; on June 22, he autographed books at the
Antin Bookstore; on July 4, he went to a party at Sylvia Beach's
to celebrate the United States publication of Henri Michaux's
Barbarian in Asia. Then his old friends Mary and Louis Wirth
visited him for a week, following which he had to help George
Plimpton, Max Steele and others launch the *Paris Review*.

The list of Wright's activities, some of which took a day, some
a week, is endless, but what matters is that he was so reluctant to
pick up his novel where he had last left off that he could no longer
resist the appeal of each new project. This time, however, he was
looking for pretexts to postpone it, not because he had let his inspiration die on him, as had been the case with "Black Hope," but

because there had not been enough time for the philosophy upon which the story was based to develop and mature in his mind. In order not to abandon it altogether, he was forced to wait, and in the meantime, he could attend to the plan for making a film of his novel, *Native Son*.

FIFTEEN

T HERE had been a great many offers to buy the movie rights to *Native Son*, but so far Wright had refused them all on the grounds that even if his message were not entirely distorted, the desire to make a profit would lead to overaccommodations to the public taste. In March, 1947, Paul Reynolds had received a typical proposal from a private producer named Joseph Fields, who wanted to change the plot of the novel somewhat. Bigger Thomas, recast as a member of a white ethnic minority, would be one of four character types—a Negro, an Italian, a Jew and a Pole—applying for the same job. The Negro and the Jew, voluntarily withdrawing in favor of the neediest candidate, the one who had a family to feed, would realize at the end of the film that they, too, could have benefited from solidarity, as could anyone who did not enjoy equality. The message of the film would be that if a minority is deprived of its civil rights, the meaning of life disappears. It was a strange way to arrive at such a laudable conclusion, and to deter any future producer from such a ridiculous idea Wright told Reynolds to ask for $75,000 for the rights.

Wright had more confidence in European producers. In December, 1946, he met Jacques Marceron who wanted to put on the play, and Roberto Rosselini wrote that he was interested in making the film, but these plans did not succeed any more than the possibility of a collaboration with Marcel Carné and Jacques Prévert.[1] Although in 1948 Wright had asked Marie-Rose Belin to adapt *Native Son* for the French stage, nothing had been formally decided when, in the fall, Wright received a proposal from the French film producer Pierre Chenal.

During the occupation of France, Chenal had been a refugee in Argentina, where he had worked with the Uruguayan Jaime Prades to make several good films. "La Maison du Maltais," "La Rue sans Nom," "Clochermerle" and, especially, "La Foire aux Chimères," with Eric von Stroheim, had earned Chenal a certain reputation

336

in France. For his part, Chenal had seen *Sangre Negro* in Buenos Aires and had been very impressed by the power of the play. He proposed that he and Wright, who would play Bigger himself, should become partners; Prades would raise the money and Chenal would direct the film. The outdoor scenes would have to be shot in Chicago, but it would be more economical to do the studio filming in Italy or France.

After the Hollywood offers Wright was, of course, pleased that Chenal intended to stick scrupulously to the novel, which even the conscientious adapter Mark Marvin had tried to soften in 1941. Prior to signing any agreement, however, Wright had Reynolds discreetly buy back the rights from the Paul Green and Welles-Houseman group for $6,000. It was a financial risk, but Wright anticipated large profits. A French company, Productions Cinématographiques, was ready to advance the money against 50 per cent of the profits. Wright himself would receive a third of what remained—that is, 17 per cent—and his expenses during the production would be paid as part of his advance. Even if Chenal and Prades abandoned the project, he counted on doing it with another producer such as Rosselini. By the middle of December, 1948, the rights had been bought back and, although Wright was thinking of asking Canada Lee to play Bigger, he was at least ready to try it himself.[2]

He quickly realized that the project would not be that easy. Political pressure immediately prevented the filming in Italy, and official American circles started to cause similar difficulties even in France. M. Genin, the director of Productions Cinématographiques, had already given his permission to go ahead when he was obliged to inform Wright on February 4, 1949, that the Centre National de la Cinématographie Française had advised him to postpone the filming indefinitely "for reasons dictated by international policy." Considering that American influence was quite strong in France at that time, there was no use protesting, and Prades decided to seek the support of Attilio Mentasti, director of Sono-Films, one of the largest film companies in Argentina. Despite his distrust of South American businessmen, Wright agreed to give Mentasti a one-month option beginning June 19, since Mentasti promised to give Chenal free rein and Chenal was ready to stop work on three films in progress in order to get started on *Native Son*. The contracts were drawn up by Reynolds in New York. By the middle of July, Wright and Chenal were working on the script in order to go to Chicago in September and be in Argentina by October. Fearing racial or political repercussions, Wright asked Reynolds to keep these plans secret. He hoped to hire as a cameraman Hackenschmidt, whom he had watched filming *The Forgotten Village* in Mexico in 1940.

Wright wrote the screenplay himself and later revised it with Chenal. Following the novel closely, Wright cut a few episodes from the trial scene and condensed others, while Chenal added several flashbacks. Wright also decided to insert several fairly long dream sequences and to concentrate ón psychological and human interest, rather than on the quasi-detective plot or ideological significance. It was "the story of a boy born amid poverty and conditions of fear which eventually stop his will and control and make him a reluctant killer," as he described it at the time.[3] After seeing him try out, Chenal insisted that Wright play the lead, and, although he had to follow a strict diet and do strenuous exercises to regain his adolescent figure, he consented—more, it seems, out of a desire to express everything that he had put in the novel, and from curiosity about his ability to do so, than from any ambition to shine as an actor.

Wright left for New York on August 20, 1949, aboard the *Queen Mary*, but only stayed long enough at the Albert Hotel to take care of some business and to sign the contracts with Chenal, who joined him there. With a cameraman, R. A. Hollahan, they went to Chicago at the end of the month to film the South Side slums and streets from which they would later construct the sets.

After an eight-year absence, not counting a few quick visits in the interim, Wright was once again in the ghetto where he had done the research for *Twelve Million Black Voices*. In contrast to his Paris life, the combined poetry and horror of this black metropolis was a shock. The absence of trees, the garbage overflowing on the streets, the tumultuous rhythm of the industrial capital depressed him, but the South Side, where the memory of his own start in life arose on every street corner, had changed somewhat. The slums were still just as poverty-stricken and dirty, but the brand-new cars parked along the sidewalks indicated a certain prosperity. New stores and a few hotels had sprung up, and Wright was especially surprised not to find the ramshackle houses where Bigger had taken refuge. As his friend Drake explained to him, the ghetto had once again broken its boundaries and now stretched all the way up to Lake Shore.

Louis Wirth had used the name of the American Council on Interracial Relations to reserve him a comfortable room at the Palmer House, on the Loop, where Blacks were generally not welcome. Besides the Wirths, who watched the filming and gave a party for him the day before he left, Wright saw some of his old friends like Horace Cayton and Sidney Williams, but once Prades and Mentasti had arrived, the filming occupied most of his time.

In the ghetto toward South Parkway Avenue and 33rd Street, and especially on Federal Street, the black passersby and observers remained on the defensive. Although the black policemen on 49th Street were cooperative, the inhabitants were afraid of being shown in a degrading light to the entire world. Prades had to bribe the Irish policemen to film in the white neighborhoods, and $10 bills worked wonders against the orders of a captain who disapproved of a film on the racial problem.

While in Chicago, Prades cast Gloria Madison as Bessie. She had already acted in *Stormy Weather* and *Cabin in the Sky* and was then studying archaeology at the University of Chicago and about to get married. Chenal finally hired the blond Jean Wallace, Franchot Tone's former wife, to play Mary after several other Hollywood actresses had refused to appear on the screen in the arms of a black man. Willa Pearl Curtiss, as Hannah Thomas, also came from Hollywood, as did Nicholas Joy (Mr. Dalton) and Charles Kane, the detective who discovers the evidence of murder.

The group arrived in New York on September 20 to depart two days later for Buenos Aires aboard the *Uruguay*. The crossing was calm and the physical education instructor took endless pains over Wright, putting him on an athlete's diet and giving him constant exercise on various apparatus, so that he finally lost thirty-five of the one hundred and eighty pounds he had weighed in July. He once again resembled the thin and timid young man who, twelve years before, had won the *Story* prize.

On September 27, the boat stopped at Port of Spain, Trinidad, where Wright gave a lecture on "The Significance of American Literature in the World Today." At Rio de Janeiro, he went to listen to sambas in a jazz club, and on October 9, in Montevideo, he spoke at length with local reporters about the racial problem. Finally, on the morning of the 11th, he disembarked at Buenos Aires, where he was met by Chenal, who had arrived by air, and a crowd of journalists. He moved into the Golden Home, a simple hotel on Posadas Street, and immediately set to work.[4]

Since the film was aimed primarily at an American audience, they had to hire from among the American tourists and residents English-speaking actors for the secondary roles. Gene Michael, a young man from California who was just visiting the country, was cast as a policeman, but he turned out to be so good that he was promoted to the part of Jan Erlone. George Green, a former nightclub dancer who had played the traitor in *Panama*, was the friend of Bigger's who discovers Bessie's body. Vera was played by Lydia Alvas, a sixteen-year-old Brazilian girl who was studying English, and Buddy by Leslie Straughn, a mechanic from New Guinea who worked at the Swift & Co. factory. George Rigaud was Farley; Ruth Roberts, Mrs. Dalton; and Don Dean, a former conductor from California who was living in Argentina, played the lawyer Boris Max. The local bridge club supplied its share of Anglo-Saxon extras, and the Blacks of the city were dressed up as "yanquis" for the street scenes.

The filming began in an aura of excitement. Gori Muñoz, the art director in charge of set design, had had a group of slum buildings constructed in the residential suburbs because the real slums of the city, located in a quarter ironically situated near the stockyards and named "Nueva Chicago," did not have suitable architecture. Wright took all these details very seriously and once had an entire night scene in front of a drugstore redone simply because the window was protected with a type of iron grating that was not used in the United States. Chenal was as demanding as Wright was painstaking. His patience alone produced a top-quality performance from Gloria Madison and made the most of Wright's talents. Wright was a model of humility and willingness. He had to light Mary's cigarette and open the door of her limousine more than ten times before Chenal stopped saying, while chewing his cigar, "No me encantó!" Although Wright knew Bigger's character better than anyone else, he felt somewhat ill at ease playing the part that Canada Lee had finally been unable to accept. He persevered nevertheless, since he wanted above all to finish the film even if he had to work "twelve hours a day, seven days a week." [5]

The filming was supposed to take only two months, according to Chenal's first predictions, but progress was slow and even the final shooting script was only half finished by the beginning of November,

Boxing on the *S. S. Uruguay*

With Mentasti,
Chenal, *et al.*

1949. Although the shooting script was almost exactly the same as the screenplay, additional suspense was created and maintained by compressing the action even more and inserting flashbacks and dream sequences between the most dramatic episodes. To give Bessie a more important role in the plot, she was made into one of the stars of the South Side night club where Bigger took Jan and Mary. The love interest was embellished and Chenal did not hestitate to transport the company 200 miles to Punta del Indio for a scene in which Bessie is supposed to go swimming in Lake Michigan.

Wright got along very well with the rest of the actors and both Jean Wallace and Willa Curtiss became real friends. The actors also enjoyed the company of the cameraman Antonio Merayo and the Argentinian staff of technicians and machinists. In fact the social life, which consisted of chatter over cups of tea, cocktail parties given for the press and official receptions given by the Countess Cuevas de Vera or the ambassador of Haiti at Christmastime, created a somewhat artificial glow, a glamorous setting for Wright's success with various women, but for once he welcomed it, since it was a relaxing break from the filming. Besides, he had decided not to do any writing for the duration except for revising a few blues that had been inspired by his recent trip to Chicago and sent to Reynolds in November.[6] "F. B. Eye Blues" is an amusing satire, which almost seems to prophesy the McCarthy witch-hunt to come.

> Breaks my heart in two, Lord,
> And I just can't forget.
> Said it breaks my heart in two, Lord,
> And I just can't forget
> Old F. B. Eye ain't ended yet.

Another of these, "The Dreaming Kind," a sentimental and unexceptional song, was to be set to music by Mrs. Charles, Gloria Madison's aunt, and sung by Bessie in Ernie's night club.

It was a splendid moonlit night on March 11, 1950, when the manhunt was filmed on the roofs of Chicago. The set was a sinister-looking warehouse illuminated by a flashing neon-lighted sign advertising "Williams Funeral Garden—24 Hour Service," with a gigantic hourglass rising above it. Hundreds of people were milling around amid the water spouting from the firemen's hoses while Bigger fled, bounding from one roof to another to the accompaniment of wailing sirens and backfiring police cars. Wright had to redo

As Bigger

Kissing Mary. *Photo by Segovia*

the scene twelve times before Chenal allowed him, enveloped in a superb white poncho, to meet the curious and enthusiastic public who stayed to watch the showing of a few scenes from the beginning of the film.[7] On another occasion American ambassador Stanton Griffiths, a great lover of films, visited the studio.

Life in Argentina sometimes lacked comfort and courtesy, which was why Wright changed hotels three times before settling in March at the Windsor on Carlos Pellegrini Street. He was very careful of what he said to the press, sticking to his thoughts on literature and steering away from the dangerous topic of General Peron's dictatorship. He did say at the time that Argentina was a proud, independent and noble country, to judge by its people, but after he had left Buenos Aires he came out against the police methods and the abuses of the regime: "I'd had to consort with the decadent nobility who sat huddled and afraid in their huge houses, cursing, swearing that the peons could not operate telephones, could not run railroads. . . !"[8] Conversations with some of the Argentinian studio technicians who had become his good friends showed how fear of the government weighed upon the people. Even Wright himself was not immune since, on Mentasti's advice, he had refrained from applying for a work permit so that he could avoid paying taxes. In addition to this irregular situation he was, like most foreign visitors, subjected to very obvious police surveillance of both his correspondence and his telephone conversations.

It was only during the filming, however, that he realized the dishonesty of his associates. Prades had misled Mentasti about the money and time needed for the filming, and in his Spanish translation of the contract he had changed certain of its original terms. Furthermore, when Wright went to refer to his copy of it, he discovered that it had been stolen from his hotel room. Wright accordingly approached Mentasti directly, and they drew up a confidential agreement giving Wright a fifth of the profits, excluding Prades and Chenal from the association and assuring Wright his twenty per cent. The financial and legal situation was so complicated that, on Reynolds' advice, Wright hired a German lawyer, Erwin Wallfisch, a former filmmaker, to defend his interests for a 5 per cent commission.

By spring the situation soon resembled a spy story and serious money problems had to be solved. On May 27, 1950, Wright, mystery lover that he was, actually went to Montevideo so that he

Carrying the body. *Photo by Segovia*

Quarreling with Bessie. *Photo by Segovia*

Scene from the
dream sequence.
Photo by Segovia

In front of a poster for
the film, Buenos Aires

could safely send Reynolds a secret code in which they would now write their letters. Number of copies sold would mean dollars and each of the parties involved was assigned a new name. Wright became "Adolph"; Reynolds, "Alexander"; Chenal, "Benjamin"; Wallfisch, "Charles." Somewhat after Wright's March 8 agreement with Mentasti, Wright had received an advance of 37,500 pesos (close to $2,500) owed him by Sono-Films for the distribution rights.[9] Since the law entitled the Argentinian government to claim a large percentage of any sum mentioned in a notarized document, they could not mention the cost of these rights in the contract that was drawn up in Buenos Aires. The money then had to be transferred secretly, because it was illegal to send money out of the country.

These precautions were useless, however, since Wallfisch's business sense left a great deal to be desired, though his integrity was unquestioned. He enjoyed the drama of his new role but did Wright little service; he had little success selling the film abroad and even less getting Mentasti to respect the terms of the contract. On his return to France, Wright had to retain another lawyer, to the mortification of Wallfisch, who deluged Wright with irate letters.

At the end of June, 1950, the film was finished and Nicholas Joy and Gloria Madison flew back to the United States, but numerous technical details and part of the editing had still to be completed. The music, which the Katherine Dunham Quintet had prepared with John Elert, was not perfect, but according to the local papers the film, which lasted more than an hour and forty-five minutes, was a credit to its producers, the most carefully executed job to have come out in Argentina for ten years. The only problem was that it had cost three times Chenal's estimated $100,000.

Nevertheless, *Native Son* was completed in October, 1950, and had its world premiere on November 4 aboard a Pan American strato-clipper, a daring publicity stunt of Mentasti's devising. Since Wallfisch's negotiations with Paramount Pictures had come to nothing, Mentasti had advised that the distribution of the film in English-speaking countries be entrusted to the Walter Gould Agency in New York. The complete version of *Sangre Negra,* which opened at the Rex Theatre in Buenos Aires on March 30, was such a triumph, confirmed by box-office receipts from the rest of the country, that Wright began to have real reason to hope for its success in America but the *Canard Enchaîné* of May 16, 1951, pointing out that Argentina was making a hit out of *Native Son*

while America was executing Willie McGee, came closer to pro-
phesying the truth.

Indeed, the New York State Board of Censors demanded extensive
cutting. Gould obeyed, amputating about 2,500 feet of film, or about
half an hour, as Wright himself realized to his horror when he
finally saw this version in July at a private showing at the Filmax,
in Paris. Owing to difficulties with the censors, the United States
premiere at the Criterion had been postponed from April 15 to
June 16. The New York film critics were far from enthusiastic. Even
the best reviews expressed disappointment with the amateur acting as well as with the cuts, to which Wright attributed the failure
almost entirely. He wrote to Reynolds on August 6, 1951:

People everywhere know that the film was cut, that the killing of
the rat was cut, that making of the homegun was cut, that the real
heart of the boys' attempt at robbery was cut, that most of the
dialogue between the newspaper men was cut. . . .

But the cut that did the greatest damage was the cutting of the
trial. As you know, the trial is shown with arms waving and
mouths moving but nothing is heard.

Wright felt that Gould had made a grave error in not defending
the original version more vehemently. He went on to say that perhaps since Gould was a naturalized citizen, he was afraid of being
labeled "un-American" in that era of nascent McCarthyism if he did
not cut the film.

Gould apparently did his best to distribute it, however. When
RKO expressed some interest, he had it shown in Trenton, New
Jersey, with great commercial success, but they insisted on some
further trial runs before closing the deal, and in the Warner Theatre
of Patterson, the receipts were only average. The local censors of
Pennsylvania, Wisconsin and Ohio still refused to allow the film to
be shown, and in Chicago, when the film finally opened, the situation was complicated by the recent racial incidents in Cicero and
the hostility of the *Chicago Defender* and a part of the black public.
On August 11, 1951, *Native Son* reached Los Angeles, but Gould
did not think that their problems would be over before the Venice
Film Festival.

The situation was somewhat reversed in Europe. Wright had been
so horror-struck at the mutilated version that he refused to give it
his approval for fear of compromising his reputation as a militant

intellectual. Past differences with Pierre Chenal faded somewhat as he now became a valuable ally; with the support of the cinema unions and the French left-wing press he was ready to boycott the cut version. But Wright felt that any Communist intervention would be unfortunate in the present tense atmosphere. There was no solution. If the complete version were shown, the American circles would certainly attack it, and Wright did not want to owe too much to Communist support, while the French Left would interpret distribution of the cut version as a concession to the Marshall Plan and would reject Wright. Accordingly, Wright dissuaded Chenal from intervening on his behalf and Gould from presenting the film in France. In any case, he had no further hope of recouping his losses, as he confided to Reynolds on August 6:

I shall not concern myself at all with what happens to the film over here. Frankly I don't think I shall see any money from it and the reviews make it plain that my reputation is not being done any good by the film being shown. . . . Chenal is really in the right and Gould is wrong. . . . Gould told me that they were planning to enter the film in some kind of festival in Venice; I've heard nothing about this; it was supposed to take place in July; I hope that they did not enter it; and if they plan to, I hope they don't. People over here are more intelligent than Gould thinks and they will not be fooled into believing that the Negro problem in the USA is what the cut version of the film tries to pretend it is.

On July 19, 1951, Wright had left with his family to spend the vacation in the Haute Savoie at Allinges near Thonon-les-Bains. Ellen had rented a manor-house, La Grange Allard, where their friends Hélène and Michel Bokanowski visited them several times. Gunnar Myrdal, who was working for the United Nations, invited Wright to spend a few days with him in Geneva, and this proved to be the beginning of a fast friendship.

Meanwhile Gould had obtained an official invitation to show *Native Son* at the Venice Film Festival through his European representative Carlo Bellotti, the director of a film company in Rome. Somewhat grudgingly, therefore, Wright went to the Cinema Palace and waited, expecting the worst. The day before the showing, he and Pierre Chenal gave a press conference to explain the origins and difficulties of the film. It was shown on August 22, 1951, and Wright was relieved to discover that some of the sound track for Max's speech had been restored and the cuts reduced to a minimum. The reviews were favorable in Italy, where his renown as a writer and intellectual bolstered his reputation as an actor. The Milan papers, *Epoca* and *Il Tempo*, even stated that Wright deserved to be thought of as a proven film star. After a short visit to Rome, Wright left for Lausanne, somewhat reassured.

In the United States, the film continued its career. In December, 1951, Jean Wallace, Charles Kane, Willa Pearl Curtiss and Jaime Prades presented it to Hollywood at the Canon Theatre in Beverly Hills. It was still definitely prohibited in several states, but Wright's family was able to see it the following spring in Mississippi.[10] The film was shown throughout Italy and Wright himself attended it in London on February 16, 1952, when it was also running in Bristol and Manchester, but it never came to France, despite the enthusiasm of the French press at the Venice Film Festival.[11]

Exclusive of the damage due to cuts and some unfavorable reactions prompted by the current political and racial situation in the United States, the critics (whose opinion will have to be respected in lieu of a firsthand judgment) were unanimous on one score: the lesser roles were played by obvious amateurs and the film suffered accordingly. Almost everyone agreed that Wright's performance was at least sincere, although he was awkward and hesitant at some times and at others, frankly poor; in any case, they regretted the absence of an actor like Canada Lee. Jean Wallace did an excellent job, but it was felt that the white characters on the whole were too lifeless and unconvincing. In addition, some divergences from the book, which the American public knew almost by heart, as if it were a classic, were criticized. Now that Jan Erlone was reduced to a simple labor organizer, he was no longer very convincing; the person who narrated Bigger's past for the benefit of the audience at the beginning of the film, lacked presence, and the summary did not clarify his motives for murder; the climactic point of Max's defense had been cut and his relationship with Bigger so reduced that the protagonist's final comprehension of his situation had little to support it. The interesting innovation of the dream sequences, which paralleled Wright's experiments in literary technique, did not attract comment.[12] The impression from the score of articles in the New York papers is that the critics, who had been well-disposed toward Wright's enterprise but very demanding after the triumph of Canada Lee in the stage version, were now disappointed. This was a severe but not unfair reaction, considering that the cuts had deprived the film of part of its message. They were expecting a passionate appeal and received a somewhat feeble replay, which, in comparison with the novel and the play, seemed boring and badly acted. Masquerading under the label of liberalism, the reactionary press enjoyed pointing out the very gaps and imperfections that were due in large part to the reactionary censorship. The European critics were more tolerant, both because they were less cognizant of the racial situation and because they had not been exposed to the play. Even though it was the cuts that had dealt the final blow to the film, and although its failure was only relative, without ever publicly blaming Gould or anyone else Wright considered it a total disaster. He had been reluctant to go to Venice and initially refused to go to London. He certainly disliked discussing the film with journalists and quickly lost interest in the project after investing a year's work in it. Not only had he lost valuable time that he might have spent advancing his literary career, but he had also lost financially, since he never received a dollar from the receipts and what he did earn was not even enough to cover the cost of buying back the rights in the first place. The final irony was that after Sono-Films went bankrupt, he was never able to obtain a copy even of the cut version of the film, from Classic Pictures.

Wright's stay in Argentina did give him the opportunity to make a trip to Haiti, a country that he had been wanting to visit for over a year. In 1949, he had told his friend William Rutherford, a UNESCO official in Paris, that he was anxious to do a report on the island, on the assumption that the UNESCO pledge to gather and disseminate information on the colored peoples of the world was sincere. The United Nations had already established a pilot project and Wright thought his services might be useful, but his offer had been refused because of his political past and his relative ignorance of the language. By July, 1950, the film had been almost completed and Wright set off for Haiti to collect some notes and impressions that he would publish as a travel journal. He had explained his intentions in January to Mr. Léger, the Haitian ambassador in Buenos Aires:

I would try to react to the life of the Haitian people as an individual, to record in words my impressions and responses to the tissue and texture of Haitian experience and living. I would expose my sensibilities to the mores, traditions, music, institutions, and landscapes of Haiti.

Léger had promised his support and Wright boarded the *Argentina* on July 7.[13] The trip was broken by many stops. He visited Rio with Stanley Marshall of the *Chicago Defender* and the Brazilian aviatrix Bobbe Morris. He went with his friend Eric Williams, the vice-president of the research committee for the Caribbean Commission, to the Port of Spain City Club to hear his first tin-can band.[14] He was in Curaçao on July 21 and finally reached Haiti in time to dine with Dr. Giles Hubert, agricultural consultant at the American Embassy, in his Pétionville house on July 28. Thanks to the several Haitian writers he met that evening, he was able to see more than he would have as a simple tourist, and he learned about the native customs, history and current problems of the island as a professional journalist.

He also made notes for representative biographical sketches of individuals like Paul Duncan, a member of the ancient and exclusive local aristocracy; the painter Max Pichinot; the young student Lazare Cornet; the doctor Yvonne Sylvain; the actor Daniel Figrolé; and the Minister of Justice and Labor, Emile Saint Jot. Other notes show that he was planning to analyze the historical and economic development of the country, the endemic poverty of its enormous peasant population and the disorientation of the young, which intrigued him more than the tin-can bands and the voodoo cult. Wright must have become dissatisfied with the material or been dissuaded from continuing with it, since he never told Reynolds of his project and once back in Paris, started to work instead on a film about the great Haitian hero and martyr Toussaint L'Ouverture, whom C. L. R. James had celebrated in *The Black Jacobins.*

This second project also derived from Wright's general ambition to rehabilitate the black peoples in the estimation of Western opinion. With the help of Mark Sharron, a press agent, Wright explained his project to Streten Maric, a cultural adviser to the Yugoslav embassy in Paris. After the outside scenes had been shot in Haiti, the film would be made in Yugoslavia with the help of Yugoslav technicians; Wright would create the dialogue, find an actor who could play Toussaint, and be responsible for the general ideological perspective.[15] The reply was not encouraging, so Wright sent Alexander Korda, the director of London Films, a more detailed plan on November 17, 1950. He could count on local support in Haiti, he wrote, because of his recent trip; one of the country's historians, General Demours, would oversee the accuracy of the material; the government could assure the cooperation of the Army and help with the necessary transportation. If they did the studio filming in Kingston, Jamaica, expenses could be kept down despite the number of sets and extras required. Wright would work on a percentage basis since he had enough confidence in the project to take the same risks as he had with *Native Son*. While waiting for Korda's agreement, he would prepare a synopsis and could soon be ready to write the dialogue.

The deal never went through, but Wright's passion for film-making continued unabated. On December 5, 1951, he submitted a screenplay to the French Association of Film Writers. "Freedom Train," or "The World Between," was the story of an engineer who detours his train to reach the American free zone in Germany. The American authorities hold the two dozen passengers in the small station for three days so that they can make the choice between East and West. One young Czech student wants to rejoin her fiancé; another woman leaves her lover to return to her husband and children; a black American, who had been thrilled to see his compatriots again ends up hanging himself after some racists humiliate him. Among the other passengers, a dedicated Communist takes the opportunity to become a spy but is denounced by a former comrade who, in turn, is sent back behind the Iron Curtain because the Americans do not have faith in his defection; a banker and a manufacturer both choose the West as the best place to make their fortunes, while the engineer himself manages to find a job as sales manager of a factory manufacturing toy trains in the United States. A doctor decides to go home for no special reason, and a peasant makes the same decision out of a pure love of the land. A widow who is incapable of choosing is sent to a psychiatrist, but a fireman who has the same difficulty breaks a window in order to have time to think about it in prison. A priest is the only person who wants to try living in the West before making his choice. The American officials debate whether or not to give him this privilege, but the observer sent by the Czech government refuses. Eventually the priest finds himself rejected by both sides, to live in "the world between."

The allegory was clear. The situation allowed Wright to criticize East and West alike. Given the terms of his choice, is the "world citizen" in fact capable of choosing? Or should he refuse to do so? From now on, Wright continued to ask this question in a variety of different ways.

2

Wright had flown from Haiti to New York, where he stayed just long enough to take care of his business with Paul Reynolds and to see the Jameses and the Werthams again. He visited the Lafargue Clinic with Frederic Wertham to reacquaint himself with the progress made against delinquency in Harlem, but he was in a hurry to return to Paris, not only to see his family, but to relax after his sojourn in Argentina. During an interview on August 18, the day before he sailed on the *De Grasse*, he was reserved in saying, "I may complain about America but still I am a citizen of the United States. The only thing that Paris has that the United States does not seem to have is humanity"; [16] but considering Wright's statements at the various RDR meetings, there is no doubt that this "humanity" was crucial. Wright primarily considered himself a citizen of the world, but Paris was his refuge from the growing hysteria of anticommunism in America and practically a second home.

Wright was therefore happy to get back to his Parisian life after a vacation in the Alps during September, when he visited Basel, Zurich and the Aoste valley, where he was a jury member for the third International San Vicente Prize Competition, along with Guiseppe Ungaretti, Paul Eluard, Louis Bromfield and several others. Europe seemed to demand that Wright participate in its cultural life. Thus, accepting an invitation from the Italian Cultural Society to speak on Afro-American literature, he gave his lecture on January 19, 1951, at the Teatro Carignano of Turin. He repeated it the next day in Genoa and again in Rome on January 23 at the Teatro Eliseo. Since he spoke in English, a résumé of the speech and the poems he cited was handed out in advance. Introduced by Antonio Baldini as "a humanist writer and social critic," Wright spoke at length about Langston Hughes and Marian Anderson, analyzed some blues, criticized the paternalism of both "Bozambo" and "Hallellujah," compared *Anna Lucasta* by Abram Hill and Harry Gribble to *'Tis a Pity*

She's a Whore—written by John Ford in 1627—traced the literature of the South from Faulkner to Flannery O'Connor, and quoted from Ellen Harper and the early Afro-American poets. He even touched upon the international political situation and, in fact, went way beyond the subject of the lecture as it later appeared in *White Man, Listen!* [17]

In Paris, of course, Wright continued to be invited to literary and cultural events. On March 6, 1951, in fact, he participated at an evening given by the Club des Lettres du Monde along with Joseph Zobel from Martinique, who had just won the prize of the Gazette des Lettres for his autobiography, *Rue Case Nègres*.[18]

In June, Wright and Jean Cocteau inaugurated the Cercle International du Théâtre et du Cinéma, organized by French radio-television, and, with Sartre, William Saroyan, Norman Mailer and Tennessee Williams, he was on the list of patrons for *New Story Magazine,* which Jean-François Bergery and David Burnett were starting in order to discover new talents and reach a young audience. James Baldwin soon had work published in this magazine, and on Wright's advice they accepted selections from *Our Lady of the Flowers* by Jean Genet.[19]

While Wright was conscientiously performing these routine functions, he was also involved in the founding of the French-American Fellowship, a new organization that used up the time and energy formerly devoted to the defunct Rassemblement Démocratique Révolutionnaire.

Possibly Wright's visit to the United States, where he learned how little the racial situation had changed in Chicago, combined with the perspective he had acquired on the French political scene, created a new set of pressures within him. He told his friend Dorothy Norman, who visited him in Paris in the autumn of 1950, that he was disappointed in having been used by the RDR and displeased with the existentialist group for not defending humanism vigorously enough against the inroads of industrial civilization.

If America lacked culture and humanity, and European traditions were weak and narrow, perhaps the talents and position of the black American who was fighting for his freedom could at the same time bring new blood to Europe and life to dying America. In an interview on William Faulkner, who had just won the Nobel Prize, Wright insisted that "the moral confusion and social decadence of the West" be clearly defined, particularly for the United States, which sought to monopolize the image of democracy and was doing such a poor job of achieving it.[20]

Wright proposed to work toward improving relations between Americans of both races and those French people who were interested in the United States, limiting his action, at the start, to the Parisian scene with which he was familiar. Wright himself had not been welcomed very cordially by most members of the American colony in Paris, probably because many of them were working for branches of private American companies and so constituted a population that was not free of racism and snobbism. If he had wanted to move in these circles (which he emphatically did not) he would have been ostracized, both because of his race and his interracial marriage. Even though the American Embassy observed the government's official policy of equality and even though Wright had some true friends among the colony, as a group they were somewhat suspicious of him even when he was not under surveillance because of his political opinions.[21]

During his first trip to Paris, Wright had certainly embarrassed embassy officials with his frankness about the American racial situation. In "I Choose Exile," Wright described his initially warm reception from the American Embassy and the motives behind it.

This sudden rainfall of official affability was clarified a few days later; at a cocktail party a strange white American took me discreetly aside and whispered in my ear: "Listen, for God's sake, don't let these foreigners make you into a brick to hurl at our windows." I realized that a bare recital, when uttered in an alien atmosphere, of the facts of Negro life in America constituted a kind of anti-American propaganda.

Wright certainly did not heed this advice and even the Communist reporters were satisfied. The headline "I feel more at home in France than over there where I was born," was not enough, and during September, 1947, Wright reported in his journal that when Miss Helen Hokinson came to interview him, he said what he thought:

. . . that the U.S. was in a period of utter confusion; that with the death of Roosevelt there was no longer any sense of direction; that emotional starvation was the keynote of the American masses; that this starvation made it possible for the masses to project their pains outward upon minorities; that the act of being an American was a fantastically self-conscious thing; that many immigrants of Europe changed even their names in order to be as American as possible and reap the benefits of American life; that in the end America was a kind of religion, but for the white protestant stock only.

His opinions did not fail to be heard in the United States.

Considering that he was a former Communist who now condemned the materialism of his country (and with it the Marshall Plan), it is not surprising that his most innocent activities, even though he was equally critical of the Soviet Union, should have been suspect during these years of cold war and McCarthyism.

In addition, Wright's self-imposed exile in Paris, followed by that of James Baldwin in 1948, Chester Himes in 1953 and other Afro-American writers and artists, undermined the assurances of American propaganda that the black problem was being solved. Wright naturally had as little contact as possible with the Establishment in Paris, although he certainly had friends within it, such as the pastor of the American Church in Paris, Reverend Clayton Williams, in particular, as well as some of the professors at the American School, which Julia attended before entering the Ecole Alsacienne. He gravitated more toward writers and artists, often black, and often antiestablishment, as well as the foreign correspondents of the progressive American newspapers.[22]

Encouraged by his contacts with intellectual, artistic and even political figures in France, Wright now undertook to extend his political activities of the late forties into a sort of unofficial protest movement against the cold war. Accordingly, he and his friend William Rutherford, who was still a UNESCO official, worked on a plan to regroup black Americans and their white friends of both nationalities. On October 5, 1950, around thirty of these people agreed to meet every two weeks until they had drawn up the statutes and defined the goals of the association, and on December 10, the French-American Fellowship was officially inaugurated with a reception at the International Center on Avenue Gabriel. Jean-Paul Sartre and Louis Fischer, the guests of honor, spoke on the problems of information and freedom in the modern world.

The goals of the organization were twofold. First, by presenting a more accurate picture of America than embassy propaganda could supply, these honest and good-willed Americans hoped to establish a more workable relationship between France and their own country. And second, the French-American Fellowship would fight the rampant job discrimination and racism in certain American businesses abroad. James Baldwin was put in charge of finding out from the U.S. embassy the working conditions for black Americans in Paris.

Wright had written most of the prospectus for the Fellowship, emphasizing how eager the American members were, as representatives of their country, to explain American thinking to the French— their artists and intellectuals in particular—since political confusion and distorted news sowed mutual mistrust and made relationships uneasy.

In a more general context, the statutes themselves are clear on this point.

This group exists to serve the mutual and personal needs of its members; to promote social and cultural relations; and to heighten the consciousness of its members in relation to the urgent issues confronting the world today. It proposes to attain these ends by dedicating its energies to an elucidation of the problem of human freedom amidst modern industrialization; to combat the deepening and extension of racist ideas and practices from whatever quarter they spring; to urge the spread of the principles of fundamental education among the non-industrial peoples of the world; to lend encouragement and support to all minorities and exploited groups in their aspirations and struggles for freedom; to promote interest in the relation of modern art, literary, plastic, and musical, to the consciousness of contemporary man; to an exposure of all those mental habits which tend to solidify racial, class, social, religious, and national divisions between men; to support those impulses which seek to express a creative concept of human freedom; to reaffirm the common identity and destiny of humankind, and the internationalism of the human spirit.[23]

When he aims "to heighten the consciousness" of the members, Wright is, in fact, joining the tradition of those American liberals of "Art as Vision" and *Twice a Year,* and the followers of Randolph Bourne and Alfred Stieglitz, who sought to use the arts in defense of civil liberties. In addition, Wright's humanist concerns, which he had already expressed at the RDR Congress and connected with internationalism by supporting Gary Davis, are formulated here in their entirety.

Cultural activities of the Fellowship included a visit to the studio of the painter Jean Hélion and lectures by Charles Delaunay on jazz, Claude Bourdet on Franco-American politics and M. Dessinge on the war in Indochina. At the beginning of 1951, there were more than sixty members, and they formed a committee to find jobs and fight against discrimination, which was particularly obvious at the American Hospital. In February, Margaret McCleveland had, without specifying her race, applied for a job as a nurse and been hired in writing, but when she arrived in person, the engagement was not honored. Wright, Rutherford and other members of the Fellowship investigated the case, only to have the hospital administration invoke a law requiring that a certain quota of French employees be hired; they promised to hire black personnel in the future, but nothing was done. On June 6, the Fellowship held a press conference following Wright's article on "American Negroes in France" in *L'Observateur*, a progressive weekly paper. Racism had grown in France as the result of increasing American influence caused by the Marshall Plan. Clashes between G.I.'s of both races became frequent, tourists loaded with dollars were encouraging hotels not to accept Blacks and the discrimination in American companies abroad continued.

American attitudes and behavior in France . . . have caused many Frenchmen to turn to American Negroes to demand explanations for such rigorous nationalistic manifestations on the part of their white fellow-countrymen.

American Negroes, in defense of their liberty and as a gesture of friendship and solidarity towards their French neighbors, organized themselves into a group. As much to aid Frenchman as themselves, they launched the French-American Fellowship whose aim is to raise again the concept of freedom, generosity, the dignity and sanctity of the individual.[24]

The French-American Fellowship also supported the Marxist historian Daniel Guérin, who had just been refused an American visa on account of his book *Où va le peuple américain?*, for which Wright had made certain corrections and suggestions. On April 26, 1951, as the guest of honor at a lunch given by *L'Observateur*, Wright had himself spoken about literature and the racial problems in the United States, mentioning the case of Guérin, and the Fellowship contributed to the distribution of his book as part of a general protest campaign. An open letter signed by more than thirty intellectuals, among them Wright, was published in *Combat,* but Guérin was never granted a visa.[25]

In February, Wright and the French-American Fellowship helped organize protest meetings and collect signatures petitioning the Supreme Court to intervene on behalf of the Martinsville Seven, who had been condemned to death for rape in Virginia. Again in May, the Fellowship became involved in the case of Willie McGee, who had been accused of raping a Mrs. Hawkins of Laurel, Mississippi, in 1945. The prisoner had appealed in vain after being twice condemned to death, and was to be executed on July 27, 1950. The Civil Rights Congress, which was considered a Communist front organization, had launched a somewhat controversial protest campaign, and they had obtained a postponement with the possibility of a new trial. Meanwhile, Carl Rowan, a black journalist, had investigated the case and discovered that McGee had been Mrs. Hawkins' lover for years, making his death sentence tantamount to a legal lynching. Communist propaganda triumphed while America's image was damaged in world opinion. President Truman did grant a postponement until May 8, 1951, after receiving more than 50,000 signatures from all countries, but the governor of the state refused a pardon because the Communists had petitioned for it. On May 15, 1951, *Le Droit de Vivre* published a moving article by Wright entitled "Behind the McGee Case," in which he explained the state of mind and the racist customs of the Old South that made this "legal lynching" as inevitable as it was immoral, although he pointed out that

the fight to save McGee resulted in a moral victory. The men who killed him were condemned at the court of world opinion and the damage done to the international image of the U.S. by this case has been so great that several high American officials have been forced to ponder the folly of racial prejudice.

The day after McGee's execution, the French-American Fellowship joined the International League against Racism and Anti-Semitism in collecting money for his family.

In March, 1951, the Fellowship sent a message of support to the Peoples' Congress against Imperialism in Rome, and in November, Claude Bourdet, Jean Cocteau, Wright, Sartre and Katherine Dunham joined Josephine Baker when she publicly called for liberty and justice regarding the trial of Grand Bassam in Africa.[26]

The cultural events provided by the Fellowship were as valuable as its political activities. Wright himself inaugurated an exhibition of the American painters McWilliams, Parker, Richardson, Dee and Wamble on July 13, 1951, and before the year was out, Fellowship members had been able to hear Roger Baldwin, Jean Cocteau, René Piquion, Louis Dalmas and Elmer Carter of the New York Commission for Equal Employment Practices. By the time the Prefect of Police granted the French-American Fellowship legal status as a "non-commercial, non-political, cultural group," Wright considered his task finished and resigned as president in order that others should define the future orientation of the organization. Unfortunately, the rent for the small office at 100 rue Réaumur and some secretarial work had used up all the money collected as dues, while a gala evening given on July 7, which most of the black artists in Paris attended, had lost money. Perhaps it was these financial difficulties, or the absence of Wright's dynamic leadership, that caused the Fellowship to cease all activity by the end of 1951.

Even so, its efforts had not been wasted. It had not only combatted the racism of certain Americans in Paris, but it had also had an effect in the United States, since *Crisis* had published in the spring of 1951 Wright's article for *L'Observateur*. Above all, the group had succeeded in strengthening the climate of sympathy among certain intellectuals and artists in Paris, particularly among the Afro-Americans and some of their white countrymen. Besides Wright there had been, among others, Leroy Haines, who soon abandoned his career as a teacher to become a restaurant owner famed for his soul cooking; Samuel Allen, a G.I. who had stayed on to continue his studies at the Sorbonne and begin his remarkable career as a poet; Ligon Buford, former Director of the World Refugee Office; Jean Maho; Edward Myers; Leopold Bonds; and the progressive journalists William Rutherford and Ollie Stewart— in all perhaps twenty dedicated members. Wright's ties with former RDR members such as Claude Bourdet, as well as with the existentialists, gave the Fellowship a wide scope in which Wright could accomplish his goal of fighting with words to humanize the world, concentrating, to begin with, on the problems confronting his black compatriots.

It might seem strange that James Baldwin, who was also an active member of the Fellowship, described Wright's endeavors with as much scorn as injustice, were it not for the fact that their personal relationship had complicated their professional dealings.[27] Baldwin had followed in Wright's footsteps, arriving in Paris in November, 1948, and at that time was open in his admiration for Wright, who had helped him get settled in a cheap hotel. But by 1950, when "Everybody's Protest Novel" was published, marking the beginning of Baldwin's career, things had changed. Wright was not a little surprised that Baldwin not only vehemently attacked the committed black novel in general, but used *Native Son* as his main target, claiming that it was merely *Uncle Tom's Cabin* in reverse. Ironically, it was Wright who had asked Themistocles Heotis to publish this controversial article in *Zero*, the little magazine that he was helping him launch.

Baldwin was then in the clutches of personal problems caused by his search for an identity and his complicated relationship with his adopted father, and he was probably hoping that Wright would be a kind of spiritual father to him. Since Baldwin had started to write under his influence, he perhaps feared that the white American critics would automatically classify him as "second generation," that he would not succeed in expressing his own originality if he were overpowered by Wright. He had, therefore, leaned over backwards to assert their differences. Wright was so irritated at being singled out by this beginner whom he had recommended for a scholarship that he did not hesitate to tell him, the day after the article was published, that he would have no more to do with him. Baldwin, however, was still fascinated by his mentor; and needed Wright's recognition of his talent in order to believe in himself. His first unfortunate attack gave rise to a need for reconciliation, and since there was no hope of that, he naturally turned hostile in his disappointment. "Everybody's Protest Novel" may have been less a deliberate attack on Wright than Baldwin's attempt to free himself from his influence, but he let the essay be published (along with Richard Gibson's attack entitled "Many Thousands Gone") in the *Partisan Review* and later in a magazine financed by the American Cultural Service called *Profils*. Since at that time the United States Government was resolutely hostile toward the leading black novelist living in exile, Baldwin was letting himself be used in an attempt to destroy Wright's reputation.

Chester Himes once witnessed a dispute between the two men. Baldwin had telephoned Wright to meet him at Saint-Germain-des-Prés because he needed to borrow some money. Himes accompanied Wright to the café, where Baldwin started to justify his past behavior, but Wright would not stand for representing the "father" whom Baldwin had to kill so that the "son" could survive. The presence of a white girl whom Baldwin had brought only aggravated the situation.

Wright did not, on this account, fail to recognize and publicly proclaim the value of *Go Tell It on the Mountain*, but he always avoided its author, who, in turn, was not satisfied until he finally took Wright's place in the eyes of the American critics, after Wright's death. The articles he wrote at that time were still further attempts to free himself from the obsessive memory of what could have been friendship between the two men.[28]

Although personal problems partially explain Baldwin's hostility, political or tactical motives are the only way to account for the attitude of other black Americans. In September, 1950, during Wright's stay in Chicago for the filming of *Native Son*, John Johnson, editor of a large black publishing company, had asked Wright for some articles on the contemporary scene for *Ebony* magazine, of which he was the publisher. The Wirths, Horace Cayton, Sidney Williams and others had provided him with enough material on recent changes in ghetto life to enable him to write "The Shame of Chicago," but Wright did not think that there had been significant progress since his departure. He was certainly not in the least sentimental about his return to the United States, except for a few moments of real happiness when listening to the blues on the South Side.

Ebony waited until December 7, 1951, over a year later, to publish this article, and only then with an editorial rebuttal by John Johnson and Ben Burns contesting some of Wright's most pessimistic statements. The second article was "I Choose Exile." After two years *Ebony* had still not published it, and Wright, who understood why the magazine might not want to use such a violent critique itself, was hoping to submit it to the *Atlantic Monthly*, which had in the meantime asked him for an essay on the racial situation. He therefore addressed a long letter to John Johnson and

Ben Burns on January 23, 1952, tactfully expressing his position:

Frankly I have come to feel, because of your silence and the non-
publication of the article, that the sentiments I expressed in that
article were a little too strong for your magazine. I don't quarrel
with you about this; you are on the home scene and you know
better than I do what kind of an impression you want *Ebony* to
make. . . . As you well know, my primary aim is to fight the
battle of the Negro in the nation's thought, and I do want to try to
deal blows where I think they will do the most good. It is therefore
advisable, on some occasions, to let white periodicals carry the
moral burden of printing articles that might harm Negro publications in the eyes of the Government.

Ebony, however, refused to return the article, although Wright
naturally offered to repay the fee and to continue to work with the
magazine. At the same time, the *Atlantic Monthly* let him know
that they did not want an article of that kind either. Wright was
less surprised than bitter to see that fear had so increased in the
United States that praising the culture of another country was
forbidden, even if it were an official ally. The anti-Communist
spirit was such that he predicted, even on the part of the liberals,
fierce attacks against what he was trying to accomplish in his new
novel. Alarmed by his pessimism, Reynolds advised Wright to
refrain from mentioning France in a coming interview for *The New
York Times*, thus avoiding any comparison of the two countries.
Nevertheless, Wright's statements to *Time* magazine reporter Curtius
Prendergast in early March, 1953, could be considered critical of
American policy on racial problems. Without denying that there
had been some slight progress in black-white relations, Wright
said that segregation in housing alone could nullify all the gains
made in employment and education. Racial prejudice existed in
Europe, but it had never become an institution there and France
remained a free country. In the United States, the burden rested
with the Whites. As for the Blacks, they had too often adopted the
least worthy elements of industrial civilization, while the Negro
press lacked courage, broadmindedness and a sense of its responsibilities.

It is not raising the issues that should be raised, the problem of
freedom in the Western world, the problem of Africa and Asia. If

the city the Negro is raised in is isolationist, he is too. Negroes constitute no menace. They are disgustingly loyal, even in the worst sense.[29]

Wright also regretted the lack of honest representatives in the government services abroad. Bad propaganda was more harmful to American prestige than the undisguised truth, he warned, since Soviet skill in this area might well win them the Third World. While Wright was aware that he could be going against the current of American opinion with his difficult new novel, *The Outsider,* the fact that he was not trying to conciliate anyone at all was harmful to him in the long run. Although his criticisms of government policy and the black press were as justified as they were courageous, America was going to resent his overstepping the limits, not only of Negro provincialism but of another form of provincialism: American nationalism.

3

When Wright had written to Reynolds on November 8, 1948, that he wanted to completely rework his novel, he was far from having conceived the story that eventually became *The Outsider.* His trips to Argentina and the United States, his renewed political activity and his new concerns as an existentialist writer, all contributed to his evaluation of modern man, which explains why it took so long for him to bring it alive in fiction. The wounds caused by his break with the Communists had been too recent for him to have assimilated that experience, while he also had to establish some independence from the existentialists in order to treat an existentialist situation. This independence he achieved by turning his attention away from Europe toward the Third World. By the beginning of 1952, he finally felt ready to return to fiction. He left for London on February 16 and, in the solitude of his room on Glenluce Road (and later in Catford, Surrey), it took him only three months—after a period of almost six years—to complete the

new version of his novel, close to 650 pages. This time the subject
was clear.

The break from the U.S. was more than a geographical change.
It was a break with my former attitudes as a Negro and a Communist—an attempt to think over and re-define my attitudes and
my thinking. I was trying to grapple with the big problem—the
problem and meaning of Western civilization as a whole and the
relation of Negroes and other minority groups to it.

Out of this searching grew the idea of *The Outsider*. It's the way
novels are born for me. It can't be said that I write books, books
happen with me. I become deeply involved with certain problems.
The way I attack them and think through is by writing books.[30]

Wright's ideological plan, which his experiences during the forties
had inspired, led him to choose a black intellectual evolving in the
same environment as his own: the South Side, Harlem and Greenwich Village. He wrote Reynolds on May 1 that he himself considered it a

character study, dealing mainly with character and destiny. There
are four murders, a suicide, an ambush murder, which ought to be
enough blood. There is a kind of love story in it, but a rather dark
and tortured one. I tell the story of this young Negro, who is 26
years of age, in a rather close-up fashion; he is in the center of the
action all the time.

As in *Native Son*, Wright used melodrama, but this time, though
the hero is black, the story is not primarily racial, and though he
is a Communist, it is not primarily political. Through his protagonist, he sought to unify and bring to life a wide range of
philosophical problems that would depend more on metaphysics
than drama or politics. He first thought of using as a title the
symbolic name of his hero—Cross Damon, a mixture of the Christian ethic of suffering and of the demonism of Nietzsche. Then, in
June, 1952, attracted by a line from *Richard III*, he called it "I Did
But Dream."

In the May 1 letter, Wright had confided his fears about the
book, which were not much different from those he had for *Black
Boy*.

I don't know if the novel is any good or not; but, good or bad, I'm
sort of full of it, got it, so to speak, in my blood, and want to get
rid of it before doing anything else.

And on June 28, 1952, he speculated on the American reception of it.

> I've been told that the atmosphere in America is hot and hysterical, and that no one wants to hear any point of view but the official one. The book is certainly not official yet I feel that it gets somewhere near what is happening in the world today. My hopes for it are not great; indeed I cannot conceive of anybody liking it, especially Americans. . . . It is grim. It is not hopeful and it travels along a path that avoids popular conclusions.

Since Wright considered it an original work, a primarily philosophical and existentialist one, he felt that the European intellectual, with his richer cultural background, would be more likely to appreciate it than the average American reader with no training in philosophy, yet it was to this reader that he addressed his novel of ideas, disguised as a melodrama.

Toward the middle of July, Reynolds received the manuscript, which Wright had corrected and slightly condensed over the past two months, and criticized a dozen or more details in addition to questioning the motivation for certain actions. Wright made the suggested changes and corrections in an effort to be scrupulously accurate so that the necessary coincidences of the plot and the often strange behavior of the hero would not make the story too difficult to believe.[31] John Fischer, Wright's editor at Harper's after Edward Aswell, then insisted that the manuscript be cut by more than a quarter and suggested how this could be done.[32]

Since Wright trusted Reynolds, who had told him on which points he agreed with Fischer, he agreed to make further revisions in order to enliven the story and lessen the ideological exposition, but his adamant refusal to consider certain of Fischer's suggestions reveals that Wright was trying "to show that Cross's crimes are part and parcel of the every day life of man and that *some* men know this." John Fischer had done only a cursory reading of the novel, as if he thought it was no more than a detective story, and Wright argued cogently for preserving what he called "the subjective side of Cross." [33]

In July, 1952, Wright reworked some episodes dealing with the draft board and Cross's philosophical knowledge, and on August 17, he started rereading the entire manuscript in order to make the necessary cuts. During a short vacation in Corrèze, which he spent with his family, he continued to correct the text. He wrote Reynolds on August 30 that he had made the designated passages more credible and cut 36,000 words in the first two books without affecting the essential structure of the work. Wright had probably never before taken into account so many of the suggestions of his agent and editors, and he had certainly never worked so hard to find a suitable title. On August 7, John Fischer had suggested seven, to which Wright added, in order, "Between Dreams," "Out of This World," "Man Upside Down," "Last Man" and "Colored Man." Later he suggested "The Outsider," "God's Slave," "Two Thousand Years" and "The Crime of Cross," and finally "Beyond Freedom" and "Innocence at Home." It was the Harper salesmen who decided upon *The Outsider* in November, 1952.[34] Apparently Wright's conception of the novel alternated. He saw the protagonist's struggle either as a life "outside of the world," a confrontation with God or an existence made up of dreams (or rather nightmares) as the title of Book II ("Dream") suggests.

According to Wright's September 29 letter to Reynolds, he had reduced the manuscript to almost 600 pages but was still revising. He was particularly unhappy about the character of Eva.

I must confess that she is still the weakest character in the book, but I cannot think of anything else to do with her. This is how I've pictured her: she is an abstract artist; she was married by Gil at the suggestion of the party in order to recruit her. She finds this out in Paris when on her honeymoon and she and Gil are at each other's throats. She wants to leave him, but the Party says no, she must stay or they'll slander her. She stays and she is in that state of mind when she meets Cross.

On October 5, 1952, a friend of Wright's who was going back to the United States took the manuscript with her. He had cut 120 pages in all, and when Fischer asked him to cut another whole scene between Cross and Hattie, he complied.[35] The manuscript finally went to the printer at the end of November, and Wright returned the corrected proofs in record time, on December 26. *The Outsider*, in fact, took up most of Wright's time during 1952; his London trip and the vacation in Corrèze were only means of isolating himself in order to concentrate better. As opposed to previous years, he refused to enter into any project that might have distracted him. The only exception occurred during the spring when, at

Maurice Nadeau's request, he wrote a brief introduction to the French translation of *Lonely Crusade* by his friend Chester Himes.

The Outsider came out on March 16, 1953, and one of the first reactions that Wright saw was, in his estimation, a "low blow" from *Time* magazine on March 31. The headline, "Native Son Doesn't Live Here," alone made clear the reproach.

Wright argues, the whole world, including the U.S., is getting worse and is in for a totalitarian age. The Soviet Union—though he now rejects it—is not much worse than any place else. As a novelist, Wright has resorted to so much ludicrous coincidence, unlikely conversation and soapbox bombast that his history becomes a bore.

And the author thus concluded.

While Wright sits out the threat of totalitarianism in Paris, an abler U.S. Negro novelist sees the problem of his race differently. Says Ralph (*Invisible Man*) Ellison. "After all, my people have been here for a long time. . . . It is a big, wonderful country. . . ."

The American critics were not, on the whole, as negative as Wright had predicted, and they certainly made an unexpected effort to understand his intentions, which were clearly stated on the book jacket. It was not always literary considerations, however, that led to misunderstanding and criticism. Wright felt that even if Cross Damon's experiences were influenced by his color, he was more representative of a type whose intelligence made him grapple with the ethical and metaphysical problems of a society which had lost the sense of the sacred and in which the collapsing of traditional values meant that everything was permitted. Unfortunately, several black critics did not understand this perspective. In the *Chicago Sunday Tribune Magazine of Books* for March 23, 1953, Roi Ottley concluded, under his headline, "Wright Adds New Monster to Gallery of Dispossessed,"

I suspect Wright is mocking us with a ghastly joke. His main character, Cross Damon, was driven by no discernible motives— racial, political or religious—even though the author would have us believe he is a rational person. Actually he is not a Negro but what Wright describes as "the psychological man."

The reviewer of *Jet*, little brother to *Ebony* in the Johnson family of publications, was perhaps pretending not to fully understand when he panned *The Outsider* as a repeat of *Native Son.*

A Negro youth, unable to adjust to his Jim Crow environment, goes berserk and winds up a killer. . . . Wright still displays his terrific gifts for writing brilliantly. But his almost psychopathic lust for violence gets the better of him . . . and his story becomes as completely phony and unreal as a cheap drugstore whodunit.[36]

L. D. Reddick, writing for *Phylon*, was more perceptive and only sorry that his friend's philosophical erudition seemed to have smothered the storyteller within him. In *Crisis*, Henry Winslow, Jr., formulated a more suitable judgment, calling it "a titan" among the great philosophical novels of the century.

The religious press was not necessarily displeased by this spiritual epic since, in a way, atheism emerged as its own victim. Of course Roland Sawyer in the April 30, 1953, *Christian Science Monitor* found this "treatise on despair" just good enough for the shelf of rejects in the Library of Congress, but the Jesuit M. D. Reagan commended in the April 4 issue of *America*, "the message of a perceptive ex-Communist who happens to be an American Negro," and seconded the voice of protest in Wright's "bold and significant book." Apart from the foreseeable, but by this time negligible, hostility of the Communist press, every critic reacted to the political message and existentialist ideas according to his own interpretation. Without denying the powerful interest of this novel of ideas, Max Eastman found the hero unconvincing because Wright was "wrestling [too] earnestly with problems torturing his own mind in passing from the Communist conspiracy to the Existentialist racket." Orville Prescott's conclusion to his perceptive and influential review in *The New York Times* cut both ways:

It is a fair assumption, I think, that Mr. Wright deplores Cross' moral weakness and irrational behavior but that he finds much cogency in Cross' philosophy. That men as brilliant as Richard Wright feel this way is one of the symptoms of the intellectual and moral crisis of our times.

John Henry Raleigh lamented in the *New Republic*:

The Outsider makes sad reading when thinking of the author—a man of determination, idealism, intelligence (he is not a genuine *writer* as compared to someone like Newby)—driven by intolerable circumstances, but, as he is the first to say, driven by himself, by his own demon, to the bleak wailing wall, there to curse the night a manchild was conceived.

Lewis V. Fogler thought that Wright's was a courageous effort indicating that "he is currently having an uneasy time of it in the Existentialist part of the maze. One suspects that the act of searching, even though it leads through all these alleys of dread, is better than attempting to ignore the labyrinth." Luther P. Jackson regretted that Wright was as incapable of steering clear of the debates on the Left Bank as he had been in avoiding the political harangues in Chicago's Washington Park, and reproached him for his elementary discovery that communism was not a solution, that, in fact, there was no solution. On the other hand, Harvey Curtiss Webster thought this very lack of commitment to a particular solution was a sign of progress:

The Outsider is one of the most tantalizingly imperfect novels of the past two decades. In its great imperfection, it belongs with those other novels that enable us to understand the cursed condition of humanity, which is born to one law and to another bound. . . . Wright has come a long way from his naive and justified resentment of white folks, a long way beyond and above Communism and existentialism, a long way toward a theory of man in our universe that may enable him to write novels better than he has yet written and as good as those that have been written by the best outsiders of our century.[37]

Granville Hicks offered perhaps the most judicious opinion, which appeared on the first page of the March 22 *New York Times Book Review* under the title "Portrait of a Man Searching."

If the ideas are sometimes incoherent, that does not detract from the substance and power of the book. It is in the description of action, especially violent action, that Mr. Wright excels, not merely because he can make the reader see but because he compels him to participate. . . .

This, he goes on to say, sustains the reader's interest even through the longest and most obscure of Cross's philosophical discourses. He claimed that *The Outsider* was Wright's "most valiant and successful effort to come to terms with his feelings about the human conditions"; it was not about a black man but about a modern man, defying the modern spirit. The word challenge appeared in most of the reviews that spoke with any understanding at all of the novel;

the book, it was agreed, was easy to take issue with, but impossible to ignore. Wright himself was rather unjust when, chagrined that none of his critics had agreed with him, he claimed that they had refused to go to the heart of the problem.

The negative comments usually concerned the form of the novel, and they were justified. Melvin Altschuler agreed with Wright's own estimation of the weakness of the portrait of Eva, and found the melodramatic plot hard to believe.[38] Gilbert Highet questioned the double character of Cross. A postman imprisoned by his milieu and a bold, intelligent murderer could, he admitted, exist in one man, but the transition from the first to the second, which Wright covers in only a few days, should have taken months if not years. Perhaps the cutting of several episodes at John Fischer's urging had actually harmed the novel by accelerating the action and leaving the characters and background too thinly elaborated. In any case, *The New Yorker* review summed up the general opinion:

. . . as the story of a flight, both physical and psychological, it is enthralling, although Mr. Wright's ideological debates get seriously in the way of the action without adding much to the power of the book. The writing is intense, garrulous, rowdy, and often flowery, and there is about many of the paragraphs an ill-at-ease air of having been too carefully worked over.[39]

The true imperfections of *The Outsider* were not, as was often assumed at the time of publication, directly caused by its ideological or philosophical content, but rather by Wright's failure to adapt realism and naturalism, so successful in *Native Son*, to a didactic novel. Without forgetting the important symbolism of the earlier novel, it is fair to say that a more symbolic, perhaps even surrealistic, form was needed to structure Cross Damon's spiritual journey.

Wright had actually opened the novel with a whole section from the then unpublished *Lawd Today* describing Cross's life in Chicago, his work at the post office and his colorful conversations with his colleagues, and leading the reader to expect a picturesque, perhaps even humorous, depiction of black life. Then Cross makes his existential choice, killing his original identity in order to reveal his second self. Although the suspense increases, the story is now somewhat lacking in substance and human atmosphere, for which the hero's ideological dissertations are no substitute. Not only is there

The Outsider, 1953

an imbalance between Cross's first and his second life, but also between the chronological account of Cross's actions, which is restricted to crucial episodes, and his sometimes verbose theoretical digressions. Granville Hicks had recognized that Wright could sustain the action by virtue of his storytelling ability, but nevertheless Wright made the same mistake here as he had at the end of *Native Son*, outlining in a professorial manner what he should have left to be suggested by the context. *The Outsider* needed either a coherent symbolism, as in "The Man Who Lived Underground," or a more fully developed realism that would have contained the ideology within it—at the expense, however, of the fast pace of the plot. The original version of the manuscript, in fact, had more of the intricacy and richness of a Dostoevsky novel. Lacking that extra 120 pages, the structure stands out like a skeleton and certain concepts seem so hastily formulated as to be almost caricatured. Cross, for example, is obsessed by woman and the female body, a leitmotif that Wright sometimes evokes rather inexpressively (as in the recurring phrase, "woman as the body of a woman," which even *The New Yorker* reviewer found strange) and sometimes in the vulgar terminology of cheap voyeurism. Either more details were needed to develop and sustain Cross's emotional involvements, or the ideological debate should have been drastically reduced. A condensed version, published with Wright's permission by Panther Books in 1960, does, in fact, restore the balance in this direction, but in the Harper edition, there is not enough description left to get beneath the surface of the events; Cross's motives are thus obscure and his behavior proportionately implausible.

Despite these limitations, *The Outsider* cleared a path for much of Wright's own future spiritual development and, what is perhaps less evident, for that of future American novelists. In exorcising the ghosts of totalitarianism, Wright was trying to find an escape for the human personality, and, via Cross, he was presenting himself with the existential choice between remaining a black American or becoming a citizen of the world. At the time, these were mutually exclusive due to current racial and historical conditions and to the incomplete development of Wright's own perspective. His originally involuntary and later self-imposed exile had conferred upon him the disquieting privilege of simultaneously observing his society from within and from without. When Wright assumed the position of an outsider he condemned himself to a lasting spiritual isolation. His reading in the existentialists (Kierkegaard, Husserl and especially Heidegger, rather than Camus and Sartre) had shown him that this exile that he had blamed primarily upon his color was, in fact, the fate of everyone, that problems are never solved except through action and that the individual is responsible for creating his own values. This was the metaphysical conquest that he accomplished with so much difficulty. At the same time, Wright prophesied the fate of industrial civilization: the advent of a dehumanized society that would give birth to amoral monsters. From this standpoint *The Outsider* is a precurser of Norman Mailer's *An American Dream* and Truman Capote's *In Cold Blood*, providing their frame of reference—a world where everything is permitted.

Wright certainly went way beyond the "Negro provincialism" so dear to the critics, and bypassed American chauvinism, religious fanaticism and political authoritarianism as well. Damon achieves a Dostoevskian liberation, but he commits a fatal error in trying to become God and in burning the bridges that link him to mankind. In his almost Conradian finale Wright condenses all the horror that he had discovered in his solitude, but he also suggests, somewhat hesitantly perhaps, that new relationships are possible. "Man is a promise he must not break"; humanism is the only solution—not the ideal of the Renaissance, the *honnête homme,* nor the ideal of the white pseudoliberals, but a worldwide humanism that would break down the barriers between races, nations and religions. It was this idealistic and noble belief that, almost providentially it seems, but also quite logically, turned Wright's attention toward the Third World.

Through the trauma of the break with Stalinism and the evolution of his own brand of existentialism, Wright developed an insight and elaborated a synthesis which, though still imperfect, meant that he could link the freedom that "societies must guarantee to men [so] . . . that man can remain human despite the factory system" with the humanity "America can start guaranteeing to its own Negroes." He therefore felt obliged to remain an expatriate in order to "bring up [his] children to feel free and dignified." [40]

He now felt obliged to formulate the problems of the modern age without ambiguity, and began openly to criticize the growth of McCarthyism. Eisenhower's victory did not bother him in the least since the Democratic party had long since ceased to be democratic, and he wrote Reynolds on November 6, 1952, that he hoped that Eisenhower would "clear out the State Department crowd and make things so that a man can get his passport without being too scared." In fact, when John Fischer suggested that he come to New York for the publication of *The Outsider,* he wrote back on December 1 refusing lest he, too, become an object of interest to the Committee on "un-American activities" and not be able to leave again. He preferred to stay put and be free to expose the effects that this policy might have on the so-called Negro problem.

This period of evolution left Wright somewhat deserted, since he could no longer depend upon the existentialist praxis for support. Once he had found his own equilibrium, it was inevitable that he should become independent of Sartre, who had been so close to him in 1948. In addition, after the failure of the RDR, Sartre had moved further toward the Communists, agreeing to attend the Vienna Peace Congress, along with Communist representatives from around the world, to prove that one could work with the Party while still criticizing it. On March 22, 1953, a brief *New York Times* article entitled "Wright You Are" quotes Wright as saying on this occasion, "What a stupid move."

"Black Orpheus," Sartre's introduction to Léopold Senghor's anthology of Negro-African poetry, had aroused some opposition among the *Présence Africaine* group because many felt it was too sentimental and primitivist; in spite of his vigorous attack on anti-Semitism, he was criticized for not coming out strongly enough against anti-Black racism and the American situation, and for giving too much space to the oppressed peoples of Central Europe and not enough to the fight against colonialism. Wright ran into this himself one day when Sartre refused to publish in *Les Temps Modernes* an article about the Third World that Wright was anxious to have appear immediately. In broad terms, it might be fair to say that Wright was already so much of a "world" intellectual that he found Sartre too exclusively European.

The composition of *The Outsider* had also proved to Wright that existentialism as a philosophy of action could not promise a solution nor even provide a unified perception of the modern world. Wright's former somewhat blind faith in the European cultural tradition had not been totally misplaced; he had gained perspective on himself as both an American and a black American, but he had outgrown this faith in the process. For Wright *The Outsider*, therefore, settled old accounts much more than it uncovered new premises from which to start afresh. Indispensable as the writing of the book had been, Wright could now give himself entirely to the non-Western nations, the emerging universe with its promise of regeneration, new blood and solutions to the problems of a struggling industrial civilization. Of course, Africa had a sentimental appeal for Wright, but he was most attracted to it at this time because the recent decline of colonialism there now left room for a liberation which the cold war and McCarthyism made impossible in the West.

At the same time that Wright had been moving toward the new equilibrium provided by the composition of *The Outsider*, he had also been writing another novel that, though superficially very different, shows some interesting parallels. It was not to be a story "in black and white," and thus it resembled "The Man Who Lived Underground." Rather, as Wright described it to Reynolds on December 26, 1952, it would be "completely non-racial, dealing with crime *per se*." Largely inspired by the Clinton Brewer case and Dr. Frederic Wertham's *Dark Legend*, Wright had made his protagonist a psychopathic murderer, who killed a woman to punish his mother by proxy for her sexual promiscuity during his childhood. The novel, which was eventually published as *Savage Holiday*, was divided into the three acts of classical drama, Wright's favorite form for most of his novels. "Anxiety," "Ambush" and "Attack" cover three days, from a Saturday evening to Tuesday morning. Erskine Fowler is a wealthy New York insurance executive, but the banquet which was to mark his apotheosis in the company actually celebrates his premature retirement. His anxiety starts to show through when, aggravated by the continuous noise of his neighbor's son playing the drums on the balcony, he has a terrible nightmare. Upon awakening, he goes out nude to collect his paper from the doorstep and a sudden draft slams and locks the door behind him. He panics, becoming an animal trapped by human convention. He steps around to the balcony, planning to climb in by his bathroom window, but the sight of his hairy body frightens the young drum-player Tony, who shrinks back against the railing and falls to his death from the tenth floor. Torn between fear and guilt, Erskine conceals the fact that he was present during the accident.

Religion does not quiet his anxiety but does help assuage his guilt: Tony's death has led his mother, the "fallen woman" Mrs. Blake, to repent, and Erskine has been the tool of this providential chastisement. Puritan that he is, Erskine both scorns and desires this disturbing neighbor whom he decides to marry, not in order to buy her silence, as he tells himself, but to possess her tyrannically. His hesitations, jealousy and even delirium—all of which indicate his dangerous mental state—lead him to stab her savagely in the kitchen; it is the only way he can possess her and punish her at the same time.

Fowler's strange behavior, like that of his real-life model, Clinton Brewer, is explained by psychoanalyzing his past. Erskine constantly recalls his childhood, the death of his father, the lovers of his mother, who was even imprisoned for her conduct. He would have liked his mother to love him, but she was impure; he identifies with Tony, who is likewise disturbed that men seem to "beat" his mother and afraid because he thinks that babies derive from this violence. Mabel Blake, therefore, as a sensuous woman and an image of his unworthy mother, represents two temptations—desire and incest—which his Puritan conscience vigorously condemns. His regression is clear. Because his nakedness startled Tony, he feels responsible for his death; as a member of society, he is convinced that he has a right to punish Mabel, whose only sin was being too attractive. When he gives himself up to the police, his illness is revealed. The four pencils that he constantly touches for reassurance hark back to an early childhood incident in which he had drawn the picture of a broken doll, representing his hostility toward his mother for neglecting him. Thus in *Savage Holiday* Fowler kills because of "a guilty dream which he had wanted to disown and forget but which he had had to reenact in order to make its memory and reality clear to him" (p. 220).

The concept of a deeply buried desire that emerges thirty years later in the form of a crime has two meanings in Wright's novel. First, it places the murder itself on another, almost secondary level, since the remembered reality of Fowler's childhood is revealed as the unreality of a dream. And it also supports Wright's claim that it was impossible to separate the act from the fantasy and life from the dream, which was, in fact, the theme of "The Man Who Killed a Shadow" and later, *The Long Dream.*

The importance thus given to delirious fantasies distinguishes Wright's novel from Frederic Wertham's *Dark Legend,* but in addition to this and the details borrowed from the Clinton Brewer story, the purely autobiographical touches in *Savage Holiday* explain two things: why Wright originally took such a great interest in Brewer's case and, more important, why he attached so much importance to the publication of *Savage Holiday.* For, in fact, when working on *The Outsider* and evoking his childhood, Wright had been forced to confront, on the written page, his own attitude toward his mother. Cross eventually repudiates his mother, ostensibly on intellectual grounds, for being too submissive and religious. Considering the autobiographical elements involved in the mother-son relationship, this intellectual rejection could mask an emotional foundation that shows up in *Savage Holiday.* Erskine, while playing with Gladys and her dolls, draws the broken doll as a way of venting his anger at his mother, who has left him to go out with a man while he is ill. When she learns of this hostile act, she tells him to look in the mirror to see how naughty he is. Might this not be a reminiscence of the cat episode in *Black Boy,* in which the mother inflicts an unbearable guilt upon the son? Gladys was, after all, the name of Richard's favorite cousin, and Mrs. Fowler's desertion of her sick child is reminiscent of Ella's severe beating of Richard which brought on a fever. Wright includes a similar episode in *The Long Dream,* where the little boy falls and burns himself against the furnace because he has been left alone. Could not Tony's drum be the same one that Richard's father confiscated? Wright of course never had the slightest reason to reproach his mother for promiscuity, but he had often interpreted her extreme severity as rejection without exactly knowing why, while his Oedipal tendencies had made him jealous of anyone his mother seemed to prefer to him, whether it was a gluttonous pastor or God himself. In a sense, Wright uses what were mere inclinations in himself to create a veritable psychosis in Fowler. It is for this reason that the theme of this psychoanalytical novel appealed so much to him. If it can be said that *The Outsider* was a repudiation of Wright's ideological past, it is just as true to say that *Savage Holiday* was a repudiation of his psychoanalytical past, and that the second novel accomplishes on an emotional plane what the first had achieved on an intellectual one. It was certainly not a coincidence that the two were written in quick succession. Wright was actually awaiting the March publication of *The Outsider* when he started to write *Savage Holiday* around Christmas, 1952. In one month he had almost completed the first version of 60,000 words, and although he had not got away from Paris to go over it at leisure, as he had planned to do, he sent the manuscript of "Monument to Memory," as it was then called, to Reynolds on March 6, 1953, with the comment:

This is a rather simple little story and is rather short, but I don't like trying to pad out things just to make them long. The length of a story sort of determines itself, and if you put more words into it, they stick out and spoil things. As I told you, this deals with just folks, white folks. I don't know how people will receive a story like this. Don't know if Harper will like my switching or not. But, as you can see, there was no sense in making this story a Negro story. . . . Do read this and tell me what you think. I was of a mind to say try to publish this under another name. What I am worried about is that people will read this in a light of saying that this is a Negro writing about whites. Which is true. But they might read it with more a desire to try to find fault than just to be moved or interested in the story. Give me your opinion.

Reynolds himself liked the story but he could not imagine it selling very well, even if *The Outsider* were a great success, because the public was no longer interested in the subject. At this time

Reynolds criticized only two specific points. First, it seemed to him unlikely that Erskine Fowler would voluntarily retire at the age of forty-three; and second, if he were to ask Mabel to marry him for fear that she would betray him, there had to be some incident to provoke this fear. Wright certainly must have had this novel well in hand, because he was immediately able to make the necessary changes. The president of the insurance company would get rid of Erskine in order to give the job to his own son. The second problem was more complicated because Wright wanted to leave the unconscious motives of his hero untouched. Thus, he had Erskine cut his hand as he climbed through the window, getting his newspaper bloody in the process. He then would substitute it for Mabel's and she, in turn, seeing the blood, would confide to Erskine that Tony's death was not an accident. He, feeling threatened, then determines to buy her silence.[41]

Harper's immediately rejected "The Wish and the Dream" because John Fischer thought the story dated. Even if Wright had been concerned with fashions in American literary tastes, which he never was, he would not have agreed with this estimate. He had once again written out of his own experience on a subject of intimate concern to him. Accordingly, he asked Reynolds to offer the story to World Publishing Company, where one of the editors, Ben Zevin, had evinced a great desire to be his publisher. Wright had also approached Collins in London at the beginning of June and initiated proceedings for original publication in Great Britain as a trial run. Meanwhile, after Pyramid Books had rejected it, Avon offered a $2,000 advance, which more than satisfied Wright, as he told Oliver Swan of the Reynolds agency on August 22:

> Let me say that I'm glad that this deal with Avon went through so quickly and at such a good price. I'm proud that my effort, which began on Xmas eve day and ended on Easter Sunday, has resulted in a little "book." I'm still stumped about the title. . . . I don't like the present one, but I'm at a standstill when trying to dream up something new.

In his impatience to learn what changes Avon might suggest, Wright only stayed in London on his way back from Africa, where he had spent the summer, long enough to see the Padmores at Cranleigh House. He was back in Paris on September 17. "The Queen Mother," Wright's latest idea for the title, needed only a few minor cuts, which he quickly took care of before having the photographs of his recent trip developed and entering the hospital for a hernia operation.[42]

The following summer he hastened to correct the proofs before setting off for Spain. The European publishers were just as interested in this novel as they had been in Wright's previous work. Fabio Coen sold it for $2,000 to Mondadori in July, 1953. In February, 1954, *Les Temps Modernes* offered to publish it in installments, as they had *Black Boy*, and after refusing the advance of Albin Michel, Wright sold it to Editions Del Duca. Although the publication was completely ignored or dismissed as a "pot boiler" in the United States when the Avon paperback came out in 1954,[43] *Le Dieu de Mascarade* was reviewed with great seriousness in several Paris papers, and Wright spoke at length about it on a radio program at this time—yet another proof of his interest in the book.[43]

SIXTEEN

BY 1953, Wright was a novelist with an international audience, an "established writer" and what could be called a Parisian intellectual—to which certain people would add, bourgeois.[1] He certainly had no financial worries at the time. From the sale of more than 900,000 copies of *Black Boy* and close to 600,000 of *Native Son*, he had a yearly income that enabled him to ignore the only moderate sale of *The Outsider*. By mid-April the novel ranked only sixteenth among United States best sellers, despite a promising 13,000-copy advance. Wright had never entertained luxurious tastes and was content to lead a comfortable but simple life on rue Monsieur le Prince, in the house formerly inhabited by the composer Saint-Saëns. He replaced the Oldsmobile that had aroused the jealousy of his neighbors in 1947 with a less ostentatious Citroën. Alice, the maid, diligently helped Ellen around the house, Julia now attended the progressive Ecole Alsacienne, and Rachel's birth in Neuilly made Wright what the French government called a "résident privilégié," which meant that he could become a naturalized citizen without difficulty.

Wright also had a well-established group of friends, admirers and literary acquaintances, and enjoyed somewhat of a reputation as a *maître* to whom young writers came for advice on their manuscripts. Although he had refused to act as James Baldwin's "spiritual father," the settling in Paris of his friends Chester Himes and Ollie Harrington, the famous cartoonist of the *Pittsburgh Courier*, and a number of younger Afro-American artists and writers supported and reassured him in his exile. He now avoided formal gatherings whether social or literary, but he adored discussing politics and literature with Blacks of all nationalities, or with the Scandinavian and American students in the Monaco and the Tournon, his regular cafés, which had completely replaced the Deux Magots and the Procope. He also visited his favorite bookstores, George Whitman's, opposite Notre-Dame, and the "Daphne Adeane," on rue de Seine, where Mademoiselle Gaité had the latest American publications for him. He was more than ever at the center of the international exchange of ideas, with the comings and goings of compatriots such as Elmer Carter, Dorothy Norman, Nelson Algren, E. Franklin Frazier, Louis Wirth and Dorothy Maynor; of the Africans Léopold Senghor and Alioune Diop; and of those unknown students who would one day be famous and who, like Frantz Fanon, wrote him respectful letters. His Parisian friends might have considered themselves safe in assuming that Richard Wright, now somewhat portly, with ready smile, and eyes sparkling behind delicate gold-rimmed glasses, had attained the summit of his career.

Yet Wright did not necessarily intend to stay in Paris forever. Although racism was greater in London, Wright had enjoyed his reclusive life there, in contrast to the obligations Paris imposed on a writer of his renown. For years Ellen had protected her husband from many of the visitors and aspiring writers wanting to obtain his support, but now she had a profession of her own. She had learned enough about writers and publishers to become a literary agent, and while Wright was in Argentina she had placed a few manuscripts with American houses. She began working with her friend Hélène Bokanowski and soon devoted herself to this new job that called upon her own talents. Since this left her less time to protect Wright from intrusions, he began to think seriously of living in England where, in addition to the more tranquil existence he and his wife could lead, Julia could get an education in her native language. Wright even mentioned this possibility during Curtius Prendergast's interview for *Time* in March, 1953.

Furthermore, considering the metaphysical impasse he had reached with *The Outsider*, his growing dissatisfaction with the French Left and his attempts to rise above the schisms of Western civilization by building bridges between intellectuals of the several continents, it is more likely that Wright was only at another turning point, comparable to his successive departures from the South, Chicago and New York. Wright did not actually leave France, but 1953 seems to mark his spiritual departure from Paris and Europe.

It therefore makes sense to group together the projects and activities that occupied him henceforth, since, despite their apparent diversity, they all proceeded from the same desire to rehabilitate the entire black world by liberating its inexhaustible human resources.

In the Café Tournon. *Photo by Gisèle Freund*

At a signing party
with Léopold Senghor

Richard Wright

In his library

Ellen, Julia and Rachel. *Photo by Richard Wright*

Julia and Rachel with Quintanilla's portrait of Wright.
Photo by Richard Wright

He had already expressed this goal succinctly in a letter to Pandit Nehru on October 9, 1950:

The changing physical structure of the world as well as the historical development of modern society demand that the peoples of the world become aware of their common identity and interests. The situation of oppressed people the world over is universally the same and their solidarity is essential, not only in opposing oppression but also in fighting for human progress.

Thus, Wright was visibly less interested in the critical reception of *The Outsider* and the revival of *Native Son* in Michigan during the spring of 1953 than in the birth of a new project, or rather the realization of a long-cherished wish to visit Africa.[2] In 1947, and again in 1949, he had alluded to this next step in his voyage of discovery, referring to it as an "exploration," which his friend George Padmore heartily encouraged. They had had the leisure to discuss the project while he was in London writing his novel. He envisioned a study that would not only evaluate the humanistic and spiritual resources of the Third World, but would induce the West to acknowledge them.

Since Padmore had been appointed political adviser to Kwame Nkrumah, the prime minister of the Gold Coast, then on its way toward independence from Britain, he was able to assure Wright of his personal support as well as an official welcome.

After a brief visit from the Padmores in December, 1952, at which the plans were consolidated, he wrote Reynolds on December 26 that he was hoping to write a long essay on native participation in the government of the colony. At that time, John Gunther was in Africa doing research for a book modeled on his earlier work *Inside Europe*, but Wright's intentions were different: he would concentrate on the apprenticeship in modern politics that Blacks still in the process of abandoning their tribal civilization were receiving. The Gold Coast was an admirable example of a nation in transition from a feudal culture to a preindustrial civilization, and Wright planned to make note of his impressions and judgment of its growth in the form of a travelogue, as he had attempted to do in Haiti a few years earlier.

Paul Reynolds encouraged him heartily. Would it not be a good idea to spend a long time in Africa, he asked, not only keeping a journal but perhaps using another form as well, in order to bring a practically unknown country alive for the Western reader, explaining its social structures, the workings of its institutions and the reasons behind its customs? While Wright considered this project part of his ideological evolution, his "mission," Reynolds suggested another excellent reason for the trip in this letter of April 6:

I am particularly keen because I think this will stimulate you. I am sort of worried about a man living in Paris and just writing novels laid in this country. I think your search for material, your going for a purpose, namely to find out, will be of great value to you.

Wright had originally thought of promising a series of articles to a magazine like the *Atlantic Monthly*, but Harper's gave him a big advance on the journal and agreed to finance a large part of the trip.

Dorothy Padmore's visit to Paris at Easter was decisive. Since she was not only up-to-date on the political situation, but also was familiar with the practicalities of living in the Gold Coast, she helped Wright plan the details of his stay. George, meanwhile, quickly got him authorization from the prime minister to enter the country.[3] In his letter of introduction Kwame Nkrumah stated that he had met Wright in the United States, had known him for a long time and considered that his past experience qualified him to investigate the history and social development of the country, where he would be treated as his personal guest. Wright immediately booked passage for the beginning of June. A letter from John Fischer, stressing the literary mission of the visit, enabled Wright to get his British visa without much trouble.

From the very moment he was certain that he would be going, Wright had started to research the history of Africa, British colonialism and the customs of the Gold Coast. Among the major works he studied at the time were the recently published *Capitalism and Slavery* by his friend Eric Williams; *A History of the Gold Coast* by W. E. F. Ward, already five years out of date; *Colonial Civil Servant of Ashanti* by R. S. Rattray; *Social Survey Sekondi-Takoradi* by K. A. Busia; and *The Sacred State of the Akan* by Eva Meyerovitz.[4] Wright met his first Ashanti warrior on May 28 at Padmore's apartment in London. Barima Otno Ochampong I, chief of Kuamawu, had come to London for the coronation of Elizabeth II. During the few hours spent with the chief, his "linguist" and his adviser, Wright caught a glimpse of the complicated tribal rites concerning food, family and religion, all of which the chief scrupulously respected. He also saw a reflection of the political tensions signaling the approaching end of British domination in the incisive criticisms of the Barima, who had been very much offended when the royal family had smiled at his exotic costume and heavy gold jewelry.[5]

Wright was the only American passenger aboard the Elder-Dempster Line ship *Accra*, which left Liverpool on the morning of June 4, 1953. His journal shows him chatting with his tablemate, a certain Judge Thomas of the Nigerian supreme court who typified the ultra-Anglicized African; or pitching and rocking on the Bay of Biscay with this sad and impassive group who whiled away the time playing bridge, table tennis and drinking; or listening on a Sunday to the far-off chant of psalms in the grand saloon. The ship stopped at the Canary Islands on June 10, and, along with the judge and a Y.M.C.A. official, Wright visited Las Palmas. He was particularly amused by their visit to a brothel, where he claims to have taken great pleasure in forcing the embarrassed judge to choose between his dignity as a magistrate and the satisfaction of his appetites.[6]

They soon hit the tropics, where the majestic sunsets moved him, in later writing *Black Power*, to long poetic passages worthy of Chateaubriand, and where the sea evoked in him strange apprehensions reminiscent of Conrad or Gide in the Congo:

The dropping sun proclaimed itself in a majestic display of color that possessed an unearthly and imperious nobility, inducing the feeling that one had just finished hearing the dying, rolling peal of a mighty organ whose haunting chords still somehow lingered on in the form of those charged and spangled lances of somber fire. The ship sliced its way through a sea that was like still, thick oil, a sea that stretched limitless, smooth and without a break toward a murky horizon. The ocean seemed to possess a quiet but persistent threat of terror lurking just beneath the surface and I'd not have been surprised if a vast tidal wave had thrust the ship skyward in a sudden titanic upheaval of destruction (*BP*, pp. 26–27).

When they stopped in Freetown, Sierra Leone, Wright had a chance to visit the public market, under an already merciless sun, before going to see Wallace Johnson, who was editor of the *African Standard*, a member of parliament, head of the League of West African Youth, as well as a practicing lawyer. He had just come back from the coronation and spoke for over an hour about himself,

the African world, the scorn of the British and the origins of the
liberation movement that he led.[7] Wright also learned a great deal
from talking to a young man named Taylor in a small, dingy bar
hung with pictures of Hollywood movie stars. Poverty, filth, "puritan" taboos conflicting with Western sexuality, black nationalism
coexisting with English domination: all these characteristics of Sierra Leone were portrayed in detail by Wright to suggest what the
Gold Coast was before the arrival of Nkrumah on the political scene.

At dawn on June 16, the boat finally reached the Gold Coast,
landing at Takoradi, a busy port with wharves covered with ware-
houses, cranes and derricks, teeming with activity. Wright was welcomed by a personal friend of Prime Minister Nkrumah, Mr. Baidoe
Ansah, director of a huge forestry enterprise, and after doing a few
errands he got a bus for Accra. It took eight hours to cover the 170
miles through the lively markets of the fishing villages, the innumerable communities of mud huts with their nude inhabitants, and
forests of cedar, cashew, cocoa, coconut and rubber trees buried in a
deepening jungle of which each new detail was registered on his
memory as in a dream.

Nkrumah's secretary, Erica Owell, was expecting Wright and installed him in a government bungalow where a trained boy served
him in silence. Wright spent the next day walking around the city,
observing the lines that formed at the public fountains for water,
the bustling markets and hordes of beggars. Nkrumah returned from
a trip in the North on June 19 and immediately received Wright,
giving him an official tour of the capital amid roaring motorcyclists
in scarlet uniforms and a crowd shouting "Freedom! Kwame! Ak-
waba!" In Jamestown, the working-class quarter of the city, Wright
attended a meeting of the women's section of the Freedom Party,
where he observed the patriotic spirit and the emotional reserves
which, though left untapped by Christianity, Nkrumah had been able
to use to his advantage by exalting, channeling and structuring them
into a ritual of libations and oaths. The evening finished up at the
Government Palace with political discussions, official reports and
folk dances.

The following day, Wright again visited this area of town on his
own, taking photographs and discovering how greatly African
customs and even ordinary concepts differed from his own. That
evening, he attended an important political meeting at the West-
end Arena at which the speakers exchanged thoughts with a

crowd of almost ten thousand people. He himself had prepared a short address, a noble, almost overexalted plea that the citizens of the future nation of Ghana lead the way for all Africa. There was very little applause, and, although Wright never knew why, the Prime Minister discreetly told a reporter from the *Daily Graphic* that he preferred not to have the speech published.[8]

In order to live closer to the people, Wright left his bungalow on June 21 and moved into the Seaview Hotel, near the beach and opposite the Jamestown quarter. As he marveled in *Black Power*: "It was the kind of hotel that one heard about in a Joseph Conrad novel and, what intrigued me most, I had only to go to the balcony and look down and there was Africa in all its squalor, vitality and fantastic disorder" (p. 80). The same day he also wrote to Reynolds:

It's hot, and, as you warned, the food is bad. But I'm well started on my diary which now runs to some 20,000 words. . . . Life here is incredible:—poverty, nakedness, and illnesses. The only redeeming feature is the strident political party, the CPP, which is fighting for self-government. . . . I'm a little slow getting under way because I must get used to the heat. But I find that I'm getting more and more active as the days go by.

By depending less strictly on the cooperation of the government, Wright hoped to mingle more easily with the people, perhaps by moving into a "compound" and plunging himself into this life to which he felt so emotionally akin, yet from which he was so culturally estranged. He was again invited to a political rally, preliminary to a partial vote at Cape Coast, the nation's cultural center, where the seat of a recently deceased assemblyman, Kwesi Plange, was being hotly contested by followers of the People's Party and the pro-British opposition. Nkrumah once again resorted to a mixture of brutal frankness and the mystic rites of ancestral religion to combat the propaganda of his adversaries, Busia and Danquah. The director of the Government Information Office, Kofi Baako, explained to Wright the origins of the People's Party and the development of the independence movement. George Padmore had already acquainted Wright with the history of "The Secret Circle" to which Nkrumah and a few others had belonged since the forties. Wright's notes accumulated complementary and contradictory impressions, but on that day he ventured: "Though the conditions of life were harsh, ridden with fetish and superstition, [the Gold Coast African] would eventually be free for he was determined and tough" (*BP,* p. 97).

He spent June 23 walking in the alleys of Jamestown. On June 24, he had a long conversation with Mrs. Hannah Cudjoe, secretary for propaganda of the women's section of the CPP. Wright studied the role of the woman in the tribe, her economic status and lack of education, but he was unable to persuade a family to allow him to share their daily life as a paying guest. On June 25, his long discussion with the secretary general of the Party, Kwame Afriyie, was on the whole disappointing. "Every time I brought up an important question, I sensed that vague reaction of timidity, fear, and mistrust among my listeners." [9]

Nevertheless, Wright succeeded in exploring all avenues of possible contacts. He accompanied a young African who had studied in the United States to "Weekend in Havana," a club where he was surprised to see men dancing with each other.

Intellectually, I understood my friend's all too clear explanation of why boys liked to hold hands and dance together, yet the sight of it provoked in me a sense of uneasiness on levels of emotion deeper than I could control (*BP,* p. 110).

Although this was nothing more than a popular open-air dancing spot, he could not help his puritan reaction. In fact, he had to combat the growing feeling that the world around him was totally irrational. He could calmly analyze the differences in culture, but he was not sufficiently detached or fatalistic to contain, for example, his indignation on seeing the dock workers running with enormous loads on their heads and struggling in their small boats against the breakers, risking their lives for a shilling a trip. While everyone around him seemed to find this natural, he rebelled.

I'd seen River Rouge and it was nothing compared to this hot, wild and hellish labor. It was not only against exploitation that I was reacting so violently; it frightened me because the men did not seem human, because they had voluntarily demeaned themselves to be spokes in a wheel. . . . There are circumstances in which human life is no longer human life, and I'd seen one of them. And for this particular barbarity I had no answer, no scheme; I would not have gone on strike if I had worked there; I simply would not have worked there in the first place, no matter what (*BP,* pp. 122–123).

Even though he knew how the Party operated, had analyzed Nkrumah's political methods, studied the economy of the Gold Coast and observed the strange life of Accra, Wright could not help being increasingly surprised, not by the novelty, but by the psychological gap between the country of his ancestors and himself. Of course he had never expected the color of his skin automatically to open the door to the soul of Africa, but now his knowledge, both from conversations with Africans in Paris and from his own past in Mississippi seemed ridiculously inadequate tools with which to apprehend African realities. On June 27, he attended a wake that seemed more like a lascivious dance, while the funeral procession he saw the next day struck him as an excuse to parade gaudy materials and nude breasts to the sound of repeated bursts of gunfire. He observed and sympathized, but could not participate. To establish a contrast, he went to a Wesleyan Methodist service on June 29, but he found the ritual merely dull and hypocritical. His sympathies were with the African paganism, but he could not identify with its way of thinking. In two weeks he had collected more than 200 pages of notes, but it discouraged him to think that he would never be able to know everything and know it intimately.

My money is melting under the tropic sun faster than I am soaking up the reality about me. . . . I'm of African descent and I'm in the midst of Africans, yet I cannot tell what they are thinking or feeling. And without the help of either the British or the Africans, I'm completely immobilized. . . . I looked like the Africans but I had only to walk upon a scene and my difference at once declared itself without a word being spoken (*BP,* p. 137).

The American consul, Mr. Cole, and the United States Information Service were helpful to Wright, but the British, foreseeing his criticism of their administration, were hardly disposed to furnish him with the revealing details of their neglect and oppression. Since he could not expect much from the Whites, he decided to discover on his own the more hidden of the facts about the inland bush and the northern regions. Until now he had restricted his attention to the coastal zone—Takoradi, Cape Town and Accra —which represented the most industrialized area. Buses inland were infrequent and slow, and the only railroad followed the coast, so after trying to buy a secondhand car he eventually had to rent one. A day-by-day account of his findings and contacts shows to what extent and purpose Wright reworked his original impressions when he wrote *Black Power*.

On July 4, enroute to Tema, a new port still being built, he visited the fishing village of Labadi, where he saw juxtaposed to the picturesque sight of women crushing fufu the pathetic specter of children decimated by malaria and pian. A conversation with an electrician provoked him to condemn heartily the missionaries, and the next day, at a religious school in Tema, he actually saw the children being taught pidgin English for reasons of expediency. What could be hoped for from a Christianity that had them repeat in unison: "I go—I go up—I no go—I go so"? When he returned to Accra on July 6 to have his typewriter repaired, he incidentally discovered that the Prime Minister's secretary believed in sorcery. Nor were his surprises for the day over. He was propositioned by a social worker, whose tranquil audacity in offering her body disconcerted him, and next he learned that no one had ever dared fill in or dry up the fetid lagoon of Korle Bu, situated only a few hundred yards from the general hospital, out of respect for the spirit of the place, who was once supposed to have helped the people of Accra.

On July 10, Wright sat in on a solemn session of the legislative assembly, presided over by Sir Emmanuel Quist, during which Nkrumah presented a motion proposing extensive constitutional amendments for greater independence. Wright was thus able to evaluate the two sources of opposition that the Prime Minister and the People's Party had to confront. First there were the colonial officials themselves: the governor, Sir Charles Arden-Clarke; the minister of defense and foreign affairs, R. H. Saloway; the minister of justice, P. Branigan and the minister of finances, R. P. Armitage; and second, there were the black intellectuals who had studied at Oxford or Cambridge, such as the jurist and philosopher Danquah and the sociologist Busia, who sided for the most part with the pro-British opposition.

At Christianborg, Wright visited the ruins of the Richter slave prison and fortress, whose ownership the black and the mulatto branches of the family were still contesting. He spent hours at the offices of various newspapers, among them the *Ashanti Sentinel* and O. B. Amankwah's *Ghana Evening News*, both Convention People's Party publications; *The African National Times*, Daniel Tackie's *Daily Echo* and the *Daily Graphic*, a "white" paper that had fostered a strong pro-African trend; but he found these papers extremely provincial, with no interest in the rest of the world. After hearing the minister of commerce, Mr. Gbedemah, speak at the Government Information Office on the plan to build a huge dam across the Volta, he endeavored to get the opinions of the natives. A conversation with the cook of Lloyd Shirer, a missionary, answered some of his burning questions about slavery on African soil.

To be a slave was proof that one had done something bad, that one was being punished, that one was guilty . . . that your ancestors had consigned you to perdition! To treat a slave harshly was a way of obeying the spiritual laws of the universe (*BP,* p. 196).

Was this not similar to the Puritan attitude toward the poor, and later, the American attitude toward the Blacks?

The next day Wright was finally able to record in his journal that he had enjoyed an open and frank conversation with someone who at least started from the same basic concepts as he did, even if he did not share his conclusions. Dr. Ampofo, the chief of a large family from Mampong, had studied at the University of Edinburgh before the war and had lived for a time in Stockholm. An enlightened and liberal middle-class intellectual himself, he considered Nkrumah too revolutionary, believing that the people were not sufficiently educated and that one could not build upon sand. Wright disagreed because he put freedom before education, yet he was happy to talk frankly with an African intellectual, even if they disagreed, because he had deplored the reticence of the People's Party leaders to whose political views he did subscribe.

For as long as his money lasted, Wright planned to explore the bush country between Takoradi, Accra and Kumasi, where three-quarters of the population and resources of the country were to be found. He hired a former middleweight boxing champion, "Battling Kojo," as chauffeur, and he got an itinerary from the Information Office. This held him up for several more days, but it meant that he could attend a party given by the head of the Information Office, Major Lillie Costello, on July 27. There he met the chief of police, who was "the most liberal-minded Englishman [he had] met so far in Africa. . . . His mind was not encumbered with bulky theories of sociology or anthropology that insisted that certain spans of time had to elapse before people could absorb knowledge." (*BP,* p. 210.)

While he was waiting, Wright visited the village of Prampram, where he witnessed the funeral of an elder. He bought *The Akan Doctrine of God* by Dr. Danquah and sought to meet the author in person, who turned out to be a lawyer whom he found "gracious, affable, generous-hearted, a man who was deeply baffled and tried to hide it, a man whose mind was desperately trying to grapple with a new and alien reality which he hated" (*BP,* p. 219). At a luncheon with the American consul, Mr. Cole, he also spoke with the chief of Odumase, a village in the province of Manya Krobo, who especially reproached the English for giving Nkrumah so much power that the chieftains' authority was diminished, a complete betrayal of their pact. He also supplied Wright with some fascinating details about the practice of magic. Wright then went to see K. A. Busia, a sociology professor at the University of Achimota. During their talk, Busia stressed the strength of the Akan traditions and religion, deplored the hypocrisy of the English—who, he declared, were only protecting the CPP to defend their economic interests—and regretted the arrival of an industrial society that was introducing a form of veritable paganism. Although Dr. Busia had a remarkably clear view of these changes, he was opposing what Wright considered to be the natural progress of a nation undergoing rapid industrialization.

With his detailed itinerary and a long list of chiefs, doctors, lawyers and businessmen to meet, Wright finally left on August 3 for Kumasi, Kumawu and Bibiani, taking

a half-gallon thermos jug for water, about 30£ worth of tinned food, a bottle of germicide to put into the water before using it for washing, a big box of DDT, cigarettes, and a five-yard length of colored cloth to use as a sheet at night when I'd been bunking in out-of-the-way places (*BP,* p. 241).

He traversed a thick, dark jungle in traveling from Mampong to Koforidua, a clean and friendly city of 25,000 people. Since there seemed to be some trouble with the gears of the Vanguard he had rented, Wright sent Kojo to get another car from Accra while he himself stayed with Mr. R. A. Eccles, the local director of the United Africa Forestry Company. That same afternoon, he met Chief Osei Kwesi, Omanhene of New Jauben, who claimed to be protected by enchanted bees. He then had to go to a cocktail party given in his honor and met various people from the city who tried to extract his opinions on the colonial question. He finished the evening in a bar with a nouveau riche African whom he did not want to offend. Despite the torrential rain, he set off with Kojo the next day in a Chevrolet for Nkawkaw, arriving in time for lunch at Ejisu, the former capital of Ashanti sorcerers; and on August 7, he began a ten-day visit in the truly African city of Kumasi, "the heart of historic Negrodom . . . less vibrant than Takoradi, moodier than Accra, dreamier than Koforidua, Kumasi has huge black vultures wheeling in its cloudy sky all day long" (*BP*, pp. 272–273).

Here Wright got in touch with John Tsiboe, editor of the *Ashanti Pioneer*, who had gone over to the opposition because he considered that Nkrumah was actually serving British policy, and he observed the compulsory formality of paying his respects to the district commissioner. He visited the strange Lake Bosomtwe, where the decomposition of organic matter caused explosions of gas every five or six hours and dead fish would float to the surface, to be collected by the natives as gifts of the local spirit.

At a dinner party, Mr. Krobo Edusei introduced him to the king of Ashanti, Sir Osei Agyeman Prempeh II, who gave him an audience. This grandson of the Ashantehene in turn presented him to the chief of Mampong, Asofo Kamtantea II, but since he did not feel authorized to speak in the absence of the elders, Wright, as a guest of the Queen Mother, simply learned about the fabrication and significance of the sacred stools. He spent the next few days visiting the different chiefs of the region, who were for the most part illiterate and often deprived of their power, but remained indispensable as mediators between the living and the dead. Wright thought the chief of Efiduasi, Kwame Dua Awere II, and a few others particularly well-informed and capable, but despite his rapid initiation into the royal and religious mysteries of the Ashanti, he still felt they were all somewhat on their guard against him. Dr. R. E. Armattoe, who had studied in England and Germany, explained the secret rites and sacrifices in detail, and at the Kumasi market he spoke to the natives who sold home remedies, but it was impossible for a non-African to delve any deeper.

On the day of his audience with the king, he was received at the palace, in the presence of a secretary. Although he was intelligent and relatively progressive, aware of the changes taking place in the world, the king appeared to be trapped by his ancestral religion and tribal customs. "He was no doubt struggling to find ways and means to let his people know that he was not akin to any mystic powers; but *could he?*" (*BP*, p. 257).

Mr. A. J. Hughes, the Information Office employee in charge of organizing Wright's trip in the Secondi-Takoradi district, accompanied him a hundred miles northwest to Berekum, where Wright collected information on funeral rites and the sacrifices made to the dead. He then visited the huge gold mine of Bibiani, in the old native city built on the edge of a swamp. The next step of the journey took him to the largest world plywood and construction wood plant run by the United Africa Company at Samreboi. At a cocktail party given in his honor by the director general, Wright (mistakenly introduced as Dr. Williams) was able to talk with over a dozen Europeans from the city but as a result had to listen to the usual complaints about the stupidity and bestiality of the natives. Wright knew that the natives were more exploited than lacking in intelligence, having found out from the Union that salaries ranged from four to ten shillings a day.

Wright then left for Takoradi, the industrial capital of the country, where he had a series of frightening experiences. First he was almost stabbed, while trying to take a photograph of a funeral procession, by a drunk who thought he was in the pay of the English; then he had great difficulty in refusing the advances of a woman without causing a scandal; and finally, a guest at the funeral advised him to get out of the vicinity before the frenzy, intended to frighten the spirit of the dead person, broke out. For the first time in Africa, Wright was really afraid, afraid of the pagan religion with its incomprehensible and bloody practices.

It was probably from Bibiani that he wrote Reynolds, on August 22, of his intention to go back to Accra, head for Tamale and briefly visit Togo and spend a week with an African family somewhere before returning to Europe. Five days later in Accra, he figured out that he had very little money left and shortened his stay considerably, moving his passage ahead to September 2.[10]

Wright spent his last few days on the Gold Coast visiting the forts along the southern coast, first at Christianborg, the official residence of the governor of the colony, then at Cape Coast, where the slave convoys were held before being shipped to Elmina. The fortress of Elmina itself, with its dungeons and thick-walled "compound," still bore the traces of its flourishing slave trade. Wright eventually chose the symbolism of these prisons and chains belonging to a bygone era to suggest, in *Black Power,* a final vision of Africa devastated by colonization.

As he boarded the *Apapa,* Wright had with him thousands of notes, more than 1,500 photographs and a whole suitcase of books, newspapers and government publications. Ten weeks had been time enough for him to see almost everything he wanted to see, but he had never attained that intimate knowledge he so desired. His intellectual and ideological discussions with the leaders of the People's Party and the country's elite had been on the whole fruitful, but the reserve of the people had thwarted him. The chiefs and the sorcerers may have vouchsafed some of their secrets, but the African "soul," which the theoreticians of negritude in Paris had evoked in a manner that Wright had always considered a little too exaggerated, too mystical, too poetic, turned out to be very difficult to capture. The Africans, in all probability, were not intrinsically mysterious, but they had treated Wright as a Westerner.

Wright's own faith in rationality was another impediment, since it rendered him incapable of sympathizing with and sharing the beliefs of tribal culture. The color of his skin turned out to be less of a bond with the Africans than the white oppression that they had separately suffered on both sides of the Atlantic, but even this was not enough to overcome certain differences.

Given the political and economic corruption caused by English domination, itself enough for a long critical discourse, Wright decided not to concentrate on the political situation beyond describing the activities of the People's Party and Nkrumah's vigorous program. The main part of his book would cover daily existence: the customs whose very antiquity explained their strangeness, the superstitions which were hardly any more irrational than the religion of the missionaries. As a reporter, he was content to expose his impressions by reorganizing his daily journal into a book that would be called "O, My People!" This, at least, is what he wrote Reynolds from Accra on August 25, 1953, but once he had left the country, he was able to express himself more freely, as in his letter of September 4:

I was shocked at what I found here, and yet I'm told that the Gold Coast is by far the best part of Africa. If that is so, then, I don't want to see the worst.

What is so sad about this is the African boys are neck deep in corruption, stealing, bribery, etc. When and if this experiment blows up, the world will say that Africans cannot rule themselves. . . . I could not write much to you from the Gold Coast, as letters are opened and read. It is the same in all hot countries; hot countries seem to be corrupt. But, unlike my experience in Argentina, I was my own boss here and went and got what I wanted.

Wright in fact worked on *Black Power* until the spring of 1954 in order to finish it before considering an offer from Doubleday to write the biography of Marian Anderson.[11] He allowed himself only enough time off to write two articles. In October, 1953, *Kiosk*, a small American magazine in Paris, published a few witty pages on cafés, in which Wright not only covered the infinite variety to be found in Paris but described how Americans behaved in France— their inhibitions and liberation, their fear of trying anything new —against the background of the French, who were unable to understand the problems of another civilization. "There's Always Another Café" could almost be called a piece of comparative cultural anthropology.

At Edward Aswell's request in March, 1954, Wright wrote an introduction to George Lamming's autobiography, *In the Castle of My Skin*. Wright found this "Black Boy" from Barbados a typical example of someone making the transition from an agrarian to an industrial civilization, a problem that never ceased to preoccupy him. The Western Black's historical mission, Wright thought, should be to attempt to lead many lives in one, to provide a link between the dying culture in which he was born and the still unreal society to which he was striving to belong. Lamming wrote about life in the tropical villages and described the native customs, somewhat as Wright was doing in his book on Africa, but even if the humorous and poetic prose, and the vivid personalities depicted in Lamming's book had not fascinated Wright, he would have welcomed the underlying message, which echoed his own quest and convictions:

I, too, have been long crying these stern tidings, and when I catch the echo of yet another voice declaiming in alien accents a description of this same reality, I react with pride and excitement, and I want to urge others to react to that voice. One feels not so alone, when, from a distant witness, supporting evidence comes to buttress one's own testimony.[12]

Meanwhile, Wright was busy organizing his report on Africa, anxious to stick as closely as possible to his original chronological narrative, consisting of numerous experiences relating to a few recurring themes, among them funeral rites, the talent and love for dancing and the scorn of the British. Each new piece of evidence would contribute to the gradual revelation of African life. Conversations and descriptions would be accompanied by the reflections and reactions which Wright had jotted down at the time, but since they were often reworked, later, he sometimes sacrificed the exotic flavor of an event in order to stress its significance. At this second stage he also added statistics and long quotations from the documents at his disposal, in order to substantiate the sociological, economic and historical premises of the book, which, despite everything, remained a travelogue, since its progression depended upon the experiences of exploration. The first version, 600 pages long, was finished by the New Year, and by January 21, 1954, Wright had reread and reduced it by forty pages. On February 21, Wright told Reynolds that the manuscript had been retyped. By March 2, when he sent the manuscript to America, the suggested titles were "Richard Wright in Africa" or "The White Man's Grave"; "Stranger in Africa," "A Journey in a Land of Pathos," and "What is Africa to Me?" had already been rejected. Wright also enclosed Nkrumah's original letter of introduction, which he thought might add something to the book.

This work represented both Wright's personal reaction to the land of his ancestors and a fairly unromantic picture of the evolving Gold Coast, an example in miniature of the overall development of the Third World, with its historical and human implications. From a country drained of its vital forces by colonization, spiritually weakened by Christianity and deprived of its tribal stability by industrialization and its attendant urbanization, Wright saw, or would like to have seen, a nation emerge. He points out the negative aspects of this process just as honestly as he portray the ravages of British exploitation and the scorn of its administrators.

Nevertheless, as an American and a Westerner, Wright had difficulty identifying with the African vision of the world. Having always rejected any exclusively racial definition, he had since his journey asked himself thousands of questions about his African heritage. That the trip was in large part a personal pilgrimage to his point of origin is evidenced by the line from Countee Cullen, which he quoted in full and considered for a time using as the title of the book. In hunting for the possibility of some "precise ancestral reality," he had, for the time being, assumed the existence of a shared identity between Africans and American Negroes, although he had always refused, as did sociologist E. Franklin Frazier, to consider the "African survivals" in Afro-American culture very significant. It was more an hypothesis, which when disproved, led him to exclaim in stupefaction: "I was black, they were black, but my color did not help me," a refrain denoting frustration, if not anxiety. Africa turned out to be a foreign country, whose customs, emotions and habits of thought disconcerted, even alienated him, and taught him that he was incurably American and Western. Blocked by the mistrust of the leaders of the People's Party on the one hand, and his own inability to appreciate the deep motivations of the tribal personality on the other, he was forced to identify either with the masses transplanted into the city, or even more, with the intellectual elite, torn between two worlds, both of which represented to Wright reflections of himself at different stages in his career.

The "new men" of the latter group, influenced by missionary ideologies to disown their primitive past, and shunned by the racism of the West, were thus torn between the two cultures to which they simultaneously belonged. In the disorientation accompanying liberation, Nkrumah embodied a transitional ideal, a kind of substitute mystique which could perhaps fill the emotional void and which was the basis for Wright's rather optimistic conclusion. Though underdeveloped, divided, bound by barbarian rites and riddled with corruption, the people still could and should unite behind the Prime Minister in a kind of permanent civil mobilization to lead the country toward a socialist nationalism. If regimented, these labile personalities would stabilize, and the economic and human resources thus mobilized would bring about the indispensable industrialization. Wright therefore advocated that the tribal system be completely abolished, along with the power of the chiefs and spirits, and the total triumph of the rational be accomplished. He was still so leery of the tainted gifts of neocolonialism that he urged Africa to accept from the West only the tools she needed, and then to adapt and change them so as not to find herself restricted by this technological and cultural loan.

Paul Reynolds was on the whole enthusiastic, but his reactions to certain points led Wright to eliminate several references to United States foreign policy, although he retained his penetrating analysis of how the African is treated in America in contrast with the prevailing attitude in France and England. Harper's considered the book too long and suggested cuts, but Wright, who lacked sufficient perspective, found it difficult to condense individual incidents. The alternative was to choose among them, perhaps keeping only one of the many descriptions of funerals, dances and markets. The repetitions, however, were essential, he explained to Reynolds on March 19.

By going from spot to spot, talking to this person and that one, I had to gather this reality as it seeped into me from the personalities of others. There might be some merit in that kind of getting and giving a reality, but it might bore the reader. Conrad wrote all of his novels in that roundabout way. It involves going back to some extent over ground already covered, but each going back reveals more and more of the things described.

Rather than artificially assemble in one section what he had slowly absorbed by osmosis, or what had only gradually become apparent to him, Wright eventually left the responsibility for the cuts to his editor, Frank McGregor, who sent him a list of changes at the beginning of April. He hastened to carry them out and, in addition, inserted a warning to the reader emphasizing his anti-Communist stand along with his Marxist perspective. In his concluding open letter to Nkrumah, he softened the words which might have given the impression that he was exhorting the Africans to use the weapons and methods of their oppressors.[13] He added a few pages to this section but cut the overall manuscript by one quarter, concentrating especially on the introductory chapters in which he had contrasted his initial expectations with what he eventually discovered to be true of Africa. By May 3, 1954, the first one hundred pages were down to thirty-nine, leaving only the episodes revealing his agnosticism. He condensed political analyses and conversations (particularly one with Mr. Hagerson, which he had originally recounted word for word), and eliminated most of his astonishment and exasperation with the oversuspicious Africans.[14] The manuscript that he finally sent back to Harper's was thus quite different, not only from his original notes, but even from the first version.

Meanwhile, Wright had selected a small number of photographs to accompany the text, but Harper's for some reason omitted them and the book was illustrated only with maps and two photographs of Nkrumah. Since they were also thinking of postponing the original October or November publication date, Wright made every effort to return the corrected manuscript before the deadline so that they would have no excuse to go back on their word.[15] Remaining problems included the risk of libel—incurred, for example, by Wright's unflattering picture of Judge Thomas—and the difficulty of finding a title. Wright had added to the original suggestions "This Heritage," "Black Brothers," "Dark Heritage," "Africa Turns Black," "Ancestral Land" and "Ancestral Home," all of which indicate his point of view, but he finally settled on *Black Power*, clearly meaning "political and state power," without racial implications.[16]

Wright had not received his usual author's copies, so it came as a surprise to read in the newspaper that *Black Power* had been published on September 22. The small, 4,000-copy advance was an omen of the poor sales, due mostly to the fact that the international situation had not yet led the American public to become interested in Africa, but also, it seems, to the hostility of certain magazines toward Wright. Neither *Time*, *Newsweek* nor the daily *Times* reviewed the book, and Michael Clark, writing for the Sunday *New York Times Book Review*, was scathing in his condemnation. Judging the book "more . . . a tract than . . . a considered study," he claimed, "[Wright's] caricature of British colonialism is drawn not from life but from the dreary old arsenal of Marxist slogans," and "nothing could be as grossly unfair as his strictures on the subject of Christian missionary endeavor," which only betrayed his "own hidden or sublimated desires for racial revenge." [17] In their eagerness to mitigate his attack on the colonial system, the magazine had even changed Wright's captions for the photographs he had obligingly lent them.

In the *Saturday Review* and the *Afro-American*, Jay Saunders Redding expressed irritation on another count, criticizing Wright's endless surprise at the customs of the black continent as well as his explanations of them. He was also alarmed by Wright's advice to militarize, and described the book as being as "extravagantly overgrown as one of Africa's own forests . . . much of it dark, strange, and impenetrable." [18] The *New Yorker* review of October 9, 1954, stressed how badly equipped Wright had been for the task, with his cumbersome Marxist and Freudian preconceptions, his ignorance of anthropology and his obsession with the slave trade, but concluded that he had, nevertheless, overcome these handicaps to produce a moving and significant book.

The majority of reviewers were actually quite complimentary. Walter White, in the *New York Herald Tribune Book Review*, called it "the most up to date, hopeful and valuable picture yet written of the most important experiment in democratic living which is taking place in Africa or anywhere else in the world." He had only two minor complaints—that Wright had neglected America's contribution to Nkrumah's political education, and had ignored the profound differences between the national and the tribal culture in his evaluation of the African personality.[19] The *Boston Globe*, the *Chicago Sunday Tribune*, the *Christian Science Monitor*, Henry F. Winslow in *Crisis* and Lewis Gannett in the daily *New York Herald Tribune*, all understood the scope of the book. Though the *New Republic* did not mention it, Joyce Cary, writing in *The Nation*, congratulated Wright for distinguishing so carefully between his personal opinions and the facts. "As reporting it is a first-class job and gives the best picture I've seen anywhere of an extraordinary situation." The review was so enthusiastic that the Book Find Club reprinted it in its monthly bulletin when *Black Power* was its October selection.[20]

Even before the publication of *Black Power* in Europe, various organizations and magazines showed interest in what Wright had to say about Africa. He first spoke on the subject to a group of foreign diplomats assembled at the International Quaker Center of Paris on April 12. Then, in September, *Encounter* published under the title "What Is Africa to Me?" passages from chapters one, seven, nine and ten of *Black Power*, chosen to highlight the cultural differences between the African and the black American. And finally, in November, *Preuves* published at John Fischer's request "Two African Portraits," an account of Wright's meeting with the Ashanti chief at the Padmore's, before he left for Africa in June, 1953, and his interview with Wallace Johnson in Freetown, both of which had been cut from the first section of the book.

The Stichting voor Culturelle Samenwerking (representing the

Congress for Cultural Freedom in Amsterdam) invited Wright to speak in mid-October. He traced the history of the liberation movement of what later became Ghana from the first meeting, in 1949, of the six founders of the Unified Convention—among them Nkrumah, Danquah and Gbedamah. For this talk Wright used the same technique borrowed from stage directions as he had for his accounts of the Joe Louis matches. The drama was set in western Africa; the period, mid-twentieth century; the cast, symbolic representatives of colonials and colonized.

At the reception following this much-appreciated talk, Wright met for the first time his translator Margrit de Sablonière, who had, the previous year, prevented Den Hollander, an editor with Sijthof Publishers, from cutting, without permission, twelve pages of *The Outsider* as an economy measure. The novel was published in its entirety, and since both author and translator found that they had in common their militant opposition to colonialism, their correspondence, thus begun, continued to flourish. Not only did Wright have such confidence in Margrit that he sold Sijthof the rights to *Black Power* only on the condition that she translate it, but this meeting was the beginning of a friendship which, several years later, developed into deep and mutual affection.

Wright was also asked to speak about the Gold Coast back in Paris, this time before an international audience of young people at the Cité Universitaire. Meanwhile, in September, 1954, Corréa had published *Puissance Noire* in France, where it was extremely well received. England reacted somewhat differently. Angus and Robertson had refused even to consider publishing the book, much to Wright's annoyance, since he had prided himself on the moderate tone of his attacks on British imperialism.[21] It was then offered to Dennis Dobson, via George Padmore, and accepted as the first volume of a larger work, later completed by volume two, *The Color Curtain*. In Germany, everyone predicted a great success, which, along with the favorable reaction of Europe in general, should have reassured Wright. Once again, however, he was more influenced by the initial response, which in this case consisted of the unfavorable, often hostile, remarks of the conformist American press. He was making a visible effort to suppress his bitterness in a letter to Reynolds on October 9, 1954: "So far as I am concerned, *Black Power* is in the past and I'm setting my eyes and mind on the Spanish job. . . . After the book on Spain, I hope to get down on some fiction."

SEVENTEEN

1

T HE "Spanish job" that was now taking up most of Wright's time and energy was not a frivolous undertaking, although it could easily be considered a diversion, or even a compensation for the unenthusiastic reception of *Black Power* in America. As one of the oldest nations of Europe, Spain seems at first glance an unlikely choice of subject matter for a writer who had recently turned away from the Old World in favor of burgeoning Africa, but in fact a great deal of time and research had gone into Wright's decision to visit the Iberian peninsula.

On May 24, 1954, Paul Reynolds had repeated his opinion that Wright had been absent too long to make present-day America the setting for a novel. He could just as well write about Americans in Paris, or perhaps use the South at the time of the Civil War for a setting.

Wright immediately rejected the second suggestion. Despite the recent court ruling to desegregate the schools, which he had greeted with enthusiasm, he did not think that the racial situation in America had changed sufficiently to inspire him with anything very new. He had once considered a brief crime story set in Paris, but this no longer interested him. Reporting on another African nation was now much more to his taste than writing a novel anyway, and he was tempted to visit French-speaking Africa, where he would run into less distrust and could observe less advanced industrialization than on the Gold Coast. He even thought of going to Madagascar, Egypt or India, since he would not be allowed to visit the Soviet Union. In other words, he was anxious to stick to nonfiction, as he finally admitted to Reynolds on May 30, 1954.

I'm inclined to feel that I ought not to work right now on a novel. This does not mean that I'm giving up writing fiction, but, really, there are so many more exciting and interesting things happening now in the world that I feel sort of dodging them if I don't say something about them.

407

Would Wright's political, racial or ideological commitment to promote humanism in promoting the Third World in fact end his
career as a novelist? His voyage to Africa had certainly shown him
the necessity of writing about the advent of the black nations and
the failure of the West, but this was no different as a cause from
what he used to consider his duty as a Communist writer. Rather,
by using his faithful "words as weapons"—Mencken's advice to
writers—he had reached the limit of the novel's usefulness. In this
light, a long theoretical essay might well have presented the dilemma
of the "marginal man" better than *The Outsider* did, but at that
time Wright had been grappling with a personal conflict which
had to be resolved in a novel, whose composition had a therapeutic
effect that the writing of an essay or a story had not. By 1954,
however, Wright was psychologically liberated. To reach the widest
possible public, by the most direct route, he now returned to journalism and lecturing as the mediums best suited to expressing his
opinions. He was, significantly, attracted only to countries in transformation, either "falling to pieces or trying to build themselves
up." Alva Myrdal had suggested Sweden to him, but in the same
letter to Reynolds he described it as "over-civilized, quiet, with no
class or racial problems, with a high rate of neurosis, insanity,
alcoholism."

In any case, he and Reynolds agreed that the next book would
be a report, not a novel, and Reynolds advised him to present
Harper's with a carefully planned outline. Once again Wright cast
his eyes around the globe. Some of his friends suggested the newly
formed State of Israel, but he had mixed feelings on the subject,
as he confided to Reynolds on June 30, 1954.

I know that a lot of building, etc., is going on. I know also that
the Jews have suffered horribly in Europe. And I know that they
consider that this is their homeland. But their claim to this seems
kind of special. It would be like my claiming Africa for the
AMERICAN Negroes. I just don't believe in that kind of claim. I
may be wrong. Then there is the problem of the Arabs, to whom
the Jews are as heartless as Hitler was to them.

As for Africa, Wright was afraid that he would have trouble entering the Belgian Congo, and before setting off to visit the French-
speaking countries or the Cameroons, he wanted to know how
Black Power would be received. Yugoslavia would present no prob-

lems, since Americans were welcomed, but he questioned how much general interest there was in such a country. Just as Nazism made him loath to consider Germany, his disapproval of Franco had so far prevented him from following Gertrude Stein's last words of advice to go to Spain. Nevertheless, he had always been haunted by her spiritual legacy. The material would certainly be colorful and rich in significance, and the black market, the secret police, the religious ceremonies, the corridas, resistance movements, the Civil War and the vestiges of the Inquisition were all subjects of natural interest to Wright. On the practical side, too, it would be convenient. He was somewhat familiar with the language after his visits to Mexico and Argentina, the cost of living was low and a visa easy to obtain. Spain, then, may not have been an ideal choice, but it was the best of the options at the time.[1]

Reynolds had no sooner obtained a verbal agreement from Harper's than Wright started to prepare for his trip. He decided to make a preliminary visit of several weeks to confirm that there was material for an original and richly documented book, so with his $500 advance, he left for Spain on August 15, 1954.

He drove the Citroën himself, crossing the border from Perthus into Catalonia to spend six days in Barcelona, where his warm reception bridged the language gap to a certain extent. Two young people who spoke French took him to visit the cathedral and found him a pension, where he met Carmen, a young girl studying to be a social worker. She told him at length about her life and her religious beliefs, and provided him with a copy of the "little green book"—the political bible of the Falange—from which the quotations woven throughout *Pagan Spain* were taken.[2] For Wright, Barcelona meant Las Ramblas and La Plaza de Cataluña as well as the slums, where, accompanied by his new young friends Miguel and André, he spoke with prostitutes and bought from them letters which they had received from American sailors.[3] Wright then went with Carmen's brother Carlos to Valencia, where he was able to study the political situation in detail, finding out about the methods and abuses of the regime. He himself had to pay a fine because a boy washed his car in public without complying with the law requiring that he ask the owner's permission. Pardo L., a Vatican translator, took him to the famous monastery of Montserrat, whose site later inspired Wright to attribute the presence of the Christian sanctuary to a primitive sexual cult.

Moving in with a middle-class family enabled him to observe the scars that the Civil War had left on individual Spaniards, such as Lola, who had become insane after witnessing the execution of her father by the Republicans.

On August 22, after André's family had entertained him for lunch, they took him to a large corrida, with Chamaco as matador. By the time he left for Madrid, he had more than fifty pages of first impressions which he later used as a basis for characterizing all of Spanish life.

Wright stopped to visit Saragossa before going on to spend the night at Guadalajara, a town of 20,000 inhabitants at the foot of the sierras. It was only an hour's drive to Madrid the next day, where he stayed in a small pension. He immediately made friends with the young American torero, Harry Whitney, who took him along with several Spanish matadors to Morata de Tajuna, where he not only witnessed several bulls put to death, but also learned about the training of the toreros and the technique and rules of the corrida.

After a sight-seeing tour of the capital and a long visit to the Prado museum, Wright spoke at length with a number of Spanish intellectuals: the Marquis of Valdegleisias; Don Mariano de Urguiz, the director of tourism; a well-known journalist; a young man who, reassured by an American friend from the British-American Club, confided to Wright all his thoughts on Catholicism; a New York architect who wanted to help Spain by Americanizing it; a doctor; a businesswoman who had become a naturalized citizen after her marriage; and a Jewish businessman. These were largely chance encounters and thus, because of the wide range of social backgrounds, beliefs, and political opinions, provided a good sampling of the diverse reactions to Franco's regime.

On Sunday, August 29, Wright left for Cordoba in a pouring rain. He arrived in time to observe Mass at the Church of Santo Dominigo d'Ocaña, where he was struck by the contrast between its sumptuous decor and the obvious poverty of the congregation. He quickly crossed the plain of La Mancha, through Madridejos, Puerto-Lapiche, Manzanares and Valdepeñas, but spent so few days around Cordoba, Grenada and Málaga that his impressions were superficial compared with those of his second trip, when he gathered the material which appeared in the book. He spent more time in Seville, making the rounds of the nightclubs and observing prostitution and the white slave trade like a professional investigator. He was back in Madrid by September 5, but only stayed five more days, pursuing some of his conversations with his varied acquaintances in Spanish society.

Wright was convinced, after covering close to 4,000 miles in three weeks and taking 150 pages of notes, that he had enough material for an original study. He intended to organize the book by subject (the corrida, the black market, etc.) and the detailed outline he sent to Harper's indicated that he was mostly interested in describing the opinions of the people and the Spanish temperament. The political situation would merely serve as a backdrop for what was primitive, irrational and mystical (what he eventually termed "pagan") in the Spanish soul. His letter of September 19 to Reynolds, stating that he would show "how a non-western people living in Europe work out their life problems," reveals that he had already established such a hypothesis to characterize the relationship of Spain to the rest of Western Europe. This paradoxical definition was perhaps not totally incorrect, but it is a little surprising to find Wright formulating it after only three weeks, and after very little reading on the subject, particularly when one compares this with the amount of research he had done prior to going to Africa and writing *Black Power*. It seems very much as if he had begun, not with a theory to test, but with a hypothesis that he was determined to verify by selecting only those features of the civilization which substantiated his point of view.

Wright returned to Paris estimating that he needed several more months to know Spain in depth. Luckily, some American friends had obtained official permission for him to investigate whatever interested him, in complete freedom, and since he had been exhausted by driving on the terrible roads, he promised himself a chauffeur on the next trip. In the meantime he accompanied his friend Gunnar Myrdal, who was passing through Paris, back to Geneva in order to get up-to-date information on the development of Spain's economy from the United Nations Library. He spent most of his time reading, consulting nineteenth-century travelogues and historical studies and, in particular, Americo Castro's *Structure of Spanish History*, which he ordered from the United States. He also worked on his Spanish so as to leave as little as possible to chance.

Since he planned to visit the provinces in the Southwest before settling down in Madrid as his base of operations for several months, Wright crossed the frontier at Irun on November 8, heading for San Sebastian and Azpeitia, where he visited the house and sanctuary of Saint Ignatius Loyola, the founder of the Jesuits. Heavy rains had cut off the electricity, but he was shown the holy relics by flashlight; later, in writing the book, he used this episode to express once again his amazement at the strength of superstition and the close link between Church and State. He quickly passed through Galicia and Asturias to reach Madrid via Burgos and Avila. On this trip, he had more time to spend and not only spoke with many members of the aristocracy and the middle class, but also to some opponents of Franco. In addition, he collected a great deal of information about the persecution of the Protestants, although only a small part of this appeared in *Pagan Spain*. By December 5, he had more than 500 pages of notes, or about half the documentation he required. He was still planning to organize the book by themes, fitting in general observations on Spain and its history between the conversations and long passages of straight reporting.

Wright wanted to celebrate Christmas with his family, as well as settle some pressing business affairs, so he returned to Paris on December 17, crossing the frontier at Behobia. He was at the time deciding whether to buy a small farm which he and Ellen had found that autumn in the village of Ailly, near the town of Gaillon-sur-Eure. They had already spent several weekends at a country house that their friends the Bokanowskis owned at Croisilles, in Normandy, and had been so taken by the area that they wanted a place of their own where they could spend vacations and Wright could work in peace and quiet. The purchase of the farm was quickly concluded, but getting from the various workmen estimates for the repairs, and the constant supervision needed to get the work well under way, were more time-consuming than Wright had planned.[4]

Meanwhile, an international conference to be held in mid-April in Bandung, Indonesia, by the free countries of the Third World was announced at the beginning of January, 1955. Since Wright immediately decided to attend it, preparations for the trip took up still more of his time, and it was already February 20 by the time he headed directly back to Madrid, intending to make the most of his remaining days there before setting off for the Bandung

Conference. He stayed in Madrid until March 2, spending a long time at Toledo, which he described later in his book as "a vast museum crammed with the past of Spain." On March 3, he visited the cathedral in Saragossa, which he had not seen on his first trip, and the next day he reached Barcelona, where he stayed for ten days. The famous Festival of the Fallas was held in Valencia from March 15–19 and Wright was able to follow the entire celebration, from the preparation of the floats and fireworks up to the burning of the enormous cardboard figures which had been part of the interminable procession. Unfortunately, his colorful description of this week was eventually omitted from *Pagan Spain*. He then headed south, arriving in Granada on March 20 and setting off from Algeciras for Spanish Morocco on the 22nd. He spent a day in Tangier and the next morning went to Gibraltar, where he was surprised to see the Spanish employees on the British base concealing contraband provisions in their clothing before going home for the day. Returning to Granada, Wright spent a few more days there and then went to Seville for Holy Week. The city was mobbed with tourists, so he returned to the pension he had found the previous summer, run by four women whose pious airs belied their libertine behavior. He also saw a one-armed friend who had taken him around to see flamenco dancers in the nightclubs, but this time he was more interested in relics, the Santa Maria de la Sede cathedral, the penitents in the streets and, above all, the procession on Holy Friday, which he watched for hours. This third visit to Seville added enough significant material to his impressions of Montserrat and Azpeitia for Wright to conclude that in Spain religion was based upon sexuality, superstition and paganism.

For various reasons, Wright did not have an extended period of time to work on this book for almost a year, but since his notes were abundant, the different chapters of his journal easy to regroup by themes, and clear guidelines provided by his firm convictions about current life in Spain, it did not take him very long once he got started in February, 1956. By March 12, his typed manuscript was 537 pages long. *Pagan Spain: A Report of a Journey into the Past* (the title chosen to parallel *Black Power: A Record of Reactions in a Land of Pathos*, and *Black Boy: A Record of Childhood and Youth*) was divided into five parts: "Life After Death," "Death and Exaltation," "The Underground Christ," "Sex, Flamenco and Prostitution," and "The World of Pagan

Power." Wright deliberately omitted the subjects of gypsies and of Republicans in exile; there was nothing he could use about the picturesque qualities of flamenco, and the Civil War was only one page of history among many others. The study only concentrated on what interested Wright personally: the relationship between superstition and faith, and instinct and spirituality, in this Catholic universe tyrannized over by a religion whose roots were buried so deep in sexuality and the subconscious that he considered himself justified in speaking of a "pagan" Spain. In criticizing the political regime, the Falange and the Catholic Church, Wright knew that he was exposing himself to numerous attacks, but he was counting on support from the American Protestant public, since the book was in a broad sense "pro-Protestant." With the manuscript, which he sent to Reynolds on April 1, 1956, he included photographs of bullfights, the Holy Week processions and the Festival of the Fallas to illustrate his argument.[5]

On May 14, he received a response from Harper's, where his new editor, Mr. Appleton, was only partially satisfied. Although Wright agreed once again to make the suggested changes, he was prey to a growing uneasiness in working with editors who did not trust him, and who wanted his manuscripts reworked to such an extent. Mr. Appleton agreed to the title, but wanted him to make some extensive cuts in the section describing his first stay in Barcelona; to reduce the long chapter on Protestantism by half; to eliminate the Festival of the Fallas altogether, and parts of the colorful chapters on Granada and Seville which also developed the themes of prostitution and poverty; and to shorten several pages on Madrid, including a story about the pirated Spanish edition of *Black Boy*. The book may have gained a little in being concise but it lost a great deal in local color, while the criticism of Franco's anti-Protestant policy was considerably weakened. Wright sent back this final version at the end of July, 1956, and offered the 150 pages he had cut to several magazines.

Pagan Spain did not come out until February, 1957, and despite the fairly encouraging reception by the critics, it was a commercial failure; only 3,000 copies had been advanced and by March 14, Harper's had sold only an additional 500. By that time, perhaps, Spain was not in fashion, and the American public probably did not think that a black man without religion had the right to dissect and judge the decadence of a white Christian nation, particularly one that was considered "friendly" by the U.S. government. This, in any case, was the almost unanimous reaction of the Catholic press and, somewhat surprisingly, certain of the Protestant daily papers. Even the Marxist Elmer Bendiner, writing in the April 1, 1957, *National Guardian*, regretted not only that Wright never mentioned the political protests against the regime which exploded periodically in Barcelona, but also that he made such an issue of sexual symbols that his description of the procession on Holy Friday had been spoiled.

On the whole, however, the critics were not hostile. Herbert L. Matthews set the tone in *The New York Times Book Review* on February 24, 1957, commending Wright's insight into the ritual and emotions of the corrida, and praising his great talent for portraying a country, unusual in tourists and journalists alike. Thomas Bergin, in the *Saturday Review*, stressed as strong points of the book Wright's deep sympathy for the oppressed, his brilliant analysis of the unconscious sources of religion and the mystical rhetoric of fascism.[6] Wright was most frequently criticized for his paradoxical attempt to make a pagan nation out of such a blatantly Christian one, and for his tendency to see phallic symbols even in the candles and rocks at Montserrat. Certain inaccuracies were also pounced upon, with some justification since he confused La Junquera with Perthus, which he put in Spain, and he placed El Greco in the Middle Ages. In addition, some people felt that he used too many quotations from "the little green book," *Formacion politica para Los Flechas*, and that it was evident that he had only stayed a few weeks in a country where he was unfamiliar with the language. Once again, Wright came to regret the cuts that John Fischer had required. Certainly the scenes in Granada and Seville, and the Festival of the Fallas would have proven the extent of his travels as well as his careful documentation, although they added nothing essential to his analysis. In any case, *Pagan Spain* represents a fascinating document on Wright himself as well as a nuanced report on Spain, and although its form limited it to the category of merely good journalism, the account of the corrida could be favorably compared with Hemingway descriptions, and the use of a psychoanalytical perspective for the anthropological passages of the study shed a new, almost sensational, light on Spanish civilization and culture.

In addition, the book was very good reading and those who knew

Spain at that time can testify that it was more exact and subtle than anything else available on the subject. Nevertheless, Wright's method, which was so successful for *Black Power*, where he stressed the strangeness of the African world and the excitement of watching a nation emerge, was not sufficient for an ancient country like Spain. To concentrate on the pagan roots of its mysticism and the depressing sight of its decay was to overlook the richness of its history and the resulting complexity of its present contradictions. Thus, Gunnar Myrdal was not being too severe when he wrote his friend on April 16, 1957, that *Pagan Spain* was "only a preamble to the serious, penetrating and revealing analysis of the country which [he] ought someday to write."

2

When Wright left Madrid in April, 1955, he was headed for what was to be the first meeting of black leaders to which the West would not be invited. His report, therefore, would fall naturally into line with *Black Power* and would, in fact, be a continuation of it. On January 4, 1955, he had submitted this idea to Reynolds, asking him to look around for the necessary financial backing from some large American foundation. He planned to write on the problems brought out in the conference and describe the outstanding personalities who would be present, emphasizing the attitude of the Third World toward the West in both interracial and international relations. He soon discovered that no help was forthcoming from American organizations, so he set about raising the necessary funds himself. He had no luck with several large European magazines and newspapers, but he finally got an encouraging response from the Paris office of the Congress for Cultural Freedom. This organization had been founded in 1950 at an international meeting of intellectuals, mostly liberals, held in Berlin, and boasted members like Theodore Heuss, Salvador de Madariaga, Léopold Senghor, Reinhold Niebuhr and Jacques Maritain. Nicholas Nabokov was the secretary general and Denis de Rougemont president of the executive committee. The Congress had organized some important round-table discussions, one of which had been held in Paris in 1950 on "The Work of the 20th Century," and was attended by William Faulkner, André Malraux, and W. H. Auden. Many of Wright's friends and acquaintances from the non-Communist Left, such as Hannah Arendt, David Rousset, John Dos Passos, Richard Crossman, John Strachey, Ignazio Silone, Arthur Koestler, Thomas Diop and Gunnar Myrdal, supported these events "in the defense of culture." Presumably as part of a campaign against the anti-Communist hysteria, the Congress had just financed the publication of *McCarthy and the Communists* by James Rorty and Moshe Decter, so it was clear that Wright's sympathies corresponded to a large extent to the declared aims of the organization:

To resist the temptations of intellectual apathy, to denounce tyranny and come to the aid of its victims . . . to organize a permanent confrontation with the problems which freedom is posing in such new and diverse terms.

Freedom is not only threatened by totalitarianism. It can also be compromised by material progress itself, which, though liberating in theory, is often spread as a result of national, ideological or private ambitions which interfere where there is anarchy regardless of existing traditions, and without the regulating force of wisdom.[7]

Wright probably saw in this a condemnation of colonialism and capitalist imperialism, as well as of the Stalinist dictatorships. Although the discovery that the organization was indirectly financed by the CIA as a means of combating Communist propaganda from the liberal Left was not made until some years later, most of the great names associated with the Congress were unaware of this at the time. Without worrying unduly about who was sponsoring the organization, Wright made sure to establish his terms in advance and communicated them to Reynolds on February 4, 1955. In order to ensure that his statements on colonialism and the Third World would in no way be controlled or censured, he would attend the conference as an independent journalist. The Congress would have the option to use any of Wright's articles in its various publications, and, in return, he would receive $500 in addition to travel expenses and retain the right to publish his entire report as a book at a later date.

After securing a visa for Indonesia, Wright immediately began to do some preliminary research on the conference and the country he would be visiting so that he would be prepared to interpret the events and reactions he would encounter. He read some books on East-West relations and used a series of prepared questions to interview a number of Dutch, Asians and Indonesians. Meanwhile, his recent contacts with the Congress led him to attend the Tuesday gatherings of its French magazine, *Preuves*. There he spoke about *Black Power* at the center for Les Amis de la Liberté, where Sidney Hook, Henry Poulaille, Thierry Maulnier and General Béthouart had also lectured, mostly on decolonization and European unity. All these activities were so time-consuming that Wright decided not to return to Paris from Spain before leaving for Djakarta.

On April 10, Wright flew from Madrid to Rome. There he caught a KLM flight for Cairo on which he encountered a group of French journalists (among them Jean Lacouture) also headed for the Bandung Conference. On April 12 he arrived in Djakarta, far from the traditions and history of the Spain he had just left. He enthusiastically proceeded to register his impressions and collect information on Indonesia; he already had certain theories about what might happen at the conference—his main prejudice, he admitted, was that he was favorably disposed toward what he would discover in this newly independent Third World nation—but this time he had no desire to go ahead before comparing his opinions with the facts.

The flags of the twenty-nine participating nations were flying at the airport where Wright received his press card and was met by Mochtar Lubis, who rapidly got his guest through customs before taking him home to Tugu, situated on the cool hills a few miles outside the city. Lubis was a young journalist, painter and novelist, but best known as editor of the *Indonesia Raya*, a socialist publication hostile to the domestic policy of President Sukarno and to the conference itself, which was considered a diversionary tactic on the part of a government unable at that time even to maintain order within the country.

Over the weekend, the P.E.N. Club invited Wright to discuss Afro-American literature with the members of a cultural circle presided over by Takdir Alisjabana. Himself a poet and a novelist, Alisjabana had founded the magazine *New Poet* in 1913, and had since made his name as a philosopher and professor at the University of Indonesia. He owned some bungalows near the Puntjak

With Mochtar Lubis in Indonesia. *Photo by Muller, Djakarta*

Pass where several times a year he liked to gather artists and intel-·
lectuals for long discussions followed by a feast of roast kid. Among
the many young Indonesian intellectuals Wright met there were the
critic H. B. Jassin, the essayist Asrul Sani, the Eurasian journalist
Beb Vuyk, the poetess Siti Nuriani, and the novelists Trino Su-
mardjo and Baruki Resabowo.

When he moved into Djakarta proper, Wright stayed with an
Indonesian engineer who was an ardent nationalist and partisan
of industrialization and modernism from whom he was able to learn
a great deal; during that time he met, among others, J. H. Ritman,
the Dutch editor of *Nieuwsgier*; Sutan Sjahrir, the former Socialist
prime minister and specialist on international affairs; and, via Lubis,
Dr. Mohammed Natsir, who favored the foundation of a Muslim
state. These varied contacts enabled Wright to collect opposing and
complementary viewpoints on the domestic situation.

Meanwhile, Wright found that many aspects of Indonesian life,
such as the lack of comfort, antiquated equipment, ignorance of
administrative techniques, and delayed industrialization, resembled
life in Africa. But in a country not divided by tribalism, nor held
back by an ancestral religion, these deficiencies could only be attributed to Dutch colonialism, whose sole aim had been to create
obedient servants. Eloquent proof of this was brought to Wright's
attention by *Bahasia Indonesia*, an elementary Malay grammar,
published in 1949, in which all the examples of dialogue were designed to teach what a master might require his help to say.

Bandung was in the mountains, some distance from the humid
climate of the capital, and Wright took a room there in the Hotel

Van Hengel from April 17–25. The opening session of the conference, to which Wright was officially invited, took place on April
18. In addition to the French journalists he had met on the plane,
he now got to know the teams from all the other countries represented. Among the Americans were his friend Ruth Fischer, the
Unitarian minister Homer P. Jack and Marguerite Cartwright. He
saw the delegates themselves only from afar, but he listened in-
tently to what they said in order to make sure he caught the full
implications of their words and the strength of their arguments. In
his report he mentioned by name U Nu, Achmed Sukarno, Ali
Sastroamidjojo, Norodom Sihanouk, Gamal Abdel Nasser, Kojo
Botsio, Prince Wan of Thailand, Sir John Kotelawala, Sami So,
Takasaki, Carlos Romulo, and El Jamali, but he analyzed in greater
detail the statements of Chou En-lai and Jawaharlal Nehru, the
only leader with whom he spoke at length in person. He had never
intended to report everything that was said, but rather to restrict
himself to his own impressions and reactions, while attempting to
extract the recurring themes of race, religion and color which later
made up the three main chapters of his report.

Wright stayed on after the conference until May 5, to familiarize
himself further with the country before embarking upon the *Willem
Ruys*, which was bound for Naples. After a stop at Colombo,
Ceylon, on May 10, Wright left the boat in Africa on May 20
and flew from Nairobi to Paris via Rome. Throughout the trip he
was busy reorganizing and clarifying his two hundred pages of notes
in order to get a first version of his manuscript off to Reynolds as
soon as possible. He continued writing when he reached Paris, and
was finished by the end of June.[8] Then, in July, *Preuves* published
"Vers Bandung via Séville," the story of Wright's last few days in
Spain and arrival in Indonesia, which was reprinted in the November issue of *Cuadernos*. *Encounter* bought the rights to "Indonesian
Notebook," which concentrated mostly on Wright's impressions of
the country's economic status as it emerged from Dutch domination.
In August, *Preuves* published "Le congrès des hommes de couleur,"
an account of the conference itself, and in September, "Le monde
occidental à Bandung," Wright's attack on colonialism, which ended
with a vibrant appeal to the conscience of the Western world.

Wright was finally free to relax a little, and accordingly spent
July–October, 1955, with his family at Ailly. The major repairs

had been completed and the little farm began to serve as a pleasant retreat. There was now a large sitting room where the cow shed had been, the loft had been converted into two bedrooms and, next to them, Richard had made himself a study whose walls were covered with maps and whose bookcases were well stocked, where he could read in comfort on his sofa. Rustic furniture had been bought to go with the brick floors, white walls and beamed ceilings of the house, but the minor details of moving in still required a great deal of time, as did the clearing of the garden and its landscaping. Richard had planned to spend the mornings writing up his notes on Spain, and the afternoons on these agreeable chores, but other worries soon cropped up to distract him.

Reynolds, with high hopes for the Bandung manuscript, had sent it on to Harper's. It met with an unexpected rejection there, but William Targ, whom Wright had known since his Chicago days, agreed to publish it with World. Edward Aswell, meanwhile, had left Harper's to become editor-in-chief at McGraw-Hill and wrote Richard, soon after Targ made his offer, to welcome him to his new company. Wright, of course, had no intention of deserting Aswell, who had always been a shrewd editor as well as a devoted friend. This meant that it was important not to give World an option on his future work. He naturally thought that this would ruin any chance of their publishing the book, which he was no longer free to offer to McGraw-Hill. But he was anxious that these personal complications should not delay its publication, since, aside from any financial considerations of his own, he felt that the American public should know as soon as possible what the first meeting of the Third World leaders, organized almost against the will of the West, really meant:

I've no illusions about how people in America feel about straight reporting like this. But I just can't whitewash the Western world when the whole issue about that world is the role it has played during the past 500 years. So you are going to have trouble with this book. . . . The world's press sabotaged Bandung and did not give the full picture.[9]

At lunch on August 10, therefore, he asked his friend Gunnar Myrdal to write a brief preface that might help him place the book elsewhere, only to hear soon afterward from Targ that World had agreed to publish it without the option; Wright then accepted a low,

$500 advance in order that his warning to the West might be heard in time.[10]

In fact, the relationship of Western civilization to the Third World had now replaced the relationship between black and white Americans in Wright's priorities. This is apparent in his statement to the French press that the recent acquittal by a Mississippi court of the murderers of Emmett Till was a "parody of justice" which, he claimed, would ultimately be a defeat for white civilization as a whole, since the Third World peoples would express their disapproval, not only of the United States but of the entire West, as a result of this incident.[11]

Because the American proofs of *The Color Curtain* were not ready in time, Calman-Lévy came out first with the French translation, a hasty and awkward job entitled *Bandoeng: 1,500,000,000 hommes*, which was nonetheless, enthusiastically welcomed by the Paris papers in December, 1955.

The Color Curtain: A Report on the Bandung Conference was published in the United States on March 19, 1956. Wright distrusted the American critics and the opinions of some of his black compatriots of the Third World so much since the publication of *Black Power* that he suggested to his editor, Donald Friede, on September 25, that "no galleys be sent to James Baldwin, Ralph Ellison or Horace Cayton, etc., these people [being] not independent enough to give their honest reaction to a book like *The Color Curtain*." But as if to show how excessive this caution had been, the book was much better received than its predecessor.

Wright began his study with a presentation of the information he had gathered between January, 1955, and the beginning of the conference in April, through the use of a questionnaire prepared for him by the sociologist Otto Klineberg, but his actual account of his stay in Djarkarta was much more impressive and far transcended the level of competent journalism. He evoked a complete atmosphere and state of mind, a mixture of racial pride, distrust (of the West) and hope; in both his report on the conference and the journal of his stay, Wright singled out race as the determining factor in the emotional reactions and political choices of the Third World. Europe and America had for centuries equated their economic and political supremacy over the colonies with racial superiority; the result was that now these newly independent nations were united by common resentment and ambition to regenerate themselves by the industrialization of their destroyed civilizations. The aim of the

The farm at Ailly.
Photo by Richard Wright

Ellen, Julia and Rachel at Ailly

conference was thus to define the cultural, political and economic themes which were common to this reconstruction and which would eventually free the Third World from economic neocolonialism. Perhaps because the West, following the example of John Foster Dulles, had neglected the importance of this meeting, Wright was more anxious to stress the common ideals of the participants than their differences. The final motion of the conference in essence offered the West one last chance. While proclaiming their pride in having liberated themselves, half a billion human beings were asking their former masters to forswear their imperialist and racist habits, (in Africa especially) and help them to industrialize. In *Black Power* Wright had advised Nkrumah to beware of Western aid, but here, in *The Color Curtain*, he closes with an appeal for it. The task was enormous, he warned, and the risk of disaster—when the religious, racial and emotional forces of these nations were finally liberated—was very high. Chou En-lai was waiting in the wings for the situation to become ripe for communism, and if the Western powers did not heed this final message addressed to its moral conscience by Asia, their refusal would sound their own death knell. But Wright was still hopeful that the West might help and that Bandung might be counted less as Red China's first victory than as the final round won by the countries who had signed the Colombo Pact.

The reviews of the book in the American papers were for the most part written by specialists or by people who had attended the conference and who therefore brought to their judgments some background knowledge. Tillman Durdin, in the March 18, 1956, *New York Times Book Review*, praised everything except Wright's tendency to exaggerate the racial and religious unity of the Third World and the importance of China. But he summed up:

In his concluding chapter, however, Mr. Wright poses correctly the crucial question highlighted at Bandung. He asks whether the sensitive and resentful people represented there are to be brought out of their present state of poverty, ignorance and economic backwardness under the aegis of a bloody Communist totalitarianism or through wise and generous aid from the West that will link them with our freer democratic system.

Homer Jack, writing in the *Saturday Review,* called Wright's analysis an "important contribution" to understanding the confer-

ence.[12] Political magazines such as *The Nation*, *The Progressive* and
The New Leader, as well as the black press and the large daily
papers, devoted entire pages to the book without making any serious
criticisms, while the Communists no longer seemed to despise the
very sound of Wright's name. Abner Berry wrote a fair article for
the *Daily Worker*, and Eugene Gordon was mostly troubled by a
certain confusion between the mysticism of color and economic realities. One of the few unfavorable reactions, which in fact pertained
only to the extracts published in *Encounter*, came, ironically enough,
from Wright's erstwhile host, Mochtar Lubis, who complained of
his "racial" point of view:

The majority of the people with whom Mr. Wright came into contact in Indonesia (one of the best-known Indonesian novelists and
others) belong to the new generation and are the least racial and
colour-conscious of the various groups in Indonesia. They are all
amazed to read Mr. Wright's notebooks in which Mr. Wright
quotes them saying things which they never said or to which they
did not put meaning as accepted by Mr. Wright.

"No," Wright replied equably, but with decision, "I did not see
Indonesia through 'colored' glasses nor did I feel it with a 'religious'
skin. For the three weeks I stayed in Jakarta and Bandung, all the
talk I heard was of race and religion. . . . To me this seemed
natural and inevitable." [13]

EIGHTEEN

1

"I FEEL that the time has come when I need a new publisher," Wright had confided to Reynolds from Indonesia on May 14, 1955, "and I'm most definitely of the opinion that I do not wish to go to World, not unless all other publishing houses are of a mind to reject my work."

In planning to follow Edward Aswell and thus sever his connection with Harper's, where John Fischer and Mr. Appleton seemed as little satisfied with what he wrote as he with their suggestions, Wright was running a certain risk. After Harper's rejection of *The Color Curtain*, Wright had felt obliged to accept the offer from World in the interests of having the book published as soon as possible. William Targ had been relatively accommodating in not requiring the customary option, but soon Donald Friede began to pressure Wright for a definite commitment on his next novel, while by this time, Aswell was no longer able to promise Wright a contract for future fiction because McGraw-Hill did not as a rule publish novels. Aswell, however, perhaps sensing that he would not remain long with McGraw-Hill, asked Wright to take a chance, and to draw up a plan, defining his fiction works for the years to come with the idea of obtaining a long range contract with yet another publisher. The regular advances he would receive in this way would replace the royalty payments from *Black Boy* which were due to end in February, 1957.

On August 21, 1955, the very day on which the sinking of a well was disturbing the habitual quiet of Ailly, Wright set to work elaborating such a plan in the course of a long letter to Aswell. It was not, in fact, an altogether new idea. Wright had let it be understood that someday he would gather a group of novels, both published and as yet unwritten, into a "magnum opus"; as early as 1941 he had

426

envisaged *Twelve Million Black Voices* as the conceptual framework for a kind of *Human Comedy* that would trace the evolution of the Blacks in America, which typified in his eyes the transition from the rigid structure of the rural and feudal world to the individualistic freedom of life in the large industrial centers. In 1945, his outline for "Voyage" further explained the psychological and personal aspects of this major theme, and ten years later, he proceeded to fill out and organize the same ideas and subjects under the general title "Celebration." In this long letter he first sketched his own philosophical and ideological evolution since his break with the Party, and then defined the essential aim of his work and the major preoccupation of his own quest, which would be to examine the individual's relationship to modern society, characterized as it was by a high rate of material progress without a corresponding spiritual and moral growth. This humanist point of view may not be original, but Wright was in effect anticipating the importance of this crucial relationship in the thought of a good number of social philosophers today.

The novels included in this series would deal systematically with the same theme that Wright had already used in his previous work: the individual's insertion into society and the conflicts resulting from it. Perhaps because *The Outsider* had been considered too didactic, Wright decided to present his point of view indirectly. Borrowing from Dos Passos his method of impersonal commentary, Wright would not resort to changes in perspective, but would create an atmosphere or a mood that would convey the positive values of life. This mood, sometimes expressed in free verse, sometimes in poetic prose, would glorify all the experiences that contribute to the blossoming of the vital elements of a being, not only of human or animal beings, but of any living organism. On this point Wright was certainly as indebted to Wilhelm Reich's orgone theory as to Walt Whitman's poetic and philosophical vision. On July 27, 1955, Wright had written to Reynolds, although he did not send the letter until October, explaining this idea.

The work I have in mind is a series of novels tied together, not as in the usual case, by plot, but by an attitude . . . under a common heading of searching for the highest and most intense moments in people's lives, moments that show the individual in violent conflict with his environment. . . . The central idea of this work would be a depiction or a dramatization of what, for the want of a better name, I'd call the "life force" at its highest expression in each life touched upon. . . . The nearest analogy I have in mind is the work of Walt Whitman; a kind of free verse would introduce each incident, story or novel.

Wright then included a long passage of free verse reminiscent of Whitman, followed by a few pages of poetic prose, suggesting the blossoming of vegetable life, the transition to the animal kingdom, and finally the advent of man in this evolutionistic incarnation of the Spirit.

For the fullness of time is every day and every hour; and of time
    I sing, time that seeks fulfillment.
And yet no song am I; my music is unheard; there is no pulse that
    can feel my rhythms;
And yet nearer to music am I than to anything amidst the millions
    of whirling suns;
And no flesh am I, and no blood;
And though I am of myself persuaded to dwell for swift moments
    in the breathing temples of men, I am not man, and with his
    ways I have I am not to be confounded.
Yet I live; yet I have my being; yet I haunt the whole of this and
    other worlds without number and without end;—
At home in the rock's deep heart, in the still, cold depths of the
    ocean's sand, on the trembling leaves of tossing trees,
In the icy stretches of stellar spaces, on the stamen of nodding
    flowers, in falling columns of light imprisoning motes and
    beams, in the darkness and silence of swamps,—
I was, I am, I will be,
Everywhere and nowhere, visible and invisible, felt and unfelt,
    there and not there, in all and in nothing, I hover, seeking to
    enter . . .
Shaping tiny spheres of plunging water into crystals of floating snow,
Touching and cracking seeds slumbering in their earthy bed and
    coaxing delicate shoots of green to peep forth,
My hot will belching upward from the tall tops of mountain peaks,
    sending lava sliding and smoking down the ragged slopes,
Nestling eternally at the cores of burning suns,
Charging the eruptions of semen jutting from the penises of amorous
    bulls,

Deforming the ocean's furious waves that dash against the sides of
    lonely cliffs,
Shaping and guiding the forms of fantasy in the timid hearts of
    maidens,
Electrically, frigidly holding the planets in their wide swings through
    black voids,
Controlling the fluttering of a baffled and curious child's eyelids,
Relating the heart's beats, each to each,
Structuring the bones of men and women,
Breathing in laughter that leaps from singing lips,
Exulting in flexed and tensed flesh,
And equally,
Suffering I am, pain, the compulsive rasping in the choked throat,
Flowing warm and red out of the fresh and stinging wound,
Throbbing in taut abcesses,
Weighing heavy limbs with final fatigue,
Ecstatically aching inflaccid muscles,
Stiffening joints that will move no more,
Swimming in waves of worms in hot carcasses that sleep in the sun,
Escaping slowly as foul scent from corpses, seeking release,
Issuing in screams from contorted lips while tugging new life from
    wombs past wet thighs,
Burning in bodies that lay in fever, seeping as pus from rotting flesh,
Proclaiming victory when the body gives its last heave and lies
    still . . .

Savage Holiday, which had already appeared outside of this poetic
context, was to be the first novel of the series, a kind of trial run,
even though he had never before described the novel as such. Of
the second novel, "Strange Daughter," Wright gave a fairly complete description in ten pages. It was to be the story of a young
American white girl who grows up to associate sex with guilt because of her strict and puritanical upbringing. She has been frustrated and filled with anxiety during adolescence because she could
not achieve satisfaction in love unless she felt humiliated, taken by
force and corrupted. She eventually meets a Nigerian whose brutality
satisfies her perverted appetites. Living with him, she gradually
works free of her childhood taboos, only to be victimized by those
of her lover who, in obedience to his tribal religion, which forbids

that his ancestors be reincarnated in the white race, kills her when he learns that she is pregnant.

After this violent study of religious and social prohibitions on the interpersonal level, Wright planned a similar analysis on a broader scale. This third novel would deal with the psychology of colonization with the Aztec leader, Montezuma, as the hero. The story would hinge on the relationship between the social and religious principles of his culture and those of Western civilization at the time of Cortez's expedition. "When the World Was Red" was not intended to be an exotic reconstruction of a historical period, but rather aimed to explore the psyche of the Aztec ruler torn between his fascination with the new ideas brought by the invaders and his horror at their bloodthirsty methods. This went far beyond the narrow psychoanalytical sphere of *Savage Holiday*, replacing the individual's repression with colonial oppression. The "men in between," the elite on the path of cultural liberation, have conflicting allegiances that allow them to choose which elements of each civilization would be suitable to the incarnation and historical development of the Spirit.

Although these plots were remarkable only for their melodramatic violence and taste for blood and death, the originality of the plan should not be overlooked on that account. Wright considered every individual tragedy as only the summary, or epitome, of a collective tragedy. He was thus trying to present, sometimes awkwardly, but with great foresight, a major problem of our age: how to establish cultural pluralism.

Wright spent more than a month just writing this letter, since it included a detailed outline of his entire plan plus the two synopses. "Strange Daughter" had been inspired by the pathological experiences of the daughter of a couple he knew in New York, but he had had to delve into history books (Prescott on the conquest of Mexico and Peru, for example) in order to elaborate "When the World Was Red." He finally sent his forty-page outline to Aswell in October, at which time he also gave Reynolds the general idea of this latest project.

On October 25, 1955, Wright received Reynolds's reactions. From a commercial standpoint he thought that interspersing the novels with poetry, which had such a limited appeal, would be disastrous. Would not a prose preface do as well or better to explicate each episode? Furthermore, the story of Montezuma would certainly not interest an American public which considered him more a historical "Wizard of Oz." And finally, he felt that "Strange Daughter" should be set in Paris:

I have a lot of doubts as to whether a man who has been nine years away from this country can successfully write novels laid in this country. America has changed in the last ten years. . . . People's attitudes have changed, dialogues have changed. We are dealing with nuances, but there are an enormous number of them.

This was the third time Reynolds had repeated this warning (on January 14, he went so far as to tell Aswell that he thought Wright's two last novels dated by fifteen years) and Wright eventually agreed to set "Strange Daughter" in postwar Europe, as well as to do away with his poetic "mood." Nevertheless, beneath the polite, even humble, tone of his reply, his disappointment shows through; it was so difficult to reconcile what he had dreamed of accomplishing with what he could hope to publish. For the time being, he postponed any definite decision until he heard from Aswell.

Since Rachel had scarlet fever in November, 1955, and had to be quarantined at home, Wright left Paris, despite the cold and fog, to get some quiet at Ailly, using the two most easily heated rooms on the ground floor. He thought that he would be able to work uninterruptedly on his book about Spain, but, upon receipt of a warning from Margrit de Sablonière, he had to write both Reynolds and his Dutch publisher, Van Looy, on December 15, and take steps to prevent sixty pages of *Black Power* from being cut from the translation. This, he explained, would destroy the delicate balance between his criticism of the British on the one hand and the Africans on the other. In order to concentrate on his writing, Wright returned to Paris only once, to speak about *Puissance Noire* at the Methodist Church of Paris and spend Christmas with his family, returning to Ailly on January 24, 1956.

He was just starting once again to tackle the composition of *Pagan Spain* when he finally received a reply from Aswell, who was no more convinced than Reynolds that the plan for "Celebration of Life" truly represented Wright's creative personality. On January 24, 1956, Reynolds had even written a blunt but honest letter suggesting that Wright's exile might be responsible for a decline in his inspiration for fiction.

Why was that the most creative period in your life up till now, and why, since then, have the sources of your creativeness seemed to dwindle? It seems to me—and of course I am only guessing now—that as you have found greater peace as a human being, living in France, and not been made incessantly aware that the pigmentation in your skin sets you apart from other men, you have at the same time lost something as a writer. To put it another way, the human gain has been offset by a creative loss. So I think that your present situation calls for some serious effort of reassessment, or re-evaluation, of discovering where you are and where you are going.

Aswell was perhaps more tactful in stating that Wright's real world had been Mississippi and the ghetto.

Wright must have been fundamentally in agreement with his two friends, judging by how quickly he decided to abandon the project; it was almost as if he had cherished it as a pipe dream rather than an attainable goal. Perhaps he had finally been forced to elicit the reactions of other people because of a need to confront his dreams with reality, to weed out the possible from the impossible. He still considered the themes he had chosen significant, but he would now be content to treat them in the essay form rather than develop them through fiction. He also had another idea for a novel in reserve, which he mentioned almost immediately. Conforming more to his past work, it would be set both in the Deep South and France, and would show how racism in America deforms the black man's personality to the point that he will continue to be conditioned even in a nonracist environment. Wright actually knew of a striking true example on which to base his story; it was the experience of a certain Ish Kelly, a black American whom the French government had expelled as an undesirable alien after he had lived for years at the expense of several women and left three of them with children. As Wright explained to Aswell on February 6, "I think that I understand what made this chap act as he did and that will be the main burden of what I'll try to say in the book. At the moment I'd like to call the book, "Mississippi." [1]

Many distractions and difficulties interrupted the eventual composition of "Mississippi" (published in 1958 as *The Long Dream*), which he did not begin until the fall of 1956, but for the time being, since Aswell was completely satisfied with the idea, Wright was sufficiently encouraged to devote himself exclusively to his much-neglected book on Spain.

2

Although his work on "Celebration of Life" had come to nothing, the summer of 1955 had seen the inception of another, very different plan, for which Wright had great hopes. On the initiative of Alioune Diop, the editorial board of *Présence Africaine* had started to lay the groundwork for a congress that would assemble black writers and artists from around the world. The meeting would permit the representatives of the different currents of thought already published in the magazine to exchange ideas and perhaps formulate a synthesis on negritude. Although Wright no longer had an official position on the board, he was a member of the group, along with Aimé Césaire, Alioune Diop, Léopold Senghor, Paul Hazoumé and René Maran, that organized the broad outlines of the meeting and composed an appeal inviting the readers of the magazine to the First Congress of Negro Artists and Writers, scheduled for September, 1956, in Paris. Since Wright was responsible for the black American contingent, he wrote on March 18, 1956, to Roy Wilkins of the NAACP, which was financing the delegates, to send some more militant spokesmen than usual, perhaps the poet Melvin B. Tolson, the sociologist E. Franklin Frazier or the historian J. A. Rogers, rather than George Schuyler or Jay Saunders Redding. Wright spared neither time nor effort on these preparations and accordingly agreed to speak himself, although he did not choose his subject until the month before the Congress. He had originally thought of examining the psychological reactions of oppressed peoples, which he had never treated in a lecture, but he substituted instead "Tradition and Industrialization: The Tragic Plight of the African Elites."

It appears that these two themes had been suggested by reading Octave Mannoni's *Prospero and Caliban*. Published in France in 1950, under the title *Psychologie de la Colonisation*, this study by the Parisian psychiatrist had just been translated into English and

The Nation had asked Wright for a review, which appeared in the October 20, 1956, issue under the title "Neuroses of Conquest." During his own trips to Africa and Asia, Wright had observed some of Mannoni's assertions for himself, but he had never made such a precise statement about the personalities of the colonial and the native. At this time, Wright also read *The Burden of Our Time* by Hannah Arendt and the galleys of *An International Economy*, which Gunnar Myrdal had just sent him, but Mannoni, who had for a long time taught in Madagascar and studied the emotional relationship between colonized and colonial, provided him with the most food for thought. From these books and his reflections on his own African experience, Wright was able to write his review for *The Nation*, his talk for the Congress and another lecture entitled "The Psychological Reactions of Oppressed Peoples." At the Congress, Wright planned to stress the social and political implications of colonization, and the mentality of the Europeans, while his other lecture traced the effects of white cultural supremacy on the psychology of both the native and the black American.

Prospero and Caliban had in fact confirmed Wright's fear that imperialism had done even more harm than Marx and Lenin had prophesied. The European adventurers of the sixteenth and seventeenth centuries were not after merely the material wealth of gold and spices. In his review for *The Nation* Wright claimed that these people had actually been social misfits and had therefore sought subjects in foreign lands who would submit blindly to them, and in so doing they turned Asia and Africa into arenas for satisfying their neurotic appetite for power and self-indulgence, a habit which they could not subsequently break without doing themselves severe psychological damage. While tribal religion persuaded the native to identify white power with his gods and ancestors (an idea that Wright had planned to develop in the story of Montezuma), the Whites could not satisfy his emotional needs. As a result, he found himself being gradually destroyed. The more he adapted to Western culture, the more he hated himself, since his newly acquired European values only revealed the extent of his so-called primitive degradation and the huge gap separating him from Europe. This view of missionary Christianity as culturally destructive was later presented in Wright's story "Man, God Ain't Like That," while the coherent and well-developed theory of the "tragic elites," already stated in existentialist terms in *The Outsider*, later became the central theme of *White Man, Listen!*

Wright left Ailly (where he had been working out the details of his novel) to attend the Congress at the same time that his family went to Amsterdam, where Ellen had to take care of some business. Dr. Price Mars chaired the opening meeting on September 19, in the main amphitheater of the Sorbonne. Wright, John A. Davis, Horace Mann Bond, William T. Fontaine, James W. Ivy and Mercer Cook made up the American delegation. Absent was W. E. B. Du Bois, who had been refused a passport on account of his Communist sympathies. He had had to content himself with sending a message, to which Wright was chosen to reply at the beginning of the evening session, open only to the sixty delegates from the twenty-four participating nations. Du Bois had implied that the Afro-Americans present were implicitly agreeing to uphold the official United States propaganda on racial problems.[2] Wright, therefore, opened by asserting his own freedom of expression and his desire to see the Congress provide valid answers to certain problems. He questioned the definition of the black American and the assertions of his links with African culture, maintaining that because the black American was a member of the Western world, this complicated any simple kinship he might feel with Africans due to their common color or heritage. While praising that morning's speech by Léopold Senghor on the richness and spontaneity of African poetry, Wright suggested that a culture so dependent on tribal customs and ancestor-worship had perhaps hindered the Africans in their fight against colonization. To what use could such religious beliefs be put in the future development of the black continent? Should they be preserved and perpetuated as vestiges of a past civilization, or should the Western ideas that were destroying them be adopted for the very purpose of resisting the West?[3] Wright was in fact questioning certain basic principles and assumptions held by the partisans of negritude, and in a way that was disturbing for many an African. Was he demanding too much rationality, too much discipline? The Haitian Jacques Alexis, who was the next to speak, proposed a distinction between the Negro-African culture in general, and specific national cultures. Then Senghor answered him at length, returning to Wright's "very moving speech" but emphasizing the African heritage of the Afro-

Americans. He claimed that *Black Boy*, as well as Wright's early poetry, showed obvious resemblances to Negro-African literature. Alexis, too, returned to Wright's speech, asserting that Wright had in fact assumed the existence of general Negro-African culture, and reducing the problem to ascertaining whether the black American should be associated primarily with that culture or with American culture. Mr. Ablemagnon then led the discussion into a cultural inventory, although Wright's second question was still unanswered by the time Louis T. Achille, from Martinique, rephrased it in writing: to what extent could animism resist the spread of scientific ways of thinking? Paul Hazoumé then gave a remarkable account of animism, concluding that the part dealing with magic proper would never fall under the sway of rationalism. Eventually Cheik Anta Diop had to adjourn the meeting because of the late hour, recommending that they continue with the cultural inventory of negritude. The questions that Wright had raised had certainly not yet been discussed.

In the next day's discussions, Davidson Nichols mentioned Wright in connection with the English-speaking literature of Western Africa; Frantz Fanon did likewise in his talk on "Racism and Culture," while Aimé Césaire of Martinique, speaking on "Culture et Civilisation," to some degree justified Wright's appeal to Nkrumah at the end of *Black Power*, and began to deal with the problem of determining the relationship between independence and the fate of ancestral customs. Again the meeting continued far into the evening, and Wright was gratified to see the discussion finally reach the heart of the problem, thanks to Césaire, although he regretted that so much time had been wasted.

We could have examined in concrete terms why African culture has been so easily shattered, and what could have been done to protect it, perhaps changing the elements which seemed too subjective in that culture purging it to make something more objective, and hence more useful as a tool. . . . I also thought that we could have left here having taken a dramatic stand towards the West, in order to cure them completely of their chronic assumption that Africa is dependent, something which the Africans themselves are forced into believing by the living conditions in their country.[4]

Wright had brought up the relationship between Afro-Americans and African culture mostly in order to elicit a redefinition of it, and he was disappointed not to have found one.

The American delegates, and in particular Mercer Cook, had been shocked to hear Césaire liken them to a colonized people. After Césaire had spoken, Wright did not repeat his second question, which had been misunderstood, but did continue the discussion with Césaire in private. Wright had always felt that they were separated by communism but as opposed to the other Afro-Americans, he agreed with Césaire on many points. By this time, Césaire was moving away from the Party anyway, and the Congress provided an opening for a fruitful meeting between the two men which Alioune Diop organized soon thereafter.

During the September 21 session, Cedric Dover stressed the importance of cultural nationalism for black literature, and referred at length to "Blueprint for Negro Writing." George Lamming, speaking about the black writer and his world, compared Amos Tutuola's *Palm Wine Drinkard* and *Brother Man* by Roger Mais with *Black Boy*, whose important place in black literature he emphasized. Wright's own speech came the day before the closing session. He read his prepared text on "Tradition and Industrialization" but inserted additional comments pertaining to the questions and answers stemming from the Congress. For instance, he pointed out that the black nationalism he had advocated during the thirties had been a reaction of defense and pride which, due to the slow but constant shift in the American treatment of the racial problem was no longer entirely justified. Wright also regretted the absence of another minority group—women—since there was only one woman delegate present. More important, in his original analysis of the causes and substrata of the colonial conquest, both psychological and ideological, he had concluded that it had in part saved the African from an irrational religion. He now questioned this, along with his certainty about what type of spiritual revolution Europe had, in spite of herself, unleashed in Africa. Colonization may not have freed Africa from her past, and her elite might not represent, as he had thought, the "freest men in the world today." These comments could easily have offended many people present, since they reveal a disenchantment with the "African personality," which he considered too mystical and therefore not politically efficient. This was not a sequel to his disappointment with the Gold Coast, but rather a more critical reevaluation of negritude. Wright also repeated his conclusion to *The Color Curtain*. The only rational course of action for the Western world was to grant the elites of the Third World the liberty and means to rebuild their countries. More than any of the other participants with the exception, perhaps, of Aimé Césaire, Wright led the discussion toward political as well as cultural issues, and he addressed not only the Third World but also the West, which was responsible for colonialism. The Congress was almost an intellectual Bandung for Wright, who called upon his colleagues to reject a useless past and to turn toward rationalism and industrialization. But was there not a tragic misunderstanding in all this? Did the West want to help Africa in her liberation, and did Africa really want to free herself from the ancestral religion, to rid herself of just those irrational and spontaneous qualities which the partisans of negritude were in fact exalting? Wright's words created a certain uneasiness, not only among all those (Christians or pagans) whose religion was being questioned, but also among those who were convinced of the indefinable and intuitive value of the Negro "soul."

At the final session of the Congress on September 22, Léopold Senghor led a "dialogue between Africa and Europe" which answered to some extent Wright's questions of the day before, in particular that of what function the black national cultures had played in preventing the infiltration of Western ideology. After several opinions delivered in French, Senghor chose Wright as the spokesman for the Afro-American delegation. Wright accordingly declared that the Congress marked the end of five centuries of Western cultural domination. Nkrumah had recently invited Afro-American engineers and technicians to work in Ghana; this was the kind of role that Wright thought his black compatriots should play in the rebuilding of the Third World. He stated in their name: "We will serve."

Despite the cultural inventory of the black world that the Congress had so successfully achieved, Wright was still sorry that no positive motion had been voted or any concrete action planned to blend national traditions with modern rationalism. In fact, his personal goal to provide a link between the cultures was turning out to be impracticable, since it was sometimes difficult to act as a simple go-between even for two groups of men. Since Wright had become better acquainted with the American delegates—and with Mercer Cook in particular—he had mediated between them and the Africans, explaining to the Americans, for instance, that Aimé Césaire's communism, which had troubled them, was not a danger,

With Senghor and others at the Congrès
des Ecrivains et Artistes Noirs, 1957

Inside, at the Congrès

since he was sufficiently independent not to support a Party decision that conflicted with the interests of the Blacks. Wright told the Africans, in turn, who were leery of the very moderate American delegation, how difficult it would be to take any action that would be both openly militant and truly effective in McCarthy's America.[5] With one foot in each camp, he set about dissipating the distrust due to mutual ignorance, and after his efforts in this area at the Congress, it was no wonder that in December, 1956, he was chosen to help found the Société Africaine de Culture and, somewhat later, to serve on its executive committee with Dr. Price Mars as president.

Since Wright was more interested in political action for the liberation of Africa than in the exploration of negritude, he naturally admired George Padmore much more than Senghor or even Césaire. Padmore was a spiritual father of pan-Africanism whom perhaps Wright loved not so much for his wealth of knowledge and advice as for his determination to continue the fight for the decolonization of all Blacks. In March, 1956, he had written an enthusiastic preface to Padmore's book *Pan-Africanism or Communism?*, in which he formulated some of the observations he later repeated in his essay on the psychological reactions of oppressed peoples, and also evoked in moving terms the ascetic simplicity of his friend's existence. Wright identified very strongly with Padmore, since even their political destinies were similar.

When George discovered that, beyond doubt, Stalin and his satraps looked upon black men as political pawns of Soviet power policies . . . he broke completely with the Kremlin, BUT HIS BREAKING DID NOT MEAN THAT HE THEN AUTOMATICALLY SUPPORTED THE ENEMIES OF THE SOVIET UNION AND HIS REFUSAL TO SUPPORT THE ENEMIES OF THE SOVIET UNION WAS NOT DICTATED BY ANY LOVE FOR STALIN. NO! HE CONTINUED TO WORK ALONE, STRIVING TO ACHIEVE THROUGH HIS OWN INSTRUMENTALITIES THAT WHICH HE HAD WORKED FOR WHEN HE WAS IN THE COMINTERN HIERARCHY, THAT IS FREEDOM FOR BLACK PEOPLE.[6]

Wright was not sure that liberation of the black people had been a goal of the Congress, and he was even beginning to doubt the efficiency of writing as a weapon, insofar as this liberation implied the necessity of being armed with real weapons. "The *Présence Africaine* Conference was a success of a sort, but it left me terribly depressed. I'd like to talk to you about it in detail," he wrote to Daniel Guérin on September 29, and, as he later revealed, he began at this time to feel that *Présence Africaine* was secretly being taken over by the French government and certain Africans who were actually opposed to African nationalism. He therefore considered withdrawing altogether, in order to free himself for this fight, and certainly his projected lecture tours to Germany and the Scandinavian countries were intended more to forward the liberation of Africa than to stimulate the sale of his books.

In spite of a longstanding disinclination to visit Germany, for fear, as he wrote Margrit de Sablonière, that he might "have to shake a hand that helped to burn up people in murder factories," Wright had finally accepted the invitation of his German publisher, Mr. Claasen, to speak in Hamburg on the publication of *Schwartze Macht*. After a brief trip to Bonn, the day after the Congress, he left for Hamburg with Ellen on October 9, to be the guest, not only of his publisher, but also of the Congress for Cultural Freedom and the Sociology Department at the University.

Wright attended a reception in his honor given by Professor Bruno Snell, and he conversed freely with the journalists before the dinner preceding his talk on "The Psychological Reactions of Oppressed Peoples." In their two days in Hamburg, he and Ellen toured the city with Wright's literary agent, Ruth Liepman, and her husband and had a chance to hear an orchestra from Ghana in a nightclub of St. Pauli. They were warmly received wherever they went and gratified by everyone's sincere desire to know more about the African situation and the racial problem in the United States.[7]

Wright had only a week back in Paris before leaving for Zurich, where he spent six days on business. He then flew directly to London where, on October 27, 1956, he went to a meeting of the Congress for Cultural Freedom organized by Arthur Koestler and attended by J. B. Priestley and George Mikes, among others. He was back in Ailly when he heard about the Franco-British invasion of Egypt, soon followed by the Hungarian revolution, news which inspired him to make dire predictions on the future relations between the West and the Third World. He wrote to Margrit de Sablonière on November 21, 1956:

I waited for someone to try and voice protests. But the whole atmosphere was so confused with lies on both sides that I did not feel that any word of mine could help. You may be sure that I feel sad today. I'm sure that what has begun in Egypt is not over; there may be a lull, but the West seems determined to impose overriding considerations which the Asians and Africans will not accept. Bandung is coming true much quicker than I feared. . . . I expect, before this issue is solved, that the Western World will burn up millions of brown, black and yellow people. . . . I've been pushed on all sides to give my name to protest against what is happening in Hungary and when I say yes, I'll sign a protest about what is happening in Hungary if you include what is happening in Egypt, my friends back off in sullen silence.

What, in fact, was there for Wright to do in view of the hypocrisy of Europe and the bad faith of his French friends who professed so much good will? He already considered himself a partisan of liberty, not so much against totalitarianism as against neocolonialism because now the Third World seemed more threatened than the West, which was the source of all new dangers.

On November 22, Wright set off, alone this time, on a lecture tour of Scandinavia. Invited by Bonniers, who had been his Swedish publisher since 1949, he repeated his Hamburg lecture on the evening of November 26—the Swedish publication date of *The Outsider*—at the Medborgarhus in Stockholm, as part of a literary event that also featured Eva Maria Lennartson reciting black poetry and Thore Ehrling performing Duke Ellington. The book sold close to 35,000 copies in four days.[8] During his brief stay, Wright cemented his relationship with his publishers and with the native country of Alva and Gunnar Myrdal, to whom he had just dedicated *Pagan Spain*. The next day, he spoke at Uppsala University before going to Oslo where, on the morning of the 29th, he was welcomed by Brita Brantzeg, the student sent to meet him from the university. He lunched at the Continental Hotel with the Norwegian Writers' Club, and then spoke with the assembled journalists before giving his talk that evening to the Student Association. After a short visit to Charlottenberg, he repeated his lecture at the Park Avenue Konferenzrum in Göteborg on November 30. He flew to Denmark the next day and spoke on December 4 at Malmö. The following day he gave his last lecture, in Copenhagen, leaving himself four days to visit the city.

In addition to the publicity and money earned from this tour, Wright came back with two ideas. Bonniers had asked to publish the lecture he gave in Stockholm, along with his others on related

With Jens Schade in Denmark

subjects, and in Copenhagen he had found material for a short story. Surely his stay in the Hotel St. Anna or else some Danish anecdote was the inspiration for "Big Black Good Man." Wright actually started writing this humorous story about the relationship between a grateful black sailor and a timid Danish receptionist on the train back to Paris on December 8, and by mid-January, Paul Reynolds had received the manuscript, which he had no trouble selling to *Esquire*. At the same time Wright also sent the text of his four lectures, which he had slightly revised and polished in the preceding month. Along with a ten-page introduction, which he finished the day after Christmas, this completed the manuscript of *White Man, Listen!*

3

In addition to this short story and the collection of essays, Wright had completed a manuscript in yet another genre in 1956, for which he was not so fortunate in finding an audience but which nevertheless represented a short period of energetic and creative production so typical of Wright whenever he became enthusiastic about a project.

Early in the summer a young Frenchman, Louis Sapin, author of several nightclub shows in collaboration with Georges Vidalie, who had adapted "Fire and Cloud" for French radio, brought the manuscript of his first play to Wright. *Papa Bon Dieu* was a sort of miracle play and Wright, as a former admirer of Father Divine, was immediately taken with the idea. The play opens in the suburbs of a large city where a junk dealer (nicknamed Papa Bon Dieu) is having a drinking contest with a friend. Papa is drinking to console himself for the misery of the human lot, while Samuel, his friend, is trying to forget his tragic love for the prostitute Lea. Papa's sole support in life is his sister, Anna, as virtuous a Christian as he is an inveterate sinner. She has always tried to convert him without daring to hope for his salvation, but one morning, soon after the play opens, she finds him lying stiff as a ramrod in front of the door, apparently dead from too much drink. Since the pastor refused to bury the miscreant (perhaps because there was no hope of his being paid for it), Samuel takes the body to the cemetery, where the real adventure begins. While Samuel, Thomas the grocer, Lea, Jeremy the gravedigger, Anna and the two lovers, David and Sarah, are standing around the grave, along with the pastor who has finally agreed to say a few prayers, the corpse begins to slide off the wagon and come to life. It is a miracle, of course, and the new religion of Papa Bon Dieu is born. He preaches love and peace, and advises everyone to enjoy paradise on earth because there is no sin where "body and soul are united." Everyone who belongs to the new sect is transformed: Lea becomes an "angel," Sarah leaves David in favor of God, and the disciples multiply, attracted by the belief that they can see God. The pastor's congregation dwindles accordingly and he dies soon afterwards, perhaps because he had threatened Papa Bon Dieu, who meanwhile has converted the mayor and escaped unhurt from shots fired by David, enraged by Sarah's desertion. Thomas administers the religious organization and distributes food, seasoned with good advice, until one day Sarah and Sem (a believer who had been miraculously cured of his blindness) run off with the funds; the poor are enraged. Thomas appeases them with a huge distribution of rum, but it must have been time for Papa Bon Dieu to abandon his flock, because he dies a second and final time. In the last scene, Thomas has taken over, Sarah and Sem are preaching the new faith, Anna has returned to a religion without miracles and, out of faithfulness to the deceased, Lea and Samuel are planning to remake their life together: their happiness will justify to the Almighty, Papa Bon Dieu's noble and daring attempt.

Wright appreciated the humor of the play, which he called "a satire on one of those social phenomenons which most authors broach only with the greatest respect, whenever they do not decide, for one reason or another, that it is foreign to artistic creation altogether." [9] The conflict between rational civilization and the human thirst for miracles, which life can never assuage; the dilemma of a messiah whose feelings of mercy and tenderness for mankind forbid him either to assert or deny his divinity: both were part of Wright's continuing interest in the roots of religious feeling, in his Grandmother's Adventist faith, and in the popular cults of Father Divine and Daddy Grace. He could, in fact, so easily imagine such a story actually taking place in the "Black Belt," that he did not need to be persuaded to adapt the play, using black American characters and setting. *Daddy Goodness* was written before he had even notified Reynolds of the project, and it was only at the beginning of July, 1956, that he felt obliged, due to an indiscretion on the part of Sapin's agent, to sign a contract covering all the adaptation rights, of which he would get 50 per cent.[10] In August, he reread and improved the text, altogether eliminating the gravedigger-prophet, Jeremy, and cutting the whole by twenty pages. The script was then shown to one producer after another, including Robert Joseph and Cheryl Crawford, but they all rejected it. The following July, a Mr. Morse offered to put it on in an off-Broadway theater under the direction of Ben Zevin, but he wanted Wright, in return, to fill out the part of Papa Bon Dieu and change the humorous satire on religion into a sort of apologia. The authors therefore declined the offer. Somewhat later, Wright got in touch with Anna Dere Wyman, a millionairess whom he had met in London and who wanted to help him make the play into a musical comedy, a second "Melody Limited" perhaps, but this plan, and the entire project, finally came to nothing.[11]

NINETEEN

THERE was nothing uncertain about Wright's literary standing in that autumn of 1956, despite the somewhat unfavorable reviews his latest books had received in the United States and his own pessimism concerning projects he cared about. He was translated, read and respected throughout Europe. Both books on the Third World came out at this time in London, where the British press were particularly true to their principle of "fair play" concerning *Black Power*, while the German reception of *Schwartze Macht* and its author had been exceptional.[1] In the Scandinavian countries he had just visited, as in Paris, Wright was considered an authority on racial problems, and even *The Color Curtain* was selling better than he had hoped in the United States. He was also secure financially; in fact he had just refused a $6,000 advance on his next novel from World, when Edward Aswell, who had since moved to Doubleday, was able to reward him for his faithfulness by assuring him on July 20, 1956, as good a contract for "Mississippi." Of course the Harper payments were coming to an end in February, and the funds that Paul Reynolds had kept in reserve for him had been almost depleted by the purchase and repairs of Ailly,[2] but it had been a good investment since the farm was not only very attractive but an ideal retreat. The garden where he liked to work during the afternoons, after a strenuous morning of intellectual endeavor, had been replanted in the spring and provided most of the family's vegetables. From time to time, Richard enjoyed distributing his crops among his Parisian friends, who were extremely surprised at his horticultural talents. The house was surrounded by a luxuriant orchard and what with the calm of the countryside, friendly chats with the neighboring farmers, and the regular, natural rhythms of life in the village, Wright could feel completely at peace.

It is therefore somewhat surprising that he was so profoundly affected by some unfortunate occurrences that he could not regain enough peace of mind to continue writing for quite a long time.

The first bad news was the death of Aunt Maggie. She had been living in Jackson for almost four years, caring for Ella at 1085 Lynch Street with the help of Richard's monthly checks. He had learned on his return from Denmark that she was dying of cancer and had immediately cabled $500 for an operation, but she died on January 20, 1957. She had been Richard's favorite aunt, although she had never understood his ambition to become a writer, and had always looked after Ella with the utmost devotion.[3] With her died a witness to his childhood and the only member of his family, aside from his mother, to whom he felt close—perhaps the main explanation for his grief.

Maggie left part of her meager fortune to her great-nieces, Julia and Rachel, which forced Wright to confront some unpleasant realities once again in dealing with the bank at Jackson that held the will. "They address me as 'Wright' and there is no salutation. That form is to avoid saying 'Mr. Wright' no doubt," he stated bitterly to Reynolds on January 25, 1957, explaining that the racist attitudes he planned to discuss in his new novel were still flourishing.

Unfortunately for the composition of "Mississippi," Wright was in the midst of a continuing feud with Ben Burns, his "white friend" from *Ebony* magazine. In the March 8, 1956, issue of *The Reporter*, Burns had attacked Wright and all the expatriate black writers. He first accused the French photographer Henri Cartier-Bresson of willfully stressing the slums of Chicago and not the modern improvements, and then recalled Wright's "unpublishable" article ("I Choose Exile") in which he obstinately refused to recognize any amelioration in the racial conditions in America:

Wright's venom, retailed constantly by expatriates at sidewalk cafes plus years of headlines about Dixie lynching has succeeded in poisoning European thinking about racial problems in America. . . . Richard Wright enjoys a good audience on the Left Bank for his hate school of literature.[4]

Burns went on to be deliberately misleading about his second point, which was that Wright ignored the racist treatment of the Algerians in France. The two men had actually discussed the question only once, in a Paris café during the summer of 1953, and Wright, without minimizing the racial prejudice of the French, had reminded Burns that he had to refrain from publicly denouncing French colonial policy if he wanted to remain in the country. The "witch

hunt" in the United States, which at that time was at its peak, meant
that he would have to face the Senate subcommittee on un-American
activities if he returned. The question remains as to why Burns considered it opportune, three years later, to start justifying American
racism by the age-old tactic of denouncing it in other countries and
why, in particular, he would want to accuse Wright of poisoning
European public opinion. Could he have been acting on behalf of
certain reactionary forces that wanted to discredit Wright? Was he
jealous that Wright was safe in exile? Or was he deliberately trying
to provoke an incident? Wright had asked himself all these questions
and had communicated his violent reactions to Reynolds on April
13, 1956:

> It is simply foolish to say that I poisoned the mind of Europe; if
> that is true, I am more powerful than either Moscow or Peking.
> . . . To my mind, subversion is a legal business and I felt that
> Ben Burns was taking the role of the Attorney General when he
> said I bordered on the subversive. . . . If you think a lawyer
> should look at the article, all right.

Wright was so incensed that when Reynolds told him that *Male
Magazine* wanted to publish "The Man Who Lived Underground"
he at first refused, thinking that Burns was somehow remotely connected with the magazine. Meanwhile, Burns had in fact become
editor of *Duke* (an imitation of *Playboy* and *Down Beat* for the
black readers) and had offered Reynolds $100 for the right to
reprint a chapter of *The Outsider*. Before Wright even had a chance
to cable that he denied his permission—he would have nothing more
to do with "that individual" under any circumstances—Burns had
paid Harper's $75, as if the deal had been made for that price. The
Harper lawyers had a great deal of trouble preventing Burns from
going ahead.[5]

Perhaps these disagreeable incidents could be blamed simply upon
irresponsible behavior, but they could also have been the result of a
concerted attempt to damage Wright's reputation. In either case
they left their mark on him, because the following year, when he
found himself the object of similar attacks, he was much quicker to
interpret them as deliberately malicious, and harmful not only to
himself but to all black writers living in Paris. He felt that the
campaign could no longer be explained merely by personal rivalries among Blacks, which he had previously always been able to

differentiate from provocation purposely instigated by racists or political enemies. By 1957, Wright began to consider all attacks against him as part of a general plot, and since later incidents tend to support this theory it would not be difficult to agree with him. For the time being, it is only important to note that such abuse had started to preoccupy him and disturb his peace of mind just when he was embarking upon his first novel since *The Outsider*. Perhaps his tendency to dramatize such occurrences drove him to take refuge in, and comfort from the writing of his novel over the period from the autumn of 1956 to the spring of 1958. Although these tensions made the composition of it proportionately more difficult, they also inspired him to be explicit about his militant anticolonialism, and uncompromising in his condemnation of both American and Western policy in general.

To do some additional research for "Mississippi," Wright had suggested to the *Pittsburgh Courier* in May of 1956 that he write a series of articles on the black Americans in the NATO forces of Western Europe and the problems they encountered in France, England and Germany. Thanks to friends on various bases, he was well informed about the subtle but continuous segregation to which they were subject, as well as the discrimination in the entertainments they were allowed.[6] With this reportage, Wright would thus be killing two birds with one stone, since whatever material he found, he could use to combat this pernicious form of racism, but he was mostly interested in getting documentation for his novel.

While waiting for their response, Wright had used his free time following the *Présence Africaine* congress and his lecture tours during the fall to write a first draft. Settled in Ailly since mid-January, 1957, he had written 644 pages by the beginning of April, and, although his main concern was to be the reactions of Fishbelly (whose name he used for a title at one point) *after* his arrival in France, he had only just managed in all those pages to trace his hero's past before bringing him to Paris. What is more, after five or six attempts, he had been altogether incapable of getting beyond this stage. He outlined what he had written so far to Aswell on April 11, 1957:

The main burden of the story centers around a father-son relation-ship. Tyree tries to steer his son in a manner that will enable him to keep what property he had amassed and avoid trouble with the whites. Tyree owns several wooden tenements which he rents to black workers, and he also owns houses which are being used for places of prostitution. For ten years or more Tyree has been collecting from the madames of the houses of prostitution and turning over half of the proceeds to the chief of police. All goes well until a dance hall, the Grove, which Tyree partly owns, burns down, causing the death of some forty Negroes. When Tyree is informed that he will have to stand trial for manslaughter, he begs his white police friends to protect him. They refuse and try to milk him of what money he had amassed. Tyree turns the evidence of police corruption over to a white reformer who, in turn, gives it to the Grand Jury. Tyree is ambushed and killed for betraying the police with whom he formerly worked.

Fishbelly steps into his father's shoes at sixteen years of age. But he lacks Tyree's experience. The police believe that Fishbelly has a hoard of cancelled checks which will prove that they had taken graft money from the hands of his father. They try to sweat it out of him and he refuses to talk; he is kept in jail for two years on a charge of attempted rape, the object of jailing him being to make him talk and disclose the evidence that will harm the city's officials. Fishbelly refuses to talk, learns slowly to practice the art of deception and is released to carry on his father's work. He cannot. He flees.

Wright knew that *Black Boy* had already covered an initiation into racism in the Deep South, and it almost seems as if he had plunged himself back into the memories of his youth all over again. But here he faltered. He did not know whether he ought to end the story with Fishbelly's flight, and create a new set of characters to describe the adventures of an Afro-American in Paris, or whether he ought to forge ahead in spite of his difficulties. Once again he consulted Aswell.

On April 16, Aswell wrote back that though he did not like the title "Mississippi," he did not see why Wright could not repeat certain of the events of *Black Boy* in a new context. He only asked that Wright provide a conclusion to the present story. The sequel to Fishbelly's adventures could easily begin with his arrival at Orly and become the subject of a second volume; there was no reason to choose another hero if the past of this one had already been discussed in detail. The two novels would be both independent and complementary if Wright were to briefly review Fishbelly's crucial experiences at the beginning of the second book. Reynolds happened to write that same day with similar advice. Accordingly, while he tried, via Austryn Wainhouse, to get more details on the Ish Kelly affair from the defense lawyer, Carrier himself, as inspiration for the continuation of the plot, Wright went back to work on a second version of the manuscript.

He also took a vacation with Ellen at this time, attending the grand banquet given in Milan for a circle of authors, critics and booksellers to celebrate the fiftieth anniversary of Mondadori Publishers and their publication of *Potenza Nera.* They first spent a few days in Switzerland, then visited Venice (in the rain) and went on to Verona after their stay in Milan, where Richard had been enthusiastically greeted. In interviews he mentioned his favorite Italian authors: Carlo Levi, Elio Vittorini and Ignazio Silone, whose *Fontamara* he had just read. He also spoke out against Catholic censorship, which had caused the Italian translation of *Pagan Spain* to be expurgated, and he deplored the fact that France was spending so much money fighting in Algeria which could be put to better use for its citizens.[7]

They were back in Paris by June 12, 1957, and in mid-July Wright visited the American-occupied zone in Germany, even though the *Pittsburgh Courier* had not taken up his offer to write some articles on the black G.I.'s. He had agreed to serve as judge for a story contest organized at the American Air Force base at Ramstein, near Kaiserslautern, his main purpose being to collect information about life on U.S. military bases in Europe for his novel.[8] His trip to Hamburg on July 22 was for the publication of *Pagan Spain* by Claasen Verlag, and he informed Reynolds on July 28 that a German radio station had asked him at that time if he would write a play for them. From Hamburg, he had to go directly to England in order to sell the rights to *Pagan Spain*, since he distrusted his representative for the British Isles, Innes Rose, who had not made a sincere effort to place *Black Power*.[9] Indeed, Wright had now to pay closer attention to financial matters in order to balance the family budget, especially since he could hope for very little from *Pagan Spain*, which had sold poorly since its February publication in the United States.

By this time, he had almost finished the second version of his new novel and thought of calling it "The Double-Hearted" or "American Shadow," when Aswell suggested "The Long Dream." He had also verified most of his facts and had actually written to the law office of Morse & Morse in Jackson for information on Mississippi's judicial procedures. He had the manuscript typed in England, where Ellen went in August, 1957, with Julia and Rachel. Although he had made an outline and taken notes for the second volume, he did not want to commit himself to any deadline for the time being. He felt completely devoid of inspiration after *The Long Dream*, and since he also had to think about his play for German radio, he admitted to Reynolds on September 18 that he was in no condition physically or mentally to undertake another long novel.

To forget his anxieties, he devoted himself completely to the revisions of *The Long Dream*, which Aswell had liked since it had the narrative power that had made *Native Son* so successful. In a letter of December 23, Aswell suggested changes, pointing out the passages which slowed the action, in order to reduce the 767 pages to about 500. The only scene which he felt should be totally omitted was a lengthy clay ball fight between the young boys (a childhood memory that Wright had extracted from "Tarbaby's Dawn") since it served only to explain their arrest.[10] Wright also had to condense a good deal of dialogue and often cut descriptions of the characters' state of mind which their words or actions made redundant. He also agreed to eliminate the four-letter words and one anecdote which was obscene without being funny, as well as to smooth the abrupt transitions from dream life to real life. Aswell also felt that the transcription of popular speech was sometimes too phonetic and needed simplifying.

By mid-February, 1958, Wright had followed Aswell's suggestions to the letter and the novel was only 506 pages long. His only difficulties had been with the final episodes, as he admitted to Aswell on February 28: "At the end of the book, I tried to weave in the reference about Fishbelly's running away to find a solution to his problem. . . . I wrote the section time and again and always felt that the author's thumb sort of showed on the page."

Since the publication of *The Long Dream* depended entirely on how quickly Aswell looked at the revised version, Wright urged him, on Reynolds's advice, to fix the date for the autumn. The beginning of the school year was bound to renew the controversy over segregation, and it would be a good moment to sell a book dealing with the long-lasting damage resulting from it. Wright also decided at this time to dedicate the novel to Edward Aswell and Paul Reynolds. Considering that it literally would never have been written if they had not discouraged him from embarking upon "Celebration of Life," this was due homage; they had guided him back to his true vein and, somewhat comforted, Wright left for Ailly at the beginning of March, 1958, to begin the second volume.

2

Aswell had been deeply moved by *White Man, Listen!* and accepted it immediately in February, 1957, for Doubleday, with an advance of $1,500. He made a few revisions with Wright's permission in order to get it out by August, and in the meantime asked him to write a short presentation of the book to be distributed to booksellers for promotion purposes. Wright thereupon tape-recorded a six-page text in which he explained his intentions in collecting the lectures.

Despite this haste on both sides of the Atlantic, various delays postponed publication of the book until October 15, 1957. First, Aswell's wife died suddenly, and he was so grief-stricken that he had trouble continuing his work. At the same time, he decided to allow the publicity department as much time as they needed to plan a strong campaign, since he was not sure that the book would be a commercial success.

For once, however, the black press was almost unanimous in its praise. In his review for the Associated Negro Press, Jay Saunders Redding said that Wright had "never written either more brilliantly nor more poignantly" than in this "measured and balanced analysis of the meaning of the world today." James Ivy in *The Crisis*, Roi Ottley in *The Chicago Sunday Tribune*, Ollie Stewart in *The Afro-American* and critics from such diverse magazines as *Jet, The Journal of Negro History* and *The College Language Association*

Bulletin agreed that Wright had presented the warning that they themselves would have liked to offer the white world.[11] The silence of most of the large daily papers in the South was partly balanced by the warm reception of those which did mention the book, generally judging it as penetrating, moderate and very objective. The only exception was the *Chattanooga News-Free Press*, which advised Wright to come back to Natchez to discover that the Blacks of the South were thinking not of revenge, but of love:

The standards are still the same, raised by the heritage of invisible hands. Before you write the next book, Wright, come home from Paris, France. Greater voices than yours shout commands, greater lives show example and greater loves walk in an imperishable fellowship with Christ, regardless of the racial hate so voluble in your book.[12]

The liberal papers, whatever their religious or political leanings, were at least attentive. The *Christian Science Monitor,* without finding the book "a complete discussion of international racial questions by any means," nevertheless thought that it broke some new ground for the average Westerner. Paula Snelling, in *The Progressive,* stressed not only the importance of the psychological and political analyses, but also the in-depth study of black poetry and the "dirty dozens." Stanley Plastrik did regret that Wright had minimized the appetite of the "tragic elites" for personal power, as well as the problems of their effecting an economic recovery, but this was only in conclusion to a whole page of favorable comments in *Dissent,* which Wright had authorized to publish a few extracts from the book.[13]

On the other hand, the Establishment press refused to heed Wright's appeal. *Time, Newsweek,* the *Saturday Review* and several large national papers did not even mention *White Man, Listen!* Oscar Handlin, in his fair and perspicacious review for *The New York Times Book Review,* criticized Wright mostly for treating the white world as a solid block, an attitude "likely to evoke an exclusive nationalism as unfortunate in its consequences as that of the racism of some white men in the past," while *The New Yorker* was uncompromisingly severe:

The author, as self-appointed spokesman extraordinary for the colored peoples of the world . . . is correct in calling white supremacy a rash and wicked anachronism . . . but the ungainly

blend of intellectual jargon and strident emotionalism in which he
has draped his message reduces it to the level of soapbox oratory.[14]

The Establishment was in fact reproaching Wright for his base
ingratitude. He had achieved a successful career in the United
States but had chosen to live elsewhere, and now he had suddenly
decided to play the moralist, digging up old grievances at a time
when the victories of the black minority were accumulating day by
day. Wright was well aware of this opinion generally held by conservative America, as his letter to Margrit de Sablonière on October
26, 1957, indicates:

I suspect that I'll have to stick to fiction for a long time now for,
as I told you, my books on world affairs are not really wanted.
. . . My book *White Man, Listen!* has been more or less nega-
tively received in the USA. They hate the book, yet it tells the
truth. Then why should I go on writing books that folks will not
read? I'm sorry to sound so depressing but one must look facts
straight in the face.

Wright was prey to incertitude and worry as he reexamined his
recent career and present situation. He realized that his point of
view on racism, colonialism and the Third World was often un-
welcome. He blamed the poor sale of his nonfiction books as much
on the Whites' refusal to face reality as on a change in his American
audience and, accordingly, his belief in his mission as a militant
and embattled writer was shaken as much as his confidence in his
talent. Ironically, this occurred just when he was planning to turn
away from fiction toward the ideological essay dealing with current
political and social events. Since the beginning of the fifties, he had
moved further and further away from purely imaginative writing.
After a period of existentialist doubting, he had discovered a larger
cause to espouse, but even if Europe paid attention to him, the
audience he most wanted to reach—the American liberals—would
not; they now refused to recognize him as anything other than the
pugnacious black novelist whose books *Native Son* and *Black Boy*
had earned him a reputation as *the* black writer of the forties. Ten
years later, literary fashion and the mass media had pushed other
black writers like Ralph Ellison and James Baldwin into first place.
Protest was no longer the fashion since McCarthyism had taught
Americans to keep silent, to affect a blasé and detached tone or,
at most, to use insinuation rather than the frontal attack to further

White Man, Listen!

a given cause. Because of his exile, Wright had not been exposed to these changes and was accordingly faithful to himself, to his own style of writing and thinking. The question remains whether his transcription of the world as he saw it was out of date, or whether his new ideological viewpoint had not put him in advance of his times. It was certain, however, that he was aware of a time lag, one way or another, between himself and his audience.

In addition to this general discouragement brought on by the first, very negative reviews of *White Man, Listen!* his physical fatigue due to extensive traveling and his prolonged work on the revisions of *The Long Dream*, Wright was reacting somewhat like a seismograph to the tensions of the international situation. The invasions of Hungary and Egypt had already shaken his hopes for a lasting peace. Back in 1956, on August 1, he had exclaimed to Margrit de Sablonière: "NASSER HAS SEIZED THE SUEZ CANAL: This could be the beginning of something serious. The people of Asia and Africa are determined to be free. They out-number the West and most of the raw materials of the world are in their countries. I am really afraid of what the West will finally do." And then on the 4th, he continued, "Nasser is a man who wants to redeem his country. He has no practical way to do it and he might resort to adventure to fill up the horrible void that is in him and his people. Let us hope that time can give us enough room for a little peace." He thought that if Europe felt she were surrounded, she would try to penetrate into the Middle East. On August 28, 1957, just a year later, the Algerian war caused him to make further depressing predictions, which were currently shared by more than a few Frenchmen: "France is sinking each day, each hour. We may have a dictatorship here before the year is over. A Fascist one! It will be strange. And it will now have to happen. Poor mankind."

On October 26, 1957, Wright had left for Ailly after his visit to London, perhaps to find a shelter there from his somber reflections and growing discouragement. Having sent off his revised version of *The Long Dream* to Edward Aswell, he turned to fiction again, sketching the broad outlines of the sequel as therapy or a "distraction," in Pascal's sense of the word. He did, however, come out of his retreat to give a long interview on the United States to *La Nef*, which they published in November, 1957. Wright spoke mainly about the racial events in Little Rock, Arkansas, going back to Reconstruction to explain the problem. Governor Faubus's defiance of the Federal Government challenged the principles at the very heart of the Constitution, which were supposed to be "one nation, one law, one people." He explained the inequalities in the educational system, but said that the Blacks were determined to enjoy their civil rights and mentioned the possibility of a new Garveyism. He stressed the relationship between race relations and the international policy of America, where his pessimism finally broke through:

Today, there is no guarantee of a rapid solution. The Negro in the United States may very well suffer the fate of the Jew in Germany. Obviously, the problem of race relations in the United States is more difficult today than it was right after the Civil War. . . . Until 1954, when the Supreme Court voted for desegregation of the schools, the nation had never made a real and honest effort to solve the racial problem. . . . The white elites finally realized that their prejudice was causing them embarrassment in the rest of the world, and they finally tried, somewhat belatedly, to show the African and Asian masses an ideal, cleansed of all racial stigma. This will be a long and difficult evolution because they have to

contend with a racial indoctrination which has been passed down
from father to son, for three hundred years.[15]

Wright was still convinced that the future of Africa—of Ghana
under Nkrumah, in particular—would be decisive, even in South
Africa, where the thirty-six militants accused of high treason were
just coming to trial in Johannesburg. He told Margrit de Sablonière
on November 14, 1957, that he had contributed a signed book to
the "Treason Trial Fund" supporting them, and that there was no
question of his unconditional support of the Third World peoples
against the West, as he wrote again on December 18:

I've read the accounts from Indonesia and I'm afraid that things
there will go from bad to worse. I suspect that civil war will soon
come there. *Racial* feeling and *religious* feeling is at the bottom of
it all. And I feel that it is impossible to make the West understand
or accept that. . . . What a problem for white men, who are
used to lording it over the human race! It is a hard decision to
make. The trouble is that the white man dislikes too much on the
earth today. Their own state of mind makes them see too many
enemies and they do not know what enemy to fight first. . . . It's
indeed gloomy.

That same fall, however, his courage and enthusiasm returned
as soon as he heard that a conference of Asian and African nations
was scheduled for December 26 in Cairo. He felt that he would
bring back an even better report than the one from Bandung if he
could get Doubleday to finance his trip, or if he could interest an
American magazine, provided he secured support from a French
one first. He was set on going and did not think that this would
interfere with the publication of *The Long Dream*, since Aswell
would not have finished reading the manuscript before he returned.
All this he explained to Paul Reynolds on October 26, somewhat
in justification for once again deserting fiction in favor of journalism: "I've just moved in this direction and my writing simply reflects
what I feel." Which shows perhaps that Reynolds was wrong in
claiming that Wright's literary career had suffered now that he lived
in such a calm atmosphere. Indeed, he had not found peace in
retreat but had merely exchanged racial tension for other preoccupations, broader interests, which did divert him from writing
novels and turn him toward nonfiction, but certainly are no reason
to believe that he was less inspired on that account.

Unfortunately, Wright's failure to find support for this trip to Cairo only strengthened his suspicion that he was "writing books that folks will not read," and he could not help but doubt himself as a result.

TWENTY

THE BOUTS of discouragement resulting from these criticisms and attacks, alternating with moments of intense creation or militant action, never left Wright any prolonged period of peace. The reverses and struggles that had marked the mid-fifties were followed by even greater disappointments, more numerous and more concerted attacks, with the result that both his writing on political and social situations and his novels were characterized by more intense and specific anxieties. The composition of "Island of Hallucinations," the sequel to *The Long Dream* and somewhat affected by the reception of the first novel, was largely inspired by Wright's own conflicts, first with other expatriate Blacks in Paris, and then with certain representatives of the American government who were not able to forgive him his strong opposition to their policies and accordingly made life difficult for him well after the tumult of McCarthyism had died down in the United States. Wright met the attacks from Blacks and Whites alike, and partially withstood them, but he was increasingly depressed to discover how powerful were the means employed to control him, if not to reduce him to silence.

In the spring of 1958, Wright was forced to go to the French police apropos of a curious matter which had actually started several years earlier and was then referred to in the American black colony as the "Gibson affair."

In 1956, Wright's friend Ollie Harrington, a former NAACP public relations officer and a well-known cartoonist for the *Pittsburgh Courier*, had rented his Paris studio while he was away on the Côte d'Azur to Richard Gibson, a young black novelist in Paris on a Whitney scholarship. Harrington was disagreeably surprised on his return to find that Gibson not only refused to vacate the apartment, but claimed to own the furniture, paintings and personal belongings that he had left behind. The argument continued for almost two years. Gibson made violent attacks which verged on the psychotic, while Harrington resigned himself to living elsewhere rather than call in the police, fearing that the American Embassy might intervene on account of his status as an expatriate with Communist sympathies. Meanwhile, the Afro-American novelist William Gardner Smith, who was working for the Agence France-Presse, had helped get Gibson a job and would not disavow his friend, with the result that the black community had slowly taken sides in the struggle. Wright naturally supported Ollie Harrington, who had been his good friend since his arrival in 1955, although he did not share all his political opinions.

In 1957, one of the letters to the editor of the October 21 issue of *Life* magazine bore Harrington's signature and, replying to a September 30 article, violently condemned French policy in Algeria. Similar letters were also sent to *The Observer* in London, in reply to articles by M. Kraf and John G. Weightman that appeared on January 20 and January 30, 1958. Harrington, however, had not written these letters. Since the French policy was to deport any foreigner who got involved with French domestic politics, someone must have used this maneuver to compromise him, and he accordingly initiated an investigation with the support of the well-known criminal lawyer Jacques Mercier. Both the French and American police found conclusive evidence that Gibson had written the letters. A memorable fight ensued in the Café de Tournon, where Harrington thrashed his opponent so thoroughly that he had to be taken to the hospital; Gibson signed a confession, but the American Embassy possibly intervened with the Sûreté Nationale to hush up the affair.

Wright became involved because he was asked to testify along with the mathematician Joshua Leslie, his wife, who was an American cancer researcher, and William Gardner Smith, but he was also an indirect victim of the affair. Personal vengeance could account for Gibson's desire to get Harrington deported, but was he not also helping to discredit certain Afro-American exiles in Paris by associating them with the F.L.N. only a few weeks before the Algerian question came up for discussion in the Security Council of the United Nations? Could he be working for an organization like the CIA, which certainly had enough reasons to dislike the idea of Blacks like Wright being reluctant to support American propaganda while living in Europe?

These questions haunted Wright, who was not this time exaggerating the ramifications of the affair. The entire fabric of his life in Paris was affected. The relations between black expatriates had never been altogether tranquil, at least since the beginning of McCarthyism, and among the writers jealousy had possibly motivated several attempts to diminish Wright's reputation.[1] In addition, the more or less discreet surveillance of the Blacks in Paris resulted in enough provocation. Now, however, suspicion poisoned many relationships in the black community; Wright could only count on a few faithful friends like Ollie Harrington, and he felt, probably with justice, personally threatened by these calumnies. There was plenty of reason for anxiety, considering his highly defensive temperament—developed by long experience of racism in the United States—and his innate tendency to dramatize. Wright actually spent weeks assembling a file of documents to protect himself if need be. He also made a list of questions designed to reveal Gibson's real motives and William Gardner Smith's true position. He wisely got in touch with Gibson himself, who wrote back denouncing Smith as a "false brother," and reassuring Wright that he was too big a figure for anybody to harm without an extraordinary amount of manoeuvering.[2] But there was no way of knowing the truth or who could be trusted, so he found no peace of mind. He thought that Smith, who was ostensibly acting as a friend, was actually attacking him, and while it was also rumored that Wright was an FBI agent, he was convinced that the CIA itself was the source of all these machinations.

Nevertheless, for Wright to consider himself one of the targets of these attacks was perhaps to overestimate the threat which his political stands and antiracism posed in an international context. Even though he never hesitated to condemn certain aspects of American policy, he could not be thought of as really anti-American.[3] His present state of mind, on the other hand, must be understood in the context of the general atmosphere of the cold war and the related long accumulation of incidents starting with the discreet investigations right after his break with the Communist party in the United States. The "witch hunt" mood in Paris during the mid-fifties was reinforced by the actions of Mrs. Agnes Schneider, who, as the head of the passport bureau at the American Embassy, could decide the fate of anyone too progressive or incautious. When Wright himself had given his passport to the American Embassy to have it renewed a few years before, he had been asked, contrary to usual practice, to come by and pick it up in person; without giving him any reason, they had kept him waiting for weeks and he had, in fact, threatened to reveal what he called their efforts at intimidation to the French press before they gave it to him.[4] As one of the few Afro-American intellectuals who refused to submit to pressure and who uncompromisingly stated his view of the truth, Wright had good reason to feel endangered, though he may have exaggerated the risks he actually ran. As the most recent and dramatic incident of this series of events, the "Gibson affair" tormented him for months, impeding progress on the adventures of Fishbelly (although it eventually provided some original material) and probably also prompting him the following year to take refuge in England from these pressures and the uncertainty of living under the unstable French government.

The political crisis in France had, by the summer of 1958, reached its height, with talk of civil war. The police were reputedly already taking up positions at strategic points, when the government decreed a state of emergency. After the events of May 13 and General de Gaulle's takeover, Wright had opposed the new regime by supporting Sartre, Simone de Beauvoir and other left-wing intellectuals in the Committee for Action and Defense of the Republic. He was ready to leave the country on a moment's notice if he had to, although French politics since his arrival in 1947 had several times proven to him that the country always solved its impossible situations at the very moment when foreign observers stated that it was on the verge of collapse.

Gibson's eventual confession and humiliation reassured Wright somewhat, without improving his opinion of American officials, and more than ever he kept his distance from the embassy. On the other hand, he gladly agreed to help out the Cultural Center on rue du Dragon since the director, his friend Rudolph Aggrey, had his entire confidence. On April 24, he was active in a Congress for Cultural Freedom discussion following a talk given by the Indian ambassador, Sandar K. Pannikar, on the problems of black Africa. From May 2 to 4 he was a special guest at a seminar on Mark Twain, Emily Dickinson, Thomas Wolfe and Ernest Hemingway organized by the American Cultural Center at Blérancourt, a château near the town of Soissons, where professors Leary, Hapgood and Unger lectured to French students.[5] The USIS then asked him to speak about the American novel on May 23 at the Sorbonne. That same month, *Preuves* published his answer to a symposium on black culture. Wright maintained that Afro-American culture was primarily determined by oppression, whose gradual decrease would inevitably cause the disappearance of what was considered the "black soul." The same would be true in Africa. Admittedly, before colonization all African culture had shared some of the same background—their pagan beliefs, in particular—but nowadays the co-existence of this culture with industrial civilization engendered more harm than good, even though the fusion of the diverse religious perspectives was a necessary phase of modernization. As for art and literature, he insisted, they resulted from a combination of personal factors and the national cultural context:

An American Negro will therefore write like the whites of his native country. It is not a question of choice. He will begin to do it before he even is entirely aware of the value of this stake on the racial level. An American Negro will write more or less like a white American, and more or less for the same reasons. If he achieves a somewhat different tone, this is explained by the way in which the Negro is allowed to integrate himself into the country where he was born, and into the culture of which he is an organic part.[6]

After the summer vacation, when Wright profited from the serenity of Ailly to work toward completing his Fishbelly trilogy, he once again returned to the sometimes painful realities of life in Paris.

The Long Dream was coming out in New York in mid-October, 1958, and the advance reviews were full of reservations, claiming that the novel was too brutal and too biased. Wright for once did not lose heart. "Sorry that folks are finding *The Long Dream* too brutal. Looks like I'm either too soft or too hard each time. But I hope that a few folks read the book," he wrote to Paul Reynolds on October 5, and indicated that he was willing, despite his coolness toward all Johnson publications, to give *Ebony* a long interview (for which his friend Ollie Harrington would do the photographs and captions) in order to publicize the novel. Unfortunately, Wright lost his optimism after reading the clippings that Reynolds had sent him on his return from Zurich on November 4. He had heard some of the general criticisms before, in relation to *The Outsider*: the novel was said to be dated, strangely disoriented and betrayed both a compulsive violence and a decline in artistic ability. This time, however, the reproach that Wright had lost all contact with America in living abroad recurred like a leitmotiv. *Time* magazine stated, "By this time, even Expatriate Wright should know that his picture is too crudely black and white. He writes as if nothing had changed since he grew up in Mississippi"; [7] under the headline "Richard Wright Wastes Talent in His Dream," Van Allen Bradley concluded with irony, "A few years ago, the author was quoted as saying, 'There is more freedom in one square block in Paris than in all of the United States.' *The Long Dream* stems from that dimension of thinking, and therein lies its weakness"; Philip Bonosky, in "Man Without a People," blamed Wright for still sticking, after twenty years, to "a point of view that cut him off from his people"; and, a few months later, Bryan Haislip recommended the book but reassured the readers of the *Raleigh News-Observer* with a typical general reaction: "There is little about his story that North Carolina readers will be willing to recognize. It may comfort them to reflect that, after all, author Wright has spent the past decade in Paris and can hardly be in touch with life in the American South."

If the white critics attacked Wright for ignoring the increase in desegregation, the improved standard of living and the civil rights now enjoyed by Blacks, the Afro-Americans would have been as justified in criticizing him for neglecting the striking new militancy of the black movement, which had arisen during the public transportation boycott in Montgomery, Alabama, foreshadowing the surge of power that Martin Luther King would give the civil rights movement. The central character of *The Long Dream*—Fishbelly's father, Tyree—was, if anything, the type of "compromise leader" with whom the black community no longer wanted to identify. Yet others like Roi Ottley, Hoke Norris and Jay Saunders Redding were not critical of this particular aspect of the novel; Nick Aaron Ford, for example, took exception to the development of the plot and the style before stating,

One who cares about the realism of fiction that pretends to be serious will find Wright's logic confusing, his motivations weak, and his conclusions not always convincing. . . . Social criticism is an acceptable ingredient of fiction only when it is caught up into an artistic design and made a necessary and natural part of

At Blérancourt, 1958. *Photo by Berand-Villars, Paris*

At Blérancourt, with panelists. *Photo by Berand-Villars, Paris*

plot development, in short, when it does not get in the way of
art. . . . In *The Long Dream* the social criticism is the central
concern; whatever art there may be is subordinate, is dragged in to
try to support the sagging weight of a clumsily-contrived thesis.[8]

It seemed as if many black critics were still punishing Wright for
stressing too exclusively the degradation of racism, which had so
disturbed them in *Black Boy*.

There were some striking exceptions to this concert of unfavorable, sometimes even malicious, judgment. In "The Power of
Richard Wright," Granville Hicks calmly reviewed the literary
merits of the novel. Dorothy Parker and Ted Poston had similar
reactions, but unfortunately most of the favorable reviews came out
somewhat late, as replies to the original attacks. Pieces by Henry
F. Winslow, Maxwell Geismar and Irving Howe all recognized the
truth and the realism of the novel, as well as the slowness of change
and the continued resistance of the racists, which, ironically enough,
was confirmed by the recent lynching of Emmett Till.[9] All this was
too late for Wright to derive much comfort from it, but when
Mrs. Jenny Bradley, who indirectly represented him in France, was
said to have reported that "Dick's book has had a terrible press in
the USA and they're saying in the USA that he ought to go home,"
Wright, infuriat ed, exclaimed in a letter of November 7 to Reynolds,
"What has my geographical position on earth got to do with the
faults or merits of a book?" although he was actually asking his
agent's opinion on the subject.

In 1953, Reynolds had stated unequivocally that no one could
live in Paris and set his novels in the United States, but Aswell did
not agree and sincerely admired *The Long Dream*. Certainly,
Robert Bone had not been able to consider the genesis of the novel
when he described it as Wright's "desperate attempt to rejuvenate
his art by returning to his Mississippi youth." [10] Admittedly Wright
sometimes got bogged down by his memories and seemed, in particular, determined to use certain chapters of "Tarbaby's Dawn"
at all costs. Nevertheless, his difficulties in extracting Fishbelly
from the American context were subsequently balanced by the
rapid composition of "Island of Hallucinations," which not only
proved his ability to set an original plot in Europe, but also char-
acterizes *The Long Dream* more as a solid foundation for this new
departure than as a return to the beaten path. Furthermore, most
of the action does not take place at the time of Wright's own youth

but as late as World War II and the early fifties (the fire in the
Rhythm Nightclub of Natchez, which inspired the central episode
of the novel, occurred about the time of his trip through the South
in the summer of 1940). The novel cannot, in fact, be criticized
for historical inaccuracy, but because it was not set in the recent
past none of the changes which were apparent by the end of the
fifties were mentioned. Because the novel was not about any recent
events, it seemed dated. There were no references to organizations
like the NAACP, the federal government was still regarded as a
remote power, and he made Clintonville a completely segregated
city. Insofar as every writer has only one story to tell, Wright may
have already said everything about the psychological, sexual and
social growth of black youth in *Black Boy*, but in *The Long Dream*,
he was also aiming to describe the complex racial relationship
symbolized by the black undertaker as the economic power of his
community and the white chief of police as the legal and political
power in the city. Here Wright succeeded admirably, with a detachment and objectivity due perhaps to exile and the passage of time.
Except for a few outdated expressions, the language is precise and
well suited to the characters, and there are none of the lengthy
tirades that were so damaging to *The Outsider*. The Whites, such
as police chief Cantley, who combines an undeniable complexity of
character with a certain humanity, are no longer the one-dimen-
sional types of his earlier novels. The great triumph of the novel
is the characterization of the relationship between father and son.
Tyree, subtly portrayed as a mixture of pride and humility, wiliness
and brutal frankness, fear and courage, represents the best incarnation of fatherhood in all of Wright's work and in many ways
is the father whom Wright would have liked to have.

There are structural weaknesses in *The Long Dream* (which
Granville Hicks very aptly assessed in his review), yet in many ways
the novel deserves to be considered the counterpart of *Native Son*
in its portrayal of a black youth being initiated into manhood
through racism. Bigger Thomas becomes a man because he kills;
Fishbelly, because his father is killed and, unable as he is to play
the game, because he has to flee. Of course, he is not a truly heroic
character, since he allows himself to be conditioned by his environment, his desire for comfort and status, and the white power.
Yet this conditioning and his attempts to escape it, which Wright
originally conceived as a mere introduction to the work, are far

from being undramatic and come to constitute precisely the subject of the novel. Wright returns to his origins and the South, but in a more subtle way and with a less self-centered orientation than in *Black Boy*. Although the literary technique of *The Long Dream* is superior to that of *The Outsider*, the overall effect is not superior to the impact of *Native Son*; yet it is fair to say that, if Wright was marking time, his last novel has given no evidence of a decline in his creative powers.

It chanced that the very day after he had read the unfavorable reactions to *The Long Dream,* he received a telegram from his brother, Leon, saying that their mother was seriously ill. He immediately cabled $100, but he had to borrow it from Reynolds. He no longer had any savings, and it did not look as if the sales of *White Man, Listen!* and *The Long Dream* would provide much income. He wrote Reynolds on November 6 that he might even have to borrow money on his holdings in France to cover these added expenses; thus, financial worries now became additional causes of daily anxiety.

As if enough had not happened already, Paul Reynolds telegraphed only the next day that Edward Aswell had suddenly died of a heart attack. The New York papers recalled his brilliant career. A former editor of the *Atlantic Monthly,* and administrator of the Eugene Saxton foundation, with such novelists as Kay Boyle and Fannie Hurst as his good friends, he was currently writing the biography of Thomas Wolfe, who had named him executor of his will. Wright, meanwhile, mourned the end of a unique friendship; he confided to Reynolds on November 6,

He was indeed a rare man, the like of which, as an editor and friend, I don't think I shall find again soon in this life. What made my relationship with Ed so wonderfully unique was that both of us were Southerners and we both knew what the subject matter down in the South was. And we both accepted that subject matter as being valid for writing. There is no better Southerner than an honest one for he has a lot to face and accept. And Ed did that. . . . I'm still sort of numb from the news.

The allusion to the South as a still "valid subject matter" was, in fact, a reference to Reynolds's opposing views on this matter.

Yet another blow fell on November 7. Wright was trying to make some money by selling his latest books in France, only to discover that Reynolds's representative had apparently been serving him very poorly. In order to pay the deposit on an apartment in 1948, the agent had obtained from Gallimard advances of 200,000 francs for each of Wright's next two novels. Gallimard had accordingly deducted half this sum from his advance on *Le Transfuge* in 1955, and, since they had not wanted to publish any of his later works, the second half had been taken from his royalties. The agent, however, was claiming that Gallimard still had an option on him. Wright did not necessarily want to change agents, but he did need to be rescued from this disconcerting situation, especially, he thought, since the agent was not doing him any good by telling everyone about the unfavorable reviews of *The Long Dream* in America.[11] A few days later, Reynolds asked her to cease her negotiations on Wright's behalf.

Wright was just getting a little nervous about *Ebony*'s proposed article on him after hearing that Ollie Harrington might not be in charge of the photographs, when an incident occurred that aggravated his worries. On November 12, 1958, *Time* magazine published an article on the black writers in Paris, entitled "Amid the Alien Corn." The author quoted Chester Himes, Ollie Harrington and William Gardner Smith on the near absence of racism in France, before continuing,

Richard Wright, the dean of Negro writers abroad, says bluntly: "I like to live in France because it is a free country. Then, there are my daughters. They are receiving an excellent education in France." What of the danger of getting out of touch with U.S. life? Snaps Wright: "The Negro problem in America has not changed in three hundred years."

The journal then cited William Gardner Smith's opposing opinion and added a remark from Richard Gibson on the "Roman exile" of William Demby and Ralph Ellison.

The week before, as it happened, Wright had refused to grant an interview to *Time* and *The American Pen*. Meanwhile, photographer Gisèle Freund, with whom Wright had been friendly in Argentina, had come to take photographs of him at the request of her New

York agent; she later affirmed that she had no idea whom the photographs were intended for. In any event Wright had made no statement to her. Aside from the last sentence, the opinions attributed to Wright in the *Time* article corresponded more or less to what he actually believed and often expressed, but the article was distinctly intended to sully his reputation, and not combat racism. In his November 14 letter to Reynolds, he quoted the cable which he had immediately sent the magazine: "Quotations attributed to me in your article Amid Alien Corn completely false and fabricated. Astounded at Time's journalistic ethics. Did not see your reporter. Are you aping Communist tactics of character assassination?"

Wright asked his friends at the embassy to be on the alert and went to the Paris office of the magazine, where they apologized profusely and claimed that the whole thing had been an error. Yet *Time* categorically refused to admit that Gisèle Freund had not interviewed him for the magazine. Wright obtained a written statement from her denying this, but despite the request he made to her on November 9, she never defended him very vigorously. Reynolds consulted a lawyer, but bringing suit would have been so time-consuming and so costly, and would in any case have procured Wright only a few symbolic cents for damages, that he abandoned the fight.[12] He later learned from a member of the *Time* Paris office that such defamatory tactics had been inspired by some letters in a British magazine written for the purpose of discrediting black writers in exile. Wright's energetic defense did win him a victory, however, since *Time* had intended to publish in a forthcoming issue comments by some readers who were hostile to Wright but subsequently refrained from doing so.[13]

In Wright's eyes there was no doubt that this recent skirmish was linked to the "Gibson affair." The quotation attributed to William G. Smith actually repeated the more or less disguised accusations of anti-Americanism which Gibson had made against Wright, Himes and Ellison, whose denial that he had gone to live in exile in Rome was eventually published on February 9, 1959. Wright was the victim of disloyal and malicious attacks which justified only too well his criticisms of America. As he concluded bitterly, "It is things like the article in *Time* which make you want to remain abroad."

2

For Wright life in France was now as strained as it had been in the United States, disproving his agent's assertion that he was too sheltered from the tensions indispensable for his writing good fiction; but Reynolds was right in supposing that adversity provided a propitious atmosphere for his client's creativity. If it was true that Wright's attention was sometimes diverted by discouraged broodings or calculations and counterattacks, then the necessity of having to fight seemed to consolidate his energies. In writing a novel he could escape and symbolically conquer his anxieties and enemies. It was certainly the freest and most satisfying way for him to exercise his will and power, and so, as soon as he could, he returned to the relative peace of Ailly, where he devoted himself to writing "Island of Hallucinations."

The French political situation had calmed somewhat, and Julia had passed her baccalaureate with flying colors, when the family finally left for the farm. In three months during the summer of 1958, Wright completed 400 pages of the first version, even though he was revising and polishing his text as he went along, which was not his usual practice. He had already been able to send 115 pages to Aswell on June 13, just a few months before his death, for his reaction.

The novel begins with Fishbelly's flight from New York to Paris, where his long meditations reveal his past to the reader, followed by an episode on his arrival in which two French crooks relieve him of half his fortune. Next he runs into a prostitute from Montmartre, Anita, before he finally meets Yvette Lafon, a girl from an upper middle-class family who is the first to succumb to his advances. Wright planned the real plot—the portrayal of Fishbelly's friendship with "Mechanical," a black American named after the very type he represented, and Fish's change into a kind of pimp providing the soldiers on the American bases with obliging women—to begin after these chapters. Wright, like Zola in the composition of *Nana*, carefully researched prostitution in Paris, and could quote, as he had done in *Pagan Spain,* from letters he had obtained in Pigalle.

Thus, intrigues and controversies did not totally disrupt the steady progress of the novel. Writing it obviously enabled Wright to put obsessions down on paper and to take revenge on his enemies by turning them into fictional characters whom he could control and unmask at will. Wright had initially intended to use Fishbelly's adventures as a means of describing the life of the black American expatriates, and the accounts of their petty intrigues as well as their political and ideological activities fitted with that intention. Once again he became so engrossed in the wealth of material that, as had happened with *The Long Dream*, even another full volume was not enough to finish the story, which was supposed to end with Fishbelly's deportation. On November 19, 1958, when Wright sent his progress report to Timothy Seldes, who had replaced Edward Aswell at Doubleday, he had written more than 500 pages and needed 100 more just to get to Fishbelly's second conquest. In addition, the reviews of *The Long Dream* had convinced him that a third volume would be a good idea. The reader could not assimilate so much emotionally charged material on race relations if it were too concentrated. He wanted, therefore, to dilute it, emphasizing the dialogue more than the plot, since the melodramatic aspect of the latter had been diminished when he moved the action from America to the freer racial atmosphere of France.[14]

By November 25, the manuscript was 514 pages long. Wright originally intended to rework the final 300 pages before taking a break prior to going back over the entire thing, but with a new surge of energy, he worked straight through on the corrections and revisions and finished this first version by mid-January. The manuscript was typed and sent to Reynolds on February 16, 1959, with a covering letter which indicated, more than ever before, Wright's doubts about the value of his novel and his future as a writer:

I've never sent you a ms. about which I had more misgivings than this. I can readily think of a hundred reasons why Americans won't like this book. But the book is true. Everything in the ms. happened, but I've twisted characters so that people won't recognize them.

I'd like as quick a reaction from Doubleday as possible and I'll tell you why. If this book flops as completely as *The Long Dream*, then I know that Doubleday won't want to publish me again under the old conditions. . . . If such should happen, then I must look about quickly for some other way of making a living. So you see that this is a crisis book. It takes me a year to turn out a novel that satisfies me and if a publisher thinks that I'm not a good investment, he will, of course, drop me.

I'm not criticizing anybody in all this. I know that it is because I live in France that I've such a bad press in the United States. But I can't change that. My children have never lived under racist conditions and they'd get emotionally ill if I brought them back. Indeed, I'd be a criminal to do so. . . .

Many white writers live here in France, but no one brings up their being in exile. It is only a handful of black Americans who attract attention, and the wrong kind.

If "Island of Hallucinations" gets the same press that *The Long Dream* did, then I must seriously think of abandoning writing for a time. One has to be realistic.

In thus apparently staking his career on the fate of his novel, Wright was rightly taking into consideration the economic conditions of the publishing world in the United States, but his pessimism could also perhaps have been an excuse to justify in advance a failure caused by certain intrinsic weaknesses in the novel, however authentic in other ways it may have been.

Since Wright had never before written about his experiences abroad, unlike William Gardner Smith and James Baldwin, who set their American characters in postwar Germany and France in *Last of the Conquerors* and *Giovanni's Room,* the novel was a departure from his usual mode. Moreover, except for his analysis of the psychological results of racial oppression, which he covered thoroughly in *White Man, Listen!*, the subject itself was new in its unraveling of the intrigues partly instigated by an American secret service desirous of controlling black citizens on French soil.

Yet many aspects of this novel, in particular the structure, are similar to *The Long Dream*, and the two were, of course, linked not only by their common hero, but by his childhood pals, now soldiers in the NATO forces, who reappear to act as advisers or ironic doubles of their young friend. Nightmares also figure in a striking way, as they did in the earlier novel. Fishbelly's terrifying dream in the plane, with mingled visions of a coffin, his father and the white temptress, sets the tone. In another dream, some Whites in underwater masks try to drown him during a ferryboat ride. After he seduces Yvette, Fish expresses his guilt in yet another nightmare, in which the Whites chase him among trains and coffins until he covers his face with flour. The coffin appears again, this time full of small change, which the chief of police, Cantley, is in the process of burying. When Fish opens it he finds Mechanical dressed as a woman, and he hastens to bury it again. These dreams and themes establish the link between *The Long Dream* and "Island of Hallucinations," which is also divided into four sections. Part one, "Phantoms" takes place entirely on the plane; "False Faces" and "Delayed Bombs" cover his love affairs and the political intrigues among the black Americans in Paris; and finally "Parenthood," much shorter, is an account of Fishbelly's final choice between his two mistresses, and the violent death of Mechanical.

The first part stresses the passionate reactions of the American passengers on the plane to Paris in the presence of a black man. A businessman from Texas loudly expresses his disgust; a student is afraid of having Blacks in his classes at the Sorbonne; a missionary headed for the Gold Coast associates color with sexuality; a respectable citizen and member of the Ku Klux Klan meditates about the virginity of his daughter. For his part, Fishbelly is so timid and cautious that he cannot conceal his fear. He is soon caught up by events and his new environment, drawn into an unbelievable labyrinth of intrigues which explain the title of the novel.

Fishbelly's interests lie in three general areas: women, money and politics. The myth of the white woman quickly impels him to seek a companion. In Pigalle he meets Anita, a strange creature with paraffin-inflated breasts and, after an operation, an invisible navel, symbol of the unnatural woman—an artificial doll, mercenary and mechanical. The group of prostitutes surrounding her exploit Fish before he eventually finds that he can sell their wares to the G.I.'s at the base in Evreux, who miss their striptease shows. In living off women, Fish in many ways is following in his father's footsteps, although he soon rises to another social echelon by associating with

Yvette Lafon, a Parisian heiress, who, like Mary Dalton, had become a Communist through idealism and rebellion against her father. She is a virgin when Fish seduces her, but she offers him much more than sensual love by suggesting that he partake of her tradition and share her past. She describes to him the horrors of the war, the bombings and the German occupation; how, as a gesture of defiance, she burned her father's supply of black-market butter, and how the Americans liberated the city. She is actually offering him the soul of France, which their trips to the country reveal in the simple pleasures of life and in figures of French history: Fish may reject Joan of Arc and her voices, Napoleon and his thirst for power, but he, like Wright, is fascinated by Fouché, the great chief of police.

Fishbelly's principal mentor is not, however, Yvette, but an Afro-American lawyer in exile who has a great deal of Wright in him. Ned Harrison explains to Fish, for the reader's benefit, that "the sex of a white woman is practically a religion" for anyone who had always been taught not to touch them under penalty of death. He also tells Fish about other Blacks who had come to Paris before him. One of them, a college graduate, was working for an American company that sent him to the Third World, where he managed to save some money by falsifying his travel expenses. He was hoping to marry his white secretary, who had gone to Vassar, but she had him fired by their boss when he had an affair with a French girl back in Paris. Another fellow named Jimmy Whitfield methodically exploited women until he was finally denounced to the American Embassy. Threatened with deportation, he chose to commit a crime and stay in prison rather than return to the United States. Ned also explained one day, after Fish had slept with Yvette to overcome his complexes, that "taking a white girl like you took Yvette is a way of proving to yourself and to the white man that you're really *mentally* white, even if the white man says you're not." [15]

One day, however, Yvette, who is now pregnant, disappears suddenly, kidnapped, as it turns out, by her brother, who has denounced Fish to the police as a dangerous revolutionary. Fish then takes refuge with a friend, where he meets another young girl, Marie-Rose. After a party he seduces her, too, so that by the end of the novel, he is forced to choose between his two mistresses. Love has not given him freedom, even if he felt much more than sexual attraction for Yvette. She could perhaps have Europeanized him, but he discovered that he was irrevocably American. Wright, who was certainly speaking in his own name, concludes, "He knew he could never be French even if he lived in France a million years" ("IH," p. 353).

Nevertheless, Fish does manage to overcome some of the inhibitions he had developed growing up in America. The episode of the "chapeau américain," published in *Soon, One Morning*—Fish thinks the crowd is going to lynch him when they are merely making fun of his wide-brimmed hat—occurs early in the novel. Soon the hero is mingling easily in expatriate circles, if not among the native French, and is exposed to the personal and political intrigues which split the little colony. He also meets his strange friend, Mechanical, the grandson of a hangman, a homosexual whose face is scarred by smallpox, and just as much of a complete masochist as his faithful dog. Mechanical comes from Detroit, where his father had been a fanatic follower of Father Divine; he had spent six months in prison for having thrown a bottle of ink at an editor who refused him a job as a reporter because of his color, and he had lived in Africa before marrying Céline, a French girl who admired his writing and had borne him two daughters. As a Trotskyist, he is playing a subtle game, working with the French police to track down Stalinists with the help of a West Indian named Juggler. This political circle is joined by a Nigerian, Saturday, and by Bill Hart, a Fascist who spies on Blacks for the American government. In order to put him to the test, Mechanical signs Hart's name to a pro-Communist article which he sends to *Life* magazine. Despite the congratulations of his fellow cell members, Hart is forced to give himself away by admitting that he did not write the article, while Mechanical has to confess these events to the French police and is arrested after a café brawl with Bill Hart. He commits suicide in the dramatic and grandiose gesture of hurling himself from the top of Notre Dame.

Fishbelly, however, refuses to become involved in these political intrigues which set the Afro-Americans against one another: "Fish respected the world too much to want to become a politician; his deeper yearning was for that world to confer upon him a recognition of his humanity" ("IH," p. 323). This attitude is shared by Ned Harrison. Disliked by the other Blacks because he scorns their petty rivalries, Ned at one time tried to found a French-American Association; he is both a pacifist and a pacifier, as well as a wise friend who testifies for Fish whom Mechanical, in his fury, had accused of kidnapping Yvette.

Wright's satire of course reflects the actions of those who had surrounded him during the years, and draws upon their trivial or heated discussions at the Café Tournon, but it is not a simple *roman à clef*, since the easily recognizable experiences and traits taken from his friends and enemies in Paris (Richard Gibson, William Gardner Smith, James Baldwin and Ollie Harrington, among others) are used in composite portraits; no one character corresponds exactly to a real person. Nowhere else, with the exception perhaps of his journal in 1947, does Wright express so openly his often extremely unflattering opinions of people he knew. This can certainly be interpreted as revenge, the striking down on paper of the puppets and phantasms that troubled him.

The desire to write in a more picaresque vein is also obvious. Fishbelly's adventures in Clintonville were tragic, or at least pathetic, even though the real hero of *The Long Dream* was his father, Tyree Tucker. In the second volume, however, the author-narrator only half-identified with Fish and his adventures. The epigraph to "Phantoms," a quotation from Mark Twain, is explicit: "I like him; I'm ashamed of him; and it is a delight to me to be where he is if he has new material on which to work his vanities where they will show him off as with a limelight." Fish in Paris is thus a kind of "schlemiel," a would-be hustler akin to Wright's earlier hero Jake Jackson, only the three *A*'s of *Lawd Today*—"automobile, alimony and abortion"—are replaced by the three *C*'s which govern the life of the expatriates—"cunt, cognac and Communism." Although Wright does not spare the Afro-Americans, he is no more merciful to the French. Landing in Shannon Airport on the flight over, Fish meets Jacques Duval, an engineer who has visited Harlem and knows how to gain Fish's confidence. He advises him to open a small hotel in Paris, with money which Fish boasts of having brought with him. At this point a pretty blond girl arrives and the two men invite her to sit at their table. It turns out that she has an apartment to let in the sixteenth arrondissement. Fish agrees to pay half the rent in advance, but when he and Jacques go to Avenue Maréchal Foch, he discovers that Nicole Rivet, the real owner of the apartment, is not the beautiful blonde. What can they do? Jacques sets off for the police station but never returns, leaving Fish to figure out, after inquiring at Orly, that he has been duped by a couple of crooks. The same sordid thirst for money reigns in Pigalle, where Fish, now rid of all scruples, goes to beat the pimps on their own ground by exploiting a troupe of stripteasers.

This does not mean that Wright was particularly desirous of portraying French life for its own sake. Paris is merely a setting, sometimes sinister, and sometimes poetic, a world of cafés and monuments, political demonstrations, financial or government scandals, solid bourgeois society. The warmth of France is more evident in the country scenes, but, with the exception of Yvette, the French characters are puppets. The Afro-American characters were more carefully drawn, but even their numerous disappointments and schemes were compiled more as proofs to fill up a dossier than as ways of making them interesting as individuals. Undoubtedly the most skillful analysis is that of the personality of Mechanical, although it is never clear whether he is supposed to be an object of pity or of laughter.[16] He is complex but naïve in his Machiavellianism, and his death is as ambitious as his life had been. Deaf to the pleas of a priest, Mechanical finally throws himself off the tower of Notre Dame, only to be caught halfway down by the net which the police have had time to stretch out. He hangs himself from it when, at the risk of his own life, the priest manages to cut the rope. Mechanical then falls to the courtyard below and, with a final irony of fate, injures two onlookers. His suicide never achieves the romantic beauty of a final act of defiance, and is merely an ignominious ending to a series of aborted or sabotaged attempts. Thus, none of the characters rise from mediocrity to the level of tragedy. Abandoning the anti-hero, represented by Bigger Thomas, as well as the metaphysical rebel, symbolized by Cross Damon, Wright seems to have restricted himself to these third-rate protagonists out of a feeling that they were the only ones who deserved to live in the cowardly universe of the fifties.

Instances of irony and humor also differentiated the novel from earlier works, and were similar to the lighter tone of his stories "Big Black Good Man" and "Man, God Ain't Like That." Nevertheless, the primary question explored in "Island of Hallucinations" was not, in Wright's opinion, that of how the black expatriates practiced their little games of espionage or indulged in petty quarrels, but rather why their exile, which was generally a liberation, did not change their lives, which continued at best like a daydream and at the worst like an obsessive nightmare.

There's nothing on earth calculated to shatter a person's faith in the ordinary reality of life better than an atmosphere like this. When you make a person feel that what he sees and lives each day and hour is not true, then it is as though you shunted him off the earth. He is on an island and this island is himself. . . . Most of the world we live in is given to us by those around us. In order to live we must trust, in a sense, even our enemies. No man can stand absolutely alone and make any meaning out of life. When you begin distrusting the images that make your world, you're standing alone. Soon you'll begin to doubt everything. Your world turns into a dream. It is as though you were having a hallucination ("IH," p. 328).

Ned Harrison thus expounds the deep meaning of the novel and its title, stressing one of Wright's favorite themes since the composition of *The Outsider*.

Society won't let men do what they *want*, what they *desire*, what they, above all, feel like doing. The basic law of social life is that we cannot act on all our feelings. So we kill those feelings. . . . Men trapped between the hot desire to destroy something and a fearfulness to act become loaded with a burden of guilt. . . . These guilty men cannot conceive that the menace that they feel is but the shadow of their renounced dream cast by the lurid light of their fears. So they start looking for the "nigger" . . . just any old thing you happen not to like ("IH," p. 329).

The serious exploration of this guilt-ridden world necessitates the creation of noble or tragic figures, but the only character of any depth in the novel is Ned Harrison. In a way Fish lives in Harrison's shadow, just as he had grown up in Tyree's, but the ambivalent personality of Tyree in *The Long Dream* seems to have provided two characters for "Island of Hallucinations." The mentor Harrison is its positive incarnation and the Machiavellian masochist, Mechanical, the negative. As Wright's spokesman, Harrison reveals and explains the action and, after Mechanical's suicide, expresses the author's own aversion to masochism.

When a man makes a cry from the depths of his heart, we ought to be able to know what he's talking about. That's the least a man can demand from his fellows. . . . There are some traits about religion that make a proud, emotionally clean man ashamed. One of these traits is the love of suffering ("IH," p. 503).

Wright deplored it as not only unmasculine, but repugnant, and once Mechanical had left the abnormal world of the South he was transformed into an object of scorn. In this way, Wright condemns the conditioning that induces the black man to scheme for survival and in so doing rid himself of his moral scruples. He wanted to see the Black become a responsible adult, master of his destiny, but, with rare exceptions, it did not seem possible in Europe. This is certainly the reason why Wright used Algeria, a revolutionary nation within the ancestral land of Africa, as the setting for Fishbelly's renaissance in volume three.

Perhaps Harrison has enough dignity to restore the tragic perspective to events, but he does not participate enough in the action, limiting himself to long comments upon it somewhat like the unsatisfactory characters of *The Outsider*. Wright often emphasized the inherent tragedy in the fact that the black American, conditioned as he was by racism, could not adapt to living in a free world. The long-term damage caused to the psyche of the oppressed is more detrimental than economic oppression. While a good part of his human comedy is based on the observation of externals, and thus ridicules the black American for being at a loss in new situations, Wright does not abandon his moralistic point of view. In fact, he is perceptibly torn between the tragic—which too often comes out as melodrama in the plot or theorizing in the dialogue—and the picaresque—which becomes more harshly ironic than humorous. The serious elements of *The Long Dream* lost their nobility in the second volume so that, in spite of his most likable traits, Fish was finally little more than a pimp and professional seducer.

If Wright could have controlled his indignant denunciation of racism and its effects, the satire might have attained greater dignity. Criticizing Americans and French, Whites and Blacks, he warns his Afro-American readers to beware the trap set by Whites who seek power by fostering rivalry within the black community. In addition, he maintains that the Blacks should no longer believe in a democracy whose leaders are secretly perfecting devices for controlling public opinion and detecting the slightest resistance to the system.

Unfortunately, however, in his anger he lacks perspective and very often descends to the level of harsh revenge, since he was still in the throes of the combats he describes. In a way, the very authenticity on which he prided himself prevented him from imbuing the puppets of the American black community of Paris with the dimension necessary for a great novel. As a result, the picaresque elements detract not only from the tragedy, but from the irony itself, since the characters are too paltry to be worthy of righteous indignation. Mediocre, ambiguous and unreal describe Wright's universe of illusions and hallucinations, but perhaps the subject itself made its treatment in the novel somewhat unsatisfactory.

"Island of Hallucinations" does have some of the power of a good picaresque novel, since Wright is still as much a master story-teller as ever, capable of writing episodes in the best style of burlesque, as well as the usual intrigues of a thriller. The innumerable digressions and anecdotes spring from the same didactic tendency that showed up in *The Outsider,* but they are more easily absorbed in a context of café conversations, and enlivened by humor, as proven by the passages which appeared in *Soon, One Morning.* In certain respects, "Island of Hallucinations" is similar to *Lawd Today,* which makes it surprising to see Wright constantly stressing the serious side of his message, not only in letters to his publisher and agent, but in the novel itself. He sometimes seems to have been unaware of the truly comic effect of certain scenes and situations, as if he keeps steering the story toward the tragic from a sort of compulsion which has nothing to do with the novel itself.

It certainly seems that at the time Wright was not able to maintain the emotional detachment and distance indispensable for achieving the necessary humor. His doubts about his own talent and the possibility of making himself heard in America were the price he was paying for his refusal to keep his opinions of American policy to himself. Since Wright took each separate attack as part of a large plot against him, he was too upset to combat it on a comic level in the novel. Nor could he help dramatizing the fact that fate now seemed to be working against him. When he heard of his mother's death on January 14, 1959, he was not surprised; he merely withdrew even further into his grief.[17] For several months, in fact, he had been greatly discouraged due to physical and nervous exhaustion, his uncertain financial situation and his profound sadness at being the object of deceit and injustice—all of which far outweighed any reasons for hope brought on by the approach of spring. How, in these circumstances, could "Island of Hallucinations" have turned out any more serene?

Reynolds showed no enthusiasm for the novel in his letter of February 4, 1959. He was sorry that Fishbelly had become essentially a spectator of the action, reacting mostly to overly philosophical speeches from his mentors. He also thought that the racial atmosphere of the United States had changed to such an extent that the references to lynching and other practices in the process of disappearing no longer rang true. Wright did not try to justify himself when he wrote back on March 2, but merely explained that even if a sociological reality disappears, its profound psychological effects still remain, which was precisely the meaning of the book. He had proof in the experience of Africa and Asia as well as in his own life: "The attempt to organize American Negroes in Paris that is described in the book was my experience; I placed it in the mouth of Ned. I could not organize them because they were still back in their Black Belts, though they lived in Paris." That, for him, was the truth in 1959. The social and political changes since World War II had not changed the reactions of the Blacks toward America; only the week before, he had spent an entire day talking to Martin Luther King, who had confirmed this opinion.[18]

The civil rights movement and the advent of Black Power during the sixties indicate that Wright was not far wrong. Martin Luther King and the new leaders were just beginning their campaigns, and the recent wave of black nationalism and racial pride had not yet arisen. The black Americans had not yet reacted with violence and strength against their conditioning, but as they started to reject the image of themselves represented by Tyree and Fishbelly, in order to strive toward their new ideal, it was inevitable that they would refuse to accept some of the painful truths that Wright was reiterating. His facts were authentic, but their truth could hardly serve the positive myths of black militancy. In hoping for a cultural renaissance and for revolutionary action Wright had placed his faith in the Third World, neglecting the Afro-American potential which was going to show itself much sooner than he expected.

Meanwhile the liberals, who had become more optimistic than the situation warranted, due to a certain amount of economic progress among the black bourgeoisie and a few legal victories for desegregation, were only willing to look on the positive side of Americanism. Wright, who was caught between both points of view—each of which opposed his for different reasons—was thus deprived of his usual audience, as he pointed out to Reynolds on March 2:

I'm sure that no one reading my novel can say that I'm for Russia, but, if they define being for America as being unable to say that America is not perfect, then they can say that I'm a bad guy who is just as dangerous as a Communist. All of this makes it hard for a writer. I have grown to feel that I would rather not write about Negroes any more; I've grown to feel that nobody, not even Negroes, wants to listen anymore. Yet I'm convinced that I'm telling some important truths. What does one do in a situation like that? Frequently, of late, I've been casting around in my mind the possibility of dropping writing about the Negro entirely. Yet that too represents a problem.

For the time being, however, Wright was anxious to hear from Doubleday on "Island of Hallucinations" (for which he was still trying to find another title [19]) and to receive a contract for volume three, somewhat for reassurance about his ability as a novelist, but mainly to secure a more regular and substantial income. Without waiting for Doubleday's decision he sent Reynolds two letters dated March 13 and March 15, outlining the third novel, in which Fishbelly finally becomes a man of action. Tyree had been the central character of *The Long Dream*, and Mechanical and Harrison had taken over in "Island of Hallucinations," with Fish becoming more than ever a mirror for the action. In volume three, he was finally to be liberated from his racial conditioning and would become the main protagonist.

Home again, Fish meets his old friends Tony and Zeke, who had himself had some trouble with a German girl. Fish tells them about his problems with Marie-Rose and Yvette, and they dissuade him from assuming his responsibilities toward these girls as he had, for once, intended to do. He therefore takes a third girl on a tour of the American NATO bases in France and Germany with his striptease show. On his return, there are now three complaints filed against him by girls whom he has seduced. On the advice of Anita, who rescues him from the police, Fishbelly decides to marry Yvette. She persuades him that they should go to North Africa, and then to black Africa. There he starts an insurance company, which fails. He asks his mother, who begs him to return to the United States, for money, and she comes looking for him, arriving just in time for the birth of her grandson. She then helps the couple to get settled in New York, which is how Fishbelly returns to his native country, hoping some day to integrate himself into American life.

Africa provides Fish with the time to catch his breath and reflect for the first time in his life. He meditates on his origins and his African heritage; he becomes aware of what is happening in politics, and of the millions of men who are liberating themselves in the Third World. Thus begins Fishbelly's moral, social and political awakening. Through Yvette, he breaks the racial spell that has shackled him since his youth, and he can now see the world in a more realistic light. The novel was to end with some thoughts on the future of Fishbelly's son. Should he remain in Europe or should he accompany his grandmother Emma to Mississippi at the risk of becoming another Fishbelly?

Some of the author's own story, up to the unresolved and agonizing problem of exile, is contained in the outlines of this trilogy, and it presents, in a somewhat different form, the theme of the "magnum opus" which had haunted him for so long. Wright had originally wanted to paint the destiny of the black people in America from their beginning through their liberation. The circle finally seems to close when he takes Fishbelly to Africa, the country of his ancestors, in order to bring him back, changed, to American soil.

Timothy Seldes mentioned the need for serious revision in his first reactions to "Island of Hallucinations," and without any precise idea of what would be required, Wright declared himself ready to follow Reynolds's advice and any that Seldes was willing to give him. On March 12, 1959, Seldes announced that he would be coming to Paris soon and the discussion of particular points could be postponed until that time, but that Wright would have to cut repetitions, some long speeches and a didactic tone which hampered the vivacity and coherence of the story.

Seldes's discussions with Wright at the beginning of June, 1959, did not clarify the situation a great deal. He said that the beginning had to be changed, the plot made more dramatic and more strongly outlined, and the didactic tirades completely eliminated. By this time, Wright was no longer in the mood to go back to the novel, since he wanted to settle his plans for another trip to French West Africa before rereading it at leisure and planning revisions. In any case, Doubleday was in no hurry to publish the book or to give him another contract, so for the time being, the matter was dropped.

TWENTY-ONE

Setbacks, disappointments and attacks had become, with time, an integral part of Wright's daily life, but he was not therefore any less upset by them. One after another, his hopes were dashed: first the plan to return to Africa to write another report; then a proposed move to London; and finally, the possibility of achieving financial security from the success of the New York stage adaptation of *The Long Dream*. After the summer of 1959, in fact, he was obliged to take on additional work to meet his expenses, while he was constantly struggling against exhaustion and sickness to continue his regular writing. In this increasing moral and physical solitude, Wright was inspired to compose some of his most delicate and polished poems, haiku born of a tormented soul confronted with hardship. Yet, although he privately seemed to withdraw into himself in search of peace, he never abandoned his constant commitment to social change, as evidenced, in this case, by his support of the anticolonial cause. Thus his last lecture, his last letter, and his last radio broadcast, only three days before his sudden death, were all aimed at revealing the sinister maneuvers of the American secret service in Paris. It is symbolic that as he was born into rebellion, this final chapter of his life should end in it.

It was Wright's intransigence—his personal honesty, which rejected compromise—that caused the failure of the project for which he had been cherishing the most hope since the beginning of the year. He wanted, essentially, to do for French-speaking Africa the kind of report that he had done for the Gold Coast in *Black Power*. In order to get the funds, he would have to approach a foundation, or some other organization, as well as a publishing house or a magazine. Mercer Cook, who represented the American Society for African Culture in Paris, knew about this project and said that he was interested. He assured Wright of his personal support and referred him to John A. Davis, the executive secretary of the New York Society.

Meanwhile, however, Wright had been keeping his distance from certain organizations that he had formerly supported wholeheartedly. Autumn of 1958, for instance, was the last time he supported the Society for African Culture, helping them to organize a meeting which took place in London then. He had also moved away from *Présence Africaine*. He thought that the magazine, now dominated by the pro-French, the pro-Catholics, and the antinationalists, was no longer working for its original goal, which should have continued to be the liberation of African culture. In the same way, he considered the American Society for African Culture, which he had helped to found, much too moderate and not sufficiently independent. Thus, he refused an invitation to attend the Society's first New York congress in March, 1959, with the excuse that he had to finish his new novel. He was also supposed to be a delegate to the second Congress of Black Writers and Artists, planned for Easter, 1959, in Rome, but the meeting was postponed to September because of the French referendum, which claimed the time and energy of all the intellectuals who, like Aimé Césaire, exercised political functions. This allowed Wright to put off until the last minute his refusal to participate. His reasons were the same, however. If the Congress took place in Rome, it would in some way be under the influence of the papacy, the Catholics and, hence, the conservative members of the organization. Nothing positive for the cultural decolonization of Africa could be accomplished.

While lunching with Ben Zevin, who happened to be passing through Paris, Wright found out that World would be willing to publish his report, and also heard from Reynolds on May 1 that Doubleday would give him an advance of $2,500. He still needed to find the rest of the $10,000 which he deemed essential for the trip, given the cost of traveling and of hiring an interpreter.

He therefore submitted a detailed and somewhat ambitious plan to John A. Davis, in a letter of May 11, 1959. Setting out in the autumn of 1959, Wright proposed to cover Sénégal, Mauritania, Sudan, Guinea, the Ivory Coast, Nigeria and Upper Volta in a minimum of six but perhaps as much as nine months. He would take notes and photographs, and record interviews on tape. Studying and weighing the influences of the various traditions and religions, he would analyze the attitude and strength of the local elites, the only ones capable of efficient government. He would thereby plan to answer the question: "What basis is there now in French West Africa for the erection of independent, stable governments?"

Through his friend Michel Bokanowski, then minister of the P.T.T., Wright was hoping to enlist the support of French authorities who could perhaps use such an essay on political anthropology. With the help of the Congress for Cultural Freedom, the local American information services and his own contacts among the nationalist leaders and African heads of state, he thought he would be able to get in touch directly with the different parties and political movements. His main problem, therefore, was financial, and John Davis's reaction was discouraging. Since the annual budget of the Society was established in June, Davis claimed that there was too little time left to study the plan. In his reply, however, on May 23, 1959, he added what was certainly the main reason for his refusal.

After you have finished the book, it may turn out that we ought not to associate ourselves with it for purely organizational reasons. Should that prove to be the case, we would be in the position of having gotten nothing for our money. . . . Your request ought to be for a smaller amount.

Wright wrote back on June 3:

I quite understand your position. Perhaps a way could be found to solve the money question, but the question of whether your organization's sponsoring me would bring good or harm to you is quite another thing. After due reflection, I've come to the conclusion that the prospect of doing "harm" would psychologically cripple me in trying to gather material in French Africa. I have no notion of just what I'd find in French Africa and no notion as to what my reactions would be. Certainly I'd not like to go there with the feeling that I'd have to inhibit myself in whatever I'd write.

Under these circumstances, I think that it is in your interests as well as mine that we don't go into this project now. I think that the wiser course for me would be to seek some more disinterested sponsorship. By doing so, I am personally responsible for what I'd write and the public's reaction.

Nevertheless, he did not lose courage. On the advice of Nicolas Nabokov, he approached Edmund Wilson and *The New Yorker*, while the Congress for Cultural Freedom led him to hope for $5000 from the Ford Foundation. In the meantime, learning that the CIA, had infiltrated organizations like American Society for African Culture, he lost his illusions and at the same time any remaining desire to have recourse to them. Finally, when his friend E. Franklin Frazier visited him in October, he learned that the Ford Foundation had refused the grant and that Frazier himself could not accept Wright's invitation to accompany him to Africa. What with Gunnar Myrdal's efforts to raise funds having failed, and the news that Ira Morris, who at that time was supporting liberal pacifist movements and was one of Wright's last hopes, could be of no help to him, the plan was doomed. Sickness, lack of money and finally death prevented him from realizing this project which meant so much to him.

There were two major reasons for Wright's growing desire to leave Paris. He was primarily disturbed by the fact that French politics seemed to be falling more and more into the personal power of one man and becoming increasingly submissive to pressure from America, but he also found the peaceful Parisian atmosphere he had enjoyed shattered by the quarrels and attacks instigated by the enemies of the expatriate black writers. Following the reception of *The Long Dream* in the United States, he thought that he might stop writing for a time and look for another profession. He seriously considered helping the African nationalist cause directly, and at the same time, getting a job in some English-speaking country, which would support his family. Through his friend George Padmore, he offered his services first to Ghana, as a consultant or a teacher, but he did not receive a reply from Kwame Nkrumah. He was also disappointed by Eric Williams, whom he had once helped after he had been fired from the Caribbean Commission. Now, as President of Trinidad, Williams could have returned the favor. Alva Myrdal, who was reprsenting Sweden in India, offered her support, but Wright was reluctant to live in India. He decided to try his luck in England.

Ever since 1953, Wright had been thinking that he might one day like to live in London. In 1957, to make sure that he would not run into any difficulties with the British government, which he had not spared in *Black Power*, he had asked his friend John Strachey, former Labour minister of national defense, to sound out the reactions of the Home Office. The evasive replies of Reginald Butler had forced Strachey to ask him officially before the House of Commons on November 20, 1958.[1] He publicly received the assurance that Wright's request, already submitted to the British Embassy in Paris, would be considered in the light of the recent loosening of the generally restrictive laws governing the immigration of colored people.

In the spring of 1959, Ellen made several trips, of a few weeks each, to London, looking for a suitable place to live. London would not only be a quieter place for Wright to work, but it would also be a more convenient base for her own activities as a literary agent. Julia, meanwhile, had decided to continue her studies at Cambridge University, after taking her second baccalaureate.

Somewhat unwillingly, Wright agreed to sell the Ailly farm, in order to pay for the new establishment in London. Although he had never had to mortgage his property to cover current expenses, it was out of the question that he keep the farm and also move to London.

Shortly after an autographing party on June 26 at the Escalier Bookstore, which marked the Calman-Lévy publication of *Ecoute, homme blanc*,[2] Wright fell suddenly ill, victim of a virulent attack of amoebic dysentery which he had probably contracted during his stay on the Gold Coast. His trip to England was postponed and his summer was subsequently divided between going to the American Hospital for treatments and numerous examinations, even spending a week there starting August 22, and visiting the Moulin d'Andé, near Saint-Pierre du Vauvray in Normandy. This magnificent place belonged to a French businessman, director of the "Verigoud" soft drink company, who had organized it for receiving guests, for the most part artists, actors and writers. On June 29, 1957, at a sale for the benefit of the little town celebrated by a gala musical evening, Wright had been there to autograph books, along with Ionesco, Hubert Juin, Francois-Régis Bastide and René de Obaldia. He had gone back several time, once as recently as April, 1959, and he was very much admired for his gifts as a storyteller and his outgoing good humor. Now that he was without Ailly, he went to the Moulin d'Andé to enjoy the tranquility and walks of the Normandy countryside.

At about this time, Wright refused to participate in a cultural festival (at which a film by Ben Davis, Jr., was supposed to be shown) put on in London by a pro-African group, partly on principle—because the Communists would be represented—it seems from a letter of July 7, 1959, to James Holness:

I have my own outlook which is allied with Black Nationalism for Africans, but if I allow myself to be seen in Communist company, then my right to fight for Africans as I see fit will be taken away from me. I am alone. I belong to no gang or clique or party or organization. If I'm attacked there is nobody to come to my aid or defense. Hence I must keep clear of entanglements that would stifle me in expressing myself in terms that I feel are my own. . . . You recall that I did not attend the Rome meeting. Now I find it advisable to withhold myself from African activities in general in Europe. I shall keep my relations with the African politicians who are now carrying the real burden of the fight for freedom.

Wright's refusal was prompted from anti-Communist sentiments and a feeling that the fight was to take place in Africa, but also from a desire to preserve his integrity by sticking to the principle of noninterference in the affairs of the country he was living in. He had, in fact, assured John Strachey on January 8, 1959: "In the event that I am granted the right to reside in England, I shall not participate in British politics or British racial problems in any shape, form or manner. . . . I feel this is the minimum courtesy which a guest should display to the host country in which he resides."

When he left the apartment on rue Monsieur le Prince because it was too big for him now that his family were in any event no longer going to live there, Wright found that the deposit he had put down ten years earlier would now enable him to buy a two-room apartment, which he planned to keep as a pied-à-terre in Paris, on the ground floor of 4 rue Régis, a quiet neighborhood of small shopkeepers near Sèvres-Babylone.

By mid-November, his health permitted him to travel again and he decided to go to London on a visitor's visa to join Ellen, who was still looking for a house that she liked. There he visited George Padmore, whom Wright had not seen since his own departure for Ghana in 1957. Although George, who had come home from Africa for a medical checkup, was seriously ill and Wright himself somewhat weak after his lengthy treatment, the two spent some happy moments discussing Wright's African trip as well as the international situation in general. In France, the growing lack of liberalism, and the tensions from the Algerian war, indicated the possibility of a crisis.[3] In Africa, the new nations were encountering such serious obstacles in their effort to become economically liberated that Padmore was pessimistic about the future of Ghana.

On his arrival at Folkestone, British customs officials had held Wright's passport for a long time, something that had never happened before, and after a Kafkaesque conversation in which Wright assured them over and over again that he would not try, during this visit, to settle as a resident in England, they had granted him a tourist visa for one week. He had, in fact, already registered his request to immigrate with the British Embassy in Paris, and although he had made it quite clear that his current visit had nothing to do with his proposed move to England, this sudden distrust and suspicion might have been connected with it.[4]

Only a few days after Wright had left England, George Padmore died and Wright returned to London for the funeral. Since Ellen had finally found the apartment of her choice, he decided to use the rest of his time in London to straighten out his position with the immigration services. On the advice of a member of the British Embassy in Paris, Wright went in person on November 29 to the Aliens' Division of the Home Office. After a long wait, he was received by an official who refused even to understand why Wright, who was not asking for the extension of his tourist visa which he had just gotten at the airport, might want to talk about his immigrant visa with anyone from that office. By closing time Wright was finally received by a high official whose name he never knew, and confronted with the landing card that he had filled out in Folkestone on September 16. This stated "Not coming here to reside" without specifying "on this trip," something which Wright was still ready to believe an involuntary omission, although he had repeated it several times to the customs official. He was then advised not to buy the apartment until he found out the decision on his case.

Back in Paris, Wright described the details of what had happened to his friend Strachey:

That evening I discussed with my wife and daughter my impressions of British officials and, after debating pros and cons, we arrived at the conclusion that if my four hassles in twelve days represented what we were likely to encounter in living in England, we were making a mistake, that it would be far wiser to abandon any desire to live in England.[5]

After all this, therefore, Wright and his family agreed that he should withdraw his request, not only because of the long delay since his original submission of it and John Strachey's initial difficulties, but mostly because of the recent incidents, which he was finally forced to interpret as deliberate attempts to make him feel, in an indirect way, unwanted. He continued in his letter of October 12, 1959, to Strachey:

What appalled us was not the coldness or rudeness of the British officials but the cheapness of their manner of trying to get me to renounce my intention to reside in England. There was something monstrously shameful in Her Majesty's civil servants debasing themselves to such a degree.

Furthermore, when he had gone to reserve a seat on the plane for Paris, Wright discovered that the Home Office had not returned his passport to him; but after an anxious night, thinking that this was another deliberate move to harm him, he got it back without difficulties. Wright took the opportunity, on this final visit to the Aliens' Division, to say everything on his mind, but the official replied that he was merely following orders. That was the end of the affair. Wright related it to Strachey, asking him to send a copy of his letter to Reginald Butler but not to bring it before the House of Commons. He concluded:

That is, in sum, what happened and seen from the outside, it may be said I should have stood my ground and seen it all through. But *what ground*? I'm an alien. I have no claim on the British except that claim that they will acknowledge. . . . Self-respect as much as anything else compelled my withdrawal.

All this as it related to me is not terribly important. I'll stay in France where I have friends. I had elected to live in England, but I was made to feel that I was not wanted. But there are larger and more important issues involved in this: Britain is a part of the white Western world and I am a part of that world. . . . Can the white West afford this kind of behavior? . . . If Britain was calculatingly seeking to spread and deepen the notion of black nationalism, then I declare that the attitudes I encountered were designed to accomplish just that. Of course, I do not credit that much Machiavellian intelligence to British actions; I suspect that those actions are short-sighted and stupid, but the consequences are just as real in the end. It is that aspect of the matter that I'd like the British to think on.

Was this, in fact, a group of unrelated incidents which Wright interpreted as a disguised refusal of his request? Was he, as in the

Gibson affair, too ready to see hidden forces gathering against him? It does not seem so. He had waited for many months and provided proofs of solvency and good conduct—an extraordinary requirement to be demanded of a novelist of international reputation whom the French government had welcomed as a distinguished guest and who had political support in Great Britain. This was, as he justly deduced, a simple way for the immigration officers to tell him, without being explicit, that he was undesirable.

One of Wright's first actions, back in Paris, was to get in touch with the embassy of Ghana to offer his services to the members of the Movement for the Liberation of Africa. Considering that the West had infiltrated the so-called pro-African organizations, and that the African nationalists were under great pressure in Europe, Wright thought that the only place for him to fight efficiently was in Africa itself, by cooperating closely with Kwame Nkrumah. Furthermore, it seems that in so doing he wanted to carry out one of the last wishes of his friend George Padmore, whose death had deeply affected him.[6]

The second result of the British rebuff was that Wright permanently settled on the rue Régis. Ellen, who during the incidents with British immigration had already rented the apartment in 2 Brompton Lodge on Cromwell Road, would remain in London. For one thing, Julia was registered at Cambridge. For another, the new apartment in Paris was too small for the entire family, adding tensions to Wright's already nervous state, and the family was expecting to buy the floor above to make a duplex. In the meantime, in order to help with expenses, Ellen took an editorial job in London near the Lycée Français which Rachel attended.

At the beginning of November, Wright's amoebic dysentery was still being treated. His doctor had allowed him to work only on the condition that he would lie down the minute he was tired. Yet he often made his own meals, although he had a regular maid to wash the dishes and clean, which he hated to do. He could, moreover, count upon a good number of friends, such as Michel and Hélène Bokanowski, Colette and Rémi Dreyfus, Simone de Beauvoir, Ollie Harrington and the Reverend Clayton Williams. He was also in touch with Ellen by telephone several times a week.

Wright certainly did not (as he had written to Reynolds on October 28, 1959, of his desire to) "make a tour of the American army camps and get more material on how Fishbelly sold shows to the G.I.'s." After autographing books at the Soulanges Bookstore, on December 16, he left for the Moulin d'Andé, where he had reserved a room, in the hopes of rewriting "Island of Hallucinations" during the winter. He wanted to use Fishbelly's efforts to make his fortune in France as a guideline for the plot, which would, though not involving complete reworking, provide a different perspective in order to bring the protagonist to the forefront.[7] He never succeeded, however, since his illness left him too tired to concentrate, and he returned to Paris for Christmas. Subsequent efforts to rewrite the novel never resulted in a second version.

By February, 1960, in fact, Wright was constantly ill. The treatment given at the American Hospital had almost cured him of his amoebic dysentery, but during his convalescence, intestinal troubles had contributed to his complete exhaustion. This is how he happened to go to a specialist, Dr. Victor Schwarzmann, who became a fast friend. Being Jewish, Schwarzmann was extremely sensitive to the problems of minority groups. During his first office visit, Wright had noticed *White Man, Listen!* on his desk. Their common interests brought them closer together, and gave Wright some much-needed psychological support, while a rigorous treatment managed to put him back on his feet. He was forced to follow a strict diet: no alcohol, spices or fried foods, and a daily dose of bismuth. He despaired of ever regaining his complete strength; he had never before been seriously sick and was impatient. Each time he thought he was cured, he had a relapse, such as that on March 10, which made the future uncertain again. Wright could, therefore, not help chafing at the fact that he was not in the process of traveling throughout Western Africa instead of languishing in his room.[8]

On February 19, 1960, Wright received news from Reynolds that was hardly designed to comfort him. The New York premiere of the stage adaptation of *The Long Dream* had received such bad reviews (and Cleveland Amory had gone so far as to chastise Wright for his exile on a radio program) that the adapter, Ketti Frings, in her indignation had decided to withdraw the play from the bill of the Ambassador.

The preceding spring, Anthony Quinn had told the Hollywood press that there was an already well-advanced plan for Ketti Frings to adapt the novel to the stage. Quinn was to have the role of Tyree in the Broadway production, while Lloyd Richards, who had just done *A Raisin in the Sun* by Lorraine Hansberry, would be the director.[9] Wright had signed a contract and, in a letter to Reynolds on April 5, 1959, declared himself on the whole satisfied with the first version of the play, pleased that it was faithful to the novel and had lively dialogue. He thought the language a bit pale, though, while he criticized the second part of the third act for weakening the denouement and found the character of Fish more mature and adult than he would have liked. While Ketti Frings was revising the adaptation, Anthony Quinn withdrew and the production was taken on by Cheryl Crawford and Joel Schenker. The rehearsals began in December, with Lawrence Winters replacing Quinn in the role of Tyree. On January 13, 1960, Wright gave his wholehearted approval of the completed version, which he had just received from Ketti Frings. The few reviews of some preview performances of the play—given at the Walnut Theatre in Philadelphia from January 29 to February 6 and at the Schubert Theatre in New Haven from the 8th to the 15th—had been favorable.[10] Wright even requested two complimentary tickets for Dr. Schwartzmann, who was supposed to go to New York in March on his way to Cuba, thus indicating that he had complete faith in the success of the play, which opened on February 17, 1960, on Broadway.[11]

The next day there were four unfavorable reviews and three lukewarm ones signed by the major New York critics. In *The New York Times*, Brooks Atkinson was extremely severe. He praised the acting and the sets by Zvi Geyra, but found the adaptation heavy, lifeless, full of clichés and not improved by the staging. Robert Coleman in the *Daily Mirror* commended the acting and the baritone voice of Lawrence Winters but described the adaptation as simplistic and unsubtle, depriving the plot of all mystery and intrigue. Walter Kerr of the *New York Herald Tribune* was more detailed. Although he felt that the text rang true and both the staging and acting brought out this quality, he criticized the too precise, heavy-handed adaptation, which deprived the play of its warmth, inhibiting the communication which was indispensable for audience participation. In Frank Aston's review for the *New York World Telegram*, he remarked that John Chapman, the critic for the *Daily News*, had left after the first act, which he considered "lascivious and vulgar." Aston continued, however, that he himself had found the performance interesting but uneven, often moving but without momentum. The first eight scenes did a good job in presenting the problem, the ninth was packed with suspense, but the tenth and last bogged down in melodrama.

Should the impressions of several critics be respected in this case, or would it be justified to say that they were unfairly prejudiced against plays dealing with the racial problem? On February 23, Warren Miller's novel *The Cool World*, adapted for the stage by the author and Robert Rossen, opened at the Eugene O'Neill Theatre. The play portrayed feelings in a gang of Harlem youths. The only major criticism that one could make of the play was that it was overly sensational. The reviews, however, were so violently critical that it closed after three performances. Stuart Little, quoting Joel Schenker in the *New York Herald Tribune* on February 25, was perhaps right in stating that a play dealing with the Negro problem inspired such a feeling of guilt and shame in the white audience that they were discouraged from going to see it.

The preceding week, *Shakespeare in Harlem* by Langston Hughes had been well received, and Lorraine Hansberry's *A Raisin in the Sun*, directed by Lloyd Richards, continued to be successful after a run of an entire year. Nevertheless John Beaufort, in reviewing these events in the February 29, issue of *The Christian Science Monitor*, pointed out that the plays of Lorraine Hansberry and Langston Hughes were both optimistic and calm, which might explain the approval of the public. The critic Marya Mannes, in an article entitled "The Dark Side of the Street," which appeared in *The Reporter* of March 17, 1960, was certainly right in remarking about *The Long Dream* that since the protagonists were not likable, there was little room for compassion, the feeling most necessary for the catharsis of a racial crisis.

Thus, critics and audiences were not necessarily against plays about Blacks, but they only wanted to see a reassuring picture, one that would allow them to leave the theater with an easy conscience.

It should be noted that although the review in the Associated Press was clearly negative, that of the United Press International was on the favorable side, and that the sarcasm of the *New York Journal American* was balanced by the admiration of Richard Watts in the *New York Post*. He praised the production as much as the adaptation, in noting that a recent racial demonstration in Mississippi justified the melodrama. He was the only one with this opinion. In the February 26 issue of the *New York Post*, in his article "Two New Plays, One Already Gone," he again came to the defense of the play, posthumously, so to speak, since it had closed after five performances. He was extremely surprised that his colleagues had found it shocking, simplistic and vulgar. This time he was not alone. In *The New Yorker* of March 7, Kenneth Tynan wrote:

It is true that the play was disfigured by a garishly melodramatic third act, ending with a gratuitous and perfunctory murder. It is also true that the action as a whole moved jerkily, hopping in haste from one climax to another and displaying a disastrous flair for eliminating minor characters as soon as we had learned enough about them to want to know more. . . . There was, I admit, a good deal wrong with the piece. Yet much of it seemed to me tense, instructive and right, and I cannot help lamenting its early departure. Fine second rank plays do not come my way so often that I can witness their extinction without a pang, and when, as in this case, they are both enlightened and enlightening, the pang tends to swell into a protest.

In spite of this belated consolation, Wright was disappointed. He wondered whether Elia Kazan, who had refused to write the adaptation, and Anthony Quinn could have saved the play, but it did no good to speculate upon it.

2

Wright considered the New York critics' adverse reaction to *The Long Dream* aimed as much at him personally as at Ketti Frings's adaptation. In a letter to Paul Reynolds on February 23, 1960, he stated, "They have no political objection to me, but they hate the idea of an independent Negro living in a foreign country and saying what he likes. I'm about the only 'uncontrolled' Negro alive today and I pay for it.[12] This independence, in fact, was beginning to be so expensive that Reynolds advised Wright not to forfeit the $1,700 which Ketti Frings still owed him for the adaptation rights, since he was, undoubtedly, poorer than she.

In France, he was running into additional problems trying to place the novel. Gallimard had rejected it, and in the same letter Wright stated "Editions Mondiales bought the book for 750,000 francs. But, I'm told in whispers that American pressures made them drop it, they gave it up." He needed money more than ever, now that he had to support his family in London and himself in Paris, which meant maintaining two apartments. The Doubleday payments had ended and his royalties were considerably lower. Yet it was a time when his health demanded prolonged rest. The absence of worries would have hastened his convalescence, insofar as his intestinal problems were to some degree psychosomatic, but Wright made every effort to work, partly because he was temperamentally incapable of inactivity and partly, of course, because he needed money.

The failure of *The Long Dream*, following upon that of *Daddy Goodness*, meant that Wright could not hope for much from the theater. In 1958, the Théâtre Populaire Africain had planned to put on *Daddy Goodness* in Paris,[13] and on February 19, 1959, the English version had been presented to an audience at the American Theatre Association in Paris, in a theater of the USIS. The parts were read by Larry Potter, Leroy Haines and Ines Cavanaugh, and it was so well-liked that Fred Hare, director of the A.T.A., chose it as their spring play, with Leroy Haines as Daddy Goodness. The rehearsals began on April 12 with a troupe of professional actors, but four of them soon abandoned the enterprise for better-paid roles, and Hare's efforts to sell stock in order to cover the cost of production—which would come to about five million francs —never came to anything. The promoters could not hope to get their money back unless the play ran for two months in Paris, and there was a possibility of a profit only if it made a tour of London or New York. A performance given without costumes and sets on May 4 at the American Embassy Theater did not succeed in interesting a sufficient number of patrons. Wright decided to abandon the project for fear that the actors would not be paid if production costs were kept low.[14] On May 27, a reading of the play at the Récamier Theater, well-presented with a stage design by Alex Costa, musical accompaniment by Darry Hall and costumes by Ellen Cramer, was its swan song.

Meanwhile Wright was supposed to be revising "Island of Hallu-cinations" in order to get a decision from Doubleday, but he could not get himself to work on it. In the spring of 1959, he became enthusiastic about writing a radio script intended, like "Man, God Ain't Like That," for the Hamburg Radio. The subject of this script, "Man of All Works," had been taken from an article that had appeared in *Jet* magazine several years earlier. A white woman has shot at her Negro servant because she found her husband making advances to her. It is discovered, however, that the wounded person is actually a man who, having been refused a job as cook, had dressed as a woman in order to be hired. Wright wrote this little racial drama in two months, using the comic tone which had achieved the brilliant effects of "Big Black Good Man." He showed how the very structure of the black family suffers when discrimination prevents a man from supporting his family, although Wright was less interested in the problems of economic castration than in white sexuality and the interracial taboo. Once again, when Mrs. Fairchild asks "Lucy" the maid to come wash her back in the bath, the black man is in the presence of the naked white woman, a repeated and crucial scene of Wright's fiction. This time the situation is not dramatic, since the fact that "Lucy" is in woman's clothing reduces the scene to comedy. Ironically, the reversal of roles satirizes the behavior of the white man toward a black woman. "Lucy" evades the advances of Mr. Fairchild just as cleverly as he replies to the questions of the Fairchilds' daughter Lily; finally, it is the white woman, not the man, who is jealous. The moral of the tale is worthy of Brer Rabbit, since "Lucy" gets out of this delicate situation with only a slight wound and $200 awarded him for damages.

Wright spent the following summer writing a seventy-page story called the "Leader Man." In part it was a reworking of "The Jackal," which he had abandoned long before, and the plot is not remarkable. The protagonist, a fourteen-year-old black boy, suddenly learns that he is an orphan, the son of a prostitute, and that the Welfare Department is planning to remove him from the family that he thought was his own. In reaction, he runs away from Harlem, but he returns after a day of discoveries and confrontations, to hide in a cellar. Here he defeats in a one-to-one fight the head of a gang of youths. He takes over the leadership and begins to lead a life outside society; he steals, attacks solitary walkers and lives with a fence. Nevertheless, his upbringing has supplied him with a now unsatisfied need for security and love, since his longing for social integration is the deep motivation for his crimes.

Wright had intended the story for *Esquire*, but it turned out to be too long. Then Reynolds suggested that it would make an excellent beginning for a paperback original, if Wright were to continue and describe the adventures of the gang.[15] However the second title, "Rite of Passage," indicates that Wright was more concerned with the boy's ordeal of passing from the stable and sure world of his adoptive family to the dangerous world of the street than with the exploits of the gang. He wanted to expose the psychology of a nascent criminal, not write a sociological study of juvenile delinquency. This idea corresponded to one which he confided to Paul Oliver at the time: he wanted to start a "serious" magazine on crime, "which presents so many affinities with art in psychological terms." [16] *Crime International* would have an editorial board of specialists and scientists, who would supply authors with outlines for stories and could suggest, for example, the true psychiatric or sociological explanations of murder.

Meanwhile Wright was planning a new collection of stories. In Italy, a few years earlier, a book of his previously published stories had been issued under the title *Cinque Uomini*, and included "Almos' a Man," "The Man Who Saw the Flood," "The Man Who Went to Chicago," "The Man Who Lived Underground," and "The Man Who Killed A Shadow." In August, 1959, he thought he could make up a book entitled *Ten Men*, which would also include his two radio plays, more recent stories like "Big Black Good Man" and "Leader Man" and, with the title "Man and Boy," the text of *Savage Holiday*. Wright was anxious to have the critics' opinions on this last, of which he was particularly fond. Reynolds advised him to leave it out, along with his new story, "Leader Man," which he considered unfinished. Thus, by January 18, 1960, the title had become *Eight Men*.

In March, Wright sold it to World Publishers, which meant, in fact, giving them the option on his future fiction. Only three years before, he had considered this a last resort, but a great deal had happened since then. Aswell had died and Wright had not found another editor in whom he had complete confidence. He had suffered from the authoritarian and sometimes misguided decisions of John Fischer at Harper's, and he had not ever got along well enough with Timothy Seldes at Doubleday to do the final work on his latest novel. Furthermore, he no longer had the time or the inclination to make the rounds of the publishers. He was cautious with World, however, because he was deeply distrustful of Donald Friede, who was an editor there. He therefore specified in his agreement that his editor would be William Targ, whom he had known since Chicago and who he could be certain was at the very least not a racist.[17]

That spring, therefore, at Targ's request, Wright began to write an introduction to *Eight Men,* tracing the genesis of each of the stories to give the collection a common theme.[18] He also wrote an introduction to *Tant qu'il y aura la peur (As Long as There Is Fear),* a first novel by the young Françoise Gourdon, dealing with school integration and interracial love in a small town in the Middle West where she had spent four years. Relating it to the protest novel and the work of Lillian Smith, Wright expressed in a few pages his complete sympathy for this book. The most surprising aspect of it, he confessed, was that a French woman had been able to write it with so much understanding.

His foreword to Paul Oliver's *Blues Fell This Morning* also came out at this time in London. The book, a historical and social study of the blues, Wright considered a critical exposition of racial conditions corresponding to what he himself had wanted to do in his lectures on Afro-American literature. He praised the work of the young Englishman with warmth and enthusiasm.[19]

Meanwhile, since *Black Metropolis* was being reprinted in paperback, Harper's asked Wright to work on a new preface which would point out the changes that had taken place in the black community since 1945. Wright spent the spring working on a long rough draft, but before continuing he wanted to ascertain the authors' own opinions. He wrote Drake and Cayton several letters to this effect, but on receiving no answer from either, he temporarily abandoned this project.[20] He then wrote a piece for the *Saturday Review* on *The Disinherited,* a novel by Michel del Castillo, a Spanish-born writer of Jewish descent, who had spent his youth in a German concentration camp. The novel was about poverty in the Spanish slums, which led the unfortunate inhabitants, either through idealism, revolt or thirst for a religion, to convert to communism. The contradictions that they discover in communism allowed the author to discuss the meaning of their personal evolution against the background of a more general historical development. Wright considered the novel from an ideological, even philosophical, point of view, and he reacted so personally that the intentions of his own work are clarified by his piece:

May it not ultimately develop that this sense of being disinherited is not mainly political at all, that politics serves it as a temporary vessel, that Marxist ideology in particular is but a transitory make-shift pending a more accurate diagnosis, that Communism may be but a painful compromise containing a definition of man by sheer default? [21]

On March 19, 1960, after a round table discussion on black theater organized by Claude Planson of the Théatre des Nations, Wright announced to Margrit de Sablonière that he had returned to poetry. His Dutch translator had become his friend through a steady correspondence, and she eventually became his confidante. She lavished advice and remedies on him, and they often discussed politics. He now called her his "sister," a spiritual sister whose al-most daily letters comforted him in his solitude. On that day, he told her, "During my illness I experimented with the Japanese form of poetry called haiku; I wrote some 4,000 of them and am now sifting them out to see if they are any good."

Wright had been attempting this in fact since August, 1959. A young South African who loved this form of poetry had described it to Wright by chance during a conversation, and Wright had imme-diately been fascinated by it. He borrowed the four volumes by R. H. Blyth on the art of haiku in order to systematically learn the complex rules of its composition. In the poetry contests at the Heian courts of thirteenth-century Japan, the competing poets would have to compose, in a witty or light vein, sometimes the first tercet, sometimes the final dystic of the *tanka*, a fixed stanza of thirty-one syllables. The cleverest improviser was declared the winner. The *haiku*, the generally used opening stanza, soon became a poem on its own; set with seventeen syllables, it moved, somewhat paradoxi-cally, considering its origins, into a more philosophic and serious genre a few centuries later, mainly with the poetry of the Buddhist monk Matsuo Basho.

Later, the painter Tanogushi Buson accentuated the impression-ism, and the poet Issa the picturesque realism of this form. Wright's research led him directly to these sources without passing through the European or American schools of haiku, which was a very fash-ionable genre in the West at the beginning of the twentieth century and had influenced Ezra Pound and certain imagists. In imitation of the Japanese models, and as opposed to many modern haiku writers, Wright made an effort to respect the exact form of the poem

—three unrhymed lines composed respectively of five, seven and five syllables. While reproducing the syllabic structure, he also tried to condense the essence of the poem into the first two lines, and to include in them an implicit or explicit reference to the chosen season of the year, designed to join emotional tone to the symbolic meaning of the description. Thus in:

> I am nobody
> A red sinking autumn sun
> Took my name away

the number of syllables is respected, the season indicates the melancholy atmosphere and the symbolism of this delicate sketch encompasses the nostalgia of the human condition.

Sometimes Wright injects humor into the haiku, or a pathetic note, which does not spoil the original mold but gives an unexpected effect, as in

> With a twitching nose
> A dog reads a telegram
> On a wet tree-trunk

Considering

> In the falling snow
> A laughing boy holds out his palms
> Until they are white

it is clear that the snow represents winter, but as a joyous season. Yet a hidden clue may reverse the symbolism. If the boy is black, his joy in touching the immaculately white flakes is perhaps accompanied by a desire to be like them, like his palms which are lighter than the rest of his body. Hence the somewhat pathetic quality of the poem read as an attempt by the boy to forget his blackness. The effect is entirely different if the snow is seen as a symbol of fundamental human equality, in that everyone, covered with snow, is the same color.

It is curious that Wright became so interested in the haiku at the very moment when he was more involved than ever in fighting against sickness and attacks. Logically he should have been tempted to turn away from "pure" literature and to use his pen instead as a weapon. In fact, it is important not to restrict the image of Wright to that of a polemicist. It may be at the moment when he is most

Portraits, taken in 1960. *Photos by Harriet Crowder*

enraged that he shows himself the most sensitive. This is not a con-
tradiction in the poet who, in the epigraph to his first novel, thanked
his mother for having taught him reverence for the imagination. The
writing of haiku was not, therefore, an artificial attempt on his part
to become reinspired by a new form, but rather the rediscovery of
his own deep powers, and, above all, a sign that his literary sensitivity had not been in the least dulled by his polemical and political
activities. He wrote to Margrit de Sablonière on April 8, 1960:

These haikus, as you know, were written out of my illness. I was,
and am, so damnably sensitive. Never was I so sensitive as when
my intestines were raw. So along came that Japanese poetry and
harnessed this nervous energy. Maybe I'm all wrong about them.
Maybe they have no value, but I'll see.

Never before had Wright, who was so often described as "writing
with his guts," written anything so directly related to his psychosomatic state.[22]

Of his four thousand haiku, a disparate mosaic composed of varying seasons, atmospheres and scenes, Wright gradually selected
enough to make a volume in which the reader could browse without
getting lost. He first had them copied by a typist who came to his
apartment for a few hours a day, and then he tried to eliminate the
less successful variations on a same theme. For example, if four or
five poems expressed the feeling of lassitude with life in a given
season, he would keep only the most perfect one which united the
most concrete image with the richest symbolism and the most evoca-
tive sounds. In order to do this, he had to divide them by seasons
as well as by moods and themes. He therefore glued them all onto
huge pieces of cardboard and later onto loose pages hung on iron
rods. After working for some time on reducing the number of
poems, he wrote to Margrit:

The problem of selecting them is agonizing. I'm trying to figure out
a scheme. But at last I can carry them around in my hands. Before, they were strung on steel bars and weighed kilos. . . . Now,
only a pound or two. What crazy things I think of. Yet the physical weight of those haikus is an important thing to me.[23]

Finally the total was brought down to 811 by mid-April, but
Wright spent almost another month changing their order within the
sequence of seasons. He had in the meantime told Reynolds about
them, but it was already June 8, 1960, by the time he sent the

eighty-page manuscript to William Targ, both to ask his advice as a friend and to find out his editorial reactions. He did not expect them to be a commercial success, and he was even uncertain of their value, but he felt a need for them to be read by those for whom he had written them.[24]

3

The consolation of writing the haiku enabled Wright to live with illness and later to endure with greater fortitude the attacks which he felt were multiplying against him. In February, he had received an unfriendly letter from Jean-Paul Sartre which soon turned out to be a forgery, as in the Gibson affair.[25] In March he construed the lack of a reply from either Drake or Cayton as an indication that they did not want him to write a new preface to *Black Metropolis*, and he lamented the fact that white hatred should induce the Blacks to distrust each other in this way. Did he not go so far as to doubt Chester Himes's friendship when he learned that he was going to publish a detective story which apparently attacked him and his friends? [26] These worries were certainly not unfounded, but his constant suspicions became obsessive. He tried to divine the motives of everyone with whom he came into contact, and he particularly distrusted anyone connected with the American government. He even warned Margrit de Sablonière on March 30, 1960:

You must not worry about my being in any danger. . . . I am not exactly unknown here and I have personal friends in the de Gaulle cabinet itself. Of course, I don't want anything to happen to me, but if it does, my friends will know exactly where it comes from. If I tell you these things, it is to let you know what happens. So far as the Americans are concerned, I'm worse than a Communist, for my work falls like a shadow across their policy in Asia and Africa. That's the problem: they've asked me time and again to work for them: but I'd die first. . . . But they try to divert me with all kinds of foolish tricks.

These "foolish tricks" came close to succeeding, since his suspicions sometimes sent him into an unreal world and even his relationships with people whom he had known for a long time were affected. This was the case with Dr. Schwartzmann. When he came back from the United States at the end of March, he found Wright in better health, and an X-ray showed that there was nothing seriously the matter with his intestinal tract. Thus, Schwartzmann suggested that he accompany him to Leiden, Holland, where he had to attend a medical congress. Wright agreed, because he would be able to see Margrit de Sablonière, who wanted to write an essay on him, and they needed an opportunity to talk at leisure. She also would introduce him to Professor Shibika, who could give his opinion on the haiku. On April 22, 1960, therefore, Wright drove the doctor and his father to Holland in his Peugeot, and although he had to rest an entire day after the fatigue of the journey, he was definitely revived by the trip. Wright, however, not only speculated for a long time on the motives of the doctor's trip, but also, through some unconscious dislike, he was actually hostile. On their arrival at Leiden, he told the doctor and his father that there was no room for them at the hotel, even though he himself had heard from Margrit that two rooms were reserved for them.[27] Was this an indication of a new ambivalence, due to his obsessions, or was it an instinctive but justified reaction?

It also became difficult for Wright to distinguish truth from falsehood. Whenever he began to believe that he was being persecuted, he could not find any irrefutable proof, but when he convinced himself that he was only dramatizing, a new incident would occur to renew his anxiety. For example, he had returned from Holland on April 25 to give a lecture at the University of Nancy on "The psychological reactions of the oppressed peoples," as Ernest Pick, an American exchange professor had asked him to do in January. He received a letter from Pick at the last minute, however, telling him that the lecture had been canceled by the president of the Royal Society with the excuse that a talk the same evening by the filmmaker Robert Bresson would not leave him a large enough audience. A friend suggested to Wright that the Americans perhaps wanted to avoid any public discussion of Africa at a time when the problems of apartheid were attracting too much attention. Wright therefore tried to have a discreet investigation made by some influential friends, but he discovered nothing.[28] Also in April, Wright's best friend in Paris, Ollie Harrington, again had trouble with the American authorities, and Wright himself suggested that he leave France for a socialist country. Wright thus lost a faithful supporter, and without him he felt even more isolated and vulnerable. Nevertheless, he did not let himself weaken, and he faced the months which followed, a mixture of victories and defeats, with as much strength as he could muster.

Hélène Bokanowski's excellent translation of *The Long Dream*, entitled *Fishbelly*, came out on April 29, 1960, in a collection published by Juillard in their series "Les Lettres Nouvelles." There were a number of good reviews in the French papers, and Wright gave several interviews where he expressed his views on colonialism and race relations, covering the world scene and the new importance of Africa.[29] A reporter from the *Express* had the headline "The reeducation of the Whites is more important than that of the Blacks," and Wright rejoiced: "I denounced the United States on all fronts." [30] At this time, the clouds seemed to be lifting. The rights to *The Long Dream* had been sold in Israel and *Eight Men* in Germany, and Wright's health had improved. To his great joy, Julia spent several days in Paris for Father's Day on May 15, and, satisfied that he had finished with the haiku, he organized his new apartment, covering an entire wall with shelves to store his files and the thousands of volumes in his library. He put his personal stamp on the room when he began using a huge farm table from Normandy as a desk.

In June, he recorded a long series of discussions for French radio dealing primarily with his books and literary career, but also with the racial situation in the United States and the world, specifically denouncing American policy in Africa.[31] He decided to leave on June 16 for the Moulin d'Andé in order to work slowly but regularly on the revision of "Island of Hallucinations," but after an initial week of voluntary relaxation, he continued in a state of unwilling idleness until his return to Paris at the beginning of July. He had planned to welcome his family, who were coming to pick up the car and drive for a vacation in the South of France, but an airline strike delayed their arrival; then he needed to have the Citroën checked over in a hurry and sleep in a hotel because the apartment was too small to hold them all. As a result, the salutary effects of the Normandy countryside were lost. He therefore spent a week of rest with his friends the Bokanowskis at Croisilles, only to return on a rainy and gloomy day to Moulin d'Andé, where bad news

awaited him. William Targ at World Publishers did not want to
publish the haiku. Only the day to day impatience of waiting for
the answer, and the fears on that score, could indicate the extent of
Wright's disappointment, which soon deteriorated into a depression
aggravated by his inactivity. "I'm rather depressed, but there seems
to be no specific reason. Maybe this is just the reaction to all the
long months of illness. But I'm relaxed. Yet there simmers down
in me a worry that I ought to be working," he confided to Margrit
on July 19, 1960; and on the 23rd, "What a stupid thing life is.
At the time when I ought to work hard to keep up my income, I feel
absolutely no energy to work. Yet I know that I must. So I sit and
fret through the days."

Finally, at the beginning of August, Wright seemed to find his
inspiration again. Abandoning the idea of writing a new preface to
Black Metropolis, he took Margrit's suggestion of writing a story
very different from his usual style, a break which might liberate him.
On August 2 he told her:

I started a brand new piece of prose, the idea of which had been
simmering in my mind for a long, long time. I'm pounding on the
machine morning and night. It makes me feel much better. You
know I think that writing with me must be a kind of therapeutic
measure. . . . Now I'm free, with white sheets of paper before
me, and a head full of wild ideas, ideas that excite me. Maybe
writing with me is like being psychoanalyzed. I feel all the poison
being drained out. I'll tell you in another letter about the theme
that has me by the throat."

In twelve days, his rough draft was 90 pages long. By August 18,
he had written 300 pages, and he did not stop to doubt its value.
All that mattered was his need and desire to write. Working tired
him less and less, and he wanted to complete a first draft quickly,
which meant writing another 150 or 200 pages of what he called
"The Law of a Father." [32] It never stopped raining at Moulin
d'Andé, but sitting in his wool sweater next to the oil heater, he
worked relentlessly, like a monk in a cell.

Nevertheless, Wright had to return to Paris to sign papers on his
apartment and see technicians from the radio studio about his recording.[33] When he returned to the Moulin on August 27, he once
again felt unable to continue his novel. He rested, read and waited.
On his birthday he could have repeated a haiku that he had written
the year before:

It is September
The month in which I was born
And I have no thoughts.

Thus, the manuscript of "A Father's Law" did not progress. In Wright's mind it was not a story but a real novel in which he was studying the relationship between two generations and the social prohibitions which create individual guilt. The first 150 pages that he wrote are sufficient not only to suggest the broad outlines of the plot, but the detail of the characters and the episodes as well.

The action is set in the present, in police circles in Chicago. A fifty-year-old Black whose record of courage and devotion has earned him promotion to chief of police, a position usually held by Whites (which means that Wright was noting a change), is in charge of solving a series of murders panicking the residential neighborhoods. His old friend and colleague, the assistant chief of police, a humorous and brilliant Jew who had given up teaching sociology and philosophy to join the police force, soon discards the hypothesis that the criminal is either a sexual sadist or a thief. The maniac always chooses people of a certain status, whose professions imply moral authority, such as welfare officials, priests, nuns, etc. Having chosen these model citizens, the criminal always signs his murders so as to somehow destroy their respectability, leaving suggestive or lewd clues; although he always commits his murders in situations where his safety is assured, the traces that he leaves are more indicative of a desire to be caught than gestures of defiance.

Meanwhile the police chief is suffering at home because, as a good father, he is upset by a conflict with his eldest son. Although a brilliant student and athlete, the son has never stopped rebelling against his father's authority, less for personal reasons (or racial ones, although the young man represents a type of militant who considers his father an Uncle Tom) than from his horror of the police. The assistant police chief has to conquer the conflict between duty and friendship when his investigation puts him on the trail of his friend's son.

The boy's strange behavior is gradually explained. His disgust for rigid social and religious authority figures leads him to destroy the image of the father, the policeman, the priest. His original guilt, however, which forces him to find expiation, is a result of his sexuality, and of the intense remorse which he has felt ever since the day that he abandoned his girl friend with the excuse that she had syphilis (a distant echo of Wright's first engagement). He had begun his criminal career in order to bring upon himself the punishment which would cleanse him of this former sin. In the same way, therefore, that Fred Daniels and Cross Damon seem to seek retribution as an attempt to communicate with others at the end of their solitary path, the boy kills again and again, and each time he is more careless, in a half-conscious desire to be caught.

There is no way of telling how Wright planned to resolve the problems of the boy's guilty conscience and the father's dilemma when faced with the revelation that the murderer is his son. Although Wright touched upon the working conditions of the police chief—the relationships with his subordinates and white colleagues that presented difficulties—and sketched a slight satire of the black bourgeoisie, he was interested above all in the character of the father, the hidden link between guilt and crime, and the process of assimilating public morality which "civilizes" a man living in society. Once again, Wright puts his finger on one of the central problems of the age—the relationship between the individual and society—and the words he uses are sometimes prophetic. "A Father's Law" is thus akin to *Savage Holiday* and *The Outsider* in reflecting Wright's lifelong interest in crime. It also evinces a somewhat new preoccupation with the gap between parents and children, which may be related to his attitude and questions concerning Julia's career and the understanding between them, but almost certainly reflects his broodings and worries concerning Bente Heeris, a Swedish girl with whom Wright had corresponded at length. The young student had been fascinated by his books and, like many other readers of *Native Son* and *Black Boy*, had opened her heart to him, confiding her fears for the future and her feeling of powerlessness to ever change anything in the world. Wright had patiently tried to comfort her, but he had not been able to prevent her from committing suicide after she had told him of her decision to do so. He had written a moving letter to dissuade her, concluding: "For God's sake, don't let anybody make you feel that you have no worth. If I, a black man from Mississippi, made my way, then you surely can make yours." Bente's death on March 18, 1960, so depressed Wright that when her mother came to visit him in October, searching for the reasons behind her daughter's suicide, he was in such despair that he could not give her the explanations and consolations which he himself needed.

In the short story the father's concern for his son, and the tragic misunderstanding between them because the father has to assume his social role whereas the youth is seeking individual values, is dealt with in a deeply sympathetic and quite delicate way, indicative of a genuinely personal involvement.

Wright had returned to Paris on September 7 to meet Julia, who was returning from vacation. He fell ill almost immediately, which caused him to lose a week's work, but Julia's presence comforted him enormously and he was happy that she had decided to leave Cambridge to study sociology at the Sorbonne. Meanwhile, talking to Dorothy Padmore, who spent two days with him in the middle of the month, revived his worries about the political situation in Africa. He never ceased to deplore the neocolonial maneuvers of the West and his letters to his friends were full of dire predictions. He brought Dorothy up to date on "the plot" of which he was the victim, so that she could speak to Kwame Nkrumah about it, but he was no longer convinced that Nkrumah had real power.[34] Did Nkrumah understand the enormous strength of the opposition to the liberation of his people? In Ghana, where Dorothy had lived and worked since the death of her husband, developing the nation's power and supporting pan-Africanism, she found herself cut off from the true areas of decision, a situation which she attributed to the pro-British influence.[35] For the entire summer, Wright had feverishly followed the news of the Congo uprising, lamenting the weakness of Ralph Bunche at the United Nations. He hailed enthusiastically the rise of Patrice Lumumba, denounced the pressures of the West and predicted a tough and bloody struggle which would herald, in ten or twenty years, the death knell of European dominance. He was planning to revisit Africa soon to collect material for a book that would detail the efforts of the continent to gain independence, and thereby vigorously combat Western propaganda. Dr. Schwartzmann, whom he took to dinner at Leroy Haines's with Dorothy Padmore, had suggested the possibility of financing the trip with the help of friends in the UNMARCO transportation company. Wright promised himself to carry out this project as soon as he felt better.[36]

Julia left to get her belongings from London on September 24, and Wright looked for a room where she could live. To cover these extra expenses he agreed to write the blurbs for some record jackets, as Nicole Barclay, the director of the largest recording company in Paris, had requested. He wrote the necessary two or three pages for a record by Louis Jordan, the material for an album entitled "Les Rois du Caf' Conc," and for another by Quincy Jones, as well as the jacket notes for a recording of the blues of Big Bill Broonzy. This task, accepted only on account of his need for money, forced him to suppress his disgust for the unscrupulous characters to be found in the popular music industry, and he took the work seriously. As he had done in the Josh White introductions, he added a personal touch, especially in his résumé of the uncompromising life of Big Bill Broonzy.[37] Perhaps inspired by this work, he himself wrote a few blues, all of them filled with melancholy. "Blue Snow Blues" is about drug addicts:

> But Lord when I see that
> White snow swirling down
> I feel that my grave is calling me
> From deep, deep in the ground,

The end of "Nightmare Blues" is also about death.

> A devil and a great big baboon
> A-standing at my bedside
> And I feel like a cold slab of ice
> Like I had gone and died.

After Dorothy Padmore's visit on September 16, Wright had some Australian guests on the 17th, and on the 25th Arna Bontemps and his wife arrived to visit Paris for the first time. Wright was happy to see Arna Bontemps again. In his recently published *Book of Negro Folklore*, Bontemps had given Wright a good deal of space, and he wanted to act as their guide. It was an agreeable but tiring interruption, and soon, after an attempt to stop his dosage of bismuth, he was again not feeling well. Toward the end of the month, too, some black artists, unhappy about the influence Wright might gain over Nicole Barclay, threatened to boycott her if she did not fire him.[38] Was this a further evidence of the "plot"? In any case, Wright gave up writing the copy for the record jackets, although he still needed the money.

In spite of his financial straits, Wright courageously refused to compromise his principles on several occasions. He was asked by

Canadian radio to participate in a series of programs bringing the public current opinions on communism and international policy; the participants would be writers who had contributed to *The God That Failed*. He was offered $300 to appear on December 8, but he refused because of his disillusionment with Great Britain. When Reynolds urged him to accept, he wrote:

My attitude toward Communism has not altered, but my position toward those who are fighting Communism has changed. I find myself constantly under attack—both me and my books—by the white West. I lift my hand to fight Communism and I find that the hand of the Western world is sticking knives into my back. That is a crazy position. I don't want it. The Western world must make up its mind as to whether it hates colored people more than it hates Communists or does it hate Communists more than it hates colored people. It cannot, without being foolish, act as though it hated both equally. I have had some bitter experiences with the British and Canada is part of the British Commonwealth. Why should I aid a people who hold toward me an attitude of disdain? I asked the British the right to live in England to educate my children there, and they were nasty, evasive and downright racist about it.[39]

Thus Wright did not forget his grievance, even if he was somewhat unfair thus to associate the Canadians with the English. Furthermore, he was afraid of finding himself in an untenable position if he spoke out against communism at a time when there was the beginning of a rapprochement between America and Russia.

At around the same time, Wright refused a proposal of the Congress for Cultural Freedom that he go to India from December 5–8 to give a talk at a conference in memory of Tolstoy. He had already refused their invitation to participate in the Tolstoy convention in Venice at the end of June. He was not personally on bad terms with the leaders of the Paris office, but he had become aware that the organization was largely financed, and thus controlled, by the American government which made it impossible for him to have anything to do with them.[40]

Wright was as interested as ever in literature. Reading *Mandingo*, which dealt in clinical, brutal terms with the economic and sexual exploitation of the slaves in the Old South, had inspired him so much that he offered his help to the author, Kyle Onstott, in getting the novel published in France. But he was saving most of his strength

for a polemical lecture which he gave on November 8 to students
and the members of the American Church in Paris, where his faithful friend Rev. Clayton Williams was still the minister. His speech,
"The situation of the black artist and intellectual in the United
States," showed how American society reduced the most militant
members of the black community to silence whenever they wanted
to question the racial status quo. Wright offered as proof various
incidents from his own life: how Ethel Waters had been afraid to
help him with the stage adaptation of "Bright and Morning Star,"
the subversive attacks of the Communists against *Native Son*, the
quarrels which James Baldwin and other authors had sought with
him. He did not hesitate to refer directly to the Gibson affair, to
describe in detail the spying which flourished in the black community in Paris and the hypocrisy of the American government
toward racial problems, particularly in its policy toward the Congo.
He described the tactics used by the system to belittle black Americans in these words:

It is a deadly fight in which brother is set against brother, in which
threats of mystical violence are hurled by one black against the
other, where vows to cut or kill are voiced. . . . Having lived
on the fringes of that system, I feel free to speak of it; I think that
I've grasped its outlines with a certain degree of objectivity. . . .
My speaking of it has this aim: perhaps I can make you aware of
the tragic tensions and frustrations which such a system of control
inflicts upon Negro artists and intellectuals.[41]

Wright perceived that the government had begun to fear the
growth of foreign, not merely Communist, ideas in the black community:

Obviously we are entering a period where complete control over
the ideology seeping into the Black Belts cannot be completely
controlled. Books, mass means of communication, the developing
tourist habits of the Negro have broken down the walls around the
Black Belts.

This explained the new methods of infiltration used by the CIA:

Negroes who harbored revolutionary ideas were not talking; they
were wary. They had to be found and identified. Hence Negroes
who could talk Communism were sent into the Black Belts. Indeed, I'd say that there is more Communism being talked among
Negroes today than ever in American Negro history, but it is a

false Communism, the language of the informer, the spy. . . . I'd
go so far as to say that most Communism in the Black Belts of
the United States today is sponsored by the American Government. I'd go further: I'd say that most revolutionary movements
in the Western world are government-sponsored; they are launched
by agent provocateurs to organize the discontented so that the
Government can keep an eye on them.

He concluded:

I think that mental health urges us to bring all of these hidden
things into the open where they can be publicly dealt with. What
have I been describing to you? I've been describing various forms
of moral corruption—corruption which has its roots in fear and
greed.

In a letter to Margrit de Sablonière on November 8 he expressed
great satisfaction because he thought that he would now bluntly and
openly declare the truth, things having reached the point where hints
and allusions were no longer sufficient. His message must have been
heard by at least a few black Americans because on November 28,
Edward Reeves of the *Chicago Defender* headlined his account of
the lecture "Richard Wright Hits US Racial Hypocrisy, Country is
Rapped," and stressed the political, even nationalist, scope of the
talk.

Wright was then planning to spend several days with his friends
the Bokanowskis at Croisilles. He felt well and his digestion had
returned to normal, but the flu kept him in bed for two weeks,
causing a recurrence of his intestinal troubles. Dr. Schwartzmann
prescribed heavy doses of antibiotics, three million units of penicillin in three days, and Wright was once again too weak to type
more than a few pages at a time. Ellen, meanwhile, was very busy
with her work in London. After the dismissal of Innes Rose, she
had begun to represent her husband in England and was working
so hard on several new contracts that she did not plan to return
to Paris in the near future. Wright was being looked after by friends,
and Julia was at his bedside. He now found himself subject to dizzy
spells. Since he did not dare go out, Dr. Schwartzmann advised him
to convalesce in the Eugene Gibez Clinic, where he could have the
extensive examinations he needed while also receiving the necessary
care. Before going there, on November 26, he saw Langston Hughes
in the morning and had time for a chat before getting into the

doctor's car. He had eaten very little in the last three days and felt a little better. He spoke to Hughes about *Daddy Goodness* with enthusiasm and gave him the manuscript.[42] Only three days earlier, on November 23, Margrit de Sablonière had told him that he was the object of another attack. Beb Vuyk, a journalist whom he had met in Indonesia, had attributed some words to him which implied that he was advocating a dictatorship for Ghana, and making him sound like a pro-Communist nationalist. His reply was in open conflict with American policy at the moment:

I think that it is clear that you understand the real meaning of that woman's attack. The Americans now do all their important work through the non-Communist left, which, as I told you, they have bought. These tactics of the Americans have caused much confusion. This woman is most definitely with Lubis. . . . SHE IS DEFINITELY NOT A COMMUNIST. Maybe she poses as one to start trouble, to act as an agent provocateur; but that too is part of the American tactic. . . . Find out what organizations this woman belongs to. Is she a member of the Congress for Cultural Freedom? Then all is clear.[43]

It was also the reply of a tired fighter, who finished, "Hell, I don't seem to have any luck this year at all!"

At the clinic, Wright regained strength while waiting to have his extensive medical examinations. His visitors found him in better health and Ellen, with whom he spoke almost daily on the phone, was not overly worried. Everyone was surprised, therefore, to read in the Paris papers the announcement that he had died of a heart attack on November 28, 1960, toward eleven o'clock at night. He had just turned fifty-two.

Conclusion

IT was not until November 30, 1960, two days later, that
the press announced the "untimely death of a great American
writer." Although Wright had been suffering the interminable symptoms of amoebic dysentery, there had not been undue cause to worry
about his health. He had been under the constant care of a specialist
whom he had come to consider a close friend, and no one had felt
any need to summon his family from London, where they had been
living for some months. Thus, there was every indication that, had
he not succumbed to this unexpected heart attack, Wright would
have picked up and continued his activities as a militant black writer.

Various questions were raised by his sudden death, however, and
when I first began my research on the career of Richard Wright,
I came across a number of conflicting opinions and rumors about it.
Some suggested that his heart attack was not due to natural causes
but was rather the final blow dealt by his enemies in a move to
eliminate a figure who had become embarrassing. For by defining
himself as a non-Communist revolutionary both in his written statements and his lectures, Wright was openly opposing American and
Western policy toward Africa. He might, therefore, have been disposed of at the Eugene Gibez Clinic, where he did, in fact, die
shortly after having been given an injection, at a time when his
health was apparently better. Others believed that Wright had become so paranoid at the end of his life that he could no longer
distinguish between reality and his own "Island of Hallucinations"; they maintained that he tended to attribute whatever happened to him to imaginary enemies but was never really threatened,
and that he simply died of a heart attack, perhaps because he was
then undergoing greater physical and mental stress than ever before.

521

It would certainly be possible to write two contradictory but reasonably convincing conclusions, one proving that Wright had been
the victim of the very phantoms he had conjured up, the other that
these fantasies were actually one step behind reality—that political
intrigue had forcibly prevented him from writing the last chapter
of his "fictional" spy story.

Although I was unable to discover the slightest proof that Wright
had been assassinated (as a literary critic and biographer, I was
admittedly ill-equipped to conduct this type of investigation), I
could not automatically conclude that Wright had not been the
victim of the "evil designs" of the CIA. It is true that his death had
apparently not seemed suspect to his family, and the strain he had
been under for nearly two years was probably enough to make his
heart attack—which his doctor, a gastroenterologist, had not foreseen—entirely plausible, and in any case, the cremation of the body
on December 3 made any medical investigation impossible. Yet I
have another, more important reason for finding it difficult to believe
that Richard Wright was assassinated. There seems to be too much
discrepancy between his supposed importance as an obstacle to
American policy and the drastic means employed to suppress him.
Richard Gibson himself had written Wright in 1957 that it would
take a great deal of maneuvering to do him any real harm and that
therefore he should have no cause for fear. Not that governments or
secret services spare themselves any trouble when it comes to getting
rid of agitators or revolutionaries. It is easy to conceive of a Lumumba, a Malcolm X or a Martin Luther King as a victim of a
political plot. Yet, in spite of my admiration for what he accomplished as a militant and my evaluation of the political repercussions
of his fight against racism, I find it difficult to believe that Richard
Wright posed such a threat in 1960 that he had become a marked
man. Neither *Black Power* nor *The Color Curtain* nor *White Man,
Listen!* had been censored or even seriously attacked on political
grounds by the Establishment critics. Even if there was something
else, some secret that Wright could have divulged in addition to the
information concerning black spies in the Paris American colony
that he had imparted in his last lecture and left with a number of
friends, this would not have been sufficient reason for killing him:
the activity of spies working for the American Embassy and secret
services in Paris was not so well concealed that several others, like
Ollie Harrington, were not well aware of it. Furthermore, the "docu-

ments" and the "plot" that Wright alluded to in his letters to Margrit de Sablonière, Dorothy Padmore and a few other friends were merely photostats of statements incriminating the forgers in the "Gibson affair." Some people suggest that Wright might have been an informer for Nkrumah at the time, but what special sources of information could the novelist have had access to? Besides, his correspondence indicates that, to his disappointment, he never enjoyed Nkrumah's confidence thoroughly enough to substantiate this hypothesis.

It is true that Wright's correspondence, in his last years, gives the impression that he knew he was threatened and that he feared the worst. This could have been the combined result of the slanderous attacks against him, his depressed moods due to long bouts of amoebic dysentery, and financial worries, and should, in any case, be evaluated in the light of his lifelong tendency to make dramatic pronouncements and dire predictions. Finally, it is to be expected that thoughts of his own death would be more frequent in the fifty-year-old demoralized man than in the acclaimed novelist of World War II, especially considering that the presence of death (that of Maggie, Edward Aswell, George Padmore, Ella, Bente Heeris) was so woven into the fabric of his later days that it appeared not only in the morbidity of "Nightmare Blues" but also in his fiction. Hence, perhaps, the gloomy exclamations at the end of some letters, such as the one he wrote to Margrit de Sablonière on March 30, 1960:

I don't want anything to happen to me, but if it does my friends will know exactly where it comes from. . . . So far as the Americans are concerned, I'm worse than a Communist for my work falls like a shadow across their policy in India and Africa.

Since something *did* happen to him, one is prompted to assume that his pessimistic statements were actually a premonition, almost an advance indictment. Would it not, however, be just as logical to believe what he had said to the same friend just eight days before— that it was "the tensions within [him] that were killing [him]"?

It is, then, much more likely that Wright died from inner conflicts and pressures engendered by racism, which sometimes caused him to explode like Bigger Thomas and which, according to medical statistics, kill a good number of black Americans each year through high blood pressure. Yet if we conclude that Wright was not enough of an international figure to merit direct assassination, it is important not to pass off his death as simply accidental, without first investigating whether racist America did not deliberately harass, to the point of madness and death, someone whom she wished to destroy.

Two questions arise from this hypothesis, one concerning whether Wright was mentally ill at the end of his life, and the other, whether the attacks directed against him were part of a real plot or largely the product of coincidence and personal jealousy.

In reading his correspondence with Margrit de Sablonière and other friends it is easier to believe that Wright had become the target of a certain American policy after he had begun openly to avow his unconditional support of Africa. In addition, it is tempting to unite all the individual incidents—the Gibson affair, the *Time* magazine campaign against him, Great Britain's refusal to grant him an immigrant visa, the possible attempts to prevent him from speaking on Africa and to hinder the publication of his books, the attacks from Beb Vuyk—as pieces of a puzzle which together form a whole: an organized plot. This is the reason why, by recounting these incidents as nearly as possible in their chronological sequence so as not to lead the reader to assume a common cause for them, I have endeavored to show that some of them could be explained by mere misunderstandings and coincidences and that others, which do reveal a deliberate desire to harm Wright's reputation, need not necessarily be laid at the door of the CIA. Nothing proves conclusively that these events which so troubled Wright were part of a single campaign. In addition, Wright's suspicions, for the most part well-founded and understandable, are sometimes frankly exaggerated, as, for instance, his negative reaction to the offer of the Canadian Broadcasting Company, which he refused without even bothering to check whether or not they would have censored his message.

I myself do not consider it unreasonable to conclude that a series of provocations was directed against Wright by the American government and that these were to a certain extent responsible for his heart attack. And I would not go so far as to say that he was neurotic enough to invent imaginary grievances (like the forged letter from Sartre) to add to the real ones. I have used the term "hallucination" in regard to Wright only because of the title he had chosen for his last novel, and not to imply that he himself suffered from such disturbances. Although he exaggerated the extent and intent of some attacks, I believe that many were expressly designed to make him lose his sense of reality. Whether caused by personal jealousy, political intrigue or racial malevolence, the desire to harm Wright was indisputable. Can it therefore be concluded that he was taken in by them, that he fell into the trap of illusion, neurosis or paranoia? I think not, since it is important to remember that his tendency to foresee the worst usually alternated with great bursts of enthusiasm, optimism and vitality. Thus, like the period 1947–52, the last years of his life could have merely corresponded to a pessimistic phase. His close friends and relatives all testify that he did not at the time suffer from even the slightest mental illness, and his work is certainly confirmation of this. The evidence, in fact, betrays nothing more than intense physical exhaustion due to recurring disease, combined with a nervous reaction to the numerous "slings and arrows of outrageous fortune." Wright's heart attack, then, can be characterized as an indirect consequence of the tensions which he suffered throughout his life, as well as the more immediate result of his recent illness and anxiety, and was not hastened or heralded by any sort of mental derangement.

Answering this last question is important in evaluating Wright's literary career because it enables us to consider whether, as some American critics claim, Wright's death may be interpreted as the natural conclusion to a period of artistic decline due to his living abroad, or, rather, as the abrupt interruption of a cyclic process of development. Even admitting that the best of Wright's fiction was written in the early forties, I am in favor of the second interpretation and would rather say that death caught him in a period of evolution.

After 1957, it was obvious that it had become increasingly difficult for Wright to concentrate on his writing while tortured by the attacks against him and the doubts and questions they raised in his mind. At first glance this fact may seem confusing, since in the past he had been stimulated by this type of adversity, not prevented from writing; such challenges had enabled him, on the contrary, to adopt his favorite role of a Mencken-like intellectual. The important distinction here is that to function well, he had always to be sure of support from at least one segment of public opinion (which is reflected in his abhorrence of addressing a hostile audience), as he had been, for instance, during the controversies with David L. Cohn and Burton Rascoe in 1940. Each time such support was wanting, it took Wright more time to regain his confidence and spiritual strength. This is probably why he let six or seven years elapse between *Black Boy* and *The Outsider*, during which his essays and extraliterary activities can be considered more as temporary distractions than as the exercise of his true vocation. He needed all that time to get over his break with the Communist Party and redefine his perspectives in existentialist terms, thereby finding another ideal to sustain him.*

A similar situation might have existed at the end of his life. He was not receiving much encouragement in his attempts to persuade the West to renounce the easy role of neocolonialism or for his sometimes awkwardly expressed defense of African nationalism. He clearly felt that he lacked support. In addition, he was once again going through a period of ideological change which, had its course been completed, might have caused him to start writing in a new vein. It is highly probable that the civil rights and Black Power movements would have given him a second wind, had he lived another five years.

Granted the lesser artistic quality of Wright's work during the last three years of his life, the importance of what he achieved should not be ignored, since it included *Daddy Goodness,* "A Father's Law" and the haiku, thus differing little in quantity from what he had achieved in the early years of his exile. Nor is there much quantitative difference, considering that he had been writing since 1930, between his output during the fifteen years preceding 1945 and the fifteen years that followed. The "American" works include four works of fiction ("Tarbaby's Dawn," *Lawd Today, Uncle Tom's Children* and *Native Son*) and two of nonfiction (*Twelve Million Black Voices* and *Black Boy*) which correspond respectively to "Island of Hallucinations," "A Father's Law," *The Outsider, Savage Holiday* and *The Long Dream* (fiction) and *Black Power, The Color Curtain, Pagan Spain* and *White Man, Listen!* (nonfiction). The haiku and *Daddy Goodness* balance the revolutionary poems and the stage adaptation of *Native Son*, while the blues, essays, articles and stories included in *Eight Men,* all fall equally into the two periods. Thus, if Wright's artistic career were traced on a graph, it would not be a single parabola reaching its peak somewhere

---

* This was also an era when incipient or actual McCarthyism damaged Wright's reputation in America because of his progressive sympathies and, by altering the American consciousness, deprived the novelist of his audience. The government's desire to win the cold war by eliminating all opposition to it partially determined America's negative attitude toward the Third World, and Wright himself often bemoaned the fact that not to be wholeheartedly pro-American, or to be simply "un-American," was interpreted as being anti-American.

around 1945, so much as a continuing sine wave with three main peaks and corresponding valleys, a pattern which he might have continued to follow in the years to come.

Since Wright was thinking beyond the European backdrop which he had just begun to use as a setting for his fiction, and heading toward the concept of the symbolic function of the black American in the liberation of the Third World, might he not therefore have created new myths and new character types, perhaps benefiting from the propitious climate of Black Power for the support he needed, in order to return to his former position as spokesman of his race? Although I can only speculate on this point, everything seems to indicate that Wright's fiction was at least headed in a new direction. On the one hand, there was "Big Black Good Man" and "Man, God Ain't Like That," in which racial beauty and pride predominate and humor is used to strike down the stereotypes created by Western feelings of superiority. On the other, there is the trilogy begun by *The Long Dream*, which Wright considered a stepping-stone to the future and not the retreat into his Mississippi childhood which was all the American critics found in it. At the same time, Wright was exploring two of his favorite interests, criminology and poetry, and the haiku were his most successful experiment in the latter domain.

It seems unfair, therefore, to limit Wright's literary achievements to two books just because critics are right in hailing them as his best. *Black Boy* and *Native Son* do not represent the extent of Wright's accomplishment and critics should beware of claiming that Wright could never find literary salvation outside of the Old South and the ghetto.

His career as a whole can be studied through the evolution of his literary and political perspectives. Because he was black, Wright first used literature in the way he would later, at times, use politics— as a means of personal survival. As a Communist, he soon discovered that politics provided a means of group survival and could work for the development of mankind, but he was, in turn, forced to choose between propaganda and literary creation. Nevertheless, his very success as a writer constantly led him, largely because he was black, to take up his pen in defense of a cause—in other words, to subordinate writing to action, with, of course, the knowledge that he could sometimes return and take refuge in literature. Literature and politics were two equally indispensable tools in the service of humanism. This is why I insist upon judging Wright's work as a whole, not separating his writing from its ideological framework, and not making a split, only artificially justified by his exile, in the unfolding of his career. It is only by respecting this unity in its ideological, racial and historical context that Wright's importance can be fairly evaluated.

Because of personal difficulties due to the poverty of his family, the severity of his grandmother's religion and the repressive racism of the South, Wright stands out as one of the American writers whose vocation was the most surprising and whose professional success and spiritual growth the most dearly won. His achievement was therefore viewed as exemplary by many Blacks who planned to make writing their career. Historically, however, Wright appears as much more than a prototype of black literary achievement in the United States. Indeed, no American novelist before him wrote about urbanization with as much depth and force. Admittedly, the problems of the ghetto are linked to the exploitation and racial oppression of the Blacks, but the reactions of a Bigger obviously transcend the color of his skin and the particular circumstances of his youth and background. Thus, Wright's first novels, and in particular *Native Son*, soon became a point of departure for a certain number of authors who sought to explore violence, poverty and the alienation of the urban setting.

The ghetto, however, represented only one stage of Wright's quest as a humanistic novelist; his path through life symbolized the individual's struggle with his environment, and he refused either to admit defeat or to play the game. His environment was of course first limited to Jackson, and then the Chicago South Side, but later expanded to New York, where society placed its favorite black writer of the day on the appropriate pedestal; France, which expected a set pattern of behavior from its intellectuals; and finally the West as a whole, which mobilized them in defense of its culture and ideology. Wright's life, and to a lesser degree his writing, betrayed an incessant desire for expansion and growth. One after another, the anchor lines of his thoughts were cut in a transcontinental and then intercontinental journey, toward ever-widening horizons. This quest for humanity made the American citizen by birth, the honorary citizen of Paris, into a citizen of the world by virtue of his innermost calling.

Wright's refusal to belong to any kind of tradition (for somewhat ambiguous reasons) made him susceptible to the existentialist view of the world, although this involvement with existentialism certainly did not begin with his Parisian exile; it was a lifelong way of thought. At twelve, he had already experienced the "tragic sense of life," which his later close association with certain philosophers merely made more explicit, and although existentialism seemed to have been relegated to second place in favor of finding a link with the Third World, it turned out to be as dear to Wright at the end of his life as it had been in 1952. Likewise, his desire to see Africa, which was not fulfilled until his visit to the Gold Coast, was not a sudden whim; it dated from many years before, and his disappointment at being greeted as an American in his ancestral land did not affect his sense of political responsibility toward it. All through his life Wright remained an American (brought up in spite of himself on Horatio Alger and the Bible), and the epithet "expatriate," which became attached to his name after a certain date, can be misleading in that it neglects his allegiance to and membership in the American society which he criticized so vehemently.

It would now appear forced to tailor Wright's career to fit into a chronological framework. There was no succession of tendencies or activities which were mutually exclusive. The most that can be said is that at different moments of his life, different elements of his political and literary personality predominated and controlled his creative powers. Whatever definition he is given—novelist, playwright, poet, polemicist, journalist, essayist, Marxist, puritan, agnostic, existentialist, non-Communist revolutionary, integrationist for America, nationalist for Africa and humanist for the world—it will not correspond to or be exhausted within any one period of his life. At regular intervals, there would reappear his obsession with the relationship between crime and knowledge, superstition and sex, race and taboos, all of which are reflected in his first and last stories. Certain concepts return more often than others: Mencken's ideal of art as a weapon of the mind; the writer as a criminal (a Prometheus twice guilty in the eyes of the white gods: the Black as an underground creature, and even more as a symbol of modern man in a universe of chaos and absurdity); and William James's theory of "unguaranteed existence," embodying the fundamental greatness of the "tragic elites." These metaphors in fact represent a constant element in Wright's attempt at ideological elucidation. In this quest for truth and certainties, *Native Son* resulted from a fierce determination to deny the heritage of Uncle

Tom. Although several literary historians use 1940 as the date that Afro-American literature reached maturity, this was only a beginning for Wright. At the very time he was working on *Black Boy* he was also (with "The Man Who Lived Underground") laying the foundations for *The Outsider,* which represented a most important advance toward existentialism for the American novel. Again, in 1952, in addition to social criticism—at which he was a master— he was also posing a metaphysical and racial challenge to our society whose scope is only now becoming apparent. Even Wright's last years, the most chaotic of his life, reflect in their very disorder and suffering his simultaneous refusal to be limited to one definition of himself—as Marxist, Westerner, or Negro.

His career not only reveals his desire and need to possess the culture which he had been denied, and later to enrich it by crossing it with other cultures, but also to describe realistically areas which were still untouched or largely unknown: the depths of his own country's violence and frustration, instincts and dreams, and the ancient traditions of nations hitherto thought to be "without history." Ultimately, Wright appears as a kind of explorer, although he never explored for the pure pleasure of it. His youth spent in poverty and his early political commitment engrained in him a need for efficiency which motivated him to try to change the world, to suggest new possibilities to his readers, to bring up problems. If he sometimes wrote to escape, to rid himself of his ghosts, his continuous exploration of the Afro-American soul, of the contemporary human soul, represents a conscious contribution to a redefinition of our entire culture.

As a result, the world of Wright's fiction derives its greatness from his controversial and humanistic intent, even if, or perhaps because, it does not present a well-ordered body of material. In this sense, it is possible to imagine his life as the "great voyage" he often dreamed of making, and to see each book as a new, somewhat solitary advance along an uncleared path. What is there to be learned from it? Sometimes horrible truths which society prefers to suppress and hide like so many skeletons in the closet. Sometimes reason to hope, to believe in the survival of man. And so, in addition to the current definition of Wright the novelist as an artist and storyteller, and of Wright the individual as militant, he can be considered as lone explorer, a philosopher, posing problems and awakening consciences. Certainly Wright's "philosophy" remains more of an intuitive

than a bookish conception of life, even if his lack of formal education did leave him with a sometimes exaggerated reverence for books
and with too much faith in ideas. Admittedly, the visceral, true-to-
life, apparently unstudied quality of his writing and the forceful
techniques of his narrative are the characteristics which account
for his success among a varied, popular audience throughout the
world. Yet while enjoying his fiction, we must not forget that
Richard Wright was attempting more than entertainment or even
political enlightenment. Uncertainly at times, but more often quite
consciously, he was grappling with a definition of man. Although
his solitary quest ended prematurely and did not allow him to find
one, his achievement as a writer and a humanist makes him, in the
Emersonian sense, a truly "representative man" of our time.

Notes

Notes to Chapter One

1. The sources for the family and childhood of Wright are certain episodes from the second draft of *Black Boy* that have not been disproven by evidence from other sources, and the recollections of the neighbors and friends of the Wilsons in Natchez and Jackson, collected in December, 1962. The most specific of these are from Mr. and Mrs. Smith, Mrs. Thurston, Mrs. Shirley, Mrs. Essie Lee Ward Davis, Rev. Cobbins, Mrs. Kersh, Mrs. Tillie Scott, Mrs. Sarah Harvey, Mrs. Minnie Farish, Joe Brown and Mr. L. V. Randolph. Other information was obtained from Miss Eleonora Gralow, Director of the George W. Armstrong Library in Natchez; from eight photostats lent by Mrs. Susan Woodson dealing with the military career of Richard Wilson; and, finally, from Wright's own correspondence with his family.

2. *Black Boy*, pp. 137–140, 151. It was Velma whom Wright visited on his trip to Natchez in 1940. Dumas Wilson, her youngest brother, was only a baby when Wright left for Memphis in 1925.

3. The portrait of Uncle Thomas in *Black Boy* is exaggerated. After living with the Wilsons, he moved next door and became a real-estate broker. In 1938, he was a member of the Executive Committee of the Citizen's Civic League in Jackson and wrote a book on the word *Negro*, discussing the superiority complex of the Whites and its effects on the Blacks. At this time, Richard put him in contact with Doubleday publishers and the uncle and nephew were completely reconciled.

Uncle Thomas, who suffered from Parkinson's disease, maintained a certain position in the community as well as enjoying a modest fortune until he was killed in an automobile accident during the fifties.

4. Addie, too, was not spared in *Black Boy*. She reacted rather well to reading the book—she stated that if Richard wrote in that way, it was to support his family—and tried to protect the privacy of the family from the intrusion of *Life* magazine reporters in 1945. Her letters, how-

ever, do reveal a woman intransigent in matters of morality and religion. She married and eventually went to live in California in 1947.

5. The story of the fire is confirmed in a letter from Fred Hoskins to Wright, dated 1947.

6. "Being between three and four years of age, I had not to my knowledge encountered such before. I know that my fear was all out of proportion to what was actually happening. Perhaps sex carries with it some racial memory; perhaps my underdeveloped body was trying to summon up from the depths of me an answering response.

"They would play with me, kiss me. As I now recall, there was a great deal of repressed sex in their fondling of me. I remember for some reason being afraid of some of the girls because of the way in which they fondled me." (First rough draft of *Black Boy*.)

7. Wright wrote to his publisher in 1938: "In Elaine, Ark., I hung around saloons, learning of the lurid exploits of Jack Johnson from proud and drunken Negroes." (Quoted by Ulysses Keys, in the *Chicago Bee,* April 2, 1939.) Was prohibition, which had become the law in Arkansas in 1915, really enforced in these saloons? It seems that the chronology implied in *Black Boy* is correct and that the scene actually took place in West Helena one or two years later. All these episodes, as well as that of Uncle Silas's drunkenness, are confirmed in a letter from Fred Hoskins, Silas's son from his first marriage, to Wright in 1947.

8. There is no evidence to confirm that Wright ever knew the "details" of Matthews's crime provided by Constance Webb in *Richard Wright: A Biography*. New York, Putnam, 1968, pp. 40–41.

9. See, for example, the reviews of *Black Boy* in the Communist papers, Chapter Thirteen, p. 279.

10. Wright seems deliberately to exaggerate his undisciplined behavior in an interview at the Mercury Theatre: "I was shipped off to an uncle in Greenwood, Miss. He soon gave up trying to stop me from fighting, lying, stealing, and cutting school, and shipped me back home to my grandmother, who predicted I would end on the gallows." (*Theatre Bulletin*, Spring, 1941, p. 1.)

Notes to Chapter Two
1. These biblical images occur in Wright's early poems, are implied in "Big Boy Leaves Home," which is a kind of parable of earthly paradise and sin, and are especially evident in *The Long Dream* and the unpublished novel "Tarbaby's Dawn."

2. Joe Brown claims that this teacher was Miss Kate Wilson, but Wright mentions the name of Alice Burnett in "Hell's Half Acre."

3. *Black Boy*, p. 111: "I did not suspect that I would never get inti-

mately into their lives, that I was doomed to live with them but not of them, that I had my own strange and separate road, a road which in later years would make them wonder how I had come to tread it."

4. The novel was published by Harper's in 1921 and then came out in installments in many newspapers. Wright states that it was just the type of story that interested him, and everything that interested him, satisfied him at that time. (*BB*, p. 112.) He was reading *Argosy All Story Magazine* then, which began publication in 1920. He mentions *Flynn's Detective Weekly* (*BB*, p. 116) but it only began to appear in 1924, so he would have been at the Smith-Robinson School when he read it.

5. *Black Boy*, p. 105. In a manuscript fragment, Wright mentions "Indian books I used to read, Indian histories—the death of a girl in the neighborhood." Elsewhere he claims that he projected his love for the elder's wife into the story. The theme of a vow and a drowning in a river perhaps comes from his promise to pray and his fear when Uncle Hoskins drove him into the middle of the Mississippi (*BB*, p. 45).

6. Wright's school friends are unanimous on this point. (Conversations with Mrs. Minnie Farish Booker and Mrs. Sarah McNeamer Harvey—December, 1962—and Mrs. Ellie Ward Davis—June, 1964—as well as a letter from Joe Brown—May 5, 1965.)

7. From August 31, 1908, to 1922, Richard Wilson and his widow vainly tried to get the pension. Their claim was rejected because "the best obtainable evidence failed to show that Richard Wilson was the man who rendered the service on which claim was based."

As late as 1946, Wright asked his uncles Lonnie and Thomas for his grandfather's papers so that he could bring suit against the government.

8. See the fascinating account of these games given by Joe Brown in the previously mentioned Constance Webb biography of Wright, pp. 53–56.

9. See page 49, the text of "Hell's Half Acre" as reconstructed by Mrs. Scott: "She would have Bigger arrested and tell my mother as soon as she came home from school. My mother was teaching at the rural. . . ."

10. On March 5, 1938, he wrote the minister of this church to ask for his certificate of baptism, which he dates between 1920 and 1922.

11. *Black Boy*, pp. 138–40. Their relationship improved with time. See *BB*, p. 88.

12. Joe Brown's recollections in Constance Webb, *op. cit.*, p. 60.

13. See Frederic Wertham, M.D., "An Unconscious Determinant in *Native Son*," *Journal of Clinical Psychopathology*, Vol. 6 (July 6, 1944), pp. 113–14.

14. See E. R. Embree, *Thirteen Against the Odds.* New York, Viking, 1944, p. 27: "He remembers the Smith-Robinson school with some gratitude. The teachers tried their best to pump learning into the pupils. 'They realized,' Wright says, 'that this was all the schooling the colored kids of Jackson were likely to get, so they gave all they had.'"

15. Conversations with Mrs. Harvey, Mrs. Booker, Mrs. Davis and Rev. Otto D. Cobbins. In a manuscript fragment, however, Wright says, "I hate English in school and made my lowest in them [*sic*]."

16. Mrs. Tillie Perkins Scott, whose brother Walter was a friend of Wright's, was then the typesetter at the paper as well as secretary to Mr. Rogers who, she said, admired Richard a great deal. She wrote this text from memory in my presence and was supposed to send me the continuation after I left Jackson, but my letters to her were never answered. In a manuscript fragment, Wright notes, "When I could not study medicine, I decided to write vaguely—My first story was of the death of a man next door who had stolen from his dogs [he is referring to Mr. Mance]—At thirteen I wrote one that was published." In an early version of *Black Boy* he stated that the heroine for the "Voodoo" was called Lily Jackson (WPP).

17. See "How Bigger Was Born," Grosset edition of *Native Son,* pp. xv–xvi. "When I was a bareheaded, barefooted kid in Jackson, Mississippi, there was a boy who terrorized me and all the boys I played with. If we were playing games, he would saunter up and snatch from us our balls, bats, spinning-tops and marbles. . . . We never recovered our toys unless we flattered him and made him feel he was superior to us. . . . He left a marked impression upon me; maybe it was because I longed secretly to be like him and was afraid." Mr. David Bakish found James Thomas alive but "largely illiterate and in a constant drunken stupor" (letter to M. Fabre, February 4, 1970).

18. Conversation with O. D. Cobbins, June, 1964; see Note 6.

19. In a review of *Struggling Upwards and Other Works,* Wright states: "The old-fashioned, morally uplifting tales of Horatio Alger were a part of the dream of my youth." (*PM,* September 16, 1945, p. m8.)

20. *Black Boy,* p. 151. Wright describes or evokes lynchings in "Big Boy Leaves Home," "Between the World and Me," "Obsession" and, most vividly, in the story of Chris's death in *The Long Dream,* which is the closest reproduction of this childhood incident.

21. One of Wright's notes says: "June 1924–September 1924, American Optical Co., Jackson, Miss—Mr. E. C. Ebert—porter and messenger boy—salary $15" (WPP).

22. See *Black Boy,* p. 152. The oldest, Velma, did not dare disobey her

father openly but played with Richard in secret. They were very close. When he returned to Mississippi in 1940, Wright visited the two sisters, who were living in the suburbs of Natchez. Later, Velma had Ella come and stay with her for a while.

23. After this incident, which is corroborated by Joe Brown, Essie Davis and other classmates, but which Rev. O. D. Cobbins claimed he knew nothing about, Wright became very hostile toward his principal and teachers. He confided to Embree in 1943: "I didn't even learn to read with any skill, certainly not with pleasure or understanding. It wasn't so much that I graduated as that in the Spring of 1925 the teachers capitulated." (*Thirteen Against the Odds*, pp. 27–28.) The story about the prayer was told to me by Rev. O. D. Cobbins in June, 1964.

Notes to Chapter Three

1. I was not able to uncover any firsthand evidence to confirm this episode except that in the earlier version, Wright talks of physical love-making and a longer affair with R—— W——, later called Bess Moss in *Black Boy*. See Chapter Ten, page 196, for the story of Mrs. Sawyer and Marion.

2. Ralph Ellison uses this same type of incident in *Invisible Man*. It was usual at the time for Southern Whites to make two or more Blacks fight, just as plantation owners had once organized matches among the slaves, but, again, I found no evidence to corroborate this particular story.

3. *Black Boy*, p. 198. Wright states in some fragments: "I wrote a story called The Memphis Monster and it captured my imagination to the extent that I began to believe in it and became frightened believing that I had committed a crime and was wanted by the police. / Was it a story I wrote about a murder, or was it a dream I told Shorty. / It seems that Shorty dictated the story of the crime to me one day while I was sitting in the cubby hole eating lunch" (WPP).

4. According to Professor Keneth Kinnamon, the editorial, entitled "Another Mencken Absurdity," appeared on May 28, 1927, in answer to Mencken's May 23 editorial in the *Baltimore Sun*. Apropos of the flooding of the Mississippi, he had written that it would be difficult to arouse the compassion of the rest of the country since no intelligent people inhabited the devastated areas. The *Commercial Appeal*, defending the South, condemned the stupidity, arrogance and ignorance of Mencken, "a charlatan or a narrow minded fool—and what he writes is largely bilge." According to an interview with Wright conducted by May Cameron ("Prize-Winning Novelist Talks of Communism and Importance of 'Felt Life,'" *New York Post,* March 12, 1938), Wright's

interest in Mencken was aroused by an editorial about an artist from Alabama who was not allowed to attend a show of his own works because he was black.

5. His name appears as Joe Beeker in the carbon of an unsigned article in WPP. Wright calls him W—— in an early version of *Black Boy*.

6. *Black Boy*, p. 219. In *A Book of Prefaces* (New York, Knopf, 1917, p. 109), George Moore's definition—"The power to tell the same story in two forms is the sign of the true artist"—is applied to *Sister Carrie* and *Jenny Gerhardt*. Later, Mencken says that Thomas Hardy, Anatole France and Dreiser are the only writers comparable to the genius of Conrad. In an early version of *Black Boy*, Wright says he also read *The Financier* and *The Titan* at that time.

7. "In Memphis, after work, I first seriously began to write, not for publication, but for myself. I'd write detached sentences like this: 'the lump of butter melted slowly and seeped down the golden grooves of the yam.' There was a roll, a period which I liked. I'd try others. Soon, I was trying whole pages of them." (Unpublished fragment, WPP.) Although he was practicing his literary style, he was still so fascinated by detective stories and fantastic tales that he chose them as subjects for his own works, as evidenced by the notes on "The Memphis Monster."

Notes to Chapter Four

1. "American Hunger," pp. 1–2. A number of details on Wright's life in Chicago come from "The Horror and the Glory," the second part of his autobiography as it was submitted to Harper's in 1943, under the title "American Hunger." When the book became a Book-of-the-Month Club selection under the title *Black Boy,* this second part was dropped. The episodes dealing with the Communist Party subsequently appeared in the July and August, 1944, issues of the *Atlantic Monthly* as "I Tried to Be A Communist," and were reprinted in *The God That Failed* (*GF*) in 1949. Other episodes appeared under the title "Early Days in Chicago" in the 1945 volume of *Cross Section*, and were reprinted in 1960 as "The Man Who Went to Chicago," in *Eight Men* (*EM*). A few other pages appeared in the September, 1945, issue of *Mademoiselle* as "American Hunger," leaving only a few pages of "The Horror and the Glory" still unpublished. In 1947, Wright gave Constance Webb permission to publish this in its entirety, in a limited mimeographed edition, which I will refer to as "AH."

Other, more personal details come from an early version of the autobiography, which did not, like "American Hunger," reach the galley stage. I will refer to this as the "earlier version" of *Black Boy*.

It is interesting to compare Wright's personal impressions in this passage with those he ascribes to the black immigrant in *Twelve Million Black Voices*, pp. 99–100.

2. *Eight Men,* p. 222. This opinion certainly expresses Wright's state of mind in 1944 rather than 1930, and at the later date he wrote letters to Gertrude Stein which contained the same criticisms of American materialism.

3. At sixty-five cents an hour, with 10 per cent for overtime, Wright could earn up to thirty dollars a week, making the family income between one and two thousand dollars a year. According to St. Clair Drake and Horace Cayton in *Black Metropolis*, 68 per cent of all Blacks never reached even this bracket.

4. Len Mallette, who was then one of the best educated of the group, remembers Wright's start at writing and his plan to compose a novel, but not his reading any of his work at that time (conversation with M. Fabre, June, 1964).

5. See Roi Ottley, *The Lonely Warrior.* Chicago, Regnery, 1955, pp. 291–95. Metz Lochard, an editor for the *Chicago Defender*, obligingly supplied me with more information on this subject.

6. *Abbott's Monthly*, April, 1931, p. 75. Some of the awkward passages to note are: "The room seemed heir to a blanket of decay and melancholy" (p. 46); "amused at the efflorescence of kisses" (p. 64); "saturated in their grief" (p. 66); "I likened myself to a spiritual ghoul ravaging the superstition-ridden souls of these pathetic people" (p. 72).

7. Compare, for example, a passage modeled on Conrad—"At that moment, the coming tragedy cast its shadow, and that shadow, like all the shadows that attend human events, was unseen by human eyes. The causes in our lives that later develop into glaring effects are so minute, originate in such commonplace incidents that we pass them casually unthinking, only to look back and marvel" (p. 64)—with Fentley Burrows's final remark, which could have come from one of Poe's protagonists: "I did not remain for the funeral. My curiosity, my confoundedly morbid curiosity had been satisfied, yes, more than satisfied!" (p. 73). See my article "Black Cat and White Cat," in *Poe Studies*, Vol. 4 (June, 1971), pp. 17–19.

8. Mr. Harper died on October 20, 1963. Hoyt W. Fuller and Margaret Danner were also friends of his. (H. Fuller to M. Fabre, November 8, 1963.)

9. Letter from Abe Aaron to J. Conroy, January 13, 1934. See Note 7, Chapter Five.

10. Len Mallette does not clearly remember the title or the subject of

the novel that Wright was working on in 1931, but he does recollect his taking notes on post-office duties.

11. This anecdote was told to me by Mrs. Fern Gayden in June, 1964.

12. In addition to Drake and Cayton's *Black Metropolis*, see William A. Nolan, *Communism Versus the Negro* (Chicago, Regnery, 1951), the issues of *New Masses* for the period and, especially, a series of detailed articles by Edith Margo entitled "The South Side Sees Red," published by *Left Front* from 1933 to 1934.

13. Wright claims, in "AH" (pp. 38–39), to have scribbled "I protest this fraud" on the bundle of ballots that he handed in for the Republicans. In *Current Biography* (1940, p. 886), he stated: "I became an assistant precinct captain in the Republican primary election. I was promised a job. I didn't get it. Next time I became an assistant precinct captain for the Democrats and was promised a job which I didn't get. So then I became a Red."

14. Joe Brown to Wright, July 1, 1945. (See also Joe Brown's recollections in Constance Webb, *op. cit.*, pp. 105–7.) Traces of this episode appear in *Lawd Today* and *The Outsider*.

15. Conversation with Mrs. Wirth, June 20, 1964. About getting Richard the job she said, "Since regular jobs were not to be had, I appealed to a personal friend, a doctor at Michael Reese hospital. . . . Richard must have impressed me a lot, as with the heavy work-load we had those years I can't remember being so resourceful for any other young man." (Letter to M. Fabre, October 14, 1963.)

16. None of the names used in the successive versions of this story seem to belong to the actual people involved. See *EM*, pp. 238–44.

Notes to Chapter Five

1. *The God That Failed,* p. 115. A special effort had to be made to increase the number of black members. At the time there were only two, M. Kersey and J. Powell, who were both painters. As far as the story of Wright's membership is concerned, I have used the version he supplied in "I Tried to Be a Communist" (reprinted in *The God That Failed* —*GF*) when it is confirmed by written documents or when several former members agree on a given point. Since it was written after Wright broke with the Party it is to be read with caution: it suffers from some reversals in the chronological sequence of events as well as significant omissions.

2. The true genesis of these poems probably differs from the account given in *GF* (p. 118). Wright confided to Edwin Seaver that he had immediately had the feeling that he could write better than the contributors to *Left Front* and that his first poems were a sort of "exercise."

(Conversation between E. Seaver and M. Fabre, March, 1964.) An unsigned article in *WPP* has some interesting details on this subject:

Two of them [young radicals] shared a room a few blocks away and asked Wright to come and listen to a little New Verse. The only strong impression he emerged with at the end of that session was however the conviction that he himself could run off something as good as anything that had been read. He singled out a half-dozen poems from a stack of *New Masses* that someone had left him, and using these as metrical models, he wrote six of his own.

The upstart literateurs who had tacitly dared him to make this try were at first ready to accuse him half-jokingly of plagiarism. But it was they who afterwards eased several of this early lot into a number of revolutionary journals—the Chicago John Reed Club's *Left Front,* the (old) *Partisan Review,* Jack Conroy's *Anvil, New Masses* and *Midland Left.*

3. *Anvil*, Vol. 5 (March–April), p. 20.

4. Possibly the line "Sweep on, O red stream of molten anger" was inspired directly by Byron's *Don Juan.* The poem also resembles the beginning of "Dark Symphony" by Melvin B. Tolson, although this appears to have been written later and was first published in 1941. Perhaps the two poems have a common source.

5. *New Masses*, June 26, 1934, p. 16. Wright's first line was undoubtedly inspired by Langston Hughes's "I've Known Rivers."

6. A mimeographed announcement reads: "Friday night 8 sept./ OPEN FORUM ON THE LITERATURE OF THE NEGRO/ by Richard Wright, Executive Secretary of the Chicago John Reed Club/ A Marxian Interpretation by a Negro Writer/ At the Club, 312 W. State Street" (WPP).

See also *GF* (pp. 121–24). Conversations with Jan Wittenber (June, 1964) indicate that the Communist members had serious reservations about Wright: he had never proved himself and he was both wary and difficult to sound out. His modesty persuaded them to accept his nomination, because they thought that they could carry out their own policies and still remain on good terms with him. Wittenber subsequently was surprised by Wright's energy and talent for diplomacy. Although he was not particularly fond of administration, Wright did recruit several Blacks (among them the painter Bernard Goss), and in addition to his work for *Left Front* he laid the groundwork for the lecture series.

7. On January 13, 1934, Abe Aaron wrote to Conroy: "I'm going to send you some of Wright's poems. I have asked him for some for you and he wants you to have some. Isn't he swell? And he is absolutely self-educated. I met him in the Post Office in 1930. . . . He also writes

short stories. On that score he considers me as a king pin compared to himself. He sees what luck I'm having. So, he never submits. . . . Once he did a blood and thunder thing in *Abbott's Monthly*. He is heartily ashamed of it . . . Incidentally, he was cheated out of his check." (Quoted with the permission of J. Conroy.)

8. He was mentioned in the May 25, 1934, *Daily Worker* apropos of "What's Doing in the John Reed Clubs of the U. S.?" Along with Hughes, Sterling Brown and Eugene Gordon, Wright found himself listed among the few black radical poets. On July 31, 1934, he signed a national petition in *New Masses* protesting the illegal arrests of workers and General Johnson's raids on the unions.

9. All of Wright's many statements on this point are in agreement. Compare "AH," p. 63, with this passage in the August 21, 1955, letter to Edward Aswell: "I was a member of the Communist Party for twelve years ONLY because I was a Negro. Indeed the Communist Party had been the only road out of the Black Belt of Chicago for me. Hence Communism had not simply been a fad, a hobby; it had a deeply functional meaning for my life." James Baldwin later used religion in a similar way to escape, both spiritually and intellectually, from the ghetto.

10. *The God That Failed*, pp. 136–37. (See also *GF*, p. 84.) In "The John Reed Clubs Meet" (*New Masses*, October 30, 1934, p. 25), Orrick Johns described Wright as "a Negro poet, impressive for his quiet gravity, a day to day worker for the John Reed Club of Chicago." Johns summarized Trachtenberg's position as follows: "He made clear that there should be no opposition between the intellectuals of our movement and the free exercise of talents, or no attempt to absorb talented people in other work; and any delegation which fails to observe this is taking the wrong line."

11. This comes from a carbon of an unsigned article in WPP, apparently written by Edwin Seaver, who interviewed Wright at length at the beginning of the forties. The link between "Commonplace" and *Lawd Today* is easily established, since this is the title of one of the sections. The novel on Jack Johnson became "Tarbaby's Dawn."

12. Wright states that he crossed the Mexican border with *Capital* in 1940, and nothing proves that he read it before then. It is impossible to know when his friend Bob Campbell gave him the English edition of Marx's *Selected Works*, published in Moscow in 1936. On the other hand, the Stalin book fascinated him (see *GF*, p. 150), and by 1940 he owned a dozen books published by the Communist Party in New York.

13. A dozen or more pages of notes on Pointdexter are preserved in WPP. Dex eventually inspired the character of Ross in "I Tried to Be a

Communist" and (along with C. L. R. James) that of Bob in *The Outsider*. (See *GF*, p. 132.) The portrait of Ed Green is modeled on Law and Harry Haywood; according to Mrs. Newton, Wright's dealings with Green correspond to those he had with Law and Herbert Newton.

14. Letter from Mrs. Davis to M. Fabre, January 7, 1963. This story about a boy's flight from the South was apparently never finished, but Wright used passages from it in "Tarbaby's Dawn" and, perhaps, in "Big Boy Leaves Home."

15. Conversation with Mrs. Davis, June, 1964. Wright wrote several sociology papers for his friend—on the New Deal and the economic crisis, and on the contribution of minorities to the national culture—as well as a literary essay on a visit to a nightclub. Mrs. Davis gave me the program of a recital of spirituals and religious music that they attended at the Metropolitan Community Church on South Parkway Avenue, on March 23, 1934.

16. Letter from William Jordan to M. Fabre, July 13, 1964. He continued: "Once I saw that his shirt was falling apart and gave him a couple of my old ones. He was grateful, but not really concerned. Writing was uppermost in his mind and he wanted to learn fast. He seldom talked to me of anything else. His father died in the South, his mother brought the children to Chicago a short time before I knew him." It is significant that Wright had led his friend to believe that his father was dead.

17. Conversation with Jan Wittenber and Jack Conroy, June, 1964. A photograph of the portrait shows it to be a good likeness. According to Wittenber, who was scornful of his timid character and lack of physical courage, Wright refused to participate in the demonstrations of the "Memorial Day Massacre" in 1935. According to Mr. Inman Wade, in an interview conducted by H. Cayton, 1969, Wright was on the contrary an active Communist orator, heard in both Grant and Washington parks. According to the Gourfains, Wright took such risks during Communist demonstrations that they were concerned for his safety. He replied, parodying the words in *Emperor Jones*, "Only a golden bullet is going to get me!" (Conversations with Ed and Joyce Gourfain, June 17–18, 1964.)

18. There was a renewed enthusiasm for Henry James in 1934. *Hound and Horn* devoted its spring issue to him; Ezra Pound, T. S. Eliot and Gertrude Stein praised him unreservedly; and the new school of critics ranked him with James Joyce and Kafka. The Left, of course, remained largely hostile.

As we know, Wright had already read some of James. In his notes for a lecture given in the forties he wrote, "Experiment in words—

Stein; experiment in dialogue—James; experiment in scenes—James; experiment in moods—Conrad."

19. Letter from Jane Newton to Michel Fabre, February 22, 1964.

20. "Prompted by random curiosity while I was browsing one day in a Chicago public library, I took from the open shelves a tiny volume called *Three Lives*, and looked at the story in it entitled 'Melanctha.' The style was so insistent and so original and sang so quaintly that I took the book home. . . . A left-wing literary critic whose judgement I had been led to respect condemned Miss Stein in a sharply worded newspaper article, implying that she spent her days reclining upon a silken couch in Paris, smoking hashish. . . . To gauge the degree in which Miss Stein's prose was tainted with the spirit of the counter-revolution, I gathered a group of semi-illiterate Negro stockyard workers and read 'Melanctha' aloud to them." In this review of *Wars I Have Seen* (*PM*, March 11, 1945, p. 5), Wright repeats a passage from "Memories of My Grandmother," an unpublished manuscript started in 1942, in which he tells how his grandmother's stories acquired a new interest for him. On April 9, 1935, *New Masses* published the unfavorable review of Gertrude Stein's *Lectures in America* to which Wright is alluding. He had perhaps discovered Gertrude Stein well before he made his literary experiment on the stockyard workers at Pointdexter's house, but everything seems to confirm that he did not read "Melanctha" until 1935.

21. "AH," p. 24. Some notes for a lecture he gave in the forties summarize his progress: "In Chicago I left off writing and began reading again, I could get hold of more books; Anderson / Dreiser / Dostoievsky / Turgeneff / Chekov / Joyce / Conrad /—Mencken's *Prefaces* [this took place between 1928 and 1932] . . . Again I tried to write, express my attitude / The labor movement / Stein's book *Three Lives* / experiment in dialogue / [around 1934–35] . . . Yet I had nothing to say / Self-discovery—reading of non-fiction / Then attempt at longer pieces of writing."

22. "I wrote about sixty pages and discovered I could not carry on. I read what I had written and discovered that it was a story in itself, and if I attempted to carry it into a full-length novel, it would be too dramatic. I therefore began to prune the long story down and it resulted in the story called 'Big Boy Leaves Home.' " (*The Writers' Club Bulletin*, Columbia University, May, 1938, p. 16.) Was this in fact the story that the *Windsor Quarterly* rejected in February, 1935? In a letter to Wright in July, Howard Nutt alluded to a story entitled "Escape," which was perhaps "Big Boy Leaves Home" but also could have been an episode from "Almos' a Man."

23. "Repeating a Modest Proposal (with apologies to old Jonathan)" signed "A Black Patriot." In the summer of 1936, an advertisement for *RACE* announced, "Richard Wright of Chicago, in an open letter to the president, proposes that we eat the Negroes and the Jews and in this way solve the race problem," but the piece was never published.

24. Letter from the editor of *Monthly Review* to Wright, January 12, 1935.

25. *The God That Failed,* p. 137. In a letter to Joseph S. Balch on February 6, 1935, Walter Snow of the New York Club stated: "In issuing the call, of the sixty-four signers, all with the exception of eleven were authors of *published books* . . . and the eleven others are well known in the magazine field."

Notes to Chapter Six

1. "Communism and Literature," quoted in "The American Writers' Congress," *New Masses*, May 7, 1935, p. 7.

2. See *American Writers' Congress*, edited by Henry Hart, New York, International Publishers, 1935, pp. 107–8. Farrell gave an excellent critique of Erskine Caldwell's *Kneel to the Rising Sun*, concentrating as much on the form and the implications of the political message as on the credibility of the plot. As for Farrell's reputation, witness this letter, dated January 13, 1934, from a Club member to Jack Conroy: "This Jim Farrell . . . I know him well. University days. He always was a little off his nut as regarded the C.P. A quotation from Dewey: a William Jennings Bryan commoner, in reverse. A style fine for picturization of physical aspects of life. A Menckenian standing on his head . . . But he does have an ear for idiom and a background which might make him a proletarian except for the fact that he is so confused philosophically that I doubt he ever will emerge."

3. *American Writers' Congress*, pp. 178–79. Specifically, Eugene Clay hailed Wright as "a poet who has developed rapidly in a short space of time. He has achieved a surer mastery of technique and image association. 'I Have Seen Black Hands' is admittedly one of the finest poems that has appeared in *New Masses*." ("The Negro in Recent American Literature," in *American Writers' Congress*, p. 145.)

4. He told all the details of his New York trip to Essie Lee Ward and stated proudly that he had marched with the writers of America on May 1. (Conversation with M. Fabre, June 19, 1964.)

5. *Writers' Club Bulletin* (Columbia University), Vol. 1, 1938, p. 15.

6. *Writers' Club Bulletin*, pp. 15–16.

7. From an interview with Wright in the *Hartford Daily Courant*, April 1, 1940. (WPP.)

8. He was then compiling a bibliography on "The Negro in Illinois," which was put in the George Cleveland Hall Library. W. E. B. DuBois used it for research during a trip to Chicago and later obtained a copy for himself. He also wrote a preliminary paper on "Ethnographical Aspects of Chicago's Black Belt." (See University of Missouri, *New Letters,* Vol. 39, Fall, 1972, pp. 61–75.) The F.W.P. research came out in 1937 under the title *A Selected Bibliography, Illinois: Chicago and its Environs.* Chicago, Illinois Writers' Project, 58 pp.

9. See Wilson Record, *Race and Radicalism: The NAACP and the Communist Party in Conflict.* Ithaca, N.Y., Cornell University Press, 1963, pp. 92–97.

10. John P. Davis to Wright, January 30, 1936. According to an early version of *Black Boy* the national leaders whom Wright refers to in "I Tried to Be a Communist" are Harry Haywood and John P. Davis. The former was secretary general of the League of Action for Negro Rights. With them, perhaps, was Tim Holmes (George Hewitt). The character of Buddy Nealson bears every resemblance to John P. Davis himself. At that time, Wright tried to appeal to the Party's secretary, but he was discouraged from doing so by Anna Louise Strong, the secretary's secretary.

Wright's trip to Europe would have taken him to the Soviet Union, a place he wanted to visit, but not just then.

11. "*Time*: an era of lynching, Jim Crowism and an era of disenfranchisement, a time when living standards of Negroes are sinking to lower and lower levels. *Place*: Chicago—the Eighth Regiment Armory, a huge black structure which houses the crack Illinois Negro 8th, a regiment whose ranks were decimated in Flanders to 'make the world safe for a democracy' the Negro people have never known." ("Two Million Black Voices," *New Masses*, February 25, 1936, p. 15.) A month later, Wright reported on the Congress before a large group assembled at the Salem Baptist Church of Champaign, Illinois.

12. The members of the group stated that it must have been a first version of "Bright and Morning Star." My information about the South Side Writers' Group comes from Wright's article "Negro Writers Launch Literary Quarterly" (*Daily Worker*, June 8, 1937); conversations with Fern Gayden (June 17, 1964), Theodore Ward (May 22, 1963) and Margaret Walker (February 28, 1972); a letter from Frank Marshall Davis to Kenneth Kinnamon (June 24, 1964); and letters addressed to Wright from Margaret Walker, Robert Davis and other club members. (WPP.)

13. According to a conversation with Ed Gourfain (June 18, 1964) and letters from Peter Pollack (August 3, 1964) and Lawrence Lipton (August 2, 1964) to M. Fabre.

14. Conversation with Jack Conroy and a letter from Philip Rahv to M. Fabre (March 22, 1963).

15. In particular, the metaphor of the hitchhikers who hear the noise of ice tinkling in glasses on a beautiful estate nearby while the luxurious cars refuse to pick them up. This was one of Wright's personal experiences. "Transcontinental," *International Literature*, Vol. 5 (January, 1936), p. 52.

16. I tried in vain to discover the real reason for this. In *Arena: The History of the Federal Theatre* (New York, Blom, 1940), Hallie Flanagan does not go into such detail and the lists of theatrical productions are incomplete. A bit more information is to be found in *Cavalcade of the American Negro*, published by the Illinois F.W.P. in 1940 (see p. 5), and even more in *Midwest*, where three articles (August, 1936, p. 36; November, 1936, p. 16; and December, 1936, p. 27) mention the prohibition. I also took into account Theodore Ward's recollections (conversation with M. Fabre, May 22, 1963) and a rough draft of an unpublished article by Wright, "Hymn to the Sinking Sun," which agrees with the account in *Midwest* and not with that of "I Tried to Be a Communist."

17. According to *GF*, p. 132. Wright had another job with the city before he returned to the Writers Project. Professor Lawrence Martin says (letter to M. Fabre, July 12, 1964): "In my evening classes in Advanced Writing Practice in the downtown school of Northwestern University, late in 1936 or early 1937, one of my students, a Negro named Oscar Hunter, told me of a young friend of his up from Mississippi working in the stockyards who, he thought, showed writing talent." It was thus, Martin claimed, that Wright got in touch with him, although a letter to Wright from Ted C. Robinson indicates that the latter recommended him to Martin.

18. *Illinois Guide*. Illinois Writers Project: American Guides Series. New York, Random House, 1939, p. 302. This style is certainly reminiscent of Wright, but although Nathan Morris is clear about Wright's work in making up the guide, he does not remember which pages he actually wrote.

19. Letters from L. Martin to M. Fabre (July 12, 1964) and T. C. Robinson to L. Martin (February 7, 1936).

The *Daily Worker* report of the reading at the University of Chicago is an undated clipping in WPP. In an early version of *Black Boy*, Wright's account is noticeably different. He says this took place in Evanston, where he had been invited to read his works and talk, and that the Communists who denounced him as a Trotskyite at the time spread the word that the audience had to leave because Wright was speaking without their permission. Wright found himself alone with William Attaway, who took him to a party among black people where they had a wonderful time.

20. Manuscript in WPP. In his long letter of August, 1955, to Aswell, Wright also takes the side of life against dehumanization.

21. See *Writers' Club Bulletin, op. cit.*, p. 18. Dan McCall's ingenious deductions in *The Example of Richard Wright* (New York, Harcourt, Brace & World, 1969, pp. 29–30) about whether the march actually took place have to be slightly corrected. Wright began the story in the summer of 1936, but it was not until 1937 that he finished reading *Let Me Live* and began writing for the *Daily Worker*, although he had been aware of the Herndon affair since 1935.

22. A scene that came after the episodes comprising "Almos' a Man," in which the hero's arrival in Memphis is described, survives only in a rough draft. Existing notes indicate that the novel never went beyond the hero's adolescence but that Wright had already revised the first version of "Tarbaby's Sunrise" before drawing his story from it.

According to the carbon in WPP, of an unsigned article, the novel would have been written before "Joe Louis Uncovers Dynamite." "He was stuck at the end of eighty pages. He returned however to another cast of the idea for two *New Masses* articles." In 1935, Wright spoke at length to Arna Bontemps about "Tarbaby" (December 29, 1962, interview with Arna Bontemps).

23. Wright places this latter incident in 1937.

According to "Negro Author Criticizes Reds as Intolerant" (*New York Herald Tribune*, July 28, 1944): "His early association with the Communists was broken in 1937 when he was 'ejected' from the Party. . . . As to what caused the Chicago rift . . . Mr. Wright said: 'It was an accumulation of many things, not so much a leaving as an ejection over a difference of opinion.' " Ed Gourfain said that at a party in 1936 he observed a Communist taking notes on a conversation that Wright was engaged in (although the subject was literature, not politics) for the sole purpose of reporting on Wright to the local authorities. Claude Lightfoot, in fact, often spied on Wright for the Party. (Interview with Ed Gourfain, June 17, 1964.) Margaret Walker is definite about the May Day parade incident. (Conversation with M. Walker, February 28, 1972.)

24. This remark was related to me by Fern Gayden (June 20, 1964)

and she, along with Metz Lochard, Len Mallette and Essie Lee Davis provided this information on Wright's life just prior to his leaving Chicago. (Interviews conducted in June, 1964.)

Notes to Chapter Seven

1. See *Thirteen Against the Odds, op. cit.*, p. 41. Embree interviewed Wright several times before writing this well-documented study.

2. The Gourfains also helped Wright financially at this time and were disappointed, later on, not to receive any word from him. (Conversation with Ed and Joyce Gourfain, June, 1964.) Henrietta Weigel distinctly remembers the elegance and reserve of the young black boy who did not dare take a shower after his exhausting journey. Wright had dinner with the Weigels that evening and spent two nights there. During this first meeting he was obviously anxious to avoid provoking any unpleasant remarks. Later, he became a good friend of Henrietta's and made her the recipient of extensive confidences. (Conversation with H. Weigel, December, 1962.) Abraham Chapman had written Wright that he could stay with him on his arrival in New York, but his small apartment at 208 West 67th Street turned out not to be available. (Correspondence between Wright and Chapman, 1937.)

3. *The Writer in a Changing World*, edited by Henry Hart, New York, Equinox Cooperative Press, 1937, pp. 226–27. This provides a very detailed report on the American Writers' Congress. See also the June issues of *New Masses*, and Dwight MacDonald's report in the June 19, 1937, issue of *The Nation*.

4. "There is a young Negro writer we saw a few times before we left New York. His name is Richard Wright and he says he has been immensely influenced by your writings. We haven't seen anything of his but he is at least a very smart person. I went as a delegate to the Writers' Congress and he was there too. There was a huddle of novelists on Sunday morning and I must say that his was the clearest and hardest of the minds present. I might say it was the only one. Anyway Harper's are going to bring out his first book before long. I think he is doubtless a left-wing writer. I know he is class-conscious to a degree and I'm looking forward to seeing what he writes. I was wondering whether you know him." Max White to Gertrude Stein, January 30, 1938. (In *Flowers of Friendship*, edited by Donald Gallup, New York, Knopf, 1953, p. 326.)

5. Conversation with Jack Conroy, June 18, 1964.

6. "Negro Writers Launch Literary Quarterly," *Daily Worker,* June 8, 1937. A similar article came out in the *San Antonio Register* of July 10, in which Wright specifies that "an organizational plan similar in structure and purpose to that of the John Reed Club which influenced

so many young writers for the past seven years is being launched with *New Challenge* as its organ."

7. "Blueprint for Negro Writing," *New Challenge* (Autumn, 1937), pp. 53–65. The version of this essay published in 1971 in *Amistad II* actually antedates the one that appeared in 1937, the result of further cutting and reorganization that Wright himself did.

8. Conversations with Ralph Ellison, February, 1963, and April, 1970.

9. Letter from Paul Edwards to Wright, August 10, 1937. Wright's departure was preceded by an extensive correspondence to ascertain whether he would be transferred to the New York F.W.P. The Chicago officials were all in favor of it, but no definite reply could be obtained from New York; Wright decided to run the risk of leaving for New York without the assurance that work would be available to him when he got there.

10. For Wright's relationship with Benjamin Davis, see Constance Webb's account (*Richard Wright*, pp. 145, 153–54), which was based on conversations with Davis.

11. Several of his friends stated that they had heard him express resentment because *New Masses* had promised him a job with the magazine while he was still in Chicago. They also say that he stayed aloof from the rest of the *Daily Worker* staff (conversations with Ralph Ellison, Willard Maas and others, which are confirmed by Wright's correspondence with Margaret Walker).

12. Wright kept in his files clippings of 45 signed and 135 unsigned articles, which he dated from June to December, 1937. He crossed his name off one article that had been attributed to him, and he did not collect all the unsigned articles from the *Daily Worker* Harlem Bureau. This implies that he wrote all the articles that he clipped and marked with a cross. A comparison of his files with the files of the paper itself for the same period indicates that Wright's collection is remarkably complete.

These articles divide up by subject as follows:

    1) 54 per cent on political events of interest to Blacks.
    2) 20 per cent political propaganda.
    3) 20 per cent on conditions of life in the ghetto.
    4) 6 per cent on cultural and artistic events.

The same categories within the group of signed articles divide up as follows:

    11 signed articles out of 109 in category #1.
    15 out of 41 in category #2.
    11 out of 40 in category #3.
     5 out of 10 in category #4.

This indicates Wright's greater interest in reporting on cultural events. In second place comes political propaganda, which is somewhat surprising, especially since this proportion does not even include his articles on the Scottsboro trial, of which only 2 out of 27 were signed.

13. On the Scottsboro trial see: "The Scottsboro Boys," in *New Masses*, November 6, 1934; *Scottsboro Boy*, by Heywood Patterson and Earl Conrad, New York, Macmillan, 1969; and especially *They Shall Be Free* by Alan K. Chalmers, New York, Doubleday, 1951. Communist leader William Patterson, who protected Wright within the Party for a long time, had served as a judicial adviser at the trial. Wright not only alludes to the case in several of his books but in 1948 agreed to advise Jean-Paul Sartre on his adaptation of *La P . . . Respectueuse*, which was partially inspired by the trial.

14. "Then she told of Oscar Hunter, a boy from the stockyards of Chicago who is now political commissar at Murcia. Oscar Hunter studied at Hampton Institute in the South and is known among the Loyalist People as 'the man who can get things done.' " "Two American Negroes in Key Posts of Spain's Loyalist Forces," in the *Daily Worker*, September 19, 1937.

15. "It hit me square between the eyes," declared Eda Lou Walton in *The New York Times Book Review* of August 29, 1937. "An excellent biographical sketch," according to Eugene Armfield in the *Saturday Review of Literature*, September 4, 1937. "The most successful material in the book," wrote Jack Conroy in *New Masses* on September 14, 1937.

16. According to Ellen Wright, some Party leaders severely criticized the novel and tried to prevent Wright from getting it published, but this almost certainly did not take place until the beginning of the forties; rejections from the publishers up until 1938 were sufficient to cause Wright's discouragement.

Notes to Chapter Eight

1. Whit Burnett to Wright, December 14, 1937. According to *The Book Union Bulletin* of April, 1938 (p. 3), it was Mrs. Gannett who was so enthusiastic that she recommended the story to her husband, who was hesitating between several at the time. Harry Scherman stated as he announced the prize: "Every sensitive white person will at once know that this is authentic Negro life in this country. Richard Wright's talent is clear and unmistakable." (*Pittsburgh Courier*, March 31, 1938.) Sinclair Lewis voted against Wright. (May Cameron, "Author, Author," *New York Post*, March 12, 1938.)

2. "He'll not squander his money on a trip to Europe in quest of material for later works. What richer material could he find anyway, he

philosophizes, than from the wealth of his own experience, gained while working in Mississippi and Chicago? . . . He will not buy a car, but shoes, an overcoat, and a nice juicy steak. 'When you're hungry, you can't really think about very much, except how a good, healthy, man-sized meal would feel under your belt. I'm none of that school that believes that art thrives on empty stomachs and cold, dingy rooms.'" (*New York Amsterdam News*, February 26, 1938.)

3. "It is a novel of Negro life in Chicago. . . . It has to be good, because I want to show that *Uncle Tom's Children* is no accident. I hope the $500 will last until I get it completed." (*Philadelphia Independent*, April 3, 1938.) "I'd like to take a leave from the project and go to Mexico. There is a changing social order there, and that's fascinating to me. I'd like to travel and study all the while." (*New York World-Telegram*, February 15, 1938.)

4. When he received the prize he invited the Weigels to drink champagne. He had bought a new suit for twenty-seven dollars at Crawford's and was carrying the package wrapped up in newspaper to disguise it, as usual, from inquiring gazes. It was the first time he had owned two suits. (Conversation with Henrietta Weigel, December 31, 1962.) The congratulation letters that he received from unknown Blacks about the prize called it "a service rendered to the entire race." The marriage proposals came from poorly educated girls who all claimed to be good Christians, pretty and responsible.

5. See in order: "Books of the Day," *Daily Worker*, April 4, 1938, p. 7; Granville Hicks (whose political viewpoint was rather narrow) in *New Masses*, March 29, 1938, p. 23; James T. Farrell in *Partisan Review*, Vol. 4 (May, 1938), p. 58; Malcolm Cowley's "Long Black Song" in *New Republic*, Vol. 49 (April 16, 1938), p. 280.

In "Four Tragic Tales" (*The New York Times Book Review*, April 2, 1938, p. 16). Robert Van Gelder compares Wright's style to Hemingway's. See also Charles Poore in "Books of the Times," *The New York Times*, April 2, 1938; and "White Fog," *Time* magazine, March 28, 1938, pp. 31, 64.

6. In "The Literary Scene," *Opportunity*, Vol. 16 (April, 1938), pp. 120–212, and "From the Inside," *The Nation*, Vol. 146 (April 16, 1938), p. 448.

7. "The Negro: New or Newer . . . ," *Opportunity*, Vol. 17 (January, 1939), p. 8. See the correspondence between Locke and Wright, WPP and Moorland Collection, Howard University.

8. Undated clipping, WPP. On March 4, she had sent her remarks to Eugene Saxton, asking him when he would prefer to have them appear in her column. In August, 1938, she repeated her feelings to Wright

himself, replying to his request for a recommendation for a Guggenheim Fellowship. Perhaps he was thinking of Mrs. Roosevelt when he spoke in "How Bigger Was Born" of the bankers' daughters who wept over his stories and whom he was hoping to deprive of this release in his novel *Native Son*.

9. "I'm trying to express the Negro's struggles, not as an isolated movement, but as part of the American working class. I owe my literary development to the Communist Party and its influence which has shaped my thought and creative growth. It gave me my first vision of Negro life in America." The *Daily Worker*, February 25, 1938. In the *New York Amsterdam News*, February 27, 1938, he says, "I have found the Negro worker the real symbol of the working class in America," which is somewhat different.

10. "Adventure and Love in Loyalist Spain," *New Masses*, March 8, 1938, pp. 25–26. Wright hailed in *The Wall of Men* "the beginning of a popular mass fiction in America, a brand which can be read with pleasure by workers, without the danger of their being duped or misled." He also reviewed *I Was a Sharecropper* by Henry Harrison Kroll for *New Republic*. The truth of the story appealed to him as much as the racial prejudice of the white sharecropper-author irritated him. ("A Sharecropper's Story," *New Republic*, December 1, 1937, p. 109.)

11. A part of this account was published in *The Writers' Club Bulletin*, Columbia University, Vol. 2 (May, 1938), p. 24.

12. "Statement by American Progressives—Leading Artists, Educators, Support Trial Verdict," *Daily Worker*, April 28, 1938. See Committee on Un-American Activities, Washington, 1938, Vol. 1, p. 375, and *ibid.,* Exhibit 114, Appendix I (1941), p. 809.

13. These engagements were as follows: On May 18, he presided over a meeting in Steinway Hall at which Granville Hicks spoke on "The Contemporary American Scene." A few days later, he was a guest at the fourth convention of the American Communist Party and, following James W. Ford's panegyric to him (ironic, considering how cordially this leader "in charge of Negro affairs" disliked the young black author), Hughes, Sterling Brown, William Z. Foster, Earl Browder and other leaders gave the signal for a general standing ovation. (Unidentified clipping in WPP.) The following week, Wright, Oliver LaFarge, Muriel Draper and George Seldes were guests of honor at a reception for the benefit of the League of Mutual Aid. On June 4, there was a cocktail dance celebrating the twentieth anniversary of the "Crusader News Agency" and Wright's appointment to the editorial board of the Literary section of *New Masses* (replacing Horace Gregory, who had not stuck close enough to the Party line). A half-dozen speeches em-

phasized that Wright had been appreciated for a long time and that the success of his recent book had nothing to do with this new honor. (See *New Masses*, June 20, 1938, and the *New York Amsterdam News*, June 25, 1938.)

Wright himself spoke at a Communist meeting on June 7, inaugurating a campaign to distribute fifteen million tracts. On June 10, with the playwright Albert Maltz and other Party members, he attended a gala evening at the Bayer Theater given by the Harlem Suitcase Players, under the auspices of the League of the New Theater, a radical group. The program was *Don't You Want to Be Free*, by Langston Hughes, and *Mighty Wind A-Blowing*, which had just won Alice Ward the drama prize at Yale University.

On October 21, he went to Boston to deliver two speeches, one on "The Negro and the Progress of American Culture" at the Beach Street Progressive Bookstore, and the other on his own writing at an author's evening sponsored by the State and City Government Workers' Union.

As a member of an L.A.W. Committee appointed to organize a reception to welcome Theodore Dreiser home from interviewing the prime minister of the Spanish Republic, he received his "master," along with Dorothy Canfield Fisher, Van Wyck Brooks, Sherwood Anderson, Edgar Lee Masters and Pearl Buck, at a party given on November 15 at the St. Moritz Hotel for the benefit of American Aid Ships to Spain. On November 19, he accompanied Alain Locke to an L.A.W. meeting where Langston Hughes, Jessie Fauset, Sterling Brown and Genevieve Taggard spoke on "The Negro, a Force in American Literature." On November 25, he participated in a debate organized by the National Negro Congress and, as a command performance, he attended (with other members of the League and Representative Vito Marcantonio) the St. Sylvester's Ball given by the Relief Committee for All Political Refugees.

14. *New York Panorama: A comprehensive view of the metropolis, presented in a series of articles prepared by the Federal Writers' Project of the W.P.A. of New York City.* American Guides Series, New York, Random House, 1938.

15. "Portrait of Harlem," pp. 132–51. Wright's research indicates the great care he took to be historically correct. Among other sources he quotes *A Story of the Negro Race in America* by G. W. Williams (2 vols., Putnam's, 1883) and *The Story of the Negro* (1909) by Booker T. Washington. He also quotes W. E. B. Du Bois, *The Suppression of the African Slave Trade 1638–1870*. He devotes a number of pages to black intellectuals and the Harlem Renaissance, which he viewed in rather personal terms: "This literary movement was notable in that for the first time the American Negro depicted his own life with a wide

and varied range of talent and feeling. For a few years, Negro writers created more than they have ever done before or since that period" (p. 142).

16. *Ibid.*, p. 143. This recalls Wright's *Daily Worker* article on the evolution of the black theater, which had been brought up to date at the time of the production of *Haiti* by W. E. B. Du Bois. The author of *Native Son* also shows through here: "It has been said that the Negro embodies the romance of American life; if that is true, the romance is one whose glamour is overlaid with shadows of tragic premonitions" (p. 151). The editors of the Guide made only a few corrections in style on Wright's text.

17. "I'm struggling with the Harlem locality story . . . for volume two of the Guide, the one covering Manhattan." Mimeographed text in WPP of a F.W.P. Editorial Conference, broadcast on April 13, 1938, p. 12a. Wright is one of the few members of the F.W.P. to be thanked for his contribution at the beginning of the book, which appeared the following year. *New York City Guide.* American Guides Series, New York, Random House, 1939.

18. He wrote on June 3, 1938, to Henrietta Weigel: "Things on the Project began to pop. They wanted to transfer us all. We had to hold picket lines, organize delegations and all around raise a lot of hell. Luckily things came out all right in the end, but while it lasted it took you from morning to night." My other sources on this point are conversations with Helen Neville (January, 1964) and Willard Maas (June, 1964), and the evidence of Edwin P. Banta in Committee on Un-American Activities, *op. cit.*, Vol. 2, pp. 1006–10. According to him, eight of the eleven members of the Workers' Alliance were Communists and certain mimeographed tracts cited the nomination of Wright and his comrades at the union office.

19. For instance, on June 24, 1938, he spoke at the invitation of the radio section of the Federal Theatre where Theodore Ward worked. His subject was "The Role of the American Writer in a Democratic Society," as part of a program called "Discovering the Arts and Sciences." (*Daily Worker*, June 19, 1938.)

Notes to Chapter Nine
1. Peter Pollack, who met Wright shortly before his departure for New York, thinks that he remembers Wright coming to his apartment on Indiana Avenue and reading some episodes which later appeared in the novel. He referred particularly to the basement scene with the menacing rumble of the furnace. (Letter to M. Fabre, May, 1964.)

During his second visit to the Newtons in the beginning of 1938,

Wright said that Whit Burnett and Martha Foley had encouraged him to write a novel, but he did not mention at the time that he had chosen Bigger for his hero, or that he had already started to write. Toward the end of February, 1938, however, he was able to give Reynolds an outline of the novel to be sent to Harper's.

2. This is Mrs. Newton's opinion. I am indebted to her for many details and for all the anecdotes concerning the writing of *Native Son*. The pages devoted to this period in Wright's life correspond very closely to her account, which she sent to me by letter on March 18, 1964. Other firsthand information was supplied by Theodore Ward, Henrietta Weigel and Ralph Ellison. The reference to Dreiser and Dostoevsky is mine.

3. "Native Son," *Book of the Month Club News*, March 1, 1940, p. 8. See also the interview in the *New York Post*, March 15, 1941: "When I was writing the book, a case which in many respects resembled the Bigger Thomas case broke in Chicago, and most of the newspaper items in the book were rewritten from those which appeared about this Chicago case. I made two trips to Chicago to check on the details of the courtroom and prison scenes."

4. A file of these clippings is in WPP. See in particular: "Brick Slayer Is Likened to Jungle Beast" by Charles Leaville (June 5, 1938) and "Science Traps Moron in 5 Murders" (June 3, 1938). The reporter quotes a letter from the sheriff of Tallulah, Louisiana, Nixon's home town, from which Wright copied the exact wording. The violence took place in the crowd just before the trial began, at the end of July. The black leaders of Chicago helped the lawyer from the International Labor Defense, but vainly protested the authorities' decision to be done with the matter as fast as possible. Nixon was executed in August, 1939. In an essay in *Phylon* (Vol. 30, No. 1, 1969, pp. 66–72), Keneth Kinnamon accurately assessed the role of these newspaper extracts in Wright's novel. He also points out that Wright borrowed another detail from the case. Nixon claimed to have taken a lipstick from the room of one of his other victims in order to avert suspicion by writing "Black Legion" in the mirror. To the same end, Bigger signs his ransom note, "Red." See "Brick Moron Tells of Killing Two Women," *Chicago Tribune*, May 29, 1938.

5. Nelson Algren to M. Fabre, March 22, 1963.

6. Wright wrote to Reynolds, October 24, 1938: "The first draft of the book is done, amounting to some 576 pages. The title at present is *Native Son*. I'm going to try to find a more colorful one before the book is published." In an interview published in the *New York Sun-Telegram* on March 4, 1940, he said: "I took the title to show that Bigger Thomas is an authentic American, not imported from Moscow or anywhere."

7. Wright had asked Marie Mencken's sister Adele, who had offered her services as typist, to write the letter asking for Mrs. Roosevelt's support. Probably out of superstition, he preferred this to be a letter "from one white woman to another." (Conversation with A. Mencken, August 20, 1964.)

8. Reynolds to Wright, March 2, 1939, and Wright to Reynolds, March 7, 1939. "I think that nine-tenths of what you say was correct. . . . The types of characters I have been using —the inarticulate Negro—and the manner of treating them which I've held to so far, made some of the weaknesses almost inevitable. My next set of characters will be more conscious, articulate, and will move in wider social areas."

9. "The entire guilt theme was woven in *after* the first draft was written" ("How Bigger Thomas Was Born," *Saturday Review*, Vol. 22 [June 1, 1940], pp. 4–20). It is possible that this happened before the second version was written, but it is more probable that it took place toward the end of the second draft. By May 5, Wright had already reread and revised 400 pages. The second version was slightly shorter than the first, which, when it was finished in October, 1938, was 576 pages long.

10. Lewis Gannett called it "a deeply compassionate and understanding novel" (*New York Herald Tribune*, March 1, 1940); Charles Poore was particularly impressed by the mastery of language and form (*The New York Times*, March 1, 1940), Clifton Fadiman compared Wright to Dreiser and Steinbeck, and even hailed the novel as an exploration of the human soul worthy of Dostoevsky (*The New Yorker*, March 2, 1940, p. 53); Malcolm Cowley thought *Native Son* was better than *Uncle Tom's Children*, and preferred the third section of the novel to the beginning (*New Republic*, March 18, 1940, pp. 382–83); Jonathan Daniels in the *Saturday Review of Literature* (March 2, 1940, p. 5) and Margaret Marshall in *The Nation* (March 16, 1940, pp. 367–68) emphasized respectively the power of the novel and the maturity of the author, superior to that of Steinbeck.

11. See "Richard Wright's *Native Son*," *Chicago Defender*, March 16, 1940, and "A Work of Genius," *New York Amsterdam News*, March 23, 1940.

12. In Alain Locke's "Of Native Son: Real and Otherwise," *Opportunity*, Vol. 19 (January, 1941), p. 4, and in James Ivy's "Whipped Before You Born," *Crisis*, Vol. 67 (April, 1940), p. 122.

13. The Book-of-the-Month Club recorded 13,719 orders during the first week. The 200,000-copy mark was reached on March 20, and 250,000 had been sold by May 6, according to *Publisher's Weekly*, which, on March 30, recorded sales of 2,000 copies a day. Sales were particularly strong in New York, Chicago, Atlanta and in Texas, where

the reviews in the *Dallas Morning News* and the *Houston Press* had been very favorable. *Native Son* was first on the best-seller list by April 1, ahead of *How Green Was My Valley* by Richard Llewellyn, *Kitty Foyle* by Christopher Morley, *The Nazarene* by Sholem Asch and Steinbeck's *The Grapes of Wrath*. During the same month it went down to number 4, where it remained for some time. It was never a great best seller like *For Whom the Bell Tolls*, or *Oliver Wiswell* by Kenneth Roberts. *Time* named it the most promising novel of the year, along with *The Heart Is a Lonely Hunter*. (*The New York Times,* April 7 and 8, 1940; the *Brooklyn Eagle*, April 14, 1940; and *Time* magazine, December 23, 1940.)

14. *Current Biography*, 1940, pp. 885–86. It was Beatrice McMurphy in *Afro-American* (March 9, 1940) who spoke of a "sepia Steinbeck." The *Memphis Commercial Appeal* (March 7, 1940) had the headline "Memphis Proud of *Native Son* Author."

15. Wright received more than a thousand letters, many of which began, "I have never written a fan letter before but . . ." Unfavorable or insulting letters numbered about one out of ten, a proportion less than that for *Black Boy*, which was a direct attack on the South. In *Native Son*, however, the South was delighted to see a Black criticize the North, and feeling was very favorable toward him, considering the fact that he was a Negro.

16. See the *Chicago Defender*, May 17, 1940. It was used by Attorney Heimberg who was defending Daniel Ellison against the Orner and Shayne real estate agency of Chicago.

17. Conversations with Ellen Wright, William Patterson, Constance Webb and Willard Maas, 1963–1969.

18. Unpublished letter from Wright to Mike Gold, May, 1940 ?, WPP.

19. "Negro Novel and White Reviewers," *The American Mercury*, May, 1940, p. 113. Wright's reply came out in the next issue, pp. 376–77, under the title "Rascoe Baiting." The July issue then printed Rascoe's second letter, as well as an opinion from a reader who was favorable to Wright.

20. *Atlantic Monthly*, June, 1940, pp. 826–28. Edward Weeks, the editor of the magazine, had to cut a dozen or more lines of Wright's more personal attacks which showed how completely exasperated Wright had become.

Notes to Chapter Ten

1. See Harry Hansen, in *O. Henry Memorial Award Prize Stories of 1938*. New York, Doubleday, 1939, pp. viii–ix.

2. See interview in the *New York Amsterdam News*, April, 1939, WPP.

Wright wanted to devote himself to writing this second novel, as well as another book. He would revise the novel while traveling, perhaps in Europe. At the beginning of the year he had discussed with Whit Burnett his idea for a novel on the domestic "slave trade."

3. On March 24, 1939, he wrote: "The plot and action of the novel will hinge upon the struggles of Maud Hampton to protect a fortune and social position which she has falsely inherited and her effort to preserve a sense of the dignity of her self amid circumstances which are essentially degrading, and her fight to maintain her ebbing health. The novel will unfold in a continuous series of dramatic scenes which will show Maud Hampton in relation to the world of politics and finance; in relation to religious women servants; in relation to the organized labor movement, in relation to her young Negro lover; in relation to white women who envy her status, and finally in relation to the warring impulses raging in her own heart."

4. Wright to Reynolds, February 6, 1940. Wright was retracing, to some extent, his own life with the help of the central ideas in *Twelve Million Black Voices*. Maud would play a similar role to that of the woman in "Song of the Prairie."

5. Wright to Reynolds, February 13, 1940: "I'm not too anxious to get tied up in Hollywood unless I was assured that I could say what I wanted to through the medium of the movies. . . . If the men in Hollywood are willing to tell the truth in relation to Washington and the Negroes generally, I might reconsider it."

6. See *Town Meeting of the Air Bulletin*, April 24, 1939, pp. 16–17.

7. On this occasion, Wright spoke for the first time at length with Dreiser. (Conversation with Dorothy Norman, who had taken him to the party, February, 1964.) See "Dreiser on Finland," *New Masses*, January 30, 1940.

8. " 'Negroes Have No Stake in the War' Wright says—Opposes Aid for Finland with Paul Robeson, Will Geer and Others," undated clipping from the *Daily Worker*, WPP.

9. In the newspapers, which were, of course, delighted to link the names of the two celebrities, there is no indication that Wright had any such desire, but in a lecture years later, he shows by retelling the incident that he had never forgotten it. ("The Negro Artist and Intellectual in the United States Today," unpublished lecture given at the American Church in Paris, in November, 1960, WPP.) The adaptation of the story had then been entrusted to the agent Audrey Wood, but nothing came of it (Whit Burnett to Wright, July 26, 1939).

10. Conversation with Willard Maas and Marie Mencken, June 10, 1964. Wright confessed to Reynolds in his letter of December 4, 1938, that he

had given the manuscript a year before to a friend to place. Wright insisted that Marie keep the commission for the sale. Wright's notes on the last manuscript page of the novel indicate that he was planning to have twelve episodes in "Almos' A Man" at the time he was thinking of including it in *Uncle Tom's Children*: among these would be the arguments with Hawkins; one love scene with Maybelle (who became Mary); the passing of the train, which suggests the possibility of escape; and a dispute with Bill, which would have preceded the purchase of the revolver.

11. According to Langston Hughes (conversation of April, 1965), Theodore Ward (conversation of February, 1963) and the Walker-Wright correspondence. See Margaret Walker's beautiful account of their relationship in University of Missouri, *New Letters*, Winter, 1971, pp. 182–202.

12. The information about the Chicago period comes from letters in WPP and an interview with Theodore Ward on May 22, 1963, at which Constance Webb was also present. Ward told me that Wright had been in love with one of the editors at *New Challenge* before finding out, to his horror, that she was a lesbian.

13. Letter from Jane Newton to M. Fabre, March 18, 1964: "He felt that he could work in the rooming house, the landlady was pleasant and he could economize on his food budget by use of the family kitchen. . . . He said [Marion's] mother considered him a respectable, steady young man, which he thought amusing. They weren't impressed by the fact that he had published a book; it was simply that he was quiet, did not get drunk or start trouble and dressed neatly that made him respectable. They were a little puzzled about how he could be living without some racket, even said things which indicated they believed he might be, but were content with his story inasmuch as he paid his rent regularly. Dick was a little embarrassed at Marion's unlettered condition, half-pleased on the other hand, that in spite of this he appeared to her desirable."

It is practically in these terms that Wright speaks about Bess and Mrs. Moss in *Black Boy*.

14. According to most people who knew her. Only one person described her as a "simple, homely type." Richard was somewhat won by her talent and self-assurance.

Wright's first wife agreed by letter to answer my questions, but never afterward showed any signs of life. I regret that I therefore had to depend exclusively upon other people's reports.

The marriage was religious because it seems that Wright insisted on conceding to the traditions of the black church.

15. Ward had left the house in Brooklyn after he had almost started a

fire with a cigarette, which strained relations between the two friends for a while. Ted had asked Richard to let him do the stage adaptation of *Native Son*, and, to illustrate his conception of the play, had acted the scene where Bigger presents himself at the Daltons'. Richard did the same, with Jane as audience, and this project occupied them for more than a week. Ward suggested Canada Lee, whom they had both seen in *Stevedore*, for the role of Bigger, but Wright exclaimed that Ted ought to play the lead. Wright hurt Ted deeply by implying that he was an actor and not a playwright.

In the spring, the Newtons' landlord, a West Indian by the name of Mr. William, evicted them in order to divide their apartment into studios. After trying to persuade him to change his mind, and then playing calypso records at full volume to annoy him, Wright moved to Room 33 at the Douglas Hotel, where Ward lived. Ward was quite impressed by Dhimah, and even more so by her mother. (Conversation with M. Fabre, February 1963.) Ralph Ellison, who knew about Wright's affair with Ellen, was more cautious, since he wondered if Wright were going to once again change his mind at the last minute.

16. She had been born Frieda Poplovicz, on September 4, 1912, and supplied the details about this episode.

17. Perhaps before the end of July. An article in the *New York Sun-Telegram*, March 4, 1940, mentions Wright and "his bride of seven months, a former dancer." Wright's last letter from St. Nicholas Avenue is dated August 2, and the first from Crompond sometime during September. The day before his marriage, Wright went to visit a former mistress and confided his dilemma. She found his hesitation to be strange, given the decision he had made. Wright apparently got married partially out of spite and discouragement. His attachment to Dhimah was real, but at another time he would not have been in such a hurry and Ellen's delay, which he interpreted as a negative decision, pushed him into taking an extreme step.

18. While the *California Eagle* of March 21, 1940, described him as "a grimfaced, cold-eyed fellow with a pugnacious jaw; a look of great, searching intelligence in his eyes, a sensitive mouth and a high forehead," the *Pittsburgh Courier* of March 29, 1940, reported him to be, "modest, affable, an excellent talker . . . just under five feet nine, [weighing] 157 lbs." They also quoted him as saying, "In all my work I intend to draw as wide a canvas as possible. I want to show the life of the Negro as it is actually lived, influenced by the many different environmental and sociological factors." In an interview with Roy Wilder (March, 1940, WPP) he stated, "Negro life as a whole in this country is unexplored, it is a virgin field for writing," and later in the same interview, he revealed, "My own stuff comes pretty slow. I live simple and can't write unless it

is quiet and simple. There are no fireworks in my life. Just work day in and day out."

19. "At once she suggested that she, her mother, her child and her pianist light out for Mexico. I fell for it." (Wright to L. Martin, January 27, 1940.) Wright certainly used to do what Dhimah wanted, as is indicated here: "Now this is what my wife says will suit us: a house, two story. . . . About a car: Dhimah has been trying to get me to buy one. . . . It all depends upon how hard she argues whether I get one or not." (Wright to L. Martin, February 5, 1940.)

20. "I'm trying to buy my folks a small home here in Chicago and finding a place is harder than I thought it would be; that is finding one without being rooked by real estate sharks. I wrote a book about the results of what real estate sharks do to Negroes and I have to see if I can apply it." (Wright to Reynolds, February 17, 1940.)

During this visit to Chicago, he was the guest of honor on February 18 at the Woodlawn Methodist Episcopal Church on Evans Avenue.

21. H. Cayton to M. Fabre, December, 1963.

22. L. Martin to M. Fabre, July 12, 1964. Wright to Reynolds, April 7, 1940: "Cuernavaca is beautiful. If I can't work here, then I'll be able to work nowhere. The house I am getting has ten rooms, a huge swimming pool, spacious grounds, flowers everywhere, fruit trees. . . ." The move was partially caused by Dhimah's having been stung by a scorpion.

23. Wright always recalled the filming of *The Forgotten Village* with pleasure. (See "How Jim Crow Feels," *True Magazine*, November, 1946.) This documentary on an ethnic minority perhaps influenced Wright in *Twelve Million Black Voices*. Viking published a book illustrated with photographs of the film in 1941. Herbert Kline, who had been published in *Left Front* in 1934, had directed several plays and had been an editor for *New Theatre*. He had encouraged Wright to write for the stage, regretting that writers like Richard and Countee Cullen had not entered the magazine's drama contest in 1935. (See *New Theatre*, Vol. 3, February 2, 1936, pp. 26–27.)

24. "I Bite the Hand That Feeds Me," *Atlantic Monthly*, Vol. 165 (June 5, 1940), p. 826.

25. Aswell was hoping to put out a special edition of *Native Son* for bookstores which would be distributed at the rate of one copy for every ten sold and which would include "How Bigger Was Born," David Cohn's article, and Wright's reply to it. Aswell even wrote on May 29, 1940, asking Wright to autograph end papers for 1500 copies, but Cohn refused his permission to reprint and the edition was never produced.

The report on the South Side for *Life* was never published, but *Look* magazine printed an article on Harlem entitled "244,000 Native Sons, the Story Behind *Native Son*," in addition to financing a series of radio programs designed to stimulate sales of the book, which had slowed in April, picked up again in May and diminished once more in June.

Life had first postponed the article because of the European situation, and later decided not to print it at all for unclear political reasons. Wright and Reynolds went to endless trouble just to be reimbursed for the expenses and to have the documents and photographs which they had lent the magazine returned to them. On October 1, 1940, Wright finally accepted $150 instead of the promised $250, remarking that he hoped "never to have to deal with those guys again."

26. See *Romance* (Mexico) June 15, 1940, WPP, and *Salud*, May 23, 1940, WPP, where Wright states: "In this hour of great crisis I feel that the creative writers of all the Latin American World should stand shoulder to shoulder with the creative writers of the English-speaking peoples in the fight for liberty and justice."

27. Conversation with Willard Maas (June, 1964) and letter from Lawrence Martin (August 2, 1964).

28. "How Jim Crow Feels," *Negro Digest*, January, 1947, pp. 44–55. Wright purposely accentuates the backwardness, stagnancy and shabbiness of existence in the rural South. A few well-chosen incidents show the stupidity and racial prejudice of the Whites with whom he was forced to deal. He concluded: "What I saw made me wonder why I had wanted to see and feel it again. I discovered that the only thing had really changed was I. The only things that were really new were the faces of the people that had grown up since I had left. And the only new developments were the astonishing number of people who had either died or who had had paralytic strokes. It took me but two hours to discover that what I had been seeking by returning was in the far-off remains of my childhood." Wright stayed in Natchez from June 15–19. (Letter to Paul Reynolds, June 19, 1940.) In Stanton, he met his half-sister, Joan Wright, and saw his uncle Salomon again. In Natchez, he visited his cousin Gladys and his cousin Hand Wright, who lived on Maple Street. On August 7, Mathilda Foley, a family friend, told him in detail of the Rhythm Club fire, material which he used much later in *The Long Dream*.

29. "How Jim Crow Feels," *ibid.*, p. 49.

30. Conversation with Jack Conroy, June, 1964.

31. The American Negro Exhibition, a section of the "Diamond Jubilee Exhibition" of Chicago, presented a history of black Americans through a series of about twenty dioramas; there was a literary display organized by Cayton, one by E. Franklin Frazier focusing on the black family, and various others on the arts, sports, etc. Essie Lee Ward and Rev.

Cobbins, who met Wright at the exhibition, both got the impression that he was now a "celebrity."

32. Conversation with Ralph Ellison, February 3, 1963. Wright even thought for a time that Ralph was living at his expense at Dhimah's invitation, but in fact, after she had lost all hope of reconciliation, she moved out overnight and the Ellisons had to pay the $60 rent by themselves.

Notes to Chapter Eleven

1. Wright had refused several offers before he became interested in Green's proposition: "It is queer that I'd not thought of Paul Green, because one of the straightest and most realistic plays of Negro life written by a white man was written by him, *Hymn to the Rising Sun*. It is true that he has not done anything of note recently, but he is a man to consider seriously. . . . He knows from first-hand just the nature of the material in *Native Son*." (Wright to Reynolds, May 18, 1940.) Although he was not originally enthusiastic about the idea of collaborating, he was attracted by the thought of working with Green: "There is only one person of the entire lot that appeals to me. I had already heard from other sources what is described as his artiness and I think I understand it. He had been writing realistic stuff for years and has not got far with it; his present attitude seems to me to be a reflex action, rationalizing that. And yet on the other hand, he possesses a knowledge and sympathy for the Negro and his life. Also, he possesses skill as a playwright. I think these things will offset the others." (Wright to Reynolds, May 25, 1940.)

2. "As I remember, I had three requirements in mind in dramatizing the book to make Communism somewhat comic, to make it clear that Bigger was partly responsible for his own failure, and that in the end he should come to the realization of his manhood. Orson Welles wanted to end the play showing Bigger as a completely pathetic character. Wright too, I remember, sided with him." (Paul Green to Edward Margolies, May 15, 1963.)

"Without seeming to realize it, for neither spoke of it, they were drawing a picture of Bigger as a distorted Black Christ—a martyr who was going to die that his race might be recognized as human beings, but, more important, that, through his crime and his death, his people might wake up to the realization of their potential power as human beings," according to Ouida Campbell, who was acting as secretary to the two authors. ("Bigger Is Reborn," *Carolina Magazine*, October, 1940, WPP.)

3. "Bigger Is Reborn," *Carolina Magazine*, October, 1940 (WPP). Wright's letters to Reynolds are quite enthusiastic about this stay at

Chapel Hill, and Green's May 15, 1963, letter to Edward Margolies evokes the atmosphere: "We often talked about literature, politics, and sparingly about the race problem. At that time, he planned, he told me, to move to Russia. I did all I could to persuade him from it. I told him that he was being appreciated in this country, his writings were a success and the struggle was here."

4. "Wright Attacks Leaders in Speech at White Rock Baptist Church," *Carolina Times*, August 3, 1940.

5. Wright thought that there were too many first names beginning with B. Houseman and Welles changed the adaptation a good deal when it came to deciding where the scenes should be cut. On October 23, 1940, Houseman wrote to Green: "The second scene is the best, but for the unnecessary entrance of Mrs. Dalton and Buckley. . . . The beginning of the second act is not right, for there is no tension because of the Bessie scene coming before the Dalton scene. . . . There is no gain in making Jan and Max the same person. And no reason for a reprieve ending if the reprieve leading to Bigger killing himself creates a different view. Bigger already found his truth before." According to a conversation I had with Paul Reynolds in February, 1963, Wright was anxious for Houseman to write this letter because he did not like Green's proposed ending. See also John Houseman's opinion in the special Wright issue of *New Letters,* Vol. 38 (Winter, 1971), pp. 71–77.

6. Wright was kept in bed by the flu until January 18 and the contracts were not signed until the end of February, at Arnold Weissberger's office.

7. "The following scenes, in my opinion, state in essence, pro and con, the issues involved in *Native Son.* Standing ideologically to the left and right of Bigger Thomas, the protagonist whose struggles you have just witnessed, are two symbolic ways of life in America: the liberal way and the status quo. In the end, having caught a vision of humanity that might have enabled him to express his life in socially valuable terms, Bigger, the victim of a snarl of fear and hate and guilt, is not in a position to accept either. There is no special pleading here; the play is merely an attempt to depict the social forces at work in our country in terms of warm human values. Bigger's point of view is presented to the fullest because he is the least known and understood." (Playbill for *Native Son.*)

8. According to *New Masses*, February 25, 1941, Welles categorically maintained that anything more than a forty second wait broke the rhythm and spoiled the effect of the play. Jean Rosenthal in "Native Son: Back-stage" (*Theatre Arts*, June, 1941, pp. 467–70) explains how the furnace of the Dalton house could descend into position in seconds, the building where Bigger hides was stored folded up to be unfolded once it was

lowered onto the stage, and the prison was arranged with an intricate system of bolts.

9. "Citizen Welles," *Direction*, Vol. 4 (Summer, 1941), pp. 9–14.

10. See the stage directions to *Native Son: A Play in Ten Scenes*. Richard Wright and Paul Green, New York, Harper & Bros., 1941. "I felt excited rather than moved," declared Stark Young (*New Republic*, April 7, 1941, p. 468) and Joseph Wood Krutch said it was "certainly the noisiest play since *Hellzapoppin*" (*The Nation*, April 5, 1941, p. 417). Rosamund Gilder had the same complaint in "Clamor and Purpose" (*"Theatre Arts*, March 5, 1941, pp. 339–342). Sidney Whipple's review was entitled *"Native Son* is another example of how director trims everything that blocks action of his play" (*New York World-Telegram*, March 28, 1941).

11. According to the *New York Journal and Guide* of April 8, 1941. Joseph Dell, a black man accused of raping his white employer, Mrs. Eleanor Strubling, was supposed to be condemned to death the day of the opening and the actress was afraid that her reputation might suffer from the coincidence.

12. Hearst learned about the movie in October, 1940, because of an indiscretion on the part of the critic Louella Parsons. He demanded a private showing of the incriminating scenes and his servants were easily able to recognize a very unflattering portrait of their employer. Although Hearst insisted that the filming be stopped, Welles ignored him, thus exposing himself to the wrath of this potentate who made every effort to harm his enterprises for many years to come.

13. See *PM*, March 26, 1941. The editor of this journal, Roger Pippett, was one of Wright's friends.

14. WNYC broadcast, April 8, 1941, at 9:30 P.M. Wright repeated the text of an article published on March 22 by the *New York World-Telegram*, "What Do I Think of the Theatre?" but he added a great deal to it. He had prepared a sort of play in the form of a dialogue between himself and Green concerning the adaptation.

15. Quoted in *Negro Digest* (Vol. 3, February, 1945, p. 79) in an article about Canada Lee, who was paid $250 a week for the first three weeks, $300 a week for the following month, and $500 for each additional week. On April 7, 1941, Bern Bernard and Lionel Stander, who had financed the production, offered him a limousine. On June 9, an entire radio program was devoted to him, with the collaboration of Duke Ellington, Paul Robeson, W. C. Handy, and others. During the McCarthy era Lee was harassed by the Un-American Activities Committee and deprived of acting jobs on account of his political opinions. His

despair at not being able to act contributed a great deal to his untimely death in 1952.

16. "*Native Son* Down Below," *New Masses*, March 10, 1942, p. 21.

17. Wright composed an introduction to the playbill for *Big White Fog*, which opened on October 22, 1940: "There lives in America," he wrote, "no playwright I know of who is better fitted for the launching of a true people's theatre for the mirroring of Negro life in America than Theodore Ward. Every literate Negro should aid with time and money for the Negro Playwrights Company. The men and women who are carrying this project forward are honest and fearless and will provide for the Negro public, for the first time in history, authentic Negro life on the American stage. And when this happens, the Negro will possess a powerful medium of expression whose potentialities are unlimited." According to Ward, Wright was disappointed not to be applauded in Harlem as much as the other stars who were present. (Conversation with Theodore Ward, May 22, 1963.) See the *Daily Worker*, September 6, 1940, and the *New York World-Telegram*, September 4, 1940.

18. "Forerunner, Ambassador," *New Republic*, October 24, 1940, p. 600. Wright was more severe in his review for the December 4, 1940, *Chicago News*, stressing the complacency of Hughes's autobiography and the middle-class values of DuBois. He later refused to review *I Wonder As I Wander* in order not to hurt his friend's feelings by attacking the book, which he considered puerile. (Carbon of an undated letter from Wright to Malcolm Cowley.)

19. Introduction to *Special Laughter* by Howard Nutt. Prairie City Press of James Decker, Vol. 3, 1940, p. x.

20. His correspondence contains references to an outline for a speech which he would have given on October 27, and according to Ralph Ellison his absence was very conspicuous. (Conversation of February 3, 1963.)

21. Conversations with Ellen Wright.

22. Wright to Claude Barnett of the A.N.P., February 5, 1941: "It is my conviction that the ultimate problems of the current war will find their solutions in these colonial and out of the way places." He cited the example of Hemingway, who had just been sent to China by *PM*. He also offered his services to Carl Murphy of the *Baltimore Afro-American*.

23. WPP. Along with William Gropper, the cartoonist; Marc Blitzstein, the composer; and his own colleague Ruth McKenney, he contributed to an auction to benefit the magazine by giving a manuscript. (Cf. *New Masses*, March 25, 1941.) For the anniversary, he stated, "For the first time during an imperialist war there exists in the world a new hope, a new workers' government, and a new magazine like *New Masses* to

give voice and utterance to the aspirations of peaceloving men." (*New Masses*, February 18, 1941, p. 26; reprinted in *New Masses*, May 6, 1941.)

24. "All of us can congratulate ourselves upon the fact that, so far, the Soviet Union has, through its strength and strategy, outwitted, out-maneuvered and outfought the imperialist warmakers. The base of world evolution, the Soviet Union, stands impregnable and indivisible, a beacon of guidance during these days of dark confusion. But the hardest task lies yet ahead. The imperialists can maneuver no longer; they are fighting and must fight for a redivision of the spoils of the world, and no man knows when the day and hour may come when they, exhausted and bit-ter, will turn from the bloody mauling of each other, and combine as common prey upon the world's lone socialist state." ("Anniversary Greet-ings to *New Masses*," *New Masses*, February 18, 1941, p. 26.)

25. The meeting took place at the Murray Hill Hotel on April 4, and was attended by Donald Ogden Stewart, Albert Maltz and others in prep-aration for the Congress, which was to be held from June 6–8. (*The New York Times*, April 5, 1941.) Wright's main L.A.W. activity that year consisted of a lecture given in January at the Malin Studios for the "Find Yourself in Writing Forum" program intended to help young writers choose their form of self-expression. Wright spoke about his interest in avant-garde techniques and a writer's problems in dealing with them.

26. At Columbia University, he had stated: "It is foolish to speak of democracy in these United States when there is a race living among its fellow Americans which does not enjoy the right of equality. . . . The only solution I can see . . . is that Negroes ally themselves to fight for their ideals and, in case of emergency, even to use drastic measures." (Quoted in *Domino*, May 8, 1941.)

27. See *The New York Times*, June 8, 1941. According to Nelson Algren and the Gourfains, he did not attend these meetings and was busy during that evening. He had given them tickets for *Native Son* but could not go with them. (Interview of June 19, 1964.)

28. "*Native Son* Wins Award for Novel," *The New York Times*, June 8, 1941. See the reports on the Congress in *Direction* (Vol. 4, Summer, 1941, p. 3); Daniel Aaron, *Writers on the Left* (New York, Avon, 1969, p. 370) and Eugene Lyons, *The Red Decade* (Indianapolis, Bobbs-Merrill, 1941, p. 385). The Randolph Bourne Prize was named in mem-ory of the great liberal who had opposed U. S. entry into the war in 1914.

Native Son was selling very well at that time. The Book-of-the-Month Club took a poll of 160 literary critics which indicated that it was in fifth place (with 57 votes and 365 points), following *For Whom the Bell Tolls* (124 votes and 1013 points), *New England: Indian Summer, Oli-*

ver Wiswell and *How Green Was My Valley*, and just ahead of *You Can't Go Home Again*. (*The New York Times*, February 10, 1941.)

29. See the *Chicago Defender*, February 8, 1941, and *Negro Yearbook*, edited by Vera C. Foster (Tuskegee, Alabama, Tuskegee Institute Dept. of Records and Research, 1947, p. 25). The Spingarn medal was established in 1934 by the president of the NAACP, Joel Spingarn, in memory of his son. Its purpose was to focus national attention on eminent black figures and to stimulate the ambition of young Blacks. The committee, made up each year of well-known journalists and religious, academic and union leaders, had already honored Walter White, Marian Anderson, Max Yeargan, and James Weldon Johnson. Wright wrote to Paul Green on February 3, 1941: "I suppose you heard about the Spingarn Award? Well, at least I think it cuts the ground from under the feet of the NAACP, which had been rather cool to *Native Son*. In fact this medal makes me almost respectable." Thus it seems that despite the friendship of Walter White, the other leaders of the NAACP had not been very favorable to Wright at this time. The black press, meanwhile, was mostly in favor of the committee's choice except for the Baltimore *Afro-American*, which, in its issue of February 15, 1941, said that it would have preferred to see a scientist or a doctor win the award.

30. Wright went to Houston with several friends including John Hammond and Horace Cayton, who both agreed on his reactions to the Party demands, according to my conversation with the former in March, 1964, and correspondence with the latter. See also Cayton's account of the trip in a round table discussion on Wright, printed in *Anger and Beyond*, edited by Herbert Hill (New York, Harper Torchbook, 1968). Later, Wright was more willing to declare himself in favor of U. S. entry into the war because he could hinge his statements on the terms of the black American participation. Thus *New Masses*, on August 5 (p. 23) published "Writers and the War," a statement signed by Wright and 130 members of the L.A.W., which specified: "The League is unalterably opposed to anti-Semitism and discrimination against the Negroes and the foreign-born." *Soviet Russia Today* also printed a telegram which Wright sent to *International Literature* after the Nazi attack.

31. Letter to the Spingarn Committee, July, 1941, WPP.

32. Undated and unaddressed telegram, WPP. On September 13, he had told Reynolds that he refused to make any public response to the United American Spanish Aid Committee, which had rented a theater for a performance of *Native Son* in Boston and requested his attendance. On October 13, he had also refused Reynolds's request to write a few lines to promote the sale of war bonds.

33. *Coronet*, April, 1942, p. 78. On December 21, 1941, Wright had written to Paul Green:

"Well, it seems we are all in for it. I did not think it would come so quickly, but since we are in this war, there's nothing for us to do but knuckle down and see it through, hoping that the world that survives will be a better one.

"Though I have been deferred in the draft because of dependents, I am anxious to serve the national democratic cause through my writing if such can be useful in helping us defeat the Axis powers. I feel that I can be of some service in popularizing and clarifying the Administration's war policy and war aims among the Negro people and among the American people as a whole. . . . In a condensation of *12,000,000 Black Voices* . . . I wrote a foreword indicating my support of the war.

"I'd like to do more, but I don't know just how or in what way. Any guidance or advice you can give me as to how I can serve as a writer (since I feel this is the best thing I can do) I'd deeply appreciate."

34. Conversations with Ellen Wright. See also Constance Webb (*op. cit.*, p. 155) who quotes Ben Davis himself as the source for this episode.

35. William Brewer, in *The Journal of Negro History*, Vol. 38 (January, 1943), pp. 107–10. At his publisher's request Wright had written an introduction to the autobiography of Jay Saunders Redding, then a professor at the University of North Carolina. Thus, Brewer went on to say: "Contrary to Richard Wright's dogmatic prediction in the introduction, *No Day of Triumph* will not 'rock on their heels, fire with anger or pour acid into the veins of any class of American Negroes.'" This was an anti-Communist reaction, although the editorial board of the magazine was not in the least so. In *Communism Versus the Negro* (Chicago, Henry Regnery, 1951, p. 263, Note 61) William Nolan stresses how hostile the Communists were to Wright after he left the Party. In the July, 1952, issue of *The Journal of Negro History* (p. 305) Vaughn A. Bornet replied that even if Wright had left the Party before the end of 1942, the critics of *No Day of Triumph* were certainly not aware of it, and furthermore, J. D. Jerome's review of *Native Son* in the April, 1940, *Journal of Negro History* (p. 251) had even then been critical of Wright.

Redding actually met Wright by chance in August, 1942, at a performance of *Othello* at Princeton. The Communists were then trying to recruit Redding and went so far as to publish a part of his book in *New Masses* without his permission, promising to make a best seller out of it. (J. S. Redding to M. Fabre, January 17, 1964.)

36. According to Dr. Frederic Wertham, who was analyzing Wright at the time, Wright was more concerned with his art than with communism or anti-communism. His break with the Party thus would have had less

importance than many others attributed to it. (Conversation of January 30, 1964.) According to Willard Maas, John Hammond and other non-Communist radicals, the rupture was most significant to Wright in that he felt alone, in relation not only to the Communists, but to the entire Left. At the beginning, he was extremely grateful that they remained friends with him and supported him after the break. It took him a long time to realize that the non-Communist Left could represent a viable force, and this loss of faith in a political ideal which had had an almost religious meaning for him led to his developing a more existentialist conception of life, but this evolution took several years.

37. Roy Fabrizzio's interview with Horace Cayton (October 29, 1963) sent to M. Fabre. According to Cayton (letter to M. Fabre, November 27, 1963): "They told me about the project and I went around with them and gave them facts about the city. Both he and Rosskam acknowledged my help, for which I am very proud. He used my files a bit, but mostly he talked and I pulled out material and talked about it. He did all of the writing." Wright acknowledged this debt in his foreword to *Twelve Million Black Voices*.

38. "Later when he was being entertained as a successful author, my husband and I met him socially at a party. I did not comment on my previous contact with him until with a sparkle in his eye he sought me out and said: 'Now, I know that a good social worker like you wants to fill in that story you started. . . .' He told me then about how he had gone to Mississippi and found his father where they had left him. . . . He visited my husband several times to discuss the things he was reading and Louis reported to me on how fast he read and absorbed the material." (Mrs. Wirth to M. Fabre, September 22, 1963.) The reading list corresponded to that of a second year sociology major. Louis Wirth had been teaching at the University of Chicago since 1926, had written two remarkable books on the ghetto and also headed a section in the Juvenile Delinquent Division. In the foreword to *Twelve Million Black Voices*, he acknowledges his debt to Cayton and mentions, among other works that he studied, *The Negro Family in the United States* by E. Franklin Frazier; *Rum, Romance and Rebellion* by Charles M. Taussig; *History of the American Negro People (1619–1918)* by Elizabeth Lawson; *Urbanism As a Way of Life* by Louis Wirth; and *Black Workers and the New Unions* by Cayton and George S. Mitchell. *Sharecroppers All*, by Arthur Raper and Ira De A. Reid. of which the introduction is dated August 20, 1940, could have helped him but it was not published until 1941.

39. At the end of the dinner with the Conroys and Algren, Wright suggested that they all act out a few scenes from *Native Son*. He himself

played Bigger, taking it very seriously, with Algren as Jan, Jack Conroy as Britten and Thora Nixon as Mary. (Conversation with J. Conroy, June 18, 1964.)

Metz Lochard, of the *Chicago Defender* came to see him at his hotel. Pollack and Hughes invited him to the Community Center where some of Hughes's one-act plays were being produced. (P. Pollack to M. Fabre, August 3, 1964.)

40. Harry Birdoff to Edward Margolies, July 4, 1965. The first drafts of the book are in WPP. The intermediate versions were made up by cutting, changing and inserting numerous passages. Wright pasted one version onto another until he reached the version (close to the final manuscript) which is in Beineke Library of Yale University.

41. In February, 1942, the *Book-of-the-Month Club Bulletin* quotes him as saying: "I want to show in foreshortened form that the development of Negro life in America parallels the development of all people everywhere." In "The Negro and Parkway Community House," a pamphlet which he wrote at Cayton's request in April, 1941, he explains: "The story of the Negro migrant's attempt at adjustment in the North is not a new story. It is but a phase of a story that is as old as man and man's effort to build a civilization. . . . The bewildered baffled faces of the migrant Negro in the northern city is but a poignant note in a theme whose variations began long before history and whose pathetic chords will resound as long as the desperate folks of the farms are forced to seek refuge in the cities." He took up this theme again in 1946 in his "Lettre sur le problème noir aux Etats-Unis" (*Nouvelles Epitres*, Paris, 1947, Lettre 2). He later modified his point of view in a letter to Aswell in 1955 on his plan for the "Celebration of Life."

42. "Twelve Million Black Voices," *Northwestern University of the Air*, CBS Network, Vol. 1, No. 8, October 18, 1941.

The book was offered free with a one-year subscription to *New Masses* in November, 1941. Samuel Sillen called it "a timely book . . . by a truly great American artist." (*New Masses*, November 28, 1941, pp. 22–24.)

43. Harper's asked him to read Henrietta Buckmaster's book on the Underground Railway, and he wrote of it: "Not only a magnificent picture of the struggle of the Negro for freedom . . . it is also an impassioned and provocative depiction of the revolutionary impulses of a nation. In an hour of national peril she resurrects and holds aloft a glorious era in our history." (Quoted on the jacket of *Let My People Go*, New York, Harper's, 1941.)

Wright advised Birdoff to approach Lee Shroyver at Viking and Keith Buckles at Random House. "As a Negro, naturally, I am concerned about how the greatest folk play of my race was received over the world. . . .

I believe you have something real here." (Wright to H. Birdoff, December 17, 1941.)

He wrote Aswell about Algren and Lipton: "I am certainly happy that the two writers I recommended are worthy of publication by Harper's. . . . If Nelson Algren can give forth a series of novels like this I think he will establish himself quite as securely as Faulkner has. Algren's ability to get into the maze-like minds of these twisted people and make them think and talk and reveal themselves is something that holds me spellbound." (Letters of July 20, and September 24, 1941.) Algren's *White Hope* appeared as *Never Come Morning* in 1942 with an introduction by Wright, and he recommended Lawrence Lipton, whose novel was *Brother, the Laugh Is Bitter,* for a Guggenheim.

44. Introduction to *Letters from the Tombs* (New York, Schappes Defense Committee, 1941, pp. v–vi). Wright had to be somewhat badgered into writing this introduction. Schappes spent three months in the sinister New York prison awaiting his release on parole, but his appeal was eventually refused and he was sent to Sing Sing in December, 1943.

45. "Dick Wright's Bigger Thomas Comes to Life in Clinton Brewer," *New York Amsterdam News*, undated clipping in WPP, by Dan Burley, which was the pen name of Wright's old friend Arthur Leaner.

46. See "Paroled Musician Enjoys the World After 19 years in New Jersey Prison," *PM*, August 22, 1941, p. 9.

47. One day Wertham took Wright with him to the prison to visit Brewer. The guard at the gate refused to admit Wright, but his superior, who was then summoned, had to respect the passes signed by the District Attorney. To Wertham's protestations he replied, "Doctor, we know you very well and you have always behaved reasonably, but you should not go to such trouble for a black man. There are no prejudices here—we have as many black prisoners as white." Wright, who was still nonplussed by this remark, had barely walked through the gate before six or seven guards jumped on him and searched him from head to toe. Wright remained cool, but Wertham, furious, got as a reply from the guards, "But didn't you know that all Negroes carry razor blades?" (Conversation with Frederic and Florence Wertham, January 30, 1964.)

48. Conversation with John Hammond, December 24, 1963; *Daily Worker*, October 3, 1941; *New Masses*, January 20, 1942, p. 30. The magazine advertised the record (Okeh Record No. 6475) which sold for thirty-five cents. Robeson's participation in the publicity campaign indicates that the Party considered the recording possible propaganda material. The final version of "Joe Louis Blues" is slightly different from that which Wright sent to Reynolds on September 25. Seven lines were shortened by one, two or three syllables and the original thirteen stanzas appeared in the following arrangement: 1-4-9-6-7-11-2-8-5-10-3-13-12.

49. This is a retranslation of "Introduction to Southern Exposure," which was published in French in *La Revue du Jazz* (April, 1949, 113) under the title "Note sur les Blues." *New Masses* called attention to the publication of White's album (Keynote, No. 107, Mercury Records) on October 2, 1940.

50. According to Robert Rice, "Broadway Report," *PM*, March 6, 1941, WPP. According to a clipping from the *New York Post* (May, 1941), Wright was collecting material on the New York "slave market." Another *New York Post* article (November 23, 1942) says that the novel was then called "Black Hope" and would not be a companion piece to *Native Son*.

51. H. Birdoff to Edward Margolies, July 4, 1964. Wright sent his notes to Aswell who wrote back on September 3, 1941: "The case histories of the domestic workers are simply extraordinary. . . . You ought to find some way to make use of this material and I am sure you will— that is, quite aside from the use you will make of it as a background in your new novel. Have you thought of writing an article for some magazine, summarizing the whole situation and perhaps citing the most interesting and the most representative of the case histories?"

52. See Reynolds to Wright, April 14, 1942: "The scene at the relief station where the man sets his clothes on fire and then is run over should not be changed an iota . . . though from an artistic point of view it could have come a little later.

"If it has a large sale, you have a fair chance of being somewhat a fixed star in the publishing firmament. Your books will vary in sales but they should hold up among the class of large best-sellers, say the way a man like Steinbeck does. . . . If 'Black Hope' doesn't sell, you will remain the author of *Native Son*. . . . You are inclined to be almost too humble and too self-doubting about your own abilities. . . . I think this is a larger and deeper book than *Native Son*."

In October, 1942, *Juvenile Book News* announced the publication of the novel for October 28, at a price of $2.50.

53. Wright owed the idea for the underground section to a piece in *True Detective* about a thief named Herbert C. Wright who got into various stores in Hollywood by digging a tunnel connecting to the basements and backs of the shops. On October 27, 1942, Wright asked the governor of California for more information ("for the purpose of fiction") concerning the motives of this man, who was being held at San Quentin on three robbery charges. (See my article on this subject in *Studies on the Novel*, Summer, 1971.) In any event, there is no evidence to prove that Wright had read *Les Miserables* at that date.

54. See "Slings and Arrows," *New Masses*, November 23, 1943, p. 20. The lack of available correspondance between Wright, Reynolds and

Aswell for 1942 makes it impossible to find out exactly why Harper's rejected the novel, nor is there any way of telling when Wright decided to eliminate the first part, which was sixty-two typewritten pages long and was never published. The second part, forty-two pages long, was included as a story in the anthology *Cross Section*, under the same title. Wright gave the manuscript as a present to Sylvia Beach, who allowed me to study it in 1962. Wright was partial to the story and, for once, was convinced of its worth.

55. *Accent* (Spring, 1942, pp. 170–76) published the passage in which Daniels covers the walls of the cave with diamonds and brand-new bills.

56. "Why I selected 'How Bigger Was Born,' " in *This Is My Best*, edited by Whit Burnett, Philadelphia, Blackiston & Grayson, 1942, p. 448. Bicek, Algren's Polish boxer hero, is also a murderer. Lover of Steffi, and friend of a number of bums and crooks, he is arrested for the murder of a Greek as he leaves the ring. Bicek is more than a subhuman or a derelict, he is the original American, genuine and not in the least contemptible because he rejects mass industrial civilization. In this sense he is related to Bigger, who kills in order to claim his own humanity.

57. To be exact, he received $17,869 from Harper's in 1940, $1,775 in 1941 and $2,268 in 1942.

58. Presided over by Wellington Roe, the White Mountains Conference gathered together writers and artists like Benjamin Appel, Alfred Kreymborg, Albert Maltz, Art Young, Marc Blitzstein and Irwin Shaw. It was over by September 2, and the Wrights left to stay with Louis Shapiro at Glenledge Cottage on Halibut Point.

59. Anaïs Nin baptized the house with this name. (Letter to M. Fabre, January 12, 1969.) The details about life at "Seven Middagh" were supplied by Mrs. Wright, Willard Maas, Carson McCullers (letter to M. Fabre, May 11, 1963), and can also be found in *Carson McCullers: Her Life and Works* by Oliver Evans (London, Owen, 1965) and *The Diary of Anaïs Nin, 1939–44* (New York, Harcourt, 1969).

60. "We were neighbors in Brooklyn and had children about of an age. . . . The one thing that stays with me is an impression of complete ease in the relationship. I felt I had from him acceptance of a kind I doubt I could have from many Negroes today." (Richard Rovere to Edward Margolies, March 10, 1963.)

61. The eight-page manuscript is interesting mostly for its international dimension. Wright wanted to "consolidate the bulwark of world colored opinion to the cause of the United Nations." Reynolds cut the first page because he felt the "oratorical plea that something be done" might deter Colonel Welles from reading the rest of the piece, since he already knew there was a problem. (Reynolds to Wright, April 17, 1942.) In

February, Wright had already attended a party given in honor of the black troops.

62. Wright to Local Board No. 178 in Brooklyn, July 7, 1942. Upon reading an article in *PM* which alluded to similar difficulties encountered by Ralph Ingersoll, Wright immediately sent a copy of *Twelve Million Black Voices* to the draft board official so that he could analyze his viewpoint, and brought his attention to "Mobilization of Negro Opinion," which had been sent on to John Houseman, then of the War Information Board.

63. Wright to Truman Gibson, July 28, 1942; Wright to Reynolds, August 22, 1942; and Wright to Reynolds, October 6, 1942.

64. According to Reynolds himself, who went to a great deal of trouble on Wright's behalf with Colonel Welles. (Conversation of January 20, 1964.) In November, Horace Cayton tried in vain to get Wright appointed to the editorial board of *YANK*, the Army magazine directed by Charles Collard and Donald Young. (Cayton to Wright, October 7, 1942.)

Notes to Chapter Twelve

1. The references to the war were added in December, 1941, shortly after Pearl Harbor. (Wright to Paul Green, December 17, 1941.) The allusions to segregation in the Army, the following spring, were characterized by remarks like, "There ain't no Jim Crow bullets." (See "Native Son Down Below," *New Masses*, March 10, 1942, p. 21.)

2. George Jean Nathan (in *The Best Plays of 1941*, "Native Son" pp. 113–15) granted the play a certain superficial melodramatic power, which he attributed to the staging and the acting of Canada Lee. The major weakness, he felt, was in the attempt to arouse compassion for Bigger because he was black.

Brooks Atkinson wrote, apropos of Lee's performance: "He had pulled the part taut and made it vibrant. . . . His voice conveys both the weakness of a boy who is terrified and the tumultuous savagery of a man who is on the loose and out of control. . . . [He is] the best Negro actor of his time, as well as one of the best actors in the country. This headlong portrait of Bigger Thomas is the most vital piece of acting on the current stage." (*The New York Times*, October 24, 1942.) Rosamund Gilder also analyzes his splendid performance in *Theatre Arts* (December, 1942, p. 744).

3. On this subject, see: *Catholic News*, December 5, 1942; *New York Post, New York Times, New York Evening Journal*, December 7, 1942; *Daily Worker*, December 8, 1942; *New York Age*, December 12, 1942; *Chicago Daily Times*, December 7, 1942.

The $400-dollar-a-week deficit was made up after the production costs had been absorbed. Wright had to call in a lawyer, Allan Taub, when the play was struck from the schedule of the Majestic. The novel itself had been exhibited at the New York Public Library, among 105 other books subjected to Hitler's purge, as part of a campaign to "Buy War Bonds and Stop Book Burning." (*PM*, November 30, 1942.)

4. Wright was cited for *Twelve Million Black Voices* and the 115 Broadway performances of *Native Son*, along with Joe Louis, Philip Randolph, Charles Johnson, the NAACP, the unknown black waiter of the U.S.S. *Arizona*, *PM magazine*, Pearl Buck and Mrs. Roosevelt.

On January 31, 1942, he was the guest of honor at a dinner given under the auspices of the Council on Negro Culture, with Count Basie, Benny Goodman, Duke Ellington, Paul Robeson, Canada Lee, Orson Welles and Josh White also attending. (Unidentified clipping in WPP.)

5. Wright to Reynolds, August 25, 1942. On October 6, Wright returned the story after making a few cuts: "The cuts are O.K. I retyped a couple of Allen's assertions and rephrased them, but I think they'll pass." The published version was read once again by Frederic Allen, who added the final paragraph.

6. "Richard Wright Describes the Birth of *Black Boy*," *New York Post*, November 30, 1944. Joyce Copper, who was then a student at Fisk, remembers the unprecedented enthusiasm which this lecture inspired among the students (interview by Horace Cayton, December, 1968).

7. The details concerning this trip come from a taped conversation between Horace Cayton and Mr. Fabrizzio, sent to me in November, 1964. Wright and Cayton had left for Nashville from Chicago, where on April 1, 1943, Wright had read some passages from his works in progress at the Parkway Community House.

8. "Black Boy was written as the result of a speech before a mixed white and Negro audience at Fisk University. . . . I believe that was the first time anyone had ever discussed the subject between both groups. The audience's reactions gave me a new sense of the value of my material and I made it into a book." ("Author Richard Wright Champion of Negro Rights," *New Haven Register*, April 8, 1945.)

The New York Times (September 17, 1944) had stated, "For 10 years, Wright has been working on an autobiography," and Wright himself declared, "I tried to write it as early as 1930; I have been working on it ever since." (*Afro-American*, March 24, 1945.)

Even when he spoke during Communist demonstrations in Grant Park and Washington Park in Chicago back in 1933–1934, Wright was already using his experiences as an adolescent to condemn racism. (Interview between Inman Wade and H. Cayton, December, 1968.)

9. "I had accidentally blundered into the secret, black, hidden core of race relations in the United States. That core is: nobody is expected to speak honestly about the problem. . . . And I learned that when the truth was plowed up in their faces, they shook and trembled and didn't know what to do. This tiny sliver of insight gave me my cue to plunge in." ("Richard Wright Describes the Birth of *Black Boy*," *New York Post*, November 30, 1944.)

10. "The handiest truth to me to plow up was in my own life." (*PM*, April 4, 1945, p. 3.)

11. *Ibid.* See also: "Richard Wright Believes Fear, not Sex, Governs Race Relations." Interview by Michael Carter in *Afro-American,* March 24, 1945.

12. *PM*, April 4, 1945, p. 3.

13. William Gardner Smith, "Black Boy in Brooklyn," *Ebony*, November, 1945, pp. 26–30.

14. "Richard Wright Describes the Birth of *Black Boy*," *New York Post*, November 30, 1944.

15. He suggested "Coming of Age in the Black South," "Coming of Age in the Black Belt," "Growing up in the Black South," "The Story of a Southern Childhood," "A Record in Anxiety," "A Study in Anxiety," "Odyssey of a Southern Childhood" and "A Chronicle of Anxiety" in his letter to Reynolds of August 20 (?), 1944.

16. In a biographical note, dated October 6, 1959, Wright is more specific: "A sharp dispute between me and the Communist Party developed over material in *Black Boy* that criticized the Communist attitude toward the American Negro and this brought about my final break with the Communist Party in 1942, but that break was not made publicly known until 1944." If this were correct, then Wright would have to have completed *Black Boy* by 1942 and shown the final chapters to the Communist leaders, but this is contrary to the evidence of his own statements in 1944 and 1945, as well as his correspondence during that time. The dates, however, are roughly correct, which means that it must not have been the manuscript of *Black Boy* which caused the break, but rather the latent conflict between Wright and the Party concerning its attitude toward Blacks, which Wright *was planning* to condemn in his autobiography.

17. "Richard Wright in Retreat," *New Masses*, August 23, 1944. The Communist attacks broke out mostly after the publication of *Black Boy*. The review of *Cross Section* in the September 26, 1944, *New Masses* was restrained in saying of "The Man Who Lived Underground," "Despite its sheer versatility, it is pervaded by a feverish unreality. A Negro fugitive, unjustly accused of murder, takes refuge in a sewer

where he enters a ghastly, gloom-haunted and demon infested world with only a tenuous relation to the sunlit regions above" (p. 31).

18. John Hammond says, "Dick felt very much like an outcast those days since the Communists had organized a powerful vendetta against him. Since I was an independent radical and was on the board of the NAACP he was surprised and delighted to find that I bore him no animus." (Letter to M. Fabre, December 24, 1963.) Wright's other friends had the same impression.

The description of a party given on December 8, 1944, by Mrs. Toy Harper, the aunt of Langston Hughes, shows Wright in the company of old and new friends, among them Ollie Harrington, the creator of "Bootsie," resplendent in his war correspondent's uniform, overflowing with savory anecdotes; Owen Dodson and Chester Himes, who were just starting their careers; and Dan Burley, who had become a jazz critic. (Clipping from the *Haitian Journal*, August 3, 1950, in WPP.)

19. The rent was high at seventy-four dollars a month, but the neighborhood was largely residential, calm and spacious, and the Wrights were the first mixed couple to be accepted in the building. After a few months, Wright organized a tenants' strike and had the rent lowered to the level authorized by the O.P.A., which of course did not endear him to the landlords in the area.

Because of Ellen's interest, Wright got involved in decorating the apartment and looking for antiques, and later continued to take an active part in furnishing their various homes. On his life in Lefferts Place, see "Black Boy in Brooklyn," *Ebony*, November, 1945, pp. 26–30.

20. "Richard Wright Feels Grip on Harlem Tension," interview by Max Schubert in *PM*, August 15, 1943, p. 4. See also *The New York Times*, August 1, 1943.

21. See *Direction*, July, 1940, p. 39. At the time there were seventy-five popular magazines and sixty literary magazines. *True Story* alone had a readership of six million.

22. The plan for "American Pages" is a typed manuscript in WPP. See p. 1.

23. This could have been the result of working with C. L. R. James, a black Trotskyist and author of *The Black Jacobins*, whom Wright had recently become friendly with, as Constance Webb, who was then the wife of James, describes using her firsthand information (*op. cit.*, p. 219). However, she creates some chronological confusion by wrongly dating "American Pages" after the idea for compiling a book on black Americans, which Wright conceived in 1944. It seems more likely that the two men worked together on the book, rather than on the magazine.

24. Wright stayed with the Caytons at the South Side Community

Center from March 21–27. He saw his old friend Essie Lee Ward and helped Alice Browning and Fern Gayden start their magazine, *Negro Story*, by putting them in touch with Jack Conroy, whose experience was valuable, and by giving them publication rights to "Almos' a Man."

25. Cayton to Wright, April 28, 1943; March 20, 1944; and March 27 (?), 1944. The manuscript of the plan for "American Pages" had been sent to Edwin Seaver, who returned it to Wright in November, 1943. Embree had promised his support in August, 1943, and in 1945 Wright was assured of the eventual collaboration of Waldo Frank. He then tried to get the magazine financed by the American Council of Race Relations but was unsuccessful.

26. On May 28, 1942, Eugene Lyons mentioned in his column for the *New York Post* that Wright was composing the script for a musical comedy, Duke Ellington was writing the music and Blarney Josephson would direct. On January 23, 1943, he again announced that Wright was working on a play, and on June 14, that he was just finishing it. On November 23, 1943, *New Masses* reported that he was hurrying to finish a novel and a play before being drafted, but there is no way of determining from Wright's unpublished manuscripts which works were being referred to. In the two latter cases it could have been "Melody Limited."

In January, 1943, Cayton declared that he was happy to learn that Wright was interested in working for Hollywood. On March 23, Wright told L. D. Reddick that the screenplay was finished. Thus he must have written it shortly after finishing "American Hunger."

27. The following year, Wright tried, also unsuccessfully, to interest Marshall Neilan of 20th Century-Fox in a film on the meaning of life for Blacks in America. (Wright to M. Neilan, July 31, 1945.)

28. Wright to Reynolds, August 28, 1944: "I'll hate to leave here. Racoons come up to the door. Bass can actually be seen in the lake. And all the books I brought along to read are unread." They were living in Mrs. Richard Craybiel's house near Ottawa. See also Wright to Reynolds, August 20, 1944.

29. Dorothy Norman published this exchange of letters between Frasconi and Wright in *Twice A Year*, No. 12–13, 1945, pp. 225–61.

30. Wright to Aswell, November 27, 1944. On November 14, Aswell had sent Wright a *Time* magazine review of *What the Negro Wants*, expressing his fear that this book might be harmful to Wright's plan. Wright accordingly explained what he intended: "It will be written by a group of Negroes who more or less hold certain basic ideas in common, which will make for a rounded presentation, a progression from subject to subject, etc. The book is not a series of appeals on race pre-

judices, but a series of essays dealing with ideas, valuations and interpretations about the American Negro and his place and meaning in the country. The whole tone of the book will be more radical than that of the Chapel Hill book. . . . The men who will write it are hot and anxious to write a book about the country and its culture as a whole from the Negro point of view." He added: "The Myrdal book (*An American Dilemma*) was what set the fellows on fire to do this job. They felt that if a white man could go that far, they ought to top him by all means; they felt honor-bound to do so."

An outline preserved in WPP gives a clear picture of the collection. To be entitled *The Negro Speaks*, it would have a preface and an introduction, and the following essays: "The American Negro Looks at History" by C. L. R. James; "History Looks at the American Negro" by M. B. Tolson; "The Meaning of the Negro in America" by St. Clair Drake; "Negro Political Action in America" by A. Philip Randolph; "The Negro's Cultural Task" by Jay Saunders Redding; "The Horror and the Glory" by Richard Wright; "Grappling with America" by Angelo Herndon; "The Folklore of Race Relations" by Horace Cayton; "The Negro's Strength and Weakness" by Eric Williams; and "What the Negro Pays to Live in America" by E. F. Frazier. "The Horror and the Glory" was the original title of the second part of "American Hunger." Wright was probably thinking of using some of these partially unpublished chapters to illustrate the acculturation problems of the American Negro.

31. "Ralph did not want to join the army because it is a Jim Crow army; he really wanted to be a sculptor, but he found that he could not say what was hotly in him to say with stone and marble. Now again he is making decisions based solely on racial identity. He has no choice." (Journal, January 22, 1945.)

32. "Negroes in Chicago," prepared by Charles Johnson (writing under the name of M. Greensfield) was in fact plagiarized from *Twelve Million Black Voices*. Cayton wrote Wright in November, 1944, stressing Embree's responsibility for this occurrence.

33. "A strange thing was revealed today at Marshall Field's . . . He seems to think that in reporting crime the word Negro ought not to be deleted as some Negroes are arguing: the motive ought to be given . . . I leaped into the discussion at this period and tried to show the Negroes present how they could turn adverse crime stories about Negroes to their advantage. But they want to be white, merely . . . I am now more convinced than ever that we Americans have subtly evolved a magic, a folklore of race relations . . . They form councils, committees, etc., and then proceed to say that their hearts are in the right places, that it must be hell to be a Negro, that this and that ought to be done. And

they wind up with nothing concretely done. The main problem of shunt-ing the Negroes into a separate life is not really touched. . . . Of these black and white race talks one can say that death is meted out to Negroes with sips from a delicate glass. I'm convinced that the problem will be solved only when these liberal and kind whites are out of the way, when their fear reaches that point where no Negro can meet a white in his drawing room." (Journal, January 12, 1945.)

34. On June 15, 1944, he wrote to judges Polier and Delaney of the Schermerhorn Street court, thanking them for their help in this matter.

35. "I think I have a scheme whereby I can foreshorten the whole idea and make it more compact à la *Native Son.* I like a straight, headlong narrative. If I can work in more about the boys' characters and then have them abduct a Negro woman, young but not too young, right away, and have them hide her for fear that she'll tell on them for their robberies if they let her go, I think I'll have the seeds for a damn good psycho-logical study." (Journal, January 10, 1945.)

"This woman, being an unwilling captive, is a damn good symbol and pole about which to group these boys." (*Ibid.*, January 11, 1945.)

"Treetop will become the pre-schizoid. I'll make some event happen to him that will leave a great emotional mark; he'll run away from home and fall in with a Harlem gang, join it; but he'll always be withdrawn when the opportunity presents itself. And he'll be able to react brilliantly when something comes up that presents a way for him to feel that he is acting out his drama, which is primarily emotional." (Wright to Aswell, November 27, 1944.)

36. He did a meticulous résumé of Egri's *How to Write a Play* and re-marked, "I tried like all hell to write a play two years ago on these rules but I didn't get anywhere. But I'll keep trying, by God." (Journal, January 4, 1945.)

37. "Watching a child grow is great fun and can teach one a lot. . . . Already there are lodged in her mind images of both me and Ellen. . . . If they influence her in any way, it will be toward action for she is sur-rounded by that. . . . Now and then, I ask her: 'Julia, what is my name.' 'Richard Wright,' she says promptly. 'What do I do,' I'll ask. 'You write books for me,' she says. 'What books?' I'll ask. '*Native Son* and *Black Boy*,' she'll answer. Then we both laugh. She's identified me with books and she's never really happy unless she's one in her hands. She seems to picture me always at my desk pounding the typewriter, which she likes to try to do." (Journal, January 22, 1945.)

38. "We left and went to a party that was given for me by Vivian Wolfert who had many folks there from the Book of the Month Club. . . . Ellen looked very sweet and beautiful; I never met a woman prettier than she

no matter where I go. She looks much younger than all the others, and so little and so pretty." (Journal, March 25, 1945.)

"Ours is a mixed marriage, yet Ellen and I never think of it as such until we are reminded that it is. There's no problem of different races marrying and living together; the only problems that may arise come from those who look on and those who look on are usually the ignorant." (Journal, January 7, 1945.)

39. Wright originally thought of borrowing from Harry Scherman or Marshall Field. He already owed $1000, which Reynolds had advanced him to pay his taxes. (Journal, January 27 and February 17, 1945.)

40. "Well, we're just technically short of being home owners. . . . Franklin Folsom lives on the top floor. I was floored. Mary Elting, his wife, introduced me to Paul Reynolds when I was looking for an agent. These people took hold of my hand to help me walk when I came to New York; they are staunch Communists; I worked with Franklin at the League of American Writers. He was the executive secretary. . . . Of course, this is an additional reason for my wanting to keep my identity hidden behind the corporate shield. But I'll be keen to know who will be the first folks to kick on my being in the building. They'll go to the corporation and ask them to get us out." (Journal, February 13, 1945.)

"Salzman has everything in hand. He said that the Communist Franklin Folsom, the top floor tenant, is threatening a rent strike. . . . He served a dispossess notice right away. When I told him who Folsom was, he was thunderstruck." (Journal, March 8, 1945.)

41. Mrs. Watkins's excuse was that she had received the farm from her first husband, who had refused to pay the taxes on it. She had given it to her second husband, who had since been reported missing in the Spanish Civil War, and the courts were making it difficult for her to sell the farm since the death of her present husband had not been proven. It was an ingenious lie and Wright never would have caught her in it if he had not read the second advertisement for the farm in *The New York Times*. He was so disgusted to discover that such racism existed in the remote countryside of New England that he gave up his plan altogether.

42. On March 25 and 26, he had been delighted to see Joseph Freeman again at the Werthams', where he also saw Dorothy Norman and was able to consult Mr. Neruman, a dealer in paintings. He collected some information on the practice of bribing psychiatrists to testify to the insanity of criminals who are actually in complete possession of their sanity.

43. Journal, January 3 and January 31, 1945. On the visit from the police, Wright added: "I disliked being involved in things like this. But I cannot help thinking how readily chickens come home to roost. James Ford and Ben Davis gave me the 4th degree, told me to climb on a limb and that they would help me and when I did climb out they cut the limb by telling Moss to keep shunt of me. Now it seems that the government has the tale from some source and is tracking down the folks involved. And what did the Communists get out of it all? They succeeded in having the War Department making a film obscuring the truth of Negro life; for that, they ditched me and put me and my whole career on the spot with the government. . . . I am glad I'm out of that mess."

In the biographical note he wrote for himself in 1959, Wright states that he refused to satisfy his military obligations during World War II because he would have had to serve in segregated units. He was placed under surveillance and had to report each week to the military authorities. He was not put in jail but had to account for all his travels, and he believed that they did not jail him simply because such a step would have damaged the already low morale of the black soldiers. These final statements are not confirmed by any documents in WPP but are perhaps based on these investigations by the military police.

Notes to Chapter Thirteen

1. See, among others, Theophilus Lewis in *America* (April 24, 1945, p. 39) and Michael McLaughlin in *Catholic World* (Vol. 161, April, 1945, p. 85).

2. "Gentlemen, This Is a Revolution," by Sinclair Lewis, *Esquire*, June 23, 1945, p. 76. "A Tragic Situation," by Lionel Trilling, *The Nation*, April 7, 1945, pp. 391–392.

3. Was (white) Ben Burns writing such things because of Communist sympathies? Despite his protestations of friendship, he was hostile to Wright throughout his career. Frank Marshall Davis's reactions are due to his belonging to the Party: "Since I knew personally that certain experiences described in the Chicago section of *Black Boy* were inaccurate and others were described as falsifications by friends of mine who were present at the times described, I pointed it out in my review of *Black Boy* for the Associated Negro Press." (Letter to Ken Kinnamon, October 24, 1964.) "I Tried to Be a Communist" was more heavily criticized than *Black Boy*.

4. In "The Black Boys" (*The New Leader*, March 10, 1945), William E. Bohn presents this problem very clearly. In "Richard Wright's Blues" (*Antioch Review*, Summer, 1945, pp. 198–211), Ralph Ellison also wanted to give Wright a "warning," but he defended Wright's in-

sistence upon the spiritual poverty of black life in America, stressing the cultural capacity of the Blacks, by whom "Western culture must be won, confronted like the animal in a Spanish bullfight."

Cayton stated, "What really got me was that Wright said that he was afraid of white people and he hated them. . . . It is the most meaningful analysis of Negro personality that I have ever encountered." ("Black Boy," *Pittsburgh Courier*, March 10, 1945.) Apropos of C. L. R. James's article in *The Militant* Wright complained, in his journal entry for April 7, 1945, "They are just like the Communists, always harping at what is left out of a book."

5. See *New York World-Telegram*, February 28, 1945, and the *New York Post*, March 6, 1945. Wright and Reynolds no longer trusted *Life* magazine after its failure to publish the piece on *Native Son*, so Aswell also asked *Look* to prepare a photographic report. On April 9, however, Wright said that he was satisfied by George Kayser and Paul Griffith's report for *Life*, which the death of President Roosevelt on April 12 prevented from appearing in the issue for which it was originally scheduled.

6. *Proceedings and Debates of the 70th Congress*: First Session, Vol. 91, No. 218, June 27, 1945, 128: 91, p. 6915. Bilbo delivered this diatribe during a filibuster against decree 8802 for integration in war industries. Wright exclaimed delightedly: "Did you see what Bilbo (THE MAN!) said about me in the U. S. Senate? Seems that the folks in Miss. are learning that a *Black Boy* once lived there. But I think *Black Boy* will be read when Bilbo is dead and his name forgotten; I really believe that." (Wright to Aswell, July 2, 1945.)

7. See *The New York Times, New York Herald Tribune, Publisher's Weekly, New York Post* from March 18 to November 11, 1945, for the best-seller lists.

8. Such debates were numerous in schools, clubs and political associations in the North. On April 29, Fern Gayden from *Negro Story* and Ben Burns of the *Defender*, along with Sylvester Watkins and some teachers at the Abraham Lincoln school, held a round table discussion in Chicago. At the end of the year, *Black Boy* received five votes for the Pulitzer Prize; *The Age of Jackson* by Arthur Schlesinger received six.

9. As part of his research for the Columbia lecture he read *The Negro Genius* by Benjamin Brawley; *The Negro Handbook*, of which he bought a copy; and some recent letters from black G.I.'s, which had been put into the Schomburg Collection. He thought J. A. Rogers's *Sex and Race* badly written, but *The Marginal Man* by Everett Stonequist provided him with much food for thought: "I AM the marginal man!" he noted on February 13. On February 2, after he had decided to write of his

travels "through the Black Belt from the Texas border to the Atlantic seaboard," he wrote in his journal, "I can talk about the extent, the height, depth, meaning, of the feeling of being a Negro."

He greatly admired Myrdal's *An American Dilemma* and recommended it, along with *Strange Fruit* by Lillian Smith, *The Winds of Fear* by Hodding Carter, *Rendezvous with America* by Melvin Tolson and *Race and Rumors of Race* by W. H. Odum. (*New York Post*, November 30, 1944, and February 1, 1945; *Brooklyn Eagle*, January 11, 1945; *Afro-American*, January 13, 1945.) Walter Winchell, who wanted to devote part of his column to the topic "What I don't know about the Negroes," asked him to make up a list of possible subjects, to which Wright also got his friends to contribute. (*New York Post*, February 17, 1945.)

10. "The problem is big and life is short. With the exception of but a few friends of mine, white and black, I stand more or less alone with this point of view. I do take time out from writing books about it— and for me writing books is a way of making a living too—to talk and travel and encourage others to go to vast masses of whites, and preach and yell and educate and talk to them. . . . I make speeches about the problem, confining myself almost always to white people, that is, white audiences. I write articles now and then. And books, stories, plays, etc. But instead of a few people doing this there ought to be a few passionate thousands doing it in a nation of 135,000,000!" (Wright to Ruth Foster, June 3, 1945.) That same day he spoke to Maxwell Hahn about "a project that would do for the inner personality, the subjective landscape of the Negro, what Gunnar Myrdal's *An American Dilemma* did for the external, social relations." This would be "the single greatest moral weapon in our fight for social justice."

11. "Don't Wear Your Sunday Best Every Day!" appeared on the jacket of the second edition of *Black Boy*. Reynolds thought that in this way he would have no trouble getting the necessary paper for the printing he wanted.

12. *Bulletins of America's Town Meeting of the Air*, Vol. 11, No. 4, May 24, 1945, p. 6.

13. Reynolds to Wright, July 12 and 13, 1945; Wright to Reynolds, July 16 and October 28, 1945. Frank Dazey and Jim Tully had written a play in 1937 based on the life of the boxer Jack Johnson and called *Black Boy*.

14. See Note 1, Chapter Four, p. 538, for publication history of "American Hunger."

15. Journal, March-April, 1945, *passim*. This was a period of intensive reading for Wright. In January, he had been too bored to finish *U.S.A.* by Dos Passos, but reading *Prejudices* had suggested the title

"The Black Flag" for "The Jackal." (Journal, February 12, 1945.) Aswell had written Mencken, asking for his impressions of *Black Boy*, and received the following reply: "Unfortunately I am forbidden to write blurbs. My pastor advises me in view of my advancing age that it would be extremely hazardous. I'll do what I can for the Wright book in other ways. It is extremely interesting stuff." (Quoted in a letter from Aswell to Wright, March 3 (?), 1945.)

16. His review of *The Brick Foxhole*, "A Non-Combat Soldier Strips Words for Action," appeared in *PM*, June 25, 1945, p. 6. Wright and other writers were ready to defend Brooks if his military superiors, from whom he had not asked permission to publish the novel, decided to court-martial him.

Of O'Hara, Wright read *Butterfield 8, Appointment in Samara, Hope of Heaven, Pal Joey* (which reminded him of *Poor Folk* and *Clarissa*, and gave him the idea of reworking *Lawd Today* in epistolary form), *Files on Parade, Doctor's Son* and *Pipe Night*, from March 30 to April 10. He was annoyed that Sterling North monopolized the broadcast, turning it in "the direction of smart cracks and jokes," whenever he tried to bring the discussion around to O'Hara's works in general. (Journal, April 16, 1945.)

17. "Gertrude Stein's Story Is Drenched in Hitler's Horrors," *PM*, March 11, 1945, p. 5. Van Vechten wrote to Stein, "I was curious about the review although I didn't expect it to interest me much. To my surprise, it is more understanding than any other review of the book that has yet appeared." (Quoted in *Flowers of Friendship*, p. 221.) For three weeks, Wright was entranced by Stein's prose and amazed, as his journal entry for January 28, 1945, shows, at their deep affinity: "Am reading Stein's *Narration* and find it fascinating. . . . How odd that this woman who is distrusted by everyone can remind me of the most basic things in my life. . . . [She] made me hear something that I'd heard all my life, that is, the speech of my grandmother who spoke a deep Negro dialect colored by the Bible, the Old Testament. Yes, she's got something, but I'd say that one could live and write like that only if one lived in Paris or in some out of the way spot where one could claim one's own soul. And I cannot do that here now. All the more reason why I dream and dream of leaving my native land to escape the pressure of the superficial things I think I know. That's why I left the South, and now I want to leave the country and some day I will, by God."

18. "The New Hope Is 'Our Sad Young Man,' " *The New York Times Magazine*, June 3, 1945, pp. 15, 38.

19. Wright to Van Vechten, July 10, 1945. See *L'Evénement* (Quebec), June 28, 1945, p. 4.

20. On July 13, 1945, he told Reynolds that, despite his desire to help the book, he would rather not use his preface at all if it meant changing it in any way, but Harcourt raised no objections. "I placed the book for Drake and Cayton when it was in a condition that no one would look at it; I argued and sold the book to Woodburn; they know now that they have a book that will sell for a long, long time, for there is no other book quite like that on the Negro." (Wright to Reynolds, August 2, 1945.)

21. Wright to G. Stein, August 23, 1945.
He wrote Reynolds, on August 20, about the lecture that Aswell had asked him to give: "I found it to be a rather elaborate place, much larger than I had supposed it would be. . . . They were rather a middle-class and blasé lot; but I suppose I've got to get used to that. I find that people dislike the Negro problem intensely but they still want to hear about it." See the review of his lecture in the *Boston Herald*, August 25, 1945.

22. For 1944, he had declared an income of $3,800. Reynolds had estimated $15,000 for 1945, but Wright declared only $10,992 because he had arranged for Harper's to spread his payments out over ten years.
At the end of 1945, *Black Boy* even won the prize of the Southern Women's National Democratic Organization. (*New York Post*, January 5, 1946.)
Wright received a telegram from *Life* in Canada, asking for the review of the play. Clippings and notes in his papers indicate that he analyzed this play by Arnaud D'Usseau and James Gow on the problems of a black soldier returning after the war to his small town in the South, but there is no trace of a review. The play had opened on October 9, and *Life* published a kind of photographic report on it, but it is unsigned and certainly not by Wright.

23. In *White Man, Listen!* in particular. He stated: "The American Negro is the only group in our nation that consistently and passionately raises the question of freedom. This is rapidly becoming the voice of America to the oppressed peoples of the world. All peoples want our testimony since we live here among the greatest pretense of democracy on earth. And we Negroes are answering straight, honestly. So the voice that America rejected is finding at last a home, such as was never dreamed of. . . . We ask you to grant us nothing. We are winning our heritage, though our toll in suffering is great." Review of the lecture, *Hartford Courant*, October 21, 1945.

About Wright as a lecturer, H. Peat wrote Reynolds on January 23, 1946: "Mr. Wright is an excellent speaker. He is utterly sincere and everywhere that he spoke his audiences and the committees liked him very much."

24. "Richard Wright Stresses Realism in Dealing with Fictional Negro Types." Interview by C. Handley Jr., *Washington Star*, November 11, 1945. See "Howard University Forum Program (1945–1946)." The three other speakers were white, and Herman Branson was the moderator.

25. On December 5, Reynolds had written to Peat: "Mr. Wright can't seem to lecture quietly and calmly and lecturing seems to get him into a condition of nervous exhaustion plus terrific indigestion and inability to keep anything on his stomach. To have him lecture was close to my heart because I thought it would be a good thing in the race prejudice business. However I wanted you to start slowly, in fact to keep it down to ten lectures this fall and winter." From November 25 to December 2, Wright had to speak in Oxford and Columbus, Ohio; Kohler, Wisconsin; Detroit, Pittsburgh and Chicago. Since Wright did not want to continue into 1946, he had to pay Harold Peat the percentage for the thirty-five lectures that he did not give. Peat's commission was 40%, and each lecture earned from $200 to $500, so that even after keeping everything Wright had earned, Peat still claimed that he was owed money; his accounts read: "Total due Harold Peat: $2,959.59. Total due Mr. Wright for completed dates: $1,427.59." (Peat to Reynolds, January 16, 1946.) On May 21, 1946, he agreed to settle the matter by keeping Wright's entire earnings, but it took all of Reynold's tact and firmness to arrange for him to let it go at that.

26. *PM,* November 25, 1945, pp. m7–m8. On the publication of *Native Son,* Himes had sent an eloquent letter to *New Masses* defending the novel. He began to see Wright fairly frequently in 1942, after Wright had left the Party, but they became particularly close during their stay in Paris. (Conversations with Chester Himes, February, 1963–January, 1967.)

27. Baldwin describes this first meeting with Wright in "Alas, Poor Richard" (*Nobody Knows My Name*, New York, Dial Press, 1961, pp. 192–93). On November 21, 1945, Aswell wrote to Wright: "You have doubtless heard from James Baldwin that the Saxton Memorial Trust has awarded him a fellowship. . . . The decision was a unanimous one. I want to thank you for your good offices in this connection. You would have been touched, as I was, by Baldwin's reaction to the good news. . . . He was so overcome with joy that he could hardly speak. He came to my office the next day to get his check and I took an instant liking to him. It seems to me that the job he is doing is an important one and

that he has the requisite integrity to carry it out." Aswell had already written to Wright about this on July 24.

28. Wright to Aswell, August 21, 1944; Aswell to Wright, December 25, 1945. The Kossas often saw the Wrights socially.

Wright had met Gwendolyn Brooks in New York in December, 1944: "On that occasion he impressed me as being a very kind person, interesting, alert-minded and somewhat shy." (G. Brooks to M. Fabre, April 2, 1963.) Wright had recommended her to E. W. Embree for a Rosenwald grant and in April, 1945, for a Guggenheim as well. Later, Wright took a great interest in Annie Allen and was instrumental in getting "The Ballad of Pearl May Lee" published in *Présence Africaine*.

As for the Greenwich Village Writers Club meetings, Wright only attended twice, on the suggestion of his friend Burton Barnett. Of Esther Carlson, he wrote in his journal for February 15, 1945: "She read the story ('The Radiant Wood') and I had goose pimples on me. . . . It was a story of symbolized incest, of a little girl who followed her father when he ran away from home. She did not know what the meaning of her story was." In February, 1945, he also praised *Who Walks with the Earth* by Dorsha Hayes.

29. Journal, January 25, 1945. "I've just finished the galleys of a novel called *Wasteland* . . . which I predict will create some talking when it is published," Wright wrote Van Vechten on December 20, 1945. See "Jo Sinclair Uses Psychoanalysis Deftly," *PM*, February 17, 1946, p. 8.

30. See Frederic Wertham, M.D., *op. cit.*, pp. 111–15. Wertham delivered this paper at the 34th Congress of the American Association of Psychopathology on June 9, 1944, after the American Association of Psychiatry had refused it without giving him any reason for its decision. (Wertham to M. Fabre, January 30, 1964.)

31. He asked himself almost a hundred questions of this kind, to be found in his own notes: "This thing of imagining myself a devil, one with a long tail—My adoration of Mrs. Wall and her mother. Did I invent these people?—When did I tell people that my mother used to send me in Arkansas down to the shit to eat?—Making 100 in every subject—Most brilliant boy in school."

32. The publication rights to the article were to go to the Lafargue clinic. *The Nation* was supposed to publish it in June or July, 1946, but then decided against it. *Freeworld* published it in September. Along with "Juvenile Delinquency in Harlem," this article also appeared in *Twice a Year* (Autumn, 1946–Winter, 1947) under the inclusive title "Urban Misery in an American City."

33. The Maltz article, "What Shall We Ask for Writers?" appeared in *New Masses*, February 11, 1946, pp. 19–22, and Howard Fast's an-

swer, "Art and Politics," in *New Masses*, February 26, 1946, pp. 6–8: "So beguiled is Maltz in his own shoddy formulation that . . . incredibly new, he drags in Engels to defend both Farrell and Wright, these gentry!" See also Joseph North, "No Retreat for the Writer," *ibid.*, pp. 8–10.

In "What Is Freedom for Writers?" (*New Masses*, March 12, 1946, pp. 8–10), Alvah Bessie stated: "It is common knowledge that not only Steinbeck, but also Farrell, Wright, Fearing and Dos Passos, have consciously repudiated the working class movement . . . and the contention should be supported with every kind of evidence that no one of them has written anything since that repudiation that is worth reading —either 'artistically' or 'politically' (and I include in this *Black Boy*, which, whatever the obvious distortions of *Native Son*, cannot hold a candle to that work)." See John Howard Lawson, "Art As a Weapon," in *New Masses*, March 19, 1946, pp. 18–20. Maltz was finally forced to condemn the "renegades," declaring, "Their anti-Soviet, anti-people, anti-labor attitudes enter their work, pervert their talents, turn them into tools and agents of reaction." ("Moving Forward," *New Masses*, April 9, 1946, pp. 8–10, 21.)

34. Horace Cayton replied with "Whose Dilemma?" (*New Masses*, June 23, 1946, pp. 8–10), noting: "Liberals and Communists advise caution and patience lest the war effort be harmed. This is what Richard Wright meant by their 'trying to change the Negro problem into something under control.' They advised the Negro to go slow. It was moral flabbiness. . . . The only justification for writing about the Negro question is to help individuals resolve their dilemmas in action. So writers (including Aptheker and Wright, Myrdal, Drake and Cayton) shame them, enrage them; encourage them and appeal to patriotism, class solidarity, idealism, etc. We force individuals to choose between the actual discomfort of a guilty conscience and the feared discomfort of inconvenience and often danger of taking a firm stand for social justice."

35. One incident is particularly revealing. Wright had been invited to lunch by Sinclair Lewis, who was staying in a hotel. Lewis, concerned because Wright was so late for the appointment, had telephoned, only to learn that Wright had decided not to persevere after being told to take the service staircase by someone at the reception desk who had taken him for a delivery boy, not imagining that Lewis would have a black man as his guest. Wright had simply turned around and gone home.

36. Wright to Gertrude Stein, April 12, 1946: "Henry Miller's book, *The Air-Conditioned Nightmare*, was published a few weeks ago. . . . Philip Wylie, who wrote a book called *A Generation of Vipers*, took Miller apart. Wylie fights America as an American; Miller fights America as an American who went to Europe. . . . I criticize America as an

American and you do too, which I think is the only real way to do the job. Miller's rejection of America seems to me to be the act of a weak man." He also said: "Money is not what is worrying me as I live in this great free land; money is fairly easy to get hold of. What is hard to get is freedom." (*Ibid.*, March 15, 1946.)

"You see we live quite simply here. Nothing is ever worked out or settled. We are wonders when it comes to making machines; we are marvels when it comes to selling things. But when it comes to just talking to each other we are scared and reach for our guns." (*Ibid.*, May 27, 1945.)

"It would help (Americans) to see that each country is not just a tight little self-contained entity. . . . There is a danger of America collapsing in a panic when she faces the problem of the Negro—as she really must some day—just as Europe collapsed when she faced the problem of the Jew. With the atom bomb hanging over us, the problem of human unity is truly terribly urgent." (*Ibid.*, Oct. 29, 1945.)

37. Conversation with Dorothy Norman, November, 1963.

38. "It is the most compact and incisive thing that you have yet written. It was a marvel how you abstracted from all the welter of aimless G.I. talk and got the essence of what they felt, what worried them, what they hoped and thought and did not know. . . . I'll write my review and leave it here behind me to be printed." (Wright to Gertrude Stein, March 15, 1946.)

39. Wright to Gertrude Stein, March 28, 1946. Sartre was representing *Combat* and *Le Figaro*, but after his first article accusing the Americans of not having helped De Gaulle because they thought him too revolutionary, *Le Figaro* broke its contract with him.

40. According to "I Choose Exile" and the well-documented and detailed article by Dorothy Norman, "Operation Richard Wright" (in the *New York Post*, June 17, 1946, p. 34). When the French Cultural Services telephoned Wright to tell him that the government was inviting him, he exclaimed in delight, "It is not possible!" which was interpreted by the French secretary as a refusal, and caused a week's delay in the plans.

41. Baldwin's *Nobody Knows My Name*, pp. 191–92. Wright's friend, about to be deported, was C. L. R. James.

On April 30, 1946, Wright dashed off a final letter to Gertrude Stein about his last experiences before he left. "Just yesterday, at 11 A.M., I got my passport. . . . It was really an agony. I had to fly down to Washington for it and fly back in time to get my visa." On May 15, 1946, he wrote Aswell the details of his departure. See also "I Choose Exile," pp. 5–7.

Notes to Chapter Fourteen

1. Conversation with Sylvia Beach, June, 1962. Wright wrote the titles of the latest novels by Algren, Jo Sinclair and Lawrence Lipton on a piece of tablecloth. He inscribed copies of *Black Boy* (on June 15), *Native Son* and *Uncle Tom's Children* (on June 20) for Sylvia Beach, and before he left he gave her the manuscript of "The Man Who Lived Underground."

2. S. Jacno, "Richard Wright," *Bref,* Vol. 2 (June 1, 1946), pp. 20–21.

3. This French translation included "Le Départ de Big Boy," "Long chant noir" and "Le feu dans la nuée." A second volume was planned but never published, but "Là-bas près de la rivière" was added to the paperback edition.

4. Anne Perlman, "Richard Wright, Negro Author, Is Here to Make Home in Paris," *New York Herald Tribune* (European edition), June 3, 1946, p. 2. Despite this headline, Wright had never to date expressed a desire to settle *permanently* in Paris; he was merely intending to come back for further visits.

5. Interview by M. Fleurent, *Paru,* December, 1946, pp. 7–8.

6. "Dans le monde entier je sais reconnaître un nègre du Sud . . . ," *Paris-Matin,* June 27, 1946. This was a translation of the article published in *True Magazine* under the title "How Jim Crow Feels" in November, 1946. See George Adam, *L'Amérique en Liberté,* Paris, Laffont, 1947, pp. 184–87.

Valéry-Larbaud, Picasso and Gertrude Stein were also involved in the Arthaud sale. See the *New York Herald Tribune* (European edition), June 8, 1946.

7. Wright to Reynolds, July 28, 1946: "I'm working on another short story; hope it turns out all right; will airmail it to you as soon as it is finished. Yes, I understand about 'The Man Who Killed a Shadow.' Just do what you can. I understand about placing my stuff. It does not do too well with the popular journals, even those that claim that they are radical."

8. Wright to Reynolds, October 1, 1946. In June, the foundation for the blind had had *Black Boy* transcribed into braille; "Silt" was reprinted in *The Second Armchair Companion*; after *True Magazine, Negro Digest* published "How Jim Crow Feels."

9. Translation from the interview in French conducted by Lucienne Escoube, *L'Ecran Français,* November 19, 1946. See also Wright's impressions in Paul Guth's interview for the *Gazette des Lettres* (September 14, 1946, p. 2), where he says, "I am learning Valéry by heart . . . in order to accustom myself to speaking exceptionally fine French vocabulary, and to train my mouth and tongue to imitate the organic rhythm

of certain difficult sounds." See also *Les Etoiles,* October 22, 1946, and "L'Amérique n'est pas le Nouveau Monde," an interview by Michel Gordey which appeared in *Lettres Françaises,* January 10, 1947, p. 1.

10. Statement made to Raphael Tardon, a West Indian who was expecting him to settle in France, in "Le Problème Blanc aux U. S. A.," *Action,* October 25, 1946, p. 2.

11. George Padmore, "Dinner of the Colored Writers' Association Held in London," *Chicago Defender,* January 23, 1947. Padmore had published numerous articles in *Crisis* during 1937–1938, among them "Fascism in the West Indies" and "Cocoa War on the Gold Coast."

12. "Why Richard Wright Came Back from France," *PM,* February 13, 1947, p. 5. In England, Wright noticed only that racial prejudice was somewhat less intense than in the United States. His opinion of the English was revised for the better when he returned in August, 1947.

13. In February, he stated: "Naturally the Board is happy to learn of this action by the Veterans Administration. We feel that it confirms our position. . . . The Lafargue Clinic has taken the first big step in implanting a new conception of social service. A year ago, experts said it could not be done. Well, it had to be done and we did it." ("Harlem Clinic Now Official V.A. Agency," John Hohenberg, *New York Post,* February 24, 1947.) See also "Psychiatry in Harlem," *Time,* December 1, 1947, and "Clinic for Sick Minds," *Life,* February 28, 1948.

14. On this subject see *L'Amérique au jour le jour* (Gallimard, 1948, p. 33 ff; American edition published by Grove Press in 1953 under the title *America Day by Day*). Simone de Beauvoir remarked: "He came to get me at the hotel, and I noticed that he was regarded with hostility in the lobby. If he were to ask for a room here, he would certainly be refused. We went to dinner in a Chinese restaurant because in the uptown restaurants, they would probably refuse to serve us."

15. Reynolds advised Wright to present his candidacy on October 15, 1946. The Committee for Action consisted of Howard Fast, Philip Van Doren Stern, Albert Halper and B. A. Botkin. Wright subsequently continued to correspond with the Guild officials on "professional" matters such as royalties and the like.

16. "E. M. Forster Anatomizes the Novel," *PM,* March 16, 1947, p. m3; "A Junker's Epic Novel on Militarism," *PM,* May , 1947, p. m3.

17. See Constance Webb, *op. cit.,* pp. 258–62.

18. Wright to Reynolds, July, 1947. Wright had declared an income of $32,175.00 in 1946.

In 1942 Ella and Maggie had left for Jackson, where Aunt Addie also stayed until 1947. They lived at 1307 Dalton Street and Wright sent them fifty dollars a month. Leon had stayed on for a while in the Vincennes Avenue house in Chicago, which was now resold for double what it had cost in 1944.

19. According to his confidences to the novelist Caroline Caro-Delvaille, Wright kept to himself on board because the snobbery and racism of the other passengers was painful to him. The Americans would ostentatiously move away when Richard and Ellen sat down in the lounge. (*Le Populaire*, July 30, 1947.) Wright found the American attitude infantile and vulgar: "Everything is democratically shoddy. The American passengers stare at us; they are still internationally wet behind the ears; they do not have the air of being at home with the world which so clearly distinguishes the English." (Journal, July 30, 1947.) "Beside the people of the continent, Americans appear like country apes. We are so young, so new, so raw a people, so crude, so lacking in human feeling and sensitivity." (*Ibid*, July 31, 1947.) In addition, the inhumanity of the sea itself, the variations of which he noted in detail in his journal, inspired him to write a short piece—never published—entitled "Sleeping and Waking."

20. "I think I'm beginning to feel fatalistic about Paris, that it is my home." (Journal, August 21, 1947.) He never managed to understand the mentality of the tradesmen, who, being closed almost half the day, did not seem to care about making a profit. In his journal he kept exclaiming, "What a country! Looks like I'm in for wasting another day!" He thought alternate-side-of-the-street parking was a joke when it was explained to him, and distrusted his garage so much that he used to leave his car in the courtyard of his building.

21. "Met Edith and we had drinks at the Café de Flore. Many people flocked around: Francis Lee, Mrs. Borcioff, Odette, a man called Rice, the Tabou crowd—Annie, her friend, Francis Lee's friends, and all. I found myself getting a little tired. Suggested that we have dinner together and we did not enjoy it. . . . Then we went to the Tabou, and the mood of fatigue that was on me settled into a mood of depression which I could not hide. First of all, I was known there and the photographers started taking pictures and I did not like it; then the music was bad and loud and an imitation of the American New Orleans style and the French boys and girls who were trying to dance and act like Americans made a self-conscious job of it. I spoke of getting home and dragged them away with me. I hated that place. It made me feel like I was living again those horrible days in Chicago when I was lonely and hungry and scared. . . . I did not really want to go home, but I wanted something that would nourish me. That is what I am missing, nourishing experiences." (Journal, August 15, 1947 and September 22, 1947.) This theme of his

incapacity to use up his energy in any pursuit except writing pervades his journal for this period.

22. A Mr. Rosinet with whom they dealt asked for an immediate decision, which made Wright suspicious, but the rent was only 196,000 francs a year, plus utilities and a deposit. The seventh-floor apartment on the rue de Lille had been sublet for one year by Maurice Grouteau, at a rent of 25,000 francs a month, including utilities. The Wrights shared facilities with Odette Lieutier.

23. "Niam N'goura or *Présence Africaine*'s raison d'être," *Présence Africaine*, No. 1 (November-December, 1945), p. 185.

24. Wright to the Baronne de Rothschild, November 6, 1948. See "In Memoriam," *Présence Africaine*, Nos. 34–35 (October, 1960), p. 297; "We still remember the numerous times when, making the sacrifice of precious hours, you went to the UNESCO with Albert Camus and other members of our movement to try and work out a program of practical collaboration."

25. See Sartre's pages on Wright in "Qu'est-ce que la littérature," *Les Temps Modernes*, March, 1947, pp. 967–69.

26. On October 18, 1947, he wrote Reynolds: "Yesterday I met Winthrop Rockefeller! We had an hour's talk, during which he said that we were already at war with Russia, but we had not yet started throwing things. How do you like that?" And on December 2: "Since the situation over here has taken a dangerous turn, I've a reservation on the *Queen Elizabeth* for the spring. . . . Just trying to be careful. Life here is incredible; but it has not touched us yet. We keep the bathtub full of water, for fear that the water will be cut off. We have candles to burn if the electric current fails; and we have a good backlog of food and coal. . . . It is sort of grim fun! But there is much suffering, that is, among the French."

27. Letter to Dorothy Norman, February 28, 1948 (published in *Twice a Year*, 1948, p. 67). On this trip, Wright met Ignazio Silone. On February 17, Silone introduced him to Arthur Koestler, who happened to be lunching at the same table at the Roi des Amis in Paris.

28. The play, cut into three acts of four, three and three scenes respectively, was produced by Colin Chandler, with Robert Adams as Bigger and Irene Worth as Mary. In spite of favorable reviews and audience enthusiasm, it did not have a long run after its opening on February 20, 1948.

29. On June 1, 1948, his friend Claude Barnett of the A. N. P. even sent him the correspondent identification card he had requested, wishing him a good trip to Africa: "It will give you a notion of how hollow the phrase 'Equality, Liberty, Fraternity' can be."

30. "Introductory Note to *The Respectful Prostitute*," *Art and Action,* 1948, p. 14. Wright had seen the play in Paris in the autumn of 1946, and five years later, in August, 1951, he served as adviser for Sartre, who was writing the movie adaptation. He made a good number of judicious comments on the screenplay, supplying an American context to justify with precise references any details which might seem strange to the American public, changes which would, then, of course, seem foreign to a European audience. His notes on the script indicate that he did a serious and thorough job.

Issue 14–15 of *Twice a Year* (Fall-Winter, 1946–47) had announced Wright's appointment as foreign associate editor. Wright had read the manuscripts for the commemorative issue in August, 1947.

31. "L'humanité est plus grande que l'Amérique ou la Russie," *Franc-Tireur,* December 16, 1948. Camus' talk, "Le témoin de la liberté," published in the same newspaper on December 20, 1948, is included in *Actuelles I.* Wright immediately brought the wrath of the French Communist Party down upon himself. "Richard Wright pronounced that sentence of unequaled baseness: 'Whoever the victor, you will be reduced to complete powerlessness, to slavery,'" stated *L'Humanité-Dimanche,* on December 19, 1948.

32. See note 10 for Chapter Six, p. 546.

33. "Richard Wright on U.S.," interview by Michel Salomon, *Labor Action,* May 30, 1949, pp. 1, 3. See also "R. D. R. Holds Antiwar Day in Paris," by Pierre Cohin, *Labor Action,* May 23, 1949, pp. 1, 4.

34. According to Farrell (conversation with M. Fabre, June 17, 1964), the message had been prepared before the Congress, and was aimed more at the section of the RDR led by David Rousset than at the American Left via Farrell and Hook. See Farrell's letter of June 11, 1949, published under the title, "Farrell Objects to Wright's Interview," in *Labor Action,* June 27, 1949, p. 2. Farrell also maintains that his relationship with Wright in Paris was very friendly, although a letter from Nelson Algren to Jack Conroy (May 15, 1949) says, "Farrell was a representative of the State Department. Neither Sartre nor Wright went along with him and Hook on their oppositionist 'Peace Congress' he and Hook recently featured." Michel Salomon recorded Wright as holding an extreme position, if the following quote he attributes to Wright is to be believed: "When the fighting starts, I am an American [i.e., opposed to the Russians], but I can't trust the white man" [i.e., opposed to the white Americans].

35. See *Freedom and Peace,* New York, New York Council on African Affairs, 1949, p. 2; and *Time,* May 2, 1949. Howard Fast, W. E. B.

DuBois and Rockwell Kent also spoke at this congress held in the Salle Pleyel.

36. The apartment consisted of a foyer, living room, dining room, three bedrooms, a kitchen, bathroom, WC, cellar and a seventh-floor maid's room. The rent was 15,300 francs a year, with a large deposit.

37. "A Parigi con Wright," F. Pivano, *Avanti* (Turin), May 19, 1948, WPP. Wright mentioned two stories—"The Man Who Killed a Shadow" and the story of a man who kills because he has not been convicted for an earlier crime and wants to be punished. Could this not be an early version of "A Father's Law?" See Chapter Twenty-one, p. 512.

The interview stressed Wright's role as a Parisian figure. In fact, the French press often mentioned his activities, such as his presence at a book sale for the benefit of the Centre National des Jeunes (December 10, 1949), or his lunch at the Crillon with Mrs. Roosevelt, who was passing through Paris (December 17). He was often referred to as a measure of the achievements of other Blacks. His witticisms—for the most part complete fabrications—were recorded, along with his indignant statements on the racial problem.

38. Translation from the French, which appeared in *L'Ordre*, January 15, 1948. In 1950, this text was used as the introduction to an extract from *Black Boy* appearing in Whit Burnett's anthology *The World's Best*.

39. Journal, September 4, 1949. Inspired by Camus' *The Stranger*, on September 16, he thought of changing his novel by using a first-person narrative. "I've learned to trust these lightning-like ideas and I shall give serious consideration to this at once. This might be the way in which I shall start writing again," but he quickly abandoned the idea.

Notes to Chapter Fifteen
1. Rosselini to Wright, December, 1946; *Liberation* mentioned this project on December 10, 1946. The French press had spoken of Carné and Prévert in conjunction with it during the summer (see *Images du Monde,* June 4, 1946) and Wright had let Reynolds know about it in his letter of May 27, 1946.

Native Son was never put on in Paris, but a radio adaptation by Albert Vidalie of "Le Feu dans la Nuée" ("Fire and Cloud") broadcast on April 25, 1948, had great success.

2. Wright to Reynolds, December 10, 1948. On November 19 Reynolds told Wright that Lee would agree to play the role, if needed, regardless of any agreements formerly made with Mark Marvin.

3. Interview by Marietta, *The Bulletin Board,* June, 1950, WPP.

4. See *La Plata* (Montevideo), October 10, 1949, WPP; *Critica* (Buenos

Aires), October 12, 1949, WPP; and an interview in *Revista Branca*, 1950 (?), WPP. Details of the film's preparation can be found in certain of Wright's letters to Reynolds and in a few articles, especially the September 2, 1950, issue of the *Chicago Defender*, and the May 20, 1951, issue of *New York Compass*. Canada Lee had originally accepted the role of Bigger, but he subsequently had to refuse because of previous engagements which conflicted with the date chosen for the filming. See Virginia Lee Warren, "Argentina Doubles as Chicago Locale for *Native Son*," *The New York Times*, May 21, 1950.

5. "*Native Son* Filmed in Argentina" (*Ebony*, January, 1951, pp. 82–86) gives the details of the filming and was largely written by Wright himself. On November 3, 1949, he wrote Reynolds: "The shooting script is about half-finished, and, on the whole, shaping more or less to my liking."

6. "He spends so little time away from the set that he scarcely has time to write to his wife and children in Paris, much less advance his literary career by a single sentence," reported Virginia Lee Warren in her May 21, 1950, *New York Times* article.

7. See *Buenos Aires Herald*, March 11, 1950, WPP. Kent Waldman and R. Neville of *Time* and *Life*, Mr. Welles of the Associated Press and Mr. Jacobsen were among the journalists present.

8. *Black Power*, pp. 204–5. He was interviewed at the time by Marietta in *Bulletin Board,* June, 1950, WPP.

9. Wright received 10,000 more of the 32,750 pesos which Mentasti still owed him. These details and the ones that follow are all taken from the correspondence between Wright, Reynolds, Wallfisch and others during the spring and summer of 1950.

10. "The film was here. Velma and Gladys saw it." Margaret Wilson to Wright, April 1, 1952.

11. See *Paris-Presse*, September 1, 1951: "In the nightmare of Bigger Thomas, the hero of 'Native Son,' Giorgio Chirico's inspired decor made up of metaphysical paintings changes into a field of cotton. Bigger . . . rushes toward the image of his father which, in turn, fades out and becomes a policeman."

12. See *The New York Times, World Telegram and Sun, Post, Daily Compass*, of June 18, 1951; *The New York Times*, June 24, 1951; and *Cue*, June 16, 1951.

13. *Chicago Defender*, September 2, 1950. His friends gave a big farewell party for him, attended by Charles Simmons, a rich Argentinian industrialist; Gordon Stretton; Baby Veronica; Irwin Wallfisch; and Madelyn Jackson, to whom Wright was quite attracted at the time.

14. "I've never seen or got such a treat. When I heard the band playing, I never thought it was a steel band. I had to get up and actually see to be convinced that it was music played on the steel heads of gasoline drums that had to be tempered by fire and tuned to individual notes. I feel it is on a par with the creative genius of the Negro which has so often proved itself in its drive for self-expression." (*Haitian Journal,* July 28, 1950, WPP.) The next day he also told the paper: "The people have a proud bearing. There is an innocence about the country!" after having chatted with John Bates and visited the capital's Artistic Center.

15. Wright to Streten Maric, October 12, 1950. A typist's receipt, dated November 15, 1950, indicates that Wright had had a detailed outline of the film typed up, but there is no trace of it.

16. "Richard Wright, Native Son Author, Returns to America," *Atlanta Daily World,* August 29, 1950, WPP. Gladys P. Graham of the A.N.P. deliberately stressed everything which attached Wright to America, rather than that which separated him from it, although his conversations with Wertham and Constance Webb James at the time clearly show how alienated he felt. It was partly this attitude which caused *Ebony* to refuse to publish "I Choose Exile."

17. The lecture was first published in 1951 by Cuaderni A.C.I. (See *Corriere de Milano,* January 26, 1951.) Wright was actually afraid that there might be a Soviet invasion during his trip to Italy and therefore told Reynolds to honor any request for money that he received from Ellen, in case she had to fly home in an emergency.

In Rome, Wright was the guest of honor at a P.E.N. reception the day before. He first stayed at l'Albergo Inghilterra and later, after two days in Capri, remained with his friends the Silones and Marguerite Caetani until February 1.

18. Zobel very much admired Wright, whom he saw often on rue Monsieur le Prince. *Black Boy* had deeply influenced him. See *Nouvelles Littéraires,* October 26, 1950.

19. Samuel Allen had recommended passages from Baldwin's first novel to *Présence Africaine* the year before in vain, but they now came out in the second issue of *New Story* (April, 1951) under the title, "The Outing."

Wright helped with *New Story* until February, 1953, and was a member of the jury for its international story contest, along with William Saroyan, John Lehman, Martha Foley and Stuart Gilbert.

Wright read the galleys of the translation of *Our Lady of the Flowers* by Bernard Frechtmann, at whose request he also wrote a couple of paragraphs recommending the book. (B. Frechtmann to K. Kinnamon, March, 1964.) He was both moved by and extremely interested in what he had read; later he met Genet, who seems himself to have been thinking of *Native Son* apropos of the white woman's murder in *Les Nègres.*

20. "Our main problem today is to enlighten man about himself," he said in an interview with Geneviève Heuzé entitled "L'Homme du Sud," which appeared in *France Etats-Unis*, November, 1950, p. 2.

In "L'Homme du Sud" (*ibid.*) Wright went on to praise Faulkner: "His hateful statements of racism will be forgotten, but the gallery of Faulkner's characters will live as long as men feel the need to know themselves, as long as troubled spirits who need peace and an opportunity for reflection, seek refuges in those books which form the reservoir of the emotional experiences of a nation."

21. At the beginning of his stay he met a certain Mr. Parsons who, he concluded, was making a secret investigation of him. "I had the feeling that Parsons was trying to let me know the many people we knew in common and also to find out just what I was really doing. He wanted to know if Dorothy was a Communist, if I was. . . . I answered in a way that pretended that I did not know what he was getting at." (Journal, August 22, 1947.)

22. Wright was already on a number of committees formed by the Americans in Paris, such as the council of the American Community School. Since 1948, he had been on the honorary committee of the American Club Theatre, where Anne Gerlette and George Voskovec put on plays by Tennessee Williams, George Courteline, and Thornton Wilder.

23. Mimeographed statutes and prospectus of the French-American Fellowship, WPP.

24. *L'Observateur*, May 3, 1951. This text was published in *Crisis* (June–July, 1951, pp. 381–83) under the title "American Negroes in France." For the McCleveland case see *Combat*, June 7, 1951; *Le Monde*, June 9, 1951.

25. Published in 1950 and 1951 by Julliard, Guérin's book was translated in 1956 and came out in London as *Negroes on the March* (Grange Publications).

26. See *La Dépêche Africaine*, November 15, 1951. A telegram of encouragement reads: "French-American Fellowship applauds your stand in the fight for liberty and justice. France and Europe watching your fight with anxiety and admiration."

27. See *Nobody Knows My Name, op. cit.*, pp. 208–12. Baldwin's evidence is largely contradicted by Chester Himes and Samuel Allen (letter to Ken Kinnamon, December 24, 1964), as well as by the minutes of the meetings, several of which he attended. Samuel Allen states: "Activist as he was, he undertook to organize a group of American Negroes to fight to achieve an inner Marshall Plan for Negroes inside the Marshall

Plan for Europeans. . . . He discovered, however, that the American Negroes in Paris felt this was not the experience they had sought in putting 3,000 miles between them and the native shores, and so the undertaking foundered. He did organize a group which was social in nature, fostering Franco-American friendship, which endured for some time."

28. See James Baldwin, *Notes of a Native Son* (New York, Dial Press, 1952), and the essays included in the section "Alas, Poor Richard," in *Nobody Knows My Name*. Baldwin himself admits that these essays betrayed a need to kill his "spiritual father." His version of the events described is on many points contradicted by Wright's last lecture, delivered in November, 1960. Chester Himes, who spoke to me about this episode which took place in the spring of 1953, stressed the moderate yet clear quality of the rift between Wright and Baldwin, and challenges Baldwin's account of the "marvelous evening" described in "Alas, Poor Richard." Wright, who had homosexual friends like George Davis and knew how to appreciate the sensitivity and finesse of their minds, nevertheless found Baldwin's attitude repugnant: "This man disgusts," he wrote to a friend, "there is a kind of shameful weeping in what he writes." The image he had of Baldwin was of a groveling, subservient person, while Baldwin regarded Wright as a scornful and self-satisfied figure.

29. "Richard Wright on the Negro Problem," unpublished interview by Curtius Prendergast (*Time*, Paris office).

On January 30, 1953, Wright wrote Reynolds, "I was a little surprised at the *Atlantic*'s reaction, but it simply means that the fear has reached even to Boston. Being far away from America gives me a kind of insight into the country which, perhaps, even those there do not have. It just means that one can't praise even the culture of an ally, and France is our official ally." On February 2, 1953, he told Reynolds that he would follow his advice and would only speak about the effects of industrialization, and even in that area he would adopt a generally neutral, "nonnational" attitude.

30. Quoted by William Gardner Smith in "Black Boy in Paris," *Ebony*, July, 1953, p. 37.

On January 5, 1950, Wright had, in fact, asked Henry Allen Moe for a second Guggenheim, which was refused. In the interval, all he had written was "The Man Who Killed a Shadow," a story of a few pages about a trans-Atlantic crossing, and a story called "The Flying Angel" or "Black Angel," about a Black who goes to heaven and, in his joy at having wings, commits so many idiocies that God cuts them off. His only remaining satisfaction is that he has been "one more flying fool."

31. On Reynolds's advice, Wright made the following changes at this

time: 1) Dot's age was lowered so that she would be a legal minor; then, if she denounced Cross he could be condemned for abduction, thus obliging him to take care of her and their child. 2) The first meeting between Cross and Houston, which originally took place in the Chicago subway, was postponed until the train trip to New York.

Reynolds had also pointed out that the draft board had to know the blood type of the draftees, and that the FBI did not necessarily intervene in nonpolitical crimes.

32. John Fischer to Wright, July 31, 1953, and Reynolds to Wright, August 4, 1952, discussing these revisions. Fischer would have liked to have the action begin with the subway accident; Cross's past, his life with Gladys, and the reasons which led her to divorce him could be covered more briefly. The scene in which Cross meets Jenny and kills Joe in the hotel would be cut out altogether to save up for the effect of the final murders. Fischer also wanted to eliminate the discussion with the priest in the dining car, Eva's journal telling of her unhappiness, the long episode following the death of Herndon and Blount, Cross's almost philosophical disquisition beginning on page 616, and the insurance agent's appearance at the end of the novel. All of this seemed either to be the result of coincidence or to slow the action. On some points Reynolds agreed with Fischer. On others he did not. Fischer, for instance, found the dispute between the waiter and the old woman in the dining car, as well as the night spent with Hattie, quite superfluous. The chance encounter of Damon and Hunter in the station, and the repeated use of the word "Fascist," also bothered him.

33. Wright to Reynolds, August 8, 1952. He was referring to the scene between Cross, Dot and Jenny, and the conversation of the attorney with the priest in the train, both of which he kept against Fischer's advice. He also kept the meeting with Jenny and the murder of Joe: "With Jenny we see that Cross is as much compelled to talk as to remain silent, and with Joe we see what can happen if and when he is confronted with danger. It is the subjective side of Cross that I'm trying to stress throughout." (Wright to Fischer, August 8, 1952.)

34. Wright had suggested *The Outsider* as a title on October 10. *Innocents Abroad* by Mark Twain had suggested "Innocence at Home" to him also. (Wright to Reynolds, November 6, 1952.) About "Colored Man" he had written, "It was Cross who made fun of the priest and Houston about the word 'colored.' I think the title becomes rather nicely ironic if used without changing anything. Not many colored people object to it; the intellectuals do to some extent, but not enough to matter." (Wright to Reynolds, September 29, 1952.) Fischer had suggested: "A Man Called Damon," "The Man with Two Names," "The Victim," "The

Man of Violence," "Second Chance," "A Name from a Grave" and "Man in Trouble."

35. "The Hattie sequence . . . does not really materially or structurally add to the story, but it does give one a sense of reality. In other words, it is atmosphere. (Maybe I do not need this atmosphere, I don't know.) Also it accounts for some of Cross's time from the day he leaves Chicago to the time he meets Bob Hunter again in Bob's flat. Also this section contains some reference to jazz music, which runs like a kind of background to the book. In trying to see how I could cut, I had in mind always retaining those few essentials. . . . If I cut in the middle, so to speak, of the Hattie sequence, cutting what Jack Fischer wants, it could be done and the other elements saved at the same time. This means, of course, cutting out the reference to Hattie at the end of the book. In that event Cross is simply ambushed and killed by the Communists." (Wright to Reynolds, November 14, 1952.) This shows how Wright's excessive compliance with his editors led him to sacrifice important elements in his work. The ideology was absolutely vital, in his opinion, but by cutting the scenes which contributed to the atmosphere, he disturbed the balance between the long theoretical development and the plot, which became too much like melodrama once it had been cut down to bare essentials.

36. "The Outsider," *Jet*, March 26, 1953, p. 42. This criticism was made elsewhere by Whites. Steven Marcus, writing in *Commentary* (November, 1953, p. 456), was sorry that Wright had depicted the life of the black American so superficially that it seemed as if the author himself had never had the experience. Milton Rugoff, in his article "Richard Wright's New Novel of Negro Life in America," says, "Wright is asserting that what was true of an illiterate Negro is no less true of an intellectual, but not by the force of fiction and the logic of drama." (*Sunday Herald Tribune Review of Books*, March 22, 1953.)

37. The articles mentioned are, in order: Max Eastman, "Man as a Promise," *The Freeman*, May 4, 1953, p. 568; Orville Prescott, "Books of the Times," *The New York Times*, March 10, 1953; John Henry Raleigh, *New Republic*, May 4, 1953, p. 19; Lewis Vogler, "Once Again Richard Wright Has Written a Controversial Novel," *San Francisco Chronicle*, April 5, 1953; Luther P. Jackson, "Wright's Outsider," *Newark News*, April 5, 1953; Harvey Curtis Webster, "Richard Wright's Profound New Novel," *The New Leader*, April 6, 1953, pp. 16–18.

38. See Melvin Altschuler, "Great Writer Wallows in Plot," *Washington Post*, March 22, 1953; Gilbert Highet, *Harper's Magazine*, May, 1953, pp. 96–97.

39. Anonymous, "The Outsider," *The New Yorker*, March 28, 1957, p. 127.

40. Quoted by William Gardner Smith in "Black Boy in Paris," *Ebony*, July, 1953, pp. 32–38. The three stories on Wright published in *Ebony* were done, curiously enough, at the three turning points in his life (in 1945, 1953 and 1960), when it was natural to do such a panorama on his career.

41. Wright to Reynolds, March 21, 1953. The day before, he had written: "The idea there was to make Erskine act out of unconscious motivations. Maybe I didn't carry it off; I don't know. But if I make the action there more precise, if I make him feel that Mabel knows more than she really does and doesn't realize how serious is her knowledge, then I'd have to toss out the unconscious motives which come out at the end of the book. . . . I had of course thought of Erskine's rashness in asking Mabel to marry him. But in doing so, he was not only trying to cover up his strange part in the death of her son, but it was really a substitute for his hate of her. And also, I had the entire thing happen within 72 hours, which was supposed to show the basis of impulsiveness that underlay his actions."

42. *Savage Holiday* was decided upon as the title on May 15, 1953. According to *Jet*, Wright owed it to a horror story by H. P. Lovecraft. They had previously thought of using "The Wish and the Deed," but Wright had also liked the idea of "The Rest Is Silence"—borrowed from *Hamlet*—"Guilt" and "Guilty Children."

43. See *Publisher's Weekly*, October 18, 1954: "Avon prepared streamers and posters for *Savage Holiday*, the first novel of Richard Wright to be published originally in paper-covered edition."

Notes to Chapter Sixteen
1. This is the impression given by an unpublished article by Chester Himes (March 1, 1954; in Yale University Library), and by "Black Boy in France," by William G. Smith, *Ebony*, July 8, 1953, pp. 32–42.

2. *Native Son* was performed for three weekends at the World's Stage Theatre at Highland Park, starting March 12, 1953, with Walter Mason, Florence Simpson and Anna Whitsitt.

3. Wright to Reynolds, April 22, 1953: "Today the letter came from the Gold Coast. The answer is yes." See Nkrumah's letter of introduction in *Black Power*, p. 3.

4. The American edition of *Capitalism and Slavery* did not come out until 1955, but Wright read the book before this date, and he quotes entire passages from it. His documentation filled two file drawers of official publications, British statistics and African newspapers, but he compiled most of it during his stay in Africa.

5. "Deux Portraits Africains," *Preuves*, November, 1954, pp. 3–6.

6. *Ibid.*, pp. 41–46. "I will accompany you, I told them, but only to watch. I have not travelled thousands of miles just to catch a 'Spanish disease' in the Canaries."

7. *Ibid.*, pp. 6–9.

8. *Black Power*, p. 103. See "Nkrumah Told, Go Ahead with Plan," *Accra Daily Graphic*, June 22, 1953, which mentions Wright's presence and talk. A little later, the paper stated that Wright would stay an entire month ("Negro Journalist on Study Tour," *ibid.*, June 24, 1953).

9. *Puissance Noire,* p. 132. Not in U. S. Edition.

10. On August 22, he wrote to Reynolds: "I'm leaving here, I think, on the 16th of Sept.; I shall spend two weeks in Monrovia; then sail on to Dakar, and will spend about ten days there; after that I shall try as quickly as possible to get to the nearest French port." On the 25th he decided to cut short his stay, however: "I've decided to call it a halt. I'm sure I've enough material for my purposes; it would have been good to see the Northern Territories but the expense would have been too much." With Kojo he had covered 2,968 miles at a cost of £220. From Accra, he had to ask Reynolds for $500 to pay for his ticket home.

11. Wright to Reynolds, October 24, 1953: "The tentative Doubleday project . . . interests me enormously. In fact it turns out that Marian Anderson is about the only Negro whose personality seems rich enough for me to want to do a job of that kind. . . . Until March or April, I shall be fully occupied with the African book and since I have invested so much money in this project I would not want to sidetrack it for anything else."

12. "Introduction," *In the Castle of My Skin*, New York, McGraw-Hill, 1953, pp. ix–xi.

13. Frank McGregor stated, in the list of suggested changes: "On page 456, in the closing letter to Nkrumah and elsewhere, [Wright] urges African would be liberators to adopt the weapons of their enemies, in effect to abandon notions of decency and fair play in their struggle. Reviewers and readers might well ask if that isn't the same argument used by McCarthy and his followers here: you can't put out a fire without wetting the furniture, etc. It could sound to some people as if Wright is saying: it's o.k. for us to play dirty, but not for the reactionaries."

14. Wright to Reynolds, May 3, 1954: "I've cut out all references to 'exasperation, pushiness.' etc. which was in the first version of the ms. Frankly, I felt that American readers ought to have had a chance to know how Americans are regarded even in Africa, but that's another subject and I let it slide. (The truth of the matter was that while in Africa, I was regarded as an American agent! That is what made my

getting information so difficult. This is the backwash of what is happening in the U.S.A.)"

15. Wright to Reynolds, March 20, 1954: "For some time now I've had the feeling that Harper's may not be too pleased with the kind of books I'm sending them. . . . Now, I feel that they ought to say that either they like or dislike this book, and not just put off publishing it for a full year."

16. *"Black Power*, this one is simple, and it describes what the book is really about" he wrote to Reynolds on April 16, 1954. In a letter to Margrit de Sablonière, Wright told her that she ought to translate "power" by "Macht" and not "Kracht": "The title: *Black Power* means political and state power. I did not have in mind any racial meaning" (June 9, 1955).

On March 29, Wright had also suggested: "Action in Africa," "And Now Africa," "Black Man's Hour," "Nervous Africa," "Africa Reaches for Power," "Black Freedom," "Battle for Africa," "Africa Divides," "Black Sun" and later, on May 15, "Black Nation."

17. Michael Clark, "A Struggle for the Black Man Alone?" *The New York Times Book Review,* September 26, 1954. "I must say that I was not prepared for the violence of the kind of attack the *New York Times* gave me. They even went so far as to alter the captions on the photos," Wright wrote to Reynolds on October 5, 1954.

18. Jay Saunders Redding, "Two Quests for Ancestors," *Saturday Review*, October 23, 1954, p. 19. See also *Baltimore Afro-American*, October 23, 1954.

19. Walter White, "A Major Report on Africa Today," *New York Herald Tribune Book Review*, September 26, 1954.

20. Joyce Cary, *The Nation*, October 16, 1954, p. 332. See also Ronnie Vulcan, *Boston Globe*, March 19, 1955; David E. Apter, *Chicago Sunday Tribune Magazine of Books*, October 10, 1954; John Allan May, *Christian Science Monitor*, September 30, 1954; Henry F. Winslow, *Crisis*, February 1955, pp. 77–80, 125; Lewis Gannett, *New York Herald Tribune*, September 23, 1954.

21. Mr. H. M. Q. of Angus & Robertson wrote to Innes Rose on January 5, 1955: "Wright's opening sentences admit complete ignorance of his subject and this ignorance could not be reversed in the short time at his disposal. He seems to sink to slum backyard intelligence as he flings his crudely poisoned spears at the British."

Notes to Chapter Seventeen
1. Wright to Reynolds, June 30, 1954. Wright was still thinking of going to French-speaking Africa and he made an effort to improve his

French, which was far from adequate, by taking a one-semester course for foreigners at the Sorbonne. (Wright to Reynolds, February 21, 1954.) He also studied Spanish before he left, but he only had enough time to learn the first twenty pages of the grammar.

2. Wright took this book back with him to France to send to Reynolds, but he asked for its return so that he could reply to critics who accused him of inaccuracies. The first names of his Spanish acquaintances (such as Carmen) are unchanged, but their last names were left out of *Pagan Spain* to spare them any annoyance.

3. A dozen or more of these letters are in WPP. It is somewhat strange that Wright should have taken such an interest in prostitutes, not only here in Barcelona but also in Las Palmas, Seville and, later, in Paris. He was planning both to study the psychological phenomenon of prostitution (for a report or a novel) and to collect information (for an investigation or a story) on the relationship of soldiers and other Americans, both black and white, with European women. Thus, his documentation on this subject was in excess of what would be considered necessary for a regular report on a given country. Some of these letters are quoted verbatim in *Pagan Spain*.

4. He wrote to Reynolds on February 4, 1955, "As you no doubt remember, my wife and I have been looking for some two years for a house in the country. Well, at last we found one; it is a farm house and I'm buying it. That was why I cabled you some weeks ago for $5,000. Instead of sending my wife and kids to England, I shall send them to the country now."

5. Wright gave these photographs to Milton Sachs to take to the U. S. He had chosen them carefully, along with an engraving of Santiago de Compostella that showed the saint overcoming a Moor; a portrait of Chamaco; and a color photograph of a strange painting of a bull jumping at the bedside of a wounded matador, which he thought might be suitable for the jacket. None of these were used.

6. "Misery and Sex," *Saturday Review*, March 16, 1957, pp. 60–61. See also: *Newsweek* (February 25, 1957, p. 59); *Crisis* (May, 1957, p. 313); *The Nation* (September 5, 1957, p. 114); *New Republic* (February 18, 1957, p. 18); *New York Post* (February 24, 1957); *The New Yorker* (March 23, 1957, p. 150); *Washington Post* (February 24, 1957).

7. *Congrès pour la Liberté de la Culture, 1950–1960*, Commemorative pamphlet, Paris, 1960, p. 2.

8. Wright to Reynolds, June 20, 1955. The definitive title was chosen in July, 1955, after Wright had suggested "East Side, West Side"; "All Around the World"; "Color Crazy"; "Actors: Asian and African";

"Black, Brown and Yellow Masks"; "Whose World?"; "The Colored Flood"; "Two Worlds"; "The Wounded World"; "The World Is Colored"; and "Black, Brown, and Yellow Men."

9. On August 23, he wrote to Reynolds: "I'm glad that things have ended that way with the Bandung ms. I've no kicks coming about the $500 advance; I'd rather take that than feel I was tied up. But I don't have any doubts about what publishing house I've chosen. It's Eddie and McGraw-Hill!" See also Wright to Reynolds (August 19, 1955).

10. See *France-Soir*, September 27, 1955, which also quoted William Faulkner's reaction. Wright's words were reported by Edgar Schneider. In his fight for the same cause, Wright had attended a meeting of the Mouvement contre le Racisme, l'Antisémitisme et pour la Paix, held at the Mutualité on January 4, 1955.

11. Homer P. Jack, "Asia's Last Call to the West," *Saturday Review*, March 17, 1956, pp. 19–20.

See also the reviews by Guy Wint (*The Nation*, April 14, 1956, p. 324); Keith Irvine (*The New Leader*, April 23, 1956, pp. 24–25); Paula Snelling (*The Progressive*, June, 1956); John Lash (*Phylon*, Winter, 1957, pp. 7, 23); Hugh Smythe (*Crisis*, January, 1957, pp. 58–59); Eugene Gordon, "Spirit of Bandung a Growing Force in the World" (*National Guardian*, July 6, 1956); Charles Wisley (*Masses and Mainstream* (June 1956, pp. 50–53); and Abner Berry in the *Daily Worker* (May 15, 1956).

12. Mochtar Lubis, "Through Colored Glasses?", *Encounter*, March, 1956, p. 73.

13. "Letter to the Editor," *Encounter*, April, 1956, p. 42.

Notes to Chapter Eighteen
1. Wright had found out about the Kelly affair from a French friend and, along with another American friend, he had written to a black newspaper in America offering to do a kind of report on it. Perhaps it was their rejection of the idea that led him to include it in his novel. Aswell, in any case, said in his February 9 reply that he was satisfied with the theme: "This is something with which you can make effective use of your own experience—even though your own experience happily is not at all the same as that of this young man. In other words, I think the subject is one to which you can apply your imagination and insight and come out with something that has the ring of truth in it."

2. The Congress was covered in detail in a special issue of *Présence Africaine* (*Présence Africaine*, Numéro Spécial, 8–10, Congrès des Ecrivains et Artistes Noirs, Juin–Novembre, 1956) from which the information in the following pages is taken. Du Bois's telegram stated: "Any

Negro-American who travels abroad today must either not discuss race conditions in the United States or say the sort of things which our State Department wishes the world to believe."

3. In May, 1957, Wright presented "De la Côte de l'Or au Ghana," an extract from Kwame Nkrumah's autobiography which *Preuves* was publishing to commemorate the new state of Ghana which had become independent on March 6. Wright pointed out the resemblances between the growth of the new state and the career of its leader, contrasting the European vision of the world with the African and once again asking his questions that had gone unanswered at the Congress: What would be the respective roles of tradition and modernization? How could the two cultures blend successfully?

4. *Présence Africaine, op. cit.*, p. 217.

5. The American delegates were upset to see the Communists publish parts of the report on the Congress which was to appear in *Présence Africaine*. After having shown them that a French Communist magazine had broken faith with Diop by obtaining the reports under the pretext of extracting a few short quotations, Wright continued: "I heard talk that the American delegation was too negative, too scared of communism to see what was really happening. To some degree I believe that this criticism was valid but I took pains to tell the critics that the American delegation did not have time to study and analyze the meeting." (Wright to John Davis, Roy Wilkins and others, November 21, 1956.)

6. "Introduction," *Pan-Africanism or Communism?*, London, Dobson, 1957. The piece was written in March, 1956.

7. The lecture was given in English and a résumé in German distributed to the audience. Ner-Tamid, in Frankfort, published it under the title "Die Psychologische Lage Unterdrückter Völker."

The press was also very favorable to Wright. See "Richard Wright Kommt" and "Die Farbige Welt muss gleichbar rechtig sein," *Hamburger Echo*, October 4 and 10, 1956; and "Vom Mississippi zur Seine," *Hamburger Abendblatt,* October 10, 1956. Ruth Liepman is emphatic about the exceptional warmth of this reception. (Letter to M. Fabre, May 3, 1963.)

Schwartze Macht (*Black Power*) sold very well and Wright signed a contract for the publication of his other books, beginning with *The Outsider.*

8. 65,000 copies of *Black Boy* and 75,000 of *Native Son* had been sold in Sweden. Wright told the press: "Jeg matte forlåte Amerika for å bli en god Amerikaner!" ("I had to leave America to remain a good American.") He mentioned his plan to write a novel on the American

soldiers in Europe, and said that he was collecting information, like Zola, on the customs and language of the prostitutes with whom the soldiers spent most of their time. Apropos of Bigger, he quoted Flaubert: "Madame Bovary, c'est moi!" He claimed that a black writer who wanted to write about what he knew should write about Blacks. Faulkner himself had never been able to put himself in a black man's skin. See, among others, *Volket i Bild* (November 1956, pp. 8–9, 47–49), *Stockholm Expressen* (November 28, 1956), *Oslo Dagbladet* (November 29, 1956).

9. "Une Pièce qui aurait ravi Voltaire," Introduction to *Papa Bon Dieu, L'Avant-Scène,* February 15, 1958, p. 4.

10. Wright to Reynolds, June 14 and 29, and July 5, 1956.

11. Wright to Reynolds, July 28 and August 6, 1957. Wright was not expecting much from Mrs. Wyman, since on the evening that he had met her he found her "so drunk that she seemed to be asleep standing up." The play was eventually produced off-Broadway in 1969.

Notes to Chapter Nineteen

1. See the *Manchester Guardian* (October 15, 1956), *London Times* (August 27, 1956), *Times Literary Supplement* (September 21, 1956) and the *Spectator* (September 14, 1956). Padmore wrote a remarkable review of *The Colour Curtain* in *Mankind* (August, 1956, pp. 91–94), while Cedric Dover, in *United Asia* (October, 1956), called it "a tortured attempt, at once sympathetic and sneering . . . of the Negro Communist . . . changed into yet another 'tragic mulatto'—clawing at 'curtains,' projecting his own infirmities and soaked in mystique."

2. Reynolds to Wright, July 20, 1956; Wright to Reynolds, August 2, 1956. Although he no longer had any reserve funds, Wright was not obliged to write anything for the sole purpose of making money. *The Color Curtain* had been sold to Mondadori in Italy and to Van Hoeve in Holland, where Sijthof was having *Savage Holiday* translated.

3. After Maggie's death, Ella stayed temporarily with one of her nieces, Mrs. Maggie Hunt, in Gloster, Mississippi. At the beginning of May, 1957, she broke a hip, which so worried Richard that he added a hundred dollars to her monthly allowance so that his cousin could hire a nurse. Once she was well again, at the end of June, she joined Leon in Chicago.

4. Ben Burns, "They're Not Uncle Tom's Children," *The Reporter,* March 8, 1956, pp. 21–25.

5. Reynolds to Wright, March 14, 1957. Wright replied, on March 19: "The man really has a lot of gall; after saying I had poisoned the mind of Europe against the U. S. A., he wishes to print my stuff. He is just

morally crooked. I don't understand him." On March 8, he had already stated categorically: "Even if he offered a thousand dollars an article, I don't want to have anything to do with him."

6. Wright to Mrs. Robert Vann, May 11, 1956.

7. Unidentified interview accorded an Italian journalist, WPP. In France itself, Wright never made a public declaration on the Algerian war, but he spoke more freely in Sweden, Germany and Italy, always against French policy, although he was careful to distinguish this neocolonial war from a racist war.

8. See *Ramjet*, Vol. 5 (July, 1957), p. 2.

9. Wright learned from Dennis Dobson, who had accepted *Black Power*, that Innes Rose had presented the book to him as being anti-British, and accordingly Wright protested violently to Reynolds (July 9, 1955): "I would accept Rose handling my work only if he wants to handle it and would not try to brand it as he hands it over to publishers."

10. This episode was taken directly from "Tarbaby's Dawn," as were both the idea of clear-cut separations between the action and the dream sequences, and the type of relationships the protagonist had with his friends. In fact this kind of opening, with the hero flanked by several (usually four) confederates, is a recurrent situation beginning with "Tarbaby's Dawn" and continuing through "Big Boy Leaves Home," *Lawd Today, Native Son, The Outsider* and finally *The Long Dream*. Just as Wright used part of *Lawd Today* at the beginning of *The Outsider,* he returned to "Tarbaby's Dawn" for *The Long Dream*. Does this indicate his reluctance to let an unpublished manuscript go to waste, a compulsive return to his beginnings, or the fact that he had exhausted his imagination? When Wright told Reynolds that he had put some personal experiences into *The Long Dream* that he had not used in *Black Boy*, was it literally true or was this merely an allusion to the fact he had used passages from "Tarbaby"?

11. Jay Saunders Redding, *Afro-American*, November 26, 1957, p. 2. See *Crisis*, December, 1957, p. 640; *Chicago Tribune*, November 10, 1957; *Afro-American*, July 6, 1957, p. 8; *Journal of Negro History*, October, 1957, p. 303; *C. L. A. Bulletin*, March, 1958, pp. 10–11.

12. In a letter to *The New York Times* (December 3, 1957), Pyke Johnson, the publicity director at Harper's, compiled a list of favorable reviews which had appeared in the following papers: *Jackson State Times, Asheville Citizen-Times, Clearwater Sun, Newport News Daily Press, Northwest Arkansas Times, New Orleans Times-Picayune, Winston-Salem Journal and Sentinel, Austin American-Statesman, Memphis Commercial Appeal* and *Norfolk Virginian-Pilot*. He also quoted the unfavorable extract from the *Chattanooga News-Free Press*. (WPP.)

13. See: Saville R. Davis, "Wright Speaks His Mind," *Christian Science Monitor*, October 17, 1957; Paula Snelling, "Warning Voice," *The Progressive*, December, 1957, pp. 40–41; Stanley Plastrik, "Lonely Outsiders," *Dissent*, Spring, 1958, pp. 191–92.

14. *The New Yorker,* October 26, 1957, p. 203. For Oscar Handlin's review, see "Patterns of Prejudice," *The New York Times Book Review*, October 20, 1957.

15. Translation from the French text of "Les Etats-Unis sont-ils une nation, une loi, un peuple?" *La Nef*, November 1957, pp. 57–60.

Notes to Chapter Twenty

1. Richard Gibson had already attacked Wright fiercely as a protest writer in "A No to Nothing," which came out in *Perspective U.S.A.*, an American Cultural Services publication, during the winter of 1953, at the same time as Baldwin's "Everybody's Protest Novel." Some people claim that *Time* and *Life,* following the publication of *Invisible Man,* made every effort to have Ellison win the National Book Award (which the novel deserved on its own merits), with the aim of detracting from Wright's reputation and establishing Ellison as *the* black novelist of the day. The photographer Gordon Parks had already agreed to cover the story, when Ralph Ellison refused to play along with the scheme. Baldwin, on the other hand, was more willing to play the role of Wright's "successor" toward 1956. In "Alas Poor Richard," published after Wright's death in *Nobody Knows My Name*, Baldwin continued to malign Wright until he finally felt that he had conquered this "spiritual father."

2. Gibson to Wright, August 22, 1958. In his letter of August 11, 1958, to Wright, Gibson intimated that Smith had double-crossed him. Among a list of thirty-one questions which Wright drew up, presumably for Gibson, appear, for example, the following: "Why were Ollie and I linked as targets of Smith? Ollie as an alleged Red and I as an alleged FBI man? . . . Could you have any idea why a girl with whom Smith was sleeping would come to my apartment on three occasions and ask to use my typewriter when she had one and could have used Smith's or could have borrowed Ollie's, since Ollie lived next door to her?" Wright also made a floor plan of Harrington's apartment, showing how the girl, Pamela, could have entered via a closet; and for the benefit of several of his friends he also had xeroxes made of the documents of the investigation, including the March 24, 1958, letter in which Gibson admitted to Harrington that he had sent the letter to *Life Magazine* and the two letters to *The Observer* with the manifest intention of compro-

mising him with the French authorities. Gibson apparently thought this was his only chance to save himself from expulsion from France. Wright eventually used most of these details in "Island of Hallucinations."

My sources for the Gibson affair are Wright's correspondence and papers, and the evidence of several people who wish to remain anonymous. In 1960, Richard Gibson sent Wright a postcard from Cuba, suggesting that he come and see the achievements of Castro's regime as if he really was in favor of it, but the Maoist magazine *Revolution*, of which Gibson had been on the editorial board for a time, openly denounced his "counterrevolutionary" activities, in its April, 1964, issue.

3. In a letter to Gertrude Stein, written on April 12, 1946, Wright had defined a position in relation to the United States which he later adopted for himself: "It is very easy to damn America by rejecting America. . . . I criticize America as an American and you do too, which I think is the real way to do the job." In "I Choose Exile," he explains: "I insist I am *not* anti-American, which, to me, is the important thing. My un-Americanism, then, consists of the fact that I want the right to hold, without fear of punitive measures, an opinion with which my neighbor does not agree; the right to travel wherever and whenever I please even though my ideas might not coincide with those of whatever Federal Administration might be in power in Washington, . . . to exercise my conscience and intelligence to the extent of refusing to 'inform' and 'spy' on my neighbor because he holds political convictions differing from mine."

4. In response to an article, "Passport Refusals for Political Reasons," published in the *Yale Law Journal*, Wright addressed a letter to the editor on May 5, 1952: "Would the writer be interested in gaining contact with other people who had their passports taken from them? If so, I can put him in touch with at least three others.

"The purpose of this letter is to beg a word of information from the writer. If the State Department notifies an American citizen living abroad that his passport has been cancelled and if the passport remains in the possession of the owner and is not stamped cancelled, and if the American citizen refuses to surrender said passport, what law is he violating? The passport in question let us suppose has just been renewed for a period of two years . . ." Wright was evidently referring to his own situation. See also Wright to Reynolds, June 13, 1958.

5. Wright took his responsibility very seriously and reread a good number of books by these four authors. He actively participated in the debates and encouraged the French students to question the importance of their cultural heritage. One of his favorite, and most disconcerting, questions was, "Would you like to have a tradition?" as if they didn't already have one. (Conversation with Michel Terrier, May, 1967.)

6. "Le Noir est une création du Blanc," *Preuves*, May, 1958, pp. 40–41. Léopold Senghor, James Ivy, Cedric Dover, Ralph Ellison, Davidson Nichols, Gilbert Gratiant and Richard Gibson also contributed to the symposium.

7. In order, the articles were: "Tract in Black and White," *Time*, October 27, 1958, pp. 95–96; *Chicago Daily News*, October 29, 1958; *Mainstream*, February, 1959, p. 49; *Raleigh News-Observer*, May 5, 1959. The critics here were merely reiterating an often-expressed opinion.

8. "The Long Dream," *C.L.A. Journal*, December, 1958, p. 143. See Nick Aaron Ford, *Phylon*, Winter, 1958, p. 453; Roi Ottley, *Chicago Sunday Tribune Magazine of Books*, October 26, 1958; Hoke Norris, *Chicago Sun-Times*, November 26, 1958; Jay Saunders Redding, *The New York Times Book Review*, October 26, 1958.

9. See Granville Hicks, *Saturday Review*, October 18, 1958, p. 13; Dorothy Parker, *Esquire*, February, 1959; Ted Poston, *New York Post*, October 26, 1958. See also: Henry F. Winslow, "Nightmare Experiences," *Crisis*, February, 1959, pp. 120–21; Maxwell Geismar, *New York Herald Tribune Book Review*, November 16, 1958; Irving Howe, *Partisan Review*, Winter, 1959, pp. 133–34.

10. *Richard Wright,* University of Minnesota Pamphlets, 1969, p. 32.

11. Wright to Reynolds, November 7, 1958: "Personal friends of mine tell me that the Gallimard family likes me and my work and wish to publish me. . . . I'd like for you to take Jenny Bradley out of this and let me see personally how Gallimard feels about me as a writer. I've never been able to get anything but vague noises from Jenny in this respect." As it turned out, Gallimard did not buy *The Long Dream*.

12. Wright to Reynolds, November 14–November 23, 1958. Gisèle Freund, among others, stated: "Contrary to the report and impression created by the representatives of *Time* Magazine, I state emphatically that I did not interview you for *Time* magazine." (Freund to Wright, November 22, 1958.)

On November 25, 1958, legal counsel for *Time* wrote to the law firm of Swigers, Chambers, Kelly and Harriman: "The photographer immediately reported the quotations to *Time*'s Paris Bureau. . . . Moreover, the quotations seem to be Mr. Wright's sentiments concerning this country . . . [and] I do not believe that [they] are in any way actionable according to our libel laws or the laws of France. In the circumstances, the editors of *Time* will not consider publishing any retraction or settling your client's claim."

13. "There is no doubt in my mind that *Time* meant harm. They claimed that they were inspired by another article appearing in a British periodical

. . . *planted* by an American to start an international fuss about American Negroes living in France." (Wright to Reynolds, November 19, 1958.)

"What is more important is that the local *Time* let it leak out that they had gathered a whole batch of letters hostile to me from their *Time* readers and they were going to run them. I think we stopped that." (Wright to Reynolds, December 8, 1958.)

14. Wright to T. Seldes, November 19, 1958. Wright explains that his use of melodrama depends upon the "racial atmosphere" he is writing about: "Negro life in the United States *is* melodramatic. I accept that. To try to dodge it would rob me of my subject matter. But since Fishbelly is now acting in a greatly less charged racial atmosphere, I find that the melodramatic element lessens."

15. "Island of Hallucinations," unpublished novel, WPP. Hereafter, I will indicate where necessary the page number of the final manuscript.

16. The character of Mechanical apparently owes much to James Baldwin and William Gardner Smith, and his experiences in Paris parallel certain of Baldwin's: "James Baldwin, in a book called *Notes of a Native Son*, describes an incident that happened in Paris. In my book, I describe a version of the same incident. This is not plagiarism. My re-recounting Baldwin's incident is to criticize what he said, put it in a normal, human light. . . . The central character, Mechanical, is a homosexual and I deal with him as delicately as I can. This, of course is a risky business." Wright to Reynolds, February 16, 1959. The incident in question was a dispute that took place at the Café Tournon.

17. Wright to Reynolds, January 15, 1959. Wright did not go to Chicago for the funeral, but he was generous in helping his brother with the expenses incurred at this time.

18. Wright to Reynolds, March 2, 1959: "I asked him point blank: 'Has the Negro's relationship to America changed?' and he said, 'No, there had been no qualitative change. It may come, but it hasn't come yet.' Now I don't agree all the way with King, but I like and admire him, and above all he tells the truth. *He* wants me to keep on writing the kinds of books that tell the truth of what he lives, but, and this is the central problem, there are not enough Negroes to buy those books. So I'm left facing a white audience that does not wish to face the general truth of the problem, even if I try to present it for their own good."

19. On March 9, he suggested "Exile Island," "Black Exile" and "Bitter Children," and on the 13th, "False Faces," "Remembering Ahead," "Dream Island," "Family Men," "Black Ghosts," "American Hunger," "Refugee Island" and "All Too Visible."

Notes to Chapter Twenty-One

1. John Strachey wrote for the first time to Reginald Butler on August 16, 1957. After a debate in the Commons (see *Hansard*, Vol. 595, No. 18, November 20, 1957, pp. 1353–54), Butler replied on January 29, 1957: "We will raise no objection . . . with supporting evidence of an acceptable financial position. . . . Assuming there is no significant change of circumstances in the meantime, Mr. Wright will be free to enter." On February 27, he confirmed this, stating that the permission to stay one year would be renewed, initially for four years and then indefinitely.

2. The translation of the book had been another worry for Wright. Having criticized Hélène Claireau's text in November, 1958, he arranged for the translation to be done by Dominique Guillet, which postponed the publication date to June, 1959. At the beginning of 1959, Wright composed a "Note for the French Reader," in which he outlined the latest problems arising from colonialism and decolonization, including a daring condemnation of European imperialism.

3. Wright to Reynolds, September 14, 1959: "Things are again looking grim here in France and if they break this time there will surely be civil war. That's why I want to be ready to move quickly."

4. He supplied a document from Reynolds on July 28, confirming his solvency, as well as a carbon copy of his contract for the adaptation of *The Long Dream*, to support his application.

5. The second harassing incident was yet another wait of one hour, on September 28 at the London airport, although no other passengers had been detained. (Letter to John Strachey, October 12, 1959.)

6. Dorothy Padmore to M. Fabre, April 13, 1963. J. E. Jantuah, the ambassador from Ghana to Paris, wrote to Kojo Botsio, the secretary of the Central Committee of the C. P. P., on October 13, 1959: "Mr. Wright appears to say that George had wanted him to ally himself more closely with the Liberation of Africa Movement led by Ghana. He therefore wishes to know in what way Ghana would like to make use of his vast experience and nationalism so that he conforms to it. He is prepared to come for discussions with the Party leaders. In any case he wonders whether he would be allowed to join the Party even now." (Carbon copy in WPP.) On October 17, 1959, Wright wrote the ambassador about the possibility of writing the preface for *Présence Africaine*'s French edition of Padmore's book *Pan Africanism or Communism?* He wanted the permission to write the preface to come directly from Accra, and expressed a great deal of suspicion of both Senghor and Mercer Cook. Regarding the editorial stance of the magazine (which, to be fair,

had approached Wright for this preface in all innocence), he said: "I consider the ideas of this magazine and the gentlemen who run it to be highly dangerous. They are strongly hostile to the idea of Black Nationalism. And there is a strong but hidden Jesuit influence in the group of men about this magazine." According to someone interviewed by Horace Cayton, Nkrumah would have agreed to have Wright gather information for him.

7. Wright to Reynolds, October 28, 1959. Only fifty pages of this documentation and the efforts to rework the novel remain, including an outline of Fish's activities on the military bases and three episodes: a trip he took with Anita and his "girls," performances at Poitiers and La Rochelle, and a dispute he had with a few soldiers.

8. "I have been ill since last July. . . . The doctors knew what was wrong but gave me the wrong medicine. I finally went to a specialist and I am now on my feet again, but I'm taking much bismuth and I must take periodic examinations." (Wright to Margrit de Sablonière, February 20, 1960.) "I took sulfa, emetine, arsenic, penicillin, etc. That was what made me raw inside. I've had some eight examinations since then and I'm free of amoebas now, but still weak. . . . I've got a good doctor, a specialist. Luckily he admires my work and does not charge me fees. He is one of the top men in France. He told me that I'd have to take bismuth for at least a year." (*Ibid.*, February 26, 1960.) "I'm slowly learning to be ill. That is the hard part. You see this is the first serious illness I've ever had and I'm not in the habit of sitting still. *When I want to move, I just tell my body to go and it goes.* But now it's different. When I tell my body to move, it hesitates and this makes you mad clear through. I had a relapse about ten days ago and had to start with vitamin B_{12}, vitamin C and sedatives. . . . I asked the doctor what caused the relapse and he said that it was a general reaction. . . . That is only half-living. . . . I ought to be in Africa. Now!" (*Ibid.*, March 19, 1960.)

9. See *Jet*, October 8, 1958, and an unidentified clipping in WPP, stating that Rosalind Hayes and Isabella Cooley were also acting in the play.

10. See H. T. Murdoch (*Philadelphia Inquirer*) and Ernie Schier (*Philadelphia Bulletin*, February 2, 1960). On February 14, an article by Lewis Funke in *The New York Times* applauded the music of Pembroke Davenport and the talent of Lawrence Winters, Joya Sherril of Duke Ellington's orchestra (Vera Mason), Josh White, Jr. (Tony), John Garth (Rev. Ragland), Gertrude Jeannette (Emma Tucker), and Al Freeman (Fish). See also Judith Crist, *New York Herald Tribune*, February 14, 1960.

11. He requested these tickets in his letter to Reynolds of January 13, 1960. "I wish I could write plays like she does," he remarked of Ketti Frings.

12. On March 2, Wright again communicated with Reynolds: "The real matter with *The Long Dream* is this: I've been informed from reliable sources here that it came under governmental taboo. You see, America as leader of the free world does not wish cruel pictures of how Negroes live shown to Africans or Asians. This is the way we fight Communism of course, this ban is never publicly or officially stated. I left Communism and I'm meeting it again in a different guise. . . . I'm willing, maybe, to die for my country, but I simply won't lie for it. If the winning of the Cold War means my destruction, then I cannot help in that war. . . . Things over here are as fierce from the American point of view. If you think you are escaping, you are dead wrong. It is here that the pressure is hottest."

13. At the beginning of 1958, Wright had agreed to be a patron of the African Popular Theatre, directed by, among others, Edouard Glissant, and at that time there was a possibility of putting the play on in Paris. When the ATA bought the rights, he tried to cancel his agreement with Martonplay, the New York office in charge of selling the rights. In this way, Wright thought he could profit from the film of *Native Son* in France by buying the rights back from Belloti, but the plan eventually came to nothing. (See Wright to Reynolds, January 6 and February 27, 1958.) *L'Avant Scène,* the magazine which published *Papa Bon Dieu* when the play was produced in Paris by Michel Vitold in November, 1958, was planning to try the American market with a first issue of 30,000 copies, which would include the text of *Daddy Goodness,* but nothing came of this either.

14. Wright to Reynolds, May 11, 1959; *A.T.A. Newsletter*, February and March, 1959, p. 1; circular by Fred Hare, May 4, 1959.

15. Reynolds to Wright, September 10, 1959. On the 14th, Wright replied: "I don't feel that I can make this story into a novel, though I've many ideas about boys' gangs. Maybe, if I had more energy at the moment, I'd do it. But I've been ill. Nothing serious, but I came down with amoebas I caught while in Africa. From the first of July I've been undergoing heavy medication and it makes me as weak as a kittten. The amoebas are gone, so the tests show, but I've got to get built up again. I'm on vitamin B_{12} and am getting stronger each day."

16. Oliver had sent *Blues Fell This Morning* to Wright, who explained his plan to him in a long letter of July 8, 1959.

17. Wright to Reynolds, September 14, 1959. The title of the collection

was definitely borrowed from Dreiser's *Ten Men*. Without *Savage Holiday* it was to be *Nine Men*.

18. He gave up this idea in August, after he had produced eight type-written pages on the role of the association of ideas in the writing of his books, and five manuscript pages on the genesis of "The Man Who Killed a Shadow."

19. See *Blues Fell This Morning,* London, Cassel, 1960, pp. vi–ix. "It is a history of the blues. Paul Oliver wrote it and it is *very good*. It is an indictment of racial conditions in America shown through the Negro's songs, something a little on the line of my 'Literature of the Negro in the United States.' " (Wright to M. de Sablonière, March 19, 1960.)

20. Wright to Reynolds, January 28, 1960. Horace Cayton and St. Clair Drake told me that they had never received such a letter from Wright.

21. See "The Voiceless Ones," *Saturday Review*, April 16, 1960, pp. 21–22. "I feel that what I've said might be a good perspective from which to see what I'm trying to do. In all of my books I've tried to weigh and feel *human possibility*, and I've tried to follow this without regard to ideology. Of course, ideologies constitute for me stages in human possibility. This is said clumsily, but the article might clear up the way I see things." Wright to M. de Sablonière, March 30, 1960.

22. Granville Hicks and Nelson Algren, among others, used this descrip-tion in a slightly pejorative way to stress the impulsive, powerful but somewhat disorderly style of his writing.

23. Wright to M. de Sablonière, April 8, 1960. "At last I've got them so that I can hold them in my hands, and that means that I'm nearly finished. Strange, that I've such signs of working, eh? Almost like super-stition," he had written her the day before.

24. Wright had already spoken about this to William Targ, who had been in Paris at the end of the summer of 1959. He wrote to Reynolds on June 8, 1960: "These poems are the result of my being in bed a great deal and it is likely that they are bad. I don't know. But don't get worried that I'm going daft. I'm turning back to fiction now."

25. Wright to M. de Sablonière, March 28, 1960: "Seeing is believing. For example, last month, I got a letter from Jean-Paul Sartre, but it turns out not to be a letter at all, but a *forgery*! Why was this letter sent to me and who sent it? I'm trying to find out. And this is not the first time forged documents have been aimed at American Negroes living in France. I know the direction from which this comes but it is hard to pinpoint it. *I have the letter in my possession. If I did not have it, I'd not speak about it, for one would not believe it!*" I did not find the letter referred to among Wright's papers.

26. "Chester Himes is writing detective stories and he had a book on the press in which he attacks me, my friends, etc. Gosh, it is strange. And I always thought he was such a good friend. He's got all his information from undercover agents of the American C.I.A." *Ibid.* The novel Wright refers to is *Une Affaire de Viol*, which did not come out until 1963. See my article "A Case of Rape" in *Black World*, February, 1972, pp. 39–48.

27. On April 7, Wright told M. de Sablonière that the doctor had suggested that Wright accompany him to Leiden. On the 16th, he had accepted, but he was worried: "I'm puzzled why he's going to Leiden and asking me along. He admits that there is nothing new at this medical conference that he can learn." On the 17th, he telegraphed Margrit to reserve three rooms for himself, the doctor and the doctor's father, and received the reply that one single bed and one double bed were all that was available. After having told the doctor that there would only be one room for himself at the hotel, he wondered: "Why in all hell did I deprive the doctor and his father of their hotel rooms? Was I reacting unconsciously to something in the doctor? I've puzzled over this for hours since I've been back. I can read: I read that part in the letter in which you told me that you had gotten me a room, but failed to read the other part. That must have been intentional; it could not have been otherwise. It was odd to feel that one is reacting intuitively. Yet the doctor and his father are friends of mine and only wish me well: *I'm convinced of this.* And this is not the first time that I've felt this deep unconscious aversion to people without knowing exactly why. There is something between me and the doctor that creates tension but I don't know what it is. Forget it, as we say in America." (Wright to M. de Sablonière, April 26, 1960.) The doctor, who says that he attached no importance to the incident, was, on the other hand struck by another of Wright's reactions. When they stopped en route at a small café in the North, and the doctor expressed surprise at the lack of hygiene, Wright retorted: "Perhaps it is dirty, but at least here they serve Negroes!" "As if the situation had not changed in the United States in the past ten years," the doctor concluded. (Conversation with Dr. Victor Schwartzmann, April, 1967.)

28. On January 8, Wright had decided to repeat his lecture, "The Miracle of Nationalism in Ghana." He changed his topic on the 15th, to avoid too heated a debate, but Pick wrote him on April 25, canceling the lecture. Wright received 150NF, but told Pick himself, on the 27th, that he intended to investigate the reasons for the cancellation.

29. See Anne-Marie de Vilaine, *L'Express*, April 24, 1960, p. 34. On May 16, *Le Figaro Littéraire* published "Rencontre avec Richard Wright," and *Le Nouvel Observateur* ran yet another interview on June 9.

30. Wright to M. de Sablonière, June 9, 1960. On June 23, he explained

to her: "You asked me what was the nature of my anti-American attacks. . . . Well, I went on the TV and explained the character of Tyree. That, of course is anti-American. I attacked the Americans for trying to control the output of Negro literature in the USA, for trying to render it harmless, etc. I pointed out that Negro literature is our testimony as to how we live our daily life and that that testimony, whether we aim it or not, is calculated to render the Asians and Africans hesitant about feeling that the American white man is a better friend to colored people than Russians or Chinese. You see, for a Negro today to cite the bare facts of his life is to make an anti-American document."

31. This series was broadcast on October 7, 14, 21 and 28, and on November 11, 18 and 25, 1960. On December 8, Hélène Bokanowski went on the air to speak about the deceased author. The tape of the last program, recorded and scheduled for December 2, was "lost," according to the French Radio Television Office. In it, not surprisingly, Wright had openly denounced the United States African policy.

32. Wright to M. de Sablonière, August 12 and 18, 1960. He did not want to discuss the subject of the novel with her until he had finished the first draft.

33. On this occasion, Wright also gave a very long interview to *L'Express* ("Entretien avec Richard Wright"), which came out on August 18, 1960.

34. "At the time, he was extremely tired, both physically, and, I sensed, spiritually too. He was working extremely hard on play, novel, articles, radio talks—all in the effort to keep separate establishments in London and Paris which were draining his resources. He also declared himself the victim of a plot, evidence of which he had gathered, and which implicated the French security, the American F.B.I. (perhaps C.I.A.) and ex-Trotskyists." (D. Padmore to M. Fabre, April 13, 1963.) The plot was almost certainly the attempt to make life difficult for Wright, which which had begun with the Gibson affair.

35. "Dorothy is suffering. It seems that the British still have powerful influence in the Ghana government and she is on the outside. . . . She still has the archives in her keeping, but that is all. She has been removed from all direct contact with African work. . . . I talked to her [about the plot]. . . . She will take it up with Nkrumah. But I'm depressed for I don't think that Nkrumah has enough intelligence to grasp the magnitude of what is fighting him and his people." (Wright to M. de Sablonière, September 18, 1960.)

36. "He talked about the possibility of making a trip to Africa for which his doctor friend would make the necessary flight arrangements through some contact he had with UNMARCO, the French travel agency and transport house. As I understand it, the doctor would also defray some

of the expenses and Richard was most anxious to come along to West Africa to see the current situation for himself at first hand, and to use his visit to present a truer picture to the world as a means of counteracting the false information that was being spread abroad about the independent African states generally and Ghana in particular. He asked if some itinerary could be arranged for him, so that he could meet the leading personalities and other sources of information." (D. Padmore to M. Fabre, April 13, 1963.) Apparently Wright was planning a twofold report in which a Black (himself) and a White (the doctor) would give their impressions on modern Africa, but it was difficult for the doctor to abandon his practice for a period of months in order to be free for what would be an expensive trip.

37. "I must increase my income. I have accepted the job of writing the text of records . . . a few hundred words for the buyer to read while trying to make up his mind if he wishes to buy or not." (Wright to M. de Sablonière, September 23, 1960.) On October 8, he wrote: "I'm not doing any serious writing at the moment, but the writing I'm doing for the records does say something. Not much, but a little something." These texts were: "Another Heroic Beginning" (unpublished); "It's Louis Jordan All the Way" (unpublished?); "So Long, Big Bill Broonzy," jacket for "The Blues of Big Bill Broonzy" (Mercury 7198 Standard); "The Past Is Still with Us," jacket for "Les Rois du Caf' Conc'" (Barclay 80818 Medium).

38. "Bel Air and Barclay have placed all public relations or goodwill programs touching the interests of Negroes in America and in France under the guidance of Mr. Richard Wright," was the reply a black artist apparently received, upon asking a favor of the recording company. This, in any case, was what a certain Eddy Wiggins was objecting to in threatening to have black American artists boycott the company if Wright continued in this position.

39. Wright to Oliver Swan, October 24, 1960. See also Wright to M. de Sablonière, November 8, 1960.

40. Wright to M. de Sablonière, November 8, 1960: "The Congress for Cultural Freedom in Paris asked me to go to New Delhi and speak on Tolstoy and I told them I was too busy fighting issues here in the Western world to go into Asia and try to sell their brand of pretense."

41. The lecture was taped but the tape is incomplete, and, in the typewritten transcription in the American Library in Paris, most of the references to the Gibson affair and Baldwin, etc., are missing. The only complete version, from which I quote, is to be found in Wright's papers, and which, in fact, Wright himself went over again after his talk, with the idea of publishing it.

42. "Wright's Last Guest at Home," *Ebony*, February, 1961, p. 94.

43. Wright to M. de Sablonière, November 24, 1960. Beb Vuyk's article, "Weekeinde med Richard Wright," had appeared on November 19 in *Vrij Nederland*, p. 19. On the 23rd, Wright wrote to Margrit: "I've been attacking here in Paris, both in writing, public speeches and on the radio (I have two more interviews to come!) and I knew that it was about time for a counterattack to start. . . . This attack is important for it means that this is the beginning of an attack against Panafricanism. A reading of *The Color Curtain* and *White Man, Listen!* ought to set out my views clearly in all these matters, but *I'm convinced that this attack was ordered by people identified with* American ideas and American aims."

Selected Bibliography

W ITH the exception of Section 1, this bibliography is limited to works devoted totally or in part to the career and life of Richard Wright, and does not include critical studies of his work. The most complete list of articles and reviews on Wright's work remains Jackson B. Bryer's "Richard Wright: a Checklist of Criticism," which appeared in *Wisconsin Studies in Contemporary Literature* (Fall, 1960), pp. 22–34 Most of Wright's letters referred to in the notes or quoted in the text will soon be published by Harper & Row in a collection edited by Edward Margolies and myself.

1. A Bibliography of Richard Wright's published works.

This is a revised and enlarged version of the bibliography published in *New Letters* (Winter, 1971), which itself is based on the bibliography prepared by myself and Edward Margolies for *The Bulletin of Bibliography* (January–April, 1956). The order is chronological within the sections; dates of composition appear between brackets when they differ from the year of publication. Reprints are indicated only when in book form or when significantly different from the original version.

A. POETRY:

"A Red Love Note." *Left Front,* No. 3 (January–February, 1934), p. 3. [1933]
"Rest for the Weary." *Left Front,* No. 3 (January–February, 1934), p. 3. [1933]
"Strength." *The Anvil,* No. 5 (March–April, 1934), p. 20. [1933]
"Child of the Dead and Forgotten Gods." *The Anvil,* No. 5 (March–April, 1934), p. 30. [1933]
"Everywhere Burning Waters Rise." *Left Front,* No. 4 (May–June 1934), p. 9.
"I Have Seen Black Hands." *New Masses,* No. 11 (June 26, 1934), p. 16. [1933]
"Obsession." *Midland Left,* No. 2 (February, 1935), p. 14.
"Rise and Live." *Midland Left,* No. 2 (February, 1935), pp. 13–14.
"I Am a Red Slogan." *International Literature,* No. 4 (April, 1935), p. 35. [1934]
"Ah Feels It in Mah Bones." *International Literature,* No. 4 (April, 1935), p. 80. [1934]
"Red Leaves of Red Books." *New Masses,* No. 15 (April 30, 1935), p. 6.
"Between the World and Me." *Partisan Review,* No. 2 (July–August, 1935), pp. 18–19. [1934]
"Spread Your Sunrise." *New Masses,* No. 16 (July 2, 1935), p. 26. [1934]
"Transcontinental." *International Literature,* No. 5 (January, 1936), pp. 52–57. [1935]

625

"Hearst Headline Blues." *New Masses,* No. 19 (May 12, 1936), p. 14.

"Old Habit and New Love." *New Masses,* No. 21 (December, 15, 1936), p. 29.

"We of the Streets." *New Masses,* No. 23 (April 13, 1937), p. 14, [1936]

"Red Clay Blues." *New Masses,* No. 32 (August 1, 1939), p. 14. Written in collaboration with Langston Hughes.

"King Joe" ("Joe Louis Blues"), lyrics for OKEH Record No. 6475. Reprinted in *New York Amsterdam Star News,* October 18, 1941, p. 16. [October 3, 1941]

"Haiku Poems." A number of haiku have appeared successively in Ollie Harrington, "The Last Days of Richard Wright," *Ebony,* No. 16 (February, 1961), pp. 93–94; reprinted in (1) Arna Bontemps and Langston Hughes, *The Poetry of the Negro,* 1964 edition. [8 poems] (2) Constance Webb, *Richard Wright: a Biography,* New York, Putnam, 1968, pp. 393–94. [4 poems] (3) Richard Wright, "Haikus," *Studies in Black Literature,* I (Summer, 1970), p. 1. (4) "Ten Haiku," *New Letters,* No. 38 (Winter, 1971), pp. 100–1.

B. FICTION:

"[The Voodoo of] Hell's Half Acre." *Southern Register* (Jackson, Miss.), circa spring, 1924. No complete version available. [1924]

"Superstition." *Abbot's Monthly Magazine,* No. 2 (April, 1931), pp. 45–47, 64–66, 72–73. Signed Richard N. Wright. [1930]

"Big Boy Leaves Home." In *The New Caravan* (eds. Alfred Kreymborg et al., New York, Norton, 1936), pp. 124–58. Included in *Uncle Tom's Children.* [1935]

"Silt." *New Masses,* No. 24 (August 24, 1937), pp. 19–20. Included in *Eight Men* as "The Man Who Saw the Flood." [1936–37]

"Fire and Cloud." *Story Magazine,* No. 12 (March, 1938), pp. 9–41. Included in *Uncle Tom's Children.* Was awarded the *Story Magazine* Prize in December, 1937. [1936]

Uncle Tom's Children: four novellas. New York, Harper, 1938, 317 pp. Includes "Big Boy Leaves Home," "Down by the Riverside" [1936], "Long Black Song" [1936] and "Fire and Cloud."

"Bright and Morning Star." *New Masses,* No. 27 (May 10, 1938), pp. 97–99, 116–24. Included in *Uncle Tom's Children* (1940 edition) and published in booklet form by International Publishers in 1941. [1937]

"Almos' A Man." *Harper's Bazaar,* No. 74 (January, 1940), pp. 40–41. Included, with slight revisions, in *Eight Men* as "The Man Who Was Almost a Man." Revised version of last two chapters of unpublished novel, "Tarbaby's Dawn." [1934–37]

Native Son. New York, Harper, 1940, 359 pp. [1937–39]

Uncle Tom's Children: five long stories. New York, Harper, 1940, 384 pp. Includes "The Ethics of Living Jim Crow," the short stories printed in the 1938 edition and "Bright and Morning Star."

Native Son, the Biography of a Young American. A Play in Ten Scenes. By Paul Green and Richard Wright. New York, Harper, 1941, 148 pp. In spite of Paul Green's recent claims, Wright's collaboration in the actual writing of the stage adaptation was important. [1940–41]

"The Man Who Lived Underground," *Accent,* No. 2 (Spring, 1942), pp. 170–76. Excerpts from a novel, differs distinctly from the novella printed in *Cross Section,* 1944. [1941]

"The Man Who Lived Underground." In *Cross Section* (ed. Edwin Seaver, New

York, 1944), pp. 58–102. Included in *Eight Men*. Second part of a novel, the first part of which is unpublished. [1941]

"The Man Who Killed a Shadow." *Zero* (Paris), I (Spring, 1949), pp. 45–53. First published as "L'homme qui tua une ombre." *Les Lettres Françaises,* October 4, 1946, pp. 1, 10. Included in *Eight Men*. [1945–46]

The Outsider. New York, Harper, 1953, 405 pp. [1947–52]

Savage Holiday. New York, Avon, 1954, 220 pp. [1953]

"Big Black Good Man." *Esquire,* No. 50 (November, 1957), pp. 76–80. Included in *Eight Men*. [1956]

The Long Dream. New York, Doubleday, 1958, 384 pp. [1956–57]

Eight Men. Cleveland and New York, World Publishing Company, 1961, 250 pp. Includes "The Man Who Went to Chicago," "The Man Who Saw the Flood," "The Man Who Was Almost a Man," "Big, Black Good Man," "Man, God Ain't Like That," "Man of All Works," "The Man Who Lived Underground," "The Man Who Killed a Shadow." [Collection prepared by Wright in 1960]

Lawd Today. New York, Walker, 1963, 189 pp. [1931–37; published posthumously]

"Five Episodes." In *Soon, One Morning* (ed. Herbert Hill, New York, Knopf, 1963), pp. 140–64. Excerpts from "Island of Hallucinations," an unpublished novel completed in 1959.

C. NONFICTION:

1. Books:

Twelve Million Black Voices: A Folk History of the Negro in the United States. Photo direction by Edwin Rosskam. New York, Viking Press, 1941, 152 pp.

Black Boy: A Record of Childhood and Youth. New York, Harper, 1945, 258 pp. [1942–43] Represents first section of unpublished "American Hunger" volume. Includes "The Ethics of Living Jim Crow."

Black Power: A Record of Reactions in a Land of Pathos. New York, Harper, 1954, 358 pp. [1953–54] From the diary of a visit to the Gold Coast. Includes "What Is Africa to Me?"

The Color Curtain. Cleveland and New York, World Publishing Company, 1956, 221 pp. [1955] First published as *Bandoeng, 1.500.000.000 hommes*. Paris, Calman-Lévy, 1955, 203 pp. (trans. Hélène Claireau). Includes "Vers Bandoeng Via Séville," "Le Congrès des hommes de couleur," "Indonesian Notebook" and "Le monde occidental à Bandoeng."

Pagan Spain. New York, Harper, 1956, 241 pp. [1954–56]

White Man, Listen! New York, Doubleday, 1957, 190 pp. Includes a slightly revised version of "Littérature noire américaine," "Tradition and Industrialization, the Plight of the Tragic Elite in Africa" and other previously unpublished essays and lectures.

2. Articles, essays, lectures, etc.:

"The Ethics of Living Jim Crow, an Autobiographical Sketch." In *American Stuff* (Federal Writers' Project anthology), New York, 1937, pp. 39–52. Included in *Uncle Tom's Children* (1940 edition). Incorporated in *Black Boy*. [1936]

"Portrait of Harlem." In *New York Panorama* (ed. New York W.P.A.), New York, 1938, pp. 132–51. Unsigned. [1937]

"Blueprint for Negro Writing." *New Challenge,* II (Fall, 1937), pp. 53–65. The text published in *Amistad II* (1970) is, in fact, an earlier version of this essay which Wright himself edited and rearranged in August 1937, and it should not be regarded as the final one.

"How 'Uncle Tom's Children' Grew." *Columbia University Writers' Club Bulletin,* II (May, 1938). [Pp. 16–18]

"Can We Depend upon Youth to Follow the American Way?" *Town Meeting Bulletin,* No. 4 (April 24, 1939), pp. 15–17. Participation in panel discussion.

"How 'Bigger' Was Born." *Saturday Review,* No. 22 (June 1, 1940), pp. 4–5, 17–20. Nearly complete version of a March, 1940, lecture later published in pamphlet form (Harper, 1940, 39 pp.).

"I Bite the Hand that Feeds Me." *Atlantic Monthly,* No. 155 (June, 1940), pp. 826–28. Reply to a review of *Native Son* by David L. Cohn in the May, 1940, issue of *Atlantic Monthly.*

"Rascoe Baiting." *American Mercury,* No. 50 (July, 1940), pp. 376–77. Reply to a review of *Native Son* by Burton Rascoe in the May, 1940, issue of *American Mercury.*

"Statement in Support of Browder and Ford." *Daily Worker,* September 30, 1940, p. 15.

"What Do I Think of the Theater?" *New York World-Telegram,* March 2, 1941, p. 20. On the stage adaptation of *Native Son.*

"Not My Peoples' War." *New Masses,* No. 39 (June 17, 1941), pp. 8–9, 12.

"U.S. Negroes Greet You." *Daily Worker,* September 1, 1941, p. 4. Reprinted as "I Support the Soviet Union" in *Soviet Russia Today,* September, 1941, p. 29. [A cable sent to *International Literature* following the Nazi attack]

"What You Don't Know Won't Hurt You." *Harper's Magazine,* No. 186 (December, 1942), pp. 58–61. Partly fictionalized Chicago memories later incorporated into the manuscript of "American Hunger."

"Twelve Million Black Voices." *Coronet,* No. 15 (April, 1942), pp. 23–93. Introduction, extracts of *Twelve Million Black Voices* and verse captions for photographs from the book.

"The Negro and Parkway Community House." Chicago, 1943, 4 pp. Pamphlet written at the request of Horace Cayton, director of this Chicago institution, in April, 1941.

"I Tried to Be a Communist." *Atlantic Monthly,* No. 159 (August, 1944), pp. 61–70; (September, 1944), pp. 48–56. Part of the second section of "American Hunger," the original manuscript of *Black Boy.* Later included in *The God that Failed* (ed. Richard Crossman, New York, Harper, 1949). [1942–43]

"Richard Wright Describes the Birth of *Black Boy.*" *New York Post,* November 30, 1944, p. B6.

"Early Days in Chicago." In *Cross Section* (ed. Edwin Seaver, New York, McClelland, 1945), pp. 306–42. Included in *Eight Men.* Part of second section of "American Hunger" manuscript. [1942–43]

"Is America Solving Its Race Problem?" *America's Town Meeting of the Air Bulletin,* No. 11 (May 24, 1945), pp. 6–7. Participation in panel discussion.

"American Hunger." *Mademoiselle,* No. 21 (September, 1945), pp. 164–65, 299–301. This is only part of the second manuscript section of "American Hunger" which was left out of *Black Boy.* [1942–43]

"A hitherto unpublished manuscript by Richard Wright being a continuation of *Black Boy.*" Photo-offset pamphlet edited by Constance Webb for private circulation in July 1946, n.p. In spite of the title, only half a dozen pages from the second section of the "American Hunger" manuscript were unpublished at the time.

"A Paris les G.I. Noirs ont appris à connaître et à aimer la liberté." *Samedi Soir,* 25 May 1946, p. 2.

"Psychiatry Comes to Harlem." *Free World,* No. 12 (September, 1946), pp. 49–51. Reprinted as "Psychiatry Goes to Harlem" in *Twice A Year,* No. 14–15 (1946–47), pp. 349–54. On the founding of the Lafargue Clinic.

"How Jim Crow Feels." *True Magazine,* (November, 1946), pp. 25–27, 154–56. First published as "Je sais reconnaître un nègre du Sud . . . ," *Paris Matin,* 27 June 1946, p. 2. On Wright's trip to Mexico and the South in the summer of 1940.

"A World View of the American Negro." *Twice A Year,* No. 14–15 (Fall, 1946–Winter, 1947), pp. 346–48. First published as "Lettre sur le problème noir aux U.S.A." in *Les Nouvelles Epitres,* Paris, 1947, lettre 32 (with facsimile reproduction of July 1, 1946 letter).

"Urban Misery in an American City: Juvenile Delinquency in Harlem." *Twice A Year,* No. 14–15 (Fall, 1946–Winter, 1947), pp. 339–45. [1945–46]

"Niam N'goura or *Présence Africaine's* Raison d'Etre." *Présence Africaine,* No. 1 (November–December, 1947), pp. 184–92. This is an adaptation, done in collaboration with Thomas Diop, of Alioune Diop's article in the same issue, pp. 7–14.

"Littérature Noire Américaine." *Temps Modernes,* No. 35 (August, 1948), pp. 193–220. Included in *White Man, Listen!* [1944] This is the text of a lecture often given by Wright in 1945 in the U.S.

"L'humanité est plus grande que l'Amérique ou la Russie." *Franc-Tireur* (Paris), December 16, 1948, p. 4. Speech given at "Rassemblement Démocratique Révolutionnaire" congress in Paris on December 10, 1948.

"L'homme du Sud." *France Etats-Unis,* December, 1950, p. 2. On William Faulkner.

"Richard Wright Explains Ideas about Movie Making." *Ebony,* No. 6 (January, 1951), pp. 84–85. On the shooting of "Native Son" in Argentina. [1950]

"American Negroes in France." *The Crisis,* No. 58 (June–July, 1951), pp. 381–83. First published as "Les Noirs Américains et la France" in *France-Observateur,* No. 56 (May 3, 1951).

"Derrière l'affaire [McGee]." *Le Droit de Vivre* (Paris), May 15, 1951, p. 1. On the trial and execution of Willie McGee.

"The Shame of Chicago." *Ebony,* No. 7 (December 1951), pp. 24–32. On Wright's return to Chicago in 1949. [1950]

"There is Always Another Cafe." *The Kiosk* (Paris), No. 10, 1953, pp. 12–14.

"What Is Africa to Me?" *Encounter,* No. 3 (September, 1954), pp. 22–31. Included in *Black Power.* [1953]

"Deux portraits africains." *Preuves,* No. 45 (November, 1954), pp. 3–6. From the first unpublished chapter of the manuscript of *Black Power.* [1953]

"Vers Bandoeng via Séville." *Preuves,* No. 53 (July, 1955), pp. 6–9. Incorporated in *The Color Curtain.*

"Le congrès des hommes de couleur." Preuves, No. 54 (August, 1955), pp. 42–48. Incorporated in *The Color Curtain.*

"Indonesian Notebook." *Encounter,* No. 5 (August, 1955), pp. 24–31. Incorporated in *The Color Curtain.*

"Le monde occidental à Bandoeng." *Preuves,* No. 55 (September, 1955), pp. 45–55. Incorporated in *The Color Curtain.*

"Tradition and Industrialization: the Plight of the Tragic Elite in Africa." *Présence Africaine,* No. 8–10 (June–November, 1956), pp. 347–60. Included in *White Man, Listen!* Paper given at the First Congress of Black Artists and Intellectuals in Paris, September 1956.

"De la Côte de l'Or au Ghana." *Preuves,* No. 75 (May, 1957), pp. 11–14.
"Le Noir est une création du Blanc." *Preuves,* No. 87 (May, 1958), pp. 40–41. Answer to a list of questions on Black culture.
"Spanish Snapshots: Granada, Seville." *Two Cities,* No. 2 (July, 1959), pp. 25–34. Part of the unpublished section of the *Pagan Spain* manuscript. [1954–55]
"Espagne Payenne." *Haute Société,* No. 3 (November, 1960), pp. 34–38. On Spanish festivals.
"Harlem." *Les Parisiens,* No. 1 (December, 1960), p. 23.
"Homage à Quincy Jones." *Les Cahiers du Jazz,* No. 4 (Spring, 1961), pp. 55–57. [1960]. This is preceded by a two-page interview of Wright.
"The American Problem." *New Letters,* No. 38 (Winter, 1971). pp. 9–16. [Early fifties]
"Ethnological Aspects of Chicago's Black Belt." *New Letters,* No. 39 (Fall, 1972), pp. 59–75. [1936]

3. Book Reviews and comments on books:

"A Tale of Folk Courage." *Partisan Review and Anvil,* No. 3 (April, 1936), p. 31. Review of *Black Thunder* by Arna Bontemps.
"Between Laughter and Tears." *New Masses,* No. 25 (October 5, 1937), pp. 22–25. Review of *These Low Grounds* by Waters E. Turpin and *Their Eyes Were Watching God* by Zora Neale Hurston.
"A Sharecropper's Story." *New Republic,* No. 93 (December 1, 1937), p. 109. Review of *I Was a Sharecropper* by Harry B. Kroll.
"Adventure and Love in Loyalist Spain." *New Masses,* No. 26 (March 8, 1938), pp. 25–26. Review of *The Wall of Men* by William Rollins.
"Lynching Bee." *New Republic,* No. 102 (March 11, 1940), p. 351. Review of *Trouble in July* by Erskine Caldwell.
"Richard Wright Reviews James Weldon Johnson's Classic 'Black Manhattan'." *Chicago News,* May 22, 1940, p. 10.
"Inner Landscape." *New Republic,* No. 103 (August 5, 1940), p. 195. Review of *The Heart Is a Lonely Hunter* by Carson McCullers.
"Forerunner and Ambassador." *New Republic,* No. 103 (October 24, 1940), p. 600. Review of *The Big Sea* by Langston Hughes.
"As Richard Wright Sees Autobiographies of Langston Hughes and W.E.B. DuBois." *Chicago News,* December 4, 1940, p. 10. Review of *The Big Sea* by Langston Hughes and *Dusk of Dawn* by W.E.B. DuBois.
Comment on *Let My People Go* by Henrietta Buckmaster, New York, Harper, 1941. On dust jacket.
"Gertrude Stein's Story Is Drenched in Hitler's Horrors." *P.M. Magazine,* March 11, 1945, p. m 15. Review of *Wars I Have Seen* by Gertrude Stein.
"A Non-Combat Soldier Strips Words for Action." *P.M. Magazine,* June 24, 1945, p. m 16. Review of *The Brick Foxhole* by Richard Brooks.
"Alger Revisited, or My Stars! Did We Read That Stuff?" *P.M. Magazine,* September 16, 1945, p. m 8. Review of Horatio Alger's *Collected Novels.*
"Two Novels of the Crushing of Men, One White, One Black." *P.M. Magazine,* November 25, 1945, p. m 7–m 8. Review of *Focus* by Arthur Miller and *If He Hollers Let Him Go* by Chester Himes.
Comment on Dorsha Hayes, *Who Walks with the Earth* (New York, Harper, 1945). Back dust jacket.
Comment on Marianne Oswald's *One Small Voice* (New York, McGraw, 1946). Back dust jacket.
"*Wasteland* Uses Psychoanalysis Deftly." *P.M. Magazine,* February 17, 1946, p.m. 8. Review of *Wasteland* by Jo Sinclair (pseud. for Ruth Seid).

"A Steinian Catechism." Back dust jacket of Gertrude Stein's *Brewsie and Willie* (New York, Random, 1946). [April 1946]

"American G.I.'s Fears Worry Gertrude Stein." *P.M. Magazine,* July 26, 1946, p. m 15–m 16. Review of *Brewsie and Willie* by Gertrude Stein in the form of a letter to Roger Pipett.

"E. M. Forster Anatomizes the Novel." *P.M. Magazine,* March 16, 1947, p. m 3. Review of *Aspects of the Novel* by E. M. Forster.

"A Junker's Epic Novel on Militarism." *P.M. Magazine,* May 4, 1947, p. m 3. Review of *The End Is Not Yet* by Fritz Von Unruh.

[Comment on] *A Street in Bronzeville,* by Gwendolyn Brooks, on back dust jacket of *Annie Allen,* by Gwendolyn Brooks (New York, Harper, 1949).

Comment on Jean Genet, *Our Lady of the Flowers* (New York, Grove, 1950). Back dust jacket. Written at the request of Bernard Frechtman in 1949.

"Neurosis of Conquest." *The Nation,* No. 183 (October 20, 1956), pp. 330–31. Review of *Prospero and Caliban* by Octave Mannoni.

"The Voiceless Ones." *Saturday Review,* No. 43 (April 16, 1960), pp. 53–54. Review of *The Disinherited* by Michel Del Castillo.

4. Prefaces, introductions, forewords, etc.:

"Foreword." *Illinois Labor Notes,* No. 4 (March, 1936), p. 2. Foreword to the special issue devoted to the first National Negro Congress meeting in Chicago.

"Richard Wright." In *The New Caravan* (ed. Alfred Kreymborg et al., New York, Norton, 1936, p. 663). Short biographical notice.

"Introduction." In Howard Nutt, *Special Laughter* (Prairie City, Illinois, Press of James Decker, 1940, pp. ix–xii). In the form of a letter, dated Spring, 1940.

Note on Theodore Ward. Pamphlet for the Negro Playwright's Company, New York, 1940, p. 3.

"Letter to International Publishers." In *Bright and Morning Star* (New York, International Publishers, 1941, p. 1). Is an introduction to the short story published as a booklet.

"Note on Jim Crow Blues." Preface to Keynote Album No. 107, *Southern Exposure* (1941). Reprinted as "Note sur les Blues" in *La Revue du Jazz,* April, 1949, p. 113. [1941]

Prefatory note. Playbill for *Native Son,* St. James's Theatre, New York, March 1941, p. 1.

"Foreword." In Morris V. Schappes, *Letters from the Tombs* (New York, Schappes Defense Committee, 1941, pp. v–vi).

[Why I Selected 'How Bigger Was Born']. In *This Is My Best* (ed. Whit Burnett, Philadelphia, Lippincott, 1942, p. 448). [July, 1942]

"Introduction." In Nelson Algren, *Never Come Morning* (New York, Harper, 1942, pp. ix–x.

"Introduction." In Jay Saunders Redding, *No Day of Triumph* (New York, Harper, 1942, p. 1).

"Don't Wear Your Sunday Best Every Day." 140-word advertisement for War Bonds on back of dust jacket of *Black Boy* (1945).

"Introduction." In Horace R. Cayton and St. Clair Drake, *Black Metropolis* (New York, Harcourt Brace, 1945, pp. xvii–xxxiv).

"Why I Chose 'Melanctha' by Gertrude Stein." In *I Wish I'd Written That* (ed. Whit Burnett, New York, McGraw, 1946, p. 234).

"Evidence de l'Art Nègre." Introduction to a pamphlet for an African art exhibition at Librairie Palmes, Paris, p. 1. [November, 1948]

"Richard Wright présente le Musée Vivant." *Le Musée Vivant,* No. 12 (November, 1948), p. 1. Introduction to a special issue on Negro art.

"Preface" to "Human, All Too Human" by E. Franklin Frazier, *Présence Africaine,* No. 6 (January–March, 1949), p. 47.

"Introducing Some American Negro Folk Songs." *Présence Africaine,* No. 6 (January–March, 1949), p. 70.

"Introductory Note to 'The Respectful Prostitute' [by Jean-Paul Sartre]. In *Art and Action, Twice a Year* (Tenth Anniversary Issue, New York, 1948, pp. 14–16).

"Introduction to 'American Hunger'." In *The World's Best* (ed. Whit Burnett, Dial, New York, 1950, p. 303). First published as "Richard Wright nous présente *Black Boy"* in *L'Ordre* (Paris), January 14, 1948, p. 3.

"Preface." In Chester Himes, *La Croisade de Lee Gordon* (Paris, Corréa, 1952, pp. 7–8). Himes's *Lonely Crusade* was published in the U.S. without a preface.

"Introduction." In George Lamming. *In the Castle of my Skin* (New York, McGraw, 1953, pp. ix–xii).

"Introduction." In George Padmore, *Pan-Africanism or Communism?* (London, Dobson, 1956, pp. 11–14). Translated and revised as a preface to *Panafricanisme ou Communisme,* Paris, *Présence Africaine,* 1960, pp. 9–12. [March 2, 1956 and September 10, 1960]

"Une pièce qui aurait ravi Voltaire." L'Avant-Scène, No. 168 (1958), pp. 3–4. Introduction to Louis Sapin's *Papa Bon Dieu,* which Wright adapted as *Daddy Goodness* the same year.

"Au lecteur français." In *Ecoute, Homme Blanc!* (Paris, Calman-Lévy, 1959, pp. xv–xxxvi). Special foreword for the French reader, dated 1959, to accompany the translation of *White Man, Listen!* by Dominque Guillet.

"Foreword." In Paul Oliver, *Blues Fell This Morning* (London, Horizon Press, 1960, pp. vii–xii).

["The Past is Still with Us"]. Introduction to "Les Rois du Caf'Conç," Barclay Album No. 80 128. [1960]

["So Long, Big Bill Broonzy"]. Introduction to "The Blues of Big Bill Broonzy," Mercury Album No. 7198 Standard. [1960, unsigned]

"Introduction." In Françoise Gourdon, *Tant qu'il y aura la peur* (Paris, Flammarion, 1961, pp. 1–3).

5. Newspaper reporting and journalism:

"Joe Louis Uncovers Dynamite." *New Masses,* No. 17 (October 8, 1935), p. 18.

"Two Million Black Voices." *New Masses,* No. 18 (February 25, 1936), p. 16.

"Negro Writers Launch Literary Quarterly." *Daily Worker,* June 8, 1937, p. 7. On *New Challenge.*

"Young Writers Launch Literary Quarterly." *San Antonio Register,* July 10, 1937, p. 4. On *New Challenge.*

"Protests against Slugging Grow, Butcher Who Attacked Negro Boy Is Fired." *Daily Worker,* July 15, 1937, p. 3.

"Negro, with 3-Week Old Baby, Begs Food on Streets." *Daily Worker,* August 4, 1937, p. 3.

"C P Leads Struggle for Freedom, Stachel Says." *Daily Worker,* August 9, 1937, p. 2.

"Huddie Ledbetter, Famous Negro Folk Artist." *Daily Worker,* August 12, 1937, p. 7.

"Communist Leader Warns on Harlem Tiger Stooges." *Daily Worker,* August 13, 1937, p. 4.

"What Happens in a C P Branch Party Meeting in the Harlem Section." *Daily Worker,* August 16, 1937, p. 6.

"Pullman Porters to Celebrate 12th Year of Their Union." *Daily Worker,* August 19, 1937, p. 3.

"Scottsboro Boys on Stage is Opposed." *Daily Worker,* August 21, 1937, p. 3.

"Born a Slave, She Recruits 5 Members for Communist Party." *Daily Worker,* August 30, 1937, p. 2.

"Harlem Women Hit Boost on Milk Price." *Daily Worker,* September 3, 1937, p. 3.

"Insect Ridden Medicine Given in Hospital." *Daily Worker,* September 4, 1937, p. 5.

"Mrs. Holmes and Daughter Drink from the Fountain of Communism." *Daily Worker,* September 7, 1937, p. 5.

" 'Horseplay' at Lafayette Fun for Children and Grownups Alike." *Daily Worker,* September 11, 1937, p. 7.

"Harlem Spanish Women Come out of the Kitchen." *Daily Worker,* September 20, 1937, p. 5.

"10,000 Negro Vets in New York Silent, but They're Talking Up at Home." *Daily Worker,* September 23, 1937, p. 4.

"Big Harlem Rally for China Tonight." *Daily Worker,* September 27, 1937, p. 4.

"2 American Negroes in Key Posts of Spain's Loyalist Forces." *Daily Worker,* September 29, 1937, p. 2.

"Randolph Urges Parley between AFL-CIO Unions." *Daily Worker,* September 30, 1937, p. 3.

"Bates Tells of Spain's Fight for Strong Republican Army." *Daily Worker,* October 1, 1937, p. 2.

"Negro Youth on March, Says Leader." *Daily Worker,* October 7, 1937, p. 3.

"Opening on Harlem Project Homes Show How Slums Can be Wiped Out in New York." *Daily Worker,* October 8, 1937, p. 5.

"See Biggest Negro Parley since Days of Reconstruction." *Daily Worker,* October 14, 1937, p. 5.

"Negro Tradition in the Theatre." *Daily Worker,* October or November 15, 1937, p. 5.

"Harlem, Bronx Sign Competition Pact." *Daily Worker,* October 19, 1937, p. 5.

"Harlem Negro Leaders Back Mayor for Liberal Views." *Daily Worker,* October 20, 1937, p. 5.

"Browder Warns of Growth of Fascism in Latin America." *Daily Worker,* October 23, 1937, p. 5.

"New Negro Pamphlet Stresses Need for U.S. People's Front." *Daily Worker,* October 25, 1937, p. 2.

"Harlem Leaders Rap *Amsterdam News,* Stand for Mahoney." *Daily Worker,* October 30, 1937, p. 6.

"Harlem Vote Swings Away from Tiger." *Daily Worker,* November 2, 1937, p. 3.

"Negro Leaders Hail Victory of ALP at New York Polls." *Daily Worker,* November 4, 1937, p. 5.

"ALP Assemblyman Urges State Control." *Daily Worker,* November 8, 1937, p. 1.

"Negro Social Worker Hails Housing, Education in Spain." *Daily Worker,* November 12, 1937, p. 2.

"ALP Assemblyman in Harlem Hails Unity of Labor at Polls." *Daily Worker,* November 18, 1937, p. 2.

"Walter Garland Tells What Spain's Fight Against Fascism Means to the Negro People." *Daily Worker,* November 29, 1937, p. 2.

" 'He Died by Them,' Hero's Widow Tells of Rescue of Negro Children." *Daily Worker,* December 6, 1937, p. 1, 6.

"Harlem East Side Honor Hero Who Died in Rescue of Negroes." *Daily Worker,* December 7, 1937, p. 4.

"Ban on Negro Doctors Bared at City Probe." *Daily Worker,* December 15, 1937, p. 1.

"Gouging Landlord Discrimination against Negroes Bared at Hearing." *Daily Worker,* December 15, 1937, p. 6.

"James W. Ford Celebrates 44th Birthday." *Daily Worker,* December 23, 1937, p. 4.

"Santa Claus Has a Hard Time Finding Way in Harlem Slums." *Daily Worker,* December 27, 1937, p. 4.

"Every Child Is a Genius." *Daily Worker,* December 28, 1937, p. 7.

"Why the Eyes of the People Turn to the Ring for the Title Bout at Yankee Stadium Tonight." *Daily Worker,* June 22, 1938, pp. 1, 4. On forthcoming Louis-Schmeling fight.

"How He Did It, and Oh!—Where Were Hitler's Pagan Gods?" *Daily Worker,* June 24, 1938, pp. 1, 8. On Joe Louis's victory over Schmeling.

"High Tide in Harlem." *New Masses,* No. 28 (July 5, 1938), pp. 18–20. On Louis's victory over Schmeling.

6. Correspondence:

"Letter to the Editors." *Partisan Review and Anvil,* No. 3 (June, 1936), p. 30. In defense of progressive writer Meyer Levin, labeled a reactionary in an article published by the magazine.

"Reader's Right: Writers Ask Break for Negroes." New York *Post,* April 5, 1938, p. 20. Letter to the Editors.

"A Letter about the War in Spain." In *Writers Take Sides* (New York, League of American Writers, 1938).

"Letter to Bruce Kaputska." *The Kaputskan,* No. 1 (Fall, 1940), p. 17. [August, 1940]

"Greetings." *New Masses,* No. 39 (February 18, 1941), p. 14. Extract of a letter encouraging the magazine.

"To Sender Garlin." *Daily Worker,* February 13, 1942, p. 7. Letter dated February 10, 1942, asking for more consideration for readers' opinions.

"From Richard Wright." In *The Flowers of Friendship* (ed. Donald Gallup, New York, Knopf, 1953), pp. 379–80. Letter to Gertrude Stein dated May 27, 1945.

"Richard Wright and Antonio Frasconi: an Exchange of Letters." *Twice a Year,* No. 12–13 (1945), pp. 256–61. [November, 1944]

"Two Letters to Dorothy Norman." In *Art and Action,* 1948, pp. 65–73. Includes a letter dated February 28, 1948 (pp. 65–71) and a letter dated March 9, 1948 (pp. 72–73) both from Paris, on the state of things in France and Europe.

"Comrade Strong, Don't You Remember?" New York *Herald Tribune* (European edition), April 4, 1949, p. 3. Letter to Anna Louise Strong in response to her article in the same newspaper.

"To Axel Lonnquist." New York *Herald Tribune* (European edition), December 19, 1956, p. 8. Letter in answer to an attack by Lonnquist published in a previous issue of the newspaper.

"Letters to Joe C. Brown." Edited with an introduction by Thomas Knipp (Kent State University Libraries, Kent, Ohio, 1968, 12 pp.) This is an unauthorized edition whose circulation has been prohibited by Mrs. Ellen Wright. [8 letters from 1938 to 1945]

"Letter to Owen Dodson." *New Letters*, No. 38 (Winter, 1971), pp. 125–27 [June 9, 1946]

2. Books dealing with the life and career of Richard Wright

MAXINE BLOCH, ed., *Current Biography*. New York, H. W. Wilson, 1940. Pages 885–86, devoted to Richard Wright, are for the most part accurate and contain certain details unavailable elsewhere.

EDWIN R. EMBREE, *13 Against the Odds*. New York, Viking, 1944. "Richard Wright: Native Son" (pp. 25–46), based upon interviews conducted by the author, is the first serious study on Wright's youth and literary beginnings.

W. E. B. DU BOIS AND GUY JOHNSON, *Encyclopedia of the Negro*. New York, H. W. Wilson, 1945. The biographical sketch of Wright on p. 161 is brief, but the style of its authors distinguishes it somewhat from other similar notices in works of this type.

REBECCA CHALMERS BARTON, *Witness for Freedom*. New York, Harper, 1948. The chapter on Wright (pp. 254–68) is a biographical sketch based exclusively on *Black Boy*.

SIMONE DE BEAUVOIR, *L'Amérique au Jour le Jour*. Paris, Gallimard, 1948. About twenty pages are devoted to the author's activities with the Wrights in New York from January to May, 1947.

B. A. RICHARDSON, *Great American Negroes*. New York, Crowell, 1956. Brief biographical sketch (pp. 126–36) based on *Black Boy*.

JAMES BALDWIN, *Nobody Knows My Name*. New York, Dial, 1961. "The Exile" and "Alas, Poor Richard," in the section also entitled "Alas, Poor Richard" (pp. 181–215) mention the meeting between the two writers, and their relationship. "Princes and Powers" (pp. 13–55) deals with Wright's contribution to the Congrès des Ecrivains et Artistes Noirs of September, 1956. Baldwin's point of view is generally hostile to Wright, and certain of his assertions are incorrect.

CHESTER HIMES, *The Quality of Hurt*. New York, Doubleday, 1972. Mentions the relationship between the two writers in New York and Paris. To be completed by John A. Williams' interview of Himes in *Amistad 1* (Vintage Books, 1970).

DAVID RAY AND ROBERT FARNSWORTH, eds., *The Life and Works of Richard Wright*. (Special number of *New Letters*, Winter, 1971, 202 pp. Reprinted as *Richard Wright: Impressions and Perspectives* by University of Michigan Press, 1973). Original biographical material can be found in personal impressions by Henrietta Weigel, Benjamin Appel, Harry Birdoff, Winburn T. Thomas, Owen Dodson, Frank K. Safford, Jack Conroy, Horace Cayton and Sidney Williams; several letters to Richard Wright and one from Wright to Owen Dodson; an article by John Houseman on his collaboration with Wright; one on Wright in Memphis by Grace McSpadden White; one by Michel Fabre on Wright's exile and one by Margaret Walker Alexander on her long friendship with Wright.

CONSTANCE WEBB, *Richard Wright*. New York, Putnam, 1968, 443 pp.

JOHN A. WILLIAMS, *The Most Native of Sons*, a biography of Richard Wright. Garden City, N.Y., Doubleday, 1970, 141 pp. Apparently written for a juvenile audience and based on Webb's book and the Himes interview in *Amistad.*

3. Interviews rich in biographical material

MARCIA MINOR, "The Author of 'Fire and Cloud' Tells How He Developed His Phonetic System." *New York Daily Worker,* February 13, 1938.

"Una conversacion con Richard Wright." *Romance* (Mexico), June 19, 1940.

"Negro Author Criticizes Reds as Intolerant." *New York Herald Tribune,* January 28, 1944.

MICHAEL CARTER, "Richard Wright Talks to the Afro." *Baltimore Afro-American,* March 22, 1945.

"How Richard Wright Looks at *Black Boy.*" *P.M. Magazine,* April 14, 1945, pp. 3–4.

FREDÉRIC STANE, "Avec Richard Wright, le romancier de la terreur sousjacente." *Gavroche,* June 2, 1946, p. 6.

PAUL GUTH, "Interview de Richard Wright." *La Gazette des Lettres,* September 14, 1946, p. 2.

RAPHAEL TARDON, "Richard Wright nous a dit le problème blanc aux Etats-Unis." *Action,* October 24, 1946, pp. 10–11.

PETER SCHMIDT, "Die Stimme des Entrechteten." *Die Weltwoche,* November 15, 1946, p. 5.

MAURICE FLEURENT, "Richard Wright à Paris." *Paru,* No. 25 (December, 1946), pp. 7–8.

MICHEL GORDEY, "L'Amérique n'est pas le Nouveau Monde." *Les Lettres Françaises,* January 10, 1947, pp. 1, 7.

FERNANDA PIVANO, "A Parigi con Wright." *Avanti,* May 19, 1948.

"Richard Wright on U. S. Politics." *Labor Action,* Vol. 13 (May 30, 1949), pp. 1, 3.

RAMUNDO GOMEZ, "Richard Wright." *El Hogar,* October 28, 1949, p. 75.

JEANINE DELPECH, "L'enfant du pays." *Les Nouvelles Littéraires,* September 14, 1950, p. 1. Reprinted in *Crisis,* Vol. 17 (November, 1950), pp. 625–26, 678, under the title, "Interview with Richard Wright."

"Entrevista con Richard Wright." *Revista Branca,* Lisbon, n.d., 1951.

RUDOLPH KUNSTERMEIER, "Ich besuchte Richard Wright." *Die Welt,* November 6, 1951.

ALAN TEMKO, "Interview with Expatriate Wright in Paris." *San Francisco Chronicle,* December 30, 1951.

HANS DE VAAL, "Interview med Richard Wright." *Literair Paspoort,* Vol. 8 (July–August, 1953), pp. 161–63.

JORGE FELIU, "Richard Wright visita a Espagna." *Imagenes,* May, 1955, p. 20.

"Je maudis le jour ou j'ai entendu pour la première fois le mot 'politique.' " *L'Express,* October 18, 1955, p. 18.

JEANINE DELPECH, "Un Noir chez les Blancs." *Les Nouvelles Littéraires,* March 8, 1956, pp. 1, 6.

BARRY LEARNED, "U. S. Lets Negro Explain Race Ills." *American Weekend,* January 24, 1959.

JOHANNES S. MARTENS, "En stor vorvatter tar bladed fra munnen." *Oslo Morgenbladet,* July 20, 1959, p. 9.

LASSE SODERBERG, "Richard Wright." *Folket i Bild,* September 18, 1959, pp. 4–5, 30.

ANNE MARIE DE VILAINE, "Richard Wright: 'La rééducation des Blancs est plus urgente que celle des Noirs.'" *L'Express,* April 24, 1960, p. 14.

B. P., "Rencontre avec Richard Wright." *Le Figaro Littéraire,* May 16, 1960.

"Avec Richard Wright." *France-Observateur,* June 9, 1960, pp. 19–20.

"Entretien avec Richard Wright." *L'Express,* August 18, 1960, pp. 22–23.

4. Major articles on various events of Wright's career

"Negro Writer Wins Story Contest." *The New York Times,* February 15, 1938.

"First Prize Winner." *Story Magazine,* Vol. 78 (March, 1938), p. ii.

JACK CONROY, "Son of the South." *Sunday Worker,* April 10, 1938.

MAY CAMERON, "Prize Winning Novelist Talks of Communism and Importance of Felt Life." *New York Post,* March 12, 1939.

ULYSSES KEYS, "Richard Wright to Receive Guggenheim Fellowship." *Chicago Sunday Bee,* April 2, 1939.

OUIDA CAMPBELL, "Bigger is Reborn." *Carolina Magazine,* October, 1940, pp. 21–24.

"Negro Hailed As New Writer: Richard Wright Comes to Town in Reality." *New York Sun-Telegram,* March 4, 1940.

FREDERIC WERTHAM, M.D., "An Unconscious Determinant in *Native Son,*" *Journal of Clinical Psychopathology,* Vol. 6 (July, 1944), pp. 111–15.

JOSEPH GOLLOMB, "Richard Wright." *Book-of-the-Month Club News,* February, 1945, pp. 8–9.

TRUDI MCCULLOUGH, "Author Wright's Life and His Works Pose a Paradox of Success and Failure." *Buffalo Evening News,* April 2, 1945.

"Black Boy in Brooklyn." *Ebony,* Vol. 1 (November, 1945), pp. 26–27.

MAURICE NADEAU, "Pas de problème noir aux Etats-Unis, mais un problème blanc!." *Combat,* May 11, 1946, p. 2.

S. JAGNO, "Richard Wright." *Bref* (Paris), 2 (June 1, 1946), pp. 20–21.

MARGARET TJADER, "Dreiser's Last Visit to New York." *Twice a Year,* Vol. 14–15 (Fall, 1946), pp. 217–27.

"Why Richard Wright Came Back from France." *P.M. Magazine,* February 16, 1947, p. 6.

JOSEPH A. BARRY, "Americans in Paris." *The New York Times Magazine,* August 18, 1948, pp. 18–19, 42.

JOHANNES S. MARTENS, "Richard Wright bosetter seg i Paris." *Oslo Morgenbladet,* December 24, 1948.

JAMES T. FARRELL, "Farrell Objects to Wright's Interview." *Labor Action,* Vol. 13 (June 27, 1949), p. 13.

GEORGE PADMORE, "Afro-American Writer Sends Greeting to African Nationalists." *Gold Coast Observer,* December 2, 1949.

RENÉ PIQUION, "Tonnerre dans la littérature." *Haitian Journal,* August 3, 1950.

GLADYS P. GRAHAM, "Richard Wright Returns to America." *Atlanta Daily World,* August 29, 1950.

GUILIELMO PIERCE, "Discorsetto a Wright sui Negri." *Il Tempo* (Rome), January 24, 1951.

WILLIAM GARDNER SMITH, "Black Boy in France." *Ebony,* Vol. 8 (July, 1953), pp. 32–36, 39–42.

J. C., "Un Bandoeng Culturel à la Sorbonne." *Demain,* September 27, 1956, p. 15.

EDOUARD GLISSANT, "Le Congrès des Artistes Noirs." *Lettres Nouvelles,* n° 43 (October, 1956), pp. 577–82.

"Onkle Tom ist tot." *Der Spiegel,* Vol. 10 (October 24, 1956), pp. 49–53.

MARIKA HELLSTROM KENNEDY, "Black Boy i Sverige." *Folket i Bild*, No. 49 (November, 1956), pp. 8–9, 47–49.

ANDERS EHNMARK, "Richard Wright will lära de förgade leva i vita världen." *Stockholm Expressen*, November 28, 1956.

"Richard Wright på Olso besøg." *Oslo Dagbladet*, November 29, 1956.

JOSEPH BARRY, "An American in Paris." *New York Post Magazine*, March 23, 1959, p. 4.

PETER ABRAHAMS, "The Blacks." *Holiday*, Vol. 25 (April, 1959), pp. 112–14, *et seq.*

BEB VUYK, "Weekeinde med Richard Wright." *Vrij Nederland*, November 19, 1960, p. 19 and November 26, 1960, p. 17.

EDWARD REEVES, "Richard Wright Hits U. S. Racial Hypocrisy." *Chicago Defender*, November 28, 1960, p. 13.

MICHEL FABRE, "Interview with Simone de Beauvoir," *Studies in Black Literature*, I (Autumn, 1970), pp. 4–5. On Wright's relationship with a few French existentialists.

DOROTHY PADMORE, "March 13, 1963, Letter to Michel Fabre," *Studies in Black Literature*, I (Autumn, 1970), pp. 5–9. An estimate of Wright's relationship to Africa and memories of his last days.

Obituary Notices

NELSEN ALGREN, "Remembering Richard Wright." *The Nation*, Vol. 192 (January 28, 1961), p. 85.

OLLIE HARRINGTON, "The Last Days of Richard Wright." *Ebony*, Vol. 16 (February, 1961), pp. 83–94.

LANGSTON HUGHES, "Richard Wright's Last Guest at Home." *Ebony*, Vol. 16 (February, 1961), p. 94.

ERWIN WICKERT, "Ein Neger in Paris." *Frankfurter Allgemeine*, February 1, 1961, p. 4.

IRVING HOWE, "Richard Wright, A Word of Farewell." *New Republic*, February 13, 1961, pp. 17–18.

OLLIE STEWART, "The Richard Wright I Knew." *Ave Maria*, Vol. 93 (May 6, 1961), pp. 9–11.

HOYT FULLER, "On the Death of Richard Wright." *Southwest Review*, Vol. 46 (Autumn, 1961), pp. 334–42.

INDEX